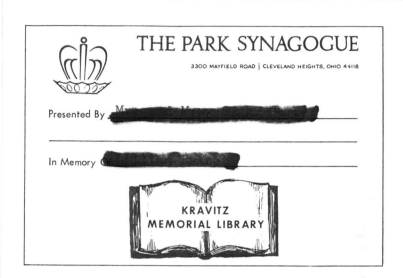

THE RELIGIOUS SITUATION

1968

Antiwar demonstrators assembled October 21, 1967, at the Washington, D. C., Lincoln Memorial.

The Religious Situation: 1968

THE FIRST IN A SERIES
OF ANNUAL VOLUMES

Edited by Donald R. Cutler

BEACON PRESS : BOSTON

Illustrations on the following pages adapted from photographs supplied by Wide World Photos, Inc.:
ii, 2, 53, 196, 451, 506, 526, 561, 577, 582, 720 (left), 745, and 886.

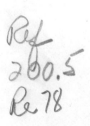

CONTENTS

Contents

FOREWORD

by Reinhold Niebuhr

A FOREWORD to this comprehensive study of religion in all the facets of its relation to our contemporary culture and to its moral and social problems is obviously both unnecessary and impossible. The table of contents immediately reveals that the study has drawn on the learning of various specialists in their respective intellectual disciplines. They have given us topical studies of realms of culture and social relations, such as the race problem in an era of Negro revolution and the population control problem in a day of population explosion, and they have considered the problem of war in a nuclear age, in which nations are trying to avoid catastrophe by the force of a precarious "balance of terror." These studies yield an account of both the successes and the failures of the religious communities to adapt themselves to a creative role in changing situations.

Other chapters try to analyze the religious situation in its historical and cultural contexts. A foreword is unnecessary in the sense that the comprehensive study speaks for itself and therefore does not require a "barker" before the tent of wealth. It is impossible in the sense that no prefatory word could possibly do justice to the wealth and variety of learning exhibited by the several distinguished authors. I cannot therefore bring myself to say anything but to contribute my little perspective on a theme which many of these studies traverse from various angles. That theme is of the religious situation in a secular age.

Modern secularism has been an all-pervasive cultural phenomenon since the rise of empirical scientific disciplines in the seventeenth century. Natural scientists have naturally been skeptical of every theory that transcended natural causes. Empirical historical investigations have also inevitably been negative about the legends with which religions embroidered their symbolic myths. Religion seemed no more than a dubious remnant of a prescientific — i.e., primitive — culture. Dr. Marty mentions one of the characteristic agnostic treatments of religion in our century: in *Treatise on the Gods*, H.L. Mencken, who made it his business to laugh at all human foibles, took particular delight in poking fun at religious foibles of his renowned "Bible Belt." It is more important to note that scientific skepticism was so pervasive that it captivated not only scientists and learned men of various disciplines, but also that it threw a shadow of doubt on the piety of the most devout religious persons.

In the light of these triumphs of secularism, which boded ill for the vitality of religious faith in a scientific culture, we must raise the significant question, Why has religious faith persisted for three centuries after the first triumphs of modern science? Could it be that wise men have overlooked some important aspects of human existence when they prematurely celebrated the demise of religion and, in our day, belatedly speak of "The Death of God"?

It may be possible to gain a clue to the mysterious survival of religious faith by consulting psychiatric analyses of the relation of a basic trust in the meaning of human existence in the human person to the instinctive will to survival in man's animal nature. One of the distinguished psychiatric philosophers in this volume, Dr. Erik Erikson, has given us valued insights on the birth of basic trust in life through the security which loving parents give the child.

But life is full of ills and hazards, of natural and historical evils, so that this childlike trust will soon be dissipated if maturity cannot devise a method of transmuting the basic trust of childhood, based on obvious security, to a faith which transcends all the incoherences, incongruities, and ills of life. Scientific and rational coherences will not restore this trust in life because human personality is assailed by all manner of ills and incoherences.

Human personality must finally come to encounter the incongruity of its own existence. Man is the most incongruous of creatures because he is a child of nature, but also transcends

nature and thus creates history. Historical sequences and coherences, however, cannot satisfy his search for meaning because man has a freedom which transcends history, as well as
nature, though this freedom never completely frees him from
either nature or history.

Religious faith is essentially the projection of a mysterious
source of order and meaning transcending all the disorders and
ills of nature and history — faith in the mysterious God who is
related to the world as creator and redeemer, the ALPHA and
OMEGA of human striving.

In the mystic faiths, so popular in the East, the penumbra of
mystery which surrounds the universe of meaning is the mystery
of an undifferentiated eternity which annuls all temporal meaning of history and of that unique and incongruous individual
who is involved in the flux of time. In those faiths the religious
problem is to escape time and one's own unique egohood.

Western culture, on the other hand, is really indebted to the
faith of Israel's prophets who insisted on including the crosspur-
poses of history and the incongruity of human individuality in
the universe of meaning. The Christian faith borrowed precious
values from the faith of the Jews. These accounted for both the
historical dynamism of western culture and its appreciation of
the dignity of man, who was immersed in time and history but
also was able to "look before and after, And pine for what
is not." The prophets insisted that the mystery of creative fulfillment was beyond human understanding. Isaiah spoke in the name
of the divine when he declared: "For my thoughts are not your
thoughts, neither are your ways my ways, says the Lord. For as
the heavens are higher than the earth, so are my ways higher
than your ways and my thoughts than your thoughts." There
was good Hebraic justification for Augustine's affirmation: "If
thou couldst comprehend him, he were not God."

There is, in short, a profound reason for guarding the meaning of human existence by asserting the mystery, not of the unknown, but of the unknowable, the MYSTERIUM TREMENDUM.
The chief error of modern empirical disciplines is their belief

that mystery is merely the realm of the unknown which will gradually disappear when science enlarges the realm of the known by triumphing over all manner of ignorance.

The open societies of the western world are culturally pluralistic and are influenced by both religious traditions and empirical disciplines. They therefore offer historical evidence of the wholesome consequences of the interaction between religious vitality and secular procedures in establishing the meaning of human existence, though this interaction is created by the reluctant partners of the mutual enterprise.

Without the religious view of the incongruous individual whose freedom transmutes all natural impulses for good or evil, there is a temptation for modern secular disciplines to try to understand man in the dimension of pure nature. They would thus misunderstand man, even if they followed Descartes and coordinated the mind to a universal intelligence and consigned man's physical nature to the coherences of nature. The unity and dimension of man's integral selfhood would be obscured. Kierkegaard's "existing individual" would be lost in either a natural or a dualistic world.

Without the constant influence of rational and empirical disciplines, however, religious life would degenerate into an obscurantist effort to restore prescientific symbols to the postscientific absurdities. Without an emphasis on the universality of natural causation, religion is tempted, in place of the simple securities of the parental frame of reference, to create childish securities under a "special" providence. This absurd sense of security is established by imagining that the divine source of being and order will interfere with natural processes for the sake of the security of the righteous devotee. Not even the radical monotheism of Hebrew faith could prevent the assurance of special securities in Hebraic devotional literature. Thus a psalm gives a radical security to the righteous man. "A thousand shall fall at thy side; and ten thousand at thy right hand. But the Evil shall not come nigh unto thee." This idea of special providence has been inherited by the Christian faith, especially in Calvinism. William James observed that, in contrast to Stoic universalism, "Christians have been engaged in lobbying in the courts of the almighty for special privileges."

Religious faith in a scientific culture was right in affirming the mystery of creation, but wrong in using confidence in this mystery as a basis for an obscurantist form of science. The mystery of creation may be defined as the mystery of novelty in the evolutionary chain of causation, since no previous cause is a totally adequate explanation of a subsequent event. But, by this issue of mystery and natural causation in the evolutionary chain, obscurantist religious faith was betrayed into denying the obvious truth that Darwin's biology in the nineteenth century had placed man in the evolutionary chain of animal species. Bishop Wilberforce in England and William Jennings Bryan in America made themselves ridiculous in challenging the biology of Darwin by the use of biblical accounts of creation.

It must be admitted that the empirical disciplines often have failed to appreciate the novel distinction between man with his dignity of rational self-transcendence and the other creatures who cannot transcend the time and nature in which they are imbedded. When modern secular culture celebrates the "dignity of man" as did the eighteenth century French Enlightenment, it is frequently too one dimensional to understand that man, "the master of things," is a creature in the very world of history in which he has become master. The mystery of the creation remains, beyond his ken, as remains God's reminder to Job about the inscrutability of the created world. Thus God challenges Job with the question wast thou there "when I laid the foundations of the earth, . . . when the morning stars sang together . . . for joy?" No, Job was not there, and it is difficult for modern man, conscious of his dignity as creator, to acknowledge the limits of his knowledge and power, and to worship the MYSTERIUM TREMENDUM, which inculcates modesty in all men, primitive or modern.

In conclusion we must, all too briefly, analyze the mutual interaction between religious faith and empirical disciplines in the realm of morals. Kant erred when he regarded the intelligible part of man as the law giver and the "sensible" part of man as law observer. For man in the integral unity of body, mind, and spirit is both law giver and law observer. Thus religion is related to the sense of moral obligation because this sense is derived, not from pure intelligence, but from an imaginative construction of an ultimate meaning of human existence.

But the religious vision of an ultimate moral fulfillment as we have it in both Jewish and Christian Messianic hopes is so pure that it seems irrelevant to the problems of human togetherness among individuals and collectives. Human nature exhibits a universal impulse of self-concern, probably more pronounced in collective than in individual behavior.

It is significant that both biblical religion and modern social learning are agreed in two facts of human nature. They agree about the social substance of human nature which makes for dependence upon and responsibility to the neighbor as embodied in the commandment "Love thy neighbor as thyself." They also agree that man's persistent self concern places him in violation of that commandment. All modern political theory takes the persistent ego striving for granted; and Christian theory as expressed in Paul, Augustine, and Luther especially has been "realistic" ever since Paul confessed: "There is a law in my members which wars against the law that is in my mind."

The primary moral and social problem is how to establish a tolerable harmony among self regarding individuals and collectives. It is increasingly important in a technical and nuclear age that standards of discriminate judgment be the indirect instruments of the love commandment. "Let love be the motive, but justice be the instrument," said the late Pope John.

Religious devotees must recognize that to make discriminate judgments on competitive human striving is more and more a matter that is dependent upon empirical knowledge of all the contingent elements which must be considered in these judgments. It follows, therefore, that learning in secular terms is more important than piety in establishing justice in the tangled common life of classes and nations. It is necessary to recognize that there is an inevitable partnership between a religious expression of trust in the meaning of human existence and the empirical procedures which are necessary to yield social and historical fruits of this basic trust. Hence we acknowledge the creativity of cultures which welcome both religious and secular components to this common enterprise of recognizing and preserving the humanity of man.

ACKNOWLEDGMENTS

GRATEFUL ACKNOWLEDGMENT is made to the following publishers for the explicit use of their publications:

"Civil Religion in America" by Robert N. Bellah is reprinted and "America's Institutions of Faith" by Edwin S. Gaustad is printed by arrangement with *Daedalus*, the Journal of the American Academy of Arts and Sciences, copyright © 1966, 1967.

"Religion as a Cultural System" by Clifford Geertz is reprinted by permission of Tavistock Publications from Michael Banton, ed., *Anthropological Approaches to the Study of Religion* (ASA Monographs), copyright © 1966.

"Pseudo-Religious Rites in the USSR" by Nikita Struve and "Orthodoxy and the Younger Generation in the USSR" by Dmitry Konstantinov are reprinted by permission of Frederick A. Praeger, Inc. from William C. Fletcher and Anthony J. Strover, eds., *Religion and the Search for New Ideals in the USSR*, copyright © 1967.

American Council on Education, Washington, D.C., for Luther A. Weigle, "The American Tradition and the Relation between Religion and Education," *Religion and Public Education* (*American Council on Education*, vol. 9, no. 22, February 1945), copyright 1945.

George Braziller, Inc., New York, New York, for Ernest Becker, *Beyond Alienation*, copyright © 1967.

The Clarendon Press, Oxford, England, for G. Lienhardt, *Divinity and Experience*, copyright © 1961.

Harcourt, Brace & World, Inc., New York, New York, for T. S. Eliot, "Four Quartets," *Collected Poems, 1909–1962*, copyright © 1963.

Harper & Row, Publishers, New York, New York, for Philip Rieff, *The Triumph of the Therapeutic*, copyright © 1966.

Holt, Rinehart and Winston, Inc., New York, New York, for Paul Tillich, *The Religious Situation*, H. Richard Niebuhr, translator, copyright 1932 and copyright © 1960.

Alfred A. Knopf, Inc., New York, New York, for Wallace Stevens, *Collected Poems of Wallace Stevens*, copyright © 1954.

XVIII

THE RELIGIOUS SITUATION:
AN INTRODUCTION

by Martin E. Marty

A SUPERFICIAL READING of the signs of the times would suggest the relevance of a study of the *secular situation*. Attention to *The Religious Situation*, then, should be obsolete and out of place. In theologian Bernard Meland's terms, "secularization is the movement away from traditionally accepted norms and sensibilities in the life interests and habits of a people — a departure from an historical order of life that presupposes religious sanctions." It is usually seen as a worldwide trend. Meland continues, it "looms upon the horizon of every culture of our time wherever there are aspirations to become modern and in tune with the events of present history" [20:3 ff].

In the Eastern world, the phenomenon of secularization has been noted particularly in India, in the development of its artistic and literary themes, in the political expression of the late Prime Minister Nehru, and in the tendency toward the evolution of India as a secular state [17, 34, 31]. For another example, the Muslim world has manifested what can be called "the irresistible progress of secularization" under Western influence [18:382 ff]. Those who discern such trends are quick to point out that the process takes different forms and proceeds at different paces in various cultures, and the movement is never without ambiguity and some signs of contradiction; yet its general direction is unmistakable.

The main lines of Western cultural development for four or five centuries, in this reading, have been toward the evolution of a new style of godless man, a self-engrossed and self-interpreting world, a cosmos in which the "god of explanation" is absent and in which notes of transcendence and mystery are disappearing. In these respects the West is then seen to be setting a pace for the world.

The main lines of Western religious thought for the past four or five decades have been based on the acceptance of this secular model and have often included an attack on residual religion. This mode of theological expression has been particularly evident in Protestantism. The Swiss thinker Karl Barth anticipated a trend when he spoke of "religion as unbelief" while Dietrich Bonhoeffer in Germany envisioned a "religionless Christianity" which would positively accept the secular model. These modest proposals have been accompanied by open and frank affirmations of a secular and "postreligious" world in the works of the American Harvey Cox, among others. Roman Catholic interest in the subject has developed more recently but no less enthusiastically, as is manifest by the popularity of Cox's work among American Catholics or by the writings of Daniel Callahan and Michael Novak as representatives of the newer generation. Dietrich von Hildebrand, in a book-length polemic against prosecular trends in world Catholicism, cites Callahan and Novak and, less appropriately, Pierre Teilhard de Chardin and Leslie Dewart as agents of these movements [14].

If there is any accuracy at all in the idea that these analyses of worldwide secular trends apply also in the religious field, only antiquarians and people with morbid necrological curiosity should be interested in a study of the religious situation. The antiquarian consigns living religion to the past and devotes himself to its lore. He tends his archaeological museums and nurtures his anthropological zoos, gathering around himself other experts who share his findings. They may collectively regret the passing of vital religion because it deprives them of new subject matter; on the other hand, it guarantees them the historical distance that scholarly objectivity relishes. They may regard all contemporary formal religion the way H. L. Mencken looked at the thought of Christianity, as something displaced by the Enlightenment: "It was in . . . The Eighteenth [century] that Christian theology finally disappeared from the intellectual baggage of all really civilized men" [21:226].

Those with necrological interests could argue with the antiquarians that religion is not yet dead and that a study of its decline and fall is a valid enterprise. After all, the title *The Religious Situation* implies some sort of contemporary existence, even if it be in the anteroom of a morgue.

Novelist Mary McCarthy in a quotation from a *Life* interview in 1963 represents the posture of many intellectuals in her abrupt comment: "My belief is nobody believes in God any more except peasants and simple people; the others just pretend to" [12]. The implication is clear: the peasants and simple people are on the wane, and pretense should be dispelled: then the world will at last be cleared of Gods and believers. To such interpreters, religion belongs essentially to the world's past and remains as a survival. The spiritual capital of the cosmos is being rapidly expended. Now, at the last minute, there may be fascination in the study of the death throe of religion in its institutional and intellectual forms.

Comment on these throes comes from differing quarters. The religious revivalist has preached as if he believed that religion is now sounding its long diminuendo. Once upon a time there were good old days, when people lived up to their covenant. Now faithlessness and immorality characterize public and personal life. The evangelist's judgment of the world situation is tempered by a kind of hope for something better. If he wishes to stimulate conversions and be successful, he must offer this hope.

At the other end of the emotional spectrum, members of the academic community have lectured at times upon this (not fully documented) interpretation of history, treating religion as an element of past culture which retains a weakening residual position in today's world. Their judgment of the place of religion in the world is tempered by their investment in historical accuracy: they must somehow allow for the fact that in some areas and respects religion seems to be a growing force. But, overall, until recently the intellectual community leaned toward the necrological approach.

Such latter-day Comteans perceive any extant religions as survivals of superstition and magic, "an inferior prelude to philosophy," as the writer of one textbook put it. As recently as

1939, F.B. Burgess' *Introduction to Philosophy* equated religion with "superstition and imagination," while Harry Alpern in his *March of Philosophy* in 1933 discounted religion because some-day it would "be rendered useless, like the appendix" [8:83 f].

Those who do study the religious situation would be in an unscholarly position if they ruled out this necrological interpre-tation of history a priori, for evidence can be produced which tends to confirm it. Other students produce counterevidence to suggest that a title such as *The Secular Situation* does not exhaust the range of contemporary reality or of human possibility, that appraisal of *The Religious Situation* is timely and perhaps urgent.

THE CRITICAL CASE OF RELIGION IN EDUCATION

This volume and those which are planned to succeed it are being published at a time when the religious situation, in America at least, is changing dramatically. During the 1960s the United States is experiencing a fundamental relocation of much that goes under the name religion. While it is not yet possible to predict the full extent of this site-changing and while it would be foolish to predict how profound the alterations will be, one can point to significant features.

Religion played a role primarily in the formation of piety and morality in the American past; today it is more involved in the appraisal of life and in that circumstance it almost inevitably takes on a more intellectual cast. This change is most demon-strable in the case of public education.

Until the recent past, religion had had at least a vestigial part in the devotional and moral nurture of most public and private school children. Sheltered nurture is a relatively insignificant aspect of formal higher education; for that reason, ritual and devotional observances had virtually disappeared from public higher education and even from much private college and uni-versity life. In most cases, the students were ministered to through tangential and intrusive chaplaincies and ecclesiastical foundations. The professor, conscious of his responsibility to help students mature and to take a critical perspective on themselves and their childhood values, would often find himself mistrustful of devotional elements in higher education if these elements were retained to reinforce unreflective childhood religious attitudes. In the curriculum, religion was treated casually and accidentally at best, and gingerly or even polemically at worst.

The legal rationale for a change came with the Supreme Court rulings in *Engel* v. *Vitale* and *Abington School District* v. *Schempp* in 1962 and 1963. In the latter case the court completed its interpretation of the Constitution. Formal devotion and prayer were ruled out in the interest of "wholesome neutrality." The Court did not find, however, the interpretive and appraising role of religion to be out of place: "It might well be said that one's education is not complete without a study of comparative religion or the history of religion and its relationship to the advancement of civilization" [11].

Supreme Court decisions are only part of the story of America's educational revolution vis-à-vis religion. Hundreds of tax-supported colleges and universities have introduced or reintroduced extensive curricula in religious studies, and private and even denominational schools have undertaken new explorations of comparative religion. Some citizens are critical: Sectarians fear that teachings contrary to their private positions might undercut the faith of their own children; secularists fear that academicians might move beyond "wholesome neutrality" toward advocacy of creedal positions, in violation of "the separation of church and state." The trend, however, has been very strong. Not too many years ago John Dewey gave classical definition to the battlelines of religion and education when he spoke of the tension between theology or religion and "science": it was "essentially a conflict of claims to exercise social authority. It was not a conflict just between two sets of theoretical beliefs, but between two alignments of social forces — one which was old and had institutional power that it did not hesitate to use, and one which was new and striving and craving for recognition against gigantic odds" [25:359].

The transition may or may not be flattering to religious forces.

Failure of secularists to oppose the new intellectual appraisal of the part religion plays in culture may be a sign that "the old institutional power" is now impotent. It may, on the other hand, be a sign that science works less diligently to screen out religion from its appropriate places in interpretive schemes. Some of the more radical educators, and not a few students, suggest there has been a reversal of roles, agreeing with the late Canon Bernard Iddings Bell that "the place of the religionist . . . today is that of the scientist in the 17th and early 18th centuries; he vigorously protested against improper curtailment of experience."

Ernest Becker, who fuses the rationalist interests of the eighteenth century Enlightenment and the theological concerns of some twentieth century ontologists, has gone further.

> It is more than simply curtailment of experience, or rather it is more concrete than that. The scientist has always been willing to admit that religion gives experience, and that science may curtail it; he has usually held, with Freud, that this kind of experience is precisely fantasy experience, and should be curtailed in the interests of hard reality. On this ground there can be no fruitful argument.
>
> But what if . . . theology were to give us concrete data that social order is not possible, nor human freedom attainable, without a theological dimension to human experience? Religion has always enjoined man to realize his "almost hopeless condition." . . . What if theology were able to show us *specifically* the ways in which man's condition was hopeless, no matter what he tried to achieve in an atheistic society? And what if theology could show us further the ways in which this hopelessness could be turned to human advantage, to the realization of greater liberty, dignity, natural creativity? This is the ultimate challenge. . . . Theology has given us the most compelling rational grounds for including it as the superordinate dimension of human experience. In fact, it is only in this way that we can actually complete what the Enlightenment began, because it is only today that we can answer one of the questions that began the French Enlightenment itself: Bayle's famous hypothesis as to whether a society of atheists was possible. . . . [Further,] Is it a desirable ideal? . . . What does it do to man? [5:166 f]

Becker and other educators are now facing this "ultimate challenge," and their explorations have consequences for the whole of our culture.

The resituating of religion in the academic world is being matched in other institutions. During the religious revival of the 1950s, most metropolitan newspapers gave greater space than before to the *institutional* dimensions of religion but isolated their reportage on a special page in the Saturday edition; in the 1960s they devote attention to the *interpretive* as well as the institutional dimensions and are quite generous in their allotments of front page space. In political life devotional religion still thrives, but it has become complicated by the controversial role the denominations and ecumenical agencies play in racial demonstrations and agitation for specific legislative programs. In the free and open dialogue characteristic of "the ecumenical age" and in a time when various organizations have stimulated interfaith conversation in celebration and enhancement of pluralist society, the intellectual and controversial aspects of religion come to prominence in cocktail party conversations as they were not likely to earlier.

"THE RELIGIOUS SITUATION" OF OUR ANCESTORS

Both advocates and opponents of religion are well advised to study the religious situation, advocates the better to plan missionary strategies and opponents the better to defend themselves against the sometimes subtle influence of religion on the framework of a society.

There is a precedent for considering it useful to appraise the religious situation. This concept goes back at least as far as the period of the witch trials in Salem, Massachusetts. At that time, lay authorities relied on "spectral evidence," and leading ministers had to complain and petition Governor Phips. They had pointed to the "need of a very critical and Exquisite *Caution*, lest by too much *Credulity* for Things received only on the Devils Authority, there be a Door opened for a long Train of miserable Consequences" [29:42].

Study of the religious situation has been born of a free society's "need of a very critical and Exquisite *Caution*" just as such studies have long been read to forestall "long Trains of miserable Consequences." This is another way of saying that, in American society, people have always had to be very alert to the religious situation, and they have always had varied motivations for their pursuit of understanding. Some have studied it for the sake of entertainment; others, for evangelistic purposes. Some have done it in order to learn about "the opposition" and others in the interest of ultimate "world integration" on a religious base. A very brief historical survey of such studies will set our present approach in a comparative context.

In the New World, foreign visitors and natives alike have tended to be reportorial in their regard for religion. They have measured, counted, assessed, projected, and reminisced about the varieties of religious responses. In part this mood may be associated with the reputed antimetaphysical and propragmatic bent of American religionists. The environment itself, however, has often been interpreted as somehow revelatory and redemptive, to the extent that one could recognize divine purpose in it without resort to theological speculation. More practical motives than these, however, have been consistently evident.

The original colonists came with at least two religious purposes in view: first, they wished to keep intact their own communities; second, in most instances they hoped to convert the Indians. The Indian provided them with the first opportunity to confront the science of comparative religion, the living presence of nonchristian and primitive traditions which had not been familiar to them in Europe. Early accounts were full of such assessments of the situation, always with practical purposes in view: "[I go] to investigate first the condition of that land, and then to enter upon the work of conversion . . . ," wrote Gabriel Diaz Vara Calderón, bishop of Cuba, on August 14, 1674, concerning Florida in an announcement which is typical of thousands of documents [32:23]. Many of the reasons were more urgent, when the practical purpose of the study of the religion of "the salvages" was to ensure survival itself.

So far as their own religious life was concerned, the colonists were no less devoted to analysis. Where theocracies prevailed, as in New England and, in a more relaxed way, in Virginia, the oligarchs had to assess the religious situation in order to manipulate order and cohesion in the colonies and to satisfy their belief that every man in his actions was responsible to and judged by a Divine Being. The records of New England synods and consociations of ministers are full of such appraisals. Dissenters against the theocratic societies had their own urgent reasons to keep their eyes open in regard to the religious situation.

By the time of the Great Awakening of the 1730s and 1740s, the beginnings of an intercolonial awareness were present. These were coupled with a strong sense of developing American destiny, a sense which encouraged obsession with the local scene as a theater for God's purposes. The greatest of the awakeners, Jonathan Edwards, announced,

> The latter-day glory is probably to begin in America. It is probable that will come to pass in spirituals, which has taken place in temporals, with respect to America; that whereas, till of late, the world was supplied with its silver, and gold, and earthly treasures from the old continent, now it is supplied chiefly from the new; so the course of things in spiritual respects will be in like manner turned [10:381 ff].

Edwards saw no purpose in antiquarianism and no occasion to chronicle religious decline and fall in such a time and place. Remembered as a metaphysician, he could also write a *History of Redemption* which culminated in New England and could patiently chronicle religious change in *A Faithful Narrative of the Surprising Work of God in the Conversion of Many Hundred Souls in Northampton, and the Neighboring Towns and Villages of the County of Hampshire, in the Province of the Massachusetts-Bay in New-England.*

By the end of the colonial period, another assessor of the religious scene was on hand: the Enlightened scholar, statesman, or salonist after the fashion of Benjamin Franklin or Thomas Jefferson. The "republican religionists" carried their tireless interest in enumeration into the religious realm; they kept a record of revivals, of sects, of legal situations, partly because everything in their environment seemed to deserve a reckoning and partly because they believed an imminent quasireligious philosophy and social pattern would help men transcend particularist follies. Among them was Ezra Stiles, who went through a "Deistical Turn" but remained Christian. He embraced Jews and Catholics, past and present, after he studied the religious situation; but this study did not mean that he discounted what he cherished most, the New England modes represented by Yale College:

> From the cursory View I made of Ecclesiastical History, I thot all the protestant Churches as well as all the Xtian Churches since the first Age, had many Usages and Doctrines which I did not find in the Bible — yet I found sincere good men in all Churches catholic and protestant. Hence I adopted and professed an extensive and universal Charity: I readily saw the Mode of Worship in the New England Churches was as conformable to the Bible as any in the World, and I thot more so [22:72].

President Stiles also learned how to approach the study of history and reporting most effectively, and his lesson still speaks to students of the religious situation:

> Fidelity in narrating *Facts* is a great and principal thing: but then only is this species of writing perfect, when besides a well digested series of authenticated Transactions and Events, the motives and *Springs of Action* are fairly laid open and arise into view with all their Effects about them, when characters are made to live again, and past scenes are endowed with a kind of perpetual Resurrection in History [22:146].

The comparative study of religion, soundly based in historical understanding, was well under way! By 1784 Hannah Adams of Boston had produced a *Dictionary of All Religions and Religious Denominations, Ancient and Modern* . . . .

Assessing the religious climate of the National period depended most of all upon the evangelist and revivalist, who, during the first half of the nineteenth century, received the call (or seized the initiative) for churching America. Much of our accounting of the religious scene on the frontier and in the new urban America derives from the chronicles of revivalists. Historians have learned to discount the extremes in such reports. The revivalist found it useful to exaggerate the bad local state of religion and to indulge in hyperbole as he spoke of the successes he had known under the Spirit. A generation in which men learned to live with the separation of church and state, religious voluntaryism, competition between denominations, and conflicting claims of entrepreneurial evangelists was a time when less scientific but even more numerous and dramatic assessments were forthcoming.

The immigrant presented a complicating feature in an environment which had been almost exclusively Protestant. The religious situation from the 1840s to the present has involved the destiny of masses of Roman Catholic and later of Jewish or Eastern Orthodox newcomers. In a climate of nativism and ethnocentrism, Protestant America produced scores of ambitious chronicles of the religious scene from Robert Baird's work *Religion in America* in the 1840s through Daniel Dorchester's *Christianity in the United States* (1888). As guests in the Protestant host culture, the inhabitants of religious ghettoes were not well equipped to generate formal studies, but for their own survival's sake they did have to produce primitive accounts of the religious situation, too.

The historical dimension which had been present in Stiles' writings waned in the nineteenth century, and studies of the religious situation had an almost exclusively contemporary orientation. John Williamson Nevin complained in 1849 that the sects were involved in

> a protest against the authority of all previous history, except so far as it may seem to agree with what is thus found to be true; in which case, of course, the only real measure of truth is taken to be, not this authority of history at all, but the mind, simply, of the particular sect itself. . . . A genuine sect will not suffer itself to be embarrassed for a moment, either at its

XXXI

start or afterwards, by the consideration that it has no proper root in past history. Its ambition is rather to appear in this respect *autochthonic*, aboriginal, self-sprung from the Bible, or through the Bible from the skies [24:499 ff].

The spirit of "now" in American religion did not militate against the spirit of "there": even while evangelists were busy churching America, the religious denominations were describing the pagan world with the practical purpose in mind of engaging in missionary work. In the middle decades of the century, several missionary-oriented works on the comparative religious situation were produced with titles like this one published by Oliver D. Cooke and Sons of Hartford: *All Religions and Religious Ceremonies: In Two Parts. Part I. Christianity — Mohometanism, and Judaism. To Which is Added a Tabular Appendix by Thomas Williams Exhibiting the Present State of the World as to Religion — Population — Religious Toleration — Government &c. Part II. A View of the History — Religion — Manners and Customs of the Hindoos by William Ward. Together with the Religion and Ceremonies of Other Pagan Nations.* No frivolous study, it concluded with a long section on "American Benevolent Institutions." This study of the religious situation was designed as a training document for missionizing in Mohometan and Hindoo cultures.

During the first half of the nineteenth century, religious Americans infrequently engaged in intellectual activity for its own sake, and the antiintellectualism of the evangelicals (thanks to the work of Richard Hofstadter among others) has become proverbial. It was in the latter half of the century that a more academic study of religion came into play; it required the prerequisites of the secularization of American colleges and the development of universities with graduate schools on the German model. Yet there was also popular American interest in the world religious scene, as evidenced by the success of the World's Parliament of Religions, which convened in Chicago at the time of the Columbian Exposition in 1893. Oriental and Occidental, creedal and free religionist, cardinal and swami — all shared the platform in an event which was given wide publicity. The Parliament was a harbinger of the day when the religious situation would be studied with the goal of promoting tolerance, brotherhood, and world integration.

During the rise of the sociology of religion as an intellectual discipline and at a time when the scientific study of religion was developing in Europe ("from Max Müller to Rudolf Otto"), American universities, for numbers of reasons, some of them already cited or implied, began to neglect situational studies of religion. Only recently has a reversal begun to occur. We have tried to demonstrate, however, that Americans have always had good reasons to be situation-conscious in the study of religion and that today they are picking up something of that tradition not only in the popular press but also in academic and intellectual circles.

Something of all the older motivations for study may remain in pluralistic America: sectarian aggression, agnostic self-defense, evangelism, ethnocentrism, and love of learning for its own sake may all be present. Even the nonreligious are finding it important to be intellectually equipped to face religious claims; few of them could be characterized in the way that Samuel Johnson spoke of Samuel Foote, an actor of his time: "I do not know, Sir, that the fellow is an infidel; but if he be an infidel, he is an infidel as a dog is an infidel; that is to say, he has never thought upon the subject" [6:95].

With such new academic resources and encouragement for intellectual appraisal of religion today, the religionist is less likely to perceive the dilemma stated by Sidney Mead: "Americans have in effect been given the hard choice between being intelligent according to the standards prevailing in their intellectual centers, and being religious according to the standards prevailing in their denominations" [19:314]. Not long ago historian Roland Bainton could write, "A Fundamentalist can take a doctor's degree in a liberal institution by being open to every fact and impervious to every idea" [4:48]; but the character of the new studies, at once intellectual and existential, makes it more difficult now than in the positivist period for students to avoid the implications of religious ideas.

My words in praise of the quality and pervasiveness of the new intellectual study of the religious situation may seem to be a diversion in every sense, a sort of verbal sleight of hand to distract readers from a point of business raised earlier. To suggest that the new study is in an honoured tradition, that it must be seen in a meaningful and practical continuity, is a misleading direction if the tradition and the continuity are themselves exhausted and at an end. If they are, then we are forced back to the perspective of the antiquarians or are forced to see the new study as being itself autochthonic. We must take a hard look at the occasions which call a study of the religious situation into question.

SIGNS OF THE END OF THE RELIGIOUS SITUATION

Many data point to the end, at last, of the human "religious situation." The most dramatic are those which have pointed to the development of a new stage of society and a new kind of man in the industrialized and affluent West. In more conventional terms, one finds evidence of an increase of unbelief and of reflective and unreflective godlessness.

Mircea Eliade, who possesses admirable credentials for seeking and finding religiousness in all quarters, has written that "modern man's originality, his newness in comparison with traditional societies, lies precisely in his wish to live in a basically desacralized cosmos" [1:267]. Roman Catholic Father John Courtney Murray enlarges: "One would have to say that the modern godless man is characterized by his will to understand and explain the world without God" [23:19]. This "godless man who is typical of the postmodern era is . . . [without] prototype in history; he is a new phenomenon" [23:21]. Father M. D. Chenu sees the godless man in the plural: the atheization of the world has "touched not only individuals but even the very structures of the new humanity" [9:12]. And Father A.M. Henry, a missionary expert, writes, "There is [a] prodigious increase of unbelief in the world . . ." [13: chap 1].

The choice of religionists, and especially of Roman Catholic scholars and missiologists, to testify on the spread of unbelief as an overt aspect of secularization may seem like a distortion of the case, and it should be qualified. Such analysts may be trying to pierce the masks a transitional society wears by attempting to ascertain whether unreflective religion serves as an ideological gloss to cover profound change. Thus, when people respond to those who take opinion polls, they may include generally positive comment on the role of religion in their lives. Theologically oriented observers of this process may, from some normative point of view or other, be charging respondents, in effect, "But you do not *really* believe that, or there would be different consequences in your lives."

We should balance these theologians' views on the end of the religious situation with those of historians or sociologists who prefer to say that world culture is undergoing one of its periodic upheavals and that public atheism is at the moment surfacing as it has in the past in similar periods. A theologian who shares this view is Herbert W. Richardson in *Toward an American Theology*. Richardson is not, however, devoted to a merely cyclical view of recurrences in history: "I do not deny that the atheism of the modern world is significantly different from manifestations of public atheism in the past; but it is not different in the fact that it is either atheism or public" [26:3 f]. Whether "public atheism" is a wholly new phenomenon or merely a quantitatively greater change within the pattern of earlier precedent, those who would help shape cultural destiny must reckon with modern unbelief, atheism, or secularism.

Second, in many portions of the world there has been a decline of inherited religious institutions. In some places this decline has been occasioned in part by suppression or discouragement on the part of political powers, some of them capable of supplanting historic churches with quasireligious political alternatives. Thus what Jules Monnerot called "the twentieth century Islam," Communism, has often contributed to the decline of Christian institutions. Based on a recent nation-by-nation survey, Kurt Hutten [16] gives much statistical evidence of such a decline.

A fairer picture can be gained from study of the Western world, where there has been less civil discouragement of institutional religious life. From a peak in about 1880 down to the present, for example, the churches in Great Britain have seen a general decline in membership, attendance, communions made, and voluntary contributions [3:23–28]. While almost all Scandinavians are nominal church members, a very small percentage of the population participates regularly in the institutional life of the churches; attendance and support of the Roman Catholic Church in France has been so low that Catholic missiologists have come to speak of it as a pagan nation in need of a fresh missionary intrusion.

Those who assess the religious situation of Canada in her centennial year have consistently remarked on signs of decline. The United States seems to be the grand exception. Down into the 1960s most graphs charting membership, attendance, and contributions indicated upward trends. During the 1960s, while the upward trends have been arrested, there has been more stability, and decline has been gradual rather than giving evidence of any sharp drops in participation. Much easily accessible useful information is contained in a section on "Facts, Figures and Opinions on Religion in the United States" in Leo Rosten, *Religions in America* [28:220–327]. In many parts of the West, much of inherited religious institutional strength has been associated with rural life, with the career of the preemancipated woman, in village and town patterns; these are being doomed by forms of urban life where organized religion has chronically been frustrated.

In addition to the spread of "godlessness" and the decline of inherited institutions, there has been the replacement of historic religions with quasireligions, which sometimes do and sometimes do not deserve to be studied under the category of "the religious situation." Here we think of modern integralist ideologies, especially when these are allied to political movements: doctrinaire Communism, Nazism, and Fascism, the religious thrusts of the American Radical Right or — on other scales — the new priesthoods of science or the cult of success. How these ideologies and quasireligions are to be regarded will vary according to the definitions of religion employed by separate critics. But because of their drama and potency they tend to displace some of the historic religions from the center of studies about the religious situation.

DISCERNING THE FUTURE

Students of the religious situation are skilled to see institutional change but they are also trained not to let this most obvious dimension of religious life exhaust the definition of religion in the modern world. The accent in any contemporary study has to be on a discerning reportage. The great philosophical temptation of students of the religious situation is to deal with the future as if it had already occurred. "We, however, shall start out from the one point accessible to us, the one eternal center of all things — man, suffering, striving, doing, as he is and was and ever shall be. Hence our study will, in a certain sense, be pathological in kind." With these words Jacob Burckhardt tried to ward off the substantive philosopher of history from study of the cultural situation [7:63].

Not that the philosopher of history is unwelcome in religious studies; rather his work must clearly be labeled for what it is. It is a kind of prophecy. If he deals with "the end of the religious era" while there is still manifestly much formal religion of every kind on hand, he is really dealing with the whole of history as if he knows its outcome, as if he has had imparted to him the secret of the future. He may be correct, and his insight may be helpful. But what he contributes can be quickly recognized for what it is: a calculated guess. The religious situation implies present mindedness, informed by a study of the past and now and then inspired by a bet on the future.

No doubt some vision of the future is involved in the often unrecognized philosophical baggage of most historians, sociologists, and analysts. When they speak of the "survival" of religious institutions or the "ascendancy" of the secular spirit, they may be tipping their hands concerning historical tendencies in ways they cannot in every case empirically demonstrate. Yet this prophetic element often serves them well for it motivates study, helps them make their way through the empirical maze toward the potentially significant, and adds color to their interpretations.

I have introduced these notes to illumine the task of contributors to these volumes. They will be engaged, consciously or unconsciously, in debate about the human future. Some of them will provide definitions of religion so inclusive and sweeping that men now and in the future cannot be exempted from involvement with them. Others will use narrower and more static institutional definitions. Some of them will be confident that, on the basis of present trends, they can predict that the human future will be secular or religious in a particular way, while others will be more nearly agnostic, content to be in suspense as each new chapter of the human story unfolds.

Readers will surely recognize the implications for the present time when a writer uses some moment from the past to describe what is normative in his definition of religion. The "myth of a golden age" when men were religious in a particular way persists not only in folk piety which looks back to an "age of faith" but also in sophisticated intellectual circles where a static definition of the religious past makes it possible for contemporary critics to rule out whatever goes on today as accommodation or secularization, not as development or religious change. Professor William Hamilton has complained of this tendency, christening it "the Walter Kaufmann syndrome," after Professor Kaufmann of Princeton, and claiming that "many secular modern men like their theological foes to be as orthodox as possible so they can be rejected as irrelevant" [2:6].

Similarly, readers will not easily be misled when analysts of the contemporary religious situation "jump tenses" on them and deal knowingly with the outcome of the human story, overconfident that the present stage of culture is normative and ultimate. Professor Harry Alpern [8:83 f] was guilty of that (see above) when he "knew" that religion would be "rendered useless, like the appendix." A third of a century later, the empirical findings do not yet bear out his prophecy. They will be suspicious of Western theologians who regard "secular man" or "secular society" as the final outcome of the human story; such a judgment is not sufficiently relativistic. "There is . . . one error which we must not impute to the philosophers alone, namely, that our time is the consummation of all time, or very nearly so, that the whole past may be regarded as fulfilled in us . . ." [7:63].

The stresses placed on students of the religious situation are enormous. But contribution to the collective appraisal of the situation does not mean that students must be clear concerning the role of religion in their personal lives. One of the greatest students of situational religion, Max Weber, wrote, "I am . . . absolutely unmusical in religious matters, and I feel neither the need nor the capacity to raise up in myself any sort of spiritual edifices of a religious character. Yet after careful self-examination I find myself neither anti-religious *nor irreligious*" [15:315]. It does mean that they dare not let elements of personal faith, personal predilection, or unexamined philosophy of history cause them to overlook secular *or* religious elements wherever these are present today.

THE MASS OF DATA

When an investigator begins from this point of view, he is astonished at the amount of data which is available. One of the tasks of experts is to help laymen sort out and render into comprehensive and even symbolic form the ill-organized and even apparently contradictory data that are perceived. As primitives, we are best equipped to approach religion with the technique which Claude Lévi-Strauss calls "bricolage." The French term comes from ball games, billiards, hunting, shooting, and riding: it refers to extraneous movements, to balls rebounding or horses swerving. But today "bricolage" is equivalent to the English "odd jobs man" who uses a heterogeneous reportoire to accomplish his task.

Not all people have occasion or time to acquire specific tools and blueprints for the task of assessing the religious situation. Yet in informal ways the situation itself confronts them constantly. Failure to organize the perceptions or the data can be problematic to the person. The newspaper serves to organize them for many.

> Motivation research undertaken for a leading American newspaper, *The Detroit Free Press*, suggested that people feel lost and anxious without a newspaper because, otherwise, they would not know what is going on in the world and, fearing the worst, they are reassured to read each day that everything is well [33:147].

But does the newspaper serve well on a matter such as religion? As religious data reach us in haphazard and random ways, can the public — religious or secular in outlook — organize the stories and effects into a coherent pattern of meaning?

Look at the flow of news in the papers in "the secular sixties." The ecumenical movement of Christians has been on the front page throughout the years of the Second Vatican Council. Is ecumenism a "great leap forward" on the part of religious communities, or does it represent a last grouping of these communities before they come to quiet death by attrition in a secular world?

During the 1960s, issues of church and state have been prominent. While four fifths of the public criticized the Supreme Court for its school prayer decisions, the religious establishments largely supported the Court, and the front pages made this clear. Why did they take this stand?

Much of the news concerning the racial revolution in this decade has been specifically religious in its orientation. "Reverends" and rabbis and nuns have led the demonstrations while denominations have worked for racial change. Do these activities represent religious initiative or accommodation, pace-setting or late hitch-hiking? Is the ethical interest a diversion from the problems of theological meaninglessness which are said to afflict the churches? Theology makes the front pages when seminary professors announce "the death of God."

XL

"What sense does that make?" asks a public which has been trained to think of seminarians as custodians, not as destroyers, of their traditions.

On the world scene, the flow of news has been no less regular or intense. India and Pakistan have been constantly on the verge of holy war over issues raised by Hindu and Muslim populations; the war in Vietnam has religious overtones, as does the Arab-Israeli conflict. Why have Buddhist monks immolated themselves? Or, for that matter, why do Quakers and members of a Catholic workers' movement resist the draft in America? What would have been the effect on the stock market of a change in papal teaching on birth control? How much would a change in tax-exemption laws of the churches benefit the general public?

Any or all of these questions could become self-conscious questions through the reading of any *New York Times* or any *Newsweek*. University curricula and public libraries contain interpretive resources for all the other sections of these journals (business, foreign affairs, medicine, the arts, and even athletics). Only in the field of religion has there been a dearth of interpretive materials for classroom or libraries. *The Religious Situation* is conceived as a contribution to making up for the lack.

TILLICH'S "RELIGIOUS SITUATION"

The title *The Religious Situation* recalls the title of the English translation of Paul Tillich's *Die religiöse Lage der Gegenwart*, but it was not consciously styled to perpetuate Tillich's ideas on either "situation" or "religion." Whether or not the borrowing was conscious on the publisher's part makes no difference: in either case a certain flattery is implied. A decent respect for the provenance of the term suggests that some notice be paid to it and, indirectly, to its author. Tillich wrote:

> A book on the religious situation of the present must deal with the whole contemporary world, for there is nothing that is not in some way the expression of the religious situation. But it is impossible for any one to write about all contempo-

rary things; we can make serious and worth-while statements about things only in so far as we have had vital contact with them. . . .

Not only the choice of material but also the position from which it is judged depend ultimately upon a personal decision [35:25 f].

The personal element goes into all analysis; in the case of Tillich, all was filtered through the mind of one person of genius; in the case of this annual, a number of editors, consultants, and spokesmen will deal with a wide range of topics from various points of view. They all grapple with the meaning of the term "religious situation." Tillich continued:

Religion deals with a relation of man to the eternal. But a relation has two sides; hence two answers can be given as we take the point of view either of the temporal or of the eternal. The first answer, which proceeds from the temporal and human, will speak of tendencies in specifically religious affairs, of churches, sects, theologies and all sorts of accompanying religious movements. Doubtless these things must be considered if the religious situation of a period is to be understood. But the questionable element in this procedure is that attention is given to just those things with which religion itself is not concerned, to the stream of events hastening out of the past into the future, while the real meaning and content of that stream, the eternal to which all things refer, is neglected. If the question be reversed so that one begins with the other side of religion, with the eternal and divine, it gains a far more comprehensive and fundamental significance. It has now become a question about the situation of a period in all its relations and phenomena, about its essential meaning, about the eternal which is present in a time [35:36 ff].

This brief passage illustrates a point we have been trying to establish: that all definition and discussion of the religious situation will involve the exposure of editors' and authors' controlling assumptions about the meaning of religion. In this case, Tillich's familiar philosophical undergirding is apparent, even though the words were written almost four decades ago. His words stand as a judgment on those who feel that by being reportorial, analytic, and "pathological" they have exhausted discussion of the religious situation. But his later words about beginning "with the other side of religion, with the eternal and divine" involve many of our contemporaries in great difficulty, for they do not share the assumption that they can speak meaningfully concerning "the eternal and divine" without claiming a special mystical or revelatory experience. Tillich's first word is a caution against trivialization; his second word represents to many an impossible ideal — indeed, to many it is not even an ideal worthy of aspiration. Even the attempt, then, to define the title of this book involves people in controversy.

Before we discuss the controversial dimensions of the adjective "religious" we can turn briefly to the noun "situation." Tillich stresses the apparently static aspect: "The term *situation* seems to mean something which is established, at rest and constant, a basic fact which lies at a deeper level than do all the visible tendencies, something which is invisible to those who live within it but which is, for that reason, all the more effective" [35:39 f]. The *Oxford English Dictionary* stresses this element: "The place, position, or location *of*. . . . The place occupied by something. . . . Place or position of things in relation to surroundings or to each other. . . . A place or locality in which a person resides, or happens to be for the time."

In a pluralistic society, however, people will be conscious of another aspect in this ambiguous term. Situation implies relationship, and "the religious situation," discussed by a variety of writers on a variety of subjects in a sequence of years, will inevitably be devoted to flux, change, and apparent relativity. *The Religious Situation* would not be conceived as an annual volume if it were felt that people could once and for all locate "the place, position, or location of religion." This premise is not acceptable to all. The mystic does not admit contingency in his experience; many representatives of Eastern religion would stress the timeless and hence situationless character of their vision; Protestant, Orthodox, and Catholic "fundamentalists" may stress the classical and finished character of their revelation and dogma. Each of these would legitimately find expression in a volume such as this while the reader makes his or her decision concerning their claims. For many readers the "sheer happenedness"

(Baron von Hügel) of Christianity can be carried over to all religion: happenedness locates and situates religion in time, in flux, in change.

While the definition of "situation" may be a threat to a few, the claims associated with the term "religion" will be a problem for all. In this introductory chapter I have made no effort at definition. Again and again in this chapter reference has been made to the visible organized institutions which call themselves religious. Concerning this usage there would be no controversy. At other times what Thomas Luckmann has called "the sacred cosmos" has come into view: this refers to the religious or quasireligious interpretive scheme which evokes symbols. Even here many could agree about the term. Beyond this would be the all-encompassing world view of a person or an era. Paul Tillich referred to a world view as religion if man or men were related to it in an unconditioned, ultimate fashion. People more expert than I on this subject will be devoting attention to this problem, and cursory treatment would be entirely unsatisfactory here.

To the cynic, everyone does what he wishes with the term. "Magic or religion: it is all one. Theologians themselves dispose of the matter by calling everything they do an act of religion . . ." [35:26]. Others besides cynics share a sense of dis-ease and disturbance. For the time being, we shall settle for the suggestion that the definition must be kept open; that it will develop and emerge in each author's usage and from year to year. Definitions will ordinarily steer between two extremes. On the one hand, they do a disservice if they overlook anything which might illumine the religious situation; on the other, they threaten the term with meaninglessness if they use it to blanket all serious dimensions of life, allowing no one and nothing an escape from "religion." The reportorial contributors can content themselves with functional definitions; the more theoretical cannot evade the philosophical problems of definition. Their discussions will manifest an important element of the religious situation!

In this introduction I have determined to be as modest as possible concerning the claims for such a study as this. It may be that the problems of pluralism and the controversial element in religion in a time of transition have been overstressed. True, many chroniclers will content themselves with noticing that

> Each torpid turn of the world has such disinherited children,
> to whom no longer what's been, and not yet what's coming,
>   belongs [27: title page].

If their pictures of reality between religious and secular epochs and spaces are accurate, they have served their readers well.

Others will seek another possibility: it may be that analysis of the religious situation, by locating problems and possibilities in the symbolic and "ultimate" realm, can contribute to understanding in a divided world. These people stand in a long tradition and share an honorable hope, a hope expressed a decade ago in Tokyo by Dr. Friedrich Heiler at the Ninth International Congress for the History of Religions. He said that it was "one of the finest hopes of the scientific study of religion" that it might contribute toward new religious tolerance and cooperation and thereby to "the realization of humanity and world peace" [30:25]. Were *The Religious Situation* to make even a modest contribution toward such a fulfillment, this would be a bonus welcomed by both editors and readers.

REFERENCES

1. Altizer, Thomas J J: Mircea Eliade and the Recovery of the Sacred, *Christian Scholar*, vol 45, no 4, Winter 1962.

2. Altizer, Thomas J J, and Hamilton, William: *Radical Theology and the Death of God* (The Bobbs-Merrill Co, Inc, Indianapolis, Indiana) 1966.

3. Argyle, Michael: *Religious Behaviour* (The Free Press, formerly of Glencoe, Illinois, now of New York, New York) 1961.

4. Bainton, Roland: The Making of a Pluralistic Society — A Protestant View, in Walter, Erich A, ed: *Religion and the State University* (University of Michigan Press, Ann Arbor, Michigan) 1958.

5. Becker, Ernest: *Beyond Alienation: A Philosophy of Educa-*

tion for the Crisis of Democracy (George Braziller, Inc, New York, New York) 1967.

6. Boswell, James: *Life of Johnson*, vol 2.

7. Burckhardt, Jacob: in Nichols, James Hastings, ed: *Force and Freedom* (Meridian Books, The World Publishing Company, Cleveland, Ohio) 1955.

8. Butler, Richard, O.P.: *God on the Secular Campus* (Doubleday & Company, Inc, Garden City, New York) 1963.

9. Chenu, Fr M D: *Cross Currents*, vol 11, no 1, Winter 1961.

10. Edwards, Jonathan: *Thoughts on Revival* in his *Works*, vol 1.

11. Frommer, Arthur, ed: *The Bible and the Public Schools* (Liberal Press, New York, New York) 1963. This book reprints the two court decisions in their entirety.

12. Grumbach, Doris: *The Company She Kept* (Coward-McCann, Inc, New York, New York) 1967.

13. Henry, Fr A M: *A Mission Theology*, Albert J La Mothe, Jr, translator (Fides Publishers, Inc, Notre Dame, Indiana) 1962.

14. Hildebrand, Dietrich von: *The Trojan Horse in the City of God* (Franciscan Herald Press, Chicago, Illinois) 1967.

15. Hughes, H Stuart: passage on "suspended judgment in spiritual matters" in *Consciousness and Society* (Alfred A Knopf, Inc, New York, New York) 1961.

16. Hutten, Kurt: *Iron Curtain Christians* (Augsburg Publishing House, Minneapolis, Minnesota) 1967.

17. Kaul, Manohar: *Modern Trends in Indian Painting* (Dhoomimal Ramchand, New Delhi, India) 1961.

18. Leeuwen, Arend Th van: *Christianity in World History* (Charles Scribner's Sons, New York, New York) 1964.

19. Mead, Sidney: Denominationalism: The Shape of Protestantism in America, *Church History*, vol 23, Dec 1954.

20. Meland, Bernard: *The Secularization of Modern Cultures* (Oxford University Press, Inc, New York, New York) 1966.

21. Mencken, H L: *Treatise on the Gods* (Alfred A Knopf, Inc, New York, New York) 1963.

22. Morgan, Edmund S: *The Gentle Puritan: A Life of Ezra*

Stiles, 1727–1795 (Yale University Press, New Haven, Connecticut) 1962.

23. Murray, Fr John Courtney: The Structure of the Problem of God, *Theological Studies*, vol 23, no 1, March 1962.

24. Nevin, Williamson: The Sect System, *Mercersburg Review*, vol 1, Sept 1849.

25. Ratner, Joseph, ed: *Intelligence in the Modern World: John Dewey's Philosophy* (The Modern Library, division of Random House, Inc, New York, New York) 1939.

26. Richardson, Herbert W: *Toward an American Theology* (Harper & Row, Publishers, New York, New York) 1967.

27. Rilke, Rainer Maria von: in Heller, Erich: *The Disinherited Mind* (Meridian Books, The World Publishing Company, Cleveland, Ohio) 1959.

28. Rosten, Leo: Facts, Figures and Opinions on Religion in the United States, in *Religions in America* (Simon and Schuster, Inc, New York, New York) 1963.

29. Shipton, Clifford K: The New England Clergy of the "Glacial Age," *Colonial Society of Massachusetts Publications* (Boston, Massachusetts) vol 32, 1937.

30. Slater, Robert Lawson: *World Religions and World Community* (Columbia University Press, New York, New York) 1963.

31. Smith, Donald Eugene: *India as a Secular State* (Princeton University Press, Princeton, New Jersey) 1963.

32. Smith, H Shelton; Handy, Robert T; Loetscher, Lefferts A: *American Christianity: An Historical Interpretation with Representative Documents* (Charles Scribner's Sons, New York, New York) 1960, vol 1.

33. Stephenson, William: *The Play Theory of Mass Communication* (The University of Chicago Press, Chicago, Illinois) 1967.

34. Symposium: *Contemporary Indian Literature* (Sahitya Akademi, New Delhi, India) 1957.

35. Tillich, Paul: *The Religious Situation*, H Richard Niebuhr, translator (Meridian Books, The World Publishing Company, Cleveland, Ohio) 1956.

The Experience and Expression of Religion

1. THE RELIGION OF BLACK POWER

by Vincent Harding

FOR SCHOLARS and ordinary citizens standing near the edges of the latest stage of America's perennial racial crisis, certain conclusions are easy to come by, especially when they are formed against the glare of burning buildings, the staccato reports of weapons, and a certain malaise verging on fear. To the observers who are at all concerned with what might be called religious phenomena, there is an especially deceptive set of circumstances and deductions surrounding the newest expression of Black Power as a force within the ancient struggle. For if movements are judged primarily by their public rhetoric and other obvious manifestations, it seems abrasively apparent that the time of singing, of preaching, and of nonviolent concern for the redemption of American society is rapidly passing, if not gone. More black love for whites evidently burns in every ghetto-shaped inferno. By certain standards, the religious elements of the struggle are to be studied only as historical manifestations from a recent and lamented past.

Such an interpretation of the present black moment is encouraged by the words of an anonymous spokesman for the current mood: "Man, the people are too busy getting ready to fight to bother with singing any more." When a song does burst forth it often proclaims,

> Too much love,
> Too much love,
> Nothing kills a nigger like
> Too much love [13:25].

Even in the presence of such compelling testimony against the adequacy of the older, more comforting religious symbols, rituals, and words, it would be myopic to miss the central issues of

3

human life and destiny which course through the current expression of blackness. Issues of anthropology, incarnation, the nature of the universe and of God, issues of hope and faith, questions of eschatology and of the nature of the Kingdom, problems concerning love and its functions — all these and more are at stake in the present situation. That they are usually disguised, often submerged, and sometimes denied does not lessen the power of their reality. Indeed the inherent power of the issues may be heightened by such camouflaging pressures. (One may even conjecture that the current black mood is in surprising harmony with much of the American trend towards a secular religion or a religionless church which, though it often overreacts to older explicit orthodox formulations, is shaped unmistakably by the life of the streets.)

BLACK POWER AND THE NEW MAN

In spite of the tendency among Black Power advocates to repress any reference to the earlier Afro-American religious expressions — especially as they were found in the nonviolent movement — the most familiar word from the past remains available to set the stage for an exploration of the religious implications of the current themes. At a forum on Black Power in Atlanta during the fall of 1966, while discussing "love," a spokesman for Black Power was heard to say, "Martin King was trying to get us to love white folks before we learned to love ourselves, and that ain't no good."

When there is serious reflection upon these words, a meaningful examination of the religious elements of Black Power may properly begin, for here is an issue which, if not the heart of the affair, is certainly very near the center of things. In spite of some public images to the contrary, it is likely that no element is so constant in the gospel of Blackness — at least as it is encountered in its native communities — as the necessity of self-love. One writer tells much that is crucial to the story when she refers to

4

"the inner power that comes with self-esteem, the power to develop to full stature as human beings" [4:29].

Healthy self-esteem has been seen in many traditions as a prerequisite to the establishment of community — whether with a spouse, a society, or a God. It has most often been the bedrock of love. It is surely this that comes through in the teaching of Jesus to love the neighbor as oneself. Black Power is a calling for black self-love, but it is not an unambiguous summons. Its clearest implications on this level are suggested by John Oliver Killens, one of the major literary spokesmen for the movement, when he writes,

> [Black Power] does not teach hatred; it teaches love. But it teaches us that love, like charity, must begin at home; that it must begin with ourselves, our beautiful black selves [11:36].

Stokely Carmichael has put this love in the context of the building of a black society "in which the spirit of community and humanistic love prevail" [2:8]. So in spite of "too much love" and in spite of the fact that Carmichael also admitted that the word was "suspect," no writer in the newest black stage fails to refer to a need for this love among black people.

Such an emphasis grows partly out of historical necessity, for all who make it are actively aware of the crushing psychological effects American life has had on the self-image of black men and women. However it may also rise out of an intuitive recognition that a call to love cuts across the deepest grain of man's being when it is addressed to an individual who is without some clear ground of self-respect.

It is precisely at this point that the ambiguity of the new black love becomes most evident, especially as it is exemplified in the writing of Killens. In the essay cited above he goes on to say that the love taught by Black Power is

> so powerful that it will settle for nothing short of love in return. Therefore, it does not advocate unrequited love, which is a sick bit under any guise or circumstance. Most black folk have no need to love those who would spit on them or practice

genocide against them. . . . Profound love can only exist between equals [11].

Killens' point of view represents much of the thinking on this subject in Black Power circles, and it is obviously a retort to what is understood to be nonviolence and to what is thought to be the teaching of Christian churches, especially black ones. However, it may be an overreaction, for, while one is eminently wise to realize that love flows out of self-esteem, one may be less than wise in demanding a predetermined response to black love. In a sense this is an interesting variation on one of the basic pitfalls of the rhetoric of nonviolence. For while the nonviolent movement promised that black love would bring predictable, favorable white responses, Killens says that, unless whites respond as they ought, love will stop. Much of the world's religion teaches that love demands nothing more than the freedom of the other to respond. Perhaps it takes the strongest love of all to continue in the path while realizing that such freedom can never be coerced.

Perhaps, however, it is even more pertinent to note that Killens speaks of love and hate as being totally irrelevant until black and white men are equals. This is the even stronger frame of mind in the ghettos today. Love for Black Power is, as Carmichael puts it, a love "within the black community, the only American community where men call each other 'brother' when they meet. We can build a community of love," he says, "only where we have the ability and power to do so: among blacks" [2:8]. At this juncture white persons are simply not considered as valid objects of black love. Such love (or, more accurately, its outward appearance) has been forced from blacks for too long; now, as one of the movement's most sensitive authors puts it, for many of the present black generation,

> the white man no longer exists. He is not to be lived with and he is not to be destroyed. He is simply to be ignored. . . .

If whites consider this relegation to nonexistence as hatred, Julius Lester says, such an interpretation "is only a reflection of [their] own fears and anxieties. . . ." As for blacks, he says, "There

6

is too much to do to waste time and energy hating white people" [13:24].

This powerful strand of Black Power thinking raises a long series of religiously oriented issues. First among many is the recurring issue regarding the control and direction of love. If it is assumed — as it surely must be — that black love must begin among black people and find its nurture there, can it be quarantined? What shall be said of a love that is willed towards some men and not towards others? Is this goal in any way related to the deadly disease that has afflicted so much of American life for so many generations?

An interim goal is now to make white men "invisible" while black men are brought into the light. Can it be brought off by blacks with any less poisoning of the spirit than occurred in whites who invented "tuning out"? If it is true that white men dream long dreams of the dark brothers they have rejected, what are the dreams in black beds? Such an exploration must also ask whether it is enough not to hate. Does our recent experience suggest that hatred might well be preferable to the creation of a new breed of nonexistent nonblack men?

The answers do not come with ease. Perhaps refusal to hate is enough to begin with when one considers the deep sources of human justification for black hatred and revenge against whites. Perhaps those who can rise out of such carefully poisoned wells of human experience with the strength not to hate their oppressors have made a major beginning, whatever their dreams may be. Of course, if anyone should dare to press on and raise the most disturbing religious issue of even loving enemies, there may be two initial responses. It must first be acknowledged that the American religious communities have offered no consistent examples of this love for enemies, especially in times of war. (Black people consider themselves at war, and they have imbibed more of American religion than they know.) Secondly it is essential that all questioners should examine the possibility that men may need the freedom to hate their enemies before love can become an authentic response. It may be that black freedom offers no less dangerous a path than any other variety.

BLACK POWER AND THE NEW COMMUNITY

In part, an answer to our questions must await the further development of the black pilgrimage in this hostile land. Now it is sufficient to note another major thrust of the Black Power movement that has deep religious moorings, a sharing in man's constant search for community. As black exiles search in an often alien world for the ground of their being, the movement is increasingly towards the building of community. Love is recognized as a necessary foundation for this structure — whatever its form.

There was a time when the vision of the community to be built was as large as America, but that is no longer the case. At least that seems no longer a task that black men can set themselves to. Julius Lester put it this way:

> At one time black people desperately wanted to be American, to communicate with whites, to live in the Beloved Community. Now that is irrelevant. They know that it can't be until whites want it to be, and it is obvious now that whites don't want it [13:25].

Now black men must build their own beloved black community, Lester concludes. Does such a statement indicate a recoil from the religious search for the fully inclusive community, or is it a more sober and therefore a more faithful estimate of the world and of the power of race?

Those persons who think of such a withdrawal into blackness as a racist or nationalist retreat from universalism would likely find comfort in the thoughts of one of the Afro-American leaders who said, "The fact that we are Black is our ultimate reality. We were black before we were born" [8:3]. When one considers some of the basic "realities" of American life, there is a certain soundness in this view, and it is supplemented by Lester's call for black men to recognize and celebrate "those things uniquely theirs which separate them from the white man."

Those who see goals of black community as falling short of the goal of universal community must recognize the fact that

8

black men in America have long been encouraged to disdain their community no less than themselves. Therefore, such a call may be the beginning of true corporate health and integrity for black people. It is surely a significant change from the major direction of Afro-American movement toward the larger society during the past generation, for that has been largely a movement away from the ghettos, away from the ground out of which we sprang. "Integration" has most often been the call to escape. (At least it was so interpreted until hard white rocks made clear the nature of its siren sounds.) Now a Karenga teaches that "Our purpose in life should be to leave the Black Community more beautiful than we inherited it" [8:27]. Now Carmichael and others like him plead with black college students to train themselves not to be siphoned out of the ghettos, but to pour themselves back into it. This direction of Black Power is one of its surest words of judgment upon the black churches of the Afro-American communities. It is the same judgment that the Nation of Islam and Malcolm X brought, for it speaks to congregations and pastors who usually have no more use for the black depths than their white Christian counterparts.

The call for communal identification among the black outcasts of America has had observable impact and will probably increase in force. It is the closest thing to a sense of religious vocation that some of the current black college and graduate students know. It is surely significant that one of them spoke in the image of John Donne's human land mass when he voiced the response of a growing proportion of his generation. In a recent article in *Ebony* magazine, Stanley Saunders, a Rhodes Scholar now in Yale's law school, confessed his former attempts to hide from his white friends the truth of his origins in the blackness of Watts. Saunders said this attempt was for him a means of gaining acceptance and assimilation into the American society. Now, with the coming of the new black consciousness, that has changed. He can say instead,

> If there is no future for the black ghetto, the future of all
> Negroes is diminished. What affects it, affects me, for I am a
> child of the ghetto. When they do it to Watts, they do it to me,

9

too. I'll never escape from the ghetto. I have staked my all on
its future. Watts is my home [17:36].

There is probably a message in these words for all who see the
call for solidarity with the black community as a call away from
universalism. For it is quite possible that the earlier liberal invita-
tions to highly selected black men — calls into the Party or into
the Church, or into some other wing of the idol of Integration —
were really deceptive, or at least premature. Perhaps we were
urged towards an identification with mankind-at-large (often
meaning white mankind) before we had learned to identify with
our black neighbors. It is likely that our humanity really begins
in the black ghetto and cannot be rejected there for an easier,
sentimental, white-oriented acceptance elsewhere. So it may be
that the question of "who is my neighbor?" is answered for us.

Of paramount importance is the fact that these questions are
being answered for persons in the ghettos who will never see
Yale. Many of the burgeoning black-oriented groups — organized in varying degrees of structural sophistication — are manned
primarily by young men who have been cast out of the restless
bowels of a technological society. Now in their teens and early
twenties, with little prospect of any meaningful work in the
larger society as it now stands, these black youths have begun
to find themselves as members of groups dedicated to the protection and development of the ghetto that has so long been their
prison. The new vision that Black Power has brought to them
may be one of the most important of all its consequences. These
were the rejected stones of integration. They had neither the
skills nor the graces demanded. They may well become the cor-
nerstones of a renewed black community.

Such a transformation may suggest that if black men are ever
to achieve to the larger universal calling, we must, like Paul,
clearly apprehend the things which are a part of our own racial
and cultural heritage. Perhaps we must be able to glory in that
past as a gift of God before we will be prepared to count it as
garbage for the sake of the new family of man [16]. For if we
begin with a conception of our ancestral community as garbage,
of our heritage as worthless, we shall be guilty of irresponsible

escapism and not growth when we move to transcend them. Isn't it taught in some circles that Jesus of Nazareth had first to explore the most profound levels of his own culture — both physically and spiritually — before he was eligible to transcend it?

So Black Power holds a healthy possibility for the coming of true religious community. It suggests the destruction of ugly and ironic caste distinctions within the Afro-American community. It encourages the discovery of roots long buried and rejected. It insists that men be true to themselves. It calls a broken people to see its own black section of the mainland. It reveals the gifts of those who were once the scorned members of the black body. Karenga may therefore be most accurate when he writes, "Until Blacks develop themselves, they can do nothing for humanity" [8:2]. Obviously, what is being suggested is that men must not only love themselves in order to love their neighbor, but they must love their communities in order to love the world.

Actually, many sections of the world are already included in the concerns of Black Power, and one has the feeling that there is intimated in these concerns a universalism that is at least as broad as that known by most western religious traditions. Black Power calls for an identification between black people here and all the wretched nonwhites of the earth. (Some leaders, like Carmichael, now expand this to the poor and oppressed of every color.) This is certainly the meaning of Lester's statement that, while a black man must now live his life in the United States

> only within the framework of his own blackness [that] blackness links him with the Indians of Peru, the miner in Bolivia, the African and the freedom fighters of Vietnam. What they fight for is what the American black man fights for — the right to govern his own life [13:25].

(Is it possible that a universalism based on suffering, struggle, and hope is more vital than some vague identification based on common links to a possibly dead Creator-Father?)

Such breadth of concern for "the broken victims" in their struggle to be free is surely another of Black Power's judgments upon American religion, especially the faith of those persons who claim a great tradition of prophetic concern for social justice, and those who claim a Master who came to set all broken victims free. For while such religious respectables stand silently or march weakly protesting, the devotees of Black Power identify themselves unambiguously with the oppressed and with the revolutions made by the oppressed. So if only by sheer numbers — the numbers of the earth's humiliated people — such identification actually brings Black Power into the orbit of a universality more authentic than the largely parochial sentiments of a "Judeo-Christian" western commitment.

Nor are the righteous delivered by pointing accurately to the fact that Black Power makes no effort to identify with the oppressors who, according to the teachings of many traditions, are also theoretically eligible for concern. The example of American religion has been poor (perhaps it will eventually prove poisonous), for its identification has been largely with the exploiters or with those who live comfortably because of the action of exploitation. Therefore black men may well sense a need to redress this imbalance, this "crookedness" that is prevalent throughout the western world — no matter how many times *The Messiah* is sung, which refers to making the crooked become straight (Isaiah 40: 3 – 4, e.g.).

Perhaps, too, black rebels remember the example of Jesus, the focus of much of western religion. For while he evidently was filled with ultimate concern for both oppressed and oppressor, he reserved his sharpest words of judgment for the politico-religious leaders and oppressors within the Jewish community, and his death came outside the gates of respectability. Black Power may well suggest that religious concern for both sides does not mean neutrality in the face of injustice. Indeed, it reminds us that the world most often will not permit that questionable luxury, even should it be desirable.

(This identification with the wretched of the earth is especially significant for the incipient struggle for leadership between Black Power adherents and the traditional spokesmen of the Negro masses — their ministers. For though there have been important exceptions, the public stance of most of the respectable pastors has been in accord with the dominant American attitudes towards

modern, radical revolution. By and large, the black church hierarchy has been no more Christian than its white counterpart on
such issues, except where the accident of race has forced it to
certain stances. Should the sense of solidarity with the exploited
peoples grow to major proportions in the Afro-American communities, it may well prove impossible for such religious leaders
to hold on to their already shaky grounds.)

BLACK MESSIAHS AND MARCHING SAINTS

The qualified universalism of Black Power is also streaked with
vivid suggestions of Messianism at many points. Indeed, Afro-
American intellectual history has long been filled with images
of Black Messiahs, either individually or en masse, rising up to
deliver Black America from its bondage and White America
from its lethal folly. Though the first event was always guaranteed, the second did not necessarily follow from it in every case
[9]. In our own century the theme was first voiced fully in the
fascinating and significant movement led by Marcus Garvey.
It was this audacious black genius who sent a Messianic promise
to the black world from his cell in the Atlanta Federal Peni-
tentiary. In 1925, Garvey said,

> If I die in Atlanta my work shall then only begin, but I shall
> live, in the physical or spiritual to see the day of Africa's glory.
> When I am dead wrap the mantle of the Red, Black, and Green
> around me, for in the new life I shall rise with God's grace and
> blessing to lead the millions up the heights of triumph with the
> colors that you well know. Look for me in the whirlwind or
> the storm, look for me all around you, for, with God's grace, I
> shall come and bring with me countless millions of black slaves
> who have died in America and the West Indies and the millions
> in Africa to aid you in the fight for Liberty, Freedom and Life
> [7:136–137].

There are still Afro-Americans in this country, the West Indies,
and Africa who attribute every movement towards black liberation to the living, vibrant spirit of Marcus Garvey.

It was so, too, with Malcolm X, and after his death there came a resurgence of the Messianic theme. The visions of an anointed leader and a Messianic people have been most recently joined in the work of a black novelist, Ronald Fair. Writing in *Negro Digest* about the meaning of Black Power, Fair moved quickly to the issue of ultimate hope, and said,

> we are the ones who will right all the wrongs perpetrated against us and our ancestors and we are the ones who will save the world and bring a new day, a brilliantly alive society that swings and sings and rings out the world over for decency and honesty and sincerity and understanding and beauty and love. . . . [5:30, 94].

Again the chosen people are black and promise a new day out of the matrix of their sufferings. Fair was not specific about the means by which the newness would come, but he said, "we fight on and we spread the love we have been told we cannot feel for ourselves to each and every black man we meet."

Finally the novelist tied the Messianic people to its leader and invoked the revered name when he said,

> We look about us and wait because somewhere, somewhere in the tenements in Harlem, or from the west side of Chicago, or from Watts, there *will* be another Malcolm and this one won't be murdered.

As Ronald Fair read the moment, "every black man in this country is aware that our time has come" [5:94].

Now is the fullness of time in many black minds; and though traditional religion is often denied, the deeper symbols and myths are appropriated to express the sense of expectation that stirs within the black communities, focused now in the ideology of Black Power. As might be predicted, the black Messianic hope expands beyond America's shores, and this aspect of it was also expressed by Killens. He wrote,

> we black Americans are no longer a "minority" but a part of that vast majority of humanity yearning to be free and struggling with every ounce of their strength to throw off the blackman's burden and the yoke of white supremacy. We are a part of that fellowship of the disinherited which will surely inherit the earth in this century [11:37].

The ambiguities of Fair's "fight" are largely discarded in Killens' vision of the way ahead. It is those who were forced to be meek (as some count meekness) who now enter into armed struggle to inherit the earth.

Another spokesman for Black Power is even less ambiguous, for Nathan Hare speaks of a "Black Judgment Day around the corner" for America. He envisions it as a possible "black *blitzkrieg* . . . making America a giant, mushrooming Watts, in which this country will either solve its problems or get the destruction it deserves" [10:01]. It is surely not presumptuous to suggest that elements of the same vision impel an H. Rap Brown to demand from the nation that it either "straighten up" or face the fire of judgment.

Within the heart of Black Power stands the perennial tension between a salvation leading to swinging and singing and love, and a day of destruction demanded by a just God. Throughout the history of black American radicalism run the themes of repentance and atonement or judgment [18:62–147]. Always there is the memory of bloodshed being connected to the remission of sins. But when the chosen, sinned-against people become both armed and anointed, when the saints march with guns, then the issues are mooted, and the day of the Lord is clouded indeed. For it may be that armed and marching black saints in Harlem are not likely to conceive of their task any differently than those who killed infidel Indians in New England, cut off unrepentant heads in old England, or now burn "suspected" children in Vietnam. Is it given to black men any more than to whites to be self-commissioned executors of Divine judgment on evil-doers? Easy replies must not suffice, for what if the Divine Judge has retired from his bench, leaving all things in the hands of men? What then? Does evil for evil become mandatory?

BLACK RESURRECTION: THE POWER AND THE GLORY

What are the means to be used in building new black men, new black communities and a renewed, black-oriented world? Already certain pathways have been suggested. The new men must come partly from a new vision of themselves. Indeed the image that has been constantly used in this century involves more than new self-image, it presumes resurrection. Ever since Marcus Garvey preached an Easter sermon on "The Resurrection of the Negro" in 1922, the theme has been constantly renewed. For Garvey, self-knowledge was a key to this resurrection.

On the occasion of his sermon he said, "We are about to live a new life — a risen life — a life of knowing ourselves" [6:88]. His central passage in the discourse was an anticipation of so much that was to come on the black scene that it merits another temporary movement back into the first quarter of the century. Continuing the crucial image of resurrection, Garvey said,

> I trust there will be a spiritual and material resurrection among Negroes everywhere; that you will lift yourselves from the doubts of the past; that you will lift yourselves from the slumbers of the past; that you will lift yourselves from the lethargy of the past, and strike out in this new life — in this resurrected life — to see things as they are [6:90].

The theme was continued faithfully in the Nation of Islam where Elijah Muhammad constantly spoke of "dead, so-called Negroes" who needed to be resurrected to their true life as black men [14]. At the current juncture the same concept finds various expressions among those who seek to build new black men. Thus Ron Karenga insists that "We must not be so busy calling the Negro dead that we can't work out methods to resurrect him" [8:17]. One of the methods is obviously the love and concern that other black men show for the "dead" brother. Another, related, path to new life is suggested by Carmichael who speaks of "the necessity to reclaim our history and our identity from the cultural terrorism and depredation of self-justifying white guilt" [3:639]. The process of teaching becomes crucial. History becomes a balm for healing and a hope for new beginnings.

The pages of recent black history are thus filled with testimonies of Afro-Americans who saw themselves as "dead" or "sick" before their contact with the healing and resurrecting power of black concern and black self-knowledge. One of Karenga's own disciples (and the word is used intentionally) recently wrote,

I can remember myself before Maulana ["Great Leader," the title assumed by Karenga] showed me the "Path of Blackness." I was so sick no one but Maulana could have saved me. Running around with no identity, purpose or direction. Maulana gave me an alternative to this white system. . . . I say, "all praises due to Maulana" . . . [8:iii].

Such dependence upon new or previously hidden knowledge for salvation is at least as old as Gnosticism and most of the mystery religions, and perhaps one also hardly needs to comment about the significance of love as a conqueror of death. Nevertheless it might be well to note that in a world where God's absence is more evident than his presence to large numbers of men, an individual's worth may no longer be sufficiently affirmed in terms of his worthiness before a Divine being. Or could one say that black love and resurrection are simply ways of speaking about and discovering incarnation where it is most needed today?

Some persons are nevertheless disturbed by what they consider a "glorification of blackness" in the healing process under discussion. In a significant sense, this is exactly what is involved in the relationship of Black Power to black and broken men who have been made ashamed of their blackness. It is indeed glorified; and a perceptive theological interpreter of this aspect of the issue offers a most helpful understanding of the action when he writes,

The glorification of blackness implicit in the term Black Power is a conscious or unconscious effort to stake a claim for the worth of those in our nation who are termed nonwhite. Essentially it is a clarification. The root meaning of the term "glorify" is to clarify, to make clear and plain and straight [19:139].

Nor does Nathan Wright confine the issue to the human sphere with this highly suggestive description of black glorification. He goes on to say,

All of life must be clarified in this sense. It must be given and seen in that dimension which sets it forth in terms of glory — now and forever. To see life as it truly is means to see it as God sees it, in its eternal dimension, in the glory appropriate to its involvement with and in the life of God [19:139–140].

If one follows this invaluable line of thought, it is obvious that Black Power has within it the possibility of setting black men in an entirely new light — the light of their Creator. They are called upon to see themselves as they were meant to be. This glorification has the potential of setting them at peace with themselves and with the creative purposes of the universe; they no longer need to curse God and die. For their blackness is now — like the rest of their createdness — a sign of His love and not His anger.

At its best, such glorification sets black men at peace whether or not the white world recognizes the reality of their dark blessedness; such clarity makes it unnecessary for them to prove to whites the facts of that glory or even to demand that they be recognized. For men at peace with the universe are at once profoundly at peace with themselves and with all others who participate in that universe. Unfortunately, such a time is not yet with us, and black men have been forced to live in shameful dependency and self-negation for too long. So the process of resurrection may well be more like three generations than three days for some of the black dead. But it is also possible that the coming forth may be unlike the quiet stories of the Gospels and more like the volcanic eruptions of the Old Testament or the fire-framed bursting of the graves in the vision of John.

One difficult aspect of the rebuilding task urged by Black Power is the break with white leadership. This has long been a subject of furious discussion among blacks, and in this century it began when several Negro members of W. E. B. DuBois' radical, black Niagara Movement, refused in 1909 to join the newly created white-dominated National Association for the Advancement of Colored People [1: vol 2, 927]. In our own time the issue was perhaps raised most sharply by SNCC, partly as a result of its Mississippi Summer experience of 1964. Even before the experiment of bringing large numbers of whites into the state had begun, it was reported that some black staff members of the organization "felt that it would destroy everything which they had accomplished." According to Julius Lester's account, the objectors were convinced that

Whites, no matter how well meaning, could not relate to the Negro community. A Negro would follow a white person to the courthouse, not because he'd been convinced he should register to vote, but simply because he had been trained to say Yes to whatever a white person wanted [13:23].

Therefore it was determined that the resurrection of black people required decisive breaks with the old patterns of life, patterns of constant dependence on whites which had been begun in slavery and then encouraged ever since. By 1966, Stokely Carmichael had put the new dictum into words, using "psychological equality" as a synonym for black mental resurrection. He wrote, "The need for psychological equality is the reason why SNCC today believes that blacks must organize in the black community. Only black people can convey the revolutionary idea that black people are able to do things themselves" [2:6].

While this decision on the part of Black Power advocates has been one of the most difficult for well-intentioned whites to abide, there is much logic in its direction if one is primarily concerned with the building of men and communities which have long been shattered, threatened, or used by forces with white faces. It is difficult for white men and women to be told to go and organize in white communities "where the racism really is," but such words are certainly worthy of serious consideration, especially if one's deepest concern is with the healing of shattered black egos more than with the bolstering of relatively intact white ones.

Even though the logic is powerful, the implications of the movement towards separation and the questions it raises are no less significant. How shall the black and white victims of American racism best find their healing before the last night settles in? What is the nature of the binding process and under what conditions shall it best take place? One wonders, for instance, if the restoration of broken, embittered spirits can take place apart from the presence — at some point — of the offending, denying, guilt-dominated brother. Or is it impossible for black men to build the necessary strength to love themselves — which must precede all else — except through studied alienation from their former oppressors, even the truly repentant ones? Perhaps an even more sobering and "practical" question is whether or not a white community without inner quietness will allow the black workers time and space to build a unique (and thereby threatening) set of structures and beings.

The models for guidance are difficult to discover, but it is evident that the ancient issue of means and ends is involved in the discussion, if one takes seriously the stated goals of some of the Black Power advocates. For instance, few members of the younger, enraged generation have any program of separate states or of Zionism on another continent. Therefore most seek to find some *modus vivendi* on the American scene. At the heart of the matter under discussion is the issue of how we can prepare black people to live with integrity on the scene of our former enslavement and our present estrangement. In examining this matter, Karenga says, "We're not for isolation but interdependence — but we can't become interdependent unless we have something to offer." In other words, he says, "We can live with whites interdependently once we have Black Power" [8:3]. So the summary response to the central question seems to be that it is only a temporary withdrawing of the black community into itself which will prepare it for interdependence, and therefore the end appears threatened by the seemingly unavoidable means.

(Somehow the black-white dilemma is often suggestive of an unhealthy and mutually destructive marriage which may require at least a period of separation for the mutual benefit of the two partners. At other times America seems to be the forever unfaithful lover of the Blues, the lover who is always lamented but never left — until the last, inevitably bloody scene. The same unclarity that marks the religious response to unhealthy love affairs and destructive marriages is likely present when one searches for guidance here. Is divorce preferable to the kitchen knife? But what would divorce mean?)

A question no less difficult arises in another step that Black Power takes towards the building of black men and the black community — the emphasis on self-defense. Speaking for his organization in 1966, Carmichael set the most obvious theme: "SNCC reaffirms the right of black men everywhere to defend themselves when threatened or attacked" [2:5]. Moving the idea from a right to an authentication of black freedom, Killens wrote, "Men are not free unless they affirm the right to defend themselves" [11:33]. But for those who would intelligently explore Black Power, even these explanations are insufficient. It was Killens who set out — largely by implication — the fuller and more profound psychological significance of self-defense for black men. He wrote in the same revealing article,

> We black folk have a deep need to defend ourselves. Indeed we have an obligation. We must teach the brutalizers how it feels to be brutalized. We must teach them that it hurts. They'll never know unless we teach them [11:34].

The issues raised by this series of statements are worthy of thoughtful consideration, for they eventually move to a level of profound moment. On the surface they seem to be nothing more than an affirmation of the somewhat disreputable "American right" to self-defense. (A right, incidentally, which most Americans have no sound moral grounds for questioning when it suddenly appears among angry black men.)

In some ways this affirmation of self-defense is an obvious response to a situation in which black people find that neither separation, respect, nor love is forthcoming from the dominant portion of the society. On another, related, level it is a repetition of the earlier theme of judgment at the hands of the injured. As we have mentioned, in a world in which God is at least obscure, and where no one else seems a dependable agent of justice for black people, black men should stand firmly on their reponsibility to do the necessary work. There is, however, an even more profound issue involved in what Killens describes so sensitively as "a deep need" for black men to defend themselves. What he seems to be implying is this: when men have long been forced to accept the wanton attacks of their oppressors, when they have had to stand by and watch their women prostituted, it is crucial to their own sense of self-esteem that they affirm and be able to implement their affirmation of a right to strike back.

The basic human search for a definition of manhood is here set out in significant black lineaments. Does manhood indeed depend upon the capacity to defend one's life? Is this American shibboleth really the source of freedom for men? Is it possible that a man simply becomes a slave to another man's initiative when he feels obliged to answer his opponent on the opponent's terms? Is there perhaps a certain kind of bondage involved when men are so anxious about keeping themselves alive that they are ready to take the lives of others to prevent that occurrence? The question is really one of the image man was meant to reflect; what is it? Certain ways of looking at the world would suggest that such questions are pointless before they come from the lips. Other religious perspectives might suggest that manhood can be discussed, but only in terms of the capacity to create new grounds for response to danger, and in the act of bringing new life into being, rather than in the animal capacity to strike back.

In his characteristically vivid way, Karenga allows no circumventing of the issue. He writes, "If we fight we might be killed. But it is better to die as a man than to live like a slave" [8:19]. In the midst of a hostile, threatening environment the Zealot pathway is often chosen by those who are in honest search of their manhood, by those who seek to protect and avenge their oppressed community. Most persons who claim to be followers of the Man who introduced Zealots to a new way of response have chosen not to follow him at this point. And here is one of the most telling witnesses to the possibility that Black Power may be more fully bound to the traditions of the western Christian world than its proponents would ever dare believe.

Now, if it is possible that the fullest stature of man was found in one who honestly and sharply opposed his enemies but finally faced them with his cross, then Black Power may have chosen far less than the best available way. If it has chosen a bondage to death, the mistake is completely understandable. It is understandable not only because retaliatory violence is deeply etched into the American grain, but also because men who have been forced up against crosses all of their lives find it difficult to take one up when the choice is fully theirs. It is understandable, too, because western society now seems unable to offer any normative response to the question, "What is man?" Moreover it appears totally without courage to experiment with possibilities beyond the old, "heroic," destructive replies.

Perhaps one possibility yet stands in the future, and Black Power's immediate choice must not be counted as its last. For who knows where the inner quest will lead black men if they are honestly in search of true manhood, true community, and true humanity? Are there not grounds for hope wherever men are soberly and devotedly engaged in the quest for new light?

OLD WHITE MODELS AND NEW BLACK HOPES

If the relationship of self-defense to the building of black manhood is crucial on the personal level, then it is likely that the kinds of "power" sought by the black community is the focal question on the broader scale. Not only is it crucial, but it faces us with another set of religious issues of considerable force. Initially one must ask: what is the power necessary to build the new black community? Perhaps Stokely Carmichael best summarized the normative Black Power response when he wrote,

> Almost from its beginning, SNCC sought to [build] a program aimed at winning political power for impoverished Southern blacks. We had to begin with politics because black Americans are a propertyless people in a country where property is valued above all. We had to work for power, because this country does not function by morality, love, and nonviolence, but by power [2:5].

Political, economic and social power, with a final recourse to armed self-defense are at the heart of the black search, even though Carmichael has since gone on to espouse aggressive guerrilla warfare. Ron Karenga, who feels the movement is not yet ready for such warfare, put the issues of power for the black community more colorfully, but no less directly when he said,

> Like it or not, we don't live in a spiritual or moral world and the white boys got enough H-bombs, missiles, T.V.'s, firehoses and dogs to prove it.

23

Therefore, he concluded, "we must move not spiritually but politically, i.e., with power" [8:19].

In some ways it is understandable to hear the avowed revolutionaries among Black Power forces refer to political, economic, and military realities as the ultimate forces in life. It is even more interesting to note that same direction in the forceful statement of an impressive group of black churchmen who wrote on the subject of black and white power in 1966. In the midst of the national furor over the newly discovered term, the churchmen published a full page advertisement in *The New York Times* which said, in part, "The fundamental distortion facing us in the controversy about 'black power' is rooted in a gross imbalance of power and conscience between Negroes and white Americans." After setting out this basic introduction to their thesis, the statement continued,

> It is this distortion, mainly, which is responsible for the widespread, though often inarticulate, assumption that white people are justified in getting what they want through the use of power, but that Negro Americans must, either by nature or by circumstances, make their appeal only through conscience. As a result, the power of white men and the conscience of black men have both been corrupted. The power of white men is corrupted because it meets little meaningful resistance from Negroes to temper it and keep white men from aping God.

Tracing the corruption of the black conscience, the churchmen attributed it to a condition in which,

> having no power to implement the demands of conscience, the concern for justice is transmuted into a distorted form of love, which, in the absence of justice, becomes chaotic self-surrender. Powerlessness breeds a race of beggars. We are faced now with a situation where conscienceless power meets powerless conscience, threatening the very foundations of our nation [15:187].

It was evident that the churchmen were convinced that "conscience," or "love" as they later referred to it, was "powerless" without the coercive forces of the society. They appeared no less disturbed than John Killens about "unrequited love," and in a

24

sophisticated adumbration, the group simply gave religious expression to the political views of Carmichael, Karenga and a host of other black spokesmen. Though it is not fully stated they seem to be saying that the ultimate weapons necessary for the building of the new black community are those now monopolized by white power leaders. Blacks have to get their hands on some of these weapons and perhaps depend upon their own consciences to "temper" black uses of the same instruments whites had used for such destructive purposes. But when blacks begin getting their proper share of the power, it would appear that they might be less dependent upon the development of "conscience" — unless it was theirs in large supplies "by nature" rather than "by circumstance." How then would black power be tempered?

A question at least as compelling is this: Does the theological position implicit in the churchmen's statement carry a doctrine of two kingdoms with it? Do these leaders seek the Kingdom of the weaponless, defenseless, homeless King at certain times, and the Kingdom of the armed, propertied, politically powerful, American, white (soon to be technicolored) King at another time? Where do the kingdoms meet? Are the guidelines to the nature of human community as blurred as those for the nature of man? On issues of ultimate power, are the insights of Christian ministers only accidentally the same as Stokely Carmichael's and Ron Karenga's?

The implications of the churchmen's statement are numerous and provocative, but it is important to supplement that statement with an even more theologically astute brief for Black Power by one of the individual signators, Nathan Wright. Dr. Wright, who is also chairman of the National Conference on Black Power, recently wrote of the image of God and its relationship to power among black men. He said,

> In religious terms, a God of power, of majesty and of might, who has made men to be in His own image and likeness, must will that His creation reflect in the immediacies of life His power, His majesty and His might. Black Power raises . . . the far too long overlooked need for power, if life is to become what in the mind of its Creator it is destined to be [15:136].

25

In a fascinating way Karenga, one of the best trained and most thoughtful of the Black Power leaders, picks up the precise line set down by Wright. In all likelihood he does it independently, so it is even more significant and illuminating that his definition of Black Power should also find its basis in a powerful deity. He writes, "God is God who moves in power; God is God who moves in change and creates something out of nothing. If you want to be God just think about that" [8:26]. (Karenga's last sentence is not random rhetoric. Evidently he has so imbibed the homocentric orientation of the American society that he upstages the Mormons by telling men that they become Gods now by entering into Godlike action. Indeed, the emphasis on autonomous black action is another of the hallmarks of Black Power ideology, a hallmark that leaves little room for any dependence on what might be called grace — a hallmark that would stamp it as far more Protestant than one might desire.)

The difficulty with the analogy evoked by Wright and Karenga is its failure to recognize another aspect of the power of God within the biblical tradition. If Wright and the other black churchmen put any serious stock in the life and teachings of Jesus of Nazareth as the clearest possible window to the face of God, then one must at least examine another way of power. That is, one must see the power of God demonstrated in weakness and in humiliation. Is it not possible that the God who dies for his enemies, who rejects their terms and their weapons — and their kind of power — is also worthy of consideration as a model for the empowerment of the black community?

Though it is difficult to propound, it would appear that such a question may have some possible validity when one remembers some of the goals of Black Power. May not one properly ask if a new black community will be created by the appropriation of the old American weapons of power? More specifically, what of Karenga's insight into the nature of racism? He said at one point,

> Racist minds created racist institutions. Therefore you must move against racism, not institutions. For even if you tear down the institutions that same mind will build them up again [8:14].

26

How does one "move against racism"? Surely not with "H-bombs, missiles, T.V.'s, firehoses . . . dogs" and all the other institutions of political power now possessed by "the white boy." And what of Stokely Carmichael's strangely religious metaphor: "For racism to die, a totally different America must be born" [2:6]? Will a black community in search of a new society really participate in the process of new birth by a reactionary fixation on all the kinds of power which have helped to corrupt the nation? How does new birth come?

Talk of weakness and death, quests for new birth, all tend to be at once sources of fascination and anathema for the current black breed. It is likely that the apparently contradictory references to such matters in their writings are largely unconscious, and that the conscious stance is one of opposition to Gods who die on crosses. As we have seen, black men have been chained to weakness for so long that any talk of voluntarily choosing a way that the society counts as weak is considered sheer madness.

Is this the scandal of the cross for the present black moment? Or is it all foolishness in the most irrelevant sense of the word? Perhaps Karenga was most true to himself and to the universe when he said, "We don't live in a spiritual or moral world." Somehow it sounds like the old black deacons who constantly joked behind the minister's back: "Praying is fine in a prayer meeting, but it ain't no good in a bear meeting."

If the world is primarily a bear meeting, and if the only way to survive in such a gathering is by becoming a bear, then the way of Black Power is evident. (Even the preachers seem to agree with elements of Black Bear Power.) Nevertheless, in such a situation, the way of human beings remains cloudy.

BLACK POWER AND RELIGION: BEYOND IMPLICATIONS

Reference to a black prayer meeting serves as a reminder that the discussion of religious issues in this essay has generally grown out of the intimations, suggestions, and tendencies one finds in the words and deeds of Black Power advocates. There has been al-

27

most no attempt to address the subject of the precise, institutionalized religious manifestations of Black Power, largely because
such an attempt would be somewhat premature. It is evident,
however, that if the ideology does institutionalize itself, a more
clearly articulated religious message and ritual will likely develop,
or rather a set of such phenomena will emerge.

Anticipation of this is present already throughout the black
ghettos. Ever since the days of Garvey's African Orthodox
Church, Black Nationalist groups have found religion to be one
of their major modes of expression. The Nation of Islam's
success is the best known indication of the power inherent in
this direction. Recently — especially since Malcolm X's appearance on the national scene — there have been many Black
Nationalist attempts to reestablish variations of African religious
practices, and one can only speculate on the mutual transformations such attempts may bring about.

None of these developments should be surprising, of course.
For instance, when the strongly nationalist Bandung Conference
of Afro-Asian peoples gathered in 1955 a resolution was passed
"to resurrect their old religions and cultures and modernize
them. . . ." Similarly at the world conference of black writers,
artists, and intellectuals held in Paris in the following year, one of
the participants said that "the main and only resolution called for
the rehabilitation of their ancient cultures and religions" [20:22].
These were significant international prefigurings of Black Power
in America, and they probably suggest the way that the Afro-
American movements will increasingly take.

Besides the plethora of Black Nationalist religious experiments
in the ghettos of the land, it is likely that Karenga's west coast
organization, US, has so far articulated the most clearly structured and self-consciously religious manifestos of all the Black
Power groups. It is representative of much of the movement's
concerns both in its rather humanistic, secular (in the most recent
religious sense of that word) orientation and in its obvious reaction to the black Christian churches. Thus Karenga teaches that
"We must concern ourselves more with the plans for this life,
rather than the next life which has its own problems. For the

next life across Jordan is much further away than the grawl [sic] of dogs and policemen and the pains of hunger and disease" [8:26].

In spite of the familiar reference to Jordan, groups like Karenga's tend to believe that men live on only through the lives of their children, and there is among them a strong emphasis on the rebuilding of the shattered black home. In such a home the role of the woman follows almost strictly Pauline lines, and some female believers in Black Power find it difficult to adjust their western indoctrination of equality to the old-new emphasis on the supremacy of the black man.

The New Testament stream that flows through their doctrine of the relationship of husband to wife does not prevent Black Power groups from engaging in constant attacks on the Christian churches. For instance, Karenga — in keeping with many other similar leaders who preceded him — says that "Christians do good because they fear — we do good because we love. They do good because God says so — we do good . . . in response to need" [8].

The issue of religion is constantly before many of the young persons who are drawn back into the ghettos by the urgent logic of Black Power. As they return — from college or from prison — to struggle against what can be reasonably described as "principalities and powers" which seem anonymously but fiercely to control the life of their people, they find themselves often insufficient as autonomous sources of inner strength. They cannot return to the Christian churches they once knew, because these churches have so often appeared irrelevant to the real needs of the community, and most often they are controlled by older men and women who seem unprepared for the competition from radical black youth. In here, strangely enough, a few black Christian churches have responded fully to the call of Black Power. In Detroit, the pastor of one such congregation, the Reverend Albert B. Cleague, Jr, of the Central United Church of Christ, preaches of a black revolutionary Jesus who came to set the nonwhite peoples free. A Black Madonna is the focal point of worship, and the church has probably attracted more persons committed to Black Power than any other single institution still connected to the Christian churches.

Even when they cannot find such havens, there is nevertheless something in the black religious tradition that continues to attract many racially conscious young people. For instance, it is most moving and revealing to watch a group of them respond totally with clapping and dancing to the Gospel songs that continue to shape the tradition that spawned them. They are at home for a time. Ideologies aside, this is still "Soul."

On what may or may not be another level of their being, some of the group also sense a strange sense of attraction to Jesus of Nazareth. They are convinced that an encounter with the historical Jesus would likely be a meeting with a revolutionary, but they have been turned off by the whiteness infused into this Jesus by the western Christian tradition. They are also able and often accurate cataloguers of the unfaithfulness of the churches — black and white. Sometimes they consider these churches as irrelevant as white persons are. A few of the seekers turn to Judaism, but often meet the reality of the Jewish middleman in the ghettos and find it an obstacle to faith. Others move towards Islamic variations of belief, often giving up their western, Christian names. This is partly another declaration of independence from slavery and its postreconstruction variations, but it is in some situations simply part of the ancient practice of men taking on new names when they find new faiths.

In the light of their search for the lineaments of a new societal order, it is surely significant that some black groups have now moved towards various forms of communitarianism. In locations like Los Angeles and Philadelphia attempts are made to find this style of life in the urban context. In upper New York state real estate has been set aside for such an experiment; while in Brooklyn a group of some sixty men and women now plan for moving back to the south, to the land. Is it likely that such actions represent more than exercises in anguished flight? Is it possible that they are really a challenge to the two settings which have been most destructive to black life — the city and the south? Are they expressions of hope in the power of resurrected black lives to conquer even these ancient foes?

There is a sense of religious ferment on the path to Black Power, a sense that is not easy to document. Mixtures of old and new approaches to the essential issues of life are being attempted. Allah and other gods of Africa enter into competition with Yaweh, Jesus, and Buddha. It is a joyously difficult time, but part of the affirmation of Black Power is "We are a spiritual people." The institutional manifestations of that affirmation are still being tested. A people separated from their past now attempt to build bridges, create new realities, or search among the ruins for whatever remains of value there may be.

So Afro-Americans enter the experience that many peoples have known before them, peoples who in time of national crisis have turned to the gods they knew before the coming of Christian missionaries, seeking for what seemed a more solid ground. Nor should it be forgotten that such searches have taken place in this century no less significantly in Ireland and Germany than in Kenya and the Congo.

As for the possible results here, one can only begin to speculate, for instance, on the impact of some African religions on a Black Power movement that is still more western oriented and Protestant than it can possibly admit. Will these religions which seek unity and harmony with the forces of God in the universe transform an ideology that is still determined to change the world around it? Can one accept the Yoruba dreams and dress without falling sway to its world view? Only the questions are available now.

Meanwhile, few adherents of Black Power deny their need for religious moorings, and, though no clear pattern has yet emerged, it must be evident by now that for many persons this movement is likely to become as fully a "church" as the earlier phase was for others. Not only does it begin to fill the need for personal commitment and a sense of fellowship with other similarly committed black persons; it also embodies impressive social concern, a call for ultimate justice, and a search to be present with the sufferers of the society. Gladly identifying with the oppressed beyond national borders, this church increasingly seeks to glorify at least that part of God which may reside in black folk.

In the midst of such developments, one central question cries out for an answer, the kind of answer that is perhaps to be found most fully in the insight of true religion. Though often articulated only in parts, if put into words by Black Power adherents, it would be, "How shall we deal with an enemy who has more power than we do, who has long controlled and destroyed our lives that are even now more fully dependent upon him than we dare confess?" Whatever religion arises from the heart of Black Power will need to address itself to such a dilemma with more honesty than most black religion has ever done before. (One of the generally unrecognized religious blessings of this movement is the honesty it has already forced into the black-white dialogue in America. It has not produced hate; it has rather revealed hate and called upon both whites and blacks to admit its sorrowful depths. There are, of course, large segments of the society who still fear this radical honesty, but it is likely that they also fear true religion.)

EPILOGUE: MARTIN LUTHER KING AND BLACK POWER

No discussion of black religion in America today can ignore the immensely important figure of Martin Luther King. In spite of statements to the contrary, he remains an individual of critical importance for anyone who would gain insights into the black experience here. Therefore it is crucial to examine King's response to a movement that has seemed to push him off the stage. The encounter may well provide unexpected illumination for some summary views.

In his most recent work, *Where Do We Go From Here?* [12] King attempts an assessment of Black Power that is significant and revealing, not for its originality or its challenge, but for the basic weakness of his response to the realities evoked and addressed by the ideology. There is in one chapter a favorable interpretation of the "positive" aspects of Black Power as a psychological healing force. Then as King attempts to define the elements which will bring the "necessary" power to the black community, he refers to power as "the strength required to bring about social, political or economic changes," and identifies this power in many of the same ways as the churchmen and the leading Black Power advocates. When the words come from Martin Luther King, however, they bear somewhat more powerful implications. He writes,

> There is nothing essentially wrong with power. The problem is that in America power is unequally distributed. This has led Negro Americans in the past to seek their goals through love and moral suasion devoid of power and white Americans to seek their goals through power devoid of love and conscience. . . . It is precisely this collision of immoral power with powerless morality which constitutes the major crisis of our times [12:37].

In religious (as well as political) terms, King's words constitute something of a crisis in themselves and raise many difficult issues. They tempt us, most importantly, to ask whether Martin Luther King was describing his own movement when he spoke of Negroes in the past who sought goals "through love and moral suasion" because no other way was available to them. If this identification is precise, then one must surely question the nature of such love and the motives of the moral suasion. And if the love was "powerless" why were so many past references made to "the power of love and nonviolence" — references found even in King's current work?

Surely the talk of love and suasion that was a kind of last resort is not in keeping with the insights of the great teachers of nonviolence, who set out this way for men who were not cowards, who had other weapons available, but who chose to put them aside for the sake of a better way. King's statements cause one to ask if there was really a nonviolent movement at any point. Was "too much love" really the problem? Could it be that nonviolence was simply impossible for a people who had never had an opportunity to affirm their manhood or to choose violence as a way of response on a widespread scale? Perhaps the late, lamented nonviolent movement can really come only after the Malcolms, Stokelys, and Raps have offered another real choice to millions of black folk.

33

Even more significant for the present discussion is King's failure to deal clearly and precisely with the central black radical conviction concerning America. Its advocates believe (and they have a growing company of fellow believers) that this nation will not allow black men the freedom, opportunity, and restitution needful for meaningful lives without a total, violent disruption of the society. Like revolutionaries before them, they believe that the national fabric must be rent before white people will believe in the validity of black demands for life. Here is the price of three centuries of racism, they say. King does not really respond to this assumption. He warns against cynicism, but fails to set out in clarity his response to a situation in which even massive, disciplined nonviolent resistance will continue to meet increasingly violent (and/or sophisticated) repression.

Somehow the night of that terror seems too dark for King to enter. His only real attempt at an answer to the Black Power conviction is a vague statement of faith, but the object of the faith also remains vague. King writes,

> Our most fruitful course is to stand firm, move forward nonviolently, accept disappointments and cling to hope. Our determined refusal not to be stopped will eventually open the door to fulfillment. By recognizing the necessity of suffering in a righteous cause, we may achieve our humanity's full stature. To guard ourselves from bitterness, we need the vision to see in this generation's ordeals the opportunity to transfigure both ourselves and American society [12:46–47].

There are missing links and false notes apparent in any religiously focused examination of this central statement. Nowhere is there any explanation of why King believes that the door "will eventually open." Is it faith in American goodness, in the power of a nonviolent movement that he hardly discusses, or faith in an abstract justice in the universe? (King's God often seems no less dead than anyone else's — at least if one judges life by appearance in the printed pages.) Without such clarification, his call could be dismissed as a Pollyanna voice attempting to challenge the whirlwind.

Even more important is his failure to discuss the possible reasons for an amorphous, variously motivated group of black people to suffer without retaliation the continued scorn and injury of people they consider at least fools and at most devils. When King referred to "powerless morality" and identified authentic power for black people with economic and political power, he was then likely obligated to ask who would be willing to live without such power once it became possible either to kill for it or to kill to protest its denial.

It would appear that, unless King is ready to face black men with the need to suffer without retaliation and also to live without the power he considered "necessary," much of his argument against violence falls apart. For the violence of revolutionaries comes not from "hatred," as he says, but from the insistence of the oppressed that they must have at least a proportionate share of the power which the oppressor insists upon keeping and defending by violent means. Leaders like Karenga say such power is absolutely necessary for black men. So does King. Black Power leaders are convinced that the country will not make such power available without armed struggle of one kind or another. What does a believer in religious nonviolence have to say to such a situation? Is it enough not to face it squarely? And if he does, must King eventually choose between armed struggle and a powerless future for black people in the United States?

In a sense this dilemma is a reminder of how much the present black situation — especially in its religious dimensions — is a microcosmic expression of the main lines of the development of American Christian ethics in this century. Within the microcosm King stands for the liberal tradition, continuing to maintain faith in American goodness, in reason, in the ordered nature of the world. Such a stance seems to require his refusing to look directly into chaos, seems to demand that he fail to trace the deepest lineaments of the nation's racist core. In a sense King appears to hope that dark "principalities and powers" in massive array are only figments of overexercised religious imagination. In their place he substitutes an eloquent dream.

On the other hand stand the proponents of Black Power, like some dark blossoms of "realism" gone beyond control. They look with cynical but not dishonest eyes at the forces of evil in the society, at their depth and their extent. They see without flinching the possibility that power will not be shared voluntarily, that atonement cannot come without the shedding of blood, and they are determined that as little of the blood as possible will flow from them. They see the night and prepare men for its terror. They refuse to dream. But like much of the realist position, they also fail to acknowledge sufficiently (perhaps because of insensitivity on certain levels of their being) the reality of creative, healing forces in the situation. Somehow the power of resurrection is totally irrelevant to the struggles they outline, except in the most personal applications to individual "dead" black men.

Moved out of the metaphorical microcosm, these two perspectives are badly in need of each other for the mutual sharing and the possible mutual growth which may well be the nation's only visible hope in the racial crisis. The necessary, relentless determination of Black Power to look fully on the evil of American life must be informed by some hope even more solid than King's, some expectation of creative possibilities (even of Messiahs), some determination not to succumb to the enemy's disease. Even more soberly put, it may be that all who speak with any seriousness about addressing the profound social and psychological distortions wrought by American racism must be prepared to experiment with totally new weapons, and be ready (how hard the words!) for complete defeat — at least as it is commonly counted.

For if racism rages as deep into American life as it appears and if violence is its closest brother, then a black revolution will no more solve the problem than a civil war did (even if Rap Brown gets his atomic bomb). So it may be most responsible to ask if it is more than despair to speak of a long, grueling battle with no victory — and no illusions — this side of the grave? Has it been important and necessary simply to learn that there are no large citizen armies of white deliverers? Was it not absolutely necessary that all trust in courts and troops and presidents be shattered? Is this part of a black coming of age, a coming which will eventually reveal that even the black God of the ghetto is dead?

36

Perhaps, though, he is not dead. Perhaps this new God has not lived long enough to die. Perhaps there is still a Beloved Community ahead. But if it is, it must be seen as the Kingdom whose realization does not depend upon whether whites (or anyone else around) really want it or not. If it comes, it may come only for those who seek it for its own sake and for the sake of its Lord, recognizing that even if He is black, the final glory is not the glory of blackness, but a setting straight of all the broken men and communities of the earth. In some strange ways Black Power may be headed in that way, but it probably needs some new and stripped-down coming of Martin King's most fervent hopes to accompany its path.

On the other hand, if the night is already too dark for the way to be found, or if society should make it impossible for these two black tendencies to live and find each other, then there seems little to expect that is not apocalyptic. This has always been a religious implication of life, especially black life. It is certainly one of the deepest implications of a wishful liberalism and an inescapable possibility for a Black Power that finally accepts not only America's weapons but also its ultimate definitions of manhood, power, majesty, and might.

Was it for this that we have come so painfully far together — and yet apart — in this strange land? Was it only for this? Is there no saving message from the drums of our homeland, or did all gods die at once?

REFERENCES

1. Aptheker, Herbert, ed: *A Documentary History of the Negro People in the United States,* 2 vol (Citadel Press, New York, New York) 1965.
2. Carmichael, Stokely: What We Want, *New York Review of Books,* vol 7, no 4, Sept 22, 1966.
3. Carmichael, Stokely: Towards Black Liberation, *Massachusetts Review,* Autumn 1966.
4. Cornwell, Anita: Symposium on Black Power, *Negro Digest,* vol 16, no 1, Nov 1966.

5. Fair, Ronald: Symposium on Black Power, *Negro Digest,* vol 16, no 1, Nov 1966.
6. Garvey, Amy Jacques, ed: *Philosophy and Opinions of Marcus Garvey* (Universal Publishing House, New York, New York) 1923.
7. Garvey, Marcus: in Cronon, Edmund D: *Black Moses* (University of Wisconsin Press, Madison, Wisconsin) 1964.
8. Halisi, Clyde and Mtume, James, ed: *The Quotable Karenga* (US, Los Angeles, California) 1967.
9. Harding, Vincent: Religion and Resistance among Antebellum Negroes, 1800–1860, in the volume by August Meier and Elliot Rudwick, ed (Atheneum Publishers, New York, New York) forthcoming.
10. Hare, Nathan: Symposium on Black Power, *Negro Digest,* vol 16, no 1, Nov 1966.
11. Killens, John Oliver: Symposium on Black Power, *Negro Digest,* vol 16, no 1, Nov 1966.
12. King, Martin Luther: *Where Do We Go From Here?* (Harper & Row, Publishers, New York, New York) 1967.
13. Lester, Julius: The Angry Children of Malcolm X, *Sing Out,* vol 16, no 5, Nov 1966, an important and eloquent contribution to our understanding of the coming of Black Power.
14. Muhammad, Elijah: *Message to the Black Man.*
15. National Committee of Negro Churchmen: "Black Power," A Statement, in Wright, reference 19.
16. Philippians 3.
17. Saunders, Stanley: I'll Never Leave the Ghetto, *Ebony,* vol 20, no 10, Aug 1967.
18. Walker, David: *Appeal* (1829) in Herbert Aptheker, ed, *One Continual Cry* (Humanities Press, Inc, New York, New York) 1965.
19. Wright, Nathan, Jr: *Black Power and Urban Unrest* (Hawthorn Books, Inc, New York, New York) 1967.
20. Wright, Richard: *White Man, Listen!* (Anchor Books, Doubleday & Company, Inc, Garden City, New York) 1964.

2. HOMELAND AND HOLOCAUST: ISSUES IN THE JEWISH RELIGIOUS SITUATION

by Richard L. Rubenstein

IT IS IMPOSSIBLE to divorce Jewish religious thought from Jewish history. The temporal vicissitudes of the Jewish people have been decisive in forming their characteristic religious responses in every age. The starting point of contemporary Jewish theology can only be contemporary history.

Two twentieth century events dwarf all others in their impact on contemporary Judaism. They are the extermination of Europe's Jews and the establishment of the State of Israel. These events have overturned much that was regarded as religiously normative by Jews for almost two thousand years.

Prof. Emil G. Fackenheim has observed that "the events that are associated with the dread name of Auschwitz" constitute the *one* experience that has proven *as yet* wholly unassimilable within the framework of normative Jewish thought [15:195]. According to Prof. Fackenheim, Jews have been grappling with the problems posed by secular liberalism for almost two centuries. The ferment among Protestant thinkers such as Harvey Cox over the religious meaning of the secular metropolis has no significant parallel in contemporary Judaism. To the extent that Jews have been at home anywhere in the western world they have been comfortable only in the urban environment. Nevertheless, they have found the secular city far more tribal and problematic than does Prof. Cox [29:145 ff; 27:199 ff]. Part of the thrust of modern Jewish experience has been to leave the city and find a place, at least for a segment of the community, on the land. This is the significance of Israel's cooperative agrarian settlements.

39

Auschwitz rather than secularity has proven to be one of the unassimilable events for normative Jewish theology. There is simply no way to harmonize Auschwitz with the biblical conception of a just God who is the omnipotent judge of the world and the ultimate author of human history. Prof. Fackenheim claims that Auschwitz is "as yet" unassimilable. If any philosopher-theologian has the sensitivity and competence to assimilate Auschwitz to the categories of normative Jewish theology, it is Prof. Fackenheim. If he cannot do it, it is not likely that it can be done. The words "as yet" reflect an understandable but pathetic hope destined never to be realized. None of the currently productive nonradical Jewish theologians have been capable of assimilating Auschwitz to their religious philosophy. The nonradical theological categories have been exploded by Auschwitz.

Like most of his theological contemporaries within Judaism, Prof. Fackenheim has very little to say concerning the *religious* significance of that other decisive and unassimilated event of contemporary Judaism, the establishment of the state of Israel. Most of the mainstream American-Jewish theologians write as if Israel were irrelevant to Jewish religious thought. Indeed, some are even hostile. Jakob J. Petuchowski, for example, is one of the most brilliant of the establishment theologians. His recent *Zion Reconsidered* [24] is the most sustained critique of Jewish nationalism written by a contemporary Jewish thinker. Writing before the decisive events of June 1967, Petuchowski rejects the role of Israel as the spiritual center for world Jewry. He concedes that Israel may become *one* of the spiritual centers but insists that this has not yet taken place. Arthur Cohen's insistence on the supernatural vocation of the Jew places him at odds with the majority of Israelis who reject the metahistorical interpretation of Jewish existence [10]. In reality, the reentry of a portion of the Jewish people into history presents almost as many problems for normative Jewish theology as does Auschwitz. It is doubtful whether the currently productive American-Jewish theologians will prove more capable of coping with the religious meaning of the state of Israel than with Auschwitz. Their theological categories are inadequate to the explosive realities of twentieth century Jewish history.

The establishment of a secular state with a Jewish majority
has turned the diaspora into a two thousand year parenthesis.
The religious values, beliefs, and aspirations of a defeated and
impotent Jewish minority, condemned to survive amidst the contempt of host nations, are no longer religiously normative, at
least in Israel. The majority of Israelis are not religious in the
traditional sense. Nevertheless, they do have a religion. They
celebrate the sacred times and seasons of the Jewish calendar.
They mark important moments in the timetable of life with appropriate rituals, often rituals historically authenticated within
Jewish tradition. They are immersed in biblical literature. They
love the land of Israel in a way which can only be described as
religious. Their religion is not the same as that of the diaspora in
fundamental mood. Neither middle-class American Judaism nor
the traditional Judaism of the ghettos of Eastern Europe has been
able to flourish in Israel.

On the soil of Israel's ancient land, Jews have once again become pagan in fact if not in name.

[It is very likely that my statement that Israel's Jews are becoming pagan in fact if not in name will be misunderstood. I
have in mind somewhat the same contrast as that suggested by
Mircea Eliade's description of the difference between archaic
religions and the religions of history — prophetic-rabbinic Judaism and Christianity. What I refer to as pagan is very much the
same religious type that Eliade calls archaic [14:1-34, 141-162;
1:44 ff].

There are two fundamental problems involved in the revital-
ization of Jewish paganism: (a) realized eschatology and (b)
the religion of nature vs the religion of history. By any reading
of classical Jewish sources, the goal of historical Judaism was
the recovery of the land of Israel and the restoration of the
exiled people to its territorial domain. For those Jews who have
returned to Israel, Judaism's eschatological goal has been partly
realized and history is nearing an end. This does not mean that
the negative aspects of existence have been dissolved. That is
too simplistic a view of archaic religion. It does mean that
Jewish religious experience will become predominantly cyclical
and ahistorical in nontechnological matters. See, for example,
my *After Auschwitz* [27:131 ff].]

Elsewhere I have argued that a reconstituted Jewish paganism is the only form of religious life adequate to contemporary Jewish experience [27:113 ff, 131 ff, 243 ff]. One of the problems yet to be placed upon the agenda of contemporary Jewish theology is the meaning of the new Jewish paganism. Only Arthur Cohen has attempted to deal with it, and he regards the new Jewish paganism as a betrayal of Israel's "supernatural vocation" [6:280 ff].

THE NEW MAJORITY

One of the more ironic results of the recent re-creation of the Jewish state is that, for the first time in almost two thousand years, Jews have some direct experience with the problems facing a national majority as it confronts a minority with a different culture and religion. Sooner or later, this perspective is bound to alter many things, not the least of which will be Israeli religion. The myths and value structure of a majority with effective political and military power are not likely to be the same as those of a minority without power. Many Israeli leaders have long insisted that the situation of diaspora Judaism is "abnormal." (On the twentieth anniversary of the Warsaw ghetto uprising, Prime Minister David Ben-Gurion declared that the only way Jews could prevent more massacres would be to "cease to be a people depending on the mercy of others." He insisted that "Hatred of Jews will not vanish until the majority of our people are reunited in their original home and until that home is secure." Georges Friedmann asserts that Israeli public opinion corresponds to Ben-Gurion's statement [16:229].)

American Jewish theologians may have little to say about the religious significance of Israel because their life situations are so different from the Israelis'. In this respect, Martin Buber must be seen as a diaspora theologian, even though he spent his last years in Jerusalem. With almost no exceptions, American Jewish theologians are very comfortable members of the upper middle class. They function in a high status profession. Their religious perspectives inevitably reflect the needs and aspirations of the class to which they belong and from which they derive their principal support. No matter how prosperous this group may be, it lacks experience with the realities of decision-making power in the upper echelons of the armed forces, the financial community, and primary industry. It also lacks intimate social contact with these groups. Middle and upper class Jews simply do not experience the world as do their gentile counterparts. American Jews are largely confined to a single stratum of society. The American Jewish ghetto may be gilded, but it remains a ghetto nonetheless.

In America Jews must constantly seek acceptance as members of a minority group, an acceptance which can never entirely be granted. In Israel, Jewish experience of the world, whether as military officers or as laborers, is far closer to that of American gentiles than American Jews. To date, most American Jewish theologians remain silent about the problems arising out of the growing hiatus between the two major Jewish communities. The social transformations which have occurred in Israel have been so great that one distinguished French-Jewish sociologist has recently explored the question of whether the establishment of the state of Israel will ultimately mean the end of the Jewish people and Judaism as we know it [16:220 ff]. The Israelis are convinced that in any military confrontation they stand nakedly alone. They have had no alternative but to become the new Spartans of the Middle East. This radical transformation will also be reflected in their religious life. The religious values of a community destined to live by its military cunning cannot be the same as those of the middle class business and professional communities of the diaspora. The contrast between the response of Europe's Jews to Hitler and the Israelis' response to the Arabs is so vast as to make one wonder whether they are one people. They are, of course, one people. Israelis are Jews who have been transformed by the catastrophic events of twentieth century Jewish history.

Even in the diaspora, there has been a massive shift in sentiment from religious belief to religious ethnicity. This shift has been given theological formulation by the Reconstructionists under the leadership of Prof. Mordecai M. Kaplan and Dr. Ira Eisenstein [21; 13]. More than any other Jewish religious group, the Reconstructionists have stressed the creative role of the Jewish people in the shaping of the character of Judaism in every age. Their assertion that Judaism must be understood primarily as the religious creation of the Jewish people rather than as a body of rigidly fixed doctrines and practices has added an important dimension of realism to Jewish religious thought. Whatever most diaspora Jews believe, they consider themselves primarily a distinctive religio-ethnic group rather than a community with a common creed. Far more Jews today accept the unity of Jewish destiny than the unity of Jewish belief. This unity was very much in evidence during the 1967 Arab-Israeli war. Jews throughout the world manifested an unprecedented emotional and practical involvement in the fate of Israel. Jewish leaders universally report that the response was of far greater intensity than they could have anticipated before the event. I can report that many Jews who had imagined themselves to be totally devoid of any inner connection with Jewish life were overwhelmed by their involvement in Israel's trial. It is difficult to describe the emotion we felt when we beheld Jews praying at the Western Wall and when we realized that the site of the ancient Temple was in Jewish hands for the first time in 1897 years. We did not feel triumphant over the Arabs. We did not believe that God had finally righted the scales for Auschwitz. We did feel profound joy and thanksgiving that a chapter in Jewish history begun in Roman times had finally been brought to a close. I must confess surprise at the depth of my own feelings. There are unconscious depths to the phenomenon of Jewishness which even those of us who have spent our lives in its study cannot fathom. No Jewish theology will be adequate which fails to take account of the response of the world's Jews to Israel's recent struggle.

CONSEQUENCES OF SURVIVAL JUDAISM

One of the most radical transformations experienced by religious Jews since the establishment of Israel has been the alteration of our sense of time and history. For almost two thousand years,

44

the goal of Jewish history was the future restoration of Zion. Ages passed. The goal was unrealized. Time seemed to drag on as a dreary theatre of almost unrelieved Jewish suffering. The restoration of Israel has transformed the destruction of Jerusalem by the Romans into a modern event. Modern Jewish history begins in Roman times. In 1948 the Jewish community in Israel reversed a historic defeat inflicted upon them by an ancient foe. In the process, they made a parenthesis of the diaspora experience. Time has ceased to be linear and future oriented for Jews. Once again, it has become archaic, cyclical, and pagan.

[Jewish theologians have yet to confront Marshall McLuhan's observations on the role of electric technology in restoring archaic, tribalized man. McLuhan has observed that "Modern man, since the electro-magnetic discoveries of more than a century ago, is investing himself with all the dimensions of archaic man *plus*" [22:69].

Perhaps the difficulty Jewish thinkers have in dealing with the phenomenon of neoarchaic man is that their culture and values are so deeply rooted in what McLuhan would describe as a linear typographical mentality. One of the most important consequences of the defeat of the Jews by the Romans in 70 was that verbal surrogates increasingly took the place of concrete experience, with a consequent shift in the ratios of sensory intake. Thus, the verbal recitation of the laws of the sacrificial cult took the place of actual sacrifice; the verbal memory of the life of the people in its own land served as surrogate for the actual life of the Jew in his own territory. In the nineteenth century, the substitution of the verbal for the real was regarded as an advance from the material to the spiritual. Most Jewish thinkers still share this estimation. I am convinced that there was at least as much loss as gain in the enforced shift.

The retribalization of the Jew and the return to the concrete experience of territory marks the return of archaic man in Israel. McLuhan sees the phenomenon of retribalization as a function of electric technology. I believe there have been more tragic, historical factors involved for Israel's Jews. One of the most striking facts about today's Israeli is his capacity to express himself with great verbal economy. The contrast between Israeli modes of expression and the verbal expressiveness of diaspora Jews is startling. For further comments on the return of archaic man in Israel, see *After Auschwitz* [27:131 ff].]

Jewish thinkers have begun to reexamine the meaning of the ancient fall of Jerusalem and the character of the resultant diaspora Judaism in the light of twentieth century experience. Whatever their racial background, today's Jews trace their psychological, cultural, and religious roots back to the Palestinian community which was decisively defeated by the Romans in two desperate wars in the years 67–70 C.E. and 132–135 C.E. As a result of these defeats, Jews were condemned to dwell as a threatened community lacking territory or power over their own destiny. Their territorial estrangement coincided with the rise of the Church and its claim that the Jews were condemned to wander about, Cainlike and degraded, until their conversion [3:57 ff; 20]. Political and military defeat was compounded by the Christian insistence that the defeat was also religious.

Exile under conditions of powerlessness and increasing degradation became normative for Jews. It became necessary to develop a strategy of survival. Normative Judaism was largely the fruit of that strategy. Although Rabbinic Judaism is rooted in biblical Judaism, the religious life of Rabbinic Jews was as different from that of the biblical Jews as was their political and social life. Parenthetically, one of the reasons why Jewish-Christian dialogue has so frequently proven difficult, especially in countries in which church and state are not separated, is that it is exceedingly difficult for those with power to talk on equal terms with those without it.

Few peoples have ever imposed upon themselves the extraordinary measure of religious discipline in every aspect of human behavior as did the Jews after the Roman wars. Many explanations have been offered concerning these disciplines. Most of the articulate contemporary theologians see the value of Judaism's commandments primarily in terms of the opportunity they provide for Jews to enter into meaningful relationship with God. "Each time I observe a *mitzvah*, and praise God for having made us *kadosh* by means of his *mitzvot*, I affirm the doctrine of the chosen people," says Petuchowski [25:161]. The theologians tend to be hostile to psychological or sociological analyses of

46

Jewish religious behavior. Most Jewish theologians reject the possibility that Jewish religious practice is rooted primarily in biological, psychological, and cultural needs rather than in a divine-human encounter. (Will Herberg, for instance, says, "Human existence, individual and social alike, is radically incomplete, fragmentary. The attempt to comprehend life in its own terms, to live it in and for itself must prove self-destructive . . ." [17:16].) They are familiar with contemporary psychology and anthropology, but they would regard as unduly reductionist the social scientist's attempt to understand belief and ritual in functional perspectives. To the best of my knowledge, none of the religious thinkers who reject the theological relevance of the social sciences have ever confronted its findings in a disciplined and systematic way. They seem content to assert that God is the ultimate source of Jewish religious teaching, as if their assertions would make it so. "Israel is not a 'natural' nation. . . . It is a *supernatural* community, called into being by God to serve his eternal purposes in history" [17:271].

I would like to suggest an alternative to the God-hypothesis as a partial explanation of why Jews willingly imposed upon themselves so wide a system of behavioral disciplines during the long night of their exile. Lacking effective power over their own destiny, Jews were compelled to control their counteraggressive hostilities. Jews were as embittered with their persecutors as any other minority. They could, however, retaliate only in fantasy, as they did when they celebrated the demise of Pharaoh at Passover, the Maccabean victory at Hanukkah, and the defeat of Haman at Purim. In reality, they had absolutely no power to prevent their periodic degradation. They were compelled to resort to prayer, petition, and pleading as their primary resources. Unable to save themselves, they were compelled to look to the compassion and restraint of others as their only hope. Surrender, appeasement, and withdrawal were the classic modes of Jewish relation to the non-Jewish world. Nevertheless, Jewish anger was vast and had to be controlled. The need to control the community against the possibility of futile explosions of aggression was undoubtedly one of the reasons for the extraordinary measure of self-repression that Rabbinic Judaism placed upon the Jew in so many areas of life. Religious Jews were convinced for almost two thousand years that the system of self-repression was divinely ordained. Most contemporary Jewish thinkers continue to regard the system fundamentally in the same light. In view of the extent to which Jews have been objects of aggression throughout their diaspora experience, it seems very strange that contemporary Jewish theologians have so largely ignored the question of the role of aggression in forming many of the characteristic religious responses of normative Judaism.

THE FAILURE OF COMPLIANCE

The rabbinic system worked with some exceptions until modern times. As long as the feudal and Christian order had compelling authority in Europe, the Jews were a degraded minority. Nevertheless, their minimal safety was usually assured by the moral and religious restraints operative within Christendom. This was evident in one of the worst catastrophes ever experienced by the Jews, the expulsion from Spain in 1492. In the light of twentieth century experience, the treatment accorded the doomed community seems almost humane. From the Spanish point of view, there was no place in Spain for non-Christians after the conquest of the last Islamic outpost in the Iberian peninsula, Granada. The Catholic Monarchs, Ferdinand and Isabella, had the power to exterminate. This was never their intention. They gave Jews the harsh choice of expulsion or conversion. In the persecutions of the twentieth century, such options were no longer available.

It is no accident that the extermination of Europe's Jews took place in the twentieth century. It is part of the characteristic myopia of our times that the Nazi regime is regarded as a throwback to an earlier age. In reality, the Nazis were the quintessence of a certain modern political spirit.

[One of the most persistent misapprehensions of Jewish thinkers has been to regard the Nazis as pagans. The Nazis profoundly rejected the fundamental insistence of the pagan world on moderation in all things. The pagans were as guilty of excess as any

48

other men, but at least they did not make a virtue out of it. Elsewhere, I have suggested that the Nazis could best be understood as satanic anti-Christians who inverted traditional values but were nevertheless dependent upon them. I have attempted to liken the Nazis to the medieval priest who celebrated the Black Mass. Such a priest was dependent upon the religious system he sought to blaspheme [27:2, 3, 19 ff]. My analysis of the Nazis as apostles of excess rests largely upon the insights of Albert Camus [8:134 ff, 9:258 ff].]

The Nazis were totally devoid of any ethical or religious restraints. They regarded the Jews as unfit for inclusion in their social order. They devised a solution, a "final solution." Unlike Ferdinand and Isabella, the Nazis did not, after 1939, permit their unassimilable minorities the opportunity of finding refuge elsewhere. They utilized a perfected technology of death to exterminate them. They were especially skilful in minimizing the psychological effects of the slaughter among the German people [18:646 ff].

The reaction of Europe's Jews to the Nazi threat was in keeping with the two-thousand-year-old strategy of compliance with, and appeasement of, those in power. The reaction was also one of the most profound misreadings of the character and intentions of an enemy by any people in all of history. European Jewish leaders tended to assume that Hitler was a medieval antisemite in modern dress. Jewish communities pleaded with the Nazis, sought to bribe them, and finally complied with their orders even to the extent of selecting victims for the camps [18:666 ff]. The strategy of the powerless failed totally with the Nazis. Jews could give the Nazis nothing they were incapable of taking for themselves. The normative Jewish posture served only to simplify the Nazi efforts. In spite of the anger and bitterness which the writings of Hannah Arendt and Bruno Bettelheim [2:4] have aroused in the Jewish community, their questions about the failure of Jewish resistance and the suicidal Jewish compliance with the Nazis cannot be ignored. I wish to disassociate myself from the singular lack of compassion which permeates Miss Arendt's book. Nevertheless, her questions cannot be dismissed.

The reaction of the Jews to the Nazis has been ignored by the theologians. Nevertheless, the problem has enormous theological relevance, especially in the domain of religious ethics. Auschwitz marks the final bankruptcy of the religious, ethical, and psychological values of diaspora Judaism. The strategy of the powerless failed completely when confronted by a technologically competent enemy determined to annihilate.

American Jews often regard Auschwitz as a temporary setback in the moral progress of the race. The shock induced by the awesome wound remains too great to be faced openly and directly. In Israel, on the other hand, the terrible lesson of Auschwitz has become the cornerstone of national psychology. Israelis are convinced that they can trust nothing save their own determination to fight to the last man should an enemy seek to annihilate them. No people has less reason to believe in abstract moral principles, human virtue, or international institutions than do the Jews. *One of the supreme ironies of contemporary religious history is that the people who gave the world the prophetic vision of universal brotherhood and peace must effectively renounce its own heritage if it is to survive.*

The first religious task of the Jews of Israel is survival in a world in which aggression between nations is deterred only by a balance of mutual terror. The death of God as a cultural fact is real and all embracing. There is no greater contrast than that between the fruitless God talk of the American-Jewish theologians and the actions of the Israelis. The death of God extends not merely to relatively inconsequential matters of whether the divine Thou encounters man in prayer or ritual; it reaches to the far more consequential matter of nuclear terror as the last remaining deterrent to acts of national annihilation.

One of the surprising aspects of most contemporary Jewish theology is how overwhelmingly God centered it remains. This is especially true of Reform Jewish theology. Man's relation to God is absolutely decisive. Following the lead taken by Will Herberg and Arthur Cohen, Eugene Borowitz posits a new Jewish fideism, which traditional Jews would find exceedingly strange. "What is ultimately required," Borowitz asserts, "is faith" [5:33]. The content of Borowitz' faith is "Judaism's trust

50

in the God who acts in history" [5:35]. He dismisses Auschwitz, almost complacently, "And before Auschwitz and Treblinka, there was Assyrian genocide, Roman savagery, Crusader zeal, and Cossack brutality" [5:35]. Borowitz claims that the Jewish people are on earth to do God's work. Should they falter, he is convinced that "God will see it (i.e. the Jewish people) through history, tough and punishing a course as that may be. He has done so until now. He does so today. He will continue to do so until the Messiah comes" [5:35].

Borowitz expressed his faith in "the God who acts in history" in the summer of 1966. One wonders whether he would do so again after the events of the summer of 1967. The bland ascription of ultimate responsibility for human history to God is as difficult in moments of victory as in moments of defeat. In defeat, such an assertion makes God the punitive author of history. In victory, such sentiments have the grating sound of *"Gott mit uns."*

THE INFLUENCE OF ROSENZWEIG

If Jewish theologians have placed too much stress on God, they have, as we have observed, placed too little on the question of power. Milton Himmelfarb has observed that no figure has more deeply influenced today's American Jewish religious thinkers than the German-Jewish thinker, Franz Rosenzweig [19:5]. Rosenzweig has achieved a kind of sanctification among contemporary Jewish theologians. His personal story is very moving. At the point of conversion to Christianity, he returned to Judaism and became its preeminent spokesman in Germany during the nineteen-twenties. Many of the German-Jewish teachers who have instructed today's American rabbis were deeply influenced by him.

Rosenzweig's last years were burdened by multiple sclerosis. It was impossible for him to move from his bed or to communicate except by a finger and a specially constructed typewriter. Rosenzweig functioned in the face of a threat of total physical

51

powerlessness unkown to any other Jewish theologian in memory. If theologies reflect the life situation of the theologian, it may have been no accident that Rosenzweig elevated the impotence of the Jewish community to greater religious significance than any other modern thinker. He stressed the contrast between the worldliness of the Church and the indifference of the Synagogue to the struggles of history. He believed that the Synagogue could remain aloof from the taint of involvement in the power struggles between the nations! He asserted that ". . . the lifework of Israel is to anticipate the eternal day, in profession and action, to be its living presage, to hallow the name of God through its, Israel's, own holiness and with its Law as a people of priests. . . . The synagogue, which is immortal but stands with broken staff and bound eyes, must renounce all work in this world, and must muster all her strength to preserve her life and *keep herself untainted by life*" [26:342, italics mine].

Rosenzweig's vision of a synagogue "untainted by life" was ironically fulfilled in a way he never anticipated. He wrote these words while forces within his native Germany were preparing their "final solution." Rosenzweig died in 1929. The Nazis were well on the road to power. Rosenzweig's theology of a synagogue "untainted by life" contains no recognition of the destructive potential of the Nazi threat. Himmelfarb is correct in stressing Rosenzweig's influence on American rabbis. I have stressed some important aspects of his thought which were simply out of touch with reality. I would not deny that much that Rosenzweig taught continues to have great value. This is especially true of his suggestion that the modern, acculturated Jew must enter Judaism with the learning and insights he has acquired in the secular world, that he must bring his special capacities to bear on traditional Jewish literature. His view can be contrasted with the traditionalist insistence that reentry into Jewish life could only occur after turning away from the secular world and returning to the ghetto. Rosenzweig's unrealistic, metahistorical interpretations of Jewish life have been taken up by his American successors. They refuse to acknowledge that issues of power and worldliness must be faced in any realistic

Israeli soldiers flying their flag June 11, 1967, from the minaret of the mosque of El Kantara in Egypt's Sinai Desert.

philosophy of religion. To speak, as they do, of the "sanctity" of the "covenant people" and its "mission" while ignoring its real life is to turn theology into a very private fantasy.

A LACK OF THEOLOGICAL FERMENT

In the spring of 1966 *Commentary* invited a number of rabbis and theologians representing all three branches of American Judaism to participate in a symposium on the condition of Jewish belief [12]. The editors were moved to do so by the obvious ferment which had been taking place in Christian theological circles, especially the spectacular prominence given by the mass media to Protestant radical theology. Thirty-eight rabbis responded. There is general agreement that *Commentary's* selection was representative. The symposium is an excellent, if somewhat dull and repetitious, introduction to contemporary Jewish thought.

In his introductory remarks to the symposium, Milton Himmelfarb comments, "What impression does this symposium give of the present state of Jewish religious thought? In general, that there is far less theological ferment than among Christians and that there are few new ideas about Judaism" [19:4]. I would concur with Himmelfarb's estimate. There is no Jewish revolt against the "fathers" comparable to that evident among Christian thinkers. Nevertheless, I cannot entirely agree with Himmelfarb's analysis of why so little revolt is manifest. Himmelfarb contends that "What is a novelty to some Christians is, as many of the rabbis remind us, old-hat to Jews. . . . Those modern Jews who want to be religious, including rabbis, have such a long familiarity with modernity-godlessness that they are less apt to be shocked by it, for good or for ill, than the Christian clerical 'country boys,' as one of the rabbis below calls them" [19:4].

Himmelfarb's statement seems surprising. I believe he underestimates Christian religious sophistication. After all, Kant, Hegel, Schelling, and Kierkegaard were Christian thinkers. Himmelfarb supports his contention that Jews have had long exposure to modern skepticism by asserting that "Spinoza was the first modern Jew." Perhaps, but he was also excommunicated by his community. There were very few "modern" thinkers *within* the Jewish community until the nineteenth century. Jewish religious enlightenment has only become relatively widespread in the twentieth century.

The absence of theological ferment among contemporary Jews may have other roots. Himmelfarb alludes to one. Theology is simply less important to Jews than to Christians. One is born a Jew. Judaism places far greater stress on ethnicity and religious behavior than upon creed. I was reminded of this indifference to theology in a highly personal way during the past year. When my radical theological views became widely known in my community, a number of Christian radical theologians warned me that I would meet with much the same kind of hostility which greeted the public exposition of their theological views. Apart from a few crank letters, I experienced hardly any reaction at all. I would have compromised my ministry far more by a lack of good taste and personal judgement in the performance of my rabbinic responsibilities than by the public enunciation of theological ideas most Jews find very strange.

I believe the threatened character of twentieth century Jewish existence has contributed greatly to the conservatism of the religious intellectuals. In addition to the holocaust, the community has been faced with widespread defection through intermarriage and indifference. This is especially true in academic circles and every year more Jews enter this subculture. Several years ago there was much discussion of the "vanishing American Jew." The posture of a minority seeking to maintain its culture is normally defensive. This has been compounded by the severe losses experienced by the Jewish world in the twentieth century. Perhaps that is one reason for Franz Rosenzweig's influence. He had, as we have noted, almost totally withdrawn from the community before turning and finding his way to Jewish faith. His personal example may have been at least as influential as his ideas. Committed Jewish thinkers normally see themselves as conservers rather than as pathfinders. They are prepared to meet the challenges of modernity, but, by and large, they reject the role of innovator. They fear that novelty will lessen the already tenuous hold of Judaism on many of its brightest sons and daughters.

Last winter, I visited a distinguished Jewish theologian. During our conversation, I expressed my conviction that it is impossible to believe in the traditional God of Jewish history after Auschwitz. I said also that our situation after Auschwitz was different from Job's. (When the establishment theologians liken Auschwitz to the testing of Job, they seek to anaesthetize themselves from its radical impact. The attempt to retreat to normative Jewish experience is understandable but futile.)

The inmates of the death camps were totally degraded, deprived of their names, and given only numbers, reduced to the status of depressed, dependent, whining children, and finally abandoned by God and man [11:179 ff]. In the bible Job suffers horribly, but he remains a person. As Job, he never ceases to be addressed as "thou" by God and man. He sat upon the dungheap. At Auschwitz, the inmates became the dungheap. I told my colleague that the only God I believe in is the cannibal Mother Goddess of Earth who brings forth her children only to consume them and take them back unto herself. My colleague did not defend the God of history intellectually. Instead, with great sadness he said, "I cannot give up my belief in the God of history and turn pagan. To do so would be to assure the final victory of Hitler's work."

His reply revealed one of the deepest reasons for the theological conservatism of today's Jewish thinkers. Judaism has been attacked so devastatingly from the outside that many perceive theological radicalism as an additional internal attack. The "Hitler theme" crops up often. I must again write in a personal vein. When my rejection of the God of history became widely known, a number of critics wrote that I was in effect doing Hitler's work, that I was placing yet another nail in the coffin of Judaism. No other comments on my theological work have saddened me as much as these. I understand the fear of radical probing, although I believe the fear is profoundly mistaken. A people is like a living organism. It is impossible to rip out a major portion of its substance without the surviving remnant's experiencing the deepest shock. The trauma of Auschwitz has yet to spend itself among Jews. It remains emotionally impossible for most Jews to deal with it. The pain and the implied threat remain too great. When an individual experiences a trauma he cannot cope with, *denial* is one of the mechanisms of defense frequently resorted to. Nor is it altogether surprising that powerless people delude themselves with pathetic myths about their importance to the human drama. A straightforward theological confrontation of the facts of recent Jewish history, painful though it may be, is an act of religious and psychological therapy urgently needed by the Jewish community. Such a labor is not, and cannot be, Hitler's mischief.

FROM SEMINARY TO UNIVERSITY

Who listens to Jewish theologians? By and large, their writings and lectures are followed by rabbis, professionals serving the Jewish community, some college students, and intellectually involved members of reform and conservative synagogues. Only one major figure, Dr. Mordecai M. Kaplan, has a large national following. His following is currently more the result of an abiding personal charisma than of intellectual contributions. Dr. Kaplan is over eighty-five years old. He maintains an astonishing schedule. He continues to write, lecture, and teach. Throughout the country, his lectures draw capacity audiences. Dr. Kaplan inspires largely because of the triumph of life that his very long career effectively symbolizes. Kaplan's insistence on the centrality of ethnicity in Jewish religious life remains one of the abiding foundations of any realistic Jewish theology. Nevertheless, Kaplan's religious philosophy was formulated *before* Auschwitz. He is the dean of American Jewish thinkers, but he is of the generation of Buber and Tillich. It is not likely that we shall see many new departures in his thinking.

Emil L. Fackenheim, Eugene Borowitz, Arthur Cohen, Arnold Jacob Wolf, Maurice Friédman, Jacob J. Petuchowski, Stephen S. Schwarzschild, and Harold Schulweis are among the younger men who have contributed significantly to contemporary Jewish thought. This list is representative but by no means exhaustive. Only two serve in pulpits, Harold Schulweis and Arnold Jacob Wolf. Both serve with distinction in specialized communities with a very high educational level among their members, Rabbi Schulweis in Oakland, California, and Rabbi Wolf in Highland Park, Illinois. Both have responded to one of the continuing dilemmas of American Judaism, the high level of secular education and the very low level of Jewish education.

A generation ago it would have been exceptional for a well-known rabbi not to occupy a pulpit. There has been a radical shift. Many of today's theologians teach at secular universities. This new development will undoubtedly grow. Even a conserving theological mentality is not always comfortable when teaching at a rabbinical seminary or occupying a pulpit. The seminaries stress scholarly competence in textual studies rather than intellectual probing. Congregations can seldom afford the luxury of an intellectually involved rabbi; they require functionaries and they are unusually understaffed. Theology is pursued only when the problematics of religious belief are deeply felt. There is a hidden skeptic within the most traditional, establishment theologian. Increasingly, Jewish theologians are finding the neutral secular universities more congenial for their work than either the seminaries or the congregations.

I know of no Israeli theologian currently making a significant impact on American Jews. This is partly due to the fact that Orthodoxy alone has official status in Israel. Israeli Orthodoxy is primarily concerned with upholding the Law and ritual observance. This antitheological Israeli bias is in contrast to the sophistication of such articulate younger Orthodox thinkers as Zalman Schachter of Winnipeg, Manitoba, and Irving Greenberg of New York.

The absence of theology among Israelis may reflect also the fact that Israelis have less conflict about their Jewish identities than do most American Jews. Here we confront again the phenomenon of the well-educated American Jew who possesses only a minimal Jewish education. Many such Jews, whether college students or synagogue members, turn to the insights of the theologians as part of their quest for identity. Their interest in theology is part of their attempt to answer the question, "Who am I?" No American Jew with any sense of reality about his personal situation can ignore the religious determinants of his identity. Sooner or later, many American Jews realize how little they know about the Jewish aspects of their identities. Theology flourishes in America largely among assimilated Jews with tenuous religious roots. There is little interest in theology among Orthodox Jews. Their folk culture still has great sustaining power.

SECTARIAN JUDAISM

When, as a rabbinical student, I made the decision to enter the strange career of Jewish theologian, I realized that a significant part of my graduate studies would have to be pursued at a Protestant seminary. In the early nineteen-fifties, there was simply no tradition of the study of contemporary theology worthy of its name in the rabbinical seminaries. The giants among American theologians were Niebuhr and Tillich. Even Buber was taken more seriously by Protestant thinkers than by rabbis [19:3]. Without a disciplined understanding of theological method, the enterprise would have been futile. To become a Jewish theologian, I had to go to school among Protestants.

The elevation of theology to significance by Jews cannot entirely be understood apart from the acculturation process. Jews have been interested in theology where Protestant influence has been strongest, in the Germany before Hitler and in contemporary America. The fideism of Borowitz, Herberg, and Cohen seems to have deeper roots in sect-type Christianity than in any authentically Jewish experience. This is true also of the hostility these men express towards their own community for its religious indifference. One of Pope John's acts of genuine humanity was his insistence that the Good Friday prayer "We pray for the

59

perfidious Jews" be altered to "We pray for the Jews." In spite of Pope John's example, Borowitz finds no discomfort in writing of his own community, "The Jewish community appears so *perfidious* (italics mine) and out for such tawdry gain" [6:31]. The righteousness of God and the sinfulness of Israel is an old prophetic theme. Nevertheless, normative Judaism never made sectarian theological distinctions between the children of light and the children of darkness. There has been a real commitment to the unity of Israel. For all of the Orthodox rejection of the legitimacy of Reform and Conservative Judaism, no Orthodox leader has questioned the full membership in the community of Jews who were not Orthodox.

Sectarianism has manifested itself less among the Orthodox than among some of the new theologians. Borowitz has suggested that Jews lacking an appropriate theological commitment ought to be encouraged to leave the community [7]. Arthur Cohen regrets that it is no longer possible to excommunicate nonbelieving Jews [10:192–193]. Jacob Petuchowski laments the inability of his rabbinical organization to exclude "on mere ideological grounds" [23]. (In fairness to Dr. Petuchowski, I must state that he has informed me that his intention was never to exclude members of the Central Conference of American Rabbis on ideological grounds but to seek for a compatible group within the larger body.)

Harold Schulweis sees three tendencies as characterizing the direction of these men [28:230 ff]: (a) an exaggerated emphasis on the individual's personal encounters with ever greater indifference to the community and those institutions which make for stability and continuity; (b) a strong tendency towards anti-intellectualism and an emphasis on the "hubris of human reason"; (c) an "aristocratic aloofness towards social and political ideology." I would add a fourth tendency, (d) a myopic indifference to the actual lives of Jews and the concrete historical situation of the Jewish community both in Israel and the diaspora.

The newer theologians are increasingly fostering a fideistic, sectarian Judaism. Their theology reflects the values of a Jewish upper middle class whose recent prosperity has not brought full acceptance in American life. Both the theologians and those they address often feel unduly guilt ridden. They are ill at ease with their good fortune and their very tenuous Judaism. They often have a compelling need to be reminded of their unworthiness. It is not surprising that they turn to a kind of Jewish Calvinism. The theological contempt heaped upon "perfidious," "natural" Jews may also be an expression of an upper middle class ideology which heightens the unspoken but very real social antagonisms within the Jewish community.

The ultimate import of theology seems to be its relevance to human self-understanding. The test of good theology would seem to be preeminently practical: *Does it deepen and help to clarify the individual's manifold insights about himself, his community, his religious and ethical values, and his place in the time-table of life in such a way that he can realistically function with minimal conflict between his biological, psychological, and cultural needs, his actions towards others, his beliefs, and his ultimate aspirations?* The wise theologian speaks about God the better to understand himself and his fellowmen. If theology does not enhance our capacity to work and to love, it is an expression of disturbed fantasy.

I think it is apparent that I cannot honestly describe the mainstream expressions of current Jewish theology as meeting the test of good theology. Of all the confusions experienced by diaspora Jews, few have been as great as the failure of many of their best religious minds to face the reality of modern Jewish history in both its agony and its triumph. Jewish history has written the final chapter in the terrible story of the God of history. The straight line of Jewish history has become the circle of eternal return. The people who gave the world the dread illusion of the angry sky-god recants its folly. The joy of Israel's Jews at the Western Wall was the joy of homecoming. After nineteen hundred years, Jews have begun to return home, to the only home they ever knew. Archaic man has reappeared in the midst of the children of Abraham the wanderer. So too have the archaic gods.

61

REFERENCES

1. Altizer, Thomas J J: *Mircea Eliade and the Dialectic of the Sacred* (Westminster Press, Philadelphia, Pennsylvania) 1963.
2. Arendt, Hannah: *Eichmann in Jerusalem* (The Viking Press, Inc, New York, New York) 1963.
3. Baron, Salo W: *A Social and Religious History of the Jews*, vol 2 (Columbia University Press, New York, New York) 1952.
4. Bettelheim, Bruno: *The Informed Heart* (The Free Press, formerly of Glencoe, Illinois, now of New York, New York) 1960.
5. Borowitz, Eugene: in *Commentary's The Condition of Jewish Belief* (The Macmillan Company, New York, New York) 1967.
6. Borowitz, Eugene: reply in the *Commentary* symposium, reference 5, p 31.
7. Borowitz, Eugene: The Jewish Need for Theology, *Commentary*, August 1962.
8. Camus, Albert: Helen's Exile, *The Myth of Sisyphus*, Justin O'Brien, translator (Vintage Books, Random House, Inc, New York, New York) 1955, 134 ff.
9. Camus, Albert: *The Rebel*, Anthony Bower, translator (Penguin Books, Inc, Baltimore, Maryland, and Harmondsworth, Middlesex, England) 1962, pp 258 ff.
10. Cohen, Arthur: *The Natural and Supernatural Jew* (Pantheon Books, Inc, of Random House, Inc, New York, New York) 1962.
11. Cohen, Elie A: *Human Behavior in the Concentration Camp*, M H Braaksma, translator (W W Norton & Co, Inc, New York, New York) 1953.
12. *Commentary*, the editors of, a symposium: *The Condition of Jewish Belief* (The Macmillan Company, New York, New York) 1967. Originally published in *Commentary*, Aug 1966, vol 42, no 2.
13. Eisenstein, Ira, and Kohn, Eugene, ed: *Mordecai M Kaplan:*

An Evaluation (Jewish Reconstructionist Foundation, New York, New York) 1952.

14. Eliade, Mircea: *Cosmos and History: The Myth of Eternal Return* (Harper Torchbooks, Harper and Row, Publishers, New York, New York) 1959.

15. Fackenheim, Emil G: On the Self-Exposure of Faith to the Modern-Secular World: Philosophical Reflections in the Light of Jewish Experience, *Daedalus* (Boston, Massachusetts) Winter 1967.

16. Friedmann, Georges, *The End of the Jewish People?* Eric Mosbacher, translator (Doubleday & Company, Inc, Garden City, New York) 1967.

17. Herberg, Will: *Judaism and Modern Man* (Jewish Publication Society, Philadelphia, Pennsylvania) 1951.

18. Hilberg, Raul: *The Destruction of the European Jews* (W H Allen & Co, Ltd, London, England) 1961.

19. Himmelfarb, Milton: Introduction, *The Condition of Jewish Belief*, a symposium compiled by the editors of *Commentary*, published in book form (The Macmillan Company, New York, New York) 1967.

20. Isaac, Jules: *The Teaching of Contempt: Christian Roots of Anti-Semitism*, Helen Weaver, translator (Holt, Rinehart & Winston, Inc, New York, New York).

21. Kaplan, Mordecai M: *Judaism as a Civilization* (The Macmillan Company, New York, New York) 1934.

22. McLuhan, Marshall: *The Gutenberg Galaxy* (University of Toronto Press, Toronto, Ontario, Canada) 1962.

23. Petuchowski, Jakob: The Limits of Liberal Judaism, *Judaism*, Spring 1965.

24. Petuchowski, Jakob, J: *Zion Reconsidered* (Twayne Publishers, New York, New York) 1966.

25. Petuchowski, Jakob J: in *The Condition of Jewish Belief*, a symposium compiled by the editors of *Commentary*, published in book form (The Macmillan Company, New York, New York) 1967.

26. Rosenzeig, Franz: a letter to Rudolf Ehrenberg in *Franz Rosenzeig: His Life and Thought*, Nahum N Glatzer, editor

and translator (Jewish Publication Society, Philadelphia, Pennsylvania) 1953.

27. Rubenstein, Richard L: *After Auschwitz: Radical Theology and Contemporary Judaism* (The Bobbs-Merrill Co, Inc, Indianapolis, Indiana) 1966.

28. Schulweis, Harold: A Religion Like All Other Religions, in *Varieties of Jewish Belief*, Ira Eisenstein, ed (Reconstructionist Press, New York, New York) 1966.

29. Schwarzschild: Steven S: A Little Bit of Revolution, in Callahan, Daniel, ed: *The Secular City Debate* (The Macmillan Company, New York, New York) 1966.

COMMENTARY

by Milton Himmelfarb

TRADITIONALLY, a Jewish commentary is a series of comments on important or difficult points in a text — often rivaling or exceeding the text in length.

A brief preface: I am sorry Rabbi Rubenstein has written this account of the Jewish religious situation, not so much because he says things I disagree with as because he has not done himself justice. Dr. Rubenstein teaches in a university department of French and knows what the French mean when they say that something is "only literature." I fear that much of what he has written here is only literature.

Auschwitz rather than secularity has proven to be one of the unassimilable events for normative Jewish theology. It is not theology alone that has been unable to assimilate Auschwitz, or theologians alone. I confess that I find it impossible to think in any sustained way about Auschwitz and all that Auschwitz symbolizes. According to Wittgenstein, whereof one cannot speak, thereof one should not speak. Since we have to speak about Auschwitz, we should speak about it reluctantly, hesitantly, with fear and trepidation, lest in some way we profane the memory of

Auschwitz by using it to prove a point — or even worse, to enhance a reputation by proving a point. In a generation contemporary with Auschwitz, none should speak of it with any pretense to authority except possibly those who have themselves survived it. I do not say this because of the conclusion that Rubenstein draws from Auschwitz, that God is not good. Rubenstein does not need Auschwitz for that.

There is simply no way to harmonize Auschwitz with the biblical conception of a just God who is the omnipotent judge of the world and the ultimate author of human history. A just God is a dogma of Judaism and has been since before the days of Jeremiah — dogma, because it is an assertion of faith and not at all a fact or reality of human life evident to eyes not illuminated by that faith. The Rabbis of the Talmud characterized the unbeliever as one who says, in their Judeo-Aramaic, *let din we-let dayyan,* there is no judgment (or, law) and there is no Judge. From Abraham in Genesis ("shall not the Judge of all the earth do justice?") to the hasidic Levi Isaac of Berditchev less than two hundred years ago, the classical literature of Judaism is full of stories of our most righteous men remonstrating about God's justice.

A little farther on Rubenstein dislikes Dr. Borowitz's statement that Auschwitz is not new. For us Auschwitz is unique because it happened in our generation, but previous generations knew horrors which made an impact upon them comparable to the impact of Auschwitz upon us. From that point of view, Auschwitz is not new. It is new for us, the Auschwitzes of the past having for us become literature or history. Not only in the 20th century could an indictment be drawn against God for His injustice.

The establishment of a secular state with a Jewish majority has turned the diaspora into a 2,000-year parenthesis. "Secular" is one of those tricky words. To be sure, Israel is a secular state; but its secularity or secularism is not the same thing as the secularity or secularism of the Soviet Union or even of the Third French Republic. As for the "long parenthesis," that is what people like Mr. Ben-Gurion have been saying. I think, however, that Israelis are increasingly coming to realize that the two thousand years of Jewish history before the establishment of the State of Israel are not to be dismissed so easily, since values created or developed in that diaspora bimillennium need to be conserved in Israel itself.

I am a bit surprised to find this notion of a historical parenthesis in Rubenstein. I would not have thought him to be of a school of Jewish theology especially apt to be influenced by the Christian theology of a Karl Barth, yet it is for Barth — as I understand it — that history is parenthetical, with the entire passage of time between the First Coming and the Second Coming of quite secondary worth.

. . . only a reconstituted Jewish paganism is the form of religious life adequate to contemporary Jewish experience. "Reconstituted" and "Jewish" do not tell us which paganism Rubenstein has in mind, the modern or the ancient. For the historian Peter Gay, in his recent *Enlightenment: The Rise of Modern Paganism*, modern paganism is atheism. To modern Jews or untraditional Jews, what would be new about atheism? Only one thing. Modern or modernizing Jews for two hundred years or more have been particularly receptive to the Enlightened "anthropological" criticism of religion: that religion breeds intolerance, persecution, superstition, obscurantism. Modern, Enlightened Jews used to be particularly fond of this argument because their own entry into the general life of the cultures and societies in which they lived and of which they wished to be part was barred by the Constantinian Christendoms of Europe in the 18th, 19th, and early 20th centuries. In the experience of many modern Jews, religion when it was Christian was reactionary, stupid, and persecuting, and religion when it was Jewish was intolerant, superstitious, and self-isolating. Only irreligion was that outlook on the world which at the same time promised to benefit mankind and was fitting for an Enlightened mind.

To the surprise of Enlightened, modern Jews in this last third of the 20th century, we find that the center of antisemitism in the world today is precisely the country in which irreligion figures most importantly as official doctrine, to be spread and imposed with the utmost energy or even violence. The Soviet Union is antisemitic as well as intolerant, persecuting, obscurantist, and, some would say, superstitious. From that point of view what is new is not a rise in the prestige of atheism but rather a decline.

If it is to ancient paganism that Rubenstein wants the Jews to return, he is not original. A good deal of "classical" modern Hebrew literature was explicitly pagan in this sense. Poets and essayists thought that Judaism had made the Jews submissive, passive, and cringing, and that the Jews could regain their masculinity or indeed their full humanity only by overthrowing the religion that had done such bad things to them. Much of this shows Nietzsche's influence. A famous poem by Saul Chernikhovsky recalls the old days when the virile, warlike Israelites' YHWH was a pagan deity like Baal or Chemosh. But, the poet laments, the Israelites became Jews and spoiled everything by "binding him [YHWH] with the thongs of their phylacteries." For Chernikhovsky, as for the authors of the New Testament, phylacteries are an outward token of much that is inwardly wrong with Judaism.

Rubenstein tells us the Israelis are becoming pagan. This makes all the more intriguing the symbolical fact that immediately after the Israeli victory in the lightning war of 1967 there was such a run on phylacteries in Jerusalem that stocks were depleted for a while. Men who had never had phylacteries, or had not had them for many years, insisted on buying their own so that they could put them on when they went to offer their thanksgiving prayers before the rewon Western Wall. If this is paganism, it is of a more subtle and unforthright kind than Rubenstein seems to believe.

Rubenstein would have it that Israelis, or perhaps modern Jews in general, are moving from traditional Judaism to paganism — moving on or moving back. I suggest that if Israeli Jews, or modern Jews generally, are moving at all, it is from modern paganism back to some measure of Judaic tradition.

. . . American Jewish theologians are very comfortable members of the upper middle class. They function in a high-status

67

profession. If this is true it is new, and I am glad to hear it. I had thought the old joke still applied: "Your son is going to be a rabbi? What kind of profession is that for a nice Jewish boy?"

. . . *this group . . . lacks experience with the realities of decision-making power. . . .* I have myself argued that this accounts for some of the abstract moralism of classical Reform Judaism and for some of the abstract, ideologized liberalism of many Jews not associated with the synagogue at all. I have also said that Israel has been a kind of lesson in reality for Jews not living in Israel, helping them to realize better than ever before the moral ambiguities of power and the inadequacies of a moralism derived from mere powerlessness. If this is true of Jews generally, it is no less true of the theologians Rubenstein is criticizing.

The religious values of a community destined to live by its military cunning cannot be the same as those of the middleclass business and professional communities of the diaspora. True, of course (though I would prefer to say "prowess." Cunning is the attribute of clever little Hebrews). But that is one of the advantages of an old, historical religion like Judaism, containing within itself elements which, if they do not actually contradict each other, at least stand in tension with each other. According to time, circumstance, and temperament, individual Jews or Jewish communities will prefer one emphasis in the tradition to another. Practically every weekday morning a Jew who prays recites the 20th Psalm, which includes this verse: "Some invoke chariots and others horses, but we the name of the LORD our God." After the Sabbath he begins the evening prayer with the 144th Psalm, which starts with this verse: "Blessed be the LORD my Rock, who trains my hand for war and my fingers for battle."

. . . *there has been a massive shift . . . from religious belief to religious ethnicity.* The trouble with this sentence lies in the auxiliary verb "has." Rubenstein would have been more correct if he had said there *had* been a massive shift. The shift is not new. The intellectual origins of Conservative Judaism in this country are usually assigned to 19th century Germany and the so-called

Historical School of men like Zecharias Frankel. Frankel broke with the Reformers on what should have been, theologically or "religiously," a minor point, their readiness to do away with Hebrew in the ritual — but not a minor point "ethnically." (There must be a better word. The New Testament *ethnikoi* renders Hebrew *goyim* and is in the English versions "Gentiles.")

Far more Jews today accept the unity of Jewish destiny than . . . of Jewish belief. Again, true, but also true of yesterday and the day before. What is really new today is, as I believe, that relatively more Jews who are modern accept Jewish belief today than a generation ago. In general, the God who died for modern Jews was less the God of Jewish tradition, who for them had died some time ago, than the God of the philosophers, The God That Failed.

Jews throughout the world manifested an unprecedented emotional and practical involvement in the fate of Israel. Yes, but the new sympathizers with Israel were recruited less from the religious than from those for whom a universalist, secularist messianism had replaced the traditional Judaism of their grandparents. What *these* were turning from when they turned to Israel and identification with the Jewish people was not theistic faith of a traditional kind. They were turning from modernist substitutes for theistic faith.

. . . *almost unrelieved Jewish suffering.* It is hard for a Jew to argue that the Jews did not suffer all that much. That would be unfeeling and might make things too easy for the antisemites. Still, as a matter of objective historical scholarship, it must be said that Rubenstein is quite old-fashioned here. "Unrelieved Jewish suffering" is part of the discredited "lachrymose interpretation of Jewish history."

Take as a standard of human welfare the distance at which a given social grouping stands from The Man With The Hoe. By that standard, in nearly every place and at nearly every time the average Jew has fared better than the average man who is not a Jew. Just one example: the Protestant historian G.G. Coulton has written that it would be unfair to compare Jew and Christian for literacy and education in medieval Western Europe. The fair comparison would be between Jew and Christian priest. Even so, Coulton says, the average Jew was better educated than the average priest.

There were massacres of Jews during the crusades, in Europe and Palestine. There was also a crusade of genocide against the Albigensians.

The historians of Jewish historiography have noted that while the lachrymose interpretation that Rubenstein likes is now popular with Zionist and Israeli contemners of diaspora powerlessness, it began as a kind of ideology of diaspora powerlessness — first a religious and then a secularist-assimilationist one.

Modern Jewish history begins in Roman times. "Only literature" — and poor history. The distinguished historian I.F. Baer advances a periodization in which the rabbinical era is a kind of autonomous unity. For him this begins not with the destruction of the Temple and the defeat at the hands of the Romans but several centuries earlier, with the Maccabees, and it ends with the end of the Jewish Middle Ages, sometime between the 14th and 18th centuries. Though this historian is an Israeli, for him the defeat at the hands of the Romans is secondary to the more overarching unity of rabbinism, which began earlier and declined later.

Time has ceased to be linear and future oriented for Jews. Once again, it has become archaic, cyclical, and pagan. More "literature." On the contrary, a major goal of Jewish linearity has been achieved in the reunification of Jerusalem. After all, that is what those old linear and future-oriented Jews prayed for all the time. That very nonpagan Jewish theologian Maimonides defined the Days of the Messiah as differing from our days in only one respect, that in the Days of the Messiah the Jews would no longer be enslaved by foreign kingdoms. Rubenstein, with his cyclical, pagan time, implies that the whole cycle of defeat and exile is inevitably going to begin again. That is possible, but not inevitable; and those Israelis whom Rubenstein considers to be pagan are not at all reconciled to its inevitability or necessity.

70

. . . self-repression. . . . Freud — whom Rubenstein may regard as a pagan Jew — thought that while repression was not a happy thing, it was a necessary thing. He believed that people could not live together in society without repression. As he said, "the ulcer is the wound-stripe of civilization." Does Rubenstein know of a culture or society, whether religious or secular, theistic or pagan, that dispenses with repression and does not attempt to have its members internalize repression in the form of self-repression?

Traditional Judaism was not only a system of repression but also a system of self-expression. Aside from the weekly cycle of sabbath contrasted to weekday and the yearly cycle of feasts contrasted to fasts, there is the question of sexuality. Rubenstein must surely realize that traditional or rabbinic or normative Judaism has been rather less repressive sexually than Christianity. Celibacy has never been a Jewish ideal, only chastity.

If traditional Judaism really imposed a grievous burden of self-repression — particularly repression of rage, violence, and resentment — we should expect to find an expression of those repressed emotions when the Jews freed themselves from the old discipline. Rabbinical law and the rabbinical outlook have been largely abandoned; in Israel, at least, Jews live without worrying about a Gentile majority; but where are the rage and violence that are supposed to have been waiting to burst out?

. . . their [the Jews'] minimal safety was usually assured by the moral and religious restraints operative within Christendom. . . . the Nazis were the quintessence of a certain modern political spirit. Exactly. The Nazis were pagans — modern and atheist, or would-be ancient. Why then is Rubenstein so convinced that paganism is a Good Thing?

The strategy of the powerless failed totally with the Nazis. Not the strategy, the fact, of powerlessness. The Communists had no strategy or philosophy of powerlessness, but the Nazis murdered every functionary of the Communist parties they could get their hands on.

. . . the people who gave the world the prophetic wisdom of universal brotherhood and peace must effectively renounce their own heritage if they are to survive. Not at all. They must only fight to keep themselves alive until the vision becomes a reality.

There is no greater contrast than that between the fruitless God talk of the American theologians and the actions of the Israelis. Of course there is a contrast between talk and action. Before the Arab-Israeli war broke out in 1967, the talking rabbis were quite active in mobilizing support for the Israelis and in helping to raise large sums of money. After the victory, those active Israelis rushed to the Western Wall to pray — that is, to talk. They gave thanks to God, by talk, for the victory that they had won, as they thought, miraculously. Among the Israelis who prayed and thanked God were many who would formerly have considered themselves to be pagans — of the modern kind.

. . . relatively inconsequential matters of whether the divine Thou encounters man. . . . Even for someone who stresses the social and communal nexus of religion, it should not be an inconsequential matter whether the divine Thou encounters man.

. . . Will Herberg . . . Arthur Cohen . . . Eugene Borowitz. . . . Rubenstein almost gives the impression that these three men are the captains of a host of powerful theologians, of a crushingly intolerant point of view, trying to bully a small but courageous minority of radical Jewish theologians of one sort or another — naturalist, or ethnicist, or death-of-God. In fact, at least until recently, Herberg, Cohen, and Borowitz represented what I think to be a minority point of view; and Rubenstein, in so far as he is a Reconstructionist and a disciple of Mordecai Kaplan, represented a more prevalent point of view — if not among theologians, then among rabbis. If Herberg, Cohen, and Borowitz sound excessively zealous, it is because they have had to take firm positions to counter what was until quite recently the dominant outlook. Herberg, Cohen, and Borowitz were trying to restore the fideist element of the Jewish tradition, which had been subordinated or had actually come to be despised. Classical Judaism, it has been said, was orthoprax rather than orthodox.

Some moderns took this as a license to say that all a Jew need do was to observe certain rituals distinctively Jewish in an ethnic sense, and not concern himself at all about such matters as God. (The various codes of Jewish law, legalistic and ritualistic, are emphatic about the primary commandment of loving and revering God.) So far had it gone that some critics of Herberg, Cohen, and Borowitz could bring themselves to say that these men's concern with God was unJewish. Rubenstein himself comes rather close to saying the same thing.

. . . *Gott mit uns*. Not necessarily. To thank God does not imply that one thinks God is always on one's side. Those Jews who have been offering their thanksgiving prayers at the Western Wall are well aware that their present joy was preceded by sorrow. Most of them know that verse from Isaiah: "I form light and create darkness, I make peace and create evil."

Rubenstein wants to have it both ways. If Jews thank God for victory, theirs is a *Gott mit uns* religion. If in their prayers they lament but justify exile and persecution "because of our sins," they are being masochistic, self-repressive.

. . . *Franz Rosenzweig*. Rosenzweig's theology was not an outgrowth of disease. His disease came upon him in the last years of his life, when his theology had been formed.

Rubenstein implies that most modern Jewish theologians agree with Rosenzweig's notion of the synagogue's renouncing this world and keeping itself untainted by life. Not so. This point of view of Rosenzweig's was a consequence of a valuation of Christianity which most rabbis do not share with him. For Rosenzweig there was a kind of division of God's labor between Christianity and Judaism, with Christianity venturing forth into the world to bring the word of God to the heathen and Judaism staying at home to guard the purity of that word: "Jacob was a quiet man, dwelling in tents." Even those American rabbis who are directly or indirectly Rosenzweig's disciples are not inclined to accept this notion.

The implication that Rosenzweig emphasized passivity over activity, and thought activity in some way immoral, is clearly

wrong. From one point of view, for a believing Jew, Rosenzweig was daringly proactivist. In discussing the false messiahs
of Jewish history, and notably Shabbethai Zevi, Rosenzweig said
that of course those who opposed Shabbethai Zevi were right,
because Shabbethai Zevi was a false messiah. But, he also said, the
danger in such opposition, right as it may have been, is that it
may finally induce an unwarranted skepticism about the claims
of all messiahs, including the true one, or that it may flow from
timidity in the face of a real possibility that the Messiah is actually at hand — a timidity which prefers the known misery of
slavery to the uncertainties of freedom. Wrong as the believers
in the false messiahs were, Rosenzweig concluded, they were at
least right in this, that they had faith the Messiah would come
and were willing to stake their all upon his coming. To this let
us add that no less a scholar than Gershom Scholem considers
Shabbethai Zevi as a precursor of Zionism — a precursor of that
revolution which transformed the Jews from passive to active
and from objects of history to subjects. But that is the revolution
Rubenstein affirms.

*To speak . . . of the "covenant people" . . . is to turn theol-
ogy into a very private fantasy.* The covenant theologians are
only trying to restore a balance overthrown by the positivist
("practice but don't believe") and ethnicist antifideists. In stressing what they feel has been dangerously neglected, they have
probably exaggerated. But, then, exaggeration itself is a traditional rabbinical device. In rabbinical literature, when each virtue
comes in turn to be spoken of and to be advocated, the rabbis
tend to say it is more important than all the others combined.
Obviously such statements are not intended to be taken as true
in any literal sense.

The positivists and ethnicists have by no means disappeared.
It is still possible to read and to hear statements like this: "The
rabbis are really going too far, talking so much about God and
religion. We Jews are primarily an ethnic group, but in America
the only place where we seem to be able to come together to
perpetuate ourselves is the synagogue. Unfortunately, Americans
see the synagogue as the Jewish parallel to a church. Really, it

isn't, or shouldn't be. We come to the synagogue — or we support it — for ethnic reasons. If the rabbis insist upon abusing our support for purposes of their own, with all that God talk, we shall have to secede." In the face of this sort of thing the fideistic emphasis of the Jewish theologians whom Rubenstein dislikes is quite understandable.

Himmelfarb . . . underestimates Christian religious sophistication. Now it is Rubenstein who is forgetting social reality and concentrating on "pure" theology. I think Christian theological thinkers, as a class, are more subtle and expert than Jewish thinkers. In *Commentary* I was talking about a contrast between social realities. In the Jewish community, ethnicists and religionists, secular messianists and theists have long been thrown together and long been aware of each others' presence and ways of thinking. There is hardly a rabbi, or hardly a rabbi who is not Orthodox, without close friends or relatives who are Jews but not religious. That is, there is hardly a rabbi who is not intimately familiar with godlessness and who has not known from his earliest days that people close to him, whom he respects for their personal and intellectual qualities, do not believe in God. On the other hand, a family of believing Christians did not typically have within it a sufficient number of unbelievers to allow a member of that family who later became a clergyman to realize that for many of those closest to him God had always or long been dead. Despite the highly developed state of Christian theology, people of Christian family background — above all from small towns — see a startling novelty in a 19th century slogan: God is dead. For nonOrthodox rabbis it is less startling or novel; and perhaps I am wrong to specify nonOrthodox.

Committed Jewish thinkers . . . reject the role of innovator. Maybe because they know that nothing is so old-fashioned as yesterday's innovation. Reform rabbis are now preparing to revise their prayer book: renovate it, bring it up to date, make it — as the saying goes — more relevant to the times. Twenty-five years ago or so, in an earlier attempt at innovation and relevance, they introduced a prayer for the welfare of coal miners. Today coal miners, as a class, are almost as irrelevant as the class of blacksmiths and buggy makers. On the other hand, the traditional Jewish prayer book is a good example of reluctance to innovate. From one point of view, it is a catch-all attic, from which nothing gets discarded. But that prayer book retains the 20th and the 144th Psalms. At the time of the Israeli war a Jew who prays found these to be quite relevant and up to date. Nor need he be troubled that the 20th Psalm speaks of chariots and horses. Somehow, he did not think it necessary to substitute tanks and airplanes.

But I suppose this is mostly a matter of temperament. Temperamentally, I am not impressed by psychedelic services in a synagogue on the eve of the Sabbath, combined with readings from Marshall McLuhan and Buckminster Fuller.

One thing more. Definition by etymology is hazardous, but "theology" must have a meaning in some way related to its origin: *logos* about *theos*, discourse or reasoning about God. Let us assume a society that believes in unicorns, in which there are specialists in the doctrine and thought about unicorns. Then the existence of unicorns comes to be denied. If a man denies unicorns, though he is expert in unicornology, is he still a unicornologian? Is he innovating in unicornology? Now substitute theology for unicornology. Couldn't we say that such a man is a historian of theology, or a sociologist or analyst of theology, but not a theologian? These questions are not new, of course, and apply to others besides Rubenstein.

There is a famous scholar — a pious believer — who does not think highly of theology. He prefers that not theology be taught, but the history of theology. Nonsense is not an appropriate academic subject, he says, but the history of nonsense can be one.

. . . *the only God I believe in is the cannibal Mother Goddess of Earth.* . . . Is the poet Robert Graves speaking or a Jewish theologian? This must be some kind of outcry. To quote a French poet, "Take eloquence and wring its neck."

"*I cannot* . . . *turn pagan. To do so would be to assure the final victory of Hitler's work.*" Of course. Rubenstein himself says that Hitlerism was paganism.

76

The fideism of Borowitz, Herberg, and Cohen seems to have deeper roots in sect-type Christianity than in any authentically Jewish experience. There are several things wrong with this statement. First, fideism — faith — is not unJewish. (In saying that, I feel almost as silly as I might if I were to say that Trinitarianism is not unCatholic.) The Jewish fideist theologians are trying to restore a balance upset by the naturalists, positivists, and nationalists. Secondly, why "sect-type"? Is church-type Christianity indifferent to faith? Thirdly, implicit in this notion of a contradiction between borrowing from Christians and authentic Jewish experience is the assumption that somehow it is wrong to borrow from a Christian theologian but all right to borrow from a Gentile philosopher: Niebuhr is wrong as an influence, but Dewey and Sartre are fine. In the Middle Ages the greatest Jewish theologians borrowed quite frequently from Muslim theologians, and sometimes from Christians.

. . . *Jews lacking in appropriate theological commitment ought to be encouraged to leave the community.* This is not really what those theologians mean. Again, we must understand that they are speaking didactically and therefore exaggerate. Then Rubenstein exaggerates them.

Their theology reflects the values of an upper middle class. . . . This is what my generation used to call vulgar Marxism. It would be easier to make a similar analysis of the relation between Mordecai Kaplan's theology, on the one hand, and the class position and Jewish ambiguities of the members of the Society for the Advancement of Judaism thirty or forty years ago, on the other hand. Anyway, this sort of thing explains equally the theology of Borowitz and the peace-of-mind theology of a Joshua Loth Liebman — more in evidence, still, than Borowitz's. What explains too much, explains nothing.

If theology does not enhance our capacity to work and to love, it is an expression of disturbed fantasy. I had always understood that theologians were rather more modest in their claims for their discipline. Theology is subordinate to faith. What theological system would have it that an expert or good theologian is more acceptable in God's eyes than a good man ignorant of theology? Maimonides' insistence on the primacy of intellectual correctness in the worship of God was not accepted by the great mass of Jews, or even by the great mass of rabbis; and at that, Maimonides was speaking less about theology than about philosophy.

I shall allow myself to tell a story here that I have told elsewhere. Before the First World War a German Jew who had returned to Judaism from unbelief was lecturing to an ultratraditionalist organization one afternoon on the philosophy of prayer. As he spoke, his auditors drifted out, until he was left almost alone with the chairman. He asked whether he had offended the people. "No," said the chairman, "they're only going out to say their afternoon prayers."

Jewish history has written the final chapter in the terrible story of the God of history. "Final"! This is apocalyptic, and it turns the tables on Rubenstein's talk about Jewish authenticity. Apocalyptic has not been a favored mode in Jewish thought. It is more Christian than Jewish. (With the exception of Daniel, it is due more to Christianity than to Judaism that apocalyptic literature has been preserved at all.)

The joy of Israel's Jews at the Wailing Wall was the joy of homecoming. But religiously this was a homecoming to Psalms and phylacteries and the *shofar.*

Archaic man has reappeared in the midst of the children of Abraham the wanderer. So too have the archaic gods. Literature; eloquence. Which gods? Moloch, for instance, as a consort for that cannibal Earth Goddess?

In the Bible the pagan gods are no-gods, they are nothing other than the material — the wood and stone — of which their idols are made: the pagan gods are wood and stone. The true God is the God both of nature and of history. Paradigmatically, history is the exodus, and the God of history is He who brought forth the children of Israel from Egypt with a mighty hand and an outstretched arm. Rubenstein's nostalgia for the pagan gods is not new among the Jews. The answer to it was given by Ezekiel, 2500 years ago: "What comes to your mind shall never happen — your thinking, 'Let us be like the nations, like the tribes of the countries, worshipping wood and stone.' As I live, says the Lord GOD, surely with a mighty hand and an outstretched arm, and with wrath poured out, will I be king over you."

COMMENTARY

by Zalman M. Schachter

THE DOMINANT Jewish theological position today is that of the rational righteous man. Rubenstein is the exception. He does not assume the stance of rational moral rectitude which was so fashionable in German-Jewish circles before Hitler and which continues to be the popular stance in our day. In calling for a theological renewal, he embarrasses the contemporary Jewish theologian by pointing to the two unassimilated events: Auschwitz and the statehood of Israel. Rubenstein is outstanding among his colleagues in his insistence that any modern Jewish theology which does not come to grips with these two issues is not relevant in our time.

There can be no doubt that Rubenstein has pinpointed two of the crucial issues which confront the Jewish theologian today. Nor can we call to question his statement that Auschwitz and Israel's statehood are unassimilated in current and relevant Jewish theological thought. (This does not mean that we can ignore the attempts to deal with the Holocaust in terms of the premessianic Armageddon, made by the late Lubavitcher Rebbe and his present-day successor, *shlita*, utilizing traditional categories, reincarnation among them, and by Rabbi J. L. Maimon, who called the establishment of the state of Israel "the beginning of the beginning of the redemption." If one rejects them because they call for a return to traditional action directives and show no readiness to encounter unprecedented forms, one must nevertheless admit that the issues were grappled with.) However, it is Rubenstein's insistence that these events are not merely unassimilated, but *unassimilable* by any other than radical means, which is our primary concern here, and which we find it necessary to take issue with.

As Weisel has remarked, the world is fascinated by Auschwitz because of the Bomb. Mankind faces its own Auschwitz if it fails to find a way out. Israel, the people of G–d, still has a mission in trying to live the working hypothesis of *t'shuvah*, renewal, turning, *metanoia*. However, it has no pattern as yet from which it can construe the return. To return to the old ways is to invite the return of the old calamity. This time the return must aim toward a state of world responsibility for the Jew. Weisel has hinted at the direction which the renewal must take. He is profoundly interested in the why of the silence of the guilty bystander and in agitating for a metanoic renewal which will do something for Russian Jewry. He looks for the cosmic laughter which can help one survive. He looks toward Pedro, his goyishe friend, and suffers for him. He wants to work to redeem not only the Russian Jew, but also the Russian goy. And here is where his intuition is true and points toward the right solution. The medium of his expression is aesthetics and not ethics, because he cannot get through to himself or to others on the straight ethical-moral line. Rubenstein knows this, and so he looks toward a nonverbal paganism for the renewal. And this is one way. To me, however, the way lies in setting up a working hypothesis as the act of faith upon which the renewal can be built.

The traditional Jewish response to calamities, "For our sins were we exiled from our land" (Traditional Prayer Book), is the only feasible one for the Jewish ethical genius. In some sense, it is a return to an examination of the causes that led to the destruction. To say, "Let us research our ways, and let us seek the underlying reason and return to our G–d" (Lamentations 3:40), is a kind of empiricism. But it is a risky one. It calls for going into unpleasant territory. It begins with an a priori: "In some way we contributed to our own calamity. What was our mistake?" But, in looking for the mistake, one risks the possibility of finding it. This then is another hang-up for the Jewish theologian. If he uncovers the reason, he turns prophet and risks being stoned or being accused of giving the final victory to Hitler. In order to avoid this, his uncovering of the reasons must be coupled with his castigation of himself and the establishment that produces and sustains him. His findings are not capable of rationalizing and defending the status quo. On the contrary, finding the cause, he shoulders the guilt together with his fellow Jews.

What Jewish guilt is there in Auschwitz? No single-valued reductive statement can serve to answer the question in a sociological frame. But, ethically and morally, our weakness was not enough righteousness toward the goyim. "What!?" I hear exclamations all around me. "*We* should have been more righteous? Why don't you preach to the Germans, why to us?" And here is the answer? Why did we not preach to the Germans (as some of us are preaching to the Johnsons about Vietnam and as many non-Jews are preaching to the South Africans)? Why did we not preach to the Arabs? *This is the point.* Thinking that we, as victims of the Nazi German oppression, somehow had no right to preach in order to save our own necks, we kept an anguished silence. In response to Nazi hostilities, we judged *all* Germans to be inhuman, predatory beasts, and the Germans returned the compliment. They were the stronger, and we, by definition, the vermin to be exterminated. In short, *the Holocaust was partially caused by Jews who did not think it worthwhile, or even possible, to reprove the Germans.*

This brings us to our next point. *Jews are responsible not only for themselves, but also for goyim. Their responsibility as the chosen people (chosen to be responsible and to be a kingdom of priests) must work paradoxically to eliminate their own chosenness by delegation of the responsibility to others who will also become G–d's people — Germans, Arabs, and Russians included.* And here halakha enters the picture.

There has been much refinement in Jewish Law. Prior to the Holocaust, the Torah of the Jew had proliferated into the most minute levels of life. But the Jewish Torah of goy, by and large, did not have any specific action directives. Those that it did have were ambiguous and self-contradictory. We, who were charged with the responsibility of reproving our neighbor when we saw him involved in a sinful act, had excluded the goy from our reproach. The goy was given the same consideration as a compulsive beast: no amount of rational reeducation could possibly help him. At best, we sought only the application of subtle pressure: "You are such a nice Minister of the Interior; please stop the pogrom." The goy who could be bought or cajoled was considered good. And so we reinforced his corruption, while maintaining that he was not good enough to hear with us the word of the L–rd. Our theology will continue to fail us as long as our halakha — that which provides us with our action directives — has not yet come to grips with our relations with goyim. *Jewish halakhists must provide us with an application of G–d's Law which will be more in the service of the total redemption. They cannot do this by recourse to old patterns, because these will bring only the old results.*

Taking this a few steps further, we meet the other matter which amazes Rubenstein. Why is it that we are so deeply moved by the Israeli crisis? Without an explicit theology to which all Jews gave assent, we acted. And this was because, in the case of the land of Israel, we still have a myth. Our myth is perhaps more civilized than most blood-and-soil myths (or so we like to think) but it is nevertheless a blood-and-soil myth and therefore dangerous.

The Middle East crisis excited us because we were threatened once more. Unconsciously, we were predisposed to new action directives. The grief and guilt over our silence in the 30s and 40s have done their unconscious work. The next step can be taken only consciously and deliberately. We must be able to see Yemen's threat at the hands of Egypt as *our* threat, or the problem of the South African Negroes as *our* problem. Arab refugee relief is our problem too; and it is our obligation as Jews not only to contribute money, but also to organize the Arab world to help their own and others. (Perhaps a penny per gallon on

82

Arab oil to help the refugees resettle and start life in the places vacated by Jews who emigrated from Iraq, North Africa, Russia, etc, is worthy of consideration by the Joint Distribution Committee.) We cannot forget that *the state of Israel is G–d's grace to Israel (the people) and affords us the opportunity to apply the lessons of Auschwitz in terms of action directives. In order for these action directives to have any reality, they must stand in a dialogical relationship with those who are part of the total redemption. They must be located, not on the continuum of a righteousness that has a precedent, but on an unprecedented, t'shuvah-centered Aggadah.*

The halakha capable of shaping the future must be t'shuvah centered. The ba'al t'shuvah is not afraid to say that what we did in the past was wrong. It is his prerogative to begin his return with a declaration of moral bankruptcy. The zadik, the righteous man, only leads us back into exile. To find fifty righteous men in Sodom is to perpetuate Sodom. But to touch the heart of the King of Nineveh, and to move him and his people to t'shuvah, is to renew the city-state of Nineveh. As Heschel has aptly observed, the primary problem confronting the Jews (who must face both Auschwitz and Israel) is the creation of a new Aggadah which will give direction to the halakhist and thus will provide the basis for new and relevant action directives. We cannot be content to accept Lorenz uncritically and allow the instinctuality of territorial defense to go undirected. Just as Judaism has shown us how to socialize sex and food instinctuality, it must also teach us to socialize our survival and territorial instincts. This we must demand, not only of ourselves, but also of others.

Elsewhere, Rubenstein has called for the resumption of the dialogue between Jew and Christian, but only by religiously committed Jews and Christians, and not by hirelings of social agencies. This is so obvious, and yet remains opaque for too many of us. Only those who have the highest values as their concern can, through dialogue, move toward a clearer grasp of the truth. It is strange, then, that we orthodox, who concentrate on action directives, restrict dialogue with goyim to that concerned

83

with social issues. This gambit only impacts the self-righteous-
ness of the upholders of the status quo, and, in their bewilderment, they must blame others, and, by that move, vacate the
platform of leadership for the renewal that will lead to a complete redemption. This self-defeating move makes them even
more defensive and anxious and negates any possibility of realistically dealing with a theology of goy. Perhaps such a theology
is really impractical. Intermarriage and assimilation corrode us
at such a rapid rate that it is only natural that we flee to hide
behind ever higher barricades. But in this our faith is tested;
and we can refuse to learn the lesson, and thus be confronted
with the same disaster again and again. But the G–d who makes
things as they are will not relent and change: *we* will have to
change, and not only ourselves, but also our fellow man. The
secular city will not allow us to retreat to a rural ghetto, and
we Jews are, at this point, committed to the cosmopolis. Here
we shall have to be the leaven and work toward the total redemption by returning to a basic concern for others. *Being open
to others as full partners in that dialogue which has as its aim
the total redemption, we must not seek easy consolation from
religion, but forsake religion and take the responsibility of a
renewed encounter with G–d, to make the covenant which will
result in a tentative, ad hoc halakha that must always stand the
test, not only of, "Is it good for Jews?" but also, "Is it good for
the total redemption?"*

The most serious attempt (and therefore the one which in-
criminates us most) to work toward the total redemption
through the love of the other which we have encountered in
this century is that manifested in Gandhi. Erich Fromm is a
theorist of the Art of Loving as a means of survival, and Martin
Luther King is the one who has translated Gandhi for the oppressed Negro in our midst. By teaching his followers to opt out
from the white supremacy games and by giving those concerned
whites who wanted to identify with the Negro struggle a chance
to do so, King showed a keen and practical understanding of the
Art of Loving in operation. For the Negro and the white, he
wrote a *"Shulkhan Arukh"* of the dropout from the bad games

84

of the white majority. That he has not been fully accepted and that Black Power people have taken an unloving attitude only show that, before our own eyes, a replication is taking place of the events before Auschwitz. If "whitey" is a devil, then there is no other way of dealing with him. But if "whitey" is as much a man as the Negro, then the Negro can call him to account. And if we see a Watts and a Newark, we can in turn call the Negro to account. No wonder then that King and his freedom workers are the same people who work for the cessation of hostilities in Vietnam. Love toward other human beings directs them in both directions.

That the Middle East crisis should turn Jewish doves into hawks was inevitable. At no point before the renewal of hostilities did we remonstrate with Nasser about the basic human situation of the right to life in the Middle East. We laughed when a lone cafe operator flew to Cairo to talk peace with Nasser. What we should have done was to go by the planeload to Cairo, and, in a peaceful manner, demonstrate for peace negotiations. Instead, we waited for the crisis, and then we acted as Jews. If Jerusalem is to be a model for the world, it will have to show the way to avoid Watts and Newark. But, as long as it is solely in Jewish hands, the goy is suffered on our soil and we have only a partial redemption. Partial redemptions, "liberations," are notorious causes for crusades. We must press for the internationalization of Jerusalem under United Nations (and hopefully World Federation) auspices and move the United Nations headquarters from New York to Jerusalem. We have a right to exact this price. Whatever the financial expense, it could not equal the Jewish-Arab blood that was shed for it. No other city can boast so much blood shed on its soil, blood of the Jebusite, Jew, the Assyrian, Roman, Moslem, Crusader, etc. We Jews object to internationalizing Jerusalem, and probably will be able to keep it for a while, but in no way will we have learned from Auschwitz, and in no way will we have made an ethically effective contribution to world peace. Rubenstein's crucial concern will be perpetuated: the event of Auschwitz will remain unassimilated, and perhaps we will have proven the validity of his statement that it is truly unassimilable. *Only when Jerusalem has been internationalized will it be a faithful city to all who gave their lives for it.*

Our Bonhoeffer has not yet entered the Jewish theological scene. He will have to say: not Jewish *religion*, which protects and mollifies the status quo, but *Judaism without religion.* In other words, he will have to find a new and meaningful encounter with the G–d who allowed Auschwitz and gave us a new chance to apply in the State of Israel the lesson derived from Auschwitz as a model for the world under the threat of the bomb.

Such an encounter will have to teach us to take responsibility for ourselves and for the goyim. That Rubenstein is right in pointing to the fact of our not having come to terms with Auschwitz and Israel is proved in the almost total absence of any significant liturgical expression of grief over the Holocaust or of the celebration of Israel's existence. Perhaps 25 years is not long enough for this to have happened.

No partial redemption will do. Hitler planned a partial redemption for the Germany he loved; but this he did at the expense of Jews, Gypsies, and others. The complete redemption is a much more difficult task. It works much more slowly. No Five Year Plan can build a Thousand Year Reich. Hegel and Marx were right in their dialectical view of history. That which enhances itself at the expense of what it oppresses begets its own downfall. No static Messianism can work, since life is dynamic, and the dialectic is infinite. The Messianic formula can succeed only if it takes into account movement and countermovement. To preach a living word to others always calls for application of the word to the preacher first. This is what Israel must achieve in order to remain G–d's people. And, in order to remain G–d's people, it must paradoxically work toward the elimination of its own chosenness by working also for the chosenness of the goyim.

COMMENTARY

by Arthur A. Cohen

THE NICE THING about the laws of physics is their imperturba-
bility. They feel nothing nor do they react. The scientist need
never worry that the physical world will alter in response to
historical exigency, unlike biology, psychology, art, literature,
philosophy, and of course theology. But why theology, one
might ask? Agreed that the law of gravity does not change; it
needs only to be discovered. But, one may reply sophistically,
If the physical substratum of the universe does not change,
should not the metaphysical origin of the universe be equally
unchangeable? This was the contention of classical theology.
The God of classical theology was the immovable mover. God
provided the occasion of history, although he had no history;
he effected the creation of all by an act of will, but was himself
unresponsive to its impact. This situation bothered classical
theology. It did not seem possible that a reconciliation could be
effected between God, the metaphysical principle, and God the
creator, lover, and redeemer of man and his history.

The God of classical theology is now dead. Part of the re-creation of contemporary American theology is rehearsing the death
agony and interment of classical theology. This is a homeostatic
enterprise; it preserves the theologian while it disposes of theology. I, for one, should be quite willing to dispose of theology
as well as most of the theologians. They strike me as a tiresome,
complaining lot at best, ponderous with gravity, striking poses,
propounding dramatic formulations. They have solved their
own problems by philoprogenitive enthusiasm, producing one
more shocking, lively, strenuous doctrine after another. We
move from the limited God, to the truncated God, to the Pro-
crustean God, from the good God to the bad God, from the
God of the universe to the God of trivial fiefdoms, from the
living God to the dead God. Fortunately people continue to

spell his name correctly, and, as the expression in the theatre goes, "Even a knock is okay, as long as they spell the name right."

Richard L. Rubenstein's "Homeland and Holocaust" is an example of mock argument. It is not simply that he doesn't like any of the Jewish theologians of the day, myself included. That's understandable, since Rabbi Rubenstein does not regard any of the theologians of the day, or any of the theologies they have represented, as possessing merit. But it is not enough in my opinion for Rubenstein to continue the reaffirmation of his eccentric *petitio principi*, as though its eccentricity was sufficient to gild its illogicality. If indeed God, religion, and classical Judaism are moribund, Rabbi Rubenstein ceases to be an effective analyst of their decease, for his conclusion does not extend the range of his premise. His is a theological Gertrude Steinism, for obviously, in his view, anything a Jewish theologian might say about God is nonsense if it does not already assume that God is dead. *Petitio principi* pure and simple. It would be one thing if the death-of-God theologians possessed the ecstatic passion of Nietzsche, for at least they would discriminate between poetry and exegesis, between vision and therapy. They do not. They are very much like the king in *Alice in Wonderland* who demanded a verdict before the first witness had been called. Rubenstein's verdict is in and presumably his essay is intended as the calling of witnesses.

All right, let's consider the evidence. If I understand him correctly, no theology can be Jewish unless it deals forthrightly with the extermination of European Jewry and the emergence of the State of Israel; no Jew can be a theologian who fails to explicate the relation of Israel to his conception of the living God of history. Even in this formulation Rabbi Rubenstein would fault me, for evidently I consider the task of theology and the Jew to be to face reality, but not necessarily to explain it. Evil can no longer be a mystery for Rubenstein; too many people have died for evil to remain mysterious. One gratuitous death may be a mystery, but six million is a gauntlet put down by history in the path of Providence. Similarly, the establishment of the State of Israel he regards as a life-affirming, natural, exultantly "pagan" assertion of strength before a life-denying world.

Rabbi Rubenstein's thetic witnesses to the hopeless inadequacy of theology before the enormity of historical evil and historical rebirth are essentially impressionistic, for he has never argued a sequential, even if unsystematic, theology of negation, nor have his writings shown forth that joy and ecstasy which hierophants of new gods usually display. It seems by and large a sad business with him: Auschwitz and the death of God.

It is admitted that, prior to the death of six million Jews in the concentration camps of Europe, the only comparable world-historical disaster of the Jewish people was the destruction of Spanish Jewry by forced expulsion. The events are not comparable. No one denies this. It is true, however, that the expulsion of 1492 and the nearly two centuries of massacres which preceded it produced a trauma of conscious which, unresolved though it remained, yielded to a mystic and messianic literature of great power. Jews were destroyed and Jewries decimated, Jews cut themselves out of the diseased body of Israel and sought the shelter of flight and anonymity, others plodded into pietism, and yet others, the few undoubtedly, believed that God could be addressed, that the effort of loving reproof would profit the conscience of God. God does not listen well, and he is a hopelessly unintelligible creator, but faith is not enforced by him nor does he make faith. *He is* as Job learned; ours is the period of enduring his presence in the world we have fashioned out of his material. No brief for God, less for man. And so then what? If we must, as Rubenstein suggests, be done with theology and theological formulations since the object of theological inquiry is no longer alive and in our midst, there is finally no response. There is perhaps the metaphoric rebuke which Elie Wiesel administered in a public lecture when he observed the grotesque incommensurability of the pious scribe who, in tradition, was obligated to purify himself by ritual ablutions and prayer before setting himself to write the name of God, and the lachrymose theologians of God's death who treat his passing as one more episode in a cataclysmic century and who apparently enjoy the *frisson* and exhibitionism which attends such well received and publicized "good news." But the rebuke of Wiesel, profound though it was, is a metaphor. It is not an answer, nor is it even an interpretation of the phenomenon.

The language of Rabbi Rubenstein's essay gives us a clue to the interpretation of the phenomenon, for his analysis depends for its impact upon the use of "power" and "powerlessness," "power" and "impotence." Theology joined to temporal authority was obviously powerful, enforceable, however ultimately demonic. Rubenstein despises such a conjunction of power and the Word of God. But theology without the sword — whether the sword be actual or only the tenacity of the will of the people to survive with dignity and honor — is equally powerless. There can be little doubt that millions of those Jews who were exterminated died with dignity and honor, no differently from those millions of their ancestors who died with the words of the *Alenu* still struggling from their lips. What Rubenstein wants is force and potency, not faith and trust. And force and potency cannot, *ipso facto*, be wrung from the language of any theology of faith, covenant, and election. Consequently it is no surprise that the only source of viable theology is the natural paganic optimism of the reborn folk, the Lawrentian phoenix of the Jewish people, who draw from blood and earth the vitalities of resurrection.

The theology of Jewish paganism redivivus is not new to modern Judaism. One has only to recall the Nietzschean discipleship of Michael Joseph Berdichevski (1865–1921) whose doctrine of Jewish transvaluation centered upon the priority of Israel to tradition, life to holiness, the natural Jew to the supernatural vocation. It was Berdichevski, although not he alone, who regarded the modern era as one which would witness the end of the Jews or the beginning of a new nation. But Berdichevski had a different distinction which marks off his radical assault upon Jewish tradition from that of Rubenstein. Berdichevski had the passion of his own potency, derived not from malaise and neurasthenic distaste for Jewish theological finickiness, but from an absolute affirmation of Jewish election and uniqueness. He could force Nietzsche to work for Jewish ethno-centricity, demanding that Jewish thought and tradition exceed themselves, transcend themselves even to the usurpation of God. Alternately Berdichevski would insist that not God, but only man, mattered and that man had not only the right, but the absolute duty, to speak with God face to face, to tell him off out of love, compassion, and anger. What passion there is in Berdichevski!

The Jewish religious situation as interpreted by Rabbi Richard L. Rubenstein has a kind of accuracy which I acknowledge. It does describe an impasse, an inability to achieve a depth of language and truthfulness which can square the living with the dead; but it fails to be remedial, except in that sense in which all rhetoric is remedial, by succeeding in the dramatic evocation of the predicament. Rubenstein describes some of our anguish. It is an anguish to be able to say nothing meaningful as yet about the enormities of this century. But is that unusual? Is it not better that we examine our wounds and take the measure of their gravity, before we administer medicaments. I prefer to be reticent with explanations. I am baffled into silence. I write fiction about God, but my fictions are another man's facts and Rubenstein's facts are for me fictions. It is not unfair. That's the way it should be. But more gentleness, more compassion, more love, Rabbi Rubenstein, for these are times when, with all our right to anger, we must also be forbearing with ourselves, with others, with God.

COMMENTARY

by Irving Greenberg

WITH the searching paradox and polemic vigor which have made his one of the outstanding voices in religious thought now, Richard Rubenstein has stated his case for the bankruptcy of current mainstream Jewish theology. He again points to the path he has painfully pioneered for us as the only way out: the radical turning from the God of History to the gods of nature. In this essay he repeats his call: Jewish theology must speak to the two great questions — Auschwitz and Israel. Rubenstein is correct that great theology can be written only in response to great questions.

We must be grateful to Dr. Rubenstein for the many brilliant and provocative insights which stud this essay and his earlier volume, *After Auschwitz*, and for offering the first comprehensive interpretation of the two overwhelming historical experiences of our times for Jews. Ultimately, however, I do not think that he has done justice to the current Jewish religious scene. And, although Judaism will have to work through his experience, I do not think that Jewish theology will adopt his course.

Rabbi Rubenstein's shortcomings grow out of the limitations of his successes. Surprisingly, his capacity for psychological insight into religion's manifest and latent content has not been employed in his reading of current Jewish theology — possibly because he is unsympathetic to it. Moreover, he has asked two of the great questions, but not a third. The third is the question of the westernization or secularization of Jewry. Only in the perspective of this issue can we grasp the significance of the new theologians and the inner connection of their theology to Auschwitz.

To put it simplistically, Jewish life and thought in the last two hundred years have been dominated by the need to modernize. The significance of current Christian theological secularity (and even of the death-of-God writers) lies in the fact that some attempt is being made to be true to both the Christian tradition and the modern experience. Were it not for the suspension of both elements in tension (with greater or lesser success) then Harvey Cox's or William Hamilton's work would hardly have attracted such attention. Were they purely in the secular context, they would be rated as belated, somewhat chastened, but rather mild liberals of a now familiar type. The key to Christianity's current vitality, then, is in its capability to relate to and not merely be assimilated by modernity. This capability stems from a number of factors. After all, Christianity is indigenous to the western world. It has had more institutional resources to draw upon to cope with the new situation. Its large number of adherents provided it with reserve, sheltered core communities (such as the Catholic Church) even after heavy losses had been sustained in the modernizing process. Out of these communities, came new responses that live in the tension.

Jewish modernization bit more deeply. Jews had to travel a longer cultural distance. Judaism's adherents had fewer reserves after the loss of the "shock troops" into the West. Jews carried the burden of minority status in their adjustment. Therefore, modernism and its categories have been the Procrustes bed of Jewish religious life in recent centuries. Most Jews went lock, stock, and barrel into the secular city, preserving little or no tension between traditional Jewish values and the new dispensation. The three denominations of Jewish life were created and molded by the process. They are lined up on a theological plane essentially by the manner in which they orient to the field of force of modernity. Rubenstein correctly praises Mordecai Kaplan's emphasis on the creative role of the Jewish people in Judaism. One might add, however, that Kaplan has also reconstructed Judaism after accepting the cultural categories of his time as normative and, well nigh, absolute. This authority of modern categories deracinated many Jews and dissolved much of Jewish folk culture and religion. In the process it impoverished the mythic and ritual aspects of the Jewish religion, as Rubenstein himself has pointed out elsewhere [7:92–111]. Its total triumph was aided by the overpowering intellectual superiority and sophistication of modern, as compared to Jewish, culture and thought. Chosenness, Revelation, Covenant, Commandment, and Halacha, and other such concepts – the life blood of Judaism historically – were excluded because of their "unacceptability" to "modern" standards. The extraordinary novelty in the new (primarily Reform) theologians lies in their capacity to "rediscover" Judaism's classical concepts – naturally in a postmodern, not premodern, fashion [13]. By doing this, they have reopened the possibility of a creative response of Jewish tradition

93

rooted in its internal resources yet firmly linked to the West. This is rife with all sorts of possibilities for the future. It is true that the group may read as excessively "God centered." It places less stress on being right with the social concerns and intellectual norms of the secular city [1]. I agree with Rubenstein in rejecting Himmelfarb's explanation that the religious Jewish thinkers are more sophisticated than the Christians. A major reason for the different attitude toward the secular world is that the Jews are reacting against their past excessive assimilation to humanism. They instinctively sense that they must first reestablish a viable theological existence. In the fullness of that identity, they can more soberly affirm in a balanced fashion what is right in the modern. Thus the "focus on divine-human encounter," "the aloofness towards social and political ideology," the "fideism" which Rabbi Rubenstein scorns is part of a dialectical movement necessary for regaining Jewish theological identity.

In the same way, Rubenstein has misread Franz Rosenzweig's appeal. I have personally heard some of the participants in the *Commentary* symposium mention that Rosenzweig's metahistorical conception is what they found unacceptable in him. Rosenzweig's main contribution and personal example were in his testimony — before the Holocaust made it more plausible — that one could live Judaism within modern culture without yielding to the tyranny of the modern categories. At the same time, he offered a method of coming to the commandments without surrendering one's judgment as it is informed by contemporary sensibility. Most of the men had to overcome Rosenzweig's rejection of Jewish involvement in history in order to accept him. To stress noninvolvement and his personal powerlessness in linking him to these thinkers (thereby to tax theology with lack of contact with reality) borders on intellectual guilt by association.

The question is, What has made possible this new theological movement? One factor is that the Jews have fully "arrived" in the West, particularly in the United States. Objectivity is possible once the anxiety of "making it" has declined. Even disenchantment shows up once people are in the Promised Land. Most of all, I would suggest that this theological reaction is made possible by the Holocaust. Rubenstein himself points out that Mordecai Kaplan wrote *before* Auschwitz. The younger mainstream theologians find Kaplan's optimism, his weak sense of the reality of evil, his simplistic love for the city of man a bit naïve after Auschwitz [8:83–92; 10:155–159]. True, the new theologians have not articulated a theological interpretation of the Holocaust. This is hardly surprising in the light of the overwhelming nature of the catastrophe. Indeed, to be as yet silent may take greater depth and sensitivity or greater radicalism of response to the experience than to offer the overt radical response of Rubenstein. Still, the Auschwitz experience clearly is the subterranean sustainer of the new theological movement.

It is Auschwitz that has mauled, if not destroyed, the humanistic eschatology which converted Jews en masse to modernism. It is the Holocaust that has neutralized the dominant field of force of modern categories and thus made possible renewed orientation to the tradition and history of Israel. What more terrible proof can there be that Jews are singled out and alone than Hitler's demonic assault on Jewry and the silence, the lack of concern even, of the democratic West about that attack? This is a silence and singling out that was repeated in June 1967 when Nasser appeared capable of annihilating Israel in the tense days that preceded the six days of war. No wonder that the Election theme sounds so strongly in recent Jewish theology.

Some of the theologians who reject Rubenstein's paganism as "another victory for Hitler" are not merely being conservative. They may see realistically that paganism is an option for and of secular man. Many Jews now alive will become purely universal men — especially in view of the risk of a Holocaust. Those who choose to remain will be particularly people who opt for their status as an election, a calling if you will. Like Rubenstein, the theologians see Auschwitz as a lesson for the world. Unlike Rubenstein, the lesson they learn is not a new paganism but a new tragic realism of man's strengths and weaknesses, of the urgency of healing and consoling mankind, of Israel as the suffering servant. Elsewhere Rabbi Rubenstein rejected this option for Jewish theology on the grounds that it must lead to a hideous assumption of guilt for Israel and divine agency for Hitler [9:47–60]. But this is a most one-sided reading of the theological alternatives. When the mainstream theological response comes, it will undoubtedly hold up three other models: Job (Rubenstein's comments [page 56] notwithstanding; I think Rubenstein does not do justice to the retention of humanity by many of the inmates, nor does he plumb the capacity of man to endure and renew; one can see a case study of what I mean in the works of Elie Wiesel); the ambivalent first part of the third chapter of Lamentations (recognition of the absence of God tempered by anger and a controversy with Him, reference 12); and the suffering servant. This last image has been too long a monopoly of Christian theology when in fact it is the essence of much of Jewish historical existence.

Rabbi Rubenstein wisely points out that the unity of Jewish destiny moves far more Jews than does a common creed. This itself is a reflection of the European catastrophe. Arthur Hertzberg has pointed out how strongly the memory of the Holocaust and the determination not to allow it to happen again operated in the outpouring of financial and moral support for Israel by American Jews [2]. This unity of Jewish destiny has given rise to the most widely and intensely practiced mitzvah in the Jewish community — giving to the United Jewish Appeal (and Israel Bonds). Rubenstein has, however, missed the operation of the Holocaust on the theological level — in the beginning of the search for Jewish religious unity. Ecumenicism among Jews has achieved notoriously less importance and involvement than the parallel movement among Christians. Much of the Jewish religious unity experience has been cooperative religious indifferentism. In recent years the first signs of a committed theological search for unity have emerged [3:131–163; 4:269–300]. As of this writing it has rarely appeared in print. However, an important group of young theologians has formed. In conferences, in community religious experiences, and in giving papers, the group has begun to seek paths of religious unity. Not surprisingly, the Holocaust has haunted the group's deliberations and, in 1967, has taken the front stage in its theological encounters [3; 4].

96

The Holocaust (and the State of Israel) dominated the deliberations of the group involved in the conference in August 1967. Although the proceedings have not been published in the past, the group (which goes under the innocuous title of the Segalls Center for the Study and Advancement of Judaism) is considering publication of the papers given. To paraphrase a central Jewish prayer: in the light of the crematoria, we are all of us as one. The original is the prayer for peace at the end of the Amidah, one of the two central prayers of the liturgy: Bless us "in the light of Your face, all of us as one."

Just as I find Rubenstein's reading of the Holocaust in his essay too narrow, his interpretation of the State of Israel strikes me as too polemic and sweeping. It may be doubted that the establishment of a secular state with a Jewish majority has turned the diaspora into a two-thousand-year parenthesis. The diaspora will continue to exist (as Babylonian Jewry did during the Second Commonwealth). The majority of Jews will live in it. The result is likely to be a bipolar or polycentered Judaism and Jewish life. This was the pattern in other great periods of Jewish history. (Two great but neglected Jewish historiographical works develop the implications of this theme. Yehezkel Kaufmann, *Golah VeNechar* and Simon Rawidowicz, *Bavel VeYerushalayim*.) Tensions and gaps will grow between the two centers but so will mutual influence.

Nor will the State of Israel lead to a swing from total submission, "compliance," and "powerlessness" of diaspora Judasim to a militaristic "renunciation" of the "prophetic vision of universal brotherhood" by the Israelis. A more finely shaded rendering is needed. In the classic period, Judaism operated with a balance of force and spirit. It was aware that divine ideals functioning in real life must operate with the categories, including force and war, of the real world. Judaism was never pacifistic. It was prophetically critical of excessive militarism, especially as an ideology. The diaspora experience distorted and twisted the equilibrium point toward the pole of submission and spiritual quietism. In Israel, the Jews again, as a people, act as agents in history. This reopens the possibility of restoring the proper balance. If religion must be purely *kultur* religion, then the thesis that it purely reflects the life circumstances would be correct. But prophetic religion has been able to lean against the tide as well. The June 1967 crisis did not prove that Israel need cast away universal brotherhood. It merely showed again that justice is possible only when there is a reasonable power balance. Jewish religion in Israel can again affirm just force where it is necessary even as it can challenge excessive militarism. (A policy of pure *realpolitik* could leave Israel vulnerable to the loss of western support as well as ultimate Arab vengeance. Excessive idealism or naïveté could lead to a similar catastrophe.)

Dr. Rubenstein so sharpens the contrast of diaspora and Israeli Judaism that he slips into an unconsciously cruel moment. I refer to his portrait of the powerless Jews cooperating in their self-destruction, which "marks the final bankruptcy of the religious, ethical and psychological values of diaspora Judaism." Like Bettelheim and Arendt, from whom he sincerely dissociates himself, he fails to make the elementary comparative study. He ignores the fact that gypsies, Russian POWs, and even Russian civilians acted the same way the Jews did when they were exposed to the same treatment [5]. This was true although they had no history of diaspora Judaism to mistrain them for that terrible moment. In fact, American prisoners acted the same way after Bataan. In 1966 a group of American nurses acted the same way as they were slain one by one by a mass killer, Richard Speck. The shattering truth is that, if the aggressor is prepared to kill without restraint or relation to significant motives, then he will probably be able to terrorize his victims into passivity, if not indeed into partial cooperation. The Israeli response to the Arab threat was that of an entire nation on its own soil, armed, not yet terrorized, and able to rise to its own defense. It is hardly fair or instructive to compare this to the response of atomized individuals, uprooted, physically and mentally weakened, and without arms. If anything was proven bankrupt by Auschwitz, it was the secular (should I say, pagan) culture whose highest expressions were in Germany — and the West — which, although physically and morally intact, did not lift a finger to help.

98

Of course, I am not accusing Rubenstein of deliberate cruelty. On the contrary. One of the valid criticisms he makes of the new theologians is that some of their writings lack compassion. They are too critical of Jews for the sake of "defending" God and the tradition. Auschwitz demands of us a theology defending Jews and justifying them — even against God. Throughout *After Auschwitz*, one feels the pain of *mittleid* in Rubenstein. The radical attack upon the God of History is, in a measure, an act of identification with the victims of the Holocaust. It is this quality that makes Rubenstein so Jewish. In any other age, Rubenstein's position, although highly significant, could be taxed with removing itself beyond the framework of Jewish existence. In our time, his position must be recognized as a possible, even plausible, authentic response for Jews — even if I think it is ultimately wrong.

Undoubtedly, Judaism will develop in new directions in Israel. The Halacha and its masters have not been faced with the dilemmas and needs of a sovereign society for more than two millennia. Neglected areas of law and policy will be revived. Other principles may be subordinated. Judaism, let us hope, may recover the fullness of its Biblical passion for social justice and the affirmation of life which has been muted in recent centuries under the influence of a certain passivity and asceticism. Thus far, the secular community in Israel has been relatively unresponsive to traditional Jewish religion. After all, it was created in part as a revolt against the exile and in the teeth of much Orthodox opposition. In recent years, the hollowness of Socialist utopias and the decline of the chalutzic ideal have led to new and widespread explorations in Jewish religious values. (Some of this material is made available in English in Herbert Wiener's *The Wild Goats of Ein Gedi* [11]. Most of this material is circulating in oral form, mimeograph and other prepublication forms. But there is a lot going on.) The Orthodox community has been too well entrenched and its spiritual leadership sheltered from modern life. But the beginnings of a religious intelligentsia and of theology can be detected. Its leadership will now have to confront the new time. The new time is not so much cyclical or archaic. Rather it is the time of the fulfillment of the two-thousand-year-old prayer that Israel and Jerusalem be available to the Jewish nation. This may well lead to the end of the fast day for the destruction of the Temple! Maimonides' conception of the Messianic time as an age of political independence and of the perfection of everyday society may now come into its own [6]. In any event, the search for values spreads. Rubenstein's argument from silence confuses the pause of the man who is thinking with the quiet of the man who has nothing to say.

This leads me to a final comment on the relative weakness and silence of Jewish theology. Jewish theology has flourished when a believing community lived in the world. Theology strives to reconcile the tensions between the rooted religious values and those generated by openness to the world. Until recently, it has not flourished because those who opened themselves to the world tended to join it totally. Only now is a *believing* remnant entering the mainstream of life. Rubenstein and the new theologians are products of this process. The Auschwitz experience itself has stirred up the subterranean depths of Jewish life and religion, giving life even as it destroyed. The truth is that we are on the brink of a great theological flowering. The new Reform theologians are a remarkable affirmation of the capacity of Judaism to regenerate itself after dissolution. Jewish Orthodoxy stands today where the Catholic Church stood seventy years ago in the pretheological phase. Then, too, the surface readings were the triumph of authoritarianism, siege mentality, and fundamentalism. But below the official levels, the remarkable renewal of the Church was germinating.

Richard Rubenstein has given us the first synthesizing statement after the Holocaust and the State. All honor to the attempt. It cannot be dismissed. At times as we brood about Auschwitz, it appears irresistible. However, the first theological synthesis after the destruction of 586 B.C. was the view that God had abandoned Israel and that, as a nation, Israel was dry bones that would never live again. The prophetic vision transcended the moment. Rubenstein has spoken first. I believe that Jewish theology will yet transcend the moment. Rubenstein betrays his own awareness of the possibility by the occasional stridency of his essay; for example, "pathetic hope [of dealing with Auschwitz through traditional Judaism] never to be realized"; "their theological categories are inadequate to the explosive revolution"; "Jewish history has written the final chapter in the terrible story of the God of History." Words like "final" and "never" are least fitting for a modern theologian.

Dr. Rubenstein's tragic realism, his psychoanalytic, religious, and human insights in *After Auschwitz* move us even when we disagree. His failure to sense the undercurrents of contemporary Jewish theology leaves a different impression. To me, it conjures up the last chapters of Job. After his controversy with God, Job falls silent. It is in the moment of the hush when Job and his friends and the entire landscape see the whirlwind rise. In this deafening silence, Elihu strides back and forth, berating Job's conception of God and man as untenable. Yet out of the silence of God and man a new encounter is born.

REFERENCES

1. *Commentary*, the editors of, a symposium: *The Condition of Jewish Belief* (The Macmillan Company, New York, New York) 1967. Originally published in *Commentary*, Aug 1966, vol 42, no 2.
2. Hertzberg, Arthur: American Jews and Israel, *Commentary*, 1967.
3. *Judaism*, a symposium on: Toward Jewish Religious Unity, *Judaism*, vol 15, no 2, Spring 1966, pp 131–163.
4. *Judaism*, a symposium on: Jewish Values in the Post-Holocaust Future, *Judaism*, vol 16, no 3, Summer 1967, pp 269–300.
5. Kuznestov, Anatoly: *Babi Yar* (Dell Publishing Co, Inc, New York, New York) 1967.
6. Maimonides, *Yad HaChazakah* (Mishneh Torah) Shofetim, Hilchot Melachim, chapter 12.
7. Rubenstein, Richard: Atonement and Sacrifice in Contemporary Jewish Liturgy, in *After Auschwitz* (The Bobbs-

Merrill Co, Inc, Indianapolis, Indiana) 1966, a brilliant tour de force.

8. Rubenstein, Richard: Reconstructionism and the Problem of Evil, in *After Auschwitz* (The Bobbs-Merrill Co, Inc, Indianapolis, Indiana) 1966, a cogent critique.

9. Rubenstein, Richard: The Dean and the Chosen People, in *After Auschwitz* (The Bobbs-Merrill Co, Inc, Indianapolis, Indiana) 1966.

10. Rubenstein, Richard: remarks addressed to Mordecai Kaplan in the Symposium on Jewish Unity, *Judaism*, vol 15, no 2, Spring 1966, pp 155–159.

11. Wiener, Herbert: *The Wild Goats of Ein Gedi* (Jewish Publication Society, Philadelphia, Pennsylvania) 1965.

12. Wiesel, Elie: especially *Night; The Town Beyond the Wall;* and *The Gates of the Forest.*

13. Wolf, Arnold J, ed: *Rediscovering Judaism* (Quadrangle Books, Inc, Chicago, Illinois) 1965.

RESPONSE

by Richard L. Rubenstein

I HAVE READ with great interest the comments of Arthur Cohen, Milton Himmelfarb, Irving Greenberg, and Zalman Schachter on my paper. I shall attempt to respond briefly to some of their observations, which seem to be important for theological discussion.

There are obviously profound differences of perspective between my position and those of the respondents. I believe Arthur Cohen has the best grasp on my fundamental concern when he writes, "What Rubenstein wants is force and potency, not faith and trust." Nevertheless, I must sadly take issue with him when he asserts, "There can be little doubt that millions of those Jews who were exterminated died with dignity and honor. . . ." I have attempted a diligent study of the Nazi extermination project, and I find myself aghast at the *indignity* of what took place. I am convinced that the wholly unanticipated character of the onslaught left Jews bereft of resources to counter the attack and to die fighting. Only at the Warsaw ghetto was Jewish honor redeemed. Elsewhere, all evidence points to the fact that the Nazis reduced the Jews to helpless, dependent subhumans who largely complied in their own undoing. I am unimpressed with the fact that other peoples in similar circumstances did not behave differently. This does not add a shred of dignity to the terminal fatality of a community with absolutely no effective power over its own destiny. I can understand why my contemporaries avoid facing this issue. I feel compelled to raise it, rather than to accept the silence they counsel, because I am convinced my community's health demands that it face without illusion the full impact of its recent past.

I originally wrote the paper for this volume shortly after the Six Day Arab-Israeli War. Its impress upon me is reasonably obvious throughout. Shortly after completing the essay, I made an extended visit to Israel and the occupied areas. I can report that the issue of power figured very largely in the preoccupations of the Israelis and has significantly affected Israeli culture. During May 1967, the Israelis were threatened with another Auschwitz. In June they exhibited their resolve that every last man, woman, and child would perish in a monumental Massada rather than suffer another Holocaust. I toured the country in a private car. I interviewed Israelis from former Prime Minister David Ben-Gurion and cabinet ministers to simple soldiers on military duty. I can report that the vast majority saw the extermination of Europe's Jews not only as catastrophe but also as indignity. There was universal resolve that there would never again be another Auschwitz.

I also concur with Mr. Cohen when he says, "And force and potency cannot, *ipso facto*, be wrung from the language of any theology of faith, covenant, and election." This is one of the most important reasons for my determination to reject covenant and election. I am aware of the fact that any expression of human potency is forever imperilled. Nevertheless, I am convinced that there is far greater dignity in accepting both the perils and the rewards of active participation in history than in the essentially passive and submissive role which the diaspora Jew was compelled to adopt in order to survive. In spite of my conviction, I do not elevate the Israeli experience to the level of exclusive validity for contemporary Judaism. On the contrary, I freely choose to live and create as an American Jew. I do question whether the religious experience of the diaspora can any longer be taken as normative. I await the theological reflections of my colleagues on the religious meaning of contemporary Israel.

Mr. Cohen and Mr. Himmelfarb point to the Nietzschean inspiration of many of my ideas. I would prefer to speak of a Nietzschean parallelism since my fundamental values derive from my experience and life history to a larger extent than from a reading of literary sources. I do owe Nietzsche a great debt in any event. I do not believe that the identification of the sources of some of my insights automatically ends debate on their validity as, apparently, does Mr. Himmelfarb. In addition to Nietzsche, I freely acknowledge indebtedness to Hegel, Freud, Sartre, and Camus, as well as to Paul Tillich and Erik Erikson.

As Mr. Cohen points out, "The theology of Jewish paganism *redivivus* is not new to modern Judaism." Mr. Himmelfarb makes somewhat the same point. I would certainly concur. At no point do I claim originality for my paganism. On the contrary, I have sought to describe a phenomenon which is as widespread among Christians as Jews. A very large part of the constructive burden of *After Auschwitz* was devoted to a defense of paganism in both America and Israel as a viable religious option.

Milton Himmelfarb, who was my high school French teacher for one unforgettable semester more than twenty-five years ago, complains that I do not specify the kind of paganism I have in mind. The fault may be mine, but I thought I had made my point clear by the last paragraph of the essay in which I asserted, "Archaic man has reappeared in the midst of the children of Abraham the wanderer. So too have the archaic gods." By paganism I do not mean irreligion, secularism, or modern atheism. Nor do I believe Nazism can properly be understood as a pagan movement. Its philosophy of excess and exclusivism derived its power from the historical religions, albeit in a hideously inverted form. When I speak of paganism, I have in mind much the same contrast as that suggested by Mircea Eliade's differentiation of religion into archaic and historical types. I am also sympathetic to Marshall McLuhan's assertion that archaic, tribalized man has reappeared in the West as a result of electric technology, although I do not regard electric technology as a decisive factor in the reappearance of Hebrew neoarchaic man.

Mr. Cohen oversimplifies my position when he implies that I am one of "the lachrymose theologians of God's death who treat his passing as one more episode in a cataclysmic century and who apparently enjoy the *frisson* and exhibition which attends such well received and publicized 'good news.' " I have consistently referred to the death-of-God event as one of immense loss and sadness. I have insisted that the death of God is a cultural fact which signals both our loss of the God of history and our return to the God of nature. Furthermore, I see an inescapable connection between the rediscovery of place and territory as Jewish religious categories after almost two thousand years and the return of the God of nature.

Mr. Himmelfarb confuses my neoarchaic religion of earth with modern atheism. As a result, he belabors me with many issues which were best directed elsewhere. I must confess that my former teacher's effort surprised me very greatly. Certainly, even an erring former pupil might have merited more charity if not justice than the suggestion that he profanes the memory of Auschwitz "to enhance a reputation."

Apparently, Mr. Himmelfarb feels that one can demolish a position simply by associating it with a prominent name, usually one that the distinguished editor of *Commentary* and his circle hold in little regard. Thus, Mr. Himmelfarb deems it a sufficient response to my contention that in Israel the diaspora has become a "long parenthesis" to assert, "That is what people like Mr. Ben-Gurion have been saying." I have much additional evidence, as a result of my recent trip, that my statement was factual. Even without it, I have too much regard for Mr. Ben-Gurion's lifelong involvement in Jewish affairs not to take very seriously his assessment of any Jewish issue. Nor do I understand what light Mr. Himmelfarb sheds on the issue of the diaspora as historical parenthesis when he suggests that I may have been influenced by Karl Barth. I have great respect for Barth, although I believe he has had a far greater impact on the fideism of the Jewish establishment theologians than upon my theological position. Speaking of fideism, in spite of its defense by the respondents, I continue to question whether a position which ultimately derives from the Reformation cry of *sola fidei* can legitimately be regarded as within the mainstream of a tradition such as Judaism, which places so great an emphasis on the religious deed.

Mr. Himmelfarb uses a similar labeling tactic when he dismisses my contention that diaspora Judaism was a history of "almost unrelieved Jewish suffering." I have some knowledge of the fact that many American-Jewish historians regard the "lachrymose interpretation of Jewish history" as discredited. My reading of Jewish history does not rest upon a quantitative analysis of the intensity and continuity of Jewish physical suffering. It rests upon the fact that the Jews were ultimately powerless and dwelt among peoples in Europe who were imbued with a mythic interpretation of Jewish destiny. The combination of Jewish powerlessness and homelessness, together with gentile myth, finally led to Auschwitz. I am unimpressed with the fact that G.G. Coulton acknowledges the superior literacy of the medieval Jew over the medieval Christian. Jewish literacy was a praiseworthy attainment, but it is not relevant to the issue of powerlessness. Similarly, I am aware of I.F. Baer's periodization of Jewish history. I would not question the great authority of his scholarship. Nevertheless, I am not nearly as willing as Mr. Himmelfarb to rest content with his judgment as final, largely because he fails to deal with the issue of Jewish powerlessness.

In my paper I confess that the only God I can believe in is the archaic Earth-Mother. In my forthcoming book, *The Religious Imagination* [1], I attempt to demonstrate that she never entirely lost her hold over the children of Israel even in rabbinic times. I am not dissuaded from my theological vision because Mr. Himmelfarb exclaims that Robert Graves has had similar thoughts. I am compelled to my belief because it seems to be the mythic image which accords most deeply with the human predicament. Mr. Himmelfarb ends his effort with a most stirring affirmation of the kingship of the Lord of history. My affirmation is more modest in expectation and more terrible in its ultimate hopelessness.

Mr. Himmelfarb sees great significance in "the symbolic fact that immediately after the Israeli victory . . . there was such a run on phylacteries in Jerusalem that stocks were depleted for a while." It would seem that in a moment of overwhelming joy some Jews wanted to express themselves through the symbolic instrumentalities of traditional Judaism. When I was in Jerusalem this past summer, I also bought a new set of phylacteries and a new prayer shawl. I used them for the first time at the Western Wall. The turning from the God of history to the God of nature and place does not cancel out the meaningful character of traditional Jewish ritual. On the contrary, my own traditionalism rests largely on the conviction that traditional Judaism preserves more of the mythic and archaic elements in Jewish religious experience than does the more rationalistic and moralistic liberal Judaism. Nevertheless, I must challenge Mr. Himmelfarb's assertion that there has been an Israeli religious revival along traditional diaspora lines. During my recent visit, I made it a point to give rides to hitchhiking soldiers and civilians wherever I drove. In Israel hitchhiking is more commonplace and more respectable than in the United States. I repeatedly inquired of my riders concerning their religious attitudes. I can report that the majority were by no means moved to return to the God of history, as Mr. Himmelfarb suggests. The consensus seemed to be that the victory was a purely human accomplishment. Here and there, some very orthodox Jews insisted on the miraculous character of the events, but they were a distinct minority. Mr. Himmelfarb's "symbolic fact" of the "run on phylacteries" would seem to be no more significant than the World War II claims that the increasing resort to prayerbooks, crosses, mezuzahs, and amulets by foxhole soldiers was the forerunner of an American religious revival. I am puzzled that so careful a scholar as the editor of *Commentary* would grasp at such a straw in view of the sources of direct information available to him.

Rabbi Irving Greenberg raises the issue of the secular city in his generous defense of the establishment theologians. He asserts that "most Jews went into the secular city, lock, stock and barrel." He insists that "many Jews alive will become purely universal secular men." But is this really so? Does not Dr. Greenberg confuse the loss of religious faith with the loss of Jewish identity? It is possible to lose the one and retain a very strong sense of the other. Dr. Greenberg's equation of religious faith and Jewish identity seems to be implicit in his comment that "those who *choose* to remain (Jews) will be particularly people who *opt* for their status as an election" (italics mine). Rabbi Greenberg apparently regards Jewish identity as a matter of choice. Is it not in reality a matter of inheritance? One does not choose to be a Jew. One is born a Jew.

Furthermore, except for a few Jews in the intellectual professions, the decision to abandon Judaism almost always involves entrance into some branch of Christianity. The "purely universal secular man" whom Rabbi Greenberg refers to looks very much like an urban, nonbelieving Jew to most gentiles. If a Jew wants out, he will not stop at the illusory halfway house of "universal secular man." He will marry a non-Jew and bring his children up as Christians. This choice will rest less upon religious conviction than upon an awareness of American social reality.

I find Dr. Greenberg's statement that "Jews have fully arrived in the West, particularly in the United States" a bit premature. In America Jews are a minority in a country with a fundamentally Protestant Christian ethos. Perhaps the view from Pittsburgh is different from Dr. Greenberg's view from New York. Nevertheless, I believe the social structure and the power relations of the Christian and Jewish communities of Pittsburgh are far more typical of the American mainstream than the special case of New York. Jews have by no means fully arrived in Pittsburgh. Their style of life, their religious and social affiliations, and their vocational opportunities are vastly different from those of their Christian neighbors. The relative prosperity of the American Jew ought not to blind us to the extent to which he remains a continuing stranger to the American mainstream.

I am not at all sure I understand what Dr. Greenberg means by "modern culture" when he writes that Jewish life and thought in the last two hundred years have been dominated by the need to modernize. If Dr. Greenberg believes that secular humanism represents the modernity that Judaism must confront, his preoccupation is probably outdated. The "turned-on," tribalized culture of our times has long since departed from the arid rationalism and the unrealistic messianic optimism of secular humanism. I would seriously question also his assertion of "the overpowering intellectual superiority and sophistication of the modern as compared to Jewish culture and thought." The theological problem of Judaism is not one of overcoming a cultural lag. If Jews must adjust to modernity, what literary work is more classically "modern" than *Finnegans Wake*? The power of this monumental achievement of modern literature consists in its dreamlike elision of mythic, archaic, and twentieth century motifs in an ever repeating cycle of human experience. The *Wake* celebrates the pagan, the archaic, and the cyclical. It leads to a renewed appreciation of the perennial power of religious myth and symbol. The River Liffey runs past Dublin's twentieth century shores in the eternally recurrent drama of man. The contemporary experience leads to neoarchaic man, rather than to an attempted renewal of fideism.

Like Himmelfarb and Cohen, Dr. Greenberg sees the silence of the establishment theologians as a token of their spiritual and intellectual seriousness before the painful issue of Auschwitz. He assures us that "the beginnings of a religious intelligentsia and of theology can be detected" and that "its leadership will now have to confront the new time." The establishment theologians have every right to delay their response. However, their silence renders questionable Rabbi Greenberg's assertion that "we are on the brink of a great theological flowering." We shall be in a better position to judge the quality of the contributions of the new theologians when they begin to address themselves to the great issues of contemporary Jewish history. Their silence would be more impressive were it not for the fact that Albert Camus addressed himself with great insight into the problem of God and evil in his novel *The Plague* shortly after World War II. The facts are in. Until we have better evidence, we must conclude that the older theological categories are in reality inadequate to the explosive events of the twentieth century.

Zalman Schachter does not remain silent before Auschwitz. He does not bid us wait yet a little while longer. He responds to Auschwitz and the rebirth of Israel in an almost totally paradoxical manner. Very wisely, he would play the religious fool. He knows that this is the only remaining option available within the framework of traditional theology. Unlike the establishment theologians, he is not embarrassed by it. The establishment theologians would do well to ponder Schachter's seemingly impractical response. They claim they are not ready to speak. Could it be that they find Schachter's mystical paradox as scandalous as my paganism and that they know of no other options? I believe Schachter fails because his vision is totally lacking in political or psychological realism. Schachter knows this as well as anybody. He has a very precise understanding of the theological options. He knows they will not magically increase with the passing of time. In the final analysis, he will not abandon the myth of the God of history. Nevertheless, he is entirely aware of the pain and the scandal required to maintain it after Auschwitz.

Only a shadow of a dialectic movement separates Schachter's position from my own, though they seem polar opposites. He urges the Jew to be the agent of the world's mystical redemption. I want my people to learn how to live wisely, realistically, and moderately in the tangled bank of luxuriant fertility and cannibalistic destructiveness. Schachter would avoid my world at all costs, although he has felt its power deeply. I can only say to him, "Reb Zalman, why do you split yourself asunder so needlessly? Accept the world in both its joy and horror without illusion. Acknowledge what in fact you already know — that in the final analysis we are of earth and to her we must be true."

REFERENCE

1. Rubenstein, Richard L: *The Religious Imagination* (The Bobbs-Merrill Co, Inc, Indianapolis, Indiana) forthcoming.

3. THE ABORTION DEBATE

by Ralph B. Potter, Jr.

MANY individuals and groups in the United States want reform of the laws governing abortion. To gain political leverage, reformers must mobilize opinion within the massive Protestant community, for in the increasingly widespread political contests over abortion law reform the mainline Protestants generally constitute a "swing vote." What basic concepts shape Protestants' attitudes toward abortion? What arguments impress them?

Protestants traditionally have disapproved of the termination of any healthy pregnancy. Amidst the present ferment and strife, however, American Protestants are showing signs of confusion regarding the proper moral and legal status of abortion. Various streams of thought have been converging to form a theological and ethical blend which is eroding the inherited Protestant position of disapproving abortion in all circumstances in which the life of the mother is not seriously threatened.

BENEFITS OF THE STATUS QUO

The first clue to Protestant confusion is the extent of the silence of the churches on the question of abortion. No one knows the exact dimensions of the abortion problem, but it is a problem of no less significance than other matters on which the churches have invested great energies. The degree of uncertainty regarding the incidence of abortion in the United States is best illustrated by the conclusion of a distinguished committee which reported to a major conference on abortion, May 29, 1957:

> Taking into account the probable trend of the abortion ratio since the interwar period, a plausible estimate of the frequency

of induced abortion in the United States could be as low as 200,000 and as high as 1,200,000 per year, depending upon the assumptions made as to the incidence of abortion in the total population as compared with the restricted groups for which statistical data are available, and upon the assessment of the direction and magnitude of bias inherent in each series of data. There is no objective basis for the selection of a particular figure between these two estimates as an approximation of the actual frequency [6:180].

During the churches' participation in a variety of civic crusades in recent decades, the practice of nontherapeutic abortion has remained morally condemned and legally proscribed, but widely practiced and perennially ignored. How has it been possible for the churches not to address themselves to the reform of abortion laws which, according to advocates of "liberalization," presently drive a million women a year to endanger life and health at the hands of criminal abortionists, engender a criminal empire, corrupt law enforcement officials, discriminate against the poor, force the cultivation of deformed embryos, ensure the birth of unwanted children, deny women control of their own bodies, and perpetuate a bogus moralism and hypocrisy? It seems out of character for the heirs of the social gospel, who frequently find it difficult to suppress their passion for prefecting the social order, to abstain from correcting a situation considered grievous by many social critics. How can we account for this unusual reticence?

The best explanation appears unduly simple and circular: Protestants have been relatively content with the status quo. They seem to have concluded that it represents the best possible balance of their conflicting inclinations towards "law" and "grace." The untidy arrangement by which antiabortion laws are retained, but enforced only sporadically against criminal abortionists and never against their clients, has allowed Protestants to employ the didactic, educative power of the law to reinforce their strong negative judgment upon abortion itself; yet relief from the stringency of the rule is afforded in individual cases by tolerating the existence of a decentralized system of illegal abortion accessible to women equipped with the resources necessary for individual enterprise in any sphere — that is, motivation, information, and money. If the resulting inequities have been unattractive, the alternatives have seemed still less attractive. Enforcement of the law would forestall relief for "exceptional cases." A weakening of the law might imply an acceptance, in principle, of nontherapeutic abortion.

NEW RECEPTIVITY

The social education and action machinery maintained by the major Protestant denominations has not been mobilized in the battle for or against abortion law reform. But it is increasingly difficult for Protestants not to become embroiled, especially in those states in which bills providing for the extension of the justifiable grounds for abortion have been introduced in the legislatures in recent years.

New legislation extending the provisions for legal abortion was passed during 1967 in Colorado, North Carolina, and California. Extensive and well publicized controversy was occasioned by the introduction of an abortion law reform bill in the New York State legislature. The bill died in committee but gave public life to the abortion issue. Abortion law reform bills have been introduced in at least twenty-four other states.

Numerous groups have been formed to promote the cause of reform. (The Association for the Study of Abortion, centered in New York, conducts the most extensive program. The Association prepares and distributes pamphlets, bibliographies, and reprints, provides speakers, conducts forums, and promotes the gathering and exchange of information about abortion.) The audience attentive to these groups has expanded; the new resonance may be attributed not so much to any novelty in the message as to changes in the sensitivities of listeners. The main elements of the abortion issue are not new; zeal for reform is not new; most of the arguments are not new. It is the receptivity of a broad segment of the "Protestant" public that is new.

Three factors have contributed most to this new receptivity. The first is the breakdown of old theological certainties which shaped Protestant opposition to nontherapeutic abortion. What has broken down is a constellation of beliefs about nature, man, and God which sustained the conviction that nascent life in the womb is, in every circumstance, a gift of God given for the realization of his mysterious purpose, and is, therefore, to be respected as inviolable from lawful human interference except in the tragic case in which the life of the fetus is pitted against the life of its mother. Protestants seldom have relied upon the natural law reasoning of Roman Catholic theologians to sustain their disapprobation of abortion. Protestant objections generally have not been grounded in a desire to avoid intervention in the biological processes of "nature," and "nature" has not been invested with a sacral immunity from pragmatic human manipulation. Protestants have feared not an "abuse of nature" but rather a direct affront to "nature's God." Abortion has been viewed as the annulment of God's special providence, the ungrateful despising of his miraculous gift, and the rejection of his summons to the vocation of parenthood.

The Protestant approach has rested upon the prevalence of Providence. When a new habit of mind now attributes new life to "rotten luck" in the practice of contraception rather than to the purposeful will of a merciful God, neglect of the countermeasure of abortion becomes irrational and superstitious retreat from the possibility of exercising control of one's destiny. Denial of accessibility to abortion comes to be seen by many as a violation of a civil liberty.

The second factor underlying the new receptivity consists of the abortion reform movement's forceful expression of themes taken from the Protestant tradition itself, particularly the themes of self-determination and rational control of nature. The principle of self-determination vindicates the attempts of autonomous individuals to shape the conditions of their existence through vigorous action. It functions as a counterprinciple, offsetting the invitation to passive acceptance of the dictates of nature conveyed in the biologically bound version of natural law philosophy underlying Roman Catholic discourses on abortion. Rational control of nature is indispensable for the realization of self-determination. As the realm in which men acknowledge the providential rule of God contracts, the scope of human control must expand. Parenthood ought to be planned because such an important matter must be submitted to purposeful control. If men are unable to believe that God has carefully planned and ordained each pregnancy, they themselves must take measures to insure that procreation is not left to "blind nature" or to chance. The status of abortion is enhanced among Protestants when it is advertised as a means of implementing rational control over nature.

The third factor contributing to the new receptivity is the dimming of the vision of a Protestant American made to conform to the dictates of Protestant conscience. Reformers assert that control over nature is a moral imperative and frequently add that self-determination in the use of reproductive powers is a civil right. Protestants, convinced of the high value of control over nature and of self-determination, feel obliged, in a pluralistic society, to concede the exercise of these powers to all men. Those who disagree concerning the specific *content* of the imperatives of conscience must, nevertheless, be afforded the freedom necessary for self-determination through control over nature. By devotion to their own principles, Protestants are obliged to tolerate a gap between what is *morally* condemned and what is *legally* proscribed.

Protestants are confused concerning the *moral* status of abortion when practiced *by Christians*. Their confusion is compounded by uncertainty regarding the extent to which the moral judgments of one segment of society should be imposed upon *others* by *legal* enactment. The unpleasant aftertaste of Prohibition lingers on. More and more Protestants acquiesce to the motto, "You can't legislate morality." They concede that there must be a sphere of privacy into which the state and its law may not intrude. But does abortion fall within this sphere? Is abortion merely a matter of "private morality"? Are the existing laws regulating abortion simply relics of an antiquated paternalism which precludes the exercise of self-determination and restricts the area to be submitted to human control? Do our abortion laws serve only to reinforce a peculiar, religiously grounded code of moral behavior which has lost power to gain voluntary assent? Or, in a pluralistic society, can some valid secular purpose establish the propriety of legal restrictions upon the practice of abortion? These have come to be the decisive issues among Protestants now forced to reconsider their stance on abortion law reform.

THE SPECTRUM OF CONTENDING VIEWS

The rallying point for those intent upon reformation of the abortion laws is the relevant section of the Model Penal Code proposed by the American Law Institute [2; 17; 31]. The suggested code would justify a physician "in terminating a pregnancy if he believes there is substantial risk that continuance of the pregnancy would gravely impair the physical or mental health of the mother or that the child would be born with grave physical or mental defect, or that the pregnancy resulted from rape, incest, or other felonious intercourse." Support for this proposal has come from disparate sources, from individuals and groups who find themselves in an impromptu alliance with others with whom they may share no other cause or belief. Even supporters of less extensive modifications can be classified, with technical accuracy, as "advocates of abortion law reform." Such a broad label may be polemically useful to opponents of reform, but it obscures distinctions between many shades of opinion concerning how lenient the law should be and prevents recognition of the many different patterns of reasoning that are employed to support these varied opinions.

If rational debate is to be promoted, careful distinctions must be made along the broad spectrum of recommendations put forward concerning abortional law reform. The spectrum may be divided into three major segments, three broad bands marking fundamentally different approaches to the issue. At the right end of the spectrum is a position that may be awkwardly referred to as "no abortion." At the left end is "abortion on demand." Those who fall within the middle range of the spectrum support the concept of "justifiable abortion."

[The term "left wing" will be used to include some who occupy the left end of the middle segment of the spectrum, that is, those who would permit very generous indications but would still require that some "reason" be given in support of a request for a legal abortion. Similarly, the "right wing" includes many "fudging Catholics" who, although formally committed to the "no abortion" position by the Papal Encyclical, *Casti Connubi*, issued December 31, 1930, nevertheless manage to make allowance for action "to prevent pregnancy" after rape and condone laws which permit therapeutic abortion necessary to save the life of the mother. The necessity of providing a flexible boundary for the right wing is confirmed by proposals advanced by Robert F. Drinan, S.J., Dean of Boston College School of Law [12:177–179].]

In their style of argument, the members of the middle or "justifiable abortion" school differ from adherents of the two extreme positions by their willingness to require and to accept certain reasons or "indications" as adequate justification for the basically repugnant act of abortion. Within this middle school there is wide disagreement concerning which indications should establish acceptable grounds for abortion under the law. But all members agree that abortion may be justifiable for certain reasons and unjustifiable for other reasons. In contrast, neither of the extreme positions deals in reasons or "indications." Those who uphold the "no abortion" position deny that there is any reason that could render abortion morally and legally tolerable. Advocates of "abortion on demand" reject the notion that any reason should be required, since all decisions regarding the use of procreative powers must be left to the unrestricted private judgment of individual women. Debate over the identity of legally acceptable indications is thus properly a characteristic of the middle range of the spectrum. It is within this range that the immediately foreseeable compromises of the law will be hammered out.

118

RALPH B. POTTER, JR. · *The Abortion Debate*

Compromise is characteristic of the middle. An intellectual compromise determines the approach and the style of debate within the middle segment. Content is drawn from the left. But the framework which determines the structure of argumentation about the limits of "justifiable abortion" is a legacy of the style of moral theology that has flourished among Roman Catholics on the right. The intellectual framework of debate is similar in form to the apparatus employed by moral theologians in assessing the claim that a particular resort to armed force represents an instance of "justifiable warfare." The burden of proof is imposed upon those who would assert, in a particular case, that an exception should be conceded from the general condemnation and prohibition. It is ironic that Roman Catholics apply this apparatus in thinking about warfare but refuse to let it structure their thought upon abortion. Protestants rely upon it in debate concerning abortion but have neglected to make conscious use of it in the analysis of the moral problem of war. The motives for neglect have been similar in the respective cases: the framework provides an apparatus for the regulation rather than for the abolition of a particular type of activity. Protestants have harbored the hope of abolishing war; Roman Catholics would like to abolish abortion.

The traditional framework, with its generally negative judgment upon abortion, has determined the shape of the abortion law reform bills modeled upon the American Law Institute proposals. Moreover, public debate has, for the most part, conformed to the pattern of delineating the proper sphere of allowable exceptions. But the sphere is expanding. Under the present compromise new content is being squeezed into the form determined by the venerable framework. In response to considerations pressed most assiduously by secular humanists, whose basic affinity is with the "abortion on demand" school, the sphere of recommended exceptions has been inflated to the extent that the encompassing apparatus is distended nearly to the point of explosion and collapse.

The compromise that dictates that new, far-reaching extensions of the allowable indications be debated within a framework designed to restrict exceptions leads to curious adaptations of the traditional vocabulary. The "Statement of Policy" of the Society for Humane Abortion, a group disposed to the cause of abortion on demand, reveals a sensitivity to the prejudicial effect of the established framework of discussion: "Because we regard abortion as a surgical procedure and not a criminal offense, we neither endorse new laws nor sponsor revision of old laws which attempt to control abortions. The underlying concept of enacting such laws simply perpetuates the idea that abortion is wrong." Nevertheless, the same Statement conforms to the pattern of offering a list of justifying indications for abortion. Even so, the list itself reveals that the conformity is a tactical, rhetorical device which conforms to the style imposed by the framework in order to subvert its strictures.

> Be it therefore resolved that the Society for Humane Abortion supports abortion for those wishing to terminate pregancy if:
> 1. There would be grave impairment of physical or mental health of the pregnant woman
> 2. Pregnancy resulted from failure of birth control devices or through ignorance of their use
> 3. Pregnancy resulted from rape or incest
> 4. The child would probably be born with a serious physical or mental defect
> 5. There exists *some other compelling reason* . . . physical, psychological, mental, spiritual or economic [36].

A resolution adopted by the Unitarian Universalist Association in 1963 parallels this statement, omitting the second item but preserving verbatim item five.

THE LEFT WING: ABORTION ON DEMAND

The further one moves to the left along the spectrum, the stronger is the inclination to treat self-determination as an absolute value. It is the master theme in a medley of arguments drawn from a variety of sources. An argument for abortion on demand is likely to be composed of the following elements arranged in differing patterns of emphasis. Abortion on demand is necessary: (1) to protect the life and health of women by making medically safe abortion available to those who cannot be deterred by rigid laws or high risks; (2) to preserve the autonomy of the medical profession; (3) to insure that only wanted children will be born; (4) to guarantee that each child will receive careful nurture within a family able to expend adequate amounts of time, money and loving care upon it; (5) to help defuse the population explosion; (6) to enable women to attain equal status through escape from the risk of unwanted pregnancy; (7) to avoid discrimination by race and social class through making abortion equally available to all at low expense; (8) to realize the promise of full civil liberty by according women unquestioned control over the use of their bodies, and couples unchallenged right of privacy [29; 18].

These themes are variously elaborated and supplemented; but they are invariably accompanied by strong emphasis upon the right of self-determination as a positive moral value which can be realized only through repeal of laws which presume to prescribe who may and who may not legally terminate her pregnancy. The central significance of the moral value of self-determination is illustrated in a passage written by Thomas S. Szasz:

> I submit that efforts to "liberalize" abortion laws by providing a broader spectrum of medical and psychiatric justifications for the procedure are, in effect, restrictive of human freedom and, therefore, truly anti-liberal. Why? Because medical and psychiatric "liberalizations" of abortion laws would only increase the number of times *other* people could provide abortions for women; they would not increase the number of occasions on which women could make this decision for *themselves*. Such measures, therefore, give assent to the proposition that it is good to deny people the right to determine for themselves how they should use their bodies [37:344].

Such an argument finds new receptivity among Protestants exposed to theological works which assure them that "Christian ethics aims, not at morality, but at maturity" [23:54].

Many younger Protestants have been nurtured in the certainty that maturity is exhibited in the willingness to accept moral ambiguity and the risk of the exercise of freedom in each new situation. Presently fashionable styles of thought simultaneously corrode the ancient tradition and create a new affinity for the major positive themes voiced by advocates of abortion on demand. (In the opening chapter of *Situation Ethics,* Joseph Fletcher illustrates the alleged benefits of the freedom and flexibility afforded by his "situational approach" to ethics by showing how it might be used to justify abortion in certain circumstances [15:37–39]. Paul Ramsey notes with irony that, "Even in *Situation Ethics* one comes upon at least one general rule of behavior, or general principle of ethics, besides love itself. . . . That rule is: '. . . no unwanted or unintended baby should ever be born.' Or, to express this for a *subject* other than the child: no woman should be forced to bear an unwanted child" [32:168].)

These intellectual currents run so wide and deep that it is certain that the present legal and political contests focused upon the American Law Institute proposals for "justifiable abortion" represent only an initial phase of an inevitable conflict between the demand for unhampered self-determination and the tradition which asserts that there is a valid basis for public regulation of the practice of abortion. The impact of the left-wing school is strong enough that one may anticipate a significant shifting of the burden of proof. In many quarters, the central question of the abortion debate is gradually being rephrased. The question becomes: "What reasons can justify the refusal of the state to grant permission for an abortion?" The form of the question preserves the style of the middle; but the content reveals the influence of the left. Eventually, the question must be faced, "Why should there be any law governing who may undergo an abortion?"

THE RIGHT WING: REALIZATION OF THE GREATER GOOD

The right wing of the spectrum is defended most relentlessly in public debate by Roman Catholic spokesmen. It should not be overlooked, however, that some members of the Protestant and

Jewish communities join in defense of the present laws regulating abortion. Nevertheless, most of the right-wing arguments stated here are to be attributed to Roman Catholic commentators who, by and large, have set the terms of debate over and against left-wing advocates.

As one moves toward the right end of the spectrum, certainty increases that it is the proper function of the state to intervene in the matter of abortion in order to prevent harm. The harm envisioned may be inflicted upon the mother, the medical profession, the family, society at large, the fetus, or what might best be described as "the cultural ethos."

The nub of the right-wing argument, as presented to contemporary Americans, is simple and stark: the condoning of widespread resort to abortion would undermine civilization. The argument is couched in theological terms; it leads, however, to conclusions in the realm of cultural anthropology. The path of reasoning sometimes twists through philosophical thickets. But the destination is a flat prediction concerning consequences for all human relationships if a significant number of people come to accept abortion in good conscience. There are many distractive bypaths along the route to be traversed in argument. But the constant goal is to convince hearers, by whatever arguments carry force in their generation, that the practice of abortion is incompatible with the attainment of man's true humanity. At stake in controversies over abortion law reform is the definition of the vision of what man should be. Urgency arises from the conviction that the content of that vision will shape the actual quality of human relationships in decades to come.

The profundity of the right-wing argument is its greatest weakness. Many of the injuries described by controversialists on the right take place in a dimension of existence unknown or unexplored by their fellow citizens. Indeed, when the particular "harms" are analyzed closely, they are seen to consist ultimately of a deprivation of a greater good, a good which may transcend the concern of a secular, pluralistic state. Can the prevention of such a harm, or the realization of such a good, be considered a valid legislative purpose sufficient to overrule the strong desires of innumerable pregnant women? Analysis of the difficulties experienced by right-wing critics in dramatizing the injuries they presume to be wrought upon mothers by abortion will suggest the perils of profundity and illustrate the dynamics of the abortion debate.

The harm that is most vivid and imaginable to typical onlookers is injury to the health and welfare of the mother. Spokesmen for the left wing generate great dramatic impact by portraying very palpable injuries to mothers. They depict vivid harm to victims with whom readers can readily identify. The power of immediacy is exploited also in their outline of causes and cures. The harm is attributed directly to the lack of legal access to medically competent abortions performed in hospital settings. A prompt remedy is offered through "legalization of abortion now." In the effort to recoup the title of "defenders of the public welfare," right-wing advocates are obliged, by contrast, to depict either very subtle injuries to real persons or somewhat less subtle harm to less vividly imaginable entities such as "society," "civilization," or "the fetus." Indeed, the attempt to overcome the seeming inability of many people to visualize the fetus as an object of real injury accounts for many of the intellectual and rhetorical maneuvers in the battle over abortion law reform.

Both the left and the right wings of the abortion spectrum would like to enjoy a reputation as guardians of the life and health of mothers. But how are life and health truly protected? Members of the left wing join with many moderates of the middle segment in urging that permission for abortion should be granted when the measure is deemed necessary by physicians to spare a woman from a nonlethal threat to her health. Going beyond that, the left wing emphasizes the need to protect women from the risk to life and health incurred through criminal abortion. The right wing asserts that true life and health are best served by guarding women from abortion in any circumstance.

To reinforce its claim to be the true guardian of the mother, each side provides empirical data concerning the incidence of abortion, both legal and illegal, and the medical and psychiatric effects of abortion performed under various circumstances. The left wing must overcome public inertia. Its spokesmen are compelled to show that a massive problem exists that ought not to be ignored. Hence, their estimates of the incidence of criminal abortion tend to be high. Moreover, their statistics must indicate that criminal abortions are very dangerous while hospital abortions are medically safe and seldom give rise to untoward psychological effects.

Conversely, statistics presented by the right wing diminish the danger gap between hospital and extrahospital abortions. Emphasis is placed by right-wing spokesmen upon the residual risk of the operation under even the best medical conditions. It is asserted that "sound medical practice" would require abortion only in exceedingly rare circumstances. With the advance of medical skill, strictly medical indications have been reduced. It is rare that life or health is seriously jeopardized in well attended pregnancy. Moreover, it is claimed, there is no strong evidence of significant therapeutic gain through abortion. There is a lack of due proportion between the undoubted risk and the uncertain gain.

The right wing's first line of defense — that abortion, as a medical procedure, is both dangerous and superfluous — seems to be crumbling under an avalanche of statistics from Eastern Europe and other regions where abortion is widely practiced and new techniques are being developed through research. The level of medical danger there is not high. Also, it can be argued that abortion is not totally superfluous. If it is seldom necessary, abortion may nevertheless be occasionally necessary, and the law should not bar physicians from attempting to preserve the life and health of their patients.

There is a second line of defense. The dangers of abortion may be more subtle. The unhappy effects may be delayed in time and buried in the recesses of the personality, accessible only to those armed with psychiatric skill. Many on the right wing insist that, no matter where, or by whom, or for what reason abortion is performed, it inflicts a scar upon the conscience of the woman and places her mental health in jeopardy by exposing her to the harsh retribution of guilt.

A considerable body of literature deals with the psychiatric effects of abortion. From this literature adherents of the left wing extract evidence that the incidence of serious psychological after-effects is relatively low. They go on to argue that the incidence would be much lower still if right-wing propaganda did not perpetuate the self-fulfilling prophecy that induces symptoms of guilt by contending that such symptoms are virtually inevitable. They hold that guilt over abortion is a cultural legacy that will become increasingly rare as societies adopt a more "enlightened" and therefore more tolerant attitude toward abortion.

The reply of those on the right wing is to make the injury from abortion appear more subtle still. They hold that some psychiatrists cannot detect the full extent of the harm to mothers because they maintain a superficial view of the full components of true health. True health involves more than "a state of complete physical and mental wellbeing." It has a spiritual dimension. The injury to the spirit of one who violates the law of nature and commandment of God by indulging in abortion may escape the notice of observers who employ less sensitive indices of affliction.

The depth of the disagreement which leads to strikingly different estimates of how harm to mothers is to be avoided comes clearly into view in debate over the meaning and function of guilt. All agree that women should be spared the experience of guilt. The left would remove the cultural inducement to exhibit this learned response. Adherents of the right wing insist that the only way to be rid of guilt is to avoid the occasion of guilt. In their view, guilt is not simply a legacy from an unenlightened past. It is a sign of latent health, a danger signal that the law of nature cannot be violated with impunity. Given the reality of abortion as the extermination of innocent life for self-centered purposes, women *ought* to feel guilty. Indeed, the *absence* of guilt is a grievous symptom which reveals that callousness and spiritual sclerosis are far advanced. Women should be spared the occasion of guilt by the refusal of abortion. But, if abortions are to be performed, the entire community must be saved from experiencing a *lack* of guilt.

The third line of defense of the right-wing claim to be the true guardian of women is the claim that the practice of abortion frustrates the realization of man's true humanity. Evidence for this is not easily given. It is difficult to muster "hard empirical data" to convince those who, on other bases, do not already share a particular view of men. The difficulty exposes the true nature of the dispute and demonstrates the burden of profundity.

With regard to the protection of mothers, as on other issues, participants in the abortion controversy talk past one another. Reformers on the left gather statistics which purport to prove that, at least in certain nations, few women experience deep remorse after an abortion. But the statistics, even if acknowledged as accurate, have little effect upon right-wing commentators. Their arguments are not grounded in such observations. Their line can be defended with the aid of statistics that show abortion *does* have ill effects. But it cannot be overthrown by empirical evidence that abortion does *not* have bad medical or psychiatric consequences. Only the outer defenses can be endangered by the attack of epidemiologists and sociologists. The inner defense is founded firmly upon theological ground. The battle is being fought over questions of theological anthropology and ethics. The issue is: What ought man to be? What style of life represents the realization of true humanity?

HIGH STAKES

The central claim of the right wing is that abortion is evil because it deprives an individual of the greater good of becoming a more selfless creature. Abortion, in killing the actual self of the fetus, kills the potential higher self of the mother. Abortion is inimical to the attainment of "a generous spirit" which welcomes new life and accepts the occasion of redemptive suffering and sacrifice.

At stake in the abortion debate is not simply the fate of individual women or even the destiny of individual nations and cultures. It is difficult to demonstrate that acceptance of the most extreme proposal for abortion on demand would establish a clear and present danger to the civil harmony necessary for the maintenance of a tranquil state. Nations that have lenient abortion laws do function. But if abortion is not an actual threat to minimal public order, it may nevertheless be a symbolic threat to the ideal moral order espoused by Christians for two millennia. Abortion does not merely contradict specific mores and moral teachings pertaining to sexuality, marriage, and procreation or endanger a system of law built upon "respect for life." It implies the rejection of a world view which has sustained a way of life, a mode of being in the world, a pattern of response to the human condition.

Abortion is a symbolic threat to an entire system of thought and meaning. The willingness to practice abortion, or even to condone resort to abortion by others, signals that the high Christian vision of selfless charity has become despised and rejected of men. The Christian portrayal of the true man as one characterized by selflessness, sacrifice, concern for the weak and the unlovely, and a willingness to accept and transcend allotted afflictions through the power of redemptive suffering has faded in public consciousness to the point that it can seldom induce willing imitation. For many people there is simply no meaning in putting up with an unwanted circumstance when recourse is available without a high probability of temporal retribution.

For Christians, an entire system of meaning may be at stake in the abortion debate; but is anything at stake for a secular, pluralistic state?

SOURCES OF THE ABHORRENCE OF ABORTION

Christians frequently are delighted to take credit for instilling into the Western tradition a deep abhorrence of abortion. This affirmation of the historical relevance of Christianity may do wonders for Christian pride and morale, but it makes it more, rather than less, difficult to maintain antiabortion laws in a secular, pluralistic setting. Norman St. John-Stevas, a British Roman Catholic barrister and member of Parliament, has celebrated the role attributed to Christian faith in the emergence of respect for the fundamental value of "the right to life."

> The respect for human life and personality that distinguishes Western society from the totalitarian societies of the East did not spring up out of nothing. It is deeply rooted in experience and history. Above all it is rooted in religion. Ultimately the idea of the right to life, as is the case with other human rights, is traceable to the Christian doctrine of man. . . . The value of human life for the Christian in the first century A.D., as today, rested not on its development of a superior sentience but on its unique character of the union of body and soul, both destined for eternal life. The right to life thus has a theological foundation. . . . Respect for the lives of *others* because of their eternal destiny is the essence of the Christian teaching. Its other aspect is the emphasis on the creatureliness of man. Man is not absolutely master of his own life and body, he has no *dominion* over it but holds it in trust for God's purposes.
>
> This respect for human life has become part of the moral consensus of Western society [34: 16, 17].

By this account, a ban on abortion might seem to be a particular application of the fundamental principle ascribed to Christian influence. But St. John-Stevas suggests that the sentiments which lead to sanctions against abortion have a more general source.

> This attitude to young life undoubtedly has in part a Christian foundation but it goes back beyond the Christian era to earlier civilizations. Rejection of abortion seems to result from the nature of man himself. . . . With the coming of Christianity condemnation of abortion was reinforced and became absolute [34: 36].

Is the rejection of abortion really rooted in the nature of man himself? Or does it derive from a response to the image of man portrayed in the Gospels? The issue cannot be settled by available anthropological data which seem to indicate a general ambivalence towards the practice of abortion within societies which differ greatly in the rate of occurrence and the severity of the sanctions imposed [8:97 – 152; 9].

The more emphasis is placed upon the distinctively Christian roots of the ban on abortion, the more difficult it becomes to argue that the restrictions can or should be maintained if the theological roots from which they sprang have now been eroded. St. John-Stevas observes that the concept of the right to life "is accepted by many who would reject the Christian doctrine on which it is based." But he implies, nevertheless, that the pillars of Christian faith are necessary props for the ban upon abortion: ". . . the right to life is ceaselessly challenged. . . . Against these attacks the Christian doctrine of man, as a being destined for eternal life, and therefore of unique value, provides the most effective bulwark" [34:127]. An increasingly shaky popular belief in man's eternal destiny is, in these days, an unsteady foundation for domestic legislation.

It seems credible that Christian apologists are correct in the historical judgment that the harsh condemnation of abortion expressed in our laws is the precipitate of Western exposure to Christian moral teaching. An evangelical vision of how men ought to behave has been imposed as the legal norm of how they must behave. The requirements of love have been confused with the demands of natural justice.

In an extensive law journal article, Eugene Quay provides an example of the extent to which Christian expectations of self-sacrificing charity have crept into Roman Catholic definitions of conduct to be required by legal enactment.

> A mother who would sacrifice the life of her unborn child for her own health is lacking in something. If there could be any authority to destroy an innocent life for social considerations, it would still be in the interests of society to sacrifice such a mother rather than the child who might otherwise prove to be normal and decent and an asset [30:234].

130

Willingness to sacrifice one's health for the sake of an unborn child would seem to many people to represent an heroic achievement rather than a minimal gesture necessary to qualify one as "an asset" to society. Quay's rendition of the natural law and the nature of man has been skewed by Christian norms; the model of charity has been taken as the mandate of the law.

Through the teaching of the church, the faithful may come to look upon self-sacrifice as "normal and decent." It is difficult to convince the unfaithful, who may not share the prior conviction that man should be something more than he is, that abortion makes man something less than he ought to be. The mother who refuses to sacrifice her health may be "lacking in something," but that something is superadded to the level of morality that the state must require in order to preserve its stable existence.

The teaching of the church generated the sentiments expressed through the ban upon abortion. Abortion is a practice which seems incongruous with the profession of faith of those who live under the sign of the cross. But the nation does not live under the sign of the cross. Why, then, should there be laws restricting abortion? Do such statutes serve any secular purpose which may invest them with binding force in a society no longer willing to submit to the tutelage of the church?

WHAT VALUES DO ABORTION LAWS PROTECT?

The harm attributed to abortion by right-wing critics of legal reform is subtle and profound; it is the deprivation of man's greatest good — a character formed by charity and humble obedience to the commandments of God. But the very nobility of the vision places it beyond the protective concern of the law.

The state cannot command charity, but it can enforce justice. If it could be demonstrated that abortion did injury to some proper subject of the law's protection, a more solid foundation for antiabortion statutes could be constructed. This is the challenge to the right wing and to the middle: they must indicate

131

a harm the law cannot ignore to a victim the law is bound to protect. The Christian commentator is goaded by a moral abhorrence of abortion derived from the charitable lesson of the Gospel. But to defend public laws against abortion he needs legal arguments derived from the universal norms of natural justice.

LATENT FUNCTIONS OF THE LAW

Society must have an appropriate and adequate reason for denying a woman legal access to a medical procedure she desires, oftentimes with great desperation. The protection of all men from the loss of the high moral stature considered by some to constitute man's greatest good is not, in itself, a suitable basis for restrictive legislation. What reasons can be given for such laws?

Left-wing spokesmen insist that the original intent of the American laws passed in the nineteenth century was to protect the prospective mother from the medical dangers of abortion which, given the state of medical art at that time, were extremely high [22:97]. Now, as medical skill has increased, the same motive requires revision of the statutes so that women who cannot be deterred by the persuasion of counseling or the threat of law can have abortions in the safety of the hospital under excellent medical care. Right-wing historians hold that the intention of the law has been to preserve the life of the unborn child and that this purpose remains a valid and sufficient basis for laws restricting abortion, for example, Quay: "Protecting the life of the unborn child has been a major concern of the earliest laws known to us. It has continued to be an object of lawmaking in every subsequent civilization which has contributed to our own because it springs from a universal feeling which in the past has ceased to move men only when a nation was in decay" [31:395].

The compromise established by the present laws realizes neither intention fully. The laws fail to deter women from risking life and health at the hands of criminal abortionists and, in failing to deter mothers, they fail to preserve the lives of the unborn children. Why then do the laws persist? Edwin Schur has searched for an answer to this sociological puzzle.

> Since present abortion laws have clearly failed to curb the unsanctioned termination of pregnancy, their persistence must be attributable to some latent function they serve for society as a whole or for certain groups and individuals [35:59].

He suggests that every social system must maintain its membership; hence, "no society has allowed uncontrolled termination of pregnancies. . . . It may be also that the members of our society feel some illusory satisfaction in maintaining a formal and ideal standard in this area, even if they are largely unable to conform to it" [35:59]. For Schur, "It is not even clear, however, just what the normative ideal embodied in present abortion laws represents." He mentions the possibility that "the proscription basically represents a direct prohibition on killing the fetus" [35:60]. But he gives greater attention to the assumption that the ban flows from the intention to prohibit illegitimacy and promiscuity or from "the insistence that woman shall not with ease voluntarily renounce motherhood as a major social role. . . . This could be interpreted as an institutionalized support of the 'maternal instinct,' a necessary sex division of labor, or a reinforcement of the subordinate social status of women" [35:60].

Portions of Schur's analysis can be bolstered and refined by close scrutiny of data from public-opinion polls. Alice Rossi's presentation and interpretation of data gathered in a National Opinion Research Center poll in December 1965 [33] can be extended to undergird the theory that public attitudes towards abortion laws can best be explained by viewing them in the light of the traditional vision of the Christian family. The vision depicts a family, faithfully trusting Providence, living as a procreative unit within which all parental sexual activity is channeled and confined.

In the Rossi data, the level of public acceptance of abortion varies sharply with the circumstances surrounding pregnancy. The more the circumstances and the reaction of the mother can be interpreted as being congruent with the ideal of the faithful procreative family, the greater is the measure of popular assent. Public reaction to the most frequently urged "indications" for abortion is recorded in Table 1.

TABLE 1
ATTITUDES TOWARD LEGAL ABORTION [33:36]
1482 respondents

"Please tell me whether or not you think it should be possible for a pregnant woman to obtain a legal abortion. . . ."

	Yes	No	Don't Know
If the woman's own health is seriously endangered by the pregnancy	71%	26%	3%
If she became pregnant as the result of rape	56	38	6
If there is a strong chance of serious defect in the baby	55	41	4
If the family has a very low income and cannot afford any more children	21	77	2
If she is not married and does not want to marry the man	18	80	2
If she is married and does not want any more children	15	83	2

The preservation of the life and health of the mother is an important precondition of the welfare of any family. Yet when the mother's health is at stake one quarter of the respondents disapprove of abortion. Even the weightiest considerations cannot overcome for some respondents the conviction that willingness to sacrifice the life of the unborn is incompatible with the "generous spirit" which must pervade the model family. As the benefits allegedly to be gained through abortion become less indispensable to the very existence of the ideal family, the rate of disapproval of abortion increases.

The belief that a mother should voluntarily accept her role provides a point of leverage for the argument that she need not accept the involuntary pregnancy imposed upon her by rape.

The norms derived from the vision of the ideal family clash dramatically when there is a serious risk of deformity. The desire to complete the family circle with the birth of a healthy, normal child is respected. Yet the refusal to be reconciled to the prospect of bearing and rearing a handicapped child violates the expectation of trust in Providence and in the power of the faithful to redeem and transcend adversity. When the same argument is lodged against the economic indication, it is not met by such a formidable counterprinciple. The level of public acceptance of abortion declines sharply at this point. As for the unmarried mother, interpretation of the NORC data would suggest that those imbued with the vision of the ideal family look upon her as one attempting to sever all the links which bind sexual intercourse, procreation, and family responsibility. The implied function of sex becomes recreative rather than procreative or unitive.

Few people in the NORC sample approve of the use of abortion as a means of birth control within marriage. Yet married women, unwilling at the moment to bear a child, constitute the largest segment of the clientele of criminal abortionists. This awkward fact is frequently skirted by reformers of moderate middle persuasion. Public reluctance to grant the healthy married woman's request for abortion cannot be accounted for convincingly by theories — frequently invoked in the case of the unwed mother — which center upon the repressed hostility of the pious toward sexual license. Nor can the condemnation be attributed to the belief that sex must never be purposefully separated from procreation, since there is evidence of widespread acceptance of contraception among those who would refuse abortion. An explanation consonant with our theory is that most people feel that the existence of a new life, or a potential new life, establishes a value and creates a presumption against abortion. The married woman who can produce no reason for her child not to be born other than her own unwillingness to receive it, seems to despise that potential life by sacrificing it to nothing more than her own convenience. Her refusal to accept the residual risk of pregnancy in marital intercourse is taken by many respondents to reveal a stubborn and selfish spirit incompatible with the generous adaptability which must sustain the true family.

THE PRESERVATION OF INDIVIDUAL CHARACTER

In order to provide a secular purpose for the legislative restriction of abortion, those sharing the inclinations of the right wing can argue that the ban on abortion functions not simply to uphold a particular code of behavior, let alone a peculiar code of sexual behavior. It upholds character, the type of character that is indispensable to good citizenship. The virtues necessary to sustain the true family are the virtues necessary to sustain the state. The virtues and vices exposed in dealing with matters of sex, family life, and procreation pervade the entire character and find expression in civic relations. The state has a stake in the promotion of self-restraint rather than self-indulgence, responsibility rather than irresponsibility, and selfless adaptability rather than selfish rigidity.

There is more to this phase of the argument than the cry that acceptance of abortion will lead to sexual promiscuity. The fear is rather that it will lead to a general decline of individual character through lax enforcement of responsibility. The issue is not whether sex is to be separated from procreation, but whether procreation can be divorced from the responsibility to nurture new life.

Most commentators at every point across the spectrum might be willing to concede that in American society, by and large, sex has already been separated from procreation. This can be accomplished, with fair reliability, by practice of the rhythm method, which is cheap, simple, available without reliance upon a supplier, and is well advertised in literature widely distributed by the Roman Catholic Church. The new sexual mores that may evolve will doubtless be labeled "promiscuous" by some moralists and welcomed by others. In either case, it is too late to suppress the knowledge that, except for occasional "accidents," sexual intercourse need not result in procreation. The small but enduring margin of error gives rise to the question, "Who will bear the risk of contraceptive failure?"

Right-wing commentators insist that the woman must bear the residual risk of pregnancy because her dismissal from that responsibility would bring on a widespread eagerness to evade every troublesome inconvenience which members of society must bear. To this, critics reply that the desire to escape the "natural consequences" of our actions is not only common and in most circumstances approved; it is, in fact, the stimulus to research and progress. The progress attained by permitting abortion as an emergency backstop to contraception would be the upgrading of parenthood and the realization of a happy family in a home in which every child would be wanted and welcomed. Men applaud the extension of human control into all other areas. Advocates of reform ask, "Why should this one act be set off as inaccessible to control?" The answer from the right wing is that life is present. No matter how tenuous the existence of a newly formed embryo, its creation is an event of moral import that cannot be totally ignored or despised.

The battle line is drawn at the point at which the relentless extension of self-determination and control over nature collides with the fundamental principle of "respect for life." Should there be no limit to willful manipulation, no inclination to concede that there are boundaries to the power that may safely be entrusted to men? The fear expressed by the right wing is that if the law does not contest a woman's claim that she has a right to dispose as she wishes of that "piece of tissue" which contains the seed of a full grown person, we shall plummet ever faster towards a brave new world in which the only barrier to the manipulation of fellow human beings will be lack of power and technique.

Opponents of abortion fear that the inhabitants of the brave new world will be possessed and driven by a type of character that will brook no interference with their ambitions from nature, man, or God. If the dystopia they envision were a certain consequence of present toleration of abortion, many moderates might reconsider their mild reformist views. But the consequences are not inevitable nor would they be horrifying to all. In light of the broad and intense demand for abortion, can the state withhold permission solely on the basis of speculation about the possible effects of abortion upon individual character?

The argument that "easy abortion" will undermine a quality of individual character necessary to uphold civic virtue suffices only to gain a place for abortion within the category of "crimes without victims." In that category, antiabortion legislation maintains a perennially perilous existence in company with laws against drug addiction, homosexuality, prostitution, and gambling. The paternalistic style of such laws is deemed old fashioned by many citizens who are only slightly to the left of the center of the spectrum. In their minds, what a man chooses to do to his individual character ought to be considered a private affair. If there is to be a justification of antiabortion legislation grounded firmly in the defense of the public interest, the search must go on.

THE POPULATION ARGUMENT: A BOOMERANG

One attempt to ground antiabortion laws in concern for the common public interest of the secular state has backfired. Throughout most of the last hundred years the strong antagonism of the churches to abortion abetted the population policies of Western nations which aimed at increasing the birth rate in order to counter the threat of underpopulation. There was a convenient alliance of secular nationalism and ecclesiastical natalism. The moral evil of abortion was also a social evil which would deny the state a citizen, a soldier, a producer. Homilies on family life frequently placed strong emphasis upon the obligation of the Christian couple, when contemplating the number of children to be brought into the world, to consider the needs of the state.

Now the demographic situation has changed. Overpopulation rather than underpopulation is a menace. The argument that couples should consider the needs of the state in deciding about their procreative behavior can prove embarrassing when public policy seeks a reduction of the birth rate. The recent demographic history of Japan is cited by many demographers as evidence that the provision of cheap and easy abortion is the most effective means of bringing about a rapid decline in the birth rate. In certain circumstances the public interest might, therefore, require the promotion rather than the discouragement of abortion.

The response of the right wing has been to deemphasize the Christian's obligation to weigh the current demographic needs of the state as a significant factor in decisions regarding family size. Instead, much labor has been expended upon the construction of a high wall of privacy which would shelter decisions regarding procreation from the influence or intervention of any public authority. Here the right wing concurs with the left. In certain contexts the Roman Catholic Bishops of the United States have expressed great deference for the principle of self-determination and the right of privacy, values central to their protagonists in the abortion debate. They invoked, for instance, "the inviolability of the right of human privacy" and "the freedom of spouses to determine the size of their families" to argue that states must abstain from exerting pressure upon the poor to practice birth control [26]. In language reminiscent of civil libertarians on the left wing of the spectrum, the Bishops have "warned of the dangers to the right of privacy." In the abortion debate, the two extreme positions seem to agree that public authority must not tamper with decisions regarding procreation.

A decision to have an abortion is viewed on the left wing simply as a particular kind of "decision regarding procreation." It falls within the sphere of private acts sheltered from public interference. As a necessary backstop to fallible contraceptive measures, abortion is indispensable to the full realization of self-determination. On the right wing, however, abortion is categorized differently. It is a decision regarding procreation, but it can never be merely private because the taking of a life is entailed. The taking of life is always a matter of public concern. It is quite properly a matter of legal restriction. This is the ground upon which antiabortion laws must rest. It is a matter of common justice and not merely of uncommon charity.

ABORTION AS A VIOLATION OF "THE RIGHT TO LIFE"

Opponents of abortion labor under the handicap of attempting to portray subtle harms to remote subjects. They find it difficult to offset the vividness of the case for abortion which can be presented on behalf of a forlorn woman whose plight can readily be discerned. There is one type of injury, however, that is vivid and is clearly within the duty of the state to prevent: murder. Right-wing authors habitually assimilate the destruction of life in abortion to the forensic category of murder. Abortion is held to violate a legally enforceable "right to life." A simple syllogism unfolds into a complex network of ideas. Human life is not to be destroyed; fetal life is human life; therefore, fetal life is not to be destroyed.

Resort to the legal vocabulary to capture the emotionally powerful term "murder" imposes an obligation to attain the linguistic precision appropriate to the legal sphere. Hence, the meaning of the major and the minor premises and the conclusion itself must be specified more closely.

The major premise represents a restriction of responsibility to protect life within confines more narrow than those implied by such terms as "reverence for life" or "respect for life." Not all life is included in the injunction, only human life. But, it is noted, even with regard to human life, the framers of the syllogism do permit exceptions. In imposing capital punishment, for example, society demands the life of one who, by his depradations upon his fellow men, is said to have forfeited his right to life. Thus the premise must be narrowed: *Innocent* human life is not to be destroyed. Again there are exceptions. In wartime, men acting in good conscience under the principle of double effect, may destroy the life of a civilian who, innocent both subjectively and materially, is tragically situated close to an impor-

140

tant military target. A further specification is required: *Innocent human life is not to be destroyed by direct, purposeful attack.*

The minor premise requires not refinement but evidence of its truth in fact. Robert Drinan, S.J., Dean of Boston College Law School, has asserted, "If the advocates of legalized abortion desire to have an intellectually honest debate about the fundamental change they seek in the moral and legal standards of American life, they should not fall back on the error of fact that a fetus is not a human being" [13:123]. What type of fact is it that a fetus is a human being? What evidence would count for or against such an assertion? What type of question is posed when one asks, "Is the fetus a human being?"

In the present context, the question is, in the first instance, a legal inquiry. It translates into the question, "Can a fetus be the victim of murder?" Murder requires a human victim. Even if the fetus is not taken to be *fully* human, a moral problem still exists. One can still ask whether or not it is right to destroy whatever it is that exists in the womb after conception and before birth. Arguments against such destruction can be given which do not hinge on the question whether murder has been committed upon a fully human fetus. If the fetus is not human, what is lost is not the moral quandary regarding abortion but the strong argument for public legislation grounded in the demands of justice. If there is no human victim to be murdered, opponents of abortion must revert to less stirring arguments.

How might one "prove" the statement that "the fetus is fully human"? In order to gain the semblance of certainty over against the seemingly arbitrary demonstration available through legal or moral discourse, many right-wing authors attempt to convert the question of when human life exists into a straightforward biological problem. The question is presumed to fall within the specialty of embryology. Eugene Quay has written:

> The Christian position against the destruction of human life before or after birth never changed, but biological thought did. . . . The development of a code of law for the Church's

own governance required definition and distinction. When are we dealing with a human life?

The answer had to be found not in moral theology or ethics but in embryology [31:426].

Such an attempt to surround a moral and legal judgment with an aura of biological factuality evades the truth that, in searching for signs of life, the biologist who does not aspire himself to be a theologian must rely upon the indices of life which the theologian has defined. If the theologian says that the drawing of breath is the sign of life, the biologist is likely to report that life is not present until a moment after birth. If human life is thought to begin when a human form is visually recognizable, the biologist must estimate the moment in gestation at which the fetus becomes so "formed." If life is defined in terms of the capacity to carry on certain biological functions, it is nevertheless the theologian who has determined that these shall serve as the appropriate criteria of life.

Nor can certainty about the fully human status of the fetus be gained by recourse to philosophical and religious thought about the soul as the animating principle or actuating cause of individual life. The question then becomes even less credibly an issue to be settled by embryologists. How would their scientific tools detect the creative act of God at the moment he animates the fetus with a living soul? Theologians again must be summoned to describe what to look for. But they have disagreed among themselves. In the last hundred years, authoritative Roman Catholic teaching has required the assumption that animation takes place at the moment of conception. But many respectable theologians, past and present, have held theories of successive animation according to which the soul develops gradually through vegetative and animal stages before the distinctively human rational soul appears. Moral theologians have disagreed precisely because there is no conclusive evidence to be brought to bear from biology or from any other discipline outside of their own field. They can neither escape the decision nor invest it with a factitious certainty. In determining what it is that is to be protected through restrictions upon abortion they define what is to be considered "human life."

To pose the questions "What is human life?" and "When does human life begin?" in the midst of the abortion debate is a roundabout way of asking whether it is morally and legally permissible to destroy the matter in the womb of a pregnant woman. The reason for taking the roundabout way is to pick up en route the emotionally powerful terms "human life" and "murder" which are necessary to an argument which draws its impact from the implication, "You and your loved ones may be next if the restraints upon the taking of life are eroded at this point." The insistence upon the continuity between fetal life and adult life makes more credible the prediction of a continuity of effect from the sacrifice of the unborn child to the murder of adults.

In discussing the question, "When does human life begin?" Glanville Williams, a prominent British advocate of abortion law reform, Professor of English Law at Cambridge University and President of the Abortion Law Reform Association in England observes, "The line is one we have to draw for ourselves. And, in the absence of divine revelation, might we not allow ourselves to draw it at a point that is humanly convenient" [40:18; 41]? The point is well taken. The abortion debate is concerned with the question, "What is humanly convenient?" Christian opponents of abortion have, in fact, drawn the line which defines when human life is present at the point calculated to provide maximum support for their argument that, from the moment of conception, the fetus is fully human; destruction of its life is, therefore, murder; and condonation of murder is not humanly convenient.

The disadvantage of this argument is that it involves a considerable straining for effect. In search of rhetorical power, right-wing publicists tend to disregard pertinent distinctions which have led to the discrimination in popular language and law between "murder" and "abortion." The lack of disciplined precision invites a counterindulgence by left-wing authors. The straining for effect is aggravated when the right wing claim that the fetus is truly human is logically extended and emotionally undergirded with a religious appeal that prospective "murderers" have concern for the eternal destiny of the soul of the fetus. The fragile fabric of argument begins to tear when stretched so far. Neither the church nor the state nor the family actually carries out the practices logically entailed by the affirmation that the fetus is fully human. The church does not baptize the outpouring spontaneously aborted soon after conception. Extreme unction is not given. Funeral rites are not performed. The state calculates age from the date of birth, not of conception, and does not require a death or burial certificate nor even a report of the demise of a fetus aborted early in pregnancy. Convicted abortionists are not subjected to the penalties for murder. The intensity of grief felt within a family over a miscarriage is typically less than that experienced upon the loss of an infant, an older child, or an adult.

It is not the fate of the fetus itself that is the troubling aspect of abortion. It is difficult for most people to imagine the fetus "suffering" either here or hereafter. Indeed, much of its vulnerability stems from men's inability to believe that the fetus has a self-conscious awareness of its own existence and prospective nonexistence. The moral outrage and fear in expectation of death ascribed to a more mature victim stirs a sense of identification which few can feel with a tiny embryo.

Glanville Williams inadvertently provides a clue to the basis of the moral condemnation of abortion: "Our comparative indifference towards the natural death of the foetus contrasts strangely with the emotions traditionally released by its artificial termination" [42:61]. The significant distinction between spontaneous miscarriage and induced abortion is that the artificial termination of pregnancy involves the intervention of human agency. The natural death of the fetus is a natural evil. Induced abortion is a moral evil. It is the doing of evil, not the experiencing of evil, that is to be condemned. It is the effect that abortion is presumed to have upon the killers rather than upon the killed that makes abortion dreadful.

But if the fetus is not harmed, how can abortion be harmful? If no identifiable subject is injured by an act, how can that act be considered evil? Perhaps the concept of "harm" has again been too crude. Legal terminology provides a means of expressing a more subtle harm, a harm inflicted by the negation of the unborn child's "right to life." Every human being, by virtue of his existence, may be invested with a natural "right to life." But in order to surround the fetus with the moral immunity from direct attack to which the possession of the "right to life" entitles him, it is necessary to assume that the fetus is human. Legal concepts such as "the right to life" and "murder" can help to dramatize the implications of the affirmation that the fetus is fully human, but they cannot establish the basic point itself, which remains a matter for affirmation rather than demonstration.

The inescapable difficulty, obscured but not erased by an overlay of biological, theological, and legal suppositions, is that many people do not consider the fetus to be fully human and there is no way that they can be logically compelled so to believe. There are undeniable differences between the nonviable fetus and the fully human adult or even the newly born infant. The nonviable fetus is physically bound to its mother and may constitute a threat to her life. It is unable to be adopted or removed to the care of another. It is totally dependent upon the mother. No other arrangement can be made for its continued life. If it should become possible through transplanting the fetus to insure its continued life and development apart from the woman who conceived it, the moral problem of abortion would be changed but not abolished. Arguments which assimilate abortion to murder would be ineffective, but the claim that, for the sake of character, women should bear responsibility for nurturing that which they have conceived might still be urged.

It is inappropriate for adherents of the right wing to deny that these basic facts are devoid of significance in reasoning about abortion. But it is equally inappropriate for those on the left wing to deny that even the newest conceptus is something more than "just another piece of the woman's tissue." It is a potential man. Abortion is not just another surgical procedure. Nor is it murder. Abortion is abortion. It is a peculiar moral problem that can neither be "solved" by clumsy analogies nor dissolved by some rhetorical sleight of hand. Abortion is the destruction of potential, potential which has already attained the form of nascent life. The rejection of abortion implies an affirmation of the goodness of creation. It gives testimony to the conviction that what is potential ought to be welcomed to actuality.

It can be replied that no one except a dyspeptic nihilist would argue that abortion is good because the destruction of life is desirable in itself. The claim of reformers is only that under extraordinary circumstances abortion may be justifiable as the lesser evil. The unknown potential of the fetus must be weighed against the actualized relationships and responsibilities of the mother. The mother, as well as her unborn child, has unrealized potential. When the balance between them must be struck how should the scales be weighted?

ASSESSING THE "VALUE" OF LIFE

Those who would indulge in such calculations can employ one of two patterns of reasoning. They may give weight to the very existence of actualized potential or to the anticipated quality of unactualized potential. The first approach could be described as the "labor theory of value." Garrett Hardin expresses an attitude that inevitably leads to preference for the mother: "The early stages of an individual fetus have had very little human effort invested in them; they are of very little worth" [20:4]. A kindred view has been baptized by a clerical spokesman for the British Abortion Law Reform Association:

> Always the interests of that which is developed and formed, i.e. the mother, must take precedence over the interests of that which is embryonic and unformed, for *in the eyes of God* it is surely the living person who is all important — that separate and independent whole, identifiable as such, who at the moment of *birth* begins that process of personality development which does not cease with the cessation of life here but continues in "other mansions" of the universe [1:4; italics added].

146

This is a curious anthropomorphic projection onto God of the difficulties finite utilitarians encounter in decision making. It is understandable that some men, bound to a tiny span of time and thus unable to predict the future of the fetus, might prefer the assessible if modest "worth" of the mother. But, if God is a utilitarian, he has the advantage of being an omniscient utilitarian. The eyes of God might foresee that certain unborn children would achieve inestimably more than the mothers intent upon aborting them. If his intention were to preserve the life that might, through a large span of time, bring the greatest good to the greatest number, preference could not automatically be given to that which at one moment happens to be more fully developed and formed. The choice of the mother is at best a tragic risk imposed by human finitude; it is foolish to bless it as a faithful and certain imitation of what God would do.

As men become more godlike in the scope if not in the employment of their powers, surprising conclusions may be drawn by application of a second mode of reasoning which, in emphasizing the quality of unrealized potential, need not lead to the automatic preference of the mother over her unborn child. By shifting the unknowables in a not uncommon decision-making formula we may perform a thought experiment which, if medically improbable, is nevertheless ethically interesting. Suppose a situation late in pregnancy where it is medically possible to save either but not both the mother and child. Suppose, further, that the state of fetology has advanced so that it can be predicted confidently that the offspring will be of very superior endowment. The mother is, by universal agreement, a wretch. Considering the potential benefit to the community and the quality of individual life that could be attained, would it not be deemed suitable to kill the mother in order to insure the realization of the superior potential of her child?

This second mode of reasoning should appeal to social engineers imbued with a perfectionist streak. It would enhance their opportunities to assist in the process of the natural selection of the fittest and thus accelerate the "improvement of the race." Indeed, it might come to be considered an indispensable argument for the

147

legitimation of "racial self-determination" if such a concept were to be challenged on behalf of the unfit and unwanted as a menace to their right of individual self-determination.

Concern for the "quality of life" or "the full realization of human potential" can be used well to stimulate efforts to prevent the occurrence of lamentable defects and deficiencies so that all may enjoy a high quality of life. But it can also lead to an inclination to derogate life which, burdened with defects and deficiencies, does not seem capable of high quality. The application of "quality control" techniques to the production of new life is a constant temptation to some. An ominous note is sounded in an article by a Protestant layman and physician Dr. H. B. Munson, who writes, "these days it seems a questionable practice even to allow an irresponsible mother to take responsibility for the rearing of a child, much less force her to do so. . . . The fact that these days we not only allow her to keep her baby, but that to a large degree we force this state of affairs by denying her an abortion would seem to make us guilty of mismanagement" [25:9]. Dr. Munson, seems to be on the verge of proposing an indication for *involuntary* abortion which would be imposed for the sake of maintaining a well managed society. One cannot repress the question, "Who will be the managers?"

It is important that the question concerning the nature of true "quality" be pressed continually. Christians, secular humanists, and other men of good will may jointly insist that the very definition of "quality of life" must include toleration, respect, and active concern for those who are aged, weak, deformed, unskilled, cantankerous, or perverse. If we are to be civilized at all, those who attain true "quality of life" must exhibit a spirit of *noblesse oblige*. (Christian theologians may properly complain that the concept of "noblesse oblige" does not do justice to the radical quality of *agape* held up for emulation in the Gospel. Those who aspire to live and die by the norm of Christian charity may be called to exhibit a higher "quality of life" in yielding convenience, health, or life itself in self-sacrificing concern to preserve the life of the fetus, just as God in Christ gave up that which was most precious to give true life to those of little worth.)

148

It seems there are few who are able to sustain the theological beliefs necessary to give meaning to the realization of potential through self-sacrifice for the sake of the life of another. But Americans habitually do glorify the sacrifice of life in defense of the nation. And heroes frequently risk and not infrequently lose their lives in the rescue of fellow men. Yet the sacrifice of a mother to save the unknown, nascent, potential life contained in a tiny tissue is not heralded on civic occasions. It is the apparent disproportion of the sacrifice that seems objectionable. The more the life of the fetus is depreciated, the more glaring is the apparent disproportion. Dr. Munson states, "After all, one can hardly equate, on the one hand, the taking of life from a breathing, thinking, full-fledged human being, with, on the other hand, the denial of life to a bit of vegetating unborn matter, that, so far as we can tell, is unable to suffer and apparently doesn't even have any awareness of its own existence" [25:9].

Behind this reaction is "the labor theory of value" which suggests that it is man's labor, his hopes and purposes, his investment of financial aid and psychological capital which bestows a value upon human life. The "worth" of a life grows as its place within the consciousness of others expands. The degree of protection to be afforded the fetus increases as it becomes more and more a focal point of others' dreams and plans. That which defines fully human existence is the capacity for social interaction which brings forth the ultimate value of "human personality." Many persons have poured their labor into the formation of the personality of a mother. To exchange that realized potential for the uncertain future of an unresponsive entity incapable of self-conscious intercourse with human beings would be to squander a scarce resource. It would be an uneconomic transaction.

This style of reasoning could leave every man uncertain whether he had attained "fully human" status. It would give little moral protection to those who might be stunted in their social development, less to the comatose, and none to the moribund.

The significance of defining "fully human existence" in terms of capacity for self-conscious social interaction is suggested in a

149

passage from a pamphlet issued by the Board of Social Ministry
of the Lutheran Church in America:

> Furthermore, in Christian decision-making, while one must re-
> gard incipient human life as precious, he will have to distinguish
> between its claims and those of more developed human life. The
> fetus or newborn infant that has been called into human exist-
> ence by God's address bears in a formal sense the image of God,
> stands in enduring relationship to Him, and has the extremely
> valuable potential for a loving human response to God and
> other human beings. Yet there is a qualitative difference be-
> tween such a being and the mature person who is a free center
> of decision and responsibility, with a history and present ca-
> pacity for full-blown, loving relationships with other persons.

The "qualitative difference between such a being and a mature
person" opens the way for the authors to recommend "compassionate abortion" for medical, psychiatric, eugenic, humanitarian,
and socioeconomic reasons. Their "proposed strategy comes close
to recent Scandinavian practice." It is intended not simply as a
reluctant concession in public law to nonbelievers but as a guide
to the "decisional life of the Christian woman considering abortion" [39:15, 25, 19].

Both the emphasis of "the labor theory of value" upon the degree of realized human potential, and the social engineering stress
upon the quality of unrealized potential represent departures
from the classical Christian account of the origin of the worth of
each human life. Christians have proclaimed that God has bestowed upon man "an alien dignity" [38:231]. Man's worth is
not to be assessed according to what he has become through
social intercourse or by an estimate of what he may yet become.
Rather, it is God's labor, his purpose, his economy which places
the price of each life so high that no transient human value can
serve as compensation. But, with the erosion of the theological
foundations of the Christian view of man's alien dignity, the
barriers to abortion built upon those foundations are crumbling
in the hearts of individuals and in the statutes of the states. The

150

trend may be lamentable, but the demands of Christian responsibility cannot be met by pouting and pining for a "age of faith." What must the churches do now in the face of a problem they will no longer be allowed to ignore?

OPTIONS FOR THE CHURCHES

The drift of the abortion debate is clearly to the left. An ironic benefit of the confusion which has beset the Protestant churches is that it has kept open several options. Different streams might be panned in the search for a new wealth of ideas.

The new receptivity of Protestants to arguments for abortion law reform has been attributed to a decline of the theological certainties which supported right-wing arguments; to the exploitation of latent Protestant themes to bolster the left-wing demand for self-determination and control over nature, including human nature; and to perplexity concerning the proper relationship between the moral beliefs of particular segments of the public and legal enactments imposed upon all of the citizenry. Alternative strategies might emerge through response to one or another of these factors.

One possibility is to attempt to reverse the tide and rebuild the eroded theological foundations of the ban on abortion so that narrow restraints might be enforced both within the church and within society. A second course is to proceed to the blessing and baptizing of the arguments of the left wing and a willing entry into a brave new world in the hope that churchmen, having supplied some of the building materials, might have a role in shaping the plan of the new city of man. A third option is to accede to the separation of the legal and the moral and withdraw into a sectarian absolutism, preserving the ban on abortion under the discipline of the church but relinquishing the determination of public policy to other voices.

Each of these three options has disadvantages. The first requires confidence in the possibility of theological reconstruction and the renewal of profound religious commitment throughout a broad segment of the American public. Even many who pray for such a revival would be startled by its occurrence. The second option entails a theological reconstitution involving the abandonment of significant elements of Christian teaching about the nature of human life and the obligation to preserve it. The discontinuity would be jarring to the churches. The changes would ramify throughout the entire system of Christian doctrine. Teaching upon related social and moral issues would have to be recast. The implications for Christian thought concerning the obligation to show respect for life in other settings might be unappealing even, or perhaps, especially to those who now advocate accommodation of Christians to the idea of abortion on demand. The third approach implies a sociological reformation of the relationship of the churches to matters of public policy in a variety of fields. If the churches withdraw from the struggle on behalf of the fetus to defend by law the most fundamental "right to life" how will they be brought back into the public arena to do battle on behalf of the rights of racial minorities, the poor, the persecuted, the victims of injustice and warfare? Whatever measure of grace, love, and justice the churches are able to mediate needs to be diffused throughout the public realm and not be confined within a sectarian enclave. It would be a bad bargain for all if the cost of removing "obstinate" churchmen from the abortion controversy were to be the diminution of their active public concern for abolition of poverty and the realization of civil rights, peace, and a more just world order.

A fourth option constitutes the most probable outcome of the churches' increasing concern with the problem of abortion. The mainline Protestant churches can be expected to provide spotty support for reform measures modeled on the American Law Institute proposals. It is doubtful that abortion law reform will become a cause promoted by a fervent Protestant crusade. But when the issue is thrust upon them, Protestants will respond with an uncoordinated but steady movement toward acceptance of moderate reform. When statewide controversies reach a critical stage in which debate is polarized between Roman Catholic spokesmen in the right wing and advocates of abortion on demand on the left, Protestants will gravitate toward the middle. They will be moved by political disposition rather than by theological exposition. After their arrival, they will need to fill in theological ground on which to stand.

To date, there has been little progress in the endeavor to shore up the position towards which Protestants seem to be edging. Extended battles over abortion law reform in New York and California have brought forth outpourings of polemic utterances. But no substantial, original study of the theological and ethical dimensions of the abortion issue has been produced by American Protestant churchmen. Readers have been forced to rely upon materials translated from German or imported from England [38; 5; 4; 7].

By the time American Protestants are prepared to address the issue of abortion in its present manifestations it is likely that new developments will have recast the current questions. The development of an abortifacient pill that might be prescribed for simple, private, inexpensive, safe use at home will alter the pattern of debate over abortion. Issues that hinge upon estimates of effects of illegal abortion upon mothers, the medical profession, law enforcement agencies, and the poor will become less salient, as will controversies regarding the utility of procedural devices such as hospital abortion committees. A new phase of debate will evolve, a phase in which polarization will be increased. Self-determination will seem to be more readily within reach. Women could abort without risky dependence upon a shady underworld and without the reallocation of scarce medical resources necessary to provide abortion on demand under present medical conditions. But the violation of the "right to life" of the fetus will be the same.

Unless the abortifacient pill is made available to all women, married and unmarried, in all circumstances, new problems of control will arise and a new debate regarding "contraindications" will evolve. It will still be necessary to balance contending values that appear to be both indispensable and incompatible. The immediate terms of debate may change. But the need for precise ethical analysis of fundamental issues will not change. Even if the tiniest sliver of life can be extinguished quietly at home by a mother uncertain of its existence, abortion will continue to be a problem worthy of Christian concern.

CAN THE DEMAND FOR ABORTION BE REDUCED?

The prospect of a safe abortifacient pill available for self-administration at home quickens awareness of the inefficacy of all external sanctions against abortion. If the demand for abortion were high, effective suppression of the pill would be difficult to achieve. But even today, when most abortions require clandestine negotiations and a costly surgical procedure, those who seek to reduce the number of abortions cannot expect success merely through more aggressive enforcement of criminal provisions or the imposition of more strict administrative procedures in hospitals. They must seek to allay the demand for abortion through a variety of social innovations which might increase a pregnant woman's inclination to bear her child by (1) easing the burden of pregnancy through the provision of better medical care and opportunities for consultation, improvement in the status of illegitimate children, and greater tolerance of unwed mothers; (2) providing assurance of proper care for the child, either *apart* from the mother, through more adequate programs for foster homes and adoption, or *with* the mother through alleviation of poverty by improved programs of social welfare, family subsidy, or tax relief, and through the creation of day-care facilities. The most popular approach to the reduction of the demand for abortion is to reduce unwanted pregnancies through better sex education and the promotion of improved contraceptive practices.

The possible effectiveness of contraception as a means of forestalling the desire for abortion has been used within the Roman Catholic Church as an argument on behalf of a more liberal attitude toward birth control programs. But many Roman Catholic commentators agree with advocates of abortion on demand that contraception and abortion will inevitably be linked in practice. Both extremes consider the hope of having one without the other to be chimeric. Believers in justifiable abortion find consolation in the anticipation that more aggressive promotion of contraception will diminish the demand for abortion by preventing unwanted pregnancies.

But the extreme schools join in the observation that, in order to motivate couples to use contraceptives, it is necessary to generate a strong intention not to have another child at a particular moment in time. By inducing this strong motivation, one simultaneously stimulates a latent demand for abortion should contraception fail. Advocates of abortion on demand conclude that "Abortion is the much-needed backstop in the system of birth control" [19:80]. Right-wing authors predict that once a "contraceptive mentality" has been cultivated and interference with the lifegiving process has been permitted a slide downward toward "murder for convenience" is inevitable.

> It is all but impossible not to feel that one has been cheated when an unexpected pregnancy arrives in spite of the prophylactic methods authorized by law. One naturally turns to the legislator who is indirectly guilty of having approved an imperfect and defective technique whose results are unexpected and disappointing. He must be asked to supplement such dubious legislation by allowing abortion to those whose belief in the effectiveness of a contraceptive technique has proved unfounded.
>
> In fact, this is precisely what we see happening in countries which have legalized contraception. Their legislation inevitably leads the way to so-called therapeutic, eugenic and social laws whose purpose it is to correct the errors and deficiencies of the prophylactic measures [24:56].

It is not unreasonable to conclude that the high demand for abortion is stimulated not exclusively by social ills but by a disposition of the spirit of the age. The clientele of criminal abortionists includes the poor and the unmarried, but it consists primarily of married women, comfortably placed, who bear neither shame nor poverty, but are resolved to preserve or extend whatever comfort they have attained. No program or policy readily at the disposal of the public can quickly change the calculations that lead women to conclude that abortion is the most convenient solution to their awkward, but not tragic, circumstance.

Abortion can be seen as a medical, legal, social, and ethical problem. It also is to be seen as a problem involving the meaning of life. No external authority can reimpose respect for the law regulating abortion. Apart from such respect, the social costs of enforcement become exorbitant. If legal restraints are to function they must be buttressed by inner conviction. But the conviction has decayed that abortion is an offense against God, nature, the state, one's higher self, the common weal, and the right to life. Can it ever flourish again?

Those who, for one reason or another, would like to reduce the incidence of abortion, must ask, "How can 'respect for life' be regenerated?" The famous Swiss Protestant theologian, Karl Barth, believes that in all but the extraordinary case in which life is pitted against life, the church must continue to urge the state to say "No" to abortion.

> The question arises, however, how this "No" is to be established and stated if it is to be a truly effective "No." In the face of the wicked violation of the sanctity of life which is always seriously at issue in abortion, and which is always present when it is carried out thoughtlessly and callously, the only thing which can help is the power wholly new and radical feeling of awe at the mystery of all human life as this is commanded by God as its Creator, Giver and Lord. Legal prohibitions and restrictions of a civil, moral and supposedly spiritual kind are obviously inadequate to instill this awe into man. Nor does mere churchmanship, whether Romanist or Protestant, provide the atmosphere in which this awe can thrive [4:417 f].

This reminder can bring both chagrin and challenge to the churches. The radical feeling of awe at the mystery of all human life can never be predictably induced. But it is best conveyed by demonstrating respect for life in all its forms through the courage of an institution or an individual to sacrifice wealth and prestige and station in defense of the poor, the sick, the homeless, the confused, the aged, the outcast in the ghetto, and the victims of war. Selective and painless opposition to evil is not impressive. The day of renewed inner restraints upon abortion will come sooner if churchmen and theologians exhibit in their relations with all men the same sacrifice of self in love which they have required of mothers menaced by their own offspring. A fetus may deserve respect because it is no less precious than a man. But neither should a man be less the object of ecclesiastical concern than a fetus. The churches must bridge their own credibility gap with costly grace, if they wish others to attain the grace to see the cost of each abortion.

The "cure" of the abortion epidemic can be no less profound than its causes. If, as right-wing critics affirm, its source is in the heart of man, its remedy must penetrate to similar depths. Neither cool debate nor heated polemics can move men at such levels. Only the example of sincere regard for others can rekindle the conviction that all life is sacred and bound together in mystery so that the death of the least diminishes each.

When a fetus is aborted no one asks for whom the bell tolls. No bell is tolled. But do not feel indifferent and secure. The fetus symbolizes you and me and our tenuous hold upon a future here at the mercy of our fellow men.

REFERENCES

1. The Abortion Law Reform Association: A Clergyman's View (pamphlet, London, England) no date, p 4.
2. American Law Institute Model Penal Code, Section 230.3 (proposed official draft) 1962.
3. American Lutheran Church: *Responsible Reproduction* (Commission on Research and Social Action, The American Lutheran Church, Minneapolis, Minnesota) 1967, paragraph 17, p 6.
4. Barth, Karl: *Church Dogmatics: The Doctrine of Creation,*

III, 4 (T & T Clark, Edinburgh, Scotland) 1961, pp 415 – 422; 417 f.

5. Bonhoeffer, Dietrich: *Ethics*, Eberhard Bethge, ed (SCM Press, London, England) 1960, pp 130–131.

6. Calderone, Mary S, ed: Report of the Statistics Committee, *Abortion in the United States: A Conference Sponsored by the Planned Parenthood Federation of America, Inc, at Arden House and the New York Academy of Medicine* (Hoeber Division, Harper and Row, Publishers, New York, New York) 1958, pp 57, 180.

7. Church Assembly Board for Social Responsibility: *Abortion: An Ethical Discussion* (Church Assembly Board for Social Responsibility, London, England) 1965, the most substantial theological and ethical analysis of abortion to be produced by a Protestant body in English-speaking nations.

8. Devereux, George: A Typological Study of Abortion in 350 Primitive, Ancient, and Pre-Industrial Societies, in Harold Rosen, ed: *Therapeutic Abortion: Medical, Psychiatric, Legal, Anthropological and Religious Considerations* (The Julian Press, New York, New York) 1954, pp 97–152.

9. Devereux, George: *A Study of Abortion in Primitive Societies* (The Julian Press, New York, New York) 1955.

10. Diocese of California: *The Pacific Churchman*, vol 98, no 4, Apr 1967.

11. Diocese of Central New York: *Abortion: a Position Paper, Adopted June 8, 1967, by the Council of the Episcopal Diocese of Central New York and Commended to Parish Groups and Vestries for Study* (Diocese of Central New York, Syracuse, New York) 1967.

12. Drinan, Robert F, S.J.: Strategy on Abortion, *America*, Feb 4, 1967, pp 177–179.

13. Drinan, Robert F, S.J.: The Inviolability of the Right to Be Born, *Abortion and the Law*, in David T Smith, ed (Western Reserve University Press, Cleveland, Ohio) 1967, p 123.

14. Fletcher, Joseph: A Moral Tension and an Ethical Frontier, *The Christian Scholar*, vol 46, no 3, Fall 1963, p 261.

15. Fletcher, Joseph: *Situation Ethics* (Westminster Press, Philadelphia, Pennsylvania) 1966.

16. Gebhard, Paul H; Pomeroy, Wardell B; Martin, Clyde E; and Christenson, Cornelia V: *Pregnancy, Birth and Abortion* (Harper and Row, Publishers, New York, New York) 1958, pp 197 f.

17. George, B James, jr: Current Abortion Laws: Proposals and Movements for Reform, in David T Smith, ed: *Abortion and the Law* (Western Reserve University Press, Cleveland, Ohio) 1967, pp 1 – 36, helpful analysis of legal materials.

18. Guttmacher, Alan F, ed: *The Case for Legalized Abortion Now* (Diablo Press, Berkeley, California) 1967, the most extensive compendium of contemporary left-wing essays.

19. Hardin, Garrett: Abortion and Human Dignity, in Alan F Guttmacher, ed: *The Case for Legalized Abortion Now* (Diablo Press, Berkeley, California) 1967, p 75.

20. Hardin, Garrett: A Scientist's Case for Abortion, reprinted from *Redbook*, May 1967, by the Association for the Study of Abortion, p 4.

21. Kinsolving, Lester: What About Therapeutic Abortion? *The Christian Century*, vol 81, no 20, May 13, 1964, pp 632 – 635.

22. Kummer, Jerome M, and Leavy, Zad: Therapeutic Abortion Law Confusion, *The Journal of the American Medical Association*, vol 195, no 2, Jan 10, 1966, p 97.

23. Lehmann, Paul L: *Ethics in a Christian Context* (Harper and Row, Publishers, New York, New York) 1963, p 54.

24. Lestapis, Stanislas de, S.J.: *Family Planning and Modern Problems: A Catholic Analysis* (Herder and Herder, New York, New York) 1961, chap 7, Contraceptive Civilization.

25. Munson, H B: Abortion in Modern Times: Thoughts and Comments, *The South Dakota Journal of Medicine*, vol 19, Apr 1966, pp 23 – 30, republished in *Renewal*, Feb 1967, p 9.

26. National Catholic Welfare Conference: Statement issued by the Administrative Board of the National Catholic Welfare Conference, Washington, D.C., Nov 14, 1966, in *The Boston Pilot*, Nov 19, 1966.

27. National Council of the Churches of Christ: *Responsible Parenthood: A Pronouncement Adopted by the General*

Board, Feb 23, 1961 (National Council of the Churches of Christ, New York, New York) 1961, p 2.

28. The National Council of the Episcopal Church: *The Family Today: The Report of Committee Five of the Lambeth Conference, 1958* (The National Council of the Episcopal Church, New York, New York) no date, p 15.

29. Pilpel, Harriet: The Abortion Crisis, in Alan F Guttmacher, ed: *The Case for Legalized Abortion Now* (Diablo Press, Berkeley, California) 1967, especially p 113.

30. Quay, Eugene: Justifiable Abortion: Medical and Legal Foundations, *The Georgetown Law Journal*, vol 49, no 2, Winter 1960, pp 173–256, see also reference 31.

31. Quay, Eugene: Justifiable Abortion: Medical and Legal Foundations, *The Georgetown Law Journal*, vol 49, no 3, Spring 1961, pp 395–538. An extensive bibliography accompanies the article, the first portion of which is in reference 30. A 73-page summary of laws governing abortion in the United States and its territories is contained in an appendix.

32. Ramsey, Paul: The Case of Joseph Fletcher and Joseph Fletcher's Cases, in *Deeds and Rules in Christian Ethics* (Charles Scribner's Sons, New York, New York) 1967, p 168; for Ramsey's views on abortion, see The Sanctity of Life: In the First of It, *The Dublin Review*, Spring 1967.

33. Rossi, Alice S: Public Views on Abortion, unpublished report of the National Opinion Research Center, Feb 1966. The paper is now available in Alan F Guttmacher, ed: *The Case for Legalized Abortion Now* (Diablo Press, Berkeley, California) 1967, pp 26–53. See also Abortion Laws and Their Victims, *Trans-action* Sept–Oct 1966. The interpretation of the poll data offered here should not be ascribed to Mrs Rossi.

34. St John-Stevas, Norman: *The Right to Life* (Hodder & Stoughton, Ltd, London, England) 1963, pp 16, 17, 36, 127.

35. Schur, Edwin M: *Crimes without Victims: Deviant Behavior and Public Policy — Abortion, Homosexuality, Drug Addiction* (Prentice-Hall, Inc, Englewood Cliffs, New Jersey) 1965, pp 59, 60.

36. Society for Humane Abortion: *Statement of Policy* (pamphlet) no date.
37. Szasz, Thomas S: Bootlegging Humanistic Values through Psychiatry, *The Antioch Review*, Fall 1962, 344.
38. Thielicke, Helmut: *The Ethics of Sex*, John W Doberstein, translator (Harper and Row, Publishers, New York, New York) 1964, p 231.
39. Wentz, Frederick K, and Witmer, Robert H: *The Problem of Abortion* (Board of Social Ministry, Lutheran Church in America, New York, New York) 1967, pp 15, 25, 19.
40. Williams, Glanville: Introduction, in Alice Jenkins, *Law for the Rich* (Victor Gollancz, Ltd, London, England) 1960, p 18.
41. Williams, Glanville: *The Sanctity of Life and the Criminal Law* (Alfred A Knopf, New York, New York) 1966, one of the most extensive recent discussions of abortion in English.
42. Williams, Glanville: Moral Issues, in *Abortion in Britain: Proceedings of a Conference Held by the Family Planning Association at the University of London Union on 22 April 1966* (Pitman Medical Publishing Co, Ltd, London, England) 1966, p 61.

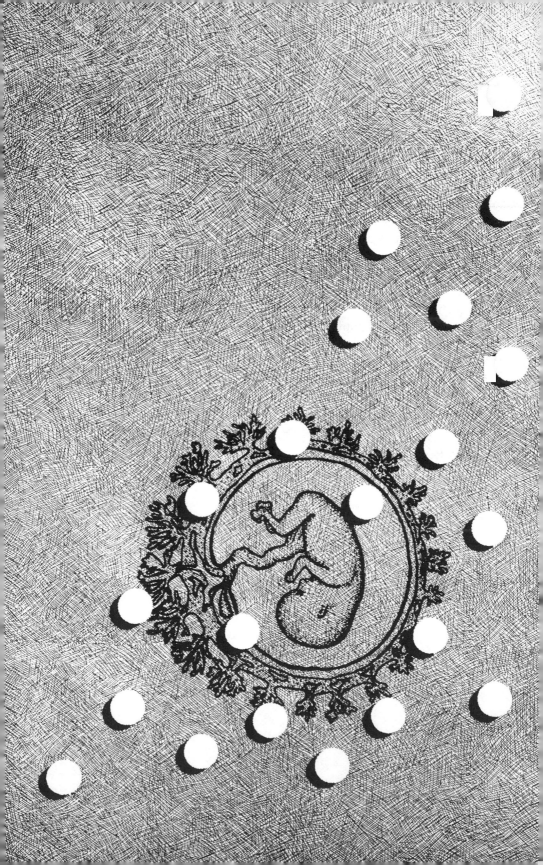

4. RELIGIOUS FACTORS IN THE POPULATION PROBLEM

by Arthur J. Dyck

CONCERN over what has been variously dramatized as "the population crisis," "the population dilemma," or "the population explosion" is now rather widespread. During the 1960s, mass media have liberally dispersed mounting demographic data documenting the increasingly rapid growth of world population. As Professor Roger Revelle has noted [41:2–9], it took hundreds of thousands of years to produce a living population of one billion people by 1850 A.D. Within 75 years, from 1850 to 1925, the second billion was added, and by 1960, in only 35 more years, the third billion. The world's population will exceed four billions by 1980 and five billions by 1990, a mere 10 years later. Barring considerable change in birth and death rates, the population increase between now and the year 2000 will be larger than the entire population presently living on this planet.

Beyond the relatively remote problems posed by the ultimate limits of sheer space, population growth rates in numerous areas of our globe are already outstripping existing capacities to provide the resources vital for human survival. Unfortunately, we cannot comfort ourselves with the thought that the minimal nutritional needs of such areas can, at least for some time to come, be met by contributions from societies now possessing fairly abundant food supplies. Calculations by Revelle [42:328–351] indicate that even an 80% increase in food production in the United States by 1985, no mean undertaking, would provide only 10% of what the underdeveloped world will require up to that time. Even if the rate of population growth of relatively underdeveloped areas should markedly diminish, the United States by tripling its food production could furnish less than

163

20% of the food needs for these areas between now and the year 2000.

These simple but sobering facts vividly pinpoint the most fundamental aspect of the population problem: the need to match population growth with food supplies. But bread alone, essential as it is, has never been seen as sufficient for the "good life." The quality of human existence is intricately tied to the quality of our total environment. Provisions for pollution abatement and for recreational, educational, aesthetic, and transportational facilities, all require some kind of rational ecological adjustment if we are to achieve more than bare subsistence on this planet or, for that matter, on any other planet.

MALTHUS' "MISERY AND VICE"

We are prone to view as strictly contemporary and unique the problems associated with the rapid growth of population. Although these problems have escalated sharply in our time, some of them are certainly not new. Scholarly reflection upon the causes and effects of population growth goes back at least as far as Malthus, whose first essay on population appeared in 1798 under the title *An Essay on the Principle of Population As It Affects the Future Improvement of Society, with Remarks on the Speculations of Mr. Godwin, Mr. Condercet, and Other Writers*. Indeed, Malthus himself, writing five years later in a revised edition of his essay, tells of the extent to which others as remote in time as Plato and Aristotle had noted "the poverty and misery arising from a too rapid increase of population"; and he expresses surprise that this subject "had not excited more of the public attention."

> In the course of this inquiry I found that much more had been done than I had been aware of when I first published the Essay. The poverty and the misery arising from a too rapid increase of population had been distinctly seen, and the most violent remedies proposed so long ago as the times of Plato and Aristotle. And of late years the subject has been treated in such

a manner by some French Economists, occasionally by Montesquieu, and, among our own writers, by Dr. Franklin, Sir James Steuard, Mr. Arthur Young, and Mr. Townsend, as to create a natural surprise that it had not excited more of the public attention [33:1–148].

But Malthus is aware of the shortcomings of what he had found in the literature:

> Though it had been stated distinctly, that population must always be kept down to the level of subsistence; yet few inquiries had been made into the various modes by which this level is effected; and the principle had never been sufficiently pursued to its consequences, nor had those practical inferences [been] drawn from it, which a strict examination of its effects on society appears to suggest [33:148].

Malthus, a minister in the Church of England and a professor of economics and history, is widely acknowledged as the founder or "father" of modern population study (including the science of demography). According to Thompson and Lewis, he earned this title because of his "continued and *highly objective* interest in the factors affecting population growth and in the relation between this growth and human welfare" [46:23].

Despite the rather extensive demographic research since the time of Malthus, much of it descriptive and relatively recent, we have yet to ascertain how, in a number of underdeveloped areas, it is possible to keep the level of population commensurate with the level of subsistence; and, as our earlier remarks revealed, the necessity for accomplishing this is fast becoming a worldwide, a *species* problem.

As Malthus observed, the human suffering associated with populations whose birth rates greatly exceed their death rates had been acknowledged for a long time. There have been several classical types of responses to the ills engendered by high rates of population growth, two of which were espoused by Malthus and a third by certain of his critics among the Marxists and Catholics. These classic responses interest us here because they still represent, in the most general sense, the alternatives confronting us today.

In his 1798 essay, Malthus took the view that "Misery and Vice," in the form of war, famine, disease, malnutrition, and other processes over which individual human beings have little or no control, determine the birth and death rates. For this hypothesis, precluding the possibility of preventing by human intervention the ravages of "Misery and Vice," Malthus was considered gloomy and pessimistic by his contemporaries. Although we shall not, in this essay, champion this first hypothesis of Malthus, it is important to bear in mind that no one is currently in a position to declare it patently false. We can envisage, and to some extent have actualized, ways to prevent war, famine, disease, and malnutrition; but we cannot claim that, as a species, man is clearly winning the struggle against them. There is evidence to suggest, however, that these forms of human suffering need not inevitably be engendered by overly rapid population growth, for, as Malthus observed after publishing his first essay, there are restraints operating upon birth rates which are within man's voluntary control.

MALTHUS' "MORAL RESTRAINT"

Malthus, therefore, revised his original hypothesis and proposed the following: "Moral Restraint" (plus or minus "Misery and Vice") determines the birth rate. By maintaining that birth rates are affected by deliberate human decisions and actions, and in this way kept at a comparatively low level, Malthus is allowing for the possibility of maintaining low death rates through good health practices and adequate nutrition without having, as a consequence, the sorts of growth rates that irrevocably lead to the syndrome of "Misery and Vice."

Students of population presently hold at least three compatible hypotheses of the type represented by the revised and final view taken by Malthus. All affirm the propositions that the birth rate and the death rate decrease with time and that the birth rate approaches the steady state death rate. This phenomenon, often described in demography textbooks and elsewhere as the Demographic Transition, has been the pattern observed in the Western world. The theoretical understanding of this pattern remains highly controversial and, as we shall try to show later, is critical for the success of any direct attempt to prevent rapid population growth where it is presently occurring.

The three hypotheses to which we are referring are the following: that large numbers of people feel a need to control the number of their children and will do so under the right conditions (the felt-need hypothesis); that the motivation to use Moral Restraint — that is, the desire to exercise fertility control — can be increased; and that the conditions favorable to the exercising of fertility control can be improved. We shall discuss each of these hypotheses in turn and, in the course of doing so, shall try to clarify the ways in which moral and religious variables relate to and affect fertility control.

The "right conditions" for the (felt-need) hypothesis are realized by providing reliable, relatively inexpensive, medically safe contraceptives, and advice on how to use them. The availability and distribution of both contraceptives and contraceptive information must furthermore be assured by setting up and maintaining effective administrative facilities and communication networks. In short, according to the felt-need hypothesis, birth rates will approach the steady state death rate when it is technically possible to have only the children one desires.

What evidence is there to confirm such a hypothesis? To begin with, it is clear that in most societies at most times, some men and women attempt fertility control, using a variety of means such as infanticide, abortion, prolonged breast feeding, partial or complete abstinence of sexual relations (including variants of the rhythm method), coitus interruptus and folk methods of contraception [32; 35; 24]. Furthermore, one finds that in certain of the less developed countries, most notably Taiwan, South Korea, and India, significant numbers of women have wanted to be fitted with intrauterine contraceptive devices (IUCD), and in India some men are willing to undergo vasectomy.

Indeed, these facts have been an important recent source of considerable optimism about the possibility of greatly reducing birth rates throughout the world. In one instance, Donald Bogue [8:449–454] is led to speak with transparent enthusiasm of the "demographic breakthrough" in the years 1963–1964: Such a shift from the "projection" to the "control" of fertility rates is brought about, he alleges, by a number of fertility control programs distributing contraceptives in various regions of the world, most of them in Asia in countries with very high birth rates. Bogue's declaration of a "breakthrough" at that time had to rest almost exclusively upon the fact that a fairly high proportion of the women contacted were accepting contraceptives provided by these family planning programs. In Taiwan, it is true, birth rates were noticeably declining. But there is no clear evidence that this decline in birth rates was brought about by a birth control program. Two recent surveys of family planning programs around the world by Dudley Kirk [25:48–60] and J. A. Ross [44:1–5] express a definite, though a somewhat more guarded, optimism about the prospects for the success of these programs.

Obviously, acceptance of the felt-need hypothesis directly determines the kind of strategy that is considered efficacious for bringing down birth rates; if birth rates can be sharply reduced by making efficient contraceptives and information concerning their use readily available, it is not considered essential to engage in research to find out *why* people have children and *why* they want to have a certain number. Establishing facilities and programs for effective distribution of contraceptives is believed to have virtually exclusive priority. That this belief has had considerable influence is evident from the money and effort expended by private organizations and, increasingly, by governments to establish birth control programs in "needy" areas around the world [44:1–5; 25:48–60].

Have these programs succeeded? Not one of these attempts to reduce birth rates has so far been *proved* to be instrumental. Where birth rates have declined, as in Taiwan, the decline had started before the program for contraception had been initiated, and, in the absence of controls, the cause or causes of the decline cannot unequivocally be determined. Although present efforts on behalf of fertility control represent "progress" for J. A. Ross [44], he candidly reports that "the missing link remains a proven fertility decline, resulting from deliberate effort." It is only fair to note that he is *hopeful* that such evidence will be forthcoming in two or three populations by the end of 1966. Dudley Kirk [25], surveying worldwide efforts at fertility control one year later, takes much the same view as Ross. It is noteworthy, however, that Kirk, in reporting three countries whose birth rates have declined (Taiwan, Korea, and Singapore), attributes the most marked declines in Taiwan and Korea largely to social change rather than to any past efforts directed toward family planning programs.

There is definite evidence, however, that the simple provision of advice and materials for contraception has, in certain cultures and under certain circumstances, proved futile. The very thorough research of Drs. Gordon and Wyon, conducted from 1953–1960 in India (the Khanna region of the Punjab) is a clear demonstration of this futility, at least for the region in question: more than half of the couples in the study accepted the advice and the contraceptives but no significant change in the birth rate resulted [50; 51]. The Lulliani study in West Pakistan, using the IUCD, obtained similar results. These findings warrant the rejection of the felt-need hypothesis as a *sufficient* account of fertility control since there are at least some populations and regions in which the behavior predicted by this hypothesis did not occur even though the conditions it posits as requisite for eliciting that behavior had been actualized.

If the felt-need hypothesis did in fact specify the necessary and sufficient conditions for bringing about birth rates that approach the steady state death rate, the moral and religious issues affecting fertility control would be relatively insignificant, limited to attitudes and doctrines regarding the use and distribution of these techniques.

FERTILITY CONTROL AND WORLD RELIGIONS

Because of its official opposition to contraceptives, the Roman Catholic Church has sometimes been singled out in the literature as the sole religious opponent of efforts to reduce birth rates throughout the world. In a survey of the demographic literature, Freedman [18] observes that many writers on underdeveloped countries stress this distinction between Catholicism and the other major religions. One might consider the Eastern Orthodox an exception here, but, as Fagley [17] has noted, their position is rather flexible.

Other major religions and religious bodies are said to form no such barrier for they do not officially condemn the use of contraceptives. Islam, in fact, has issued theologically authoritative pronouncements permitting their use under certain circumstances. In 1937, the Mufti of Egypt released a *fatwa* proclaiming, "It is permissible for either husband or wife, by mutual consent, to take any measures to prevent semen from entering the uterus, in order to prevent conception" (English translation in *Human Fertility*, vol 10, no 2, June 1945). The *Fatwa* Committee of El Azhar University in 1953, the Directorate of Religious Affairs in Turkey in 1961, and the Grand Mufti of Jordan in 1964 also issued *fatwas* of that kind.

Thus, with premises such as these linked to the felt-need hypothesis, the *Washington Post*, for example, editorialized: "To the non-Catholic world, population control is not a religious matter; it is a quite practical matter of finding an effective means of bringing birth into harmonious relation to the ability of parents to discharge the obligation of parenthood" [28:1433]. Restricting the role of religion in this way distorts our understanding of its actual significance for the solution of the population problem. It overlooks two very important considerations: the disparity between official doctrine and actual behavior, whether this disparity is promoted by the abundance or the relative lack of some form of local piety, and the scope of moral and religious variables affecting fertility control. Failure to take the first consideration into account exaggerates the importance of Catholic doctrine and, at the same time, minimizes the importance of folk beliefs currently held within the various religious traditions. Failure to take the second consideration into account means that no recognition is made of the point at which the influence of religion upon fertility control is most decisive for the population problem.

As Ralph B. Potter has convincingly argued [38], official church doctrines in the form of papal and church pronouncements have, at best, a modest effect upon practice. One finds, for example, that the percentage of Roman Catholic women in this country complying with the Church's ban on "artificial means" of contraception declined from 70% in 1955 to 62% in 1960 and to 47% in 1965. The attitudes recently expressed by both Catholic theologians and laymen mirror these changes in behavior [3; 4; 6]. In a national sample interviewed before and after Pope Paul's visit (October 1966) to the United Nations, 58% of the Catholics, compared with 55% of the non-Catholics, felt, before the Pope's visit, that the Catholic Church should ease its disapproval of contraceptive methods; directly after the Pope's visit, 55% of the Catholics and 52% of the non-Catholics still felt the same way. Catholic opinion was, however, influenced somewhat more than non-Catholic opinion by Pope Paul's statement at the United Nations calling upon the United Nations to ensure "enough bread on the tables of mankind and not to encourage artificial birth control."

There is, furthermore, no predictable relation between Catholic affiliation per se and birth rates. Some predominantly Catholic countries around the world exhibit very low birth rates.

[Note this sample of low birth rates among some countries that are more than 80% Catholic: Argentina (21.8), Belgium (16.4), France (17.7), Ireland (22.2), Luxembourg (15.6), Austria (17.9), and Italy (19.2). By comparison, the United States has a birth rate of 19.4 and Bulgaria, with the lowest among countries for which data is available, has 15.4. Ireland represents a special case in that this birth rate is achieved by delayed marriage and a low proportion of people married, methods that permit obedience to the Catholic doctrine concerning the use of contraceptives without, at the same time, experiencing rapid population growth. (Ireland's population is stable at present, partly because of out-migration.) Traditionally Catholic Latin American countries, with some exceptions, have very high birth rates with rates as high as 47–51 in the Dominican Republic, Ecuador, and Venezuela. (All of the birth rates cited in this essay represent number of births per thousand population; they are taken from the world population data sheet for 1966 compiled by the Population Reference Bureau in Washington, D.C.) In order to grasp the impact of such birth rates upon growth rates, one should note that these countries will double their populations in 20, 23, and 21 years respectively. These figures contrast sharply with countries like Belgium and Italy that will double their population in 117 and 100 years respectively.]

In view of these low birth rates in certain Catholic countries, we cannot explain the generally higher birth rates of Catholics as compared with Protestants within the same society simply by citing the Church's condemnation of contraceptives. (Ireland is an exception; Protestant Northern Ireland had a slightly higher birth rate in 1965 than Catholic Eire.)

Neither Hinduism nor Buddhism has any explicit teachings concerning the moral acceptability of contraceptives; Islam does, as we noted, officially approve their use. Nevertheless, this more official lack of opposition is not necessarily in accord with the religious beliefs held locally by great masses of people or even by some religious leaders. Reviewing what is known about the factors affecting fertility among the rural Sinhalese of Ceylon, Nag [35] notes that these Buddhists considered immoral the prevention of conception by means other than abstinence. Although some women expressed preferences for small families, almost all of them objected to any conscious attempt to prevent conception or birth. Nag describes the typical response as follows: "It is a great sin to try to prevent pregnancy. You must allow those to be born who are to be born" [35:47]. Men uniformly favored large families and wanted no control of births. Similar accounts have been given of the folk beliefs of followers of Islam. Edith Gates, recently retired from her position with the Pathfinder Fund, found that many Egyptian women did not know of the existing *fatwa* and believed that their religion forbade the use of contraceptives. Once advised of the *fatwa*, they were receptive to contraceptives and contraceptive advice.

Ryan [45] documented discrepancies among Ceylonese Buddhist Bhikku (priests) with respect to their moral assessment of contraception: the more educated tended to reconcile Buddhist principles with contraceptive practices; the less educated tended

172

to find them irreconcilable. This same difference has been observed among Islamic religious leaders.

What about birth rates associated with these religions? Though Moslems have official permission to practice contraception, their birth rates are uniformly among the highest in the world. Two notable examples are Egypt (41–44) and Pakistan (49–53); Egypt is expected to double its population within 26 years, Pakistan in 22 years. No country in Asia has higher birth rates than Pakistan; a few countries in Africa exceed it but not by much. Among other major religious groups, Hindus are most comparable to the Moslems, but the Moslems of the Indian subcontinent have higher reproduction rates than their Hindu neighbors. India, 85% Hindu, has a birth rate of 40–43 and is expected to double its population in 31 years. Buddhist birth rates, according to Dudley Kirk [26], are more variable than those of Hindus and Moslems. In some countries, however, they are as high as the highest achieved by Moslems; note Burma (43–40) and Cambodia (47–53), countries due to double their population in 35 and 24 years respectively. Clearly the failure of these religions officially to condemn contraception is not correlated with low birth rates. As we pointed out earlier, even where, irrespective of folk beliefs, use of contraceptives has gained wide acceptance among Hindu and Moslem villagers of India and Pakistan, this factor by itself did not reduce the existing high birth rate.

It should be evident by now that, if we limit the study of the influence of religion upon fertility control to the influence exerted through promulgated doctrines and if among these doctrines we focus only upon those specifying acceptance or rejection of contraceptives, religion will not be interpreted as extremely important in understanding or solving the population problem. But religion has a much more significant and diverse relation to both fertility control and fertility rates.

Harvey Leibenstein has singled out the point at which fertility attitudes and practices must be changed if birth rates are to be sharply reduced. With startling directness, he reminds us of what should be obvious: "For the most part people have large

173

families because they want them" [29:31]. *Desired* family size does not on the average deviate very much from *actual* family size. Whereas, in general, desired family size is higher than actual family size in developed countries, desired family size is lower than actual family size in underdeveloped countries. The difference between desired and actual family size in many of these underdeveloped countries is such that the introduction of perfect contraceptive knowledge and a perfect contraceptive device would reduce birth rates by less than 20%. The desired family size of the underdeveloped countries implies a doubling of the population roughly every generation and a very rapid population growth rate of more than 2% per year. The difference between desired and actual family size is considerably smaller than the difference between desired family size and replacement size. In order to reach a level at which the birth rate approximates the steady state death rate, birth rates in most underdeveloped countries like India and Pakistan would have to be reduced by more than 50%. Thus contraceptive control, without changes in motivation in the direction of desiring smaller families, cannot in underdeveloped countries result in birth rates that approach the steady state death rates. The felt-need hypothesis must definitely be supplemented by hypotheses concerning how we can increase the motivation to practice fertility control. What motivates us to want families of a certain size needs to be understood.

RELIGIOUS FACTORS AND OTHER FACTORS

Hypothetical analyses of factors related to increased fertility control have generally identified four sorts of situational inducements: considerable reductions in infant and child mortality; increased urbanization, industrialization, and the economic factors associated with these processes; a sense of group responsibility; and various kinds of education and information. In order to clarify more precisely the way in which religion relates to these inducements, it is essential to know what is entailed by the concept of *fertility control.*

So far this discussion of fertility control has been limited to the issues raised by the contraceptive techniques used to achieve some kind of control of birth rate. But "fertility control" refers more inclusively to public policy decisions about "population control" and to family planning by spacing births and controlling family size.

Many characterizations of religious positions have been confusing because they have lacked sophistication at this very juncture. Roman Catholics have generally, at the official level, opposed public population control although there are presently signs of change on this matter [52; 31]. Among the more thoughtful attempts at reformulation is that of Louis Dupré [15] as well as the three volumes resulting from the Notre Dame Conference on Population Problems edited by D.M. Barrett [3; 4]. Witness also Pope Paul VI's encyclical *Populorum Progressio* quoted in Dupré [15].

Family planning, however, has been condoned, even encouraged in the forms both of controlling size and spacing. The economic situation of the family and the health of the mother have been put forth as circumstances relevant to such planning. Catholic thought has stressed that family size must be determined by the family in its own circumstances and not by social or political agencies, not even by the Church.

[Family planning *in principle* was explicitly acknowledged in the frequently quoted passage from Pope Pius XII's Address to the Midwives, October 29, 1951: "Serious reasons often put forward on medical, eugenic, economic, and social grounds can exempt from that obligating service (the duty of providing for the conservation of the race) even for a considerable period of time, even for the entire duration of the marriage." However, the church has never delegated the authority, nor presumed to have the authority within itself to determine *when* such conditions exist. William Gibbons has observed that: "Unlike some advocates of planned parenthood, the Catholic Church has learned that ultimate decisions in this matter should be arrived at by the married people themselves" [20:122]. Testifying before the House Committee on Foreign Affairs, Louis Dupré made this same point. While acknowledging that information and technical means for family planning should be made

available to all, he nevertheless insisted that "the right to determine the size of the family belongs to the family alone" [15:7].]

It is fair to add, however, that the Church does promote the moral
desirability of large families where having a large family is within
the means of the couple involved.

[This point is unfortunately completely lost by Westoff,
Potter, and Sagi. In their attempt to pinpoint whether religion
can be regarded as a predictor of fertility, the following question was posed: "As far as you know, does your religion take
any stand on size of family? What?" When 72% of the
"active" Catholics and 61% of the "other" Catholics said that
their church took "no stand," the researchers leapt to the conclusion that their data could be regarded as "largely refuting
the theory that rejection of birth control is perceived by the
Catholic population to reflect an official encouragement of large
families" [47:85].

As we have noted above, the Catholic Church has been very
careful to *avoid* specifying what family size ought to be. One
"proper" answer to the ambiguous question posed in the authors' survey should have been precisely the one made by 72%
of the "active" Catholics. From this, however, one cannot infer,
as the authors do, that this same 72% believes that the Roman
Catholic Church does *not* encourage large families. In fact,
quite the opposite is the case, as Judith Blake has clearly documented. Amassing relevant passages from marriage manuals
which denigrate the small family on the one hand and which
eulogize the large family on the other as well as pertinent papal
statements that unquestionably underscore the large family
ideal, she concludes that: "So completely does this goal appear
to pervade Catholic mass media, standard Catholic marriage
manuals and the reward systems in Catholic culture that it
hardly seems subject to misinterpretation" [7:27]. She observes
also that, "during a ten year period ending in 1963, the mean
family size of the Catholic Mother of the Year was 8.2 children.
None of the mothers had fewer than five children and half had
nine or ten offspring" [7:32].]

In the endeavor to specify the way in which religion affects
the motivation to practice fertility control, a distinction has to

be made between controlling birth intervals (spacing) and controlling family size. It is virtually meaningless to ask whether any given religion or culture does or does not favor or practice family planning. Spacing as a form of planning appears to be a more or less universal phenomenon. It has the sanction of religion because it helps to safeguard the health of mothers. A variety of traditional methods, especially breast feeding and restrictions upon intercourse, have served this purpose. The ready acceptance of modern contraceptives by people of various religions and cultures may very likely be bound up with the desire to increase the efficiency of spacing and thereby more predictably assist the mother to maintain her energy and health; one cannot, however, assume that those who accept contraceptives for these reasons will wish also deliberately to limit the size of their families beyond the limits set by the demands for spacing. In a personal communication, the Egyptian anthropologist Laila Shukry El Hamamsy has told of the Moslem peasant women who are shocked at even being asked whether they are trying to control the size of their families or to cease having children. Such matters are in God's hands. As the interviews and clinical experience show, these women have come to the birth clinic for a more dependable respite — offered by more efficient techniques — from the exhaustion of frequent childbearing.

Folk beliefs, religious and otherwise, do not uniformly condone or encourage self-conscious efforts to avoid having more than a certain number of children. Indeed, this is one of the most significant points at which religious variables become relevant for hypotheses that try to predict how motivation to control fertility can be increased. How, then, does religion affect the decisions to control family size? In somewhat "Tillichian" fashion, we prefer to think of religious beliefs as a fundamental value orientation to the whole of reality; religious beliefs entail a cognitive and emotional commitment to what is perceived to be of ultimate concern or value. Religious beliefs or belief systems can influence the person's perceptual and behavioral responses to his environment in at least two very basic ways: they induce the believer to have certain definite expectations of his environment both in the form of circumstances that permit the perpetuation of his religion through ritual and in the form of blessings or rewards for piety; secondly, they provide the believer with an orientation to the environment both in the form of more or less explicit views of the role of man and of God in shaping events in nature and in history and in the form of a stable pattern of responses, that is to say, in the form of a certain personality type. Each of these religiously prompted relations to one's environment has bearing in one way or another upon the motivation governing the decisions to control family size and, hence, upon actual birth rates.

One of the most critical rituals observed within Hinduism, demands that a father be buried by one of his sons. "The soul of a Hindu can depart in peace from its body only if the skull is opened by a son, who at the same time succeeds him as heir to the authority and obligations of his father" [32:153]. As long as relatively high mortality rates prevail, the religious requirement of a son who will survive and bury his father will serve as an incentive to have families large enough to provide "insurance" against the probable loss of some children. The realistic nature of such planning is forcefully brought home to us by the findings of Gordon and Wyon [50]: of the mothers they studied in the Punjab, half of those over 45 years old had lost a *minimum of three* live-born children. Under these circumstances, the reduction of mortality rates would seem to be a requisite condition for making reductions in family size feasible. Moslems also require sons for religious duties at and after death [26] and therefore experience the same kind of restraint upon limiting family size just ascribed to Hindus. Doctrinal injunctions to marry and multiply are found in all the major religions with the exception of Buddhism. Fagley [17] has given us a brief discussion of this in the major religions. The Protestant view on this is most thoroughly discussed in Fagley's *The Population Explosion and Christian Responsibility* [16]; the Catholic view, including ancient and medieval Christianity, in Noonan's *Contraception* [36].

For Moslems and Hindus, children and large families are among the highest blessings God can bestow. Buddhists also reflect the folk beliefs of the predominantly rural Moslem and

Hindu populations by putting a premium upon large families. In his study of Ceylonese priests, Ryan found that, "a minority of all priests believed that Buddhism directly supports the large family, although the view is rather widely held by the poorly educated. Thus slightly over half of the latter believed that the Buddha had favored large families of children over small, but only one of the (33) highly educated Bhikku agreed" [45:100]. The prevalence and significance of religious folk beliefs, including those of large numbers of relatively poorly educated religious leaders in the underdeveloped countries, needs to be better known and understood. Studies of this sort are increasing, however.

RELIGIOUS VALUES AND FAMILY SIZE

How potent and abiding are these religious values? What are the prospects for change in the direction of small family ideals? We have already seen that the reduction of mortality rates is, in any event, one of the motivational prerequisites for such changes. We must now consider the interaction between religious views of large families as blessings from God and the processes of urbanization and education, processes that demographers see as positive inducements to limit family size.

Demographers have generally maintained that, as urbanization increases, fertility rates decrease and, likewise, as education increases, fertility rates decrease. This overall pattern of association between urbanization or education on the one hand and fertility rates on the other has been observed in connection with the shift from high to low fertility rates, the demographic transition, in the West. This same pattern of association is now, to some degree, present in some of the less developed countries. Excellent reviews and analyses of the literature on this are to be found in Freedman [18] and more recently in Beshers [5].

With respect to the present differential in fertility between Catholics and Protestants in the United States, Beshers [5] expresses confidence that it will disappear once the Catholics have lived somewhat longer in the urban setting; similarly Judith

Blake [7] documents what she sees as a progressive "Americanization" of Catholic reproductive ideals. There is some evidence to suggest, however, that the Catholic to Protestant differential in fertility rates will, at least in the immediate future, persist, even increase, implying that the Catholic approbation of large families is retaining its influence.

[Whelpton, Campbell, and Patterson [48] apparently disagree with Beshers [5] and Blake [7]. As they interpret their data, the Protestant to Catholic differential in fertility is widening: Young Catholic wives expect more children than older Catholic wives; younger Protestant wives expect fewer than older Protestant wives. The authors specifically question the assumption that the differences between Catholics and non-Catholics will disappear once Catholics more nearly approximate the rest of the population in social and economic status because they found that the Catholic to Protestant differentials in family-size expectations are usually in the higher social and economic groups. This is, of course, what one would anticipate if Catholics are being obedient to the teachings of their Church; large families are only for those who can afford them. Time will tell whether *expected fertility* is, under prevailing conditions, a powerful enough predictor of actual fertility to prove the authors correct. Many fluctuating factors in the total environment can affect such a measure, and the effects upon Protestants and Catholics need not be the same. Changes in Catholic doctrine, for example, could be among them.

Westoff, Potter, and Sagi [47] found that the best predictor of higher Catholic rates was the amount of education in Catholic institutions, an indirect measurement of loyalty and involvement in the Church and of exposure to Catholic doctrine as well.]

But gross generalizations about the effects of urbanization and education upon fertility rates are not really extremely helpful. Where the so-called "western fertility pattern" is found in underdeveloped countries — where, in such countries, the better educated urban couples have considerably fewer children than their less educated rural counterparts — the educated urban group is so small that the overall birth rates are not greatly altered. India does not consistently exhibit the western fertility pattern; the Mysore study revealed the existence of this pattern but studies of Central India did not [5]. What is still more important is that speaking in this very general way of a "western fertility pattern" obscures some important facts about demographic behavior in both the East and the West. Paul Demeny [14] has found that low fertility within marriage first emerged on a large scale in Hungary within a *fundamentally peasant setting;* this occurred at a time when fertility within marriage was very high in the *cities* of the Austrian-Hungarian region. Regarding India, Kingsley Davis, in response to questions during a faculty seminar at Harvard in 1966, expressed profound doubt that urbanization and industrialization are having the expected effect on demographic behavior. According to Davis, England had attained a shift to markedly lower birth rates by the time it was as industrialized and as urban as India is now; India, however, shows no sign of such a shift in birth rates.

What is it about urbanization or education that has come to be generally associated with low fertility within marriage, but could be true of some peasant cultures and could also fail sometimes to be true in an urban setting, even sometimes among the educated? The following general conditions would meet these criteria: (1) circumstances in which there are decided advantages, both to the parents and to the children, in having few children in one family; (2) a mode of orientation toward one's circumstances that permits and facilitates rational and purposive responses to them. These conditions may not be sufficient to ensure small family size but they are among the *sine qua non* for making it desirable.

In an urbanizing and industrializing society, large families tend to be economic liabilities rather than assets; the labor of children is much less needed and their opportunities to become financially independent and successful tend to increase with the careful budgeting of their parents. In a money economy, in contrast to a subsistence economy, children are economic liabilities. Money is required for food, clothing, and education. Housing and living space are at a premium, and crowding is undesirable to parents and children alike. Careful budgeting can provide many special cultural and educational benefits, privileges, and opportunities for an urban family; children are a critical part of such budgeting. Small families tend to be mutually advantageous to parents and children under these conditions so typical of urban settings in the West.

But comparable conditions have arisen and do exist in rural settings as well, even in peasant cultures. In rural areas, land of a financially viable size can become extremely scarce. Coupled with the absence of alternative economic and vocational opportunities, a situation is created that one could very well describe as "population pressure." Of two different castes living in the same villages of the Punjab region of India, the farming caste had a relatively lower fertility rate than the leather-worker caste [39]. This same farming caste limited also the number of married sons in order to avoid an undue fragmentation of their farms. Fertility rates, however, even for the farming caste were still high; wives aged 45 and over averaged 7.0 live births. Yet the members of this caste seemed already to be making rational and purposive responses to their particular situation. On the basis of intensive research in this region of India, Gordon and Wyon [50] have hypothesized that people in such an area would be motivated to reduce their birth rates if: mortality rates for infants and children were sharply decreased; local social units were stimulated to measure their own population dynamics and to draw inferences from them concerning their own welfare and aspirations; and efficient methods of birth control were introduced. Introducing these conditions would substantially increase the opportunities of each family unit to reduce family size without undue fear, to assess in a more exact and realistic way how fertility goals would affect themselves and their community, and to plan with more realistic hopes for success in attaining their goals. Whether birth rates would be markedly lowered by bringing about these conditions alone would depend not simply upon the extent to which people in that region start to benefit from such a reduction but also upon the extent to which people actually perceive such benefits and believe that they are attainable.

The gathering of vital statistics is, therefore, crucial: Not until statistics were introduced did the first vaccines gain general acceptance in the West. Without accurate information, a sense of group responsibility cannot exist on a rational basis and will have no perceptible dividend to the individual members. The eventual achievement of "replacement level" fertility rates through the voluntary exercise of fertility control is contingent upon providing the conditions for perceiving the desirability of that level.

The proposal of Gordon and Wyon for the Punjab assumes that rational and purposive behavior more or less exists already and can be intensified by modifications in the environment which make the intensification of such behavior more beneficial and more attainable. This assumption is plausible enough and may very well turn out to be justified, at least for certain regions and cultures.

But modes of orientation to life, and the personality types associated with them, have a hardy and independent existence of their own. And, as we noted previously, they have their say in determining how the circumstances of our lives will look to us and what kinds of responses we consider appropriate to various events in nature and in history.

It is one thing to try to make people aware, when the situation warrants it, of the benefits of planning a small family. It is quite another to try to elicit the control of family size per se where *exerting such control* is viewed as grossly impious, unmanly, or undesirable.

Our orientation to nature and to historical circumstances is very much bound up with our understanding of the relationship of man's actions to the powers that shape events in nature and in history. Florence Kluckhohn [27] has specified the following five basic value orientations that order and direct the solutions to problems that must be solved by peoples at all times and places: (1) the orientation to human nature; (2) the orientation to the relation of man to nature (and supernature) — the man-nature orientation; (3) the orientation to time; (4) the orientation to human activity; and (5) the orientation to man's relationship to other men. At present we are discussing (2) and shortly we shall take up (3).

Beliefs concerning God's active sphere of dominion and participation in human affairs directly affect attitudes toward controlling family size and define the limits of propriety with respect to taking matters into one's own hands. Thus, as Richard Fagley has noted,

> A principal pro-natalist factor in Islam stems from a strong belief in the active providence of Allah. It is Allah who creates sexuality and determines procreation or barrenness. . . . A tradition quotes the Prophet as saying, "whichever soul is destined to come to this world shall come." This concept of predestination gives a strong sense of *kismet*, fate, to the ethos of Islam, which undoubtedly does much to sustain high fertility patterns. Since it includes trust in the beneficent character of divine providence, any question of restricting the number of offspring tends to appear as lacking in piety [17:81].

These beliefs in the will of Allah do indeed find their expression in folk piety. Rural Moslems speak of having as many children as God wills and restrict the use of contraceptives, where they are used, to the demands of spacing. Hinduism and Buddhism have doctrines of *ahimsa*, noninjury, and of the cycle of *karma*, the law of cause and effect or of sowing and reaping in human affairs. In the popular mind, the conscious endeavor to prevent a conception or a birth other than by abstinence has often been interpreted as injury to life and as an interference in natural and morally inviolable cosmic processes.

Interesting parallels to these religious beliefs can be found in certain subcultures. The Gaucho of South America, who works on ranches as a cowboy, considers it unmanly to take rational forethought. For him, rational forethought is cowardly, a failure to face what "life" or "fate" has in store for each of us. Some coeds in the United States play a kind of Russian roulette by deliberately refusing to use contraceptives, claiming that thereby they obtain an "authentic sexual experience." Among working-class wives in the United States there is a tendency described by Lee Rainwater [40] to be sceptical of thinking and planning ahead.

Each of these orientations to the environment shares one very important ingredient: the tendency to eschew, for one reason or another, the future-time perspective characteristic of the purposive-rational type of personality. This personality type was first identified by Max Weber. In *The Protestant Ethic and the Spirit of Capitalism* Weber traced the religious origins of this type of personality within Calvinism and espoused the thesis that the origin of such a personality type was an essential part of the development of the social system that precipitated and sustained capitalism. Banks [1] has noted the critical role of this future-time oriented, budgeting, type of person for bringing down fertility rates within marriage in Victorian England. Lately both Banks [2] and Beshers [5] have called attention to the significance of this personality type for favoring and actualizing small family ideals. They also make the point that future-time orientation is an ingredient of religious belief within Christianity; Banks [2] develops a plausible set of hypotheses regarding the mechanisms by which Christianity gives rise to the rationalistic-purposive orientation.

Beshers [5] maintains that there are three types of social constraints upon decision-making about family size within the family unit: mode of orientation to time (personality type); budget calculation; and communication within the family. The first and second factors are combined in the purposive-rational personality type. Beshers finds also that there are three basic personality types differentiated by their future-time orientation: traditional; short-run hedonistic; and purposive-rational. The traditional personality type tends to be oriented to the past and is not prone to make use of new information for assessing the present or looking to the future. Rural Moslems, Buddhists, and, perhaps to a somewhat lesser extent, Hindus tend to exhibit this mode of orientation. The Gauchos, the coeds, and the working class in the United States tend toward the short-run hedonistic type of orientation. Both types, as we noted above, are deficient in the future-time perspective of the purposive-rational type, lacking therefore the predisposition to plan and budget for the future and to limit family size in accord with such calculations.

The religious origins, within Christianity, of the purposive-rational mode of orientation, have already been mentioned.

Especially significant for the development of this type of person were Calvin's doctrines of providence and of vocation. Every act of man had a purpose in God's scheme and, what is still more important, every action of man was a joint venture in achieving God's purpose for man and the whole cosmos. Through purposive and rational activity man could share in the mighty works of God in nature and in history. By such activities, a man could gain assurance of divine favor and of participation in a community of faith and purpose within which membership was not determined by blood relationships or geographical origins. This community was seen to have a glorious future — one of brotherhood and equity — which could be secured only by diligent and efficient dominion over the goods of this earth.

Weber believed that the purposive-rational personality type needed this ideological basis for its origin but that, once bureaucratic structures arose, they would in turn perpetuate the personality type. Hence the process often called "secularization" is set in motion and a purposive-rational pattern of behavior persists without explicit religious rationalization.

Critical questions, therefore, arise about the possibilities of fostering universally the kind of behavior characteristic of the purposive-rational personality spawned in western society. If such behavior is to be induced, will it be necessary, both morally and practically, for the people of nonwestern countries to find the resources for fostering it within their own great religious traditions? Or will economic development by itself create bureaucratic structures that will by themselves elicit the desired personality type? Since the religious and value systems of these countries are not directly comparable to those within which bureaucratization took place in the West, the answers to these questions are not clear.

It is possible that, at least in some societies, the conditions posited above in the Gordon-Wyon hypothesis will suffice. Certainly they represent certain *sine qua non* for making the control of family size a rationally feasible enterprise. In any event, demographers and others concerned with the population problem must learn much more about religious beliefs at the folk level and must learn to respect both their motivating power and their appropriateness to the settings within which they occur. In every religious tradition God is conceived as being on the side of his people, and, when many children are needed, God favors his people. Calvinism, with its emphasis on man as a coworker with God, could easily shift from the blessings of the large family to the blessing of relatively few well-educated, prosperous children with a future. One should not presume that other major religions cannot make similar adjustments.

We have now completed an assessment of the felt-need hypothesis and of hypotheses as to how the motivation to control fertility within marriage can be increased. Now we wish only briefly to touch upon the third contemporary type of variation on Malthus' hypothesis that Moral Restraint (plus or minus Misery and Vice) determines the birth rate, limiting ourselves to those measures concerned with the postponement of the age of marriage of women.

When the average age of marriage of women is increased, birth rates are reduced. This is true because the average length of the fertile period is shortened while the age-specific fertility rate after marriage does not appreciably rise. Delayed marriage, along with low proportions of married women, were initially important for the demographic transition in the West.

Postponement of marriage, apart from its general significance for western birth rates, including in a very special way those of Ireland, can be expected to help lower fertility rates in a number of underdeveloped countries. Wyon et alia [49] have documented this for India. There is a trend toward later marriages in what Dudley Kirk [26] calls "the more progressive Moslem countries." In such countries, postponement of marriage can be accelerated by providing women greater independence and self-confidence, and improved status outside of marriage. Accomplishing this requires better education of girls and enlarged opportunities for employment for girls and women outside the home. The provision of education for women would tend also to induce the purposive-rational pattern of behavior needed for efficiently controlling fertility.

MARXIST AND CATHOLIC POLICIES

We have yet to examine the Marxist and Catholic response to Malthus. In both of these instances, the whole idea of "overpopulation" was rejected. Marxists and Catholics alike initially objected to any explicit attempt on the part of governments to control or seek to control population growth. The classic Marxian formulation of the problem of population is found in Engels' "Outlines of a Critique of Political Economy" (1844):

> The area of land is limited, — that is perfectly true. But the labour power to be employed on this area increases together with the population; and even if we assume that the increase of labour is not always proportionate to the latter, there still remains a third element — which the economists, however, never consider as important — namely, science, the progress of which is just as limitless and at least as rapid as that of population . . . in the most normal conditions it also grows in geometrical progression — and what is impossible for science?

Although the Chinese communists have adhered rigidly to this Marxian assertion that "overpopulation" per se can never exist in the socialist state and that any inequity in resources as over against demand — what Catholics often refer to as "relative overpopulation" — is but a consequence of the capitalist mode of production, nevertheless the Chinese have demonstrated a marked capacity for flexibility with regard to the question of birth control. Thus, whereas official policy concerning birth control has undergone more than one volte-face in the last decade, Malthus' theory is consistently rejected. Arguments justifying the restriction of family size are invoked such as "the protection of women and children . . . the up-bringing and education of the rising generation . . . and the health and prosperity of the nation" (speech by Chou-en-lai, September 1956) as well as insisting on sexual equality and the need to devote one's energies to the development of the state. These restrictions include such measures as mandatory late marriages (men must be 30, women 25) and severe sanctions against having more than two children per couple.

Like the Chinese, the Russians have retained the traditional, categorical rejection of malthusian and neomalthusian thought while at the same time implying by their policies that the regulation of the size and growth of population is well within the scope of governmental authority [22].

The classical Catholic objections to Malthus as well as the shift to more realistic responses can, appropriately enough, be documented by reference to separate statements by Pope Paul VI. In the first statement made at the United Nations on October 1965, the Pope called for food for the hungry rather than programs to encourage contraception.

> [Zimmerman quotes a strong expression of the conservative Catholic reaction to public encouragement of family planning: "The Church has never advised an individual *family* and much less a whole nation to use the Rhythm method . . . . The organizations that recommend birth limitation on a large scale, it does not matter under what form, are relying upon the erroneous opinion that the family is for the State. It is the contrary that is true: the State is for the family and it cannot be admitted that the family must, in its most intimate life, submit itself to considerations of a demographic nature. The State, on the contrary, must assure all families of the country of the possibility of providing a becoming livelihood and education not only for one or two children but for the normal family as willed by God. To save a nation from the threat of famine it is possible to see solutions other than of limiting births, no matter how this is accomplished" [52:204–205].]

In the Pope's later statement, contained in the encyclical *Populorum Progressio*, the problems associated with rapid population growth, as well as the urgency of government policies with respect to it, are acknowledged and a plea is made for preserving the voluntary nature of family planning.

> [It is true that too frequently an accelerated demographic increase adds its own difficulties to the problems of development: the size of the population increase more rapidly than available

resources, and things are found to have reached apparently an impasse. From that moment the temptation is great to check the demographic increase by means of radical measures. It is certain that public authorities can intervene, within the limit of their competence by favoring the availability of appropriate information and by adopting suitable measures, provided that these be in conformity with the moral law and that they respect the rightful freedom of married couples. Where the inalienable right to marriage and procreation is lacking, human dignity has ceased to exist. Finally, it is for the parents to decide with full knowledge of the matter, on the number of their children.]

No more than Marxism has Catholicism prevented governmental contributions to family planning. In 1966 the Agency for International Development contributed $5.5 million toward the support of family planning programs in Pakistan, Turkey, South Korea, Jamaica, and, significantly, in the primarily Roman Catholic Latin American nations of Brazil, Costa Rica, Ecuador, El Salvador, and Honduras. Futhermore, lay Catholic opinion is keeping pace with the shift in official thought. A Gallup Poll taken in October 1965 revealed that a majority of the Roman Catholics in the United States supports the idea of Federal aid for family planning clinics.

The Catholic insistence upon the voluntary nature of decisions regarding family size is a most laudatory one. Although it is not always easy to discover why, in a given region, a sense of group responsibility for population growth is essential, efforts must be made to discern and make known any erosion of the quality of our lives due to population pressures. And, as we have argued earlier, if we are to evoke voluntary reductions of family size which are in accord with the needs of one's population group, we must not only learn to work with and respect the particular circumstances of that region, but also learn to respect the potentiality of the cultural and religious heritage of these groups for working out the most viable and likely sources of deep and abiding motivation to accomplish such reductions of family size and, hence, of rapid population growth.

REFERENCES

1. Banks, J A: *Prosperity and Parenthood* (Routledge & Kegan Paul, Ltd, London, England) 1954.
2. Banks, J A: Historical Sociology and the Study of Population, *Daedalus* (paper presented at the International Conference on Historical Population Studies, Bellagio, Italy) forthcoming.
3. Barrett, Donald N, ed: *The Problem of Population*, vol 1, 2 (University of Notre Dame Press, Notre Dame, Indiana) 1964.
4. Barrett, Donald N: *The Problem of Population*, vol 3 (University of Notre Dame Press, Notre Dame, Indiana) 1965.
5. Beshers, James M: *Population Processes in Social Systems* (The Free Press, New York, New York) 1967.
6. Birmingham, William, ed: *What Modern Catholics Think about Birth Control* (Signet Books, The New American Library, Inc, New York, New York) 1964.
7. Blake, Judith: The Americanization of Catholic Reproductive Ideals, *Population Studies*, vol 20, 1966, pp 27–43.
8. Bogue, Donald J: The Demographic Breakthrough: from Projection to Control, *Population Index*, vol 30, 1964, pp 449–454.
9. Cobb, John C; Raulet, Harry M; and Harper, Paul: An I.U.D. Field Trial in Lulliani, West Pakistan (paper presented at the American Public Health Association) Oct 21, 1965.
10. Coale, Ansley J: The Decline of Fertility in Europe from the French Revolution to World War II, *Daedalus* (paper presented at the International Conference on Historical Population Studies, Bellagio, Italy) forthcoming.
11. Cox, Harvey: *The Secular City* (The Macmillan Company, New York, New York) 1965.
12. Davis, Kingsley: Values, Population, and the Supernatural: A Critique, in G F Mair, ed: *Studies in Population* (Prince-

ton University Press, Princeton, New Jersey) 1949, p 137.

13. Davis, Kingsley: Fertility Control and the Demographic Transition in India, *The Interrelations of Demographic, Economic, and Social Problems in Selected Underdeveloped Areas* (Milbank Memorial Fund, New York, New York) 1954.

14. Demeny, Paul: Some Factors Associated with the Early Decline of Marital Fertility in Austria-Hungary, *Daedalus* (paper presented at the International Conference on Historical Population Studies, Bellagio, Italy) forthcoming.

15. Dupré, Louis: in Chakerian, Charles G, and Dupré, Louis: *Two Theological Views on Population Control* (Population Reference Bureau, Inc, selection no 21) reprinted from *McCormick Quarterly*, vol 20, no 2, Jan 1967.

16. Fagley, Richard M: *The Population Explosion and Christian Responsibility* (Oxford University Press, New York, New York) 1960.

17. Fagley, Richard M: Doctrines and Attitudes of Major Religions in Regard to Fertility, *World Population Conference, 1965*, vol 2 (United Nations, New York, New York) 1967.

18. Freedman, Ronald: The Sociology of Human Fertility, *Current Sociology* (Basil Blackwell) vol 10/11, 1963, pp 35–121.

19. Freedman, Ronald; Whelpton, Pascal K; and Campbell, Arthur A: *Family Planning, Sterility, and Population Growth* (McGraw-Hill Book Company, New York, New York) 1959.

20. Gibbons, William J: The Catholic Value System in Relation to Human Fertility in G F Mair, ed: *Studies in Population* (Princeton University Press, Princeton, New Jersey) 1949, p 138.

21. Hauser, Philip M, ed: *The Population Dilemma* (Prentice-Hall, Inc, Englewood Cliffs, New Jersey) 1963.

22. Heer, David: Abortion, Contraception, and Population Policy in the Soviet Union, *Soviet Studies*, vol 17, 1965, pp 76–83.

23. Henry, Louis: Some Data on Natural Fertility, *Eugenics Quarterly*, vol 8, 1961, pp 81–91.

24. Himes, Norman E: *Medical History of Contraception* (Gamut Press, Taplinger Publishing Co, Inc, New York, New York) 1963.

25. Kirk, Dudley: Prospects for Reducing Natality in the Underdeveloped World, *The Annals of the American Academy of Political and Social Science*, vol 369, Jan 1967, pp 48–60.

26. Kirk, Dudley: Factors Affecting Moslem Natality, *World Population Conference, 1965*, vol 2 (United Nations, New York, New York) 1967.

27. Kluckhohn, Florence, and Strodtbeck, Fred L: *Variations in Value Orientations* (Row, Peterson & Co, now Harper & Row, Publishers, New York, New York) 1961.

28. Langer, Elinor: in *Science*, Dec 10, 1965, p 1433, quoting an editorial in the *Washington Post*.

29. Leibenstein, Harvey: Population Growth and the Development of Underdeveloped Countries, *Harvard Medical Alumni Bulletin*, vol 41, 1967, pp 29–33.

30. Lenski, Gerhard: *The Religious Factor* (Doubleday and Company, Inc, Garden City, New York) 1961.

31. Lestapis, Stanislas de: *Family Planning and Modern Problems* (Herder and Herder, New York, New York) 1961.

32. Lorimer, Frank: *Culture and Human Fertility* (I.F.M.R.P., Unesco, Paris, France) 1954.

33. Malthus, Thomas Robert: *On Population, 1798 and 1803* (Modern Library, Inc, New York, New York), 1960.

34. Mudd, Stuart, ed: *The Population Crisis and the Use of World Resources* (Indiana University Press, Bloomington, Indiana) 1964.

35. Nag, Moni: *Factors Affecting Human Fertility in Nonindustrial Societies: A Cross-Cultural Study* (Yale University Press, New Haven, Connecticut) 1962.

36. Noonan, John T, jr: *Contraception* (The Belknap Press of Harvard University Press, Cambridge, Massachusetts) 1965.

37. Novak, Michael: *The Experience of Marriage* (The Macmillan Company, New York, New York) 1964.

38. Potter, Ralph B: Religion, Politics, and Population: A Time

for Change, *Harvard Medical Alumni Bulletin*, vol 41, 1967, pp 14–21.

39. Potter, Robert G, jr; New, Mary L; Wyon, John B; and Gordon, John E: A Fertility Differential in Eleven Punjab Villages, *Milbank Memorial Fund Quarterly*, vol 43, Apr 1965, pp 185–201.

40. Rainwater, Lee; Coleman, Richard P; and Handel, Gerald: *Workingman's Wife* (Oceana Publications, Inc, Dobbs Ferry, New York) 1959.

41. Revelle, Roger: The Problem of People, *Harvard Today*, Autumn 1965, pp 2–9.

42. Revelle, Roger: Population and Food Supplies: the Edge of the Knife, *Proceedings of the National Academy of Sciences*, vol 56, 1966, pp 328–351.

43. Rizk, Hanna: Social and Psychological Factors Affecting Fertility in the United Arab Republic, *Marriage and Family Living*, vol 25, no 1, Feb 1963.

44. Ross, John A: Recent Events in Population Control, *Studies in Family Planning* (a publication of The Population Council) no 9, 1966, pp 1–5.

45. Ryan, Bryce: Hinayana Buddhism and Family Planning in Ceylon, in *The Interrelations of Demographic, Economic, and Social Problems in Selected Underdeveloped Areas* (Milbank Memorial Fund, New York, New York) 1954.

46. Thompson, Warren S, and Lewis, David T: *Population Problems* (McGraw-Hill Book Company, Inc, New York, New York) 1965.

47. Westoff, Charles F; Potter, Robert G, jr; and Sagi, Philip C: *The Third Child* (Princeton University Press, Princeton, New Jersey) 1963.

48. Whelpton, Pascal K; Campbell, Arthur A; and Patterson, John E: *Fertility and Family Planning in the United States* (Princeton University Press, Princeton, New Jersey) 1966.

49. Wyon, John B; Finner, Stephen L; Heer, David M; Parthasarathy, Nadipurum R; and Gordon, John E: Delayed Marriage and Prospects for Fewer Births in Punjab Villages, *Demography*, vol 3, no 1, 1966, pp 209–217.

50. Wyon, John B, and Gordon, John E: The Khanna Study, *Harvard Medical Alumni Bulletin*, vol 41, 1967, pp 24–28.
51. Wyon, J B, and Gordon, J E: *The Khanna Population Study* (Harvard University Press, Cambridge, Massachusetts) forthcoming.
52. Zimmerman, Anthony: *Catholic Viewpoint on Overpopulation* (Hanover House, Garden City, New York) 1961.

5. THE NEW RELATIVISM IN AMERICAN THEOLOGY

THE NEW RELATIVISM IN AMERICAN THEOLOGY
by Michael Novak

I T IS THE MARK of a creative era that the observer sees initiatives in many directions but cannot yet define the shape of things to come. Definition is possible only when a wave has attained a shape, and, from the moment the wave crests, it begins to descend. Thus historians will tell us more about the shape of the present than anyone now can. For the prospect offered to theology is today so vast that no one yet has been able to glimpse the entire range of possibilities. An amazing, an astonishing, breakthrough has been achieved. The question is whether, and how, such vast possibilities can be absorbed.

In this essay, I would like to chart some of the important lines of discovery and invention. If the present generation of theologians does its work well, the bounds of theology tomorrow, by comparison with recent theology, will be immeasurably expanded. The grip of confessional theology and particularly of seminary theology, where these are conceived of as arguments within a given set of traditions, has been broken. Before we turn to other issues, the reasons for this new openness might well be stated.

THE NEW OPENNESS

Faith comes by hearing, but how do huge metropolitan populations hear? The humble catalyst responsible for opening the horizons of theologians has been the enthusiasm of the producers, editors, and correspondents of the mass media for theological subjects. Theological books and journals follow now, rather than lead, the events of public consciousness which constitute what

Teilhard de Chardin [14] called the noösphere. Whereas Paul Tillich and Reinhold Niebuhr, not to mention their less well known colleagues, spoke a special theological language whose sense eluded many ordinary Christians and nonchristian intellectuals, today theologians find both popular and academic audiences hungry to participate in theological discussion; moreover, they are beneficiaries of a humanistic language newly fashioned for carrying on that discussion. There have, of course, been writers like Norman Vincent Peale and preachers like Billy Graham to keep theology in contact with ordinary people; such writers and preachers tried to maintain the conceptual structure and images of eighteenth century theology alongside the structures and images of contemporary popular life. The newer theologians have much more ambitious purposes: they hope to create new structures and new images which will transform ancient Christian beliefs analogically and, by doing so, initiate both a radical celebration and a radical criticism of contemporary life.

What is new, then, is that the younger theologians are far bolder (a) in breaking from traditional symbols and images in order to try new ones, just as hellenistic Christianity, Latin Christianity, Germanic Christianity, and other creative movements in Christian history did and (b) in breaking from traditional concepts, distinctions, and methods of theological discourse in order to allow into theology the rich varieties of discourse available in our culture. Theologians have long been separated either from the best secular intelligence or from popular consciousness or from both. Lately they have been drawn into prolonged contact with the public consciousness, both ordinary and professional; the much disdained mass media fashioned the vital link between real public issues and theologians.

The mass media could not raise real issues unless real events were happening. The problem of God is profound and serious in our culture and was so long before the media forced theologians to confront it publicly. There is probably no major institution in our culture — not government or the universities or labor unions or business corporations — that has shown itself in recent years as willing as the churches to undertake radical reform.

Consequently, when the media began to look to the churches to see what was happening, they found nuns on picket lines, ministers supporting migrant worker protests and inner city projects; they found trenchant critics of repressive sexual morality and scholars able and willing to criticize religious ideas heretofore held sacred. In one sense it was the scholars of the *last* generation, working and teaching in relative obscurity, who inspired many students with the vision of a new relationship between theology and culture. But we would have to add that these students knew themselves to be a minority (and usually were made to feel "too advanced" in their respective churches); the mass media have given them a hearing before millions of people (and before academic colleagues) that they had not had before. The mass media have both uncovered and promoted changes in public religious consciousness and have made the theologian aware — and a little shaken by the knowledge — that people are listening.

Academic consciousness is, in its own right, shaped by a peculiar set of prejudices and values, often circumscribed by the bounds of the academic community. But theologians cannot so easily as scholars in other disciplines be oblivious to the power of their words in the lives of ordinary people. For the subject matter of theology is the relation of man to God in the center of the personality, whose nourishment comes from all the activities, projects, and relations of men to one another. In order to interpret human life according to the light given them, theologians, at their best, reflect upon what men are actually doing and experiencing. They deal with "meaning" [43:3; 26:41–49]. But this meaning is neither stable nor disembodied. Hence, theology must always be a creative act; when it is not, it not only becomes academic in a pejorative sense but dysfunctional as well. Theology which does not deal with the present activities and experiences of men (reinterpreting history and Scripture from an ever changing viewpoint, for example) loses its claim to be an interpreter of human life. To be sure, no one theologian can do everything that needs to be done; specialization is both necessary and fruitful, and some tasks are properly more remote than others from the front lines. But it is important for supporting units to know where the battleline is: the discernment of what is happening to men. This can be contrasted with Paul Lehmann's phrase, "What *God* is doing in the world" [21]. How, empirically, do we discern what *God* is doing except in what *men* are doing and through human discerners?

The word "theology" today bears, sociologically, a new meaning. To say that the center of gravity in American theology is shifting from the ecclesiastical seminary to the secular university is to say that theology is the handmaiden no longer of the church (narrowly conceived) but of the human community. The theologian in the secular university is not so much carrying on the tradition of his ecclesiastical community, as, under new conditions, he is transforming that tradition. All five of the American writers associated with radical theology have been teaching at secular universities: Altizer at Emory, Hamilton at Rochester, Van Buren at Temple, Vahanian at Syracuse, and Rubenstein at Pittsburgh.

The inadequacy of the word "God" was discovered in America when theologians ceased lecturing to captive audiences in churches and seminaries and began speaking both to the university community and to the mass media. Speaking *and listening*. Once theologians began to listen, the weakness both of liberal theology and of neoorthodoxy became apparent and had to be faced.

The scientific frontier for theology is no longer physics; the frontier is the absorption of the social sciences [46:106–117]. The social sciences have opened American theology to a new understanding of the theological task. It has become apparent to theologians that language is a social institution; that the context for what is said in language is the life forms, the symbols, and the expectations embodied in social institutions; that reality itself is a social construct [7:3–16; 8]. When theologians in the past talked about "what Christians believe," they usually articulated what Christians *should* believe (or what theologians thought they should believe). But sociologists are beginning to learn how to inquire into the attitudes which huge populations actually share. Thus theologians are becoming sensitive to the difference between a theoretical analysis and an empirical study of creeds and attitudes.

How do "religious" people pray? Theology is no longer the same when the question is taken to be empirical as well as normative. To what extent can Christianity be said to be unique? To what extent does the relativity introduced by the methods of the social sciences remove the intellectual scandal from Christianity and from Judaism by treating them exactly like other world religions? A functional analysis of religion [43; 55] seems, in particular, to understand Christianity and Judaism as culture religions and to interpret them as filling social and psychological needs.

Moreover, the impact of the ecumenical movement has deeply affected the social consciousness of men and communities that had been isolated from one another. Confidence in the rightness and the adequacy of limited traditions has been shaken by discovery of the power of other traditions. Whereas churches and denominations used to boast of their own advantages, now they are recognizing the advantages of others. The same mutual respect — or mutual modesty — seems to be growing between theists and atheists [39; 40]. A great many supposed theological differences appear, in this new light, to have been based on sociological differences.

A lack of social interaction led to misunderstandings and polemical misjudgments, and divergent emotional responses were made to certain forms of words or practices. It is not always the case that those in dialogue discover themselves to have been "saying the same thing in different words." But it is always the case that an affective, empathetic entry into the other's horizon reveals reasons why his words make sense to him.

The discovery of the richness and variety of human beliefs leads to a new appreciation of the relativity of human life and values. Yet so accustomed have theologians become to relativity that some have recognized, in John Donne's phrase, "the relativity of relativity." To see that there is no absolute standpoint does not mean that one must absolutize relativism. It is true that men differ and that each man must define his own horizon; it does not follow that one horizon is as adequate as another, but only that there is no way of appealing to some umpire outside the playing field. A Jew, for example, believes that his way of interpreting human life, given through the history of the prophets and of his people, is *a* realistic way or perhaps even *the* realistic way; and he may try to show why he believes that and to demonstrate the fruitfulness of so believing. What he cannot do is point to some absolute measuring stick outside the struggle which proves to others (or even to himself) that his interpretation of human life is correct.

Possibly the greatest factor in the opening of theology, however, is the dissolution of the modern form of Western culture. A world is collapsing around us, and a new one is being born. Some persons still find sustenance in the forms of the receding age; others are intolerably restless. New forms have not yet taken shape. To describe the present situation, then, the most useful strategy appears to be to single out the places where disintegration is most noticeably occurring and to point to the lines of exploration whence the new integration will somehow derive its character.

THE POINTS OF DISINTEGRATION

There appear to be four sources of disintegration — or at least of widespread malaise — experienced by religious persons in the United States. First, there is the collapse of the shared meanings which for a long time characterized "the American way of life." Secondly, folk religion — the traditional modality of the world religions — is becoming increasingly difficult to support. Thirdly, the impossibility of simply affirming ("celebrating") the contemporary secular world is painfully obvious. Fourth, the dominating theological tension between the liberalism of Rudolf Bultmann and the neoorthodoxy of Karl Barth has come to the end of its fruitfulness; it was, on the one hand, too Germanic in its presuppositions and, on the other, too easily and simply Christian to be of much use to American culture.

The Collapse of "the American Way of Life." Until recently, "the American way of life" was white, Protestant Christian, and middle class. Successful image makers usually adopted Anglo-Saxon names. The nation had so long lived under Protestant hegemony [3] that "American" seemed synonymous in the eyes of many with "Christian" and perhaps also with "good," "true," "reliable," "free," "brave," etc. Moreover, a pragmatic religio-cultural consensus had developed which blunted the edge of ideological differences. Yet Daniel Bell's *The End of Ideology* [6] had hardly appeared when the forces which were generating new tensions and new ideologies in American life began to break the placid surface. The year 1960, it appears, was the watershed year for American theology. In that year the powerful national symbol of the presidency passed from Eisenhower to Kennedy; old America, Protestant, folksy, and moralistic, yielded to a new America, pluralistic, sophisticated, and young. The balance of psychological authority passed from the older generation to the younger.

Attacks upon America insofar as it had become a Protestant symbol proceeded from all sides. As early as *Advertisements for Myself*, 1959 [28:379–380], Norman Mailer linked "Catholic" with "hipster" and "Protestant" with "square," and in *Cannibals and Christians*, 1967, he voiced the longstanding bitterness of the Jewish intellectual against the complacency of white Christian America, especially in the essay on the Goldwater convention of 1964 [29].

James Baldwin excoriated American Christianity in *The Fire Next Time*, 1963 [2] as did Malcolm X in his *Autobiography*, 1964 [30]. By contrast, the Republican convention of 1964 appeared to be, symbolically, the recognition by many who once stood foursquare at the heart of America that the country had spiritually passed them by. Those who wildly applauded their candidate under a snow of gold foil that July in San Francisco were applauding a code that had long felt right in their hearts and had long been taken for granted [29:34]. They were applauding the eminence of a white, Christian, achieving, acquisitive way of life. They were opposing the "treason" whereby the

Supreme Court, the President, the New Deal coalition of the intellectuals and the nonachievers (Lyndon Johnson's "welfare state"), the members of the press, radio, and television, and other assorted groups had set this nation upon a new course.

During and after 1964, President Johnson himself was to become a symbol of further division, whose cultural — and theological — roots run very deep. When the Mississippi Freedom Democratic Party was urged by Michael Harrington and other members of the left to accept a compromise at the Democratic convention of 1964, many of the leading young people who had for four years worked in Mississippi at the risk of their lives discovered their own separate identity [37:139–141]. The "old left" and the "party of consensus," they now saw, also inhibited the justice so amply proclaimed by American rhetoric. Perhaps on other matters compromise could have been tolerated. But those who had worked in Mississippi, who knew the corruption of law enforcement agencies, who had seen the naked violence and the biting hunger, who had tasted what it was like to live in an oppressed and underdeveloped region [13; 37:100] of a basically affluent society could not tolerate compromise on so serious a matter. The aftermath was to prove them correct: the United States was not serious about speedy reform in Mississippi or anywhere.

In 1964, a major student revolt broke out at the first-rank Berkeley campus of the University of California. Clark Kerr had written in 1959 of his students: "The employers will love this generation. They aren't going to press many grievances. They are going to be easy to handle. There aren't going to be any riots" [20; 37:25]. The literature on the unexpected student revolt has by now become voluminous [15; 23; 34]. A major spiritual change in the life of young Americans became increasingly apparent, especially in California. It was the young who, encouraged by the brief administration of John F. Kennedy, had turned their energies to the politics of the civil rights movement and to the international experience with "the third world" promoted by the Peace Corps and by the almost universal United States involvement abroad. It was the young who began to turn away from "the Protestant ethic" in what has come to be called "the hippie movement" [42]. In place of "dutiful," their key ethical word is "beautiful." In place of "conformity to society," they choose to try to be truthful to themselves. They have begun to use what the medievals called "the transcendentals" — truth, beauty, being, and good — in a modern, contemplative, non-activist way. They have attempted to establish "the brotherly community" apart from the rush of the world around them, like medieval religious communities or Reformation sectarian groups. Not aware that Christianity and Judaism have a mystical, contemplative tradition, the young turn eagerly to Eastern religions.

The two movements, that of the New Left and that of the hippies, must be kept distinct, though both are united in their opposition to the "liberal establishment" (the conservative establishment is, for them, beyond discussion). It is sometimes assumed that the hippies are nonpolitical; thus Jack Newfield, who has written the most perceptive book on the New Left, grossly underestimates the hippies [36:809–810; 37]. The New Left and the hippies have chosen divergent strategies for revolutionizing American life. The activist students hope to build up "parallel structures" — the free universities, the antidraft league, and other organizations — in order to create an effective political movement.

The hippies have decided to skip several steps in the political process and simply to construct their own "brotherly communities," whose political purpose is to attract people by admiration and emulation. It was thus that the Benedictines in their cloistered communities established centers that nourished European towns for centuries and became communicators of economic and political processes otherwise unknown. The hippies do not reject the world as, for example, the Mennonite Brethren do; the hippies depend upon the general affluence but believe that the age of the business ethic that produced that affluence is past. Civilization, they say, is not for work but for enjoyment; there are machines to do the work. The gentleness and nonviolence of the hippies are a token of high spiritual achievement, and are a hopeful forerunner of the future. When society is sufficiently affluent to take care of men's needs, Freudian theory suggests [11; 12; 31; 47], the acquisitive asceticism of an earlier stage of culture becomes obsolescent. How may men best live under conditions of affluence? It is amazing, but not distressing in the least, that the answer of the hippies in San Francisco should be so Franciscan.

Two theological prejudices prevent many observers from understanding the new underground culture of the young. On the one hand, there is a "realistic" prejudice that all genuine human progress begins by accepting the status quo and working pragmatically and by compromise from within its system. The value of this prejudice is its check on fanaticism; those conditions which especially recommend it are conditions of crisis and despair, in which utopian hopes seem wholly improbable and even dangerous. But, under other conditions, realism is a shortsighted and timid prejudice. Sometimes the health of society depends upon a qualitative leap; not every step of evolution is gradual and consistent with the past. Consequently, the claim that both the New Left activists and the hippies are "unrealistic" may arise only from a failure to grasp the point [32:1–199]. For these new movements have broken with "realism" on the strength of their case that "realism," under present conditions, makes an indispensable contribution to perpetuating the ills that plague us: the business ethic, the cold war, an antirevolutionary foreign policy, etc. To overcome this objection, the realist must justify his own position and not merely reassert it.

There is, on the other hand, the "pelagian" prejudice that spiritual achievement is proportionate to personal effort. Those who share this prejudice cannot conceive of the possibility that the Creator may have graced his creation with drugs which, discovered in due time, might be instrumental in preparing people to understand the gentleness, brotherhood, and peace of the gospels. Spiritual achievement is not won only through will and effort; often, it is a grace. Drugs humble the spiritual pretensions of men, effecting through the psychoneural organism what conscious effort does not bring about [52:3–24].

One effect of taking drugs appears to be the capacity to perceive the world in a way that is "not American"; for the first time, some users of drugs report, they are able to look at things outside the perspective of "usefulness." It seems to be as if blinders had fallen from their eyes. Sometimes the psychological reorientation is painful and terrifying. But often, as well, the user reports feeling liberated, seems to feel as if he were at one with the universe, and is able to notice the rich complexity and variety present even in prosaic things like a tabletop, a candle, a tree. The users of drugs report the experience not as if the world appeared suddenly chaotic and "subjective," but as if *they* could now see it "more objectively." These remarks are based immediately on term papers written by my students at Stanford and on conversations and observations of related phenomena in the San Francisco area. Incidentally, the resemblance of the new California man to Camus' Mediterranean man is worth working out.

The possibility has been raised that what seems "realistic" to the ordinary, well educated, pragmatic, technologically oriented American is highly "subjective"; the world is perceived only insofar as it suits his purposes. The user of drugs feels liberated to perceive the world more nearly as artists, mystics, and primitive people perceive it; the world is more alive, more personal, more resonant with unity, more terrifying, full of variety, of complexity, and of astonishing surprise. The language of *function* recedes; the language of *being* expresses the experience more accurately.

The Collapse of Folk Religion. Since World War II, American society has undergone changes which undermine the ways in which religion was formerly communicated to the young. Religion in America — Protestant, Catholic, and Jewish — has not been for some time, among the vast majority of people, an intellectual enterprise. Even the ordinary clergyman, as observers like Wilhelm Pauck [45:270] have amply testified, appears to have a minimal understanding of his faith. Popular piety appears to be mainly devotional and conventional, rather than creative and discerning. The unpretentious theology of widely heralded preachers is often that of the "last half of the eighteenth century" [50:19]. The ordinary religious person depends very little on theologians for deepening his faith, and, when he hears what theologians say about things he takes for granted, he is often shocked. By "folk religion," I mean, positively, a modality of religious life whose strength derives from family sentiment, local customs, and national inheritance; negatively, a modality whose strength does not come from the drive to raise questions.

Folk religion is, consequently, exceedingly vulnerable to cultural upheavals. It lacks the understanding which would allow it to perceive what is indispensable to its faith and to translate those elements from one cultural context to another. A major cultural transition tempts those who live by folk religion to abandon some elements of their faith because the new cultural forms are emotionally and imaginatively powerful. Similarly, the confusion occasioned by cultural change tempts them to cling to some of the old cultural forms which no longer express the faith but which retain nostalgic associations. Folk religion, because it resides in feelings, images, and associations is a powerful social force. For the same reason, it is blind. In an age of transition, it is partly in tune, partly out of tune, with its cultural matrix. In the name of the faith of the past it often opposes cultural movements which may, in fact, be vehicles of that faith in the present. Meanwhile, it often accepts in the name of faith present cultural movements which a more astute understanding would diagnose as blasphemous or idolatrous. Carl Amery has described one recent whipsaw which has torn folk religion in *Capitulation: The Lesson of German Catholicism* [1]. The situation of folk religion in the United States on questions of race, war, and acquisitiveness led Bonhoeffer to construct his critique of "religion," as opposed to genuine Christianity, both in Germany and in the United States [9:231].

Because folk religion is communicated to the young by way of family sentiment, the censorship of local customs, and the rhetoric of a national way of life, folk religion is highly vulnerable in a mobile urban society. Young people escape the grip of folk religion simply by turning on television or going to the movies or walking down to the corner or getting into an automobile or leaving home for college. Electronic stimulation, in particular, shapes their imagination and their emotions [27], so that even

208

while they live in the same household with their parents, their inner life develops along quite different lines than did that of their parents some years before. The meaning which they give to words used by their parents and teachers is bound to be different, since their imaginal and emotional experience is different. Young people are apt to find more understanding among their peers than from their families. Thus the Beatles sing: "She's leaving home after living alone for so many years" [5].

It is no doubt true, of course, that the vast majority of young people are motivated by fundamental insecurity to conform as closely as possible to the rules of life laid down by the competitive world into which they have been born [33:11–12]. But the actual conditions of the society in which they are growing up are so far removed from the rules they are learning that the potential of violent rebellion is very high. Even young people who go to church are not so shocked as their parents to find out that the Beatles are more popular than Jesus. The God of whom their religious teachers speak is not, in fact, functional in the world of their experience, except as a crutch in time of need. It is not difficult to persuade young people that such a God may be, at best, an idol invented to relieve man of his insecurities. Moreover, in the pluralism of American experience, the young encounter some atheists who are more open, more honest, more compassionate than many "religious" people they have known. The word "God" comes for many to be surrounded with connotations of hypocrisy, narrowness of view, and repression. The more "religious" the environment, the more emotional resistance there appears to be; the more "secular" the environment, the more openness to frank discussion of religious themes. As Bonhoeffer said:

> While I often shrink with religious people from speaking of God by name — because that Name somehow seems to me here not to ring true, and I strike myself as rather dishonest (it is especially bad when others start talking in religious jargon; then I dry up completely and I feel somehow oppressed and ill at ease) — with people who have no religion I am able on occasion to speak of God quite openly and as it were naturally [10:165].

209

The experience of living in American society provides a lived relativism. No one view of life, no one set of values, can be taken for granted. The conclusion to be drawn is not that one view is as good as another; it is that each view must prove itself under the critical eye of others. Since most people live by sentiment, folk religion remains strong. But the power of other sentiments is, on account of electronics, inescapable; and, wherever the critical faculties awaken, a deeper religious maturation arises than folk religion can satisfy: the insatiable appetite for raising questions [39: chap 4, 5, 7].

The Impossibility of Simply Affirming the Modern World. Center stage among American theologians was held in 1965– 1966 by "radical theology" — by Altizer and Hamilton, by Van Buren, and (in a different way) by Cox. But radical theology appeared to be radical only in respect to the church; it did not offer a radical criticism of our society. Since no institution today appears to be so willing to receive criticism as the church, the ecclesiastical criticisms of the radical theologians were heard, reflected upon, and absorbed by scores of thousands of persons. What were the sociological underpinnings of this discussion? Peter Berger, in a penetrating analysis already cited, has articulated a presupposition common to the secular theologians: They seem to hold that traditional religious affirmations are no longer tenable, either because they do not meet certain modern philosophical or scientific criteria, or because they are contrary to a modern world view that is somehow binding on everybody [7:5]. The fascinating point about this presupposition is that it has both academic and popular variants [7:6]. It is in the air, and so widespread an ideology naturally attracts the curiosity of the sociologist. Berger wryly points out that existentialist *Angst* and alienation are "not limited to seminary professors who have read Heidegger. To a remarkable extent, these experiences seem to be shared by suburban housewives" [7].

Since social factors establish the context of intellectual work, theology and ecclesiastical practice, naturally enough, must meet the way in which the man on the street views reality. To be sure, there are significant variations within the species "man on the street," and different theologies develop for different target audiences (civil rights workers vs corporation executives) [7:7]. The remarkable feature of radical theology today, however, is that almost invariably the religious tradition is made to conform to the cognitive and normative standard of what is taken to be modern consciousness. The radical movement "thus replicates to an amazing degree, in form if not in content, Feuerbach's program of reducing theology to anthropology" [7].

It is uncritical for theologians to assume that people who use electricity and radios are in an epistemological position superior to that of the people of the New Testament. The possibility that contemporary Western men do not represent the cutting edge of human progress, and have lost important modes of awareness, must at least be considered by a consistent relativist; Peace Corps personnel working among "underdeveloped" peoples have certainly had to face it. Contemporary urban consciousness is merely an empirical datum; it is not, unless we wish it to be, a standard of cognitive validity [7:8]. From the point of view of the sociology of knowledge, all thinking is done from a standpoint, and the characteristic of a standpoint is that the social context which supports it inhibits the standpoint itself from being brought into question. It may be necessary to penetrate through the mythical structure and standpoint of the authors of the New Testament in order to bring into relief the novelty and power of their message. But it is *also* necessary to penetrate through the mythical structure and standpoint of our urban scientific and technical apparatus [7]. The radical theologians have recognized the need for a radical transformation, but their diagnosis of the symptoms and their prescription seem to be affected by the disease they would cure. Perceiving the relativity of the forms of the Christian message, they have not perceived the relativity both *of* modern consciousness and *within* modern consciousness. There is not, in fact, any one form of modern consciousness shared by all men in our century or even by all men in urban societies. In our situation "discrepant worlds coexist within the same society, contemporaneously challenging each other's cognitive and normative claims" [7:9]. No one, today, has "any monopoly in the definition of reality." Consequently, reality does not lie still, tamed and obvious, in a general social perspective that everyone shares. Religion, *like everything else*, has been plunged into a crisis of credibility. Radical theology seems to misconstrue the situation, assuming that "modern man has some intrinsically superior access to the truth" [7:10], rather than that sociocultural forces have brought about an inescapable relativism that afflicts all standpoints.

Consequently, it seems to me, the fundamental modification to be urged upon radical theology is not that it is excessively optimistic about modern consciousness, although that is a serious modification [35; 48:32–40]. Rather, theology needs to grasp "the relativity of relativity." There is nothing absolving us of effort, nothing absolute, about standing in a culture painfully aware of historical, cultural, and social relativism. That merely happens to be where we begin our inquiry. And once we allow a doubt or a question to arise in our minds, about any matter whatsoever (even about whether we can have a question), there is in fact an *eros* of the spirit that attracts us down a never ending network of inquiries. There is a drive to question; it is as powerful as any human drive, but also as vulnerable to repression. It is this drive to raise questions (not necessarily verbally) that is the ever fertile ground of genuine religion [39].

> Is man alone in reality: Yes or no? If one is certain that the answer is "Yes," then, it seems to me, one could do better things with one's time than theology. . . . But if one is *not* so certain that the religious proposition of an *other* confronting man in reality is only a gigantic illusion, then . . . in one way or another, inside or outside the traditional religious institutions, one will want to continue pursuing the question [7:16].

Man is a question-asking and a symbol-making animal. Under certain sociocultural conditions, some men are — by the standards of others — sexually inhibited; under other conditions, the sort of wonder which gives rise to religious reflection is more or less systematically repressed. We in America live in a society in which, popularly, the work ethic and, intellectually, the view that to know is to be able to predict and to control, operate as censors which block the flow of other perceptions about the self and the world. Given such censors, it is not surprising that for many people the springs of religious experience have run dry [47]. It is a merit of the hippies that they have diagnosed and rebelled against both these censors; not by accident, religious wonder has reemerged in their experience.

I would not wish to argue that there is any single, definable religious experience. Empirically, the varieties of religious experience cover an extraordinarily wide range. In the context of a highly rationalized and pragmatic culture, however, I would like to propose that the principle of openness toward new experience, toward new understanding, toward new critical judgment, and toward new effective decisions is a contemporary and sophisticated version of the religious impulse. It is religious because it is rooted in basic trust [16:69, 89, 179–180] — its supposition is that reality is not hostile and that to be open to experience, understanding, judging, and deciding is to develop, whereas to be closed to any or all of these operations is to decline. It is religious for a second reason also; viz, that the principle of openness includes the principle that there is no ultimate division between the subject and object. Subject and object are mutually constituted by the selfsame operations of experiencing, understanding, judging, deciding. In each of these operations, "the world" impinges on "the subject" and "the subject" on "the world."

In our culture, we are taught to make a sharp division between the self and the world, as if the world stood opposite us "out there" whether we noticed it or not, and as if the self were an observing consciousness trapped in a bag of skin. The cocktail party is our ritual symbol of the atomic isolation of the self, each particle left free to move whither it is attracted, each required to be mobile and to "mix." Moreover, selves are imagined to be objects whose function is to fill the needs of other objects in some social mechanism. In this perspective, there is of course no self, as Hume [19:633–636] and Skinner [49:283, 285] pointed out. For practical purposes, however, there is that damned awareness that people have of their own states of mind, and particularly (in the Anglo-Saxon utilitarian tradition) of the equilibrium of pleasure and pain that they experience. The triumph of the therapeutic [47] occurs when man imagines himself to be a kind of seismic consciousness, recording nuances of pleasure and pain, and able enough to manipulate his own mechanism to assure the preponderance of the former.

By contrast, the principle of openness does not understand man by way of the model of a machine, or through functional analysis alone, or with the supposition that the object world is separate from the subject world. It assumes that subject and the range of the subject are twin poles of one horizon and that changes either in the subject or in his environment affect the other. The principle of openness states that the more the subject exercises the above-mentioned operations, the more the world, so to speak, enters into him and he into it. The world becomes real to the subject in proportion as he experiences, understands, judges, decides; in the same proportion, the subject becomes more real (realizes himself) through extending the range of these same operations: through further experiencing, understanding, judging, deciding.

To become thematically aware of the dialogue between self and world that occurs through adherence to the principle of openness is to become aware of the unity of self and world, to overcome the alienation between self and other which afflicts unreflective Western consciousness. This thematic awareness is, I believe, deeply rooted both in Eastern and in earlier Western traditions. Alan Watts suggests that reflection upon current field theory in the physical sciences leads to a sense of harmony between the subject and his world akin to that of Eastern mysticism and that induced by drugs [52].

My point is that, contrary to the tendency of the radical theologians, the way to overcome a falsely "religious" Christianity is not by way of a "religionless" Christianity [38], but rather by way of more penetrating reflection upon human drives and human experiences in whatever modalities they occur in our time. In countless records of contemporary experience, unreflected upon, unthematized, and unpenetrated, there lie testimonials to the perennial power of the human being to marvel at his own identity, to question it, and to delight in its elusiveness. Perhaps for the generation over thirty, the sheer mechanization of American life had rendered this religious impulse sterile. But at the center of the experiences of love, community, authenticity, and autonomous courageous action there lie the superabundance, the creative élan, the mystery, of human identity: the beyond in the midst, not at the periphery but at the center.

The Inadequacy of German Categories. In the last few years American theologians have come to appreciate their mutual religious, educational, regional, and other differences in an unprecedented way. Ecumenical conversation has generated friendships and sympathies where none existed before; but it has also sharpened each participant's awareness of the limitations and inadequacies of his own point of view. In contemporary Anglo-American philosophy, the question of justification is becoming a central one: [53] How does one justify one's point of view, one's presuppositions, one's way of life? Theologians and philosophers both, then, are arriving in the same area at the same time. The task is to find a way of speaking intelligently and intersubjectively ("objectively" would be both impossible and, if possible, undesirable) of one's own intellectual commitments. I have spoken elsewhere about the concept of "intelligent subjectivity" [39].

The fundamental relativity of each personal starting place has been obscured, however, by one central debate in recent German theology. German-speaking writers have dominated theological discourse in this century; in particular, the tension between the liberalism of Rudolf Bultmann and the neoorthodoxy of Karl Barth has dominated serious Christian thinking both in Europe and in America [50]. To put the issue between Bultmann and Barth in a far too simple way, Bultmann wishes to begin from man and "build a bridge" to God, whereas Barth wishes to "begin from God" [4:217; 27:60–61, 70; 44:31]. Both thinkers try to deal with the problem of historical relativity. Both recognize that the sociocultural context of the twentieth century is not that of the sixteenth or of the first century and that, in consequence, the essential meaning of Christianity must be interpreted afresh.

The difficulty with the problem of relativity as it travels from the German setting to the American is that it becomes a different problem. The German theological tradition appears to be fond of the chasm between Barth and Bultmann; God is set over against man, and the authentic Christian gospel is contrasted with all mere "religion." In the United States, by contrast, the situation is much more fluid, and there appears to be a closer rapport between theologians and members of other faculties of the universities. The American theologian is constantly struck by the wisdom, insight, and courage of many colleagues who, far from being Christians, are atheists of possibly three or four generations' standing. All that he considers to be signs of the presence of grace often seem to be as manifest in such colleagues as they are in Christians. Moreover, even these signs themselves seem, upon reflection, to be forms of human conduct, manner or style: compassion, patience, joy, kindness, longsuffering, and the rest. Why, then, does one remain a Christian? What does it mean to be a Christian?

The context for an American theologian, in short, is less and less the context of theological schools of thought; the context is that of the whole academic community: philosophy and the humanities, the social sciences and psychology, law and business and medicine, the physical and engineering sciences. But in the United States, the wider public also becomes involved in theological discussion; theologians soon become aware of the different interpretation given the same words by whites and blacks, upper middle class and poor, resident of Westchester and resident of Lowndes, graduate of Dartmouth medical school and the woman who left school after the fifth grade. Whether one begins with Bultmann or begins with Barth, other difficulties arise which appear both more formidable and more germane to the American theological enterprise.

Professor Smart has recently studied the early careers of Bultmann and Barth; his work documents the extent to which in Germany, before World War I, Christianity was identified with the sentiments, customs, and traditions of Western culture. Christianity was perceived by the teachers of Barth and Bultmann as more or less continuous with the progress of Western culture

216

[50:25 – 56]. Both Barth and Bultmann wished, by contrast, to emphasize the category of "revelation," of the "inbreaking" or "disruptive" word of God — though, of course, it appears that Barth emphasized the discontinuity much more thoroughly.

It is true that in the United States in our decade there is also a pronounced tendency for countless Americans to identify Christianity with "the American way of life." This identification is fostered by public officials; in 1967, after a week of widespread rioting in Negro ghettoes, President Johnson called upon the nation to observe a Sunday of prayer. A Christian day was chosen, and atheists were as overlooked as if they were invisible. Such a reliance upon an easily evoked sentiment, coupled with the avoidance of secular responsibilities (the Congress had just refused to pass a rat-control act aimed at one of the terrors of ghetto living), makes the Germanic distinction between a "religionless Christianity" and "religion" a tempting one. For, according to this distinction, religion is a sentiment of evasion and smugness, whereas genuine Christianity is unsettling and unsentimental; far from being an opiate, it is an agency of responsibility for shaping the future city of man.

The trouble with this distinction is that it does not take the secular saint, the humanistic atheist, into account. The social activist, the writer, the professor, the laborer that the American theologian meets are not likely to be "religious," but neither are they always "Christians," not even of the "religionless" sort. In a perfectly good sense, in fact, without quotation marks, they may well be religious: ultimately concerned about human openness and human responsibility and moved by the vision of a city in which men are ends and never means. Thus their religion may seem wholly immanent and wholly articulable in secular, historical terms.

What fascinates the American theologian is that the particular kind of transcendence important to Judaism and to Christianity is *also* wholly immanent and wholly articulable in secular, historical terms. The relativity that interests the American theologian is that which links the heavily humanistic and trusting atheism so common in America and the theism of those who recognize that God is not to be conceived as one more object to add to the inventory of things, but rather as a kind of intelligent force or vitality *in* all things. The atheist who believes that man by his own efforts may affect the course of evolution for the better is, from the point of view of one who observes his behavior, in this belief at least very like the Christian who believes that a God whom no man sees lives in him and directs him to be cocreator of the future.

To be sure, cases may be constructed — or encountered in experience — in which the beliefs of atheist and Christian are so divergent that their behavior, too, is opposed. But increasingly one encounters a sense of wisdom and modesty on both sides, such that the profile of belief and action becomes increasingly identical. Anthony Levi, S.J., has argued that the behavior of a good Christian or a good Jew, acting as a good Christian or a good Jew ought to act, is from an empirical point of view indistinguishable from the behavior of a good secular humanist [22:7 – 30]. From personal experience, one can but concur. Thus Christian theologians are presently attempting to create a language for Christian beliefs which is, in one sense, wholly immanent. According to that sense, every word employed has at least a correlate in human experience. Meanwhile, human experience is itself envisaged as dynamic, open ended, and at least potentially melioristic. There is nothing inevitable about human progress; periods of decline occur and man's annihilation of his own world is all too possible. But man always finds it possible to develop beyond the stage he at present occupies; he can increase in knowledge, wisdom, power, and love. Such open enededness might be called man's ability ever to transcend himself; but it is easily restricted to description in secular terms.

What fascinates the Christian theologian is that he knows that the old duality of "nature" and "grace" was, in fact, an abstraction [18; 24: vol 2, 289–324, vol 3, 69–88, 375–402, 533–578; 25]. In the concrete world of actual events, no event has ever been, is, or will be (from a Christian point of view) purely "natural"; every event takes place within the field of God's presence and love. This view might just as well be stated in the

218

optimistic, secular language of American naturalism. From the point of view of the behavior to be expected from those who share such views, the meaning of the assertions that "grace is everywhere" and that "nature is all there is" will in certain contexts so overlap as to be virtually identical. Both Christian and naturalist might face evils and joys with virtually identical behavior, resting on virtually identical assumptions stated in different language. *In the American context*, then, the project of interpreting Christianity in a wholly immanent language has a pronounced plausibility; the orientation of American thought toward the future provides the lever of criticism against the present required of the traditional notion of the transcendent.

Thus American theology is free to reject the Germanic polarity between God and man, and to achieve the same effect by being certain that every reference to God has a secular experiential correlate. No one has ever seen God. No one save God speaks for God. From the point of view of the sociology of knowledge, moreover, men speak from within communities which rest upon given social infrastructures. Even the preachers of the gospel differ from one another according to their different communities or places within the communities. No man escapes from the conditions of human language, culture, social and economic conditions, temperament, and nervous system. There is no way, then, for men to hear the voice of God pure and limpid, but only by way of other men or through written texts or through the ambiguous deliverances of their own consciousness. God (if Christianity and Judaism are to be believed) speaks *through* men and *through* instruments; He does not now show Himself face to face. Consequently, there is no genuine polarity between the primacy of man and the primacy of God. Instrumentally and empirically, all that Christians and Jews have to deal with directly are human words and human deeds. While it may be true that Christians and Jews listen for *more* than the human word, *more* than the human deed, that "more" is neither easily discovered nor free from ambiguity and conflicting interpretations.

If an impartial observer studies carefully the language of those who speak of God as acting in the world, he will notice that in every case of such usage the referent for "God" is actually a human deed or an historical occurrence. To talk about "God acting in the world" is to talk about the values and the meaning which some persons attach to human actions or human situations. No one actually sees *God* acting in the world. They merely see things happening which, according to their interpretation, appear to gain in meaningfulness if viewed in the perspective of their tradition and their Scripture. Thus "divine revelation" is experienced as a living presence in the observer, a living light, whose resonance acts upon the concrete socially structured man to form his vision of life and its unfolding. By comparison with other elements in the infrastructure of his perceptual apparatus, this living presence may on occasion appear to be "shattering." But it is so because the Jew and the Christian allow themselves to be conditioned by yet one other social community: the historical, living church (people). That community with its pluralistic history offers them leverage against the biases of their present culture. When Barth wrote his revolutionary 1919 commentary on *Romans*, he gained a perspective beyond that of his immediate teachers from assiduous reading in the obscure commentaries of the four previous centuries [50:66–67].

In one sense, no man speaks *for* God. In another sense, every man does. Yet in every man there are also countless voices of chaos, of conformity, of nervous impulsion, of merely conventional wisdom. No easy theological formula teaches anyone the discernment of spirits. How, then, do we know when a man speaks for God or for the gospels or for the people of Moses and the prophets? Here too, within the church or outside it, we have come to be aware of a fundamental relativism. Each of us chooses his favorite authors, his traditions, his teachers, his leaders, his emphases, his prior values, his "style." What we now hope is that in the concert of voices there will emerge the voice of prophecy, judgment, and creativity. Yet in the middle of the battle, at the moment when it is imperative to hear the authentic and the fruitful voice, that voice is often indistinguishable in the general clamor. Looking back into history, it is at least a little easier (but not much) to discern who was speaking most fully for the gospels. The opposition of Bonhoeffer and Barth to the Nazis is a badge of honor, now, in the same Germany where once their voices were but one side of a confused argument.

Consequently, the fundamental battle rages in the hearts of each of us. To whose voices shall we attend? On which side ought we to throw our weight? Many are ready with good will and with energy, but lack light and certainty about which way to run. What one Christian sees as betrayal, another sees as the only hope of advance. Jesus was in his own day a sign of contradiction. Relativism is the rule of life, not only outside, but also inside, the church.

Twentieth century German theology, it appears, in its effort to break from the cultural religion of nineteenth century liberal theology, has tended to adopt too parochial a notion of Christianity, revelation, and the Word. It remains true, for a Christian, that salvation comes only through Jesus. But Jesus is not only the historical figure, a Jew, who lived, died, and rose again in an underdeveloped country in the first century. He is, rather, the Word who was at the beginning, through whom, by whom, and with whom were made all the things that are made. There are, then, two sources of knowledge about Jesus. One is through the tradition of that historical community which is nourished by His living presence, through the preaching of the *kerygma* and the celebration of the meal of remembrance and unity. The other is through reflection upon the dynamism of nature and history: through faithful attention to the things made in His image and progressively through the ages revealing more about Him. For not all that can be known of the Word will be known until all the things made by Him have unfolded. The Eastern church — manifestly in Berdyaev and Dostoevsky and indirectly through its influence upon Teilhard de Chardin — has kept this cosmic notion of the Christ more adequately than the Western church [17:155–156].

Consequently, the parochialism of Christianity is properly to be "shattered" by a loving and eager study of other religions, other cultures, and the whole of nature itself, in which the Word reveals Himself. To be sure, He is not there called by the name "Jesus." It is not those who cry "Lord, Lord!" who enter the kingdom of heaven, but those who do the will of the Father. Erik Erikson has pointed out that the wisdom of "the golden rule" is cross cultural [16:221]. Surely, the primacy of understanding and loving, the primacy of community, is given witness in other cultures besides Christian cultures, sometimes more effectively. In brief, attention to the Jesus of the Christian church and to the Word of that tradition can also be idolatrous; grace is operative in more places and in more ways than Christian theologians customarily map.

In this context, one must disagree with Bonhoeffer's words about Jesus. He wrote in *Letters and Papers from Prison:* "The world's coming of age is then no longer an occasion for polemics and apologetics, but it is really better understood than it understands itself, namely on the basis of the Gospel, and in the light of Christ" [10:200]. It may well be that special spiritual graces broke into history through Judaism and Christianity, and especially the graces of hope and the sense of responsibility for co-creating the future of earth. It may even be that the resurrection of Jesus gave large numbers of men a pledge that the ultimate victory over evil had already been won and that, no matter how deep the historical crisis, reasons for despair could no longer overcome reasons for hope. There is no need so to "spiritualize" and to "universalize" the church that we neglect the concrete historical reality of the resurrection and the concrete historical community whose faith is founded upon it. But even if we were to assert that God has revealed himself in a privileged and unequaled way in Jesus Christ and remains present in the church, it does not follow that the only path to recognizing that God is love, understanding, mercy, and reconciliation is through the historical Jesus and His church. It seems patent in our pluralistic experience, that these graces are lavished among all cultures and, in our own culture, among atheists as well as among Christians. The Christian is, in daily experience, often embarrassed to find others teaching him more adequately the meaning of the Word than he can teach them, though they do not call the Word by the name of Jesus.

Thus it happens that many who understand full well the *empirical* meaning of the wisdom of the Christian faith and realize it in their lives — love of God, love of neighbor, purity of heart, courage unto death — do not, nevertheless, interpret the meaning of their lives through that name which for Christians is above all names, the name of Jesus. If our preference is for what people actually *do* rather than for what propositions they hold, can we accuse such people of misunderstanding the meaning of their own lives? When one has seen the degradation committed in the name of Christian doctrines and recognized the daily distortions done to Christian stories and attitudes, one becomes sensitive to the variety of ways in which fundamental wisdom can be articulated. What do they lack, these atheists who love their neighbor and all the rest, to distinguish them from being Christians, except that they do not preach in pulpits? One is not going to insist upon pronouncing the correct words, or standing in the proper ranks — not at least, while a hundred million human beings have been violently killed in a century that is not at an end.

Thus Bonhoeffer, I believe, insisted too much upon the need which other men might have for Jesus and the church. With him, one may assert that the church is a concrete, historical community of power and grace, for whose continued efficacy it is worth laboring. More extensively than he, one might also see many other communities not only of power and grace, but also of revelation, accurate interpretation, and illuminating symbols of the one same Word. It will be the task of prophetic spirits in all the world religions, in the common noösphere we are already coming to share, to bring together all the wisdom about man and God that they are faithful to. The dangers of an easy syncretism will be as acute as ever. But Christians, in particular, may look to the wisdom of other peoples for further light on that *Logos* whose traces they track throughout the universe. Wisdom grows in concrete traditions, where it has been watered with the blood

223

of a thousand witnesses and has brought reconciliation to ten thousand cries of anguish in ten thousand nights. It is as mistaken to abandon these concrete traditions as to stand within one of them arrogantly, unwilling to enrich one's own by learning from another.

The Christian missionary enterprise has too often consisted not of the gentle telling of parables, which learned as much from the wisdom already proper to the people as it taught dialogically, but of the preachment of an alien and one-sided monologue. Teaching the death and resurrection of Jesus is scandal and stumbling block enough, without arrogance being added to the style of the *kerygma*. When the preacher is willing to die to his own feelings of superiority in order to enter into dialogue, then, perhaps, he can commend the death and resurrection of Jesus Christ as a penetrating illumination of how God manifests himself among men. In dialogue, one can and must remain faithful to oneself. Where such fidelity is open to the Word who speaks everywhere, one need not be afraid to learn from others the many things that are lacking in oneself.

THE IMPORTANCE OF STYLE

Younger theologians in the United States living, of necessity, both inside and outside the social conditioning of their churches, have come to recognize that there is no overarching myth, language, or set of symbols by which one can speak to all of men's many communities. Seminary theology, even ecumenical theology, is insufficient. Since one cannot go by the route of abstraction and the universal, theologians are tentatively seeking a way through the concrete and the autobiographical. In this sense, there is a reemergence of analogical thought. Your life is not like mine, and the social conditioning that shaped me did not shape you. Yet if I can describe how I deal with my social conditioning and how I perceive you, then perhaps we can communicate. The *content* of our experience may be different, but many of the concrete *relationships* between me and my communities are *similar* to those between you and yours. "We have our problems, too," Methodists may nod who attended the Vatican Council. Neither atheists nor theists are vainglorious about their ability to make sense out of the times in which we live.

As existence is to essence, so is style to role [41]. As soon as we give up role playing and attempt to be honest each with himself, the concrete texture that separates one human person from another begins to become paramount. No longer is a man to be labeled "Catholic," "Atheist," "Unitarian," "Buddhist," or "Jew"; no longer is a man only a role. We each live in several communities with different companions in each. Consequently, the possibilities of self-definition are significantly enhanced. "Theologian *x* is married to a stunning wife; they like night clubs; he is fascinated by auto racing; he devours Nietzsche; he went to school with *y*, the famous linguistic analyst, near whom he spends his summers. . . ." Amid the vast possibilities open to theology today, amid the innumerable methods, starting places, and libraries of books, such autobiographical facts as these illuminate why a man does as he does, and how he is to be understood. One would not wish to say that all theology is autobiography. But one could say that in a world so socially complex as ours a man who would speak to other men cannot stand within one social community only; since there is not even a circle of communities which would furnish a *lingua franca* accessible to all, reference to the self becomes the base of a communicable analogy. Thus Sartre, Camus, and many others of the most successful communicators of our time have written often in the first person. Even when a writer employs an impersonal method, the attentive reader listens for the personal voice in order to learn how to interpret the words. Let me say, guardedly: the person is the message.

But what is the human person? In the last chapter of *Life Against Death*, Norman O. Brown quotes Thoreau: "We need pray for no higher heaven than the pure senses can furnish, a purely sensuous life. Our present senses are but rudiments of what they are destined to become" [11:308]. Brown adds: "The human body would become polymorphously perverse, delighting in that full life of the body which it now fears." Brown interprets history as the process of abolishing repression and points out that for both psychoanalysis and Christian theology "the resurrected body is the transfigured body" [11]. Psychoanalysis is the heir to a mystical tradition [11:310]. With Whitehead, history protests against the spirit of abstraction and calls for "a science based on an erotic sense of reality, rather than an aggressive dominating attitude toward reality" [11:316]. For at present [Brown citing Bachelard] it is "of the essence of the scientific spirit to be mercilessly ascetic, to eliminate human enjoyment from our relation to nature, to eliminate the human senses, and finally to eliminate the human brain" [11]. Moreover, the resurrection of the body is not merely a personal matter; it is "a social project facing mankind as a whole, and it will become a practical political problem when statesmen of the world are called upon to deliver happiness instead of power, when political economy becomes . . . a science of enjoyment instead of a science of accumulation" [11:317–318].

Which side is Christianity on, that of the concrete human being with his concrete body or that of asceticism and competitive striving that depend upon repression? The Protestant image of Catholicism is that Catholicism is both too ascetical and otherworldly [11:309], and also sunk in the fleshpots of corruption. The Catholic perceives the Protestant as underdeveloped in his capacity for sensuality and the delights of the flesh; as preoccupied with the asceticism of historical responsibility, rather than able, like Camus' Mediterranean man, to delight in the enjoyment of nature [38]. The Catholic, in this respect, feels much closer to the frank this-worldliness of the Jew. From both Catholic and Protestant theologians, Brown's challenge requires response:

> The time has come to ask Christian theologians, especially the neoorthodox, what they mean by the resurrection of the body and by eternal life. Is this a promise of immortality after death? In other words, is the psychological premise of Christianity the impossibility of reconciling life and death either in "this" world or the "next," so that flight from death — with all its morbid consequences — is our eternal fate in "this world"

and in "the next"? For we have seen that the perfect body, promised by Christian theology, enjoying that perfect felicity promised by Christian theology, is a body reconciled with death [11:308–309].

The younger theologians seem to be aware of living in a new era, in which most of the rules have been changed and whose horizons have suddenly been expanded by a factor as yet undetermined. With other men, although standing within and benefiting by received traditions of discourse, theologians are trying to understand under new and quite complicated conditions what is involved in being a man. Such a concern is an ultimate concern and, predictably, man is such a mystery to himself that many wonder whether, and how, man participates in an understanding and loving beyond his own. A younger generation unsatisfied by the achievements of pragmatism, scientific method, and technology, and coming to new perceptions of its own, is in an unexpected way concerned about the mystery of man.

Feuerbach proposed that theology is reducible to anthropology. It seems, by contrast, that concern about man, under conditions of affluence, reawakens man's sense of his own inexhaustibility. Affluence permits enjoyment and enjoyment leads man to feel at one with nature.

> I am content to live it all again
> And yet again, if it be life to pitch
> Into the frog-spawn of a blind man's ditch,
> A blind man battering blind men; . . .
>
> I am content to follow to its source
> Every event in action or in thought;
> Measure the lot; forgive myself the lot!
> When such as I cast out remorse
> So great a sweetness flows into the breast
> We must laugh and we must sing,
> We are blest by everything,
> Everything we look upon is blest [54:232].

Both autonomy and joy in the body stir the embers of theology. And the experience of human community comes to many as such an unexpected gift that the language of theonomy spontaneously reappears. Christians whose Christ pointed so resolutely to a communal bond between men as the empirical sign of God's presence should not be surprised if, as history unfolds, many other markers point in that same direction.

REFERENCES

1. Amery, Carl: *Capitulation: The Lesson of German Catholicism* (Herder and Herder, New York, New York) 1967.
2. Baldwin, James: *The Fire Next Time* (The Dial Press, New York, New York) 1963.
3. Baltzell, E Digby: *The Protestant Establishment* (Random House, New York, New York) 1964.
4. Barth-Thurneysen correspondence, 1914–1925, *Revolutionary Theology in the Making,* translated by Smart (John Knox Press, Richmond, Virginia) 1964. Quoted in Smart [50:60–61].
5. The Beatles: *She's Leaving Home* (Columbia Records) 1967.
6. Bell, Daniel: *The End of Ideology* (The Free Press, New York, New York) 1960.
7. Berger, Peter L: A Sociological View of the Secularization of Theology, *Journal for the Scientific Study of Religion,* vol 6, no 1, Spring 1967.
8. Berger, Peter L, and Luckmann, Thomas: *The Social Construction of Reality: A Treatise in the Sociology of Knowledge* (Doubleday, Garden City, New York) 1966.
9. Bonhoeffer, Dietrich: *The Way to Freedom* (Harper & Row, Publishers, New York, New York) 1967.
10. Bonhoeffer, Dietrich: *Letters and Papers from Prison* (The Macmillan Company, New York, New York) 1962.
11. Brown, Norman O: *Life Against Death* (Random House, New York, New York) 1959.
12. Brown, Norman O: *Love's Body* (Random House, New York, New York) 1966.
13. Burlage, Robb: *The South as an Underdeveloped Country.* Pamphlet. Cited by Newfield. See reference 37.
14. Chardin, Teilhard de: *The Phenomenon of Man* (William

Collins Sons & Co. Ltd, London, England) 1959, rev ed 1965.

15. Draper, Hal: *Berkeley: The New Student Revolt* (Grove Press, New York, New York) 1965.
16. Erikson, Erik: *Insight and Responsibility* (W. W. Norton, New York, New York) 1964.
17. Evdokimov, Paul: *The Struggle with God* (Paulist Press, Glen Rock, New Jersey) 1966.
18. Fuchs, Josef: *Natural Law: A Theological Inquiry* (Sheed and Ward, New York, New York) 1965.
19. Hume, David: Appendix in *A Treatise on Human Nature*, Selby-Bigge, ed (Oxford University Press, London, England) 1960.
20. Kerr, Clark: Quoted by Newfield, reference 37.
21. Lehmann, Paul: *Ethics in a Christian Context* (Harper & Row, Publishers, New York, New York) 1963.
22. Levi, Anthony: *Religion in Practice* (Harper & Row, Publishers, New York, New York) 1966.
23. Lipset, Seymour Martin, and Wolin, Sheldon S, ed: *The Berkeley Student Revolt: Facts and Interpretations* (Anchor Books, Doubleday and Company, Garden City, New York) 1965.
24. Lonergan, Bernard: St. Thomas' Thought on Gratia Operans, *Theological Studies*, vol 2, 1941, vol 3, 1942.
25. Lottin, Dom O: *Au Coeur de la Morale Chrétienne* (Desclée, Belgium) 1957.
26. Luckmann, Thomas: The Anthropological Condition of Religion, *The Invisible Religion* (The Macmillan Company, New York, New York) 1967.
27. McLuhan, Marshall: *Understanding Media: The Extensions of Man* (McGraw-Hill Book Company, Inc, New York, New York) 1964.
28. Mailer, Norman: *Advertisements for Myself* (The New American Library, Signet, New York, New York) 1959.
29. Mailer, Norman: *Cannibals and Christians* (The Dial Press, New York, New York) 1966, especially pp 1–45.
30. Malcolm X: *The Autobiography of Malcolm X* (Grove Press, New York, New York) 1964.
31. Marcuse, Herbert: *Eros and Civilization* (Beacon Press,

Boston, Massachusetts) 1955 (Reprinted by Random House, New York, New York).

32. Marcuse, Herbert: *One Dimensional Man*, Parts I and II (Beacon Press, Boston, Massachusetts) 1964.

33. Maynard, Fredelle B: The Minds of High School Seniors, *The New Republic*, vol 156, no 20, May 20, 1967.

34. Miller, Michael V, and Gilmore, Susan, ed: *Revolution at Berkeley* (Dell Publishing Co, Inc, New York, New York) 1965.

35. Murchland, Bernard, ed: *The Meaning of the Death of God* (Random House, New York, New York) 1967. See essays by John Warwick Montgomery, Robert Adolfs, O.S.A., and Eugene B. Borowitz.

36. Newfield, Jack: One Cheer for the Hippies, *The Nation*, vol 204, no 26, June 26, 1967.

37. Newfield, Jack: *A Prophetic Minority* (New American Library, Signet, New York, New York) 1967.

38. Novak, Michael: The Beauty of Earth, to be published in *Proceedings of the American Catholic Philosophical Society*, 1967.

39. Novak, Michael: *Belief and Unbelief* (The Macmillan Company, New York, New York) 1965.

40. Novak, Michael: Christianity: Renewed or Slowly Abandoned? in *A Time to Build* (The Macmillan Company, New York, New York) 1967.

41. Novak, Michael: Reflections on Style, *Una Sancta*, vol 24, No 2, Pentecost 1967.

42. Novak, Michael: The Secular Saint, *Journal of Illinois State University* (Normal, Illinois) 1967.

43. O'Dea, Thomas: *The Sociology of Religion* (Prentice-Hall, Inc, Englewood Cliffs, New Jersey) 1966.

44. Ogden, Schubert M: *Existence and Faith: Shorter Writings of Rudolf Bultmann* (Meridian Books, New York, New York) 1960. Quoted in [50:70].

45. Pauck, Wilhelm: Theology in the Life of Contemporary American Protestantism, in Leibrecht, Walter, ed, *Religion and Culture: Essays in Honor of Paul Tillich* (New York, New York) 1959.

46. Richardson, Herbert W: The Nature of Unbelief, *Continuum*, vol 5, Spring 1967.

47. Rieff, Philip: *Triumph of the Therapeutic* (Harper & Row, Publishers, New York, New York) 1966.

48. Rubenstein, Richard L: Thomas Altizer's Apocalypse in Beardslee, William A, ed, *America and the Future of Theology* (Westminster Press, Philadelphia, Pennsylvania) 1967.

49. Skinner, B F: *Science and Human Behavior* (The Macmillan Company, New York, New York) 1960.

50. Smart, James D: *The Divided Mind of Modern Theology: Karl Barth and Rudolf Bultmann, 1908–1933* (The Westminster Press, Philadelphia, Pennsylvania) 1967.

51. Smart, James D, translator: *Revolutionary Theology in the Making* (Barth–Thurneysen correspondence, 1914–1925) (John Knox Press, Richmond, Virginia) 1964.

52. Watts, Alan: *Joyous Cosmology: Adventures in the Chemistry of Consciousness* (Random House, New York, New York) 1962.

53. White, Morton: *Toward Reunion in Philosophy* (Harvard University Press, Cambridge, Massachusetts) 1956.

54. Yeats, William Butler: A Dialogue of Self and Soul, *The Collected Poems of W.B. Yeats* (The Macmillan Company, New York, New York) 1956.

55. Yinger, J Milton: *Religion, Society and the Individual* (The Macmillan Company, New York, New York) 1957.

COMMENTARY

by Harvey G. Cox

MICHAEL NOVAK'S essay puts with singular clarity the mood of the younger theologians in 1968. Already the Death of God Movement seems to be deceased. The songs of secularization have been sung, but now found a little too familiar. Books on the renewal of the church have begun to elicit more yawns than huzzas. In general there is a mood of disquietude and dissatisfaction, but it is also tinged with openness and promise. It is this mood that Novak so correctly describes and so effectively incarnates in his essay.

There are one or two places where I might take a small exception to Novak's thinking. The first concerns his section on the inadequacy of German categories. While it should serve as a welcome warning to us not to rely as much as we have in the past on the latest word from Marburg or Tübingen, it does not take into adequate consideration the freshest currents in Germany. German theology cannot be reduced to the heritages of Karl Barth and Rudolf Bultmann. In fact the most significant development of interest in recent German theology is precisely the departure of the younger theologians from this rich and ambiguous but ultimately limiting tradition. I have been greatly impressed, for example, with the work of Jurgen Moltmann, Johannes Metz, and Wolfhart Pannenberg.

Moltmann, whose book *A Theology of Hope* appeared in American translation in the Fall of 1967, seems himself to have left behind the very German categories that Novak criticizes. He discards both the "transcendental subjectivity of God," which he identifies with Karl Barth, and the "transcendental subjectivity of man," which he rightly associates with the work of Bultmann. Moltmann correctly senses the fact that in both of these positions we are left with God and man but with very little that could properly be called "world." Moltmann knows that we need a theology of the world, of the corporate structures of human life and consciousness, and he believes this sort of theology can be worked out only through a conscious departure from the positions of Barth and Bultmann. Along with Metz and Pannenberg, Moltmann believes that a theology of the future, one based on a radical reappropriation of Christian eschatology, is now desperately needed.

This recent discovery of eschatology points the direction for an answer to Novak's criticism of the so-called "radical theology" in recent American religious thought. Novak contends that one of the principal weaknesses of the radical theology was that, although it was highly critical of the church, it proposed no really significant critique of the society. Incidentally I would not accept Novak's criticism fully as far as my own work is concerned. *The Secular City* is devoted more to a theological critique of the society than to a critique of the church. It includes criticisms of the American antiurban bias, the "religion of work" in American middleclass society, and the traditional sexual conventions of American culture. Still the problem of any theology of secular culture is that it needs some point of critical distance, some perspective from which to evaluate the culture on which it is commenting. For me, this perspective can no longer be provided by a supernatural God. Here Novak would seem to agree since he really no longer accepts the traditional distinction between natural and supernatural. Where then does this sort of criticism, renewal, and evaluation come from for the theologian of the secular era?

It is precisely here that the new emphasis on eschatology, the study of the Christian hope for the future and its base in reality, becomes so highly relevant. If Christian faith is in fact an affirmation of what we hope God has done and will do, in cooperation with man, to renew the world, then the future becomes preeminently important in theological thought. What is the future anyway? Is it merely a vacuum into which the hopes and fears of man are projected? Is it a predetermined fate about which we can do very little? Or are we to understand the future as the very source and ground of human creativity and imagination, that which makes it possible for man to engage in fantasy, to dream, and to take responsibility for the realization of his hopes?

Interestingly enough this discussion about the character of the future has also come to the fore in recent dialogue between Christians and Marxists. After preliminary talk about less significant issues, Christians and Marxists generally come to the nub of that which seems to separate them. The question is whether man's aspirations for a future of peace and justice are simply wishful thinking or whether they are elicited by and sustained by a reality beyond even the sum total of all of man's hopes. Among some young Marxists there has even emerged the recognition that there must be some basis in material reality for man's seemingly indefatigable capacity to hope and to strive. This insight led a young Marxist thinker from Prague to write recently an essay entitled "God Is Not Completely Dead."

Novak is certainly correct in seeing the broad human community and not just the seminary or the church as the proper setting for theology. Sometimes, however, I think he expects a little too much from the academic community as such. We have learned in recent years that all creativity does not necessarily come from the halls of academe. Still he is right that theology must proceed within the broadest possible cultural setting. We as theologians are learning to innovate new images and symbols and to attack problems which have not come to us from the tradition of theological study but from the world around us. I personally believe that it is precisely this new way of asking questions which will keep theology alive and interesting in the period ahead. More and more we as theologians occupy ourselves not with the refinements of traditional dogmas but with issues posed for us by the world. This does not mean that we ignore the theological tradition. It means rather that we utilize this tradition to illuminate present concerns and to uncover new possibilities.

Novak describes a new and welcome openness in theology. His essay suggests that the future of theological work will find its place in the common effort of all the disciplines to answer the question of how man will remain alive and free and human in the days and years ahead. This in turn suggests that the future that God makes possible for man is in fact the appropriate object of theological inquiry.

COMMENTARY

by Daniel Callahan

SINCE I THINK it true, as Mr. Novak contends, that autobiography has a significant place in theology, let me begin with a personal note. Michael Novak and I have been close friends for some years; we have spent countless hours talking about the problems he discusses in his essay. Along the way, he has influenced me to a considerable degree, and maybe I have also influenced him. Our relationship has been rich and creative because we share some common inclinations and interests, but also because we have some significant temperamental divergences. What we share, in distinction from many other "younger" theologians, is a strongly philosophical bias and a predilection for doing theology by way of cultural analysis. You won't find many scriptural references in our writings, little mention of kerygma and salvation-history, and practically nothing about liturgy and the sacraments. All of this is a real bond, especially in a Catholicism that follows the Vatican II Council, that is caught up in an enthusiastic rediscovery of Scripture, history, and the liturgy and that, therefore, does not speak very strongly to our interests and concerns.

Where we persistently differ, it seems to me, is emotionally and temperamentally. He is inclined (to use William James' terms) to be tender minded, and I am inclined to be tough minded. He is often enthusiastic where I am wary, embracing where I am cool, aroused where I am skeptical, affirming where I am questioning.

Now I won't dare to suggest that anyone should be interested in these emotional differences so far as they concern Michael Novak and myself. But I think there is a wider issue at stake in the tough-minded/tender-minded distinction which I see constantly at work in our relationship. It is the issue of what, in the first place, one should be looking for in theological analysis and speculation and what one's criteria should be for knowing if one has found it. The tender minded, it strikes me, see more hopeful signs than the tough minded; they look for hints of a new future and usually manage to find them. The tender minded are prone to find hints of religious insight and redemption in the most resolutely areligious or antireligious writings and movements. They seem to have a keen nose for religious impulses and stirrings, a nose lacking in the tough minded, who are more prone to see and emphasize the overtly unreligious themes. The tender minded seem more easily able to entertain utopian visions, to get·caught up in fresh enthusiasms, to see everything working together for good. The tough minded are more prone to entertain the pessimistic possibilities of life.

My intention here — a very resolute intention — is not to suggest in any way that the tough-minded (usually my way) is superior to the tender-minded way. I am convinced, against my own nature, that the latter is the superior way; it's just that I can't manage it very often. But I think it is at least a way which has to be taken account of when one is speaking of contemporary theology, for many disputes come down to a conflict of the tough minded versus the tender minded; and these disputes have comparatively little to do with the categories of conservative-liberal or reactionary-progressive. Rather, it is a division within the camp of the younger theologians, most of whom would qualify as "liberals" or "progressives" by most standards.

I would like to illustrate this division by providing a brief tough-minded critique of Mr. Novak's essay.

First, I would have one observe the hopeful note on which Mr. Novak ends his essay: "man's sense of his own exhaustibility" has been reawakened, and this reawakening is embodied in a "younger generation." Happily for the Christian, Mr. Novak implies, we can expect that what is happening in this younger generation will point in the same direction as that of the Christian impulse. I wouldn't say that: how do we know that this younger generation will not end by showing the Christian that what he has taken as "the empirical sign of God's presence" — a "communal bond between man" — has been a sign without a referent and that the communal bond carries its own legitimacy and value and points to nothing but itself? Mr. Novak, in a word, sees the younger generation as recalling Christians to some of their own basic values and hence as a salutary contemporary development. My tough-minded response is that this younger generation — which I admire almost as fervently as Mr. Novak does — may teach the Christian just how mistaken and credulous he has been. Where Mr. Novak sees a confluence of basic Christian values and the values of the younger generation, I am prone to be more skeptical. We may, in the end, see a very radical divergence and I want, for my part, to wait a bit and see.

Second, I would have the reader observe the extent to which Mr. Novak's essay is permeated by many of the elements of folk religion (which, in others, he deplores). Thus, while he speaks of the "scandal" of "the death and resurrection of Jesus," he is, oddly enough, willing to commend that part of the American experience which demands that "each view must prove itself under the critical eye of others" and, more broadly, the "lived relativism" provided by life in American society. But I would want to say that it is just this public demand that "each view must prove itself under the critical eye of others" which must be resisted and, along with it, the "lived relativism." For it should be clear enough that those who accept the scandal of Christ's death and resurrection cannot prove their view to the critical eye of others; there would be no scandal if they could. And it should be equally clear that the "lived relativism" that Mr. Novak commends poses a serious challenge to that Christianity which stakes its belief on the possibility of a divine revelation which does break through man's relativistic status.

Why do I call Mr. Novak's failure to see this an indication of folk religion? Precisely because he allows "local customs and national inheritance" to determine his own viewpoint to a far greater extent than he seems to realize. For what is more resolutely local and American than the contention that all views have to pass public inspection and that everything is relative, including relativism? Mr. Novak deplores that tendency in folk religion to "accept in the name of faith present cultural movements," yet is ecstatic about the hippies and the new student left — a present cultural movement if ever there was one. A tough-minded person will have trouble at this point with Mr. Novak's argument or, more accurately, with his enthusiasms and affirmations.

Third, Mr. Novak's "principle of openness" seems to me a most dubious "version of the religious impulse." Briefly put, I take the religious impulse to be twofold: it is the quest for meaning and the quest for human community. The "principle of openness" would be an essential principle to espouse (better, to live) as one engaged in this dual quest. But there must come a point, as the price of maturity, where one makes some decisive choices, where one chooses between experiences and between critical principles of judgment. One can't be infinitely open to everything; the hardest choices of life are those in which one chooses to close off possible avenues of experience and development. For it is at this point that one runs the risk of error, of spiritual impoverishment, of living with one's finiteness – the risk of being human. "The principle of openness" is too easy, too flexible, too escapist – and, I would add, too "sophisticated." The same objection applies to Mr. Novak's "drive to question." I don't doubt the existence of such a drive but would want it complemented by the drive to find and live with answers, even if – and especially if – this latter drive required us to cease asking questions and to make permanently restrictive decisions.

Here the tough minded and the tender minded meet in a head-on crash. The tender minded see reality as promising ever and ever greater meaning and experience: infinity and transcendence are open to people if only they will be open. My tough-minded response is to say that openness guarantees nothing, that asking questions guarantees nothing – perhaps one can grow by being closed and knowing when not to ask questions. It is the enthusiast, the romantic, the visionary versus the skeptical, the pessimistic, and the nonvisionary. There is no resolution of conflicts like that.

Fourth, I would point out that a number of the people whom Mr. Novak quotes favorably hold positions which, in the end, fly in the face of his central theses. Peter Berger's article "A Sociological View of the Secularization of Theology," while sharply criticizing the disposition of radical theologians to make the modern consciousness normative (the point seized upon by Mr. Novak), is equally critical of the "deobjectivation" which he sees at work in contemporary theology. Mr. Novak's affirmation of relativism, and especially the relativism of relativism, is, I think, a prime example of what Prof. Berger was criticizing. Similarly, Berger's argument that the "essence of religion has been the confrontation with an *other*, believed to exist as a reality in the universe external to and vastly different from man . . ." — the note on which he concludes his article — directly challenges Mr. Novak's religious principle "that there is no ultimate division between the subject and object." Likewise, Mr. Novak's admiration for Norman O. Brown fails to take account of Brown's espousal of a total dissolution of the ego, an espousal which frontally assaults man's drive to ask questions by interpreting this drive as neurotic and evasive of the "polymorphously perverse." Again, I would interpret Philip Rieff's "triumph of the therapeutic" as a critique of those still enamored with the search for meaning and hope; and the "openness" which Mr. Novak espouses sounds suspiciously like the stance of psychological man, a man ever open to experience but closed to binding commitments.

What I, playing the tough-minded role, notice about the writers mentioned is how fundamentally they call into question the basic religious presuppositions of Mr. Novak's essay; what he, more tender-minded, sees is their contribution to a richer conception of religion. Put another way, what Mr. Novak sees in many contemporary movements and writers is progress toward a more encompassing, less closed view of religion. What I see, by contrast, is a rising pressure to make a fundamental choice for or against religion. For Mr. Novak the "religious impulse" retains its validity and human worth as long as people remain open and continue asking questions; that is what religion is for him. My tough-minded self says this is just not enough to constitute religion; if nothing else, it makes the human concern with religion identical with philosophical concerns.

So much, then, for my "tough-minded" criticisms. I want to insist, however, that it would be a mistake to take these criticisms as telling against Mr. Novak's article. The point is not so much that he is wrong in the line he has taken but only to point out that it is a line which springs from an essentially tender-minded stance toward man, religion, and reality. Within that framework, his article is convincing and appealing. But one gets very different results when one looks at the same data from a tough-minded stance. Some human beings find it natural to soar in great sweeping arcs, taking in the beauty and possibilities of life; others find it more natural to crawl along, no doubt missing much but also seeing some things too small and unattractive for the eye of the visionary. That is a major difference between Michael Novak and myself, and it is a difference which cuts through the center of contemporary theology. William Hamilton has discerned a "new optimism." I discern a "new pessimism." And so it goes.

COMMENTARY

by Thomas J. J. Altizer

MICHAEL NOVAK's challenging essay offers a programmatic analysis of a good deal of the terrain now being entered by American theological thinking. Its optimistic spirit, however, is not shared by all American theologians, if only because many of us lack his confidence in the secular university and the contemporary human community. Indeed, few theologians today would attempt to speak theologically to such a wide spectrum of human problems. While one can only admire the boldness of Novak's goal, it is nonetheless essential to question the legitimacy of his program for contemporary American theology and to do so with the determination that genuine theology must cease to be an ideological instrument for the ruling forces of our society.

Let us agree that theologians are now striving to initiate both a radical celebration and a radical criticism of contemporary life. We do so not with the illusion that we are therein embarking upon a new theological goal but rather with the conviction that history itself is passing through such a revolutionary transformation that theology can only fulfill its intrinsic purpose by undergoing what must appear to us to be a total metamorphosis. Our first task must be to face the broader dimensions of our dilemma. We must acknowledge that our inherited theological language

240

has been placed in question, and it is precisely when we speak most easily in terms of that language that we speak most falsely and perversely. The theologian, like the artist before him, is learning that our most exalted words are no longer speakable, except by those who speak the language of coercion, domination, or repression. We are not simply embarrassed when we hear such words as "love," "justice," "community," and "person": we are outraged, for these words have not simply become emptied of their former meaning, they have become filled with the reality of our contemporary darkness.

A simple example will illustrate this point. The conceptual discipline of ethics as we once knew it has virtually ceased to exist. Words such as "good" and "evil" have become empty of conceptual meaning not because of any deficiency in the words themselves but rather because their historical ground and origin have been eroded with the result that they no longer possess for us a fundamental meaning and can easily pass into the semantics of our languages of alienation and repression. Every theologian knows that it is the most demonic forces in contemporary Christianity which speak most readily of "good" and "evil," just as the only ethical systems which are still alive in Christianity are those which are the residues or the consequences of a reactionary and life-negating human or subhuman choice. Children may still speak of "good" and "evil," or of "love" and "brotherhood," as witness the hippies, but for adults to utter such words is to give fair warning of vacuity or danger, as the case may be.

Theologians bear a peculiar responsibility inasmuch as they are the product of a tradition which has so largely given itself to worldly power that the ruling voices of society almost spontaneously employ the language of theology in their efforts to sanction a given state of affairs. True, the language of domination employs an outdated theological language, but it is theological nevertheless, and its purpose is to sanction or to make holy a given structure of power. Once words pass out of disciplined and coherent theological discourse, and, in my opinion, this has happened to such words as "love" and "person," they are then vacuous enough to become primary words in the language of domination, and such meaning as they have becomes if anything the opposite of their original meaning. Most of us have learned how to respond when we hear the phrase, "Come, let us reason together," and we are learning to have a similar response when enjoined to "love our neighbor." Our task as theologians is to strive to discover a language which cannot be spoken by the forces of domination.

Here, an easy pragmatic test might be: a theological word or phrase is illegitimate if it can successfully be employed in a political speech, an advertisement, a television serial, or in any institutional statement whatsoever. If only on the basis of this test, many of us have decided that "God" must be dead, or our faith is in vain. How fortunate the Jew that his very tabu upon pronouncing the name of "God" has spared him the destiny of living through the disintegration and reversal of everything which faith once knew as "God." As the plates of Blake's *Jerusalem* ever again remind us, we become what we behold, and no less do we become what we speak. To speak the name of God or the promise of God or hope in God at a time when God at best can be known and envisioned only as the totally Other, or most easily and immediately as an alien and oppressive Other, is to sanction the alien otherness of our time and our world with the sacrality of the divine name, and thereby to give witness to the compelling reality of God's epiphany to us and for us as Satan. "God is love" may be appropriate language for the S.S. at Auschwitz, but for the Christian it can be at best little more than a nostalgic memory of a former faith or at worst the most demonic form of blasphemy.

It is my conviction that the contemporary theologian is most dangerous when he attempts to maintain that the ancient and traditional form of faith can be spoken in our situation or, for that matter, that it has even a latent or potential meaning which can bring life to our world. Nothing delights the enemy of faith so much as the idea that faith is ever the same, yesterday, today, and forever, with the obvious corollary that faith is hopelessly archaic and irrelevant today. The theologian enhances the charge of irrelevance when he identifies faith with its ancient form or even presumes that we can know an ancient faith in a living form. Moreover, I am persuaded that, at whatever point we employ a traditional theological form or language, we are therein engaged in the process of annulling the contemporary reality of faith, thereby not simply diluting but also assaulting a faith which can and does speak in our time. Therefore I must dissociate myself from Novak's God language, although recognizing that it has a Catholic ground, a ground which I shall certainly never fully understand, intriguing as his apparent suggestion is that ultimately theological language is identical with anthropological language, a thesis which is certainly not atheistic in the common sense and may well prefigure the coming form of Catholic theology.

COMMENTARY

by David Little

THERE is a popular image abroad that the theological thinking to be found in seminaries and divinity schools is primarily governed by what is traditional and established, while the theological thinking that goes on in secular contexts is new, fresh, and creative. Professor Novak reenforces this image: he claims that "the center of gravity in American theology is shifting from the ecclesiastical seminary to the secular university . . . [and that the] theologian in the secular university is not so much carrying on the tradition of his ecclesiastical community, as, under new conditions, . . . transforming [it]" (page 200).

Above all, as this statement implies, it is assumed that seminary theologians are part of an established pattern of thought and life that prevents, or at least greatly impedes, appreciation of the root-and-branch transformation taking place all around. "Possibly the greatest factor in the opening of theology . . . is the dissolution of the modern form of Western culture. A world is collapsing around us, and a new one is being born" (page 202).

"The younger [nonseminary] theologians seem to be aware of living in a new era, in which most of the rules have been changed . . ." (page 227).

Now even one whose mental and spiritual faculties have been benumbed by several years' association with a divinity school can, with supreme effort, recognize that what Novak is saying must be taken seriously. As with many aged and decrepit people, the seminary professor sometimes startles you with his bursts of awareness. Novak has identified some serious problems for church theologians, and these problems must not be minimized. It is clear that some kind of changes are indeed taking place in the forms of thought and behavior that characterize life in this decade. A mood has descended over important segments of Americans (in universities and elsewhere) which seeks immediacy of experience, as well as immediacy of social and political accomplishment. Theologians, and others, ignore these alterations in mood and outlook at their peril.

Furthermore, it is a fact that, as Novak implies, the church — and with it the seminary — is like other institutions in that it settles down into ways of thinking and doing that become their own reason for being. Simple recognition of this commonplace is, of course, not enough. Institutions must often be shocked into cognition by the threat of events; and it is by no means certain that the present forms of church life, like the forms of political life, can cope with the threat of events that confronts us today.

Nevertheless, to identify the problems is one thing. To interpret them accurately and "solve" them is quite another. I will admit that the cast of mind cultivated by living in or near "the establishment" has not fitted us very well for coping with the new moods and directions. Still, I suggest, this cast of mind has fitted us for raising pertinent questions about some of the "new" and "fresh" interpretations of the contemporary world offered by people like Professor Novak.

To qualify as "new," "fresh," and "creative," a proposal, such as Novak's, ought to suggest options and solutions that depart in some serious way from the established patterns of thought and action. The proposal ought to prove its own radicality. At least in this essay, Novak's proposals do not, in my judgment, pass this test. His suggestions about embracing the "relativity" of religious belief and openness to truth "among all cultures" (page 222) immediately called to my mind similar recommendations made by professors and students at a very churchly college way back, of all things, in the "silent 50s." People in those days would have been quite happy talking about "the common noösphere" (page 223) that all the world religions are beginning to share. Like Novak, they loved to dwell upon the fact that "attention to the Jesus of the Christian Church and to the Word of that tradition can also be idolatrous . . ." (page 222), and they emphasized that all creeds have something to contribute to one another.

Of course, the desire to diminish the exclusivism and arrogance of Christianity in favor of appreciative encounter goes back a good deal further than the 50s. It is part of the whole liberal religious tradition. For example, one prominent figure who began recommending in the early 20th century a "new relativism" in theology was Ernst Troeltsch. "[Troeltsch] contends that the [established Christian church] alone retains . . . the conception of Truth as essentially *monomorphous*. Against this he holds that while God, indeed, is one, and all Truth, as it is in Him, is but one, that Truth as apprehended, or even as apprehensible, by man varies indefinitely from race to race and from age to age, and does so in *quality* no less than in quantity" [1:20–21].

If I understand Novak, Troeltsch's general position is very much the same as Novak's. On the other hand, it is difficult to tell specifically just how far Novak wishes to identify himself with the liberal tradition, since he is so caught up *in announcing* the brandnewness of his approach. One wishes that, instead of devoting most of his time rejecting "neoorthodoxy," Novak might have shown with some care and precision both the points at which liberal relativism was on the right track, after all, as well as the points at which that tradition must be revised. Were he to have done that, he would possibly have moved the discussion ahead. As things stand, we simply get a few *all too familiar* generalizations about tolerance and pluralism dressed up in the rhetoric of "radical newness."

I myself feel that the problem of theological relativism posed by liberal theology is a severe problem, one we have on our hands and must come to terms with. I am convinced also that, while Barth's particular solutions to this problem are not entirely acceptable, he succeeded in pointing up equally unavoidable aspects of the Christian tradition which do not fit simply into a live-and-let-live mold. Without giving careful justifications, it will not be easy, in my judgment, to reject outright the arguments of either side on the questions of tolerance and conviction.

In any case — and most important of all — we need a moratorium on the use of the word "new" in theological discourse. I have no doubt — as I said above — that new forms of thought and action are demanded. But we shall not find these new forms by pretending that old, established ideas are fresh and creative simply because they have not been popular for a while. In short, we have a right to be shown *how and in what specific ways* a proposal is in fact new.

This leads me to add a broader concluding note about Novak's view of the contemporary world. Just as Novak's own argument does not persuade me that theology must now go on in a way that is entirely divorced from traditional modes of thought, so I am not persuaded by his bald assertions regarding "the dissolution of the modern form of Western culture" or his claim that "a world is collapsing around us and a new one is being born." Lots of people say these things, and, for all I know, they may be correct. But we have a right to know "how and in what specific ways" these claims are true. Certainly, Novak's mention of the Hippies and New Leftists is not sufficient to prove the "world is collapsing around us," for it is not yet clear just what it is that is "radical" about these groups. Some of the New Left people may be radical only in the intensity of their demand for genuine attainment of quite traditional social and political values. But precisely because I am not certain about this, I plead for careful discriminating discussions of these matters rather than rhetorical assertions.

246

REFERENCE

1. Hügel, Baron von: Introduction to Troeltsch: *Christian Thought* (New York, New York) 1957.

COMMENTARY

by Brian Wicker

IF THIS COMMENT on Michael Novak's article seems to register a significant disagreement, I want to insist at the outset that it is a disagreement within a large area of shared ground. It is just because he has so deftly touched the nerve that registers that pain of being a christian in today's world that I am stimulated to my own, rather different, remarks. For what seems to me so unbearable about the situation as he sees it, and as he exposes it, is that if he is a surgeon he has no treatment to offer and if he is a torturer he has no cause to serve. The pain is all. It is in that experience that true religion comes into being. But if so, then the pain can only be made bearable if we are certain that we *have* to bear it, and if we know very clearly why we have to bear it.

I want to fasten on one main point: that christianity must recognize not only its own relativity, but also the relativity of even that relative condition. I want to agree with this point, but to insist that another one needs to be laid alongside it. There is a contrary pull to be recognized. This opposing pull, which is elicited just because of the need to emphasize the "relativity of relativity," might be called the "absoluteness of the absolute." The more we stress the relativity of the christian (or any other) stance, the more the absoluteness of the absolute rises up against us, with all the inertia that reality, as it stands over against us, always presents.

Novak notes two moments in the recognition of relativity: relativity of expression and relativity of culture. (These are my own terms.) Relativity of expression is merely the understanding that there are different ways of saying the same thing. At its simplest, relativity in this sense means the possibility of paraphrase or translation. But it is not always so simple. Different media may convey the same message — a gesture can be the equivalent of a word; and various customs can carry the same meaning in different cultures. The core of a message may be surrounded by a mass of expendable irrelevancies. In some sense a film, or even the book of the film, does bear the same significance as the original novel from which both were taken. In the very widest and most complex sense, Novak insists that the radical American theologians, for all their radicalism, are relativists only in the expressive sense. Their object is to restate the christian gospel in a language, style, and mode that is relevant and intelligible to *modern Western man*. They want to cut away any modes of expression, any conceptual categories, any myths or presuppositions, that stand in the way of this central task. In some sense, however broad, they want to continue the christian tradition.

Now it is precisely this implicit notion of the christian tradition that Novak rightly draws attention to in his critique of modern theology. His primary emphasis is that christianity, even, or perhaps especially, in this modern radical form (Cox, Van Buren, Altizer, etc) takes for granted as normative the contemporary Western, if not American, mode of thought, feeling, and organization. It is at this point that the expressive relativism of the radical theologians meets its unacknowledged absolute. The fundamental weakness of this limited recognition of relativity is that it involves a tacit, unconscious religious Western imperialism. It stems from the innate arrogance and technological self-inebriation of modern Western civilization. The recognition of this arrogance for what it is rightly leads to such anti-western cults as the "hippy" movement within the body of Western culture. This cult reveals and underlines the relativism of that culture itself. It challenges, not just the modes of expression that arise from the cultural context, but the whole world in which they grow.

Here is the second kind of relativity that Novak discusses: the

248

relativity of cultures themselves (of which "Western civilization" is one, and of which the "American Way of Life" is a prominent example) within a culturally pluralistic world. Christianity is one expression of a particular culture and seems, to the modern sociologist or anthropologist, to stand or fall with it, because the two are too closely intertwined to be wholly separated. It is no longer possible to regard christianity from some absolute point of view, as the one means of "salvation": it is just one way, out of many, by which man may achieve his religious objectives. Even to refer to these objectives in terms of union with *God* is misleading, for "God" is a word which has a meaning only within some religious cultures. To define man's religious objectives in terms of "God" is therefore already to prejudge in favor of the cultural systems that give the word "God" a meaning and against those which do not. Cultural relativism means refusing to make such prejudgments. Of course, Novak insists that this relativity, which has to be recognized as a fact whether one likes it or not, does not mean that all systems are equally "adequate." It means only that their adequacy cannot be measured by any wholly objective, external yardstick. It can be tested only by personal experience.

It is at this point that I want to enter my caveat. It is not enough, I think, to say that the relative "adequacy" of different cultural systems can be tested only from within, so to speak. What needs to be examined is the concept of "adequacy" that is being, perhaps too unobtrusively, slipped into the discussion at this point. Novak's motive here is, of course, unexceptionable. He wants to respect logic, which tells him that the fact that there are several candidates for a constituency does not mean they are all equally good. But the question that must be faced is this: to what are the various religions and cultures adequate or inadequate? Or — to focus the point more sharply — what is religion for? There seem to be two possible answers, neither of which quite fits into the relativist view. The first would suggest that cultures, and the religions that express their inner life, are adequate or inadequate in view of some universal acknowledged basic human needs. One might attempt to distinguish these needs scientifically — in Freudian or other terms — or one might try to deduce them from first principles, as St Thomas did. But both projects run counter to the very concept of relativity itself. Both Freud and St Thomas were Europeans, inescapably caught in the Western cultural net. Who is to say they have a normative status in a pluralistic world? An alternative interpretation of adequacy would be to link it — as I suspect Novak may, consciously or unconsciously be doing — to a notion of truth. That is to say, a religion is adequate if it is true to reality: to the way things are. But here we are back with the old scholastic metaphysics of subject and object, of myself, with my formation, language, and a lifetime's luggage set over against the "facts," the external world. And this seems to be just the metaphysic which is being explicitly repudiated in Novak's article.

I am not going to suggest that anyone can produce a *solution* of the problem that is being raised here. On the contrary, what I want to insist on is the theoretical impossibility of any solution and the significance of this impossibility for a discussion of the religious situation today. It seems to me clear that, the more one puts weight on the side of relativity, the more strongly does the very language one has to use pull down the opposing side of the scale correspondingly. The more firmly one insists, as one must of course, that "to become thematically aware of the dialogue between self and world that occurs through adherence to the principle of openness is to become aware of the unity of self and world," the more is this unity of self and world betrayed by the very language in which it is asserted. For conceptualization

> imposes a pattern, and falsifies,
> For the pattern is new in every moment
> And every moment is a new and shocking
> Valuation of all we have been.
> — T. S. Eliot, East Coker II

The concept of my unity with my world is still a concept, and my actual unity with that world cannot be stated without it. "Myself" and "world" are still distinct words. In standing between the concept and the fact, the words are themselves a living refutation of the possibility that this unity of self and object might one day be fully articulated. As Merleau-Ponty put it, "the most important lesson which the reduction teaches is the impossibility of a complete reduction" (*Phenomenology of Perception*, Preface). Or, to put it another way, every proposition that says something about the nature of truth is itself open to the question: is it true? We cannot help chasing our own tails.

Taken to the limit, absolutism and relativism become identical. If one were to say that every religion has an equal — but not more than equal — claim to be thought true, then to the person within his own tradition his religion would be absolute. If I am assured that my tradition is as good for me as yours is for you, there is no reason why I should not consider my position impregnable as far as I am concerned. Why should I bother to listen to what you say — except as a matter of courtesy or idle curiosity? Your tradition would have no claim on my attention; it would present no challenge to me.

Now it is clear that this is an almost impossible position to adopt. But why? Because an emphasis on cultural relativity — to use a shorthand phrase for this second moment of relativism — only has any meaning, any cutting edge in the present debate. if it stops short at some point. That is to say, if it claims to be a service to *truth*. I would entirely agree with Novak that it is a gross defect that the point at which relativism stops short, in current "radical" theology, is the point where the values and forms of Western civilization might be brought into question. But it is not wrong to put the limit there because this "absolutizes" relativism, but only because it does so at the wrong place. In other words, the religious imperialism that this kind of Westernized theology rests upon is, in itself, a disservice to truth. It sets up as absolute a manifestly partial and relative presupposition.

The fundamental problem for the religious situation at the present time is to decide *where* relativism should stop short. In a brief comment I cannot possibly begin to solve that problem, even if I were equipped to do so. I can only say that I think much of Novak's analysis of the shortcomings of the American theological scene applies to Britain also and that basically the same general direction for forward movement is required. The main point I would wish to make, however, is to insist that there can be no permanent fixing of the limits to relativity. The limit, the point at which it must stop, is itself historically conditioned and subject to perpetual evolution. At any moment, there has to be a limit *somewhere* if relativism itself is to be significant. But it does not have to be at the same point for all time. To take one example: *if* the metaphysic of Thomism were true and if the Five Ways which are built upon it were valid, then that metaphysic and its arguments would be as true now as they were in the middle ages. Time does not by itself invalidate a logical process. But the total significance, the relevance, the usefulness, the interest, the cultural value of such "truths" may be so eroded by time as to be eventually worthless. Just as it is impossible for us to take a palaeolithic handax out of the museum and restore it to its original place in human culture, so it is impossible to restore a philosophical or religious museum piece to its old lustre. And — to pursue the analogy further — the cultural and religious museums are never full; their collections are forever expanding, and many of the tools that people are still using in the outside world have already found their way into the museum, which is their proper place. In this sense, there is no *final* boundary to relativity: but it is a sense in which the openness is in the temporal dimension only. If the act of faith is an act of self-definition, by which I discover who I am and where I stand, it must be an act by which I draw a boundary around myself and, in order that it may have any meaning, there must be something outside this line that cuts me off from the meaningless expanse of unmapped territory beyond myself. But this boundary has to be constantly drawn and redrawn. The process of self-definition is never ending.

Perhaps this admission brings me much closer to the new relativism than has hitherto appeared. I must therefore end by saying why this relativism worries me. It is because intellectually, simply as a theological position (I make no reference here to those who hold it) it is liable to sell the pass. To be open to everything, to see everything under the aspect of cultural conditioning, may lead to a readiness to tolerate everything. What stands in the way of such a possible capitulation is the cultural inertia of religious institutions. If the church, under its "folk religion" aspect, made capitulation easier for the theologically docile in Germany, it may make capitulation more difficult for the theologically sophisticated in Britain or America precisely for the same reason.

We have here just two sides of the same coin. By making a claim on one's allegiance in the name of something more exclusive than a "relative adequacy" — i.e., in the name of *truth* — a religious institution sets up the love-hate relationship that is at the heart of genuine religion. It is an essential part of christianity to loathe and detest the church as well as to love, honor, and obey it. This is the tension that religion flourishes on: the tension of life itself. Institutionalism is the social embodiment of the absoluteness that relativity itself requires as its polar opposite. Relativity has meaning only in relation to the absolute it wants to demolish. It needs its enemy and cannot do without it. Part of the role of the church, as the embodiment of the absoluteness that the quest for truth entails, is to be a target for attack, an object to be demolished if possible. Religion needs the coercion of an institution in order to assert man's personal freedom from it.

6. IDOLATRY AS A MODERN RELIGIOUS POSSIBILITY

FOR RABBI DAVID HARTMAN

by Emil L. Fackenheim

[A first draft of this essay was read as a paper at the second annual meeting of the Canadian Center of Advanced Jewish Scholarship. The final version here submitted is much indebted to the inspired discussion which followed the reading of the original paper.]

THE JEWISH religious thinker is in and of the present. He cannot be in and of the present alone. He is obliged to confront the classical sources of Judaism — Bible, Talmud, Midrash — even if he ends up with a modern dissent from the ancient wisdom. Nothing less than a genuine self-exposure to the past can lend Jewish authentication to his modern thought.

There are, however, a good many subjects on which it may well seem a mere waste of effort to engage in an "encounter" or "confrontation" of this kind. Foremost among these is surely the subject of idolatry. Surely in this modern, technological, demythologized world ancient idol-worship is dead and buried, making it romantic folly to expect any relevance in ancient wisdom.

Random examples from rabbinic literature confirm this judgment. The Talmud views idolatry as one of three deadly sins which must be resisted even on pain of death, the two other sins being murder and incest. Today, the necessity for this particular martyrdom does not arise. According to the Midrash, one who repudiates idolatry is as though he were faithful to the whole Torah: "Whosoever acknowledges idols repudiates the whole Torah, but whoever repudiates idolatry is as though he accepted the whole Torah" [*Sifre*, Deut. Re'eh #54].

By this standard any modern Jew would be wholly faithful. Rabbinic law regards the worship of graven images as so dangerous a temptation as to prohibit ownership even when no worship is intended. This is in application of the rabbinic admonition to "build a fence around the Torah" [*Pirke Abot* I, 1]. A modern man, far from himself being tempted, cannot understand how there could ever have been an attraction. In fact, this apparently once desperately serious business has become a mere joke, as in the story of the parishioner who informs his minister that, whereas he has broken nine of the ten commandments, he has, he is proud to say, never worshiped graven images. Can one doubt, then, that on this subject at least any recourse to the classical sources of Judaism is mere folly? Is it to be denied that here at any rate the whole truth is with the dogmatic modernist who asserts that the past can at best only confirm what the present already knows and that, in any conflict between past and present, the present is *ipso facto* right? So it must seem, at least as long as one takes idolatry in its literal ancient sense as the worship of trees, rivers, statues, Roman emperors, and the like. And one must take it in this literal sense before one can argue the legitimacy of taking it in any other.

The impression of the irrelevance of the traditional Jewish teaching deepens as one considers contemporary Jewish religious life. The theme of a nineteenth century East European story could still be the conflict between aesthetic appreciation of a statue and the traditional religious strictures. In the story the hero buys a statue but ends in smashing it. In twentieth century America this story has lost all poetic truth. Idol worship is no longer a real possibility, and a statue looked at, or even owned, tempts no one to worship it. This much is true even of orthodox Jews. Nonorthodox Jews go further. They have not hesitated to bring images if not statues into the house of worship itself. It occurs to nobody that a stained-glass window depicting Abraham or Moses might become an idol. The very idea is preposterous.

Equally significant is the change in Jewish attitudes toward religions that are not Jewish. For millennia, this attitude was one of reserve and even suspicion. This was not motivated, as popular liberal Christian mythology had it, by "particularism" but, rather, by the fear of idolatry. That this fear has now vanished is evi-

255

denced by the Jewish willingness to engage in interreligious dialogue, which is widespread, and by the Jewish interest in interfaith cooperation, which is universal. No modern Jew would regard another religion as idolatrous simply because images or statues are part of it. So long as the one imageless God is the intended object of worship — and of what "higher religion" is that not true? — the images and statues are at worst symbols with which a Jew, even as visitor, cannot be comfortable. (He is not comfortable, but he can still be a visitor.) But "symbol" is a modern concept, and it reflects the fact that the old idolatry has become nonexistent, or at least quite harmless.

This harmlessness suggests that, when the old idolatry existed, it was nothing more serious than a species of superstition and that this superstition, like all others, is destroyed by modern enlightenment. In the Jewish theologian, this belief is apt to produce a spirit of self-congratulation. The ancient rabbis had to wage war on idolatry. His modern descendents can beat the swords of this particular warfare into plowshares. For, whereas the ancient superstitious world was full of "polytheists," in the enlightened modern world one is a "monotheist" if one believes in God or gods at all. The traditional *Aleynu* prayer, for example, anticipates a messianic future "when Thou wilt remove idols from the earth, and the nongods shall be wholly destroyed." The corresponding passage in the modern liberal *Union Prayer Book* still is: " . . . when superstition shall no longer enslave the mind, nor idolatry blind the eye. . . ."

This spirit of self-congratulation over liberation from superstition was widely current in the eighteenth and nineteenth centuries, and not among Jewish thinkers alone. In the twentieth century, however, this spirit is wholly destroyed. No one detects a resurgence of ancient idolatry. Yet something obscurely related seems to survive in the modern world, erupting in the present age with such power as to compel universal notice. This is illustrated by the fact that a metaphorical use of "idol," "worship," "false god" has forced itself into the language of serious thinkers, both religious and secularist; even in popular usage money, success, sex, and the nation are all referred to as objects of "worship." Something is therefore wrong with the view that idolatry is a mere past superstition, now safely surpassed. Somehow idolatry survives.

Yet, what *is* a modern "idolatry"? It is not, in the first place, actual worship, and its "gods" are not literal gods: it is a modern phenomenon. In the second place, it has something in common with ancient idolatry, at least if the metaphors used have any meaning. And it surely is, in the third place, something more serious than a mere lapse into anachronism and something more specific, as well as more serious, than sin-in-general. However, to judge by the evidence of thought both academic and popular, we do not yet understand modern idolatry. We define it either too narrowly, as a folly surpassed by modernity, or too widely, as a sin not in principle different from any other. But the effect of both errors is the same: the scandalous particularity of modern idolatry is lost.

To the Jew of this generation, this is no mere academic failure. For he has been the prime victim of the most horrendous idolatry of modern times and, perhaps, of all time. Yet Nazism might never have won its frightful victories had it not been belittled, on the one hand, by good enlightened liberals (who viewed it as a mere lapse into premodern "prejudice") and, on the other hand, by good Christians (who classed it with other sins, their own included). The Jew, if anyone, knows the frightful uniqueness of Nazi idolatry. He cannot escape into the false comfort that Nazism was a case either of prejudice-in-general or of sin-in-general. On him, if on anyone, weighs the heavy task of transfiguring unique suffering into unique testimony.

One cannot, however, bear witness without understanding. How must modern idolatry be marked off, on the one hand, from mere prejudice, which enlightenment is sufficient to destroy and which is not sin at all, and, on the other, from other sins which, however grave, fall short of idolatry?

This question raises the hope that ancient rabbinic wisdom may not, after all, be irrelevant to modern realities. For in their own age rabbis did achieve a precise identification of ancient idolatry. They had surpassed idolatry, but they marked idolatry

257

off from follies surpassed. They took a serious view of all sin, yet they set idolatry apart from every other sin. For the Jewish thinker of today, there is an experiment of thought, therefore, that is well worth attempting; its object is to discover whether ancient rabbinic wisdom can be made relevant to the idolatries of the present age.

CLASSICAL JUDAISM AND IDOLATRY

Why does classical Judaism take idolatry seriously? We shall ask this question of the rabbinic sources only. A Jew in any case reads the "written Torah" — the Hebrew Bible — in conjunction with the "oral Torah" — Talmud and Midrash. In addition, it is wise in the present case to abstract from the complicating fact that in Biblical times Judaism was still in a state of genesis. There was then still serious competition with the cults native to Canaan, and, for all a nonspecialist knows, those scholars are right who believe that the earlier parts of the Bible are not yet free of polytheism. In the rabbinic age, however, polytheistic remnants have wholly disappeared. The rabbis are in no doubt that the God of Israel is the One universal God, the Sovereign of all men, and that idolatry is the worship of nonexistent deities. Why then do they take seriously such foolish thraldom to empty phantoms? The Midrash writes:

> "Thou shalt have no other gods before Me" [Exod 20:3]. Why is this said? Because it says: "I am the Lord thy God." To give a parable. A king of flesh and blood entered a province. His attendants said to Him: "Issue some decree for the people." He, however, told them: "No. When they shall have accepted My reign I shall issue decrees upon them." Likewise, God said to Israel: "I am the Lord thy God, thou shalt have no other gods — I am He whose reign you have taken upon yourself in Egypt." And when they said, "Yes, yes," He continued: "Now that you have accepted My reign you must also accept My decrees. Thou shalt have no other gods before Me" [12:237 ff].

258

We are faced, to begin with, with a startling connection between idolatry and divine jealousy. Whether or not idolatry would be possible if there were no God, or if He were not jealous, idolatry in any case achieves its full religious meaning only in the context of a covenant with a jealous God. The first commandment concerns Him who led Israel out of Egypt. It is because His is an exclusive lordship that the first commandment is followed by a second, which contains the prohibition of idols.

Divine jealousy *is* startling to modern man. We can understand that one "particularistic" god is jealous of others. Can we understand jealousy in a God who is universal and without rivals? For Hegel, God is "not envious," that is, God is universally tolerant. For Hegel this characteristic of the Christian God has become fully actual only in the modern world and is anticipated in the ancient world only by the philosophies of Plato and Aristotle. For Arnold Toynbee, Old Testament views on idolatry are mere abuse, heaped by the god of the in-group on the gods of the out-group. The coupling, here, of Hegel and Toynbee is by no means to suggest that they are thinkers of comparable rank, but much rather to exemplify the extremes of profundity and shallowness. Hegel's universalism is an unequaled synthesis nourished by a desire to do justice to every historical phenomenon. Toynbee's universalism is a mere watery syncretism, nourished by the platitude that men may rise on the stepping stones of their dead "particularistic" selves to higher, more "universal" things. It is thus not surprising that Toynbee not only fails to show the slightest historical understanding for the Biblical war on idolatry but can actually assert that the Biblical belief in the chosenness of Israel is "the most notorious historical example of . . . idolization of an ephemeral self" [21:310].

Is the rabbinic notion of divine jealousy, then, a mere remnant of an outmoded "particularism"? Were the rabbis nothing better than "chauvinists" when they refused to place their God into the "universalistic" Roman pantheon?

But terms such as "particularism" and "universalism," in any case mere platitudes of Enlightenment ideology, cannot do justice to rabbinic faith and thought. Under Vespasian, Rabbi

Yohanan Ben Zakkai made his peace with Roman political universalism, became a traitor by the standards of zealot particularism, and saved Judaism. But, when Hadrian tried to enforce idolatry, Rabbi Akiba died a martyr. Since earliest Biblical origins, the God of Israel had been the all-important God. This all-importance remained when He had beyond all doubt become the only-existing God. His universalism, in short, was not and never would be one of indifference. He still cared and always would.

But why care about idols? Why be jealous of idolatry, of all sins, when this is worship of no-gods? The question remains. It becomes still more puzzling when we proceed from the first element of rabbinic doctrine to the second, which asserts that the divine is a *discriminating* jealousy, which singles out idolatry *alone*. The Midrash already cited continues:

> For I the Lord thy God am a jealous God. Zealously do I exact punishment for idolatry, but in other matters I am merciful [12:244].

Also, Moses Maimonides points out, "In examining the Torah and the prophets, you will not find expressions such as 'jealousy' . . . applied to God except in reference to idolatry" [14:I, 36].

We could understand an all-important, and hence totally-committing, God who remained indiscriminately jealous even after He has become universal. We could certainly understand a God whose jealousy is focused on sins which are serious temptations. But can we understand a God who has become merciful of transgressions which remain serious realities and who yet remains jealous of empty conceits?

The question becomes still more baffling when we add the third element in rabbinic teaching that is essential to our purpose. *God's jealousy of idolatry extends to Gentiles as well as to Jews.* Conceivably the rabbis might have taught that among Gentiles idolatry is either inevitable or impossible, inevitable in case the Sinaitic covenant alone saved men from idolatry or impossible in case it alone raised men from an otherwise total religious ignorance. In fact, however, the rabbis firmly reject both these alternatives. Idolatry does not inevitably flow from the human condition, for, whereas sin begins with Adam, idolatry begins only with Enosh [15]. Nor is man's native condition religious ignorance, if only because God made a covenant with Noah as well as with Israel, and Noah is the father of all men now living. But *the very first commandment given to Noah concerns idolatry* [16].

The God of Israel, then, has become merciful as regards sins in Israel. He has, moreover, extended His love to Gentiles as well as to Jews, entering into a covenant with both. But He concentrates all the passion of an undiminished jealousy on the single sin of idolatry, in the case of Jews and Gentiles alike. Yet the object of idol worship is a mere nothingness, the figment of a foolish imagination! Here at last we have the whole enigmatic question.

The following passage (which contains the fourth and final element of rabbinic doctrine required for our purpose) is as if designed to answer the question:

> When someone in his anger tears his clothes, breaks utensils, throws away money, this should be viewed as though he worshiped idols. For this is the cunning of the evil inclination: today it says "do this," tomorrow, "do that," until it finally says, "go and worship idols," and he goes and does it. Rabbi Akin said: this is indicated in Ps. 81:10: "there shall be no alien god within you. . . ." What is the alien god that dwells in a man's body? The evil inclination [2].

Here, we say, we have the answer to the question. *Idol worship is a possibility implicit in the human condition.* It is a possibility even though the idols are no-gods. It remains a possibility even when men know that they are no-gods. It is and remains possible because sinful passion can reach a point at which it becomes an independent power — as it were, an alien god within — a point at which the ordinary relation is reversed and passion no longer belongs to man but man to passion. This is why the rabbis refuse to belittle idolatry by defining it too narrowly, as a folly safely surpassed, or by defining too widely, as indistinguishable from sin-in-general. This is why the rabbis disregard the "fool who saith in his heart, there is no God" (Psalm 53:2) but build elaborate fences around the prohibition of idolatry. This is why the God of the rabbis has become merciful with respect to other sins but concentrates all the passion of His jealousy on the sin of idolatry.

But precisely the doctrine which reveals why the rabbis take ancient idolatry seriously reveals also the veritable abyss between them and us, for *we* cannot take ancient idolatry seriously. To a sin more widely or loosely defined we might find ourselves attracted; to idolatry in the exact ancient sense, not at all. That it should fascinate some benighted ancients we might understand; that its lure should extend to moderns as well as ancients seems simply laughable. Imagine the evil inclination, say, to a modern man, first, "steal your neighbor's money," then, "seduce his pretty wife," and, finally, "prostrate yourself before a graven image!" What to the rabbis was the ultimate in evil fascination and the most devastating sin comes to us as a ludicrous anticlimax.

PROTESTANT CONCEPTS OF IDOLATRY

What is this abyss between ancient and modern experience, and what is its cause? The ancient world is "full of gods" (Thales). The modern world is, as the current expression puts it, "demythologized." In the ancient world finite external objects can be higher than man, so much so as to demand and receive worship. In the modern world, these objects have all tumbled from their exalted position. Rivers and hills are lifeless objects, and trees, monkeys, and cows are forms of life lower than the human, and statues are the mere work of human hands. Even the stars are not, as Aristotle thought, divine in themselves but at best only, as Kant believed, "sublime" in relation to us. Not even the universe as a whole is divine, for the myth of a World-Soul, a "likely story" to ancient philosophers [17], is now only a poetic conceit. This much is plain and indisputable fact.

What is the cause of this abyss between ancient and modern experience? One must not think of modern science alone but, rather, of the "modern," "enlightened" way of life as a whole, for one way of life can be replaced or destroyed only by another. It will be useful to compare this modern way of life with two ways of life in the ancient world which, each in its own way, demythologized the idols. Ancient Rome turns Greek poetry into prose; in the pantheon, the gods are all assembled and, because made subservient to human use, all destroyed. The Hebrew Bible too empties the earth of gods, and here too human use enters, for the earth is placed at the disposal of man. But whereas in Rome the gods are destroyed by a human empire, in the Bible their destruction is by the presence of God.

These two forms of ancient "enlightenment" differ greatly. How does modern enlightenment differ from both? Rome destroys the gods but makes human emperors into gods. The Hebrew Bible destroys false gods in praise of the true God and, having done so, must live with the persisting danger of idolatry. Modern enlightenment alone is radical. To be sure, there is disagreement as to the meaning of this radicalism. To some it means the demytholization of both God and gods. To others it means that God is expelled from the world, into the irrelevance of a sheer, Deistic transcendence. To others again it means that, whatever the effect, God can enter into the modern no less than into the premodern world. All agree that in the modern, secular, demythologized world literal worship of finite external objects — idolatry in its ancient sense — is impossible.

What, then, *is* idolatry in modern eyes? Is it a mere superstition confined to the ancient world and safely surpassed in this day and age? But we have seen that this long-popular view is no longer tenable in the twentieth century — that, while the old idolatry is safely dead, something different, and yet obscurely related, is terrifyingly alive. Even those who deny reality to all literal gods admit that metaphorical ones are all too real. Even those for whom no true worship exists see "false worship" on every side. These facts suggest that ancient idolatry was more than mere superstition when it was alive as well as that ancient rabbinic wisdom may possibly be relevant to modern as well as ancient experience. Can the concept of idolatry be so expanded

263

as to make the God of Israel as jealous of the modern metaphorical "gods" now as He was once of graven images?

In pursuit of this question, we must first consult modern
Protestant, rather than ancient rabbinic, thinkers. Of all forms
of Biblical faith, Protestantism alone is exclusively modern, and
Protestant thinkers may well spare us labor since they will deal
with modern idolatry if they deal with idolatry at all. It will
turn out, however, that, unlike the rabbis, they define idolatry
either too narrowly or too widely. We shall in the end have no
choice but to resort to the ancient rabbis. Thus we will have to
try so to bridge the gap between the ancient and modern worlds
as to make them speak to modern realities.

We begin, as we must, with Martin Luther, who writes:

> Idolatry consists not only of the worship of idols but above all
> exists in the heart which looks elsewhere for help and comfort,
> to creatures, saints and devils. . . . It is also the kind of worship
> which seeks help, comfort and blessedness in one's own works,
> and is arrogant enough to wish to force God to yield His
> heaven [13].

Luther expands the concept of idolatry. He rejects the view
that idolatry is a folly that has been surpassed in the modern
world. Indeed he does so before that view has made an explicit
appearance in man's thinking. This great virtue, however, is
bought at a price fatal by any standard, and altogether unacceptable by the standard set by the ancient rabbis. *Luther so
expands the concept of idolatry as, in effect, to make all sin
idolatrous.* For the rabbis, idolatry begins with Enosh, for
Luther idolatry already begins with Adam's pride. The rabbis
single out idolatry as one of three sins which must be resisted
unto death. Luther singles out all sin and no sin at all. Luther's
virtue, his radicalism, becomes a vice when he elevates all sin to
the status of idolatry and thus trivializes *actual* idolatry.

A Jewish thinker may well wonder whether this vice in
Luther's doctrine is not responsible for fatal consequences. It
would be absurd to blame Luther for a contemporary "German-
Christian" church which did not hesitate to accept Hitler as a
kind of divine revelation. But is it absurd to connect Luther with

a strange and fatal contemporary Christian impotence (by no means all Protestant or all German) which, while opposed to Nazism, failed to identify it as idolatry, classifying it instead with such sins as nationalism (not confined to Nazism), dictatorship (not exemplified only in Hitlerism), and, indeed, with the normal failings of good Christians?

We turn next from the first Protestant to contemporary Protestants, confining ourselves to Karl Barth and Paul Tillich. Both are great theologians, and representative, because they are at opposite poles of the spectrum. Both have shed liberal illusions and face the fact of modern idolatry. Both are opposed to Nazism and indeed bear brave personal witness against it. Yet neither is able to match personal testimony with theological comprehension.

Barth writes:

> . . . In the Old Testament the reference to the unfathomable wisdom of God is adduced as a proof of the impossibility, and therefore of the utter folly, of all idolatry. If the wisdom of God and therefore God Himself could be known by man in the created world . . . there would be no real reason why the adoration of God in images of all kinds should not be a justifiable and even necessary result of this natural knowledge of God. But the Old Testament says, quite rightly from its standpoint, that all idolatry is folly. It is not [sic!] of course sin, but only sin in the sense of folly [5:431].

The negation ("it is not of course sin") is obviously a slip. In view of the following, one is almost tempted to regard the slip as Freudian. The viewpoint expressed by Barth is not the way that the rabbis read the Hebrew Bible. In Barth's understanding, those within the covenant — old or new — cannot relapse into idolatry, for it is a folly surpassed. Those outside the covenant either know God through nature (in which case idolatry is inevitable) or not at all (in which case it is impossible). In each case what remains, in the view of the rabbis, as a deadly, yet resistible, temptation has reduced itself in Barth to a bagatelle. Is this because, like Luther, Barth defined idolatry too widely, as sin-in-general? Or too narrowly, as a folly surpassed with the advent of Christ?

We find no clear answer to this question, for we can detect in Barth's theological work no sense or urgent need for expanding the concept of ancient idolatry so as to make it encompass modern realities. Thus one passage startles us by classing German church proclamation of Hitlerian "revelations" with American church tolerance of racial discrimination, but, of course, the subject of the passage is not idolatry but rather sins against the universality of the church [6:703]. Another passage confuses and shocks us by listing "Nero, Caligula . . . , Nietzsche, Hitler" among the "monstrous caricatures produced by world history." We are confused because to class Hitler with Nero and Caligula is to obscure the difference between modern and ancient idolatry, and we are shocked because Nietzsche is included in the list at all. But, then, we have little right to be shocked, and none to be confused, for the subject is not idolatry, but rather man's self-alienation from God [6:433]. We are thus left with no choice but to conclude that, on the subject of modern idolatry, we are failed by Barth the theologian. This failure is all the more poignant in a theologian who did not fail us as a witness and a man. In 1948 Barth wrote:

> . . . National Socialism . . . was a spell which notoriously revealed its power to overwhelm our souls, to persuade us to believe in its lies and to join in its evil-doings. . . . We were hypnotized by it as a rabbit by a giant snake. We were in danger of bringing, first incense, and then the complete sacrifice to it as a false god. . . . We had to object with all our protestantism as though against *the* evil. It was not a matter of declaiming against some mischief, distant and easily seen through. It was a matter of life and death, of resistance against a godlessness which was in fact attacking body and soul, and was therefore effectively masked to many thousands of Christian eyes [4:115].

We turn now to the opposite end of the theological spectrum. Paul Tillich writes:

> Idolatry is the elevation of a preliminary concern to ultimacy. Something essentially conditioned is taken as unconditional, something essentially partial is boosted to universality, and

something essentially finite is given infinite significance (the best example of contemporary idolatry is religious nationalism) [20:13].

This definition for the first time opens up real possibilities. As it stands, however, it has serious difficulties, of which some reflect mere conceptual obscurity whereas others concern doctrine — a doctrine which, at least to a thinker inspired by rabbinic wisdom, will turn out to be unacceptable.

To understand the definition at all, one must bear in mind two well known Tillichian doctrines: one, religion is man's ultimate concern, two, all men necessarily have an ultimate concern. In the light of these two doctrines, what is idolatry? One cannot ascribe to Tillich the foolish view that whatever is *in fact* made an ultimate concern is *truly* ultimate, for then idolatry — the elevation of a preliminary concern to ultimacy — is by definition impossible. What, then, is the standard of *true* ultimacy? If it is exclusively Christian, all nonchristians — Jews, Mohammedans, Marxists, agnostics — are *ipso facto* helpless idolaters. Is it, then, religious-in-general? But this makes nonreligious humanism idolatrous, and idolatrous religion, not. Is it the standard of an "authenticity" which may take both religious and nonreligious forms? But this makes the terms "conditioned" and "unconditional," "partial" and "universal," "finite" and "infinite" so fluid as to raise doubt whether they can still serve as standards. Moreover, it provokes protests from atheists and agnostics who will wish to be classified, neither as "religious" despite themselves nor as idolaters despite themselves. Must a theologian embrace this dichotomy which, to put it plainly, smacks of misguided religious apologetics? The rabbis in their day did not. They certainly did not make professed unbelievers into believers. But — and this is the crux — neither did they make them inevitable idolaters, and for the doctrine that each man must have an ultimate concern — either genuine or idolatrous — one can find no rabbinic warrant. Has Luther's fatal error crept into Tillich's thinking? Is this what induces him, in the case of modern idolatry, to make the God of Israel too indiscriminate in His jealousy?

If too indiscriminately jealous in the modern world, Tillich's God is, of ancient idolatry, not jealous enough. Tillich writes: "Apollo has no revelatory significance for Christians" [20:128]. It appears that, so long as Apollo speaks at all, his voice is, however inadequately, the voice of the true God, and that, when he speaks no more, he has become a harmless work of art. Between these two alternatives, has the possibility of an ancient idolatry disappeared?

As emerges in further, subsequent exposition this dilemma is not wholly fair to Tillich, which is why we put it in the form of an open question. The context of the Apollo passage shows that Tillich is himself aware of the dilemma, but it also suggests that he can escape it only by means of a quasihegelian turn which (1) defines ancient idolatrous religion as a partial truth whose idolatry lies only in its claim to comprehensiveness, and (2) defines nonidolatrous truth in terms of comprehensiveness. Within such a framework there can be no such thing as *absolute* idolatry, and one might well ask Tillich (as, incidentally, Hegel himself) whether he would grant to Ba'al and Moloch what all of us would like to grant to Apollo.

Protestant thinkers, then, have failed to provide an acceptable conception in which ancient and modern idolatry are both comprehended. (This is true at least if the above representative examples are representative enough.) From a Jewish standpoint, is this failure due to some quality in their Protestantism? Or in their Christianity? Perhaps it is as much due to the gap between ancient and modern idolatry, which requires bridging, for this is suggested by the fact that Jewish thinkers too have their difficulties. Thus Will Herberg makes all pride idolatrous [10:75]. This is closer to Luther than to the rabbinic sources. A. J. Heschel abandons the rabbis, and makes divine jealousy indiscriminate, when he writes that "man cannot live without [an ultimate object of worship, and that this is either] God or an idol" [11:119]. Yet Heschel is an outstanding student of the rabbinic sources. His example shows, as eloquently as any other, the need for the Jewish thinker to make every effort to bridge the gap between the ancient and modern worlds in the hope that rabbinic wisdom might then speak to the present day.

THE PROCESS OF DEMYTHOLOGIZING

To do justice to both ancient and modern idolatry we must frame a concept of demythologizing more subtle than that thus far used. The required concept must satisfy three conditions: it must allow that the old idols are now dead; it must allow that they once had a terrifying power; and it must make possible the assertion that this power has now not simply vanished but rather passed into something else. These three conditions must all be satisfied: the first, unless we are to ignore the qualitative difference between ancient and modern idolatry; the second, if we are to assume that the rabbis in their ancient day had any genuine wisdom; the third, if we are to assume that their ancient wisdom is capable of modern application. It is true that the second and in particular the third of these conditions satisfy what may well be unfounded assumptions; indeed, they suggest that we shall be presupposing what we shall try to establish. Against this, however, we can stake the fact that our proposed concept of demythologizing is no mere *ad hoc* invention. It is a more or less common property of modern philosophers, among them Hegel, Feuerbach, Marx, and Nietzsche. This does not, to be sure, solve all methodological unclarity and, in particular, raises questions of priorities, such as between faith and reason or between ancient tradition and modern thought. But these questions can here only be mentioned and must otherwise be left aside.

We begin with the great stumbling block that we can no longer hope to understand ancient idolatry. More is involved than the fact that it is long past. The crux is that it ceases to be intelligible the moment it is demythologized. One no longer *really* knows what it is like. Hence even the Bible no longer fully understands the ancient idols, which is why it can speak of them as mere "silver and gold, the work of men's hands" (Psalm 115:4). Surely only fools would worship such things, and there is thus some truth to Barth's above-criticized view that, for the Bible, idolatry is folly. It is not, however, either the whole truth or the most important truth. To the idolater himself, the idol is *no* mere work of men's hands, and the Bible, while failing to understand, is *aware* of its own failure. Why otherwise take idolatry seriously? In the Bible, it is the atheist who is the fool, which is why he hardly appears on the Biblical scene. Idolatry, in contrast, is a constant temptation in the Bible, all the more terrifying because it is unintelligible. The temptation remains even when it has lost all traces of intelligibility — in rabbinic times, when the truth that there is no god but God has been established beyond all possible doubt.

If then neither Bible nor Talmud understand ancient idolatry, how can modern men hope to understand it? The idolater *actually believes* that the idol can hear, speak, and act. More, he *actually hears* it speak, *sees* it act, and *responds* to what he hears and sees with a degree of passion and sacrifice which leave no doubt as to his sincerity. All this is unintelligible to us, and we are therefore apt to regard ancient idolatry as mere superstition, that is, as a phenomenon without rhyme or reason, which the light of reason destroys without leaving a trace.

But ancient idolatry is not without a rhyme and reason of its own, and it need not remain totally unintelligible. We cannot understand it, if by this we mean entering into the experience. We can understand it if all we seek is abstract concepts which enable us to comprehend how the concepts that are now dead could once have had a terrible life.

Such a concept is the familiar one of *projection*. The ancient idolater projects a feeling — fear, hope, pleasure, pain — upon an external object, and he worships the object on which the feeling is projected. The object, on its part, remains no *mere* object; the projected feeling gives it a life of its own, and there may, or even must, be a special rite of consecration during which this life is conjured into it. There is, then, *worship* because the object is *other* and *higher* than the worshiper, and the worship is *idolatrous* because the object is *finite* — if only because it *is* an object. (The idolater does not, of course, recognize his projections in the worship object. If he did, he would withdraw projections, demythologize the object, and cease to worship it.)

But — and this is why Freud does not appear in the above list of sources of inspiration — the concept of projection is not by it-

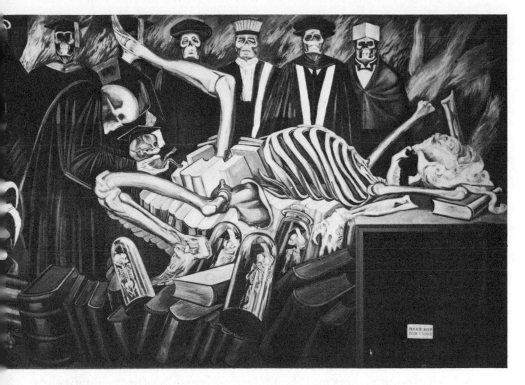

"Gods of the Modern World," a fresco by José Clemente Orozco,
reproduced by permission of the Trustees of Dartmouth College.

self adequate for the present purpose. What is to be grasped is the *religious* nature of idolatrous worship. This cannot be done so long as the feelings that we understand are no more than animal fear, limited hope, a pleasure and a pain which are mere "need." For so long as nothing more than these is projected there is no such thing as *genuine* worship. The idolatry in question being in fact mere superstition, the withdrawal of the projected feelings, if and when it occurs, leaves no trace. A doctrine, however, which in effect regards all religious idolatry as only pseudoreligious is guilty of reductionism and fails in its explanations. (Thus Freud never did manage to explain why the frustrated need for nothing more than a human father should produce the projected image of something more than a substitute human, i.e., a Father who is divine.) What must actually be reckoned with is a fear which is numinous terror, a hope which is geared to infinite bliss, a pleasure and a pain transported into total sacrifice — and an idol with a life explosive enough to inspire such terror, bliss, and sacrifice.

To reckon with these we must bestow on the concept of projection a *dimension of infinity:* what is projected by the idolater upon the finite object is an *infinite* fear, hope, pleasure, or pain. Only because the feeling is infinite is there a *religious* — not a pseudoreligious — relation to the finite object. Only because the finite object is made infinite is the object endowed with its shattering powers and the idolatrous worship of it, qualitatively distinct from mere superstition. Only because the finite object is *both other* than the worshiper *and made infinite* does the idolatry take the *form of worship*. Here at last we have grasped ancient idolatry to the extent to which abstract thought can grasp it.

But we have also grasped something else, crucial for our entire purpose. *The withdrawal of finite feelings leaves no trace; that of infinite feelings produces a dialectical transformation.* The demythologization of ancient idolatry, to be sure, destroys the possibility of idolatrous *worship*. But only the form of idolatrous worship is destroyed, and this very process of destruction creates the possibility of idolatry in a new form.

Demythologization withdraws the infinite feeling; thus the

object is reduced to its proper finitude and loses the power to command worship. But, because the withdrawn feeling is infinite, it does not vanish but rather is transformed in the inner realm into which it is withdrawn. It thus acquires the power of generating what may be called *internalized idolatry*. This is a thraldom to no alien other, but rather to what *is* within, *remains* within, and is *known* to be and remain within. It does not and cannot take the form of worship. Yet, though a Hitler did not and could not demand religious worship, the passion of Nazi idolatry matches any ancient idol worship.

The new, internalized idolatry is dialectically related to the old. It is wholly like the old in that it is composed of the same essential elements; wholly unlike the old in that these elements are totally reorganized. The new idolatry is, further, more "mature" than the old in that it presupposes and arises from its demythologization. Common speech notes all these characteristics but fails to relate and thus to understand them. As regards the first two, we speak of the new idolatry as the "worship" of "gods" and "idols," indicating likeness by the terms used, and unlikeness by the fact that their employment is consciously metaphorical. As for the third characteristic, this is recognized in part by the speech of the new idolater. He does not, of course, recognize his own idolatry. His "worship" of *Volk* and *Fuehrer* is in his mind no idolatrous thraldom but rather a new freedom, for his very self is part of the *Volk* and the *Fuehrer* embodies the *Volk*. But the truth in this new false "freedom" is that it does indeed negate all worship and hence all idolatry in the form of worship. *This new idolater takes himself as an enlightened modern.* (He does so even when he hankers after long-dead pagan myths. For he does not return to the old myths but rather resorts to concocted "myths" — "myths" which spell the final death of all genuine myths if only because they are deliberately, "creatively" invented.) And, shocking though this is to Enlightenment-liberals, there is truth in this self-appraisal. The new idolater is certainly not enlightened, but he is most decidedly modern. The new idolatry is not a relapse into premodern superstitions. It is a bastard child of the Age of Enlightenment.

273

So much for the concepts needed for the present purpose. Before we try to apply them a word of caution must be addressed to theologians. In addition to a new, internalized idolatry, the dialectical process sketched in the preceding pages has given rise to a variety of internalized religions, all of them rivals to the Biblical God. Idealistic faith in a higher Self, humanistic hope for a Man potentially infinite in perfection, the Nietzschean and Marxist dreams of a superior Man and Society, these all internalize or deny the Biblical God who remains other than human, and this fact tempts Jewish and Christian theologians to respond with an indiscriminate charge of idolatry. There is, however, no warrant for such a response in rabbinic wisdom. In their day, the rabbis refused to brand all sin against or ignorance of God as idolatry, and in the light of this restraint a modern doctrine of "either God or idol" is a clear case of misguided apologetics. The concepts developed in the present section entitle the modern Jewish thinker to assert the *possibility* of a modern, internalized idolatry. They do not justify the view that wherever God is not worshiped there is *actual* idolatry. Indeed, such a view is fatal in the light of rabbinic wisdom. Making idolatrous what is in fact at most sin, ignorance, error, or indeed partial truth, it reduces actual idolatry to a mere bagatelle.

THE MODERN IDOLATRY

What, then, is *actual* idolatry? In the light of the concepts furnished in the preceding section, how shall we identify the qualitative leap that occurs when the evil inclination no longer says "do this" or "do that," but "go and worship idols," and a man goes and does it?

With regard to ancient idolatry, we shall fail totally if we mistake the idol for a mere "religious symbol." A religious symbol, if and when it points to Divinity itself, expresses inadequately the Inexpressible, *and this inadequacy is part of the religious consciousness.* There is, for this reason, no idolatry where this gap both exists and is known to exist, which is why the Hebrew Bible, while opposed to idolatry, is full of religious symbols. A burning bush can reveal the divine Presence, for it is not itself that Presence. A divine Voice can be heard even though the divine Face cannot be seen, for it but points to the divine Speaker. Then why can "revelatory significance" attach to symbols such as these but not to the statue of Apollo? Why is the statue not a partial truth but, rather, an absolute falsehood?

Because the statue is not a "symbol" at all. The ancient idol is not a finite object which distinguishes itself from the divine Infinity even as it points to it. *The idol is itself divine. The idolatrous projection of infinite feeling upon finite object is such as to produce not a symbolic but, rather, a literal and hence total identification of finiteness and infinitude.* Only thus can we explain the inexplicable facts that the idolater believes that the idol can literally hear, speak, and act; that he actually hears it speak and sees its actions; and that, rather than merely toy with the fantasies of worship and sacrifice, he in fact sacrifices to Moloch, not this or that, but his all. This is the behavior which the rabbis knew to be possible, and to be a terrible temptation, although they did not pretend to understand it. This is why, to them, the ancient idol was not an irrelevance but rather the demonic rival of the One of Israel, and radically intolerable.

But we in our modern tolerance balk at this ancient intolerance, especially when it is directed, not against Moloch, but against dear, beloved Apollo. Hence, like Tillich, we read modern harmlessness back into the ancient idol, and reduce it to a mere symbol, that is, to a partial albeit no longer relevant revelation of truth. This tolerance, however, has its bitter nemesis. We deny God's ancient jealousy of idols, which no longer hurt or threaten, and we become impotent adequately to identify modern "idols," whose threat is all too real. We are then inclined to assert an ultimate and hence religious concern where none is in consciousness and/or to brand as idolatry what is in fact mere dissent, error, or sin which falls short of idolatry. Having become not jealous enough of ancient idolatry, the God of Israel becomes too indiscriminate or uncertain in His jealousy of modern idolatry.

To avoid this danger, we shall use the criterion that we established in the exposition of ancient idolatry as we make an attempt to identify its modern heir and successor. Idolatry is the *literal* identification of finiteness and infinity.

Is the modern scientific agnostic an idolater? In his own self-understanding, he suspends all infinites and confines himself to finite affirmations. May the theologian go behind the back of this suspension and assert an infinite affirmation, or ultimate concern, where none is in consciousness? The rabbis give no warrant for such a procedure. There is in any case little sense in affirming a commitment where there is explicit suspension. As for affirming an unconscious idolatrous commitment, this would appear to be contrary to anything found in rabbinic wisdom. Not until there was actual worship of idols in the ancient world was the evil inclination, though potentially idolatrous, in fact idolatrous. Not until finiteness and infinity are actual identified is there modern idolatry. Yet this identity is explicitly denied by the agnostic's suspension. To the believer, agnosticism is doubtless error; but not all error is idolatry.

What, next, of the atheist? He is a more likely candidate, if only because he ends the agnostic suspension. There are, however, two kinds of modern atheist, at least one of whom is no idolater. The true God known to religious faith and experience is infinite, and shows His infinity by His all importance, His demand for a total commitment, and His capacity for saving Presence. The God denied by the atheist presently under consideration, however, is a mere "God-hypothesis," unable to demand commitment, incapable of saving Presence, and important only for the limited purpose of scientific or pseudoscientific explanation. He is, in short, a mere finite postulate, and to deny Him is to make a mere finite denial. To be sure, the atheist fails to distinguish between God and God-hypothesis, believes himself to be denying the one when in fact merely denying the other, and in this shows, to the believer, religious ignorance. But ignorance is not idolatry.

But what if the divine Infinity is *knowingly* denied, by a self that is raising itself to infinity in this very act of denial? With this question we come at once upon two modern phenomena: inter-

276

nalized "religion" and internalized idolatry. It would be, however, a fatal error to confuse these two phenomena. Faith must doubtless disagree with both, but whereas the one is an authentic challenge likely to bring out the best, the other is a demonic perversion which tempts to the worst. Faith may have dialogue with modern internalized "religions" and indeed must have it unless it is to shut itself off from the modern world. Internalized idolatry, in contrast, represents, not the modern world, but rather its specific possibilities for radical evil.

To recognize this distinction we turn briefly to six modern philosophers, Fichte, Schelling, Hegel, Feuerbach, Marx, Nietzsche. These thinkers all explore the modern theme of internalized religion and are thus exposed to the danger of modern internalized idolatry. Yet not one of their philosophies is in fact idolatrous. Indeed, one may say that what makes these philosophies great is precisely the care with which the possibility of idolatrous thought is both recognized and avoided.

This is true of the first group of thinkers. These are idealists because their denial of divine otherness issues, not in an atheistic rejection of the Divine, but rather in its internalization. Divinity comes to dwell, as it were, in the same inner space as the human self, and this is enough to raise the spectre of a modern, internalized idolatry. It is therefore all the more significant that finiteness and infinitude are nevertheless kept firmly apart in the internal space they jointly occupy. Fichte's moral self becomes divine only in infinity — forever aimed at but never reached. Hegel reaches the Fichtean goal, but does so in the realm of thought alone: existentially man and God remain apart [9]. Schelling alone yields to the romantic temptation to fuse the finite and the infinite — but only for a brief period and only to set them the more firmly apart after the period is ended.

Idolatry is as firmly (if not as obviously) rejected by the second group of thinkers. These are humanistic atheists, made so by the fact that Divinity vanishes in the process of internalization, to be replaced by a humanity potentially infinite in its "freedom." Yet despite so Promethean an atheism they are not idolaters, for the potentiality never seems to become quite actual.

277

Feuerbach's man is not yet quite free, Marx's society, as yet far from classless. Even Nietzsche, for all his recklessness, does not declare himself to be Overman but merely to be Overman's fragmented prophet. And though he beholds the blessed vision, he accentuates the anguish to which he remains confined. In short, just as the first group of thinkers holds fast to the ideal divine infinity, so the second holds fast to real human finitude, prepared, if they must, to project infinity into an elusive future. With thinkers such as these, the theologian can have dialogue, and he must have it if he is to expose himself to the profoundest challenge of modernity. But with idolatrous ideologies, dialogue is impossible.

We face this ineluctable fact as we turn, next, from genuine modern philosophies to ideologies which are their idolatrous parodies. Among the grimmer facts of modern intellectual history is that almost all the philosophies mentioned, and a good many others, have become prey to ideological perversion. Fichte's thought became rabid Teutonic nationalism when his risky proposition became inverted, and goodness was no longer the standard of the true German but true "Germanness" became the standard of goodness. Hegel's thought became statism when the Prussian state became divine. Marxism became totalitarianism with the apotheosis of the present party line in place of that of the future society. Nietzsche's dream of a future innocence was defiled when it became a present barbarism "beyond good and evil." All these ideologies have two things in common: they are not philosophies at all, for they lack all honest rationality, and they are idolatrous.

These two characteristics are not unrelated. These ideologies are all the product, not of reason, but of passion, and the passion at work in them is idolatrous, at least if the ideologies themselves are accurate reflections of it. For these are blueprints for nothing less than the actual, literal identification, within the inward space of the individual or collective self, of finiteness and infinity. Through them speaks unmistakably, albeit in modern terms, the evil inclination when, tearing off its mask, it makes the ultimate, unspeakable, idolatrous demand.

278

THE LEAP FROM IDEOLOGY TO EXECUTION

But one can toy with idolatrous feelings and fantasies. One can play with ideologies about God's being dead and everything being permitted, about the need to exterminate lower races, and about a charismatic *Fuehrer* who can do no wrong. This, to be sure, is a game both evil and dangerous. Yet there is a qualitative leap between idle feeling and the passion of actual belief, between fantasy and serious plan, between what remains "theory" and actual, literal, total execution.

Such an execution boggles the mind. A proverb which was much quoted in Germany in the thirties is to the effect that the soup is not as hot on the table as on the stove. Among statements reflecting inability to take the leap from "theory" to execution, one must surely reckon Heidegger's "the Fuehrer himself and he alone is German reality and its law, today and henceforth" [18:530]. One can somehow still grasp idolatrous ideology, and indeed a certain bogus rationality can attach to works such as *Mein Kampf*, making possible at least the parody of a serious discussion. But can one understand that anyone might seriously believe the fantasies of that work? Or that they might be executed with the utmost literalness? If Hitler was not believed by the world, the best excuse is that he was incredible.

He is still incredible. Before Nazism happened we thought it could not happen. Now that it has happened, we resort to explanations which explain it away. We take it, in the style of Enlightenment liberalism, as a mere lapse into atavistic prejudice, superstition, or neurosis, ills which should not happen in this day and age and for which — soon if not now — there can be a cure. Or we take it, in neolutheran style, as a mere case of national pride, lust for power or xenophobia, sins which will always happen because we are all sinners. Possibly we take it as a mixture of the two. We in any case resist confronting it as a modern idolatry; one might say, as *the* modern idolatry because, being unsurpassable, it reveals all that idolatry can be in the modern world.

Nazism was not nationalism or imperialism: these have limited

279

goals. Nor was it a plausible reaction to defeat and depression, if only because no other nation ever reacted like Nazi Germany to these traumas. Nazism was more like pannationalism, totalitarianism, and antisemitism, for all these are nurtured by a groundless hate, have unlimited goals, and are hence insatiable. Nazism, in fact, could look like all these things before it happened. After the event, we may not ignore the difference between Nazism and pangermanism or other forms of totalitarianism. The distinction between Nazism and Italian fascism is admirably developed by Hannah Arendt [1]. In contrast to Soviet communism, Nazism could never have survived either a turn to a policy of coexistence or a repudiation of the cult of personality. Nor may we ignore the fact that no other antisemitism ever made the murder of every available Jewish man, woman, and child on earth an unshakable principle.

To come anywhere near grasping the scandalous particularity of Nazi idolatry, we must take the incredible leap from mere ideology to literal execution. The historian Alan Bullock writes of Hitler:

> Every single one of his ideas, from the exaltation of the heroic leader, the racial myth, anti-Semitism, the community of the *Volk*, and the attack on the intellect, to the idea of a ruling elite, the subordination of the individual and the doctrine that might is right, is to be found in the anti-rational and racist writers (not only in Germany but also in France and other European countries) during the hundred years which separate the Romantic movement from the foundations of the Third Reich. By 1914 they had become the commonplaces of radical anti-Semitic and pan-German journalism and cafe-talk in every city in Central Europe. . . . *Hitler's originality lay not in his ideas, but in the terrifyingly literal way in which he set to work to translate fantasy into reality, and his unequaled grasp of the means to do this* [7:64, italics added].

How can we understand this "translation of fantasy into reality"? — by no means the work of one individual only but implicating, for twelve years, a whole people and much of Europe. Notions arising in connection with ancient idolatry crowd back into the mind: the "alien god within" who becomes an independent force when idolatrous passion and fantasy, toyed with too long and too seriously, have undermined both the understanding and the will; the serious belief, immune to all evidence, that the idol can hear, speak, and act; the final act of worship which no longer toys and plays but does not shrink from overt, total sacrifice. Yet a gulf separates Nazi from ancient idolatry. Nazi idolatry involves no worship and indeed denies and destroys all forms of worship. The *Fuehrer* is no emperor-god, and there are no gods beside or above him. "The myth of the twentieth century" is a phrase which, of course, alludes to the title of the notorious book by the Nazi Alfred Rosenberg, a work second in the Nazi canon only to *Mein Kampf*. This is no genuine myth at all but, rather, a "creative" invention, known to be so by inventors and believers alike. Belief, therefore, is not belief at all. There is, on the contrary, a total lack of all serious belief, and in its place there is make-believe. Yet this make-believe commands infinite passion and has the power to exact unlimited sacrifice.

All this is because Nazism has internalized the idolatrous identification of finiteness and infinitude. The *Fuehrer*, no emperor-god, embodies the *Volk*, and the *Volk*, no worshiping community, realizes its selfhood in blind obedience and total sacrifice. Because Nazism internalizes Divinity, it is an "idealism." But, because it idolatrously identifies finiteness and infinitude, it is an idealism totally without ideals. As for finite ideals — family love, vocation, the relation between finite but real men — these are all dissolved in an infinite, "idealistic" passion. As for infinite ideals — the True, the Good, the Holy — these are defiled and destroyed by subjection to the will of a *Fuehrer* which obeys no principle but is, rather, the extreme in finitude, namely, absolute whim. Indeed, destroyed are even those idolatrous ideals to which Nazism pretends so long as it is mere ideology — destroyed when the point is reached at which fantasy no longer controls reality but the passion of reality overwhelms all "theory." Hence there is a grim logic in the fact that, when all was finished and the Third Reich was ashes and ruins, Hitler expressed ghoulish satisfaction at the apparently imminent demise, not of his enemies, but of the "master-race."

Yet, as has been said, the *Fuehrer* whose whims demand all

281

and receive all is neither god nor worshiped. He is, in fact, a nothing who becomes something only at the *Sieg Heil* of the *Volk*, and then he becomes everything. The *Volk*, on its part, is no ordinary mob. It is a mob which has destroyed every vestige of private reserve, every remaining trace of individual personality, in order to become an actual infinity through the shout of *Sieg Heil*. A demonic circularity thus exists between *Volk* and *Fuehrer*. Ancient idol worship, too, showed this circularity, for the idol owed its divinity to the worshiper, yet held him in thrall. In the modern Nazi idolatry, however, this circularity is a conscious compact. For there is no otherness between *Volk* and *Fuehrer*. Theirs is a relation of mutual self-realization; in deadly fear of the finite, something which each might be, they are both nothings which seek to become everything in their relation.

For this reason, this demonic compact between *Volk* and *Fuehrer* — two nothings — can express itself only in a passion for infinite destruction. In its own fantasies, to be sure, the lived unity of *Volk* and *Fuehrer* is an exorcism of nothingness and, indeed, the *creatio ex nihilo* of divinity. In fact, however, it can occasion no surprise that, even by the standards of its own idolatrous ideology, Nazism left behind not a single positive accomplishment. In the end, Nazism achieved but one specific goal, and that was negative: the murder of six million Jews.

IDOLATRY IN AMERICA

But the "idealistic" idolatry which is unsurpassably manifested in Nazism is alien to the spirit of America. America, and indeed the "empirical" West as a whole, suspects all absolutes and is thus largely immune to all false absolutes — the deified nation, the totalitarian state, the cult of personality, the pseudomessianic goal, the romantic longing for long-lost gods. Its goals are finite, naturalistic, and pragmatic, not infinite, romantic, and idealistic, and the thinkers looked to are not Marx and Nietzsche but Dewey and Freud. Even the theologian in America ignores existentialist anxiety, guilt, and despair and gives proximate answers to ultimate questions.

This contrast between "empirical" America and "metaphysical" Europe has given rise to a spirit of triumphalism among recent American theologians, some of whom I have criticized elsewhere [8:193–219]. The modern world has demythologized ancient idolatry. The modern American world has demythologized modern idolatry as well. The original Age of Enlightenment withdrew the infinite feelings projected upon the finite objects. The present American Age of Enlightenment is reducing these infinite feelings to their proper finite size. American democracy has already done away with the "worship" of nation, state, and charismatic leaders, and American psychiatry is doing away now with those neuroses which all along had been the true ultimate cause of all idolatry everywhere. God may or may not be dead in America. Dead are, in any case, all grounds for His jealousy — except in such dark pockets in which either ancient or modern European superstition still survives.

It would be a mistake to respond to "empirical" America with an indiscriminate charge of idolatry. As we have seen, there are no just grounds for asserting the inevitability of an infinite affirmation, or an ultimate concern, where none exists in consciousness. Much less are there any grounds for asserting that the affirmation or concern is idolatrous. The formula "either God or idol" being a case of misguided religious apologetics, Freud and Dewey are no more idolaters than were Hegel, Nietzsche, or Marx. To deny the inevitability of idolatry, however, is by no means to concede its impossibility. An American triumphalism — theological or other — must be rejected.

This is because *elevation of the finite individual or collective self is only one of two forms which idolatry may take in the modern world. The other is degradation of the infinite aspect of selfhood to a false finitude.* A society which has achieved a degree of immunity from the one has done so at the price of greater vulnerability to the other. Freud's thought is not idolatrous; the ideology currently summed up with the slogan "Freud is a fink" certainly is.

Why is Freud a fink? He demands no "idealistic" sacrifice, no worship — literal or metaphorical — of true or false gods. He sets before us no more than finite, "naturalistic" goals, and the pursuit of these is counseled by enlightened self-interest. Yet Freud *is* a fink. (So presumably would be Dewey, if his thought still aroused passion and interest.) He becomes the target of attack not because of the nature of his goals but, rather, because he has goals at all. Even the most naturalistic of philosophies still remains with the one imperative that man should make himself into the natural being he is. A type of idolater currently at large in the secular city wants simply to *be*.

Of this ideology-become-actual a haunting portrayal is given in a recent work, *Last Exit to Brooklyn* [19]. The heroes, or rather antiheroes, of this work are all slum victims; hence their idolatry implicates the society which creates, perpetuates or permits the slums. What makes them idolaters, however, is that they are not *mere* victims but rather willing and indeed passionate participants in their own degradation. No love exists between husband and wife or parent and child, no religion except for a grim farce, and the single attempt at poetry is pathetic by virtue of its very solitariness: thus no "higher purpose" ever appears. As for natural purposes, all energy is spent not on their pursuit but on their defilement. For just as "idealistic" idolatry is an idealism without ideals so this "naturalistic" idolatry is a naturalism without nature. No desire remains innocent, no animal lust, clean. For, whereas sex is all pervasive, it is permeated by a universal pleasurelessness, joylessness, and, above all, by a groundless hate. Infinite despair lurks everywhere, yet no one ever screams the infinite scream which would make it human. So, totally and completely, the antihero of *Last Exit to Brooklyn* uses his human powers to deny every trace of his own humanity.

So complete a negation would not be possible for an individual in his solitariness. There is, therefore, a society or rather antisociety. Each is related to the other in a compact of mutual destructiveness. Negro is object of white contempt and himself despises Jew. There is rage between husband and wife, whether the cause is vital or trivial. Father starves child to lavish his plenty on illicit sexual conquest, yet the conquest is no affirmation of self but negation of the other. Need does not seek fulfilment but is rather a club with which men and women beat each other, with children reduced to mere objects in the struggle. This need, in short, forms a circle of mutual hate, and the circle is unbreakable because the hate is groundless. The rabbis teach that the first temple was destroyed because of idolatry. Why then, they ask, was the second temple destroyed, when at that time no idolatry existed? Because of groundless hate, is the reply, for groundless hate is equivalent to the worship of idols [3].

The possibility of idolatry does not vanish in a society which suspects or spurns all absolutes, true or false, and assumes the form of radical secularity. For even if God is denied or ignored and in fact is remote from human experience, men must still live with what the Bible describes as the divine image. The idolatry still possible, and perhaps more threatening than ever, is the desecration of that divine image.

COVENANT WITH A JEALOUS GOD

One need not be a religious believer, and certainly not a Jewish religious believer, to be appalled by and opposed to the idolatries of the modern age. However, for the Jewish believer, today, as in ancient times, a testimony against idolatry has its full meaning only in the context of a covenant with a jealous God. But, while inspired by ancient wisdom, he must take care lest he mistake the modern object of the divine jealousy. Like its ancient predecessor, modern idolatry is the work of the "strange god within"; but, unlike its ancient predecessor, it *remains* within. It is not literal worship of external gods but metaphorical "worship" of metaphorical "gods."

Testimony against such an idolatry must shift its source of inspiration. With the false gods of ancient idolatry, the true God shared the form of worship, and He disclosed His truth and their falsehood in the fact of actual speech, for their speech was but the figment of the imagination of the heart. The false "gods" of the modern age, however, speak only too loudly, for they are not silver and gold worshiped by the heart but, rather, what is in and of the heart. Against false gods such as these, there is need for a different emphasis — on the fact that the true God is not in and of the heart but rather other than the heart, even though He may speak to it.

For this reason, a strange irrelevance attaches to a current "theology of relevance," which would empty church and synagogue, assimilate God to the secular city and, indeed, go so far as to declare that unless God is so reinterpreted as to become a wholly internalized, metaphorical "God," He is dead. An older group of theologians — Buber, Rosenzweig, Barth, Niebuhr, to name but a few — was wiser in its generation. It understood that the source of a modern religious testimony against modern idolatry is literal worship, not "worship"; and that it is in praise, not of "God" but of God.

REFERENCES

1. Arendt, Hannah: *The Origins of Totalitarianism* (Meridian Books, The World Publishing Company, Cleveland, Ohio) 1958.
2. *Babylonian Talmud*, Tractate Shabbat 105 b.
3. *Babylonian Talmud*, Yoma 9 b. The passage cites, in addition to idolatry, harlotry and murder among the causes of the destruction of the first temple.
4. Barth, Karl: *Against the Stream* (S C M Press, London, England) 1954.
5. Barth, Karl: *Church Dogmatics*, II, 1, T H D Parker and others, translators (T & T Clark, Edinburgh, Scotland) 1957.
6. Barth, Karl: *Church Dogmatics*, IV, 1, C W Bromiley, translator (T & T Clark, Edinburgh, Scotland).
7. Bullock, Alan: quoted in Luethy, Herbert: Der Fuehrer, in *The Commentary Reader* (Atheneum Press, New York, New York) 1966.
8. Fackenheim, Emil L: On the Self-Exposure of Faith to the Modern-Secular World, *Daedalus*, Winter 1967.
9. Fackenheim, Emil L: *The Religious Dimension in Hegel's Thought* (Indiana University Press, Bloomington, Indiana) forthcoming, 1968.

10. Herberg, Will: *Judaism and Modern Man* (Farrar, Straus and Young, New York, New York) 1951.
11. Heschel, A J: *God in Search of Man* (Farrar, Straus and Cudahy, New York, New York) 1955.
12. Lauterbach, Jacob Z, editor and translator: *Mekilta de-Rabbi Ishmael*, vol 2 (Jewish Publication Society, Philadelphia, Pennsylvania) 1949.
13. Luther, Martin: *Grosser Katechismus*, commentary on the first commandment.
14. Maimonides, Moses: *Guide for the Perplexed*, I, 36.
15. Maimonides, Moses, *Mishneh Torah*, Book I, IV, 1.
16. *Midrash Genesis Rabba*, Noah, XXXIV, 8.
17. Plato: *Timaeus*.
18. Proverb: written in 1933, quoted in Friedman, Maurice, ed: *The Worlds of Existentialism* (Random House, New York, New York) 1964.
19. Selby, Hubert, jr: *Last Exit to Brooklyn* (Grove Press, New York, New York) 1965.
20. Tillich, Paul: *Systematic Theology*, I (The University of Chicago Press, Chicago, Illinois) 1951.
21. Toynbee, Arnold J: *A Study of History*, abridgement of vol 1–6 by D C Somervell (Oxford University Press, New York, New York) 1947.

7. THE CATHOLIC CRISIS: SECOND CHANCE FOR WESTERN CHRISTIANITY

by Thomas F. O'Dea

THE ROMAN CATHOLIC CHURCH is a unique religious phenomenon. It is the largest of the Christian communions and indeed the most "catholic" of them judged in terms of its geographical dispersion and its accommodation to a diverse set of historical and social circumstances. It possesses a historical and theological uniqueness. It continues in our day the structure and tradition of the medieval Church, and its dogmatic and theological positions stand in unbroken continuity with the Fathers of the early Church. An understanding of the religious condition of this vast and ancient organization cannot but be of the first importance for the understanding of the contemporary religious situation as a whole.

Moreover, the Catholic Church has just emerged from one of the most important councils of its long career. Vatican II undoubtedly represents a great watershed in Catholic history, and its consequences will be felt for several generations. Many of them are beyond the capacities of our prevision at this time. Nevertheless, certain outlines reveal themselves, certain issues become visible, and certain tensions stand disclosed. These appear to be of diagnostic significance for an understanding of the future course of Catholic development. We shall attempt to analyze these elements of the current Catholic picture and to estimate their significance for the future.

The present situation in the Roman Church is interesting for an additional reason. It is in important respects diagnostic of the position of Christianity as a whole in the contemporary world. The Second Vatican Council represents more than a massive effort for renewal and *aggiornamento* on the part of Roman

288

Catholicism. It was that, and that in itself is of very great significance. But the more profound meaning of the event can be grasped only by viewing it in its full ecumenical context. Not only did non-Catholic observers play a large part in the informal theological discussions that surrounded the Council meetings and not only did non-Catholic world opinion have a tremendous, if hidden, effect upon Council decisions, but the updating efforts which came to fruition in the Council represent the precipitate of a long history. Within the Catholic Church again and again in the last century and a half, significant minorities have advanced proposals for renewal and reform. They brought forth proposals for radical reconsideration of the way the Church had up to then been meeting the challenges, problems, and dilemmas of its encounter with modernity. To have the Church take a fresh look, to have it abandon its defensive posture, to aid it in confronting the new world that was coming to be — these were the aims of these minorities, who were so frequently discouraged and repressed by ecclesiastical authority.

Thus the Second Vatican Council represents a continuation of developments that had been going on for over 150 years. It marks the fruition of insights of long standing. There is one great difference, however, whose significance needs only to be pointed out. Whereas in the previous efforts at *aggiornamento* such proposals came into conflict with and were usually suppressed by the authority of the Church, they were now adopted by the Church assembled in General Council and promulgated with all the legitimacy and even splendor of the papal approval.

THE FIRST GREAT CHANCE: LIBERAL PROTESTANTISM

This rootedness of the "new" stand of the Vatican Council in the past points to an even more notable dimension of the total ecumenical setting of the Council. It points to the fact that the insights of the Council were present in the Church before the Council. But, equally important, the great efforts made now by Catholicism toward a more adequate confrontation with the world represent the second great attempt by Christianity to face modernity and adjust itself to the challenge of today's conditions.

Protestantism has tended to divide into two major tendencies, two significant groupings, in the last century and a half. One of these tendencies clung to a premodern understanding of the scriptures and of theology and stubbornly refused to make a conscious accommodation to the requirements of science and modern thought. The more impressive Protestant phenomenon of this period, however, is that which we designate roughly under the label "liberal Protestantism." Central here were the biblical research and the theological and historical studies of German Protestant scholars. This movement attempted to understand Christianity anew and to reinterpret it in a way which its new interpreters thought would render it understandable and acceptable to the age in which they lived.

The Second Vatican Council itself and the vast ferment which it has inspired in Catholic circles — the aspirations for renewal and reform — represent a second major attempt to bring the Christian religion into a relevant relationship with the evolving modern world, characterized by science, technology, the demise of traditional social and political entities, the vast expansion of knowledge, rapid communications, and a new valuation of secular activity.

The great Protestant effort and its counterpart in present-day Catholicism are modern versions of a kind of activity long to be seen in the history of the Church. In all periods it has been the task of Christian thinkers to restate the Christian faith so that their contemporaries would find it meaningful. This task requires a confrontation with the leading ideas of the age.

> The early apologists were faced with the challenge of pagan philosophy; Thomas Aquinas by that of the Averroism of the medieval universities; Butler by that of deism. All of them by the skillful use of contemporary philosophical ideas restated the historic Christian faith in such a way as to win a hearing for it in their own time. But more than that, it may be said also that all of them made contributions of permanent value to theo-

logical thought, because they themselves won a deeper understanding of Christian truth through their work [7:3, 4].

In this sense, there is ample legitimate precedent in the Christian
tradition for what liberal Protestantism did and for what is now
attempted by postconciliar Catholicism.

Such a course, though necessary, is fraught with danger. To
Macquarrie this danger is threefold.

> Preoccupation with a secular philosophy and the employment
> of it in the interpretation of the Christian faith may easily lead
> to the distortion of Christian teaching through the over-
> emphasis of those elements in it which happen to be specially
> congenial to the philosophy concerned. Or again, ideas quite
> foreign to Christianity may slip into its theology while mas-
> querading under the guise of traditional Christian terminology.
> At worst, there may be a plain accommodation of the Christian
> faith to the prevailing philosophical fashion of the age [7:4].

The Protestant rethinking of Christian meaning in the light
of historicism, science, and biblical research stands as one of the
great achievements of the western mind. Liberal Protestant
scholarship and theology and its successor phenomenon, neoorthodoxy, did indeed probe aspects of the Christian faith to
win a deeper understanding of it in important respects. But it
may also be asserted that Protestantism did not escape the dangers
suggested by Macquarrie. There is alas some truth in the allega-
tion that liberal Protestantism often succeeded in reversing the
miracle at Cana, transforming the wine of Christian faith into
the water of scholarly opinion. These Protestant efforts too often
won contemporaneity at the price of vitality. As a consequence,
they can hardly claim to have made Christianity relevant to
the age.

Conservative Protestantism on the other hand — so-called Fundamentalism — tended to become sectarian, overliteralist, and
superficially verbal. Often it occupied itself and expended its
energies in defensive reactions to the modern world.

Within Catholicism as it emerges into the postconciliar epoch
are tendencies which resemble in general character and stance

both of these Protestant responses. Up to the time of the Council, the liberal groups constituted the weaker party and one whose legitimation rested upon weak supports. Liberal efforts were often the target of conservative attack and of authoritative censure. Yet such tendencies continued to exist and, if not to prosper, at least to grow. In the years following World War II, European Catholicism saw a kind of intellectual renaissance once again, which, coinciding with the rise of an articulate lay Catholic intelligentsia in the United States, found meaningful resonances in this country. To some observers, however, it seemed a repetition of what had happened in Europe after World War I. Then, too, there was a stirring, intellectual and social, among the Catholics of the continent. So shrewd an observer as the late Paul Tillich suggested that this renaissance would come to little of significance [11].

[Writing over three decades ago, Tillich said, "Wherever there are movements which might develop into real revolts against Counter-Reformation Catholicism they are tolerated only so long as they are of value for purposes of propaganda. As soon as they become dangerous to the centralization and the absoluteness of the church they are destroyed. When and how this fate will come upon the romantic Catholicism of our time cannot be predicted. But it is certain that unless romantic Catholicism calls a halt to its development in time this fate will visit it also" [11:187].]

It was Tillich's opinion in the early 30s that the postwar Catholic renewal would be made use of by the Roman Curia, then in full control of Church management, for apologetic purposes and, to the extent that it was useful for such purposes, it would be tolerated. If it became significant beyond that function, if it seemed to promise or presage real efforts toward internal change in the Church, Tillich thought, the renaissance would be repressed.

The war interrupted these developments, but also it stimulated them in important respects. Following World War II, continental Catholic theologians were affected by a greater familiarity with and involvement in philosophy, sociology, history, and science. They came under the impact of the postwar reaction to the Europe which two wars had created. Under these influences, Catholic theologians continued and expanded the Catholic renaissance. The effect of contemporary thought and of contemporary realities on these men is apparent. Roger Aubert speaks of their interest in three significant and quite timely areas: "the theology of earthly realities, the theology of history, and the theology of the Church." But, he pointed out, even more striking than the topics of this new concern was the "new spirit" that inspired it.

> This has two different and at first sight somewhat paradoxical aspects: the desire to draw fresh vigor from contact with the source material — chiefly the Bible, but also the writings of the Fathers of the Church and the documents of the liturgy — and the desire to make the Catholic presence felt in the world by firmly confronting the Christian message with its aspirations [1:66–67].

In the 1940s Pope Pius XII had issued an encyclical on biblical studies and their place in the Church. This was generally considered to be a great victory for genuine scholarship over the suspicions and strictures of the conservatives, although some conservatives thought it so liberal that they never really accepted it. Also, during the war and immediately thereafter, liberal political statements came from Rome, as, for example, in the 1942 Christmas message of the same pontiff. But by the 1950s the effects of the conservative hostility to the new developments were becoming apparent. It looked as though Tillich's earlier prediction might soon be realized. Says Roger Aubert,

> From 1950 onward the reaction against some imprudent measures, against developments regarded as too precipitate and compromises felt in high places to be injudicious, brought a spate of admonitions on points of doctrine (the encyclical *Humani generis*, a number of warnings related to moral questions, increased activity of the Index and the Holy Office, and the matter of the progressive catechism in France), on pastoral

subjects (particularly with reference to the worker-priests), and in the political and social field (concerning the "progressive Christians" and even the advocates of an "opening to the left") [1:53].

THE ADVANTAGES OF THE SECOND CHANCE

Our earlier references and characterizations of conservative and liberal Protestantism were of course greatly oversimplified. They reduced to a more or less clear-cut dichotomy a range of tendencies. The same thing must be said with respect to contemporary Catholicism. It is too easy to make pat distinctions and, once having made them, to take them too literally. Yet, despite the variation and range of tendencies involved, there are in fact two main tendencies here exhibited.

What is particularly important about the new Catholic efforts at updating is that they take place within a unified ecclesiastical body, within an as yet unbroken community of faith and tradition. Protestantism, in its earlier attempt to make a relevant relationship to modernity, broke apart into groups which became increasingly out of communication with each other. If Catholicism is to succeed in this second chance, it will do so only by preserving its own unity, for only a unified body can provide the setting for genuine dialogue among the various tendencies and perspectives which are found in this great historic process. It has been recognized on all sides that ecumenical dialogue between Catholics and others outside the Roman Church is an important prerequisite for success in this matter. Such cross fertilization of thinking is of the first significance. Equally crucial is the maintenance of ongoing dialogue between the groups within Catholicism itself. Indeed, it is of great consequence that "liberal-conservative" dialogue within the Catholic body be raised to the highest possible intellectual level. (The most interesting work in this respect is Jeremiah Newman's *Change and the Catholic Church* [8]. Based upon a considerable knowledge of contemporary sociological theory, it is solid and conservative and worthy of careful attention.)

294

When we examine the position of the Roman Catholic Church today, what discloses itself to us is this: Catholicism stands as representative of and surrogate for Christianity as a whole in its second great historic attempt to confront modernity. Can the Catholic Church succeed? Can the Catholic Church actually update Christianity? Can it adapt to the mentality of modernity, Christian ideas and values, Christian conceptions of God and man, Christian convictions of the reality and seriousness of the religious life? Can it accomplish this by giving to the challenging aspects of modernity the full valence they demand and at the same time not lose Christianity's deeper character and basic identity in the process? Can Catholicism confront the consequences, intellectual and spiritual, of modern developments in science and scholarship and in political, social, and economic life and adapt to them and still preserve its own lively sense of God's reality and presence?

Writing in 1933, Dr. F. L. Cross, an Anglican churchman, identified himself with "those who look forward to a worldwide Catholicism with its arms open to modern intellectual and cultural needs. . . ." The situation in 1933 did not appear particularly auspicious, but Dr. Cross nevertheless recognized the position of the Roman Church as historically strategic. He said, "Upon the development and success of a second Modernist Movement in the Roman Catholic Church, the ultimate future of Christian culture in western Europe, humanly speaking, depends" [quoted in 14:268]. The term "a second Modernist Movement" may appear to some as unfortunate in view of the upsetting connotations it has for all parties and most observers. Yet it is time to emancipate ourselves from the psychological residues of the past. Dr. Cross's point is clear enough. The kind of updating of Christianity requisite for its survival as more than a marginal phenomenon in the West may depend upon the ability of the Catholics to confront modernity. They have the faith for it; only if they have the intelligence and courage as well can it be done.

The great historic task of relating Christianity and modernity reveals itself as full of promise and fraught with peril. The

Serigraph by Sister Mary Corita,
courtesy Botolph Gallery, Boston.

Tablet of London, a conservative and highly intelligent Catholic periodical, has pointed to some of the dangers. There is the danger of

> taking the modern world too much at its own valuation . . .
> [of not allowing enough] . . . for the way the world we live
> in has been made for us, in such great measure, by the sin as
> well as by the virtues of our predecessors . . . [and that its]
> . . . cultural reality . . . has left their descendents with warps
> in their outlook, blind spots and lost perceptions, so that con-
> temporary society with its pre-occupations is not to be elevated
> into a norm to which the Church must learn to adapt herself,
> instead of bearing a witness precisely where it is least likely to
> be immediately understood or accepted [quoted in 8:315].

What thoughtful man, regardless of his own particular religious preferences and philosophical position, can doubt the general wisdom of the *Tablet* admonition? What thoughtful man can doubt the utter necessity of the kind of effort toward renewal and reform now being made within the Roman communion?

THE FINAL OPPORTUNITY?

The Catholic attempt at *aggiornamento* does then represent a great and indeed probably final opportunity for Christianity. It represents the chance to confront modernity within the context of a unified religious community which possesses great creative energies and which, at the same time, has maintained genuine and currently operative ties with the past. Roman Catholicism alone has the basic characteristics without which success in this venture can hardly be deemed attainable: unity of various tendencies and the possibility of communication among them; a depth and reality of faith on both the popular and the elite levels; a worldwide communion reflecting, potentially at least, a great variety of cultures; a real rootedness in the past. Roman Catholicism has also the advantage of making a second attempt, of being able to learn from both the achievements and the failures of the first.

An additional advantage enjoyed by this second effort is the changed character of the secular world. The long process of the secularization of culture was in many significant respects an anti-Christian phenomenon — at times and in some ways openly and even militantly anti-Christian; at other times and in other ways, indirectly and covertly so. Voltaire's "crush the infamy," Nietzsche's "absolute no," and Marx's emancipation from illusion exemplify many of the attitudes of the educated from the eighteenth century to our day.

It cannot be denied as well that the process of secularization, though it did empty out much substance from traditional Christian culture, was also a process of emancipation. In our day, religious thinkers have come to appreciate more and more the positive aspects of this emancipation, while many secular thinkers have become concerned with the genuine loss of substance that it entailed. The antireligious attitudes of the Enlightenment, the this-sided narrowness of the rationalism of the 18th and the scientism of the 19th century, and even the this-sided historicism of Marxism and related ideologies tend no longer to be sufficient to satisfy modern men. (Roger Garaudy [4] presents an example of a new openness toward Christianity on the part of a Marxist.)

There is a growing inclination for men to transcend their own personal, and indeed the general cultural, adolescent rebellion against important values of traditional religion. Such rebellion may once have been necessary for emancipation, but a definite movement beyond it is now appearing. The world seeks for meaningful orientation as it faces the stupendous tasks of our century. The question arises, "Can Christianity speak meaningfully to this quest?" The final answer to that question will be fatefully affected by the success of Roman Catholicism in its current venture.

THE PASTORAL CONSTITUTION ON THE CHURCH
IN THE MODERN WORLD

Writing in 1922, shortly before his death, Ernst Troeltsch felt that the position of Christianity was a precarious one, that its future was unpredictable. Christianity was, he thought, "at a critical moment of its further development." Moreover, if Christianity was to have any future, "very bold and far-reaching changes were necessary, transcending anything that had yet been achieved by any denomination" [12:60]. The nearly half century that separates Vatican II from Troeltsch's observation saw two important developments in Protestant theology. Again to oversimplify, we may suggest the substance and significance of these developments with the names of Karl Barth and Rudolf Bultmann.

Barth called for a return to the basic meaning of the Bible as the Word of God, for the abandonment of the *Kulturprotestantismus*, whose sociological and cultural bases had been demolished by the First World War. In contrast to the complacent liberalism of the dominant prewar theology, Barth called European man back to transcendence — to an accounting. The uneasy peace ended in 1939 with a second catastrophe, greater even than the first, and the old world, with Europe as its crown and liberal Protestantism its fairest jewel, vanished forever.

In this situation Bultmann came forward in an attempt to free the New Testament message from those archaic and mythical elements that made it incomprehensible to the men of our day. Several centuries of secularization, of scientific development, of technological revolution, and a half century of total war, had deprived western civilization of its older institutional and cultural substance and had removed it from world dominance. The world itself was being "demythologized": its consensually validated convictions were disappearing. Bultmann tried to demythologize the scripture so it could speak once again to the men of this age.

Were Barth's emphasis upon transcendence and Bultmann's attempts to shear off the culturally specific elements in Christian understanding the beginnings of the "very bold and far-reaching changes" which Troeltsch thought necessary? And does the Second Vatican Council represent the "beginnings of these beginnings" within the historic Church of Rome?

To ask these questions is to suggest the magnitude of what needs must be involved in an *"aggiornamento* in depth." We must not think of the Roman Catholic Church as an unchanging monolith, standing recalcitrant and intransigent across the path of history, which has suddenly as by some intervention from on high become an engine of progress and a force for liberation. The preconciliar Roman Church was not unchanging. Indeed, in many of the matters dealt with by the Council — liturgy, the Bible, attitude toward democratic civil government, and others — alterations of considerable scope had been introduced, often on curial initiative and with curial approval. The preconciliar Church was rather the locus of a struggle in which a new spirit attempted to bring about the renewal of the Church and in which the forces and structures of that ancient organization were, almost of historical necessity, "rigged" or "loaded" against such renewal. Yet whatever historical accidents attended the decision to call a council, the fact is that the time was fast approaching when Rome had to consider what Troeltsch called "very bold and far-reaching changes."

In the century and a half preceding this Council many attempts to advocate *aggiornamento* had been put forward by thoughtful Catholics. Although most of them were suppressed, they did have some degree of influence and did create a kind of officially disavowed sub-rosa tradition. Such semirejected traditions, however, are hard to transmit. They do not have at their disposal the resources of the general ecclesiastical community. Consequently there is an element of reinvention in their continual reappearance. What keeps such a tradition alive is much more the continuing need for what it suggests and prescribes than the transmission of its own ideas and perspectives from one generation to another. Authority could condemn and proscribe, but it could not conjure away the reality of the dilemmas to which the proto*aggiornamentists* addressed themselves. Whatever astigmatisms of time and cultural setting — and they were many, of course — may characterize the list from Lamennais and Möhler to Loisy, Tyrrell, and Murri, it becomes more and more clear that they were responding to real existing dimensions of modern civilization, real elements of the human situation as it was experienced by men in the new society which revolution and technology were bringing into the world. The tradition they inaugurated and supplemented never achieved genuine legitimacy. Their ideas had to be either consciously sought or met with by fortuitous accident. Yet from the end of the French Revolution to the close of the Second World War, Catholics invented modernization over and over again. They made repeated attempts at *aggiornamento*. They did not do so because of the institutionalization within the Church of a legitimate opposition party to authoritarian episcopal and ultramontane conservatism. They did so because the meaning of the Catholic faith and the realities of modern life stood in a state of reciprocal challenge in the minds of the educated and intelligently devout. The modern conditions could not be dismissed. They continued to issue their challenge. In fact those elements of modernity which the Church saw as particularly threatening to its traditional institutional and intellectual positions became ever more salient aspects of modern society.

This century and a half came after many previous centuries of change and saw an intensification of it. It was a time of political revolution, of unprecedented technological advance, of social transformation, of scientific development, and of intellectual metamorphosis. It was the time of the German historians — of Ranke, of Harnack, of Troeltsch; of Wellhausen, of Bauer, of Schweitzer. It was the time of the sociologists, from Auguste Comte and Saint-Simon to Emile Durkheim; from Ferdinand Toennies and Max Weber to Karl Mannheim. It watched the development of cultural anthropology from Tylor to Boas. It was the era of Marx, Darwin, Freud, and Einstein. It was a time in which both Whig and Liberal England and Revolutionary and Bourgeois France passed away, together with Catholic Austria and Spain. Pitt and Gladstone, Robespierre and Bonaparte, Metternich and Thiers — all were gone. The time had witnessed the decline of Europe, torn by two bitter world wars, and the rise of America; the end of Czarist Russia and the rise of a new Marxist orthodoxy. It saw the end of empire and the development of the third world.

The third quarter of the twentieth century found a less structured, more insecure, less stable, more open world than man had perhaps ever been in before. It was a world shedding the institutions within whose context it had lived for decades, for centuries, and in some cases for millennia. It was a world being denuded of its illusions and its assurances. It was a world being demythologized. It could become a world come of age, or it could become the scene of frightened and frantic attempts to escape the freedom into which man was emerging. It was also a world full of chaos and suffering and under the threat of nuclear destruction. But it was at the same time a world in which man began to realize that, together with the dissolution of the older contexts of his vanished security and the enormous dangers surrounding him, he was offered also greater promise than at any previous time in his history. Science put within his grasp the instruments for making life truly humane, the tools, material and intellectual, not only for subduing the earth to human designs but also for transforming himself.

To the evolution of this world the Church, officially and in terms of its ordinary teaching, had juxtaposed Gregory XVI, Pius IX, Leo XIII, Pius X, and Pius XII. To this world the Church responded by proclaiming the dogmas of the Immaculate Conception, Papal Infallibility, and the Assumption. To this world the Church had presented the two syllabuses — that of 1864 and that of 1907.

The Church had made a palpably inadequate set of responses, yet to human observation they appear almost inevitable under the circumstances. Small wonder that within its ranks the semi-outlawed forces of modernization began to gather momentum once again. The defensive position assumed by the Church, though seemingly inevitable and the predictable consequence of historical conditioning and sociological situation, was becoming obviously less and less tenable. The Church was reaching that point in its development when to remain in its own self-enforced isolation was to lose its catholicity. As Abbot Butler said, "Aggiornamento in depth" became "a pastoral necessity." He wrote,

> A species, when no longer adapted to its actual environment, can evolve, or it can perish. The Church cannot perish. But there is a third possibility. Sometimes a species succeeds in

taking refuge in a backwater of existence, where — in diminished numbers and with no further relevance except to historians of past evolution — it prolongs an insignificant story. As we look back on the Church before 1962, do we not sometimes seem to be catching a glimpse of what might have become a monumental irrelevance? [2:7]

It is not easy to understand the multitude of factors that influence such a major restructuring of outlook. The Church's defensive behavior of the previous 150 years is precisely what a sociologist would have predicted had he known all the conditions and had been able to look at them with some objectivity. But the interesting question is, Why did that defensiveness give way to a radical shift of attitude at this point in the Church's history? We have argued that the time was fast approaching when the choice was between change and irrelevance. But that it was recognized was a surprise to all. An Anglican historian had written in 1961,

If the full measure be taken of the revolutionary changes that have taken place in the worlds of thought and invention, in political and social structures, and in the conditions of living and working, and if the rootedness of the Churches in the pre-revolutionary order or the *ancien regime* be borne in mind, then their survival with so many of their ancient characteristics and appurtenances intact is remarkable, to say the least. They have not survived because they were well-prepared for the turmoil in which they were to be ineluctably involved, nor because, when it came upon them, they showed ready powers of adaptation to new circumstances and of taking time by the forelock. On the contrary, we have seen how recalcitrant they were to change, how blind or short-sighted in the days of visitation, how disposed to stone or silence or jettison the would-be prophets in their midst, and how lacking in the imaginative compassion and sensitive humanity that might have given them a secure standing in the hearts of peoples when they were deprived of earthly privileges and the active support of governments [13:270].

But recognized it somehow was. There were many influences, many changes of conditions. There was, of course, the older liberal Catholic position, quite in the background. There were the slow thaw in theology and biblical studies and the new developments of the postwar years. There were the continuing external conditions, the continuing challenge, the brute facts of reality that could be conjured away neither by the prayers of the pious nor by the regulations of the authoritarians.

Most important was the fact that the "defeats" suffered by the institutional Church did have the end effect of uprooting it. The Church was no longer a part of the traditional culture, no longer integrated into a conservative institutional complex central to civil society. It was now "freed" from that earlier outmoded "incarnation" — freed against its majority will, no doubt, but not less free for that. The greater part of its "vested interests" had been taken away from it by history. It was now free to seek new ways to embody itself in the life of twentieth century man. In Europe the Church was no longer part of the old order. In the mission regions of the world, the breakup of imperialism put churchmen in touch with the most advanced and at times the most chaotic realities; in America and throughout the entire "Oceanic" Church, the Church was functionally a denomination in a pluralist society.

Shortly before his death in 1878, Pope Pius IX, who had fought so valiantly to preserve the Church in the only way he knew how — by defending its concrete form of organization and doctrine — is reported to have said the following: "I hope my successor will be as much attached to the Church as I have been and will have as keen a desire to do good: beyond that, I can see that everything has changed; my system and my policies have had their day, but I am too old to change my course; that will be the task of my successor" [13:153]. Pius IX did not find his true successor until John XXIII, who called the Council in which the great change came to fruition.

In this Council the Fathers gathered to *discuss*, a fact that was to increase the influence of intellectuals on policy making — both the intellectuals among the episcopate and among their advisers. In this Council the Fathers soon came to feel their own collegial status and responsibility. As we have indicated, reflection might well suggest to the more thoughtful the bankruptcy which threatened the defensive policies and rigid postures of the past. In this Council the Fathers met within view and within earshot of a world favorably disposed to expect something worthwhile from them, a world which would hold them responsible in a new way. They were, in a sense, on trial.

In this situation the modernizers, who had come into existence with the slow thaw of the antimodernist mentality, came into their own. The context threw the balance in favor of the intellectuals, but conservative theologians were prepared to do scarcely more than repeat the older positions. They had little to offer except further condemnations of the well known sources of threat: communism, atheism, etc. Yet John XXIII had called the Council in the spirit of dialogue, of pastoral concern, of updating the Church, and not of polemic and anathema. The conditions within the Church and the position of the Church in the world — the total context — cried out for something new. In this situation the new theologians — those who, under official discouragement and disapproval, explored the theology of the secular world, of the Church, of history, and of the Bible — had something to offer. Not surprisingly, they were more and more called upon. It was a great moment of fulfillment for a century and a half of unsuccessful efforts at *aggiornamento* when the progressive theologians emerged as the most influential *periti* at the Council. It meant that the Church would meet the trial it faced, that it would begin the massive task of reorienting itself by rational discussion and fraternal dialogue. The molting of the old Church would begin.

Thus the Council was called and thus it became occupied with *aggiornamento* in depth. Its results record the beginning of such an *aggiornamento*, genuine though in a sense — in relation to the magnitude of the tasks — modest. "The Council marked the decisive beginning of the aggiornamento, it established the renewal, it called us to the ever necessary repentance and return; in other words, it was only the beginning of the beginning" [9:19 f]. Yet in view of the condition of the Roman Catholic Church in the late eighteenth and nineteenth centuries, in view of the historical burdens with which it entered the modern period, a decisive beginning of the beginning represents a tremendous historical accomplishment. In braving the "terrifying, threatening, unknown future facing the Church" [9:39], the Fathers considered the two most fundamental questions concerning ecclesiology. The first, as Pope Paul VI put it, was "What is the Church? This has been the great question of the Council." And the second was "the other theme, which inquires as to how the Church, in its turn, views the world" [quoted in 10:745]. Paul observes that the conciliar answers to this second "immense question" are marked by "optimism." A "beginning" begun with "optimism" of a genuine "aggiornamento in depth" could indeed point to the "very bold and far-reaching changes" necessary if Christianity in our day is to survive with relevance. It is against the background of these considerations that one should attempt to evaluate the *Pastoral Constitution on the Church in the Modern World*.

Judged according to a variety of criteria, this Constitution is without question the most typical Council document. It is the only major document to arise out of a suggestion made by a bishop speaking on the floor of the aula of St Peter's Basilica. It expresses more directly than any other conciliar document the new spirit of dialogue between the Church and the world, which all observers agree is the distinguishing characteristic of the Council.

The Pastoral Constitution is the product of a long process of preparation in which commissions, mixed commissions, subcommittees, and general floor debate made a series of drastic and fundamental alterations in it. Many of the concerns it takes up can be found in the more than 70 schemata drawn up by preconciliar commissions but scattered throughout the various documents. Curiously enough, the Council called to effect *aggiornamento* had no single prepared statement on the Church in the world. After the first session, Pope John appointed a Coordinating Commission to reduce the number of prepared documents to a manageable number. The result was 17 schemata, the last bearing the title *De Presentia Activa Ecclesiae in Mundo* (*On the Active Presence of the Church in the World*). Under the

guidance of Leon-Joseph Cardinal Suenens, whose original remarks in the first session had set the project of such a Constitution afoot, the document started its long evolution. Its number,
its contents, and even its name changed in the course of its preparation. With a further reduction of the number of documents
it became schema 13. Reworked, reformulated, restated many
times in committee and on the floor, it finally emerged, as Archbishop Garrone said in presenting it to the Fathers for their
approval, as a genuine endeavor "to place the Church in dialogue
with the world, truthfully and realistically" [6:398]. It represented, he said, "the very heart of the Council." It had come
through its long preparatory and revisory history as a statement
which recognized the condition of the modern world and strove
to speak to its problems in a language that world could understand.

Its preface stresses the intimate ties binding the Church to
mankind, stating that the Church shares the "joys and the hopes,
the griefs and the anxieties of the men of this age" (art 1). Its
basic approach is empirical, and it attempts to understand the
modern situation before all else. Only then does it try to relate
Christian values to the contemporary scene. Its empirical realism
and its spirit of dialogue are most striking. It eschews altogether
the old attitude of ecclesiastical eminence — what is sometimes
called "Constantinianism." Says Donald Campion, SJ, "The
most distinctive note sounded in the text, many already agree, is
that of the Church putting itself consciously at the service of the
family of man" [3:185].

At long last the Roman Catholic Church was putting together
a document which reflected the true condition of the Church in
the world in our time. As Bishop McGrath put it, "Here, at last
. . . for the first time in a Conciliar document, a biblical Catholic synthesis of the meaning of Christian man and Christian
society on earth and in time striving toward eternity" was presented [6:408]. In this longest conciliar document in the entire
history of the Christian Church, there evolved a most striking
attempt to take the world of secular man seriously and to relate
it in depth to the concerns and teachings of the Church. Here,

to quote Bishop McGrath again, we find "a frank pursuit of the proper values of the things and structures and situations of which the life of man is made, values which are theirs of themselves, and which must be understood to be lived and to be offered to God through the men who live them together in their striving for him" [6:410].

In this document the Church lays aside an older defensiveness for open confrontation; an older ecclesiasticism for service to man; an earlier pessimism about what Cardinal Antonelli called "the chief errors and false doctrines of our most unhappy age" [5:267] for a marked tendency, despite qualifications and cautions, "to accentuate the positive in a realistic appraisal of trends and movements at work today in the City of Man" [3:185]. In this document also the Church faces up to experience, instead of repeating its own stock formulas, and adheres with scrupulous care to a marked respect for the autonomy of the social science disciplines in observing and interpreting their data. It would appear to the thoughtful reader that Lamennais, Montalembert, Döllinger, and even perhaps Loisy and Tyrrell had not lived in vain. And this first impression is strengthened rather than dissipated by a more careful reading of the Constitution.

The Constitution begins with the preface we have quoted above and then moves to an introductory statement dealing with "The Situation of Men in the Modern World," which recognizes that today "the human race is passing through a new stage in its history" and characterizes this new stage as "a crisis of growth" (art 4). Then follows the Constitution proper, divided into two parts. The first part consists of four chapters dealing with the Church and man's calling in the world; the second, of five chapters, concerning "Some Problems of Special Urgency" dealing with contemporary problems, from those affecting the family to those concerning the dangers of total war. The first section represents the more general teaching of the Church; the second applies it to specific current problems. While this is a pastoral constitution attempting to develop and set forth the Church's relation to the world, the first part may be considered, not without some justification, a more dogmatic statement — a presentation of basic ideas on the Church in the modern world. We shall here summarize, analyze, and comment upon this important first section.

The text of the Constitution rests upon two fundamental insights concerning man in our age. It recognizes that men have now achieved the capacity to control and direct the external conditions of their lives; they have, in fact, unprecedented power over the environment. Science, as Descartes predicted, is about to render man "master and possessor" of nature. Toward this development the Church was long caught in an odd ambiguity. Its positive Old Testament evaluation of the creation as good, and its acceptance of human rationality, tended to line up the Church on the side of human progress. As Alfred North Whitehead pointed out, science developed out of the mentality that the Church had formed in the Middle Ages. But the defensiveness of the Church against secularization and the need to defend the closed formulations of its faith against new ideas placed it in opposition. Humanism was in some respects the revolt of Prometheanism against this effort to contain man's endeavors. Now the Church recognizes the nobility of and justification for human efforts. It recognizes also, however, that the process of external mastery, the achievement of rational control, has at the same time dissolved the older cultural contexts and disrupted the older social structures within which men found security, meaning, and identity itself. The development of the modern world, with its urbanized society based upon scientific technology, is the simultaneous development of scientific mastery and social anomie. Man has subdued the earth, but he is not as a consequence the master of his fate or the captain of his soul.

Man's outward triumphs have placed him in a position to remake the world. "Technology is now transforming the face of the earth, and is already trying to master outer space" (art 5). Man's technical accomplishments have set off "profound and rapid changes," which are now "spreading by degrees around the whole world. Triggered by the intelligence and creative energies of man, these changes recoil upon him, upon his decisions and desires, both individual and collective, and upon his manner of thinking and feeling with respect to things and people" (art 4). The impact of his mastery has torn up the established traditional context of life, annihilated the older provincialism so protective of his traditional beliefs and values, and brought a new interdependence and a new cosmopolitanism. The "traditional local communities . . . experience more thorough changes every day. The industrial type of society is gradually being spread, leading some nations to economic affluence, and radically transforming ideas and social conditions established for centuries" (art 4). Urbanization brings a "multiplication of cities and their inhabitants" and "a transplantation of city life to rural settings" (art 6). The modern revolution in communication not only spreads a "knowledge of events" but also gives "the swiftest and widest circulation to styles of thought and feeling" (art 6). Moreover, the "destiny of the human community has become all of a piece, where once the various groups of men had a kind of private history of their own" (art 5).

Yet the modern Prometheus remains at war with himself. Despite a great increase in power for both construction and destruction, the rivalries, competitions, and animosities characteristic of earlier stages of human history remain with us. "Although the world of today has a very vivid sense of its unity and of how one man depends on another in needful solidarity, it is most grievously torn into opposing camps by conflicting forces. For political, social, economic, racial, and ideological disputes still continue bitterly, and with them the peril of a war which would reduce everything to ashes" (art 4). His genuine progress has denuded man of traditional values to a considerable degree. "As happens in any crisis of growth, this transformation has brought serious difficulties in its wake. Thus while man extends his power in every direction, he does not always succeed in subjecting it to his own welfare. Striving to penetrate farther into the deeper recesses of his own mind, he frequently lays bare the laws of society, only to be paralyzed by uncertainty about the direction to give it" (art 4). External victories are purchased at the price of unsureness and indecision, precisely at the time when both the avoidance of tremendous dangers and the accomplishment of

310

great good make a sure sense of orientation more important than ever. Moreover, even the fruits of the external victories remain spottily distributed, thereby contributing to a greater instability and danger for man at large. "Never has the human race enjoyed such an abundance of wealth, resources, and economic power. Yet a huge proportion of the world's citizens is still tormented by hunger and poverty, while countless numbers suffer from total illiteracy" (art 4).

Man is thus not only changing the earth, his dwelling; he is changing himself. Aspects once considered part of an unchanging human nature are now seen to be altered by the historic experience of external mastery, which experience becomes at the same time a profound modification of the modes of thought and feeling. "The institutions, laws, and modes of thinking and feeling as handed down from previous generations do not always seem well adapted to the contemporary state of affairs. Hence arises an upheaval in the manner and even in the norms of behavior" (art 7). The mind and outlook of modern man are "increasingly based on the mathematical and natural sciences and on those dealing with man himself, while in the practical order the technology which stems from these sciences takes on mounting importance" (art 5). Further, "biology, psychology, and the social sciences not only bring men improved self-knowledge. In conjunction with technical methods, they are also helping men to exert direct influence on the life of social groups" (art 5).

"Finally, these new conditions have their impact upon religion. On the one hand a more critical ability to distinguish religion from a magical view of the world and from the superstitions which still circulate purifies religion and exacts day-by-day a more personal and explicit adherence to faith. As a result many persons are achieving a more vivid sense of God" (art 7). The desacralization of the world is regarded as having a positive religious significance, and man's critical abilities, so highly perfected in modern times, are thought of as providing the basis for a purer faith.

Here the Council sees the maturation function of modern developments. Old contexts — social and cultural — are dissolved, and the individual emerges in a new freedom. Knowledge advances, and the individual emerges with a new understanding. This at least is the case with some, and such is the promise, although it is accompanied by a new insecurity and too often by a lack of orientation. Yet the positive possibilities of emancipation in this molting process are acknowledged.

The Council is also quite aware that desacralization, criticism, external mastery, and the evolving social and cultural disorganization of which these processes are a part have affected religion in a negative way.

> On the other hand, growing numbers of people are abandoning religion in practice. Unlike former days, the denial of God or religion, or the abandonment of them, are no longer unusual or individual occurrences. For today it is not rare for such decisions to be presented as requirements of scientific progress or of a certain humanism. In numerous places these views are voiced not only in the teachings of philosophers, but on every side they influence literature, the arts, the interpretations of the humanities and of history, and civil laws themselves. As a consequence, many people are shaken [art 7].

Thus does the Council perceive the "true social and cultural transformation" (art 4) which, like all great changes, "calls accepted values into question." It is also aware of the self-transforming aspects of the modern experience. "To a certain extent, the human intellect is broadening its dominion over time: over the past by means of historical knowledge, over the future by the art of projecting and planning" (art 5). Men are learning "to exert direct influence on the life of social groups. At the same time, the human race is giving ever-increasing thought to forecasting and regulating its own population growth" (art 5).

Commenting on all this, the Council most significantly recognizes that "the human race has passed from a rather static concept of reality, to a more dynamic, evolutionary one" (art 5). It notes that the rapidity of the changes and the "disorderly fashion" in which they often occur "beget contradictions and imbalances, or intensify them" (art 8). Men are "more conscious than ever of the inequalities in the world," and this has an upsetting effect (art 8). There are imbalances within the person and within society, between practical achievement and "the demands of the moral conscience," between the demands of theory and of practice, between the individual and the group — "the conditions of collective existence and the requisites of personal thought" — between the demands of specialization and the need for "a comprehensive view of reality" (art 8). Quite apparent are "the mutual distrust, enmities, conflicts, and hardships" so characteristic of human life as phenomena of which man is "at once cause and victim."

In this difficult, distraught, but developing world, the Council sees mankind seeking "to consolidate its control over creation" and identifies itself with the human aspiration to "establish a political, social, and economic order which will to an ever better extent serve man and help individuals as well as groups to affirm and develop dignity proper to them." The Council is aware of the growing demand of all men for the material conditions of a decent life and their equally significant need for human dignity. It is also cognizant of aspirations for freedom and selfhood. "Now, for the first time in human history, all people are convinced that the benefits of culture ought to be and actually can be extended to everyone" (art 9).

Thus "the modern world" is "at once powerful and weak, capable of the noblest deeds or the foulest. Before it lies the path to freedom or to slavery, to progress or retreat, to brotherhood or hatred" (art 9). But beneath all of these phenomena "lies a deeper and more widespread longing. Persons and societies thirst for a full and free life worthy of man — one in which they can subject to their own welfare all that the modern world can offer them so abundantly" (art 9). In this state "man is becoming aware that it is his responsibility to guide aright the forces which he has unleashed and which can enslave him or minister to him" (art 9).

Thus has the Second Vatican Council recognized all those trends in the modern world which in the past were the bane of the Church's existence — those which it tried to resist, those to which it reluctantly attempted to adapt itself, changing itself as little as possible in the process, and those which it chose to ignore. The development of modernity involved both secularization and emancipation, the improvement of the means of life and the destruction of traditional culture and social structure, an increasing individuation and an increasing interdependence – in short, liberation and genuine opportunity together with the threat and real possibility of chaos. It is admitted that old modes of thought and feeling and old forms of social relations are passing away and are being replaced by emerging new forms, even "new social relations between men and women" (art 8). And all this is suffused by men's aspirations for and efforts to achieve "a full and free life worthy of man" (art 9).

To subdue the earth and make its forces minister to human welfare, to build a genuine human community, and to realize man's own full and free development – this the Council recognizes as central to man's purposeful activity on the earth. Such recognition modifies much in the earlier formulations of man's destiny in the practical teaching of the Church. It brings a new specificity and a new historical character to the Catholic view. It replaces the older static view with a dynamic one in which men not only change their circumstances but continually transform themselves. The importance of experience in shaping man, of immanent forces in man seeking expression and fulfillment, of the involvement of life in a historical process, of the situational conditioning of human consciousness is made plain in this characterization of the situation of men in the modern world with which the Constitution begins.

Every one of these elements was argued for by the liberal Catholic movements which in the last 150 years advocated *aggiornamento*. The Church now knows that in some way man is in fact a historical being. In some profound sense he is emerging or evolving. That realization supplies the context for the perennial questions of meaning for man, arising anew, and with renewed poignancy, in our age. "For in man himself many elements wrestle with one another. Thus on the one hand, as a creature he experiences his limitations in a multitude of ways. On the other, he feels himself to be boundless in his desires and

summoned to a higher life" (art 10). Many expect a "total emancipation of humanity wrought solely by human effort," while
others "despair of any meaning to life and praise the boldness
of those who think that human existence is devoid of any inherent significance and who strive to confer a total meaning on it
by their own ingenuity alone" (art 10). "Nevertheless, in the
face of the modern development of the world, an ever increasing
number of people are raising the most basic questions or recognizing them with a new sharpness: What is man? What is this
sense of sorrow, of evil, of death, which continues to exist despite so much progress? What is the purpose of these victories,
purchased at so high a cost? What can man offer to society, what
can he expect from it? What follows this earthly life?" (art 10).
It is to these questions in particular that the Constitution addresses its message in its first section. The introductory statement
of the document closes with the wish "in the light of Christ . . .
to speak to all men in order to illuminate the mystery of man
and to cooperate in finding the solution to the outstanding problems of our time" (art 10).

Part One of the *Pastoral Constitution on the Church in the
Modern World* looks at the present situation in the light of faith,
to "decipher authentic signs of God's presence and purpose in
the happenings, needs, and desires" with which the Church today and all men are involved. "For faith throws a new light on
everything, manifests God's design for man's total vocation, and
thus directs the mind to solutions which are fully human"
(art 11). Next are presented the three basic questions which the
Fathers will seek to answer in this document. "What does the
Church think of man? What recommendations seem needful for
the upbuilding of contemporary society? What is the ultimate
significance of human activity throughout the world?" (art 11).

"What does the Church think of man?" The Fathers assert
the dignity of the human person made in God's image in a brief
section (art 12) studded with references to and quotations from
Genesis (1:26, 27, 31), Wisdom (2:23), Ecclesiasticus (17:
3–10), and Psalms 8:5–6). They see him appointed "as master
of all earthly creatures that he might subdue them and use them

315

to God's glory." They then restate the doctrine of original sin in that "made by God in a state of holiness, from the very dawn of history man abused his liberty, at the urging of personified Evil. Man set himself against God and sought to find fulfillment apart from God." The result has been "man split within himself," his relation "to his own ultimate goal" disrupted, and "all of human life, whether individual or collective," showing itself "to be a dramatic struggle between good and evil, between light and darkness" (art 13).

Yet, "obliged to regard his body as good and honorable since God created it and will raise it up again on the last day," man "is not wrong when he regards himself superior to bodily concerns." For though "wounded by sin," by "his interior qualities he outstrips the whole sum of mere things" (art 14). His mind "shares in the light of the divine mind," and through it he "has won superlative victories, especially in his probing of the material world and in subjecting it to himself." His mind can know "reality itself" though "in consequence of sin" his certitude "is partly obscured and weakened." He can rise "through visible realities to whose which are unseen" (art 15). In particular is man's dignity related to his conscience — "the most secret core and sanctuary" — in the depths of which he "detects a law which he does not impose on himself . . . summoning him to love good and avoid evil" (art 16). The dignity of man's mind and conscience requires freedom; it demands the right to act "according to a knowing and free choice" (art 17).

But man is the creature who must die and who knows that he must die. Despite his dignity and worth, he faces death, and "it is in the face of death that the riddle of human existence becomes most acute." The problem is constitutive to man's very being. "Tormented by pain" and "by a dread of personal extinction," man "rebels against death because he bears in himself an eternal seed which cannot be reduced to sheer matter" (art 18). To this knowing and choosing being, this being of "grandeur" and "misery" (art 13), this man who feels "that desire for a higher life which is inescapably lodged in his breast" (art 18) — to him the Church brings its message of salvation from sin. It announces that

316

"the Lord Himself came to free and strengthen man, renewing him inwardly" (art 13), and expresses its hope "of a divine life beyond all corruption," for "Christ won this victory when He rose to life, since by His death He freed man from death."

There follows a consideration of atheism, "accounted among the most serious problems of this age." This treatment has been often remarked upon because it attempts to understand an aspect of the modern mentality as found in large numbers of our contemporaries, not simply to present prepared counterarguments. It points out that the Church "cannot cease repudiating" atheism as a human option but sees the answer as being given "chiefly by the witness of a living and mature faith" (art 21). The variety of atheists is recognized, from those who never knew the Christian way to God to those who "never get to the point of raising questions about God, since they seem to experience no religious stirrings" (art 19). An article is devoted to "systematic atheism," which "stretches the desire for human independence to such a point that it finds difficulties with any kind of dependence on God" and wishes thereby to give "man freedom to be an end unto himself, the sole artisan and creator of his own history." For people who embrace this view, such human freedom is considered irreconcilable with "the affirmation of a Lord who is author and purpose of all things" (art 20). Again, the Church proclaims its ancient *kerygma*, "the mystery of the incarnate Word," "Christ, the final Adam," in whom "God reconciled us to Himself and among ourselves" (art 22).

Accepting atheism as a modern problem, the document calls for "sincere and prudent dialogue," and at the same time advocating "that all men, believers and unbelievers alike, ought to work for the rightful betterment of this world in which all alike live" (art 21). In the hearts of "all men of good will" Christ's reconciliation has its effect, and "grace works in an unseen way. . . . For since Christ died for all men, and since the ultimate vocation of man is in fact one, and divine, we ought to believe that the Holy Spirit in a manner known only to God offers to every man the possibility of being associated with this paschal mystery" (art 22).

317

In Chapter II, "The Community of Mankind," the Constitution begins by noting once more "the growing interdependence of men one on the other" as "one of the salient features of the modern world" (art 23) brought about by modern technical advance. This process, in which "reciprocal ties and mutual dependencies" increase, is called "socialization," a term from the works of Teilhard de Chardin (art 25). The process can be such that "the human person is greatly aided in responding to his destiny, even in its religious dimensions," but it can divert men from that destiny as well (art 25).

In the face of this development the Constitution advocates the "full spiritual dignity of the person" (art 23) and the common good of society as the conditions that will allow "social groups and their individual members relatively thorough and ready access to their own fulfillment" (art 26). Man "is the only creature on earth which God willed for itself." At the same time, man is by nature social and can "find himself" only in a "sincere gift of himself." All men are "called to one and the same goal, namely, God Himself" (art 24). Social institutions are justified in terms of their contribution to the fulfillment of the human person (art 25), but man possesses social responsibilities and must follow "the laws of social life which the Creator has written into man's spiritual and moral nature" (art 23).

The Constitution repeats (art 28) the admonition of the gospel to love one's enemies (Mt 5:43–44) and points to the importance of man's essential equality. It states that because of this "equal dignity of persons," which remains the case despite "rightful differences," it is necessary that "a more human and just condition of life be brought about" (art 29). Man cannot "content himself with a merely individualistic morality." Rather, it is a "sacred obligation to count social necessities among the primary duties of modern man and to pay heed to them" (art 30).

Chapter II closes with a call for self-cultivation in "the moral and social virtues" (art 30) and the careful education of youth "from every social background" (art 31). Only then can it be hoped that, "with the needed help of divine grace, men who are truly new and artisans of a new humanity can be forthcoming"

318

(art 30). Only then "there can be produced . . . those great-souled persons who are so desperately required by our times" (art 31). The Fathers assert that man's personal dignity together with his "communitarian character" are fulfilled in Christ, "who sanctified those human ties, especially family ones, from which social relationships arise" (art 32).

By this time the Constitution has laid the ground for answering two of the three questions raised in article 2. It has presented its view of man, attempting to put together its classical heritage, the indications of modern thought and contemporary science, and the message of the Christian *kerygma*. It will develop these ideas further in Part Two, where are set forth more specific proposals. It has also stated its view of society, which will be enlarged upon in Part Two. In Chapter III of Part One the Constitution addresses itself to the third question, concerning the "significance of human activity throughout the world."

> Throughout the course of centuries, men have labored to better the circumstances of their lives through a monumental amount of individual and collective effort. To believers, this point is settled: considered in itself, such human activity accords with God's will. For man, created to God's image, received a mandate to subject to himself the earth and all that it contains, and to govern the world with justice and holiness; a mandate to relate himself and the totality of things to Him who was to be acknowledged as the Lord and Creator of all [art 34].

In all this men may be assured that "by their labor they are unfolding the Creator's work" and that their triumphs are "the flowering of God's mysterious design" (art 34). Moreover, by his work man not only changes things and society; he "develops himself as well," going beyond himself and developing his endowment and resources. Indeed, such growth "is of greater value than any external riches." The Constitution proclaims this "norm of human activity" that, "in accord with the divine plan and will, it should harmonize with the genuine good of the human race, and allow men as individuals and as members of society to pursue their total vocation and fulfill it" (art 35).

Here we see how the Council strove to assert its recognition of "man's total vocation" (arts 11 and 35), how it attempted to combine its recognition of the importance, the legitimacy, and the nobility of man's worldly vocation with its own conception of the true calling of the Christian. To subdue the earth, to build community, and to develop himself — this is what man is doing on earth, and it "accords with God's will" (art 34). The Constitution can assert that legitimation; it can assert that it is consistent with man's destiny to "a divine life beyond all corruption" (art 13). Working out the implications of these assertions will be the task of a theology of history and of vocation. In this case too the Council is but the "beginning of a beginning."

Christianity has never been able to solve this problem; Catholicism has never developed a model of the lay Christian, and the only Reformation group which achieved a measure of success attained it at the cost of two significant elements. First, in Puritanism it was achieved for a while at the price of massive repression, which could not but render the solution short lived. Such a repressive, overdisciplined, and narrowly focused solution had little to offer as a permanent answer to the long-range problems of man, society, and culture. The element of transcendence that it strove to maintain does, however, point to an element in the Calvinist solution which must not be lost from sight. Second, the Calvinist solution also was attained in a way which led in a few generations to something rather like total secularization — to an odd combination, in fact, of secularization without emancipation.

Thus the problem involved in putting together the idea of a fully legitimate vocation in the world with the transcendent call of the New Testament is a difficult and complex one. The failures to solve it cannot be attributed simply to human stupidity or perversity — always ample, no doubt. There is a built-in ontological problem of how a religious life is harmonized with a life in the world, how the response to the call of something "beyond" can be maintained amidst concentrated concern with tasks. Some rhythm of involvement with the world and return to a relation to transcendence would seem to be required, a rhythm to be worked out concretely in different social and cultural settings. Troeltsch has suggested how this major point of tension and balance affected the history of the Church. We have found it a central element in the great problems faced by the Church since the Middle Ages. Catholic theology now faces the great task of working out the implications of the stand taken by the Council. It must come to appreciate and indeed illuminate the worth of the dramas acted out by individuals, by classes, by nations, and by larger groupings of men in the world.

The recognition of man's vocation at the same time justifies autonomous human activity. Vocation is seen to involve earthly affairs, which means "that created things and societies themselves enjoy their own laws and values which must be gradually deciphered, put to use, and regulated by men." Such activity possesses a rightful autonomy, "required by modern men" and in harmony with "the will of the Creator." Again the Council is dealing with an aspect of the problem which vexed Christians and plagued the Church for centuries. While temporal affairs do "depend on God" and man cannot participate in them "without reference to their Creator," nevertheless a sphere of legitimate autonomous human action in the world is proclaimed.

We have seen that in the nineteenth century the Church could not accept freedom of scholarship but sought to continue the long-obsolete situation of the Middle Ages, when all learning was conceived in a hierarchy of sciences with theology at the apex. Thus in the realm of learning was found the structural equivalent of the hierarchy in society in which the Church was preeminent. But now the Fathers recognize the freedom of the human mind.

> Therefore, if methodical investigation within every branch of learning is carried out in a genuinely scientific manner and in accord with moral norms, it never truly conflicts with faith. For earthly matters and the concerns of faith derive from the same God. . . . Consequently, we cannot but deplore certain habits of mind, sometimes found too among Christians, which do not sufficiently attend to the rightful independence of science. The arguments and controversies which they spark lead many minds to conclude that faith and science are opposed [art 36].

This statement is followed by an official annotation to the two-volume study by Monseigneur Pio Paschini, *Vita e Opere di Galileo Galilei.*

The Constitution raises the question of sin, noting that man's worldly accomplishments also bring temptation to evil and that "a monumental struggle against the powers of darkness pervades the whole history of man." Caught in this conflict, man is obliged to wrestle constantly if he is to cling to what is good. Nor can he achieve his own integrity without "valiant efforts and the help of God's grace." The Christian concern is not simply with the world as the arena for man's total vocation, which is activity in accordance with God's will. There is also that world of which Paul speaks in the Epistle to the Romans when he says, "Be not conformed to this world" (Romans 12:2). The Constitution defines that "world" as "that spirit of vanity and malice which transforms into an instrument of sin those human energies intended for the service of God and man" (art 37).

The Constitution sees man with his worldly vocation, his human capacities, his involvement in sin, and his call to grace. In trying to indicate how these characteristics of the human condition can be put together in a consistent piece, it recognizes a central element in man which the Church long resisted grasping. Here the Fathers retain their ancient Hellenic heritage of natural law, but they implicitly suggest its restatement in terms of personalism. The person — existence, development, and realization — is placed first as the core of man's earthly vocation and made one of the chief ends of the political and social community. This suggests that man has a structure and that whatever violates that structure is antipersonal and therefore unethical. In the best tradition of the Greeks, ethics is seen as conventions not simply agreed upon to maintain order but derived from genuine dimensions of the human situation — of man in his relation to the world. It is now restated, however, in terms of a personalism rather than the biologism of Aristotle.

Even more significant, the Church now sees that this structure has a certain openness and flexibility about it. Formerly the Church took the static view, saw man and society as a static — and historically a conservative — archetype. Right reason, with the aid of the magisterium, was thought capable of understanding that ahistorical model. Now man's unformedness, his open

322

potential, his flexibility and manysidedness are confronted. History reveals possibilities in him which, realized in part, in part have been suppressed by conditions and even distorted in ways such that man is both "cause and victim." Man's entelechy is now perceived as open. The Church seeks to relate this openness to its own call to an ultimate destiny.

Yet the Council does not abandon the Christian insight concerning sin. Man is not simply foreshortened by the conditions of his existence which limit and distort his self-realization; he is not simply victim. He is also limited and truncated by his own short-circuited motivations; he is also cause. Self-interest, resentment, fear, the inordinate desire for security — these influence his action and its consequences. We earlier quoted the London *Tablet* to the effect that there was a danger of "taking the modern world too much at its own valuation," and of taking insufficiently into account "the way the world we live in has been made for us, in such great measure, by the sin as well as by the virtues of our predecessors" [quoted in 8:315]. It is not simply the world of the past that is so affected, the Council recognizes, but the present, evolving world. Men act out their hopes and aspirations in the dramas of earthly existence. Their efforts express elements of the greatest nobility. But they reflect those aspects of foreshortening which Christianity calls sin.

This section of the Constitution closes with a statement relating man's progress to the eschatological hopes of the Church. "Earthly progress must be carefully distinguished from the growth of Christ's kingdom. Nevertheless, to the extent that the former can contribute to the better ordering of human society, it is of vital concern to the kingdom of God" (art 39). For indeed, "Christ is now at work in the hearts of men through the energy of His Spirit. He arouses not only desire for the age to come, but by that very fact, He animates, purifies, and strengthens those noble longings too by which the human family strives to make its life more human and to render the whole earth submissive to this goal" (art 38). "For after we have obeyed the Lord, and in His spirit nurtured the earth, the values of human dignity, brotherhood and freedom, and indeed all the good fruits of our nature and enterprise, we will find them again, but freed of stain, burnished and transfigured. . . . On this earth that kingdom is already present in mystery. When the Lord comes, it will be brought into full flower" (art 39).

Chapter IV of Part One deals with the role of the Church in the modern world. It sees that role primarily as one of exchange and dialogue with the world. The Church, "a visible assembly and a spiritual community" (art 40), "serves as a leaven. . . . That the earthly and the heavenly city penetrate each other is a fact accessible to faith alone. It remains a mystery of human history, which sin will keep in great disarray until the splendor of God's sons is fully revealed." But in this state of things, the Church should strive to have a "healing and elevating impact upon the dignity of the person, by the way in which she strengthens the seams of human society and embues the everyday activity of men with a deeper meaning and importance. Thus, through her individual members and her whole community, the Church believes she can contribute greatly toward making the family of man and its history more human" (art 40). The Church would contribute to human fulfillment.

After expressing its "high esteem" for "the things which other Christian Churches or ecclesial communities have done" for this goal, the "Council now sets forth certain general principles for the fostering of this mutual exchange and assistance in concerns which are in some way common to the Church and the world" (art 40). The Council believes that by revealing God to "modern man," who is "on the road to a more thorough development of his own personality," the Church helps to meet "the deepest longings of the human heart." Only God "provides a fully adequate answer to these questions" — what is the meaning of man's life, of his activity, of his death (art 41). The Council holds that "the Church can anchor the dignity of human nature against all tides of opinion, for example, those which undervalue the human body or idolize it. By no human law can the personal dignity and liberty of man be so aptly safeguarded as by the gospel of Christ which has been so entrusted to the Church." The Church "proclaims the rights of man," yet eschews "any kind of false autonomy," while at the same time defending "the rightful autonomy of the creature, particularly of man." The Church does so because "the gospel announces and proclaims the freedom of the sons of God, and repudiates all the bondage which ultimately results from sin" (art 41).

The Council sees the "union of the human family" as "greatly fortified and fulfilled by the unity, founded on Christ, of the family of God's sons" and states unequivocally that Christ "gave His Church no proper mission in the political, economic, or social order," but rather set before her "a religious one." But it is asserted that "out of this religious mission itself" can come "a function, a light, and an energy which can serve to structure and consolidate the human community according to divine law." Moreover, the "Church further recognizes that worthy elements are found in today's social movements, especially an evolution toward unity, a process of wholesome socialization and of association in civic and economic realms." The Church seeks to sustain what is best in man's nature and in his attempts to build community. "Bound to no particular form of human culture, nor to any political, economic, or social system," the Church "can inject into the modern society of man . . . faith and charity put into vital practice." It wishes to "assist and promote" the human institutions which men establish to increase human welfare (art 42).

The Christian laity are urged to perform as faithful practitioners of their life's work and citizens of their countries. They are to be "citizens of two cities," capable of gathering "their humane, domestic, professional, social, and technical enterprises into one vital synthesis with religious values." In this way they will overcome the split between religious values and daily life, "which deserves to be counted among the more serious errors of our age."

Bishops and priests are exhorted to "preach the message of Christ" so that "all the earthly activities of the faithful may be bathed in the light of the gospel." At the same time it is humbly recognized "how great a distance lies between the message" the Church "offers and the human failings of those to whom the gospel is entrusted" (art 43).

Chapter IV thus puts before us the vision of a Church of

service. It is appreciated, however, that the Church profits from the advance of modern society. By the science of our day, "the nature of man himself is more clearly revealed and new roads to truth are opened." Moreover, the Council advocates a "living exchange," to be developed "between the Church and the diverse cultures of people." The Constitution states, "Indeed, the Church admits that she has greatly and still profits from the antagonism of those who oppose or persecute her" (art 44). Service, dialogue, and exchange – these are the basis of the role of the Church. Humble, made up of sinners, needing to be purified while holy, being aided by antagonism – these are characteristics of the Church in the world today. Overcoming much in the heritage of its history and much in its contemporary situation, the Church approaches the world in genuine fraternity.

The first section of the Constitution closes by proclaiming anew that "while helping the world and receiving many benefits from it, the Church has a single intention: that God's kingdom may come, and that the salvation of the whole human race may come to pass," for the Church is asserted to be, in the words of the *Lumen Gentium*, "the sacrament of salvation" (art 45).

TWO PROBLEMS

What is most striking at first about this document is the forthrightness, the lack of archaic language, and the humility – the lack of ecclesiastical arrogance – with which it sets forth the answers to the questions it raises. In terms of the background against which we have considered it, one is struck by the radical change in attitude and posture that it represents. With utter realism, it assesses both the situation of man today and the relation of modern man and his problems and aspirations to the historic Church.

Yet the questions posed earlier occur to us again. Is there here an equivalent of Barth's calling of modern man to transcendence? Is there here an attempt to shed the accretions of the centuries that is the equivalent to Bultmann's demythologization? The effects of the molting process, the uprooting of the Church from its embeddedness in the old order, are clearly apparent. Compared to the agonies of the past, the present situation seems to show the Church to be emancipated, freed. We are, of course, aware that the setting of the Council favors the intellectuals and gives those striving for a more liberal and up-to-date policy the support of world opinion. Yet once the bishops returned to their sees to be surrounded by the old bureaucracy, once the problems were faced again in the administrative mode of decision making, once the compromises of everyday ecclesiastical life were operative again, once the old habits and mental sets were reactivated — in short, once the Council was over — the forces recalcitrant to change were strengthened. But the changes have been started. The beginning of the beginning had been made.

The Church faces two sets of problems: the inner conflict between conservatives and the advocates of *aggiornamento,* and the evolving of its new position without loss of the intensity and reality of its faith. A prime requisite for success is the preservation of its unity, the development of true inner dialogue. But the intellectual problems confronting Catholic theology are tremendous. It is to be hoped that the Church will be able to work upon them without too great a harassment from the rearguard of intransigent forces in the Church, some of whom, no doubt, are now after the Council more frightened than ever. We are entitled to ask whether the "very bold and far-reaching changes" necessary to the survival of Christianity in our day are forthcoming. Or, more modestly, Do we have here the "beginning of the beginning" of such changes? Is the Church of Rome embarking upon the troubled waters of the great transition by which it may be able to lead Christianity to the contemporary relevance it has sought in vain and western men to a deeper and nobler vision of fulfillment?

Note: The essay Professor O'Dea was commissioned to prepare for the volume rapidly grew to book length. We have excerpted one entire chapter and part of a second to publish in *The Religious Situation: 1968.* For a considerably more comprehensive historical analysis and an interpretation of several other critical documents from Vatican II relating to Christianity and modern culture, the reader is referred to Thomas F. O'Dea, *The Catholic Crisis* (Beacon Press, Boston, Massachusetts) 1967.

REFERENCES

1. Aubert, Roger: The Catholic Church, in Guy S Metraux and Francois Crouzet, ed, *Religions and the Promise of the Twentieth Century* (The New American Library, Inc, New York, New York) 1965.
2. Butler, Abbot Christopher: The Aggiornamento of Vatican II, in John H Miller, CSC, ed, *Vatican II: An Interfaith Appraisal,* International Theological Conference, University of Notre Dame, March 20–26, 1966 (University of Notre Dame Press, Notre Dame, Indiana) 1966.
3. Campion, Donald R, SJ: The Church Today, in Walter M Abbott, SJ, general ed, and Joseph Gallagher, translation ed, *The Documents of Vatican II* (Guild Press, Inc, American Press, Association Press, New York, New York) 1966.
4. Garaudy, Roger: *From Anathema to Dialogue: A Marxist Challenge to the Christian Churches,* Luke O'Neill, translator (Herder and Herder, Inc, New York) 1966.
5. Hales, E E Y: *Pio Nono* (Image Books, Doubleday & Company, Inc, Garden City, New York) 1962.
6. McGrath, Mark G, CSC: The Constitution on the Church in the Modern World, in John H Miller, CSC, ed, *Vatican II: An Interfaith Appraisal.* International Theological Conference, University of Notre Dame, March 20–26, 1966 (University of Notre Dame Press, Notre Dame, Indiana) 1966.
7. Macquarrie, John: *An Existentialist Theology: A Comparison of Heidegger and Bultmann* (Harper & Row, Publishers, New York, New York) 1965.
8. Newman, Jeremiah: *Change and the Catholic Church* (Helicon Press, Inc, Baltimore, Maryland) 1965.

328

9. Rahner, Karl: *The Church After the Council* (Herder and Herder, Inc, New York, New York) 1956.

10. *The Sixteen Documents of Vatican II*, with commentary by the Council Fathers, NCWC translation (Daughters of St Paul, St Paul Editions, Boston, Massachusetts) no date.

11. Tillich, Paul: *The Religious Situation* (Meridian Books, Inc, New York, New York) 1956. Published in 1932 by Henry Holt & Co, Inc.

12. Troeltsch, Ernst: *Christian Thought: Its History and Application*, Baron F von Hugel, ed (Meridian Books, Inc, Living Age Books, New York, New York) 1957.

13. Vidler, Alec R: *The Church in an Age of Revolution* (Penguin Books, Inc, Baltimore, Maryland) 1961.

14. Vidler, Alec R: *The Modernist Movement in the Roman Church* (Cambridge University Press, Cambridge, England) 1934.

8. CIVIL RELIGION IN AMERICA

by Robert N. Bellah

Wʜɪʟᴇ some have argued that Christianity is the national faith, and others that church and synagogue celebrate only the generalized religion of "the American Way of Life," few have realized that there actually exists alongside of and rather clearly differentiated from the churches an elaborate and well institutionalized civil religion in America. This article argues not only that there is such a thing, but also that this religion — or perhaps better, this religious dimension — has its own seriousness and integrity and requires the same care in understanding that any other religion does.

Why something so obvious should have escaped serious analytical attention is in itself an interesting problem. Part of the reason is probably the controversial nature of the subject. From the earliest years of the nineteenth century, conservative religious and political groups have argued that Christianity is, in fact, the national religion. Some of them have from time to time and as recently as the 1950s proposed constitutional amendments that would explicitly recognize the sovereignty of Christ.

In defending the doctrine of separation of church and state, opponents of such groups have denied that the national polity has, intrinsically, anything to do with religion at all. The moderates on this issue have insisted that the American state has taken a permissive and indeed supportive attitude toward religious groups (tax exemption, et cetera), thus favoring religion but still missing the positive institutionalization with which I am concerned. But part of the reason this issue has been left in obscurity is certainly due to the peculiarly Western concept of "religion" as denoting a single type of collectivity of which an individual can be a member of one and only one at a time. The Durkheimian notion that every group has a religious dimension, which would be seen as obvious in southern or eastern Asia, is foreign to us. This obscures the recognition of such dimensions in our society.

THE KENNEDY INAUGURAL

Kennedy's inaugural address of 20 January 1961 serves as an example and a clue with which to examine this complex subject. That address began:

> We observe today not a victory of party but a celebration of freedom — symbolizing an end as well as a beginning — signifying renewal as well as change. For I have sworn before you and Almighty God the same solemn oath our forebears prescribed nearly a century and three quarters ago.
>
> The world is very different now. For man holds in his mortal hands the power to abolish all forms of human poverty and to abolish all forms of human life. And yet the same revolutionary beliefs for which our forebears fought are still at issue around the globe — the belief that the rights of man come not from the generosity of the state but from the hand of God.

And it concluded:

> Finally, whether you are citizens of America or of the world, ask of us the same high standards of strength and sacrifice that we shall ask of you. With a good conscience our only sure reward, with history the final judge of our deeds, let us go forth to lead the land we love, asking His blessing and His help, but knowing that here on earth God's work must truly be our own.

These are the three places in this brief address in which Kennedy mentioned the name of God. If we could understand why he mentioned God, the way in which he did it, and what he meant to say in those three references, we would understand much about American civil religion. But this is not a simple or obvious task, and American students of religion would probably differ widely in their interpretation of these passages.

332

Let us consider first the placing of the three references. They occur in the two opening paragraphs and in the closing paragraph, thus providing a sort of frame for the more concrete remarks that form the middle part of the speech. Looking beyond this particular speech, we would find that similar references to God are almost invariably to be found in the pronouncements of American presidents on solemn occasions, though usually not in the working messages that the president sends to Congress on various concrete issues. How, then, are we to interpret this placing of references to God?

It might be argued that the passages quoted reveal the essentially irrelevant role of religion in the very secular society that is America. The placing of the references in this speech as well as in public life generally indicates that religion has "only a ceremonial significance"; it gets only a sentimental nod which serves largely to placate the more unenlightened members of the community, before a discussion of the really serious business with which religion has nothing whatever to do. A cynical observer might even say that an American president has to mention God or risk losing votes. A semblance of piety is merely one of the unwritten qualifications for the office, a bit more traditional than, but not essentially different from, the present-day requirement of a pleasing television personality.

But we know enough about the function of ceremonial and ritual in various societies to make us suspicious of dismissing something as unimportant because it is "only a ritual." What people say on solemn occasions need not be taken at face value, but it is often indicative of deep-seated values and commitments that are not made explicit in the course of everyday life. Following this line of argument, it is worth considering whether the very special placing of the references to God in Kennedy's address may not reveal something rather important and serious about religion in American life.

It might be countered that the very way in which Kennedy made his references reveals the essentially vestigial place of religion today. He did not refer to any religion in particular. He did not refer to Jesus Christ or to Moses or to the Christian church; certainly he did not refer to the Catholic Church. In fact, his only reference was to the concept of God, a word which almost all Americans can accept but which means so many different things to so many different people that it is almost an empty sign. Is this not just another indication that in America religion is considered vaguely to be a good thing but that people care so little about it that it has lost any content whatever? Isn't Eisenhower reported to have said, "Our government makes no sense unless it is founded in a deeply felt religious faith — and I don't care what it is" [8:97], and isn't that a complete negation of any real religion?

These questions are worth pursuing because they raise the issue of how civil religion relates to the political society, on the one hand, and to private religious organization, on the other. President Kennedy was a Christian, more specifically a Catholic Christian. Thus, his general references to God do not mean that he lacked a specific religious commitment. But why, then, did he not include some remark to the effect that Christ is the Lord of the world or some indication of respect for the Catholic Church? He did not because these are matters of his own private religious belief and of his relation to his own particular church; they are not matters relevant in any direct way to the conduct of his public office. Others with different religious views and commitments to different churches or denominations are equally qualified participants in the political process. The principle of separation of church and state guarantees the freedom of religious belief and association, but at the same time clearly segregates the religious sphere, which is considered to be essentially private, from the political one.

Considering the separation of church and state, how is a president justified in using the word *God* at all? The answer is that the separation of church and state has not denied the political realm a religious dimension. Although matters of personal religious belief, worship, and association are considered to be strictly private affairs, there are, at the same time, certain common elements of religious orientation that the great majority of Americans share. These have played a crucial role in the development of

334

American institutions and still provide a religious dimension for the whole fabric of American life, including the political sphere. This public religious dimension is expressed in a set of beliefs, symbols, and rituals that I am calling the American civil religion. The inauguration of a president is an important ceremonial event in this religion. It reaffirms, among other things, the religious legitimation of the highest political authority.

Let us look more closely at what Kennedy actually said. First he said, "I have sworn before you and Almighty God the same solemn oath our forebears prescribed nearly a century and three quarters ago." The oath is the oath of office, including the acceptance of the obligation to uphold the Constitution. He swears it before the people (you) and God. Beyond the Constitution, then, the president's obligation extends not only to the people but to God. In American political theory, sovereignty rests, of course, with the people, but implicitly, and often explicitly, the ultimate sovereignty has been attributed to God. This is the meaning of the motto, "In God we trust," as well as the inclusion of the phrase "under God" in the pledge to the flag. What difference does it make that sovereignty belongs to God? Though the will of the people as expressed in majority vote is carefully institutionalized as the operative source of political authority, it is deprived of an ultimate significance. The will of the people is not itself the criterion of right and wrong. There is a higher criterion in terms of which this will can be judged; it is possible that the people may be wrong. The president's obligation extends to the higher criterion.

When Kennedy says that "the rights of man come not from the generosity of the state but from the hand of God," he is stressing this point again. It does not matter whether the state is the expression of the will of an autocratic monarch or of the "people"; the rights of man are more basic than any political structure and provide a point of revolutionary leverage from which any state structure may be radically altered. That is the basis for his reassertion of the revolutionary significance of America.

But the religious dimension in political life as recognized by Kennedy not only provides a grounding for the rights of man

335

which makes any form of political absolutism illegitimate, it also provides a transcendent goal for the political process. This is implied in his final words that "here on earth God's work must truly be our own." What he means here is, I think, more clearly spelled out in a previous paragraph, the wording of which, incidentally, has a distinctly biblical ring:

> Now the trumpet summons us again — not as a call to bear arms, though arms we need — not as a call to battle, though embattled we are — but a call to bear the burden of a long twilight struggle, year in and year out, "rejoicing in hope, patient in tribulation" — a struggle against the common enemies of man: tyranny, poverty, disease and war itself.

The whole address can be understood as only the most recent statement of a theme that lies very deep in the American tradition, namely the obligation, both collective and individual, to carry out God's will on earth. This was the motivating spirit of those who founded America, and it has been present in every generation since. Just below the surface throughout Kennedy's inaugural address, it becomes explicit in the closing statement that God's work must be our own. That this very activist and noncontemplative conception of the fundamental religious obligation, which has been historically associated with the Protestant position, should be enunciated so clearly in the first major statement of the first Catholic president seems to underline how deeply established it is in the American outlook. Let us now consider the form and history of the civil religious tradition in which Kennedy was speaking.

THE IDEA OF A CIVIL RELIGION

The phrase *civil religion* is, of course, Rousseau's. In Chapter 8, Book 4, of *The Social Contract*, he outlines the simple dogmas of the civil religion: the existence of God, the life to come, the reward of virtue and the punishment of vice, and the exclusion of religious intolerance. All other religious opinions are outside the cognizance of the state and may be freely held by citizens. While

336

the phrase *civil religion* was not used, to the best of my knowledge, by the founding fathers, and I am certainly not arguing for the particular influence of Rousseau, it is clear that similar ideas, as part of the cultural climate of the late eighteenth century, were to be found among the Americans. For example, Franklin writes in his autobiography,

> I never was without some religious principles. I never doubted, for instance, the existence of the Deity; that he made the world and govern'd it by his Providence; that the most acceptable service of God was the doing of good to men; that our souls are immortal; and that all crime will be punished, and virtue rewarded either here or hereafter. These I esteemed the essentials of every religion; and, being to be found in all the religions we had in our country, I respected them all, tho' with different degrees of respect, as I found them more or less mix'd with other articles, which, without any tendency to inspire, promote or confirm morality, serv'd principally to divide us, and make us unfriendly to one another.

It is easy to dispose of this sort of position as essentially utilitarian in relation to religion. In Washington's Farewell Address (though the words may be Hamilton's) the utilitarian aspect is quite explicit:

> Of all the dispositions and habits which lead to political prosperity, Religion and Morality are indispensable supports. In vain would that man claim the tribute of Patriotism, who should labour to subvert these great Pillars of human happiness, these firmest props of the duties of men and citizens. The mere politician, equally with the pious man ought to respect and cherish them. A volume could not trace all their connections with private and public felicity. Let it simply be asked where is the security for property, for reputation, for life, if the sense of religious obligation *desert* the oaths, which are the instruments of investigation in Courts of Justice? And let us with caution indulge the supposition, that morality can be maintained without religion. Whatever may be conceded to the influence of refined education on minds of peculiar structure, reason and experience both forbid us to expect that National morality can prevail in exclusion of religious principle.

337

But there is every reason to believe that religion, particularly the idea of God, played a constitutive role in the thought of the early American statesmen.

Kennedy's inaugural pointed to the religious aspect of the Declaration of Independence, and it might be well to look at that document a bit more closely. There are four references to God. The first speaks of the "Laws of Nature and of Nature's God" which entitle any people to be independent. The second is the famous statement that all men "are endowed by their Creator with certain inalienable Rights." Here Jefferson is locating the fundamental legitimacy of the new nation in a conception of "higher law" that is itself based on both classical natural law and biblical religion. The third is an appeal to "the Supreme Judge of the world for the rectitude of our intentions," and the last indicates "a firm reliance on the protection of divine Providence." In these last two references, a biblical God of history who stands in judgment over the world is indicated.

The intimate relation of these religious notions with the self-conception of the new republic is indicated by the frequency of their appearance in early official documents. For example, we find in Washington's first inaugural address of 30 April 1789:

> It would be peculiarly improper to omit in this first official act my fervent supplications to that Almighty Being who rules over the universe, who presides in the councils of nations, and whose providential aids can supply every defect, that His benediction may consecrate to the liberties and happiness of the people of the United States a Government instituted by themselves for these essential purposes, and may enable every instrument employed in its administration to execute with success the functions allotted to his charge.
>
> No people can be bound to acknowledge and adore the Invisible Hand which conducts the affairs of man more than those of the United States. Every step by which we have advanced to the character of an independent nation seems to have been distinguished by some token of providential agency. . . .
>
> The propitious smiles of Heaven can never be expected on a nation that disregards the eternal rules of order and right which Heaven itself has ordained. . . . The preservation of the sacred

338

fire of liberty and the destiny of the republican model of government are justly considered, perhaps, as *deeply*, as *finally*, staked on the experiment intrusted to the hands of the American people.

Nor did these religious sentiments remain merely the personal expression of the president. At the request of both Houses of Congress, Washington proclaimed on October 3 of that same first year as President that November 26 should be "a day of public thanksgiving and prayer," the first Thanksgiving Day under the Constitution.

The words and acts of the founding fathers, especially the first few presidents, shaped the form and tone of the civil religion as it has been maintained ever since. Though much is selectively derived from Christianity, this religion is clearly not itself Christianity. For one thing, neither Washington nor Adams nor Jefferson mentions Christ in his inaugural address; nor do any of the subsequent presidents, although not one of them fails to mention God.

[God is mentioned or referred to in all inaugural addresses except Washington's second, which is a very brief (two paragraphs) and perfunctory acknowledgment. It is not without interest that the actual word *God* does not appear until Monroe's second inaugural, 5 March 1821. In his first inaugural, Washington refers to God as "that Almighty Being who rules the universe," "Great Author of every public and private good," "Invisible Hand," and "benign Parent of the Human Race." John Adams refers to God as "Providence," "Being who is supreme over all," "Patron of Order," "Fountain of Justice," and "Protector in all ages of the world of virtuous liberty." Jefferson speaks of "that Infinite Power which rules the destinies of the universe" and "that Being in whose hands we are." Madison speaks of "that Almighty Being whose power regulates the destiny of nations" and "Heaven." Monroe uses "Providence" and "the Almighty" in his first inaugural and finally "Almighty God" in his second [17].]

The God of the civil religion is not only rather "unitarian," he is also on the austere side, much more related to order, law, and right than to salvation and love. Even though he is somewhat deist in cast, he is by no means simply a watchmaker God. He is actively interested and involved in history, with a special concern for America. Here the analogy has much less to do with natural law than with ancient Israel; the equation of America with Israel in the idea of the "American Israel" is not infrequent. For example, Abiel Abbot, pastor of the First Church in Haverhill, Massachusetts, delivered a Thanksgiving sermon in 1799, *Traits of Resemblance in the People of the United States of America to Ancient Israel*, in which he said, "It has been often remarked that the people of the United States come nearer to a parallel with Ancient Israel, than any other nation upon the globe. Hence OUR AMERICAN ISRAEL is a term frequently used; and common consent allows it apt and proper" [9:665].

What was implicit in the words of Washington already quoted becomes explicit in Jefferson's second inaugural when he said: "I shall need, too, the favor of that Being in whose hands we are, who led our fathers, as Israel of old, from their native land and planted them in a country flowing with all the necessaries and comforts of life." Europe is Egypt; America, the Promised Land. God has led his people to establish a new sort of social order that shall be a light unto all the nations.

That the Mosaic analogy was present in the minds of leaders at the very moment of the birth of the republic is indicated in the designs proposed by Franklin and Jefferson for a seal of the United States of America. Together with Adams, they formed a committee of three delegated by the Continental Congress on July 4, 1776, to draw up the new device. "Franklin proposed as the device Moses lifting up his wand and dividing the Red Sea while Pharaoh was overwhelmed by its waters, with the motto 'Rebellion to tyrants is obedience to God.' Jefferson proposed the children of Israel in the wilderness 'led by a cloud by day and a pillar of fire at night' " [14:467–468].

The theme of Israel has been a continuous one also in the civil religion. We have already alluded to it in the case of the Kennedy inaugural. We find it again in President Johnson's inaugural address:

They came here — the exile and the stranger, brave but frightened — to find a place where a man could be his own man. They made a covenant with this land. Conceived in justice, written in liberty, bound in union, it was meant one day to inspire the hopes of all mankind; and it binds us still. If we keep its terms, we shall flourish.

What we have, then, from the earliest years of the republic is a collection of beliefs, symbols, and rituals with respect to sacred things and institutionalized in a collectivity. This religion — there seems no other word for it — while not antithetical to, and indeed sharing much in common with, Christianity was neither sectarian nor in any specific sense Christian. At a time when the society was overwhelmingly Christian, it seems unlikely that this lack of Christian reference was meant to spare the feelings of the tiny nonchristian minority. Rather, the civil religion expressed what those who set the precedents felt was appropriate under the circumstances. It reflected their private as well as public views. Nor was the civil religion simply "religion in general." While generality was undoubtedly seen as a virtue by some, as in the quotation from Franklin above, the civil religion was specific enough when it came to the topic of America. Precisely because of this specificity, the civil religion was saved from empty formalism and served as a genuine vehicle of natural religious self-understanding.

But the civil religion was not, in the minds of Franklin, Washington, Jefferson, or other leaders, with the exception of a few radicals like Tom Paine, ever felt to be a substitute for Christianity. There was an implicit but quite clear division of function between the civil religion and Christianity. Under the doctrine of religious liberty, an exceptionally wide sphere of personal piety and voluntary social action was left to the churches. But the churches were neither to control the state nor to be controlled by it. The national magistrate, whatever his private religious views, operates under the rubrics of the civil religion as long as he is in his official capacity, as we have already seen in the case of Kennedy. This accommodation was undoubtedly the product of a particular historical moment and of a cultural background dominated by Protestantism of several varieties and by the Enlightenment, but it has survived despite subsequent changes in the cultural and religious climate.

CIVIL WAR AND CIVIL RELIGION

Until the Civil War, the American civil religion focused above all on the event of the Revolution, which was seen as the final act of the Exodus from the old lands across the waters. The Declaration of Independence and the Constitution were the sacred scriptures and Washington the divinely appointed Moses who led his people out of the hands of tyranny. The Civil War, which Sidney Mead calls "the center of American history" [12:12], was the second great event that involved the national self-understanding so deeply as to require expression in the civil religion. In 1835, de Tocqueville wrote that the American republic had never really been tried, that victory in the Revolutionary War was more the result of British preoccupation elsewhere and the presence of a powerful ally than of any Great military success of the Americans. But in 1861 the time of testing had indeed come. Not only did the Civil War have the tragic intensity of fratricidal strife, but it was one of the bloodiest wars of the nineteenth century; the loss of life was far greater than any previously suffered by Americans.

The Civil War raised the deepest questions of national meaning. The man who not only formulated but in his own person embodied its meaning for Americans was Abraham Lincoln. For him the issue was not in the first instance slavery but "whether that nation, or any nation so conceived, and so dedicated, can long endure." He had said in Independence Hall in Philadelphia on 22 February 1861:

> All the political sentiments I entertain have been drawn, so far as I have been able to draw them, from the sentiments which originated in and were given to the world from this Hall. I have never had a feeling, politically, that did not spring from the sentiments embodied in the Declaration of Independence [6:39].

342

The phrases of Jefferson constantly echo in Lincoln's speeches. His task was, first of all, to save the Union — not for America alone but for the meaning of America to the whole world, so unforgettably etched in the last phrase of the Gettysburg Address.

But inevitably the issue of slavery as the deeper cause of the conflict had to be faced. In the second inaugural, Lincoln related slavery and the war in an ultimate perspective:

> If we shall suppose that American slavery is one of those offenses which, in the providence of God, must needs come, but which, having continued through His appointed time, He now wills to remove, and that He gives to both North and South this terrible war as the woe due to those by whom the offense came, shall we discern therein any departure from those divine attributes which the believers in a living God always ascribe to Him? Fondly do we hope, fervently do we pray, that this mighty scourge of war may speedily pass away. Yet, if God wills that it continue until all the wealth piled by the bondsman's two hundred and fifty years of unrequited toil shall be sunk, and until every drop of blood drawn with the lash shall be paid by another drawn with the sword, as was said three thousand years ago, so still it must be said "the judgements of the Lord are true and righteous altogether."

But he closes on a note if not of redemption then of reconciliation — "With malice toward none, with charity for all."

With the Civil War, a new theme of death, sacrifice, and rebirth enters the civil religion. It is symbolized in the life and death of Lincoln. Nowhere is it stated more vividly than in the Gettysburg Address, itself part of the Lincolnian "New Testament" among the civil scriptures. Robert Lowell has recently pointed out the "insistent use of birth images" in this speech explicitly devoted to "these honored dead": "brought forth," "conceived," "created," "a birth of freedom." He goes on to say:

> The Gettysburg Address is a symbolic and sacramental act. Its verbal quality is resonance combined with a logical, matter of fact, prosaic brevity. . . . In his words, Lincoln symbolically died, just as the Union soldiers really died — and as he himself was soon really to die. By his words, he gave the field of battle a symbolic significance that it had lacked. For us and our

country, he left Jefferson's ideals of freedom and equality joined to the Christian sacrificial act of death and rebirth. I believe this is a meaning that goes beyond sect or religion and beyond peace and war, and is now part of our lives as a challenge, obstacle and hope [11:88–89].

Lowell is certainly right in pointing out the Christian quality of the symbolism here, but he is also right in quickly disavowing any sectarian implication. The earlier symbolism of the civil religion had been Hebraic without being in any specific sense Jewish. The Gettysburg symbolism (". . . those who here gave their lives, that that nation might live") is Christian without having anything to do with the Christian church.

The symbolic equation of Lincoln with Jesus was made relatively early. Herndon, who had been Lincoln's law partner, wrote:

> For fifty years God rolled Abraham Lincoln through his fiery furnace. He did it to try Abraham and to purify him for his purposes. This made Mr. Lincoln humble, tender, forbearing, sympathetic to suffering, kind, sensitive, tolerant; broadening, deepening and widening his whole nature; making him the noblest and loveliest character since Jesus Christ. . . . I believe that Lincoln was God's chosen one [4:162].

With the Christian archetype in the background, Lincoln, "our martyred president," was linked to the war dead, those who "gave the last full measure of devotion." The theme of sacrifice was indelibly written into the civil religion.

The new symbolism soon found both physical and ritualistic expression. The great number of the war dead required the establishment of a number of national cemeteries. Of these, the Gettysburg National Cemetery, which Lincoln's famous address served to dedicate, has been overshadowed only by the Arlington National Cemetery. Begun somewhat vindictively on the Lee estate across the river from Washington, partly with the end that the Lee family could never reclaim it [3:60–67], it has subsequently become the most hallowed monument of the civil religion. Not only was a section set aside for the Confederate dead, but it has received the dead of each succeeding American war.

344

It is the site of the one important new symbol to come out of World War I, the Tomb of the Unknown Soldier; more recently it has become the site of the tomb of another martyred president and its symbolic eternal flame.

Memorial Day, which grew out of the Civil War, gave ritual expression to the themes we have been discussing. As Lloyd Warner has so brilliantly analyzed it, the Memorial Day observance, especially in the towns and smaller cities of America, is a major event for the whole community involving a rededication to the martyred dead, to the spirit of sacrifice, and to the American vision. How extensive the activity associated with Memorial Day can be is indicated by Warner:

> The sacred symbolic behavior of Memorial Day, in which scores of the town's organizations are involved, is ordinarily divided into four periods. During the year separate rituals are held by many of the associations for their dead, and many of these activities are connected with later Memorial Day events. In the second phase, preparations are made during the last three or four weeks for the ceremony itself, and some of the associations perform public rituals. The third phase consists of scores of rituals held in all the cemeteries, churches, and halls of the associations. These rituals consist of speeches and highly ritualized behavior. They last for two days and are climaxed by the fourth and last phase, in which all the separate celebrants gather in the center of the business district on the afternoon of Memorial Day. The separate organizations, with their members in uniform or with fitting insignia, march through the town, visit the shrines and monuments of the hero dead, and, finally, enter the cemetery. Here dozens of ceremonies are held, most of them highly symbolic and formalized [18:8–9].

During these various ceremonies Lincoln is continually referred to and the Gettysburg Address recited many times.

Just as Thanksgiving Day, which incidentally was securely institutionalized as an annual national holiday only under the presidency of Lincoln, serves to integrate the family into the civil religion, so Memorial Day has acted to integrate the local community into the national cult. Together with the less overtly religious Fourth of July and the more minor celebrations of Veterans Day and the birthdays of Washington and Lincoln, these two holidays provide an annual ritual calendar for the civil religion. The public school system serves as a particularly important context for the cultic celebration of the civil rituals.

THE CIVIL RELIGION TODAY

In reifying and giving a name to something that, though pervasive enough when you look at it, has gone on only semiconsciously, there is risk of severely distorting the data. But the reification and the naming have already begun. The religious critics of "religion in general" or of the "religion of the 'American Way of Life'" or of "American Shinto" have really been talking about the civil religion. As usual in religious polemic, the critics take as criteria the best in their own religious tradition and as typical the worst in the tradition of the civil religion. Against these critics, I would argue that the civil religion at its best is a genuine apprehension of universal and transcendent religious reality as seen in or, one could almost say, as revealed through the experience of the American people. Like all religions, it has suffered various deformations and demonic distortions. At its best, it has been neither so general that it has lacked incisive relevance to the American scene nor so particular that it has placed American society above universal human values.

I am not at all convinced that the leaders of the churches have consistently represented a higher level of religious insight than the spokesmen of the civil religion. Reinhold Niebuhr has this to say of Lincoln, who never joined a church and who certainly represents civil religion at its best:

> An analysis of the religion of Abraham Lincoln in the context of the traditional religion of his time and place and of its polemical use on the slavery issue, which corrupted religious life in the days before and during the Civil War, must lead to the conclusion that Lincoln's religious convictions were superior in depth and purity to those, not only of the political leaders of his day, but of the religious leaders of the era [13:72].

346

William J. Wolf of the Episcopal Theological School in Cambridge, Massachusetts, has written:

> Lincoln is one of the greatest theologians of America — not in the technical meaning of producing a system of doctrine, certainly not as the defender of some one denomination, but in the sense of seeing the hand of God intimately in the affairs of nations. Just so the prophets of Israel criticized the events of their day from the perspective of the God who is concerned for history and who reveals His will within it. Lincoln now stands among God's latter-day prophets [19:24].

Perhaps the real animus of the religious critics has been not so much against the civil religion in itself but against its pervasive and dominating influence within the sphere of church religion. As S. M. Lipset has recently shown, American religion at least since the early nineteenth century has been predominantly activist, moralistic, and social rather than contemplative, theological, or innerly spiritual [10: chap 4]. De Tocqueville spoke of American church religion as "a political institution which powerfully contributes to the maintenance of a democratic republic among the Americans" [15:310] by supplying a strong moral consensus amidst continuous political change. Henry Bargy in 1902 spoke of American church religion as "la poésie du civisme" [2:31].

It is certainly true that the relation between religion and politics in America has been singularly smooth. This is in large part due to the dominant tradition. As de Tocqueville wrote:

> The greatest part of British America was peopled by men who, after having shaken off the authority of the Pope, acknowledged no other religious supremacy: they brought with them into the New World a form of Christianity which I cannot better describe than by styling it a democratic and republican religion [15:311].

Later he says,

> In the United States even the religion of most of the citizens is republican, since it submits the truths of the other world to private judgment, as in politics the care of their temporal interests is abandoned to the good sense of the people. Thus every

man is allowed freely to take that road which he thinks will lead him to heaven, just as the law permits every citizen to have the right of choosing his own government [15:436].

The churches opposed neither the Revolution nor the establishment of democratic institutions. Even when some of them opposed the full institutionalization of religious liberty, they accepted the final outcome with good grace and without nostalgia for an *ancien régime*. The American civil religion was never anticlerical or militantly secular. On the contrary, it borrowed selectively from the religious tradition in such a way that the average American saw no conflict between the two. In this way, without any bitter struggle with the church, the civil religion was able to build up powerful symbols of national solidarity and to mobilize deep levels of personal motivation for the attainment of national goals.

Such an achievement is by no means to be taken for granted. It would seem that the problem of a civil religion is quite general in modern societies and that the way it is solved or not solved will have repercussions in many spheres. One needs only to think of France to see how differently things can go. The French Revolution was anticlerical to the core and attempted to set up an antichristian civil religion. Throughout modern French history, the chasm between traditional Catholic symbols and the symbolism of 1789 has been immense.

American civil religion is still very much alive. Just five years ago we participated in a vivid reenactment of the sacrifice theme in connection with the funeral of our assassinated president. The American Israel theme is clearly behind both Kennedy's New Frontier and Johnson's Great Society. Let me give just one illustration of how the civil religion serves to mobilize support for the attainment of national goals. On 15 March 1965 President Johnson went before Congress to ask for a strong voting-rights bill. Early in the speech he said:

Rarely are we met with the challenge, not to our growth or abundance, or our welfare or our security — but rather to the values and the purposes and the meaning of our beloved nation.

348

The issue of equal rights for American Negroes is such an issue. And should we defeat every enemy, and should we double our wealth and conquer the stars and still be unequal to this issue, then we will have failed as a people and as a nation.

For with a country as with a person, "What is a man profited, if he shall gain the whole world, and lose his own soul?"

And in conclusion he said:

Above the pyramid on the great seal of the United States it says in Latin, "God has favored our undertaking."

God will not favor everything that we do. It is rather our duty to divine his will. I cannot help but believe that He truly understands and that He really favors the undertaking that we begin here tonight [16:4924, 4926].

The civil religion has not always been invoked in favor of worthy causes. On the domestic scene, an American-Legion type of ideology that fuses God, country, and flag has been used to attack nonconformist and liberal ideas and groups of all kinds. Still, it has been difficult to use the words of Jefferson and Lincoln to support special interests and undermine personal freedom. The defenders of slavery before the Civil War came to reject the thinking of the Declaration of Independence. Some of the most consistent of them turned against not only Jeffersonian democracy but Reformation religion; they dreamed of a South dominated by medieval chivalry and divine-right monarchy [7: part 4]. For all the overt religiosity of the radical right today, its relation to the civil religious consensus is tenuous, as when the John Birch Society attacks the central American symbol of Democracy itself.

With respect to America's role in the world, the dangers of distortion are greater and the built-in safeguards of the tradition weaker. The theme of the American Israel was used, almost from the beginning, as a justification for the shameful treatment of the Indians so characteristic of our history. It can be overtly or implicitly linked to the idea of manifest destiny which has been used to legitimate several adventures in imperialism since the early nineteenth century. Never has the danger been greater than today. The issue is not so much one of imperial expansion,

349

of which we are accused, as of the tendency to assimilate all governments or parties in the world which support our immediate policies or call upon our help by invoking the notion of free institutions and democratic values. Those nations that are for the moment "on our side" become "the free world." A repressive and unstable military dictatorship in South Vietnam becomes "the free people of South Vietnam and their government." It is then part of the role of America as the New Jerusalem and "the last hope of earth" to defend such governments with treasure and eventually with blood. When our soldiers are actually dying, it becomes possible to consecrate the struggle further by invoking the great theme of sacrifice. For the majority of the American people who are unable to judge whether the people in South Vietnam (or wherever) are "free like us," such arguments are convincing. Fortunately President Johnson has been less ready to assert that "God has favored our undertaking" in the case of Vietnam than with respect to civil rights. But others are not so hesitant. The civil religion has exercised long-term pressure for the humane solution of our greatest domestic problem, the treatment of the Negro American. It remains to be seen how relevant it can become for our role in the world at large and whether we can effectually stand for "the revolutionary beliefs for which our forebears fought," in John F. Kennedy's words.

The civil religion is obviously involved in the most pressing moral and political issues of the day. But it is also caught in another kind of crisis, theoretical and theological, of which it is at the moment largely unaware. "God" has clearly been a central symbol in the civil religion from the beginning and remains so today. This symbol is just as central to the civil religion as it is to Judaism or Christianity. In the late eighteenth century this posed no problem; even Tom Paine, contrary to his detractors, was not an atheist. From left to right and regardless of church or sect, all could accept the idea of God. But today, as even *Time* has recognized, the meaning of the word "God" is by no means so clear or so obvious. There is no formal creed in the civil religion. We have had a Catholic president; it is conceivable that we could have a Jewish one. But could we have an agnostic president?

Could a man with conscientious scruples about using the word "God" the way Kennedy and Johnson have used it be elected chief magistrate of our country? If the whole God symbolism requires reformulation, there will be obvious consequences for the civil religion, consequences perhaps of liberal alienation and of fundamentalist ossification that have not so far been prominent in this realm. The civil religion has been a point of articulation between the profoundest commitments of the Western religious and philosophical tradition and the common beliefs of ordinary Americans. It is not too soon to consider how the deepening theological crisis may affect the future of this articulation.

THE THIRD TIME OF TRIAL

In conclusion it may be worthwhile to relate the civil religion to the most serious situation that we as Americans now face, what I call the third time of trial. The first time of trial had to do with the question of independence, whether we should or could run our own affairs in our own way. The second time of trial was over the issue of slavery, which in turn was only the most salient aspect of the more general problem of the full institutionalization of democracy within our country. This second problem we are still far from solving though we have some notable successes to our credit. But we have been overtaken by a third great problem which has led to a third great crisis, in the midst of which we stand. This is the problem of responsible action in a revolutionary world, a world seeking to attain many of the things, material and spiritual, that we have already attained. Americans have, from the beginning, been aware of the responsibility and the significance our republican experiment has for the whole world. The first internal political polarization in the new nation had to do with our attitude toward the French Revolution. But we were small and weak then, and "foreign entanglements" seemed to threaten our very survival. During the last century, our relevance for the world was not forgotten, but our role was seen as purely exemplary. Our democratic republic rebuked tyranny by merely existing. Just after Word War I we were on the brink of taking a different role in the world, but once again we turned our back.

Since World War II, the old pattern has become impossible. Every president since Roosevelt has been groping toward a new pattern of action in the world, one that would be consonant with our power and our responsibilities. For Truman and for the period dominated by John Foster Dulles, that pattern was seen to be the great Manichaean confrontation of East and West, the confrontation of democracy and "the false philosophy of Communism" that provided the structure of Truman's inaugural address. With the last years of Eisenhower and with the successive two presidents, the pattern began to shift. The great problems came to be seen as caused not solely by the evil intent of any one group of men, but as stemming from much more complex and multiple sources. For Kennedy, it was not so much a struggle against particular men as against "the common enemies of man: tyranny, poverty, disease and war itself."

But in the midst of this trend toward a less primitive conception of ourselves and our world, we have somehow, without anyone's really intending it, stumbled into a military confrontation where we have come to feel that our honor is at stake. We have in a moment of uncertainty been tempted to rely on our overwhelming physical power rather than on our intelligence, and we have, in part, succumbed to this temptation. Bewildered and unnerved when our terrible power fails to bring immediate success, we are at the edge of a chasm the depth of which no man knows.

I cannot help but think of Robinson Jeffers, whose poetry seems more apt now than when it was written, when he said:

> Unhappy country, what wings you have! . . .
> Weep (it is frequent in human affairs), weep for
>   the terrible magnificence of the means,
> The ridiculous incompetence of the reasons, the
>   bloody and shabby
> Pathos of the result.

But as so often before in similar times, we have a man of prophetic stature, without the bitterness or misanthropy of Jeffers,
who, as Lincoln before him, calls this nation to its judgment:

> When a nation is very powerful but lacking in self-confidence,
> it is likely to behave in a manner that is dangerous both to itself
> and to others.
>
> Gradually but unmistakably, America is succumbing to that
> arrogance of power which has afflicted, weakened and in some
> cases destroyed great nations in the past.
>
> If the war goes on and expands, if that fatal process continues
> to accelerate until America becomes what it is not now and
> never has been, a seeker after unlimited power and empire,
> then Vietnam will have had a mighty and tragic fallout indeed.
>
> I do not believe that will happen. I am very apprehensive but
> I still remain hopeful, and even confident, that America, with
> its humane and democratic traditions, will find the wisdom to
> match its power [5].

Without an awareness that our nation stands under higher
judgment, the tradition of the civil religion would be dangerous
indeed. Fortunately, the prophetic voices have never been lacking. Our present situation brings to mind the Mexican-American
war that Lincoln, among so many others, opposed. The spirit of
civil disobedience that is alive today in the civil rights movement and the opposition to the Vietnam war was already clearly
outlined by Henry David Thoreau when he wrote, "If the law
is of such a nature that it requires you to be an agent of injustice
to another, then I say, break the law." Thoreau's words, "I
would remind my countrymen that they are men first, and Americans at a late and convenient hour" [1:274], provide an essential
standard for any adequate thought and action in our third time
of trial. As Americans, we have been well favored in the world,
but it is as men that we will be judged.

Out of the first and second times of trial have come, as we
have seen, the major symbols of the American civil religion.
There seems little doubt that a successful negotiation of this third
time of trial — the attainment of some kind of viable and coherent world order — would precipitate a major new set of

symbolic forms. So far the flickering flame of the United Nations burns too low to be the focus of a cult, but the emergence of a genuine transnational sovereignty would certainly change this. It would necessitate the incorporation of vital international symbolism into our civil religion, or, perhaps a better way of putting it, it would result in American civil religion's becoming simply one part of a new civil religion of the world. It is useless to speculate on the form such a civil religion might take, though it obviously would draw on religious traditions beyond the sphere of biblical religion alone. Fortunately, since the American civil religion is not the worship of the American nation but an understanding of the American experience in the light of ulti- mate and universal reality, the reorganization entailed by such a new situation need not disrupt the American civil religion's con- tinuity. A world civil religion could be accepted as a fulfillment and not a denial of American civil religion. Indeed, such an out- come has been the eschatological hope of American civil religion from the beginning. To deny such an outcome would be to deny the meaning of America itself.

Behind the civil religion at every point lie biblical archetypes: Exodus, Chosen People, Promised Land, New Jerusalem, Sacri- ficial Death, and Rebirth. But the civil religion is also genuinely American and genuinely new. It has its own prophets and its own martyrs, its own sacred events and sacred places, its own solemn rituals and symbols. It is concerned that America be a society as perfectly in accord with the will of God as men can make it and a light to all the nations.

In times past the American civil religion has often been used and is being used today as a cloak for petty interests and ugly passions. It is in need — as is any living faith — of continual ref- ormation, of being measured by universal standards. But it is not evident that our civil religion is incapable of growth and new insight.

The civil religion does not make any decision for us. It does not remove us from moral ambiguity, from being, in Lincoln's fine phrase, an "almost chosen people." But it is a heritage of moral and religious experience from which we still have much to learn as we formulate the decisions that lie ahead.

354

REFERENCES

1. Arieli, Yehoshua: *Individualism and Nationalism in American Ideology* (Harvard University Press, Cambridge, Massachusetts) 1964.
2. Bargy, Henry: *La Religion dans la Société aux États-Unis* (Paris) 1902.
3. Decker, Karl, and McSween, Angus: *Historic Arlington* (Washington, D.C.) 1892.
4. Eddy, Sherwood: *The Kingdom of God and the American Dream* (Harper & Row, Publishers, New York, New York) 1941.
5. Fulbright, Senator J William: speech of 28 April 1966 as reported in *The New York Times*, 29 April 1966.
6. Goodhart, Arthur Lehman, in Nevins, Allan, ed: *Lincoln and the Gettysburg Address* (University of Illinois Press, Urbana, Illinois) 1964.
7. Hartz, Louis: The Feudal Dream of the South, in *The Liberal Tradition in America*, part 4 (Harcourt, Brace & World, Inc, New York, New York) 1955.
8. Herberg, Will: *Protestant-Catholic-Jew* (Anchor Books, Doubleday & Company, Inc, Garden City, New York) 1955.
9. Kohn, Hans: *The Idea of Nationalism* (The Macmillan Company, New York, New York) 1961.
10. Lipset, Seymour Martin: Religion and American Values, in *The First New Nation* (Basic Books, Inc, Publishers, New York, New York) 1964.
11. Lowell, Robert, in Nevins, Allan, ed: *Lincoln and the Gettysburg Address* (University of Illinois Press, Urbana, Illinois) 1964.
12. Mead, Sidney: *The Lively Experiment* (Harper & Row, Publishers, New York, New York) 1963.
13. Niebuhr, Reinhold: The Religion of Abraham Lincoln, in Nevins, Allan, ed: *Lincoln and the Gettysburg Address* (University of Illinois Press, Urbana, Illinois) 1964.
14. Stokes, Anson Phelps: *Church and State in the United States*,

355

vol 1 (Harper & Row, Publishers, New York, New York) 1950.

15. Tocqueville, Alexis de: *Democracy in America*, vol 1 (Alfred A Knopf, Inc, New York, New York) 1954.

16. United States: *Congressional Record, House* (Superintendent of Documents, Government Printing Office, Washington, D.C. 20402) March 15, 1965.

17. United States Congress, 82d, 2d Session, House Document No. 540: *Inaugural Addresses of the Presidents of the United States from George Washington 1789 to Harry S Truman 1949* (Superintendent of Documents, Government Printing Office, Washington, D.C. 20402) 1952.

18. Warner, W Lloyd: *American Life: Dream and Reality* (University of Chicago Press, Chicago, Illinois) 1962.

19. Wolf, William J: *The Religion of Abraham Lincoln* (The Seabury Press, Inc, Greenwich, Connecticut) 1963.

COMMENTARY

by Denis Brogan

ONE OF THE MOST REVEALING slogans of current American politics was displayed on Fifth Avenue, New York, in the spring of 1967. It called for the support of the United States in its war in Vietnam "against atheistic Communism." This somewhat irrelevant slogan revealed how deeply embedded in the American political consciousness is the belief that the United States is committed to a theistic interpretation of the Universe; for, if it is true that an orthodox Marxist like Ho Chi Minh *must* be an atheist, is it true that a Buddhist ally of the United States can be a theist? To ask this question is, I think, to reveal the truth that the opposite to "Atheistic Communism" is "Theistic Americanism." It is, as Mr. Bellah has convincingly argued, a "civil religion" in the sense that Rousseau used the term and in the sense that a citizen of Rome or Athens would have understood a commitment to the "Gods of the City," to Jupiter or Pallas Athene and, of course, "their cousins and their sisters and their aunts."

But the character of this civic religion (as it seems to me, a foreigner) is more specific than that. If it is wrong any longer to call the United States a "Christian country," it is not wrong to call it a "Protestant country": the emblems, the metaphors, the "note" (as Newman might have put it) of public civil religion is Protestant, even when those symbols are used by Catholics, Jews, Greek Orthodox and, possibly, even by adherents of a faith not in any way connected with the "Good Book," i.e., the Bible. There has been one Sikh congressman though his holy book, the Granth, is not yet legitimized as a holy object of the national religion. There may have been a Moslem congressman though the Koran is not part of the civic religion *yet*. About the two main American scriptures, the *Book of Mormon* or *Science and Health*, I am not sure; but, as one promising candidate for the Republican nomination for the presidency is a "Saint" and another a "Scientist," the question may come up soon. However, both Mormons and Scientists are people of two Books and we may assume that it is *the* Book they share with most other Americans, not the book that marks them off from other Americans, that they use politically. For the central function of the American civic religion is not the doing on earth of the will of the Christian or Jewish God, but of securing for the United States the blessing of the God whose Chosen People is the American People. Beginning in New England with the belief that the English emigrants were the new Israel, it has become, in modern times, the belief in a God whom the Holy People have chosen, one is tempted to say, have elected to be their God.

In believing that they are especially worthy of God's benevolence and have been habitually doing his work, modern Americans are like many other peoples. It has been a long time since the Crusades were described as "Gesta Dei per Francos" and France claimed to be "the eldest daughter of the Church." "Holy Russia" was not a mere piece of pietistic rhetoric. Sixteenth-century Spaniards saw themselves as the swordsmen of God

357

against the heathen in Mexico and heretics in Germany and England.

Behind these naïve assumptions, however, lay a prenational past. There was "the Church" before there was the State. The Archbishop of Canterbury is, he asserts, heir to the missionary sent by Pope Gregory the Great (so called because he recognized the angelic character of the English). "The Most Christian King" of France, "the Catholic King" of Castile and Aragon, the "Apostolic King" of Hungary testified in their titles to something outside: something older, bigger than the nation. As I have pointed out before, the soundly Presbyterian University of Glasgow still gives degrees "by royal *and* apostolic authority." But what can be greater, older, more venerable than the United States itself? Alone among great nations, it dates its great official documents by "the Year of the Lord and of the Independence of the United States."

The reason why the American state and people behave thus is obvious. Religion has been a notorious dividing force where it was not identified with the State. Hence the Inquisition, the Penal Laws in Ireland, the waves of persecution and counter-persecution in France. The division of Germany, even today, is largely a religious one.

It is clear, however, that the new American Union, on its troubled way to becoming a nation, could not take these bold steps. What kind of religion could be enforced? The freedom that de Tocqueville saw and admired was partly based on the philosophy of the Enlightenment, exemplified in the Federal Bill of Rights. Partly it was a reluctant acceptance of necessity — very reluctant in the Puritan commonwealth of New Hampshire and, in another way, in Maryland. *But*, a neglected point, the only genuine examples of religious persecution in modern American history were the treatment of the politically as well as sexually heretical Mormons and the *political* persecution of the Protestant churches in the Confederacy and in some border states, during and after "the War of the Rebellion." The very acute, German-trained theologian, Nevin of Mercersburg, before the Civil War noted not only that patriotic ceremonies were the equivalent of purely religious commemorations in Europe but that, for President Timothy Dwight of Yale, the Eucharist itself was a kind of religious Fourth of July. Which was the more sacred? Dwight could not have answered and Nevin, who thought *he* could answer, was consciously working against the American grain.

It is true that a kind of civic religion is embodied in American political practice and in American life. Dr. Bellah's numerous examples of the profession of a Theistic and basically Protestant view of life and ritual might have been set off more clearly against the complete agnosticism of the *federal* Constitution. All attempts to "put God into the Constitution" have failed, possibly because the Confederate Constitution *did* put God in, and look what happened to it! The slogan "In God We Trust" which appears on the coinage was an administrative invention of that conspicuous Episcopalian, Salmon P. Chase, during the Civil War. It was after the Second World War that the "pledge to the flag" added "under God"; and it is in 1967 that the war in Vietnam is seen either as a crusade of God's People or a desperate sin by that People, defying God who is really — as He was in the Second Inaugural — a God above the American people, ready to condemn and punish as well as praise and reward. Lincoln's God is certainly not the God of the American Legion, of the D.A.R., of the John Birch Society. He is an ally; one almost says an employee. Again, the new God of the highly diversified people is a vaguely Protestant God: a jealous God indeed, but not the severe punishing, condemning God of the Old Testament.

The civic religion has its rituals. There are many, but one is unknown in the other "Christian" countries which I know at first hand. It is the ritual of flag worship. There are flags in European churches, tricolors beside usually horrible statues of that Saint of Patriotism, Joan of Arc. There are battle flags even in so austere a building as the medieval cathedral of my native city of Glasgow. But the ritual of the flag — the rabbinical rules about raising it and lowering it — is unknown in Britain, where most people neither know nor care, and, so, innocently offended Americans in England during World War II by treating Old

359

Glory as casually as they treated the Union Jack. This is only one instance among many of the public rituals of the American civic religion. The absurd and odious decision of the Minersville School Board meant that the children of Jehovah's Witnesses were punished for not performing an act that not only their parents but the Jews of the time of the Maccabees and the Christians of the time of Trajan would also have thought idolatrous. The people of the Qumram scrolls identified their enemies as people "who worshipped their standards," i.e., the Romans. The members of the Minersville School Board were more foolish and dogmatic than Trajan or Pliny; but they were worshiping variants of the same God. "Senatus Populusque Romanus" has become "We, the People of the United States."

But the civic religion is under attack from an older or, at any rate, a different religion, which denies the omnipotence of Caesar. Even in what is perhaps the most "patriotic" of American churches, the Catholic, there are more and more voices attacking the very concept of a "just war," more and more voices expressing agreement with Paul VI rather than with Cardinal Spellman. If such dangerous thoughts spread, the civic religion may have to fight for the things that are Caesar's against more and more men and women concerned with the things that are God's — a God who may condemn the American nation as, so the Bible tells us, he has condemned other nations just as confident of his favor.

COMMENTARY

by Leo Pfeffer

It may be true, as Bellah asserts, that his "civil religion" has until now "escaped serious analytical attention," yet the idea itself is hardly new. A quarter of a century ago its recognition and incorporation into the public school curriculum was advocated, by not a few religious educators, under the name "common core." Its premise was the same as Bellah's: that "Although matters of personal religious belief, worship, and association are considered to be strictly private affairs, there are, at the same time, certain common elements of religious orientation that the great majority of Americans share" and that these "have played a crucial role in the development of American institutions and still provide a religious dimension for the whole fabric of American life, including the political sphere." The common-core advocates took the next logical step: since it exists and is good, it should be taught in the public schools. Here is how the argument was presented by one of its chief promoters, Luther Weigle, then dean of Yale Divinity School:

> Underlying all our differences, America has a common religious faith — common not in the sense that everybody shares it, for there are some among us who deny or ignore God; but in the sense that it is common to the three great religious groups — Protestant, Catholic, and Jewish — to which the great majority of American citizens profess to belong. These citizens — Protestant, Catholic, and Jew — worship one God, Creator of all things and Father of men. They believe that His will has been revealed in the life and literature of the Hebrew people as this is recorded in the Bible, and that it is discernible in nature about us and in conscience within. They acknowledge the principle of human duty set forth in the Ten Commandments, in the teachings of the Hebrew prophets, in the Golden Rule, and in the law of love to God and to fellow men. They sing hymns and psalms that transcend differences of creed. They can all unite in the Lord's Prayer: "Our Father who art in heaven . . . Thy kingdom come. Thy will be done . . . ."
>
> There is nothing in the status of the public school as an institution of the state, therefore, to render it godless. There is nothing in the principle of religious freedom or the separation of church and state to hinder the schools' acknowledgement of the power and goodness of God. The common religious faith of the American people, as distinguished from the sectarian forms in which it is organized, may rightfully be assumed and find appropriate expression in the life and work of the public schools [12].

I am not as sanguine as Bellah that the established religions do not view this civil religion as a competitor, a bad religion which if it does not drive out the good requires them to cheapen their own wares to meet the competition, resulting in what may be called a lowest common denominator faith. Thus, the National Council of Churches of Christ, the closest thing to an authoritative voice of American Protestantism we have, states in a policy statement adopted in June, 1963:

> While both our tradition and the present temper of our nation reflect a preponderant belief in God as our Source and our Destiny, nevertheless attempts to establish a "common core" of religious beliefs to be taught in public schools have usually proven unrealistic and unwise. Major faith groups have not agreed on a formulation of religious beliefs common to all. Even if they had done so, such a body of religious doctrine would tend to become a substitute for the more demanding commitments of historic faith.

Bellah writes as a religious sociologist, and his essay presumably is intended to be a value-free analytical description. Yet, his approach is manifestly sympathetic, and it is therefore not unfair to suggest that there may be some validity to the National Council's concern. As Bellah notes, his civil religion expresses itself in a "set of beliefs, symbols, and rituals," and these compete with what must be viewed as more deeply spiritual counterparts in the traditional faiths. The civil religion, in its efforts to find a ritual that does not transgress the conscience of adherents of the traditional faiths, has come up with such doggerel prayer, recited in many kindergartens before partaking of cookies and milk (and hence popularly known as the "cookie prayer") as:

> We thank you God for the food we eat,
> We thank you God for the flowers so sweet.
> We thank you God for the birds that sing.
> We thank you God for everything.

Somewhat on a higher level but no less typical of the spirit of the civil or public religion is the following "nonsectarian" prayer formulated by the Regents of the State of New York for recitation in the public schools of the state: "Almighty God, we acknowledge our dependence upon Thee, and we beg Thy blessings upon us, our parents, our teachers, and our country."

Nor can I agree with Bellah that the civil religion is consistent with the spirit of our Constitution and its fathers. According to him, central to American civil religion is the existence of God. In support, he quotes from Kennedy's inaugural address: "For I have sworn before you and Almighty God the same solemn oath our forebears prescribed nearly a century and three quarters ago." For a moment I thought that a typographical error had been made; certainly "proscribed" would have been closer to accuracy than "prescribed," for the Constitution specifically forbids prescribed religious oaths for office, even those addressed to God. Indeed, nowhere in the Constitution is the word "God" to be found, an omission which was not inadvert but deliberately reflective of a universal consensus among the constitutional delegates [9:121–124].

In our system of government, the Supreme Court is the final interpreter of the Constitution, and the Court's decisions, I think, are remarkably consistent with this consensus. The Court rejected as unconstitutional a state's requirement of a belief in God as a qualification for public office [10]. It disallowed public school recitation of the nonsectarian Regents' Prayer quoted above [2]. It accorded the privilege of conscientious objection exemption to military service to young men who did not profess a belief in the existence of God [11]. In a number of other decisions it imposed a mandate of neutrality upon government in its dealings with religion and nonreligion [3; 7].

Yet, I agree with Bellah that there is such a thing as an American civil religion. Its existence, however, is *de facto* rather than *de jure* [5:11], at least if the latter term is equated with constitutionality as interpreted by the Supreme Court. This civil religion is a function of American compulsion toward conformity in a multireligious community, a compulsion exemplified by the incident of an out-of-town Christian lawyer who entered Temple Emanuel in New York at the beginning of a service on Sunday morning and did not discover that he was in a synagogue until a chance remark of the preacher betrayed it [4:46]. No doubt the civil religion serves a useful purpose in a nation where everybody considers religion a good thing but few take it very seriously.

My most serious disagreement with Bellah lies in his espousal of the use of civil religion as an instrumentality to achieve national goals. He deplores such use where he disagrees with the particular national goal involved, as in the "manifest destiny" drive, but warmly endorses it where the national goal is noble or commendable, such as in waging the Revolutionary War and the Civil War and, paradoxically, in not waging the Vietnam war. The use of religion, even so universal a religion as Bellah's civil religion, as a means to achieve political ends is at odds with our constitutional resolution of the problem of the proper relationship between religion and government. Madison, the father of our constitution, called it "an unhallowed perversion of the means of salvation" [6:185], and another great statesman and jurist, Jeremiah S. Black, stated that the fathers of our constitution "built up a wall of complete and perfect partition" between church and state in order that "one should never be used as an engine for the purpose of the other" [1:53].

As a practical matter, when religion is used to pursue a political purpose it is far more likely to be an ignoble than a noble purpose. History, I believe, supports this conclusion. It was no accident, to cite one example, that it was during the McCarthy era that civil religion made its most prominent appearance with the insertion of "under God" in the Pledge of Allegiance, televised Cabinet meetings opened with prayer, equating left-of-centerism with atheistic communism, etc.

Nor is it an accident that the elaborate Memorial Day ritual cited by Bellah is almost universally sponsored and conducted by veterans' organizations and used as a means of promoting narrow nationalism and military power.

Corruption results when religion, traditional or civil, allows itself to become the handmaiden of national purposes. Idealistically, not realistically, it is true, as Bellah asserts, that "the American civil religion is not the worship of the American nation but an understanding of the American experience in the light of ultimate and universal reality," and the more civil religion is used to pursue national purposes, the less true will it be.

364

REFERENCES

1. Black, Jeremiah S: *Essays and Speeches* (New York) 1885.
2. *Engel* v. *Vitale*, 370 U.S. 421 (1962).
3. *Everson* v. *Board of Education*, 330 U.S. 1 (1947).
4. Glazer, Nathan: *American Judaism* (University of Chicago Press, Chicago, Illinois) 1957.
5. Howe, Mark DeWolfe: *The Garden and the Wilderness* (University of Chicago Press, Chicago, Illinois) 1965.
6. Hunt, Gaillard, ed: *Writings of James Madison*, vol 2 (New York) 1900–1909.
7. *McCollum* v. *Board of Education*, 333 U.S. 203 (1948).
8. Madison, James. See reference 6.
9. Pfeffer, Leo: *Church, State and Freedom* (Beacon Press, Boston, Massachusetts) 1967.
10. *Torcaso* v. *Watkins*, 367 U.S. 488 (1961).
11. *United States* v. *Seeger*, 380 U.S. 163 (1965).
12. Weigle, Luther A: The American Tradition and the Relation between Religion and Education, *Religion and Public Education, American Council on Education* (Washington, D.C.) vol 9, no 22, Feb 1945.

COMMENTARY

by John R. Whitney

THREE DAYS before Christmas, 1965, the Pennsylvania Legislature provided, in *Act of the General Assembly No. 442*, "for a secondary course in the study of religious literature." Thus Section 1515 of Public Law 30, as amended, reads:

Section 1515: Religious Literature. — (a) Courses in the literature of the Bible and other religious writings may be introduced and studied as regular courses in the literature branch of education by all pupils in the secondary public schools. Such courses shall be elective only and not required of any student.

(b) Such courses shall be prepared and adopted according to age levels by the Department of Public Instruction with the advice and counsel of the Council of Basic Education and the approval of the State Board of Education.

APPROVED – The 22nd day of December A.D. 1965.

WILLIAM W. SCRANTON

According to Robert Bellah the religious reality of civil religion has marked America since the days when Washington and his associates acted as founding fathers of the United States.

One sees a connection between this concept of civil religion and the Act of the Pennsylvania General Assembly quoted above. We will consider that connection by dealing with such questions as these:

Is the idea of civil religion a helpful concept when we attempt to understand the significance of teaching the subject matter of religion in American public schools?

What groups take a special interest in the results of such an undertaking and why?

What is the possibility that such courses may promote or excite new approaches to the meaning of religion for contemporary American thought?

We will treat the idea of civil religion primarily in terms of its relation to concepts of sovereign authority, sovereign agency, and sovereign community, a triad whose interrelationships civil religion may be said to describe.

When we refer to sovereign authority, we mean God, as understood through two different kinds of religion, civil and transcivil. These oppose each other by their conflicting understandings of how God's sovereign authority is expressed in history through a sovereign agency.

When we refer to a sovereign agent, we have in mind the supreme historical power which mediates the authority of God to a community and which also mediates the loyalty of that community to God. For the civil religion, this agency is the state. For the transcivil religions, this agency is a prophetically revealed entity other than the state. We understand community itself to

366

be a human situation in which people voluntarily live together in loyalty to the same sovereign authority through the same sovereign agency.

We will assume at the start that the civil religion described by Bellah constitutes in fact the religion of the American civil community. The function of the civil religion consists in expressing and informing the reality of the civil community in relation to God's authority and to the state which pertains to it as its agent. The whole complex of public and private institutions integral to the civil life stems from, and relies upon, the existence of this willing and loyal civil community.

Civil religion conceives of the state as a sovereign agency acting to express a covenant relationship between God and the civil community. Its spokesmen typically proclaim and defend the civil community's faith that the current state excels any alternative agency that men may propose to represent God and the people. They equally affirm the duty of every citizen to uphold and defend the state against any attempt to destroy it by an alien community, whether it be a foreign power or a domestic insurgent community.

Civil religion in America proclaims God to be the sovereign authority who gives warrant to the existence and perpetuation of the American civil community. It affirms the view that God authorizes the constitutional state to act as the historical sovereign agent uniting God's authority and the United States as a civil community. The civil religion thus upholds and defends the American state as a covenant between God and the American civil community. The sovereign state expresses, according to the faith of the civil religion, the *unity* of God's sovereign authority and the sovereign civil community.

The purpose of this paper is to explore the meaning of a particular Commonwealth project in education which specifically authorizes the teaching of the literature of religion in the public schools. Does this project reflect the reality of the civil religion? We will argue that it does. Is it a reflection of anything more than the reality of the civil religion? We will say that it is. Does this mean that we must clarify a distinction to be made

367

between the civil religion and what we have referred to above as transcivil religion? We will say that it does, because in fact the study matter of a course in religious literature does not affirm inherently the civil religion but rather affirms the views of transcivil religion. We will indicate that the course serves the interests of the civil religion *in its context*, while at the same time it serves the interests of the transcivil religions *in the texts of the literature itself*. To approach these matters, we turn first to a description of the Pennsylvania project as an objective basis for interpretation.

THE PENNSYLVANIA MANDATE FOR COURSES
IN RELIGIOUS LITERATURE
AS AN OBJECT OF INTERPRETATION

The Internal Structure and Sequence of the Project. Receiving its mandate from the General Assembly, the Pennsylvania Department of Public Instruction turned to the Religious Studies Department of The Pennsylvania State University to negotiate a contract to produce a first course. By the fall of 1966 such a contract was signed. With funds provided through the Department of Public Instruction, the Penn State Department of Religious Studies proceeded to produce during the winter and spring of 1966–1967 a syllabus-commentary for an eleventh or twelfth grade course in the Literature of Western Religions. It determined the scope of this course, confining it to the classical writings of Judaism, Christianity, and Islam. This meant four distinct bodies of literature, namely, the Hebrew Bible (Old Testament), the Rabbinic Writings through the Talmud, the New Testament, and the Qur'an.

The Department made final textual selections to be included in the students' reading for the course from lists provided by prominent scholars in the four fields. These scholars made their own selections against the two following criteria: (1) Does this passage represent richly the ethos of the religion, and (2) does this passage enjoy a relatively wide influence in literature generally?

368

The Department arranged with the local school district at State College, Pennsylvania, for an experimental class during the high school year 1966–1967 in which the selected texts might be read and the syllabus-commentary employed as the basis for a first teaching of the course. Thirty-four students in all worked with the materials. The State College Area Schools also provided a teacher qualified in English to teach the course experimentally as the textual and syllabus-commentary sequence was produced. The Department maintained close communication and guidance for the teacher through the teacher's membership on a working committee related to the course and through his twice-weekly conferences with the authors of the commentary.

Under the provisions of the contract with the Department of Public Instruction, the Department of Religious Studies organized the course project with advice from the expert scholars, the working committee, and an advisory panel. The expert scholars, as we have said, provided the initial selective lists of textual readings for the students.

The working committee met weekly throughout the school year while the course commentary was being written and the experimental class remained in progress. It included a representative from the Penn State College of Education, the head of the Department of Religious Studies, the Assistant Superintendent for Instruction from the local school district, the English Coordinator from the local school district, the authors, the experimental teacher, and various representatives from the Department of Public Instruction. It offered close advice to the authors and the experimental teacher and received from them equally detailed information and opinion.

The advisory panel consisted of scholars and experts more remote from the daily business of the project. Its purpose was to provide an evaluative point of view with respect to the project from persons sensitive not only to the scholarship involved in the course but also to the teaching methodology and to whatever religious bias the course might seem to contain. The advisory panel met once in the late fall of 1966 and again in the summer of 1967.

Also under the general arrangement, the Department of Religious Studies conducted an Orientation Institute for Teachers of Religious Literature in the Public Schools. This course occupied four weeks of midsummer 1967. Thirty-one English teachers, selected by the Department of Public Instruction from secondary public schools throughout the Commonwealth, attended the institute, which was held at Penn State. Eleven of the participant teachers were men, the rest women. Most of them are teachers of senior status in their systems. Each is slated to teach the course in Literature of the Western Religions during the school year 1967–1968 as a field-test project. The senior author of the syllabus-commentary taught the sessions of the institute daily. The members also listened to a sequence of scholars in Hebrew Bible, Rabbinics, New Testament, Qur'an, Church and State Relations, and English Literature, all as a part of the course program.

The External Considerations Impinging on the Project. The structure and sequence described above did not develop in a vacuum. On the contrary, they reflect a variety of value judgments and social anxieties on the part of all concerned. Perhaps we can portray that external complex of concern by modeling a scheme to show what kinds of communities exhibit an interest in the project and what the nature of that interest seems to be in each case. One can count four such communities, broadly conceived.

(1) The *civil community* shows its interest through the action of the state in mandating the course offering in the public (i.e., state) schools. The interest of the state focuses on the possibility that such courses can serve to enhance the civil cohesion of the people of the Commonwealth. The state provides an opportunity for all students to learn academically the religious literature which no longer can be presented liturgically in the schools, since to do the latter implies incorrectly that such literature is specifically that of the civil religion.

(2) The *transcivil communities*, whose memberships may extend far beyond the domestic civil boundaries, take a different

interest in the course project. They seek to judge whether in practice the course may enhance or decrease the integrity and security of their respective religions and whether the content of the course can be useful to their members as a mode of religious education. This concern involves not only the relative relationship of the transcivil communities with each other but also the common position of them all with respect to the state and the civil community which it represents.

(3) One should also be aware of another kind of community interest in this, or any other, sensitive development within the sphere of the American culture, namely, the interest of *alien communities*, whether within or beyond the domain of the American state. These alien communities constitute any foreign or domestic communities which find the American state to be fundamentally inimical to their own existence. These alien communities seek opportunities to displace the civil status quo.

(4) In addition to the interest that people have taken in the project as members of the civil and transcivil communities, many of them also take an interest in the course from the points of view of certain *professional communities*. These are people who act as ancillary agents. They work across the tensions caused by the relationship between the civil and transcivil communities expressed in the principle of separation of church and state. These ancillary agents represent such groups as officials of ecclesiastical institutions (transcivil); public school administrators; public school teachers; professional scholars in literature, religion, and education; and civil officeholders. To name some of the concerns of the ancillary agents:

(a) Ecclesiastical leaders must deal with the problems of ecumenism and church-state relations, and they see an acute form of the problem in the teaching of religious literature in the public schools.

(b) School administrators are concerned that such a program of study does not cause hostility within or toward the school system but rather that it promotes understanding as well as scholarship.

(c) Classroom teachers prospectively involved in the course

worry that they may antagonize students, parents, politicians, or ecclesiastical leaders by what they say or omit to say in class. At the same time, they remain ambitious to teach the course as a responsible effort in literary scholarship.

(d) Professional scholars, especially in religion, take an acute interest in such courses. They raise the question whether in fact the public school English teacher can do a creditable job of teaching such literature without extensive graduate work in religious studies. They express considerable sensitivity to the possibility that such teachers, as members of one specific religion, or none, can provide only a grotesque and biased interpretation of the literature generally. On the other hand, many such scholars express a keen interest in, and may be threatened by, the possibility that the secondary school English teacher in fact may be able to provide a very useful general introduction to the field, perhaps with less training than one might suppose to be necessary.

(e) Civil officeholders find the primary source of their concern in the fact that they must explicitly uphold the claim of the civil community to include all the people under the sovereignty of the state while recognizing at the same time the limitations which the transcivil religions put upon state sovereignty. Most of the people belong both to the civil and to some transcivil community, and their loyalties fluctuate between the two according to circumstances.

THE COURSE PROJECT AS AN EXPRESSION
OF CIVIL RELIGION

The relationship of the internal structure of the religious literature project to the external pattern of community interests focused upon it supports the reality of a civil religion. Initiated by the state, the project clearly protects the self-interest of the civil community and reflects a cardinal requirement of civil religion regarding religious intolerance.

Bellah, in describing the civil religion, says, "The phrase *civil religion* is, of course, Rousseau's. In Chapter 8, Book 4, of *The*

Social Contract, he outlines the simple dogmas of the civil religion: the existence of God, the life to come, the reward of virtue and the punishment of vice, and the exclusion of religious intolerance."

The full import of how the civil religion relates religious intolerance to the interests of the sovereign state appears in this fuller quotation of the paragraphs from which Bellah's points are abstracted:

> There is, however, a purely civil profession of faith, the articles of which it is the duty of the sovereign to determine, not exactly as dogmas of religion, but as sentiments of sociability, without which it is impossible to be a good citizen or a faithful subject. Without having power to compel any one to believe them, the sovereign may banish from the State whoever does not believe them; it may banish him not as impious, but as unsociable, as incapable of sincerely loving law and justice and of sacrificing at need his life to his duty. But if any one, after publicly acknowledging these dogmas, behaves like an unbeliever in them, he should be punished with death; he has committed the greatest of crimes, he had lied before the laws.
>
> The dogmas of civil religion ought to be simple, few in number, stated with precision, and without explanations or commentaries. The existence of the Deity, powerful, wise, beneficent, prescient, and bountiful, the life to come, the happiness of the just, the punishment of the wicked, the sanctity of the social contract and of the laws [omitted from Bellah's listing of the dogmas]; these are the positive dogmas. As for the negative dogmas, I limit them to one only, that is, intolerance; it belongs to the creeds which we have excluded.
>
> Those who distinguish civil intolerance from theological intolerance are in my opinion, mistaken. These two kinds of intolerance are inseparable. It is impossible to live at peace with people whom we believe to be damned; to love them would be to hate God who punishes them. It is absolutely necessary to reclaim them or to punish them. Wherever theological intolerance is allowed, it cannot but have some effect in civil life; and as soon as it has any, the sovereign is no longer sovereign even in secular affairs; from that time the priests are the real masters; the kings are only their officers.

> Now that there is, and can be, no longer any exclusive national religion, we should tolerate all those which tolerate others, so far as their dogmas have nothing contrary to the duties of a citizen. . . . [2:124–125].

We find, then, in the course project as initiated by the state, a positive effort by the civil community to offer students an experience with the literature of religion in such a way that no intolerance on the part of the transcivil religions may be exercised. The central criterion by which the worth of the course will be measured by the state would appear to be the extent to which it may either weaken the civil community by providing an occasion for the expression of religious intolerance, or strengthen it in being an occasion for building tolerance between the transcivil communities on the basis of their common involvement in the greater civil community and its schools.

The dogmatic presupposition behind the offering of the course consists in the understanding that the civil community, as an accomplished status quo, commands a responsibility among the people to give their ultimate loyalty in history to the sovereignty of that civil community and that state. The civil community and state value and encourage the formation and continuation of transcivil communities only insofar as they work in harmony rather than in opposition to the comprehensive sovereignty of the civil community and state, a sovereignty affirmed by the civil religion and enforced by the laws of the land.

THE TEXTS OF THE COURSE IN THE LITERATURE
OF THE WESTERN RELIGIONS AS EXPRESSIONS OF
TRANSCIVIL RELIGION

While the very offering by the state of courses in the literature of the transcivil religions reflects the civil community's self-understanding in terms of civil religion, the content of the literature thus offered reflects a religion of quite another sort. Each of the Western religions treated in the first course, i.e., Judaism,

Christianity, and Islam, violates the express dogmas of the civil religion. In the first place, each expresses its own dogmas in an extensive and highly interpretable way and with lengthy explanations. Second, each can agree with the civil religion as to the existence of God, the principle of moral retribution, and the hereafter; however, each would diverge from the civil religion in the latter's claim that men's ultimate responsibility in history is to the civil community and the state law, and to the sovereignty of the community and law as warranted by the sovereign and transcendent authority of God. For each of these religions, the sovereignty of the Torah, the Christ, or the Qur'an, as a prophetically revealed agency of God's authority, stands quite transcendent to any such sovereignty in history on the part of the state. Furthermore, each one of them sees the community *not as participating in that sovereignty*, but as finding its being in obedience to it. Third, as for the matter of intolerance, each of these religions, as part and parcel of its own existence, places limits upon its tolerance toward the revealed agencies of other transcivil religions, and all put limits upon their tolerance of the civil state's claims concerning the absolute significance of its own sovereignty.

Thus, in the presence of the civil community, the transcivil religions express the existence of autonomous communities that understand themselves not as civil institutions subordinate to a state, but as communities of transition toward an eschaton, communities for whom the notion of a perpetual civil status quo in history always arouses suspicions of idolatry.

We reiterate, therefore, the claim that a religious literature project such as the one we see in Pennsylvania constitutes at one and the same time both an expression of the civil religion and also of the transcivil religions. The mandate for the project, plus the structure and orientation of it, reflect the interests of the civil community. The study matter of the proposed courses nevertheless expresses the ultimate commitments by the transcivil communities to historical agencies of divine authority which stand or act quite free of the civil community and the state and quite transcendent to both in the minds of the faithful.

THE INTERACTION BETWEEN CIVIL AND TRANSCIVIL
RELIGIONS WHICH BEARS UPON PUBLIC SCHOOL
COURSE OFFERINGS IN THE LITERATURE OF RELIGIONS

How the Civil Religion Treats the Transcivil Religions. One can find in the civil religion a tendency to modify the doctrines of the transcivil religions in such a way as to remove the sovereign agency of God's will from the Torah, the Christ, or the Qur'an and to relocate it priorly in the state.

As a first instance, one can observe that the spokesmen for the civil religion tend to substitute the concept of *providence* for the concept of *revelation* as the decisive way of God with men and their affairs. As Bellah points out, the Declaration of Independence speaks of "a firm reliance on the protection of divine Providence." In Washington's first inaugural address, we read words referring to "that Almighty Being who rules over the universe, who presides in the councils of nations, and whose providential aids can supply every defect. . . ." And Bellah furthermore incorporates a quotation from Franklin which includes, "I never doubted, for instance, the existence of the Deity; that he made the world and govern'd it by his Providence. . . ." Recourse to providence appears to be a way of speaking which never raises the problem of revelation and its requirement that the faithful community lodge its historical obedience not primarily in the civil state, but in a Torah or a Christ or a Qur'an.

Second, the civil religion works to make transcivil religion, which might be called *revealed* religion, a matter of purely private concern. The implication is that the God of the Jews, the Christians, or the Muslims is a household God who is dangerous when let out on the civil street. As Rousseau said, "Subjects, then, owe no account of their opinions to the sovereign except so far as those opinions are of moment to the community" [2:123]. Here his reference is to the sovereign state and civil community. The statement suggests a danger to civil order stemming from the public broadcast of opposing religious prejudices. The civil religion, as Bellah says, leaves "an exceptionally wide sphere of personal piety and voluntary social action" to the churches. But, if the attitude of Rousseau is reflected here, the personal piety is private in nature, and the social action may not impinge on the security of the civil community or the stability of the state. In this sense, civil religion tends to put the transcivil God under benign sequestration in the inner sanctum of the individual believer's heart.

Third, as a corollary to the privatizing tendency, one can observe that the civil religion teaches the pluralism of the transcivil religions. In benign acceptance of all transcivil religions under the aegis of the civil community, inasmuch as they are private and personal concerns, the civil religion can laud them as expressions of individual freedom and as a patent demonstration of the Civil Peace. Their very plurality proclaims the open security of the civil community.

Fourth, the civil religion provides liturgical rituals and ceremonies which focus sentiments and attitudes, of the same kind that in the transcivil religions are focused upon Exodus-Sinai and Incarnation-Pentecost, upon such civil memories as the Birth of the Nation and the Civil War. As examples, Bellah describes the holidays of Memorial Day, Veterans Day, and the Fourth of July.

Fifth, the civil religion of America draws upon the resources of the biblical traditions to find prophetic allegories demonstrating the significance of cardinal events in the civil history of America. Thus the story of Exodus-Sinai or of the Joshuan assembly at Shechem becomes an illustration of the truth of the American colonization and revolution. By these stories, the civil religion dramatizes the *origin* of America. The civil religion can employ stories like those of the Babylonian Exile and Restoration, or the Crucifixion and Resurrection, as prototypes for the *consolidation* of America, which could not be achieved without someone's paying a profoundly sacrificial price. One can find, in the manifold contemporary employment of such concepts as "mission," "crusade," and "global responsibility" on the part of civil spokesmen,

377

the importation of vocabulary from the transcivil traditions to sacralize the multitudinous *expansion* of the civil community's aegis, both at home and abroad.

Bellah refers to these three phases of American civil development as "times of trial":

> The first time of trial had to do with the question of independence, whether we should or could run our own affairs in our own way. The second time of trial was over the issue of slavery, which in turn was only the most salient aspect of the more general problem of the full institutionalization of democracy within our country. . . . But we have been overtaken by a third great problem which has led to a third great crisis, in the midst of which we stand. This is the problem of responsible action in a revolutionary world. . . .

Contemporary American activity suggests the possibility that a fourth phase in America's civil history may require a vocabulary of interpretation as yet not gleaned from the Bible. This would be a phase of *retrenchment*, demanding a civil interpretation based on scripture, of such phenomena, for example, as an American withdrawal from certain foreign commitments like Vietnam. Or, it might require a radical revision of the stance of the American civil community in the face of countercommunities of a civil nature, comprising ghetto people born *sui generis* as a domestic but alien community of people previously nourished in one or more of the transcivil religions.

One can take heed also of the fact that throughout the developing history of American education the subordination of the lore of the transcivil religions to the purposes of the civil religion has proceeded apace with the transfer of the control of the educational process from the institutions of the churches to those of the state. Bellah points to the currently pervasive influence of the civil religion within the institutions of the transcivil religions themselves, implying the basically civil orientation of the sedate modern American parish or American synagogue. This reflects Emile Durkheim, "If religion has given birth to all that is essential in society, it is because the idea of society is the soul of religion" [1:419].

378

How the Transcivil Religions Treat the Civil Religion. We have indicated already the strong trend in the direction of a complete civil-ization of the traditional religions in America. Nevertheless, much remains to be said in observation of a continuing self-assertion on the part of the transcivil religions. Transcivil religion continues to maintain and develop a language of understanding which provides a radical alternative to the language of the civil community.

In the first place, the transcivil religious communities insist on the centrality and supremacy of those sovereign agencies of God's authority (i.e., Torah, Christ, Qur'an) that have been given to them as a gift from God to be the foci of their communal submission and obedience in history.

Second, we can say that each of these transcivil religions presupposes *at least the equality* before God of its agency of God's sovereignty in relation to the other transcivil agencies; in each case, they claim *the certain superiority* of their agencies over the agency of the state as the expression of their people's covenant with God.

Third, each transcivil community persists in its own community building and in its conviction that peace with God as a quality of the community life transcends in meaning the peace with Society required by the state. Thus both social evolution and social revolution typically gestate within the nourishing environment provided by these communities.

Fourth, the transcivil communities persist in cultic activities that clearly assert an opposition to any state claims upon their people's absolute loyalty. They study the Torah, they commune with the Christ, they contemplate the words of the Qur'an. In these practices they further assert the independence and creative priority in their lives of their revealed sovereign agencies over any agency pertaining to the civil community.

Fifth, each of these transcivil religions treats its own mythology of sovereign authority and sovereign agency as impinging directly on historical events, and not as something private and apart from history. It denies the ultimacy of any civil status quo in history and looks forward to an eschatological consummation of history that will supersede all civil communities and states. It refuses to allegorize its own history merely in order to support the claims of civil religion. Indeed, it sees all civil history as ultimately under the judgment of God.

The transcivil religions see the ebb-and-flow history of civil communities largely in terms of the origins, consolidations, expansions, and retrenchments of the nations. For them, God values the civil communities as only relatively useful to him and to his people. They remain useful as status quos, not sempiternal, but pro tem.

CONCLUSION

A first possibility to note, when considering the significance of religious literature as study matter in the public schools, is that the religious tradition already has been so *civil*ized within the churches and synagogues themselves that the average American, as Bellah puts it in a slightly different context, sees "no conflict" between religion as expressed by the churches and synagogues and as otherwise expressed by the spokesmen of the civil religion.

Beyond this, however, such courses as the one being offered in Pennsylvania may be the occasion for a vital experience in living with perhaps life's most compelling antinomy. Such an antinomy requires that a person must loyally obey the God-revealed agent (e.g., Torah, Christ, Qur'an) that claims his whole life as a Jew, Christian, or Muslim, while at the same time he must obey with equal loyalty the God-provided agent (e.g., the American state) that claims his whole life as a citizen. The living of such an antinomy constitutes an ineradicable ambivalence in the interaction between the civil and the transcivil communities.

Faithful believers in both kinds of religion may learn something new, however, about how individuals generally can live this antinomy *as experience itself* when they confront the courage to teach and the courage to learn that marks a state-sponsored class in the literature of religion. For here both teachers and students deal with these equally compelling ultimate claims upon the faith and obedience of each human life. They live with them not only as a *textual* study in literature but also as a matter of *contextual* encounter in the personal dynamics of the classroom situation.

REFERENCES

1. Durkheim, Emile: *The Elementary Forms of Religious Life* (George Allen & Unwin, Ltd, London, England) 1915.
2. Rousseau, Jean J: The Social Contract in C M Andrews, ed, *Famous Utopias* (Tudor Publishing Co, New York, New York) no date.

COMMENTARY
by Phillip E. Hammond

By its lucidity, its timeliness, its palpability, Professor Bellah's essay on America's civil religion stakes its own claim to greatness. That many others [4; 7; 11; 13], including this writer [6:97–106], have attempted to circumscribe the matter at issue indicates the interest it holds for a number of us, but not until "Civil Religion in America" was there a reasonably detailed and dispassionate portrait of this American "theology." For above all, Bellah takes seriously the idea of a national faith, locating its parameters without resorting to charges of syncretism, and tracing its history as a parallel, rather than a substitute, religion in American society.

The task needed doing — for social scientists because of ancient and revered notions regarding the inevitability of common values in any viable society, for churches because of confusion over their tangential relationship to the moving forces in American culture, and for citizens because of frequent misunderstanding of the volatile nature of this nation's faith. One does not exaggerate in saying that this civil religion has now been identified.

381

Its central tenet, located, as Bellah notes, "very deep in the American tradition," is Old Testament in form, calling for the nation and its members to "carry out God's will on earth," to "establish a new sort of social order that shall be a light unto all the nations." Once identified, the notion helps in understanding the American experience of expanding frontiers, of massive immigration, of Manifest Destiny, indeed of effective warfare! Are we not the most heterogeneous and differentiated people on earth, but has not some unifying idea held us together during the times when we might easily have split asunder?

Accepting as I do the essential correctness of Bellah's argument, I want in these pages to suggest several ideas which seem to flow from his discussion of America's civil religion. The comments to follow, therefore, represent not revisions of a thesis, but extensions.

In the finest sense, Bellah's is a *cultural* analysis. That is, he identifies a set of ideas, demonstrates their interrelatedness, and illustrates their appearance in American life. The parallel *structural* analysis receives considerably less attention. Apart from a brief section of "manifestations" — including the Revolution, Civil War, the Presidency, national cemeteries, holidays, foreign wars, and foreign policy — nothing is said about the social structures through which this "culture" lives. Yet, it is axiomatic that for any ideas (and certainly religious ideas) to exist, there must be social positions, expectations, institutions, even laws for the origin, preservation, transmission, and revision of those ideas. What might be such social structures in the case of America's civil religion?

Churches, of course, are candidates. As Herberg and others have charged, The American Way of Life enjoys a gospellike position in most of this country's religious organizations, Catholic and Jewish as well as Protestant. But churches, it is fair to say, are not unique in this regard; virtually all organizations — economic, political, voluntary, educational — celebrate the civil theology. The one place where more people, more often, for greater lengths of time are confronted with the nation's faith is in public schools. Has it not been free public education that largely turned successive waves of immigrants into American "believers"? Is it not in elementary and secondary classrooms and on school playgrounds that Protestant and Catholic, Christian and Jew, theist and atheist have met and competed? And, as foreign observers have noticed, does not the high school dominate the community landscape in mainline America in much the same way that the cathedral does in Europe? Pictures of Moses or Jesus would be considered inappropriate in the hallways of America's public schools, but portraits abound of Washington, Jefferson, and Lincoln, their names identify the buildings, and their words are studied in the classroom and intoned in the assembly hall. After his essay "Protestant-Catholic-Jew," Herberg wrote on the strategic role of the public school in inculcating the American Way [8:11–51]. Public schools, it seems clear, supply major structural support for America's civil religion.

It is possible, certainly, to overestimate the didactic effect of public education; on the other hand, its total effect is much broader than formal instruction. There is, for example, from elementary grades on, the ubiquitous student government with its training for political achievement in a context of fair play and egalitarianism. There is a range of student-run extracurricular activities. And, most importantly, there is competitive athletics. No other nation has organized its participant sports so much around public schools, nor, probably, does any nation surpass the United States in the proportion of youngsters involved in serious competitive play.

What relationship, it might be asked, does sport have to the American faith? The civil religion, Bellah states in his concluding paragraph, "does not make any decision for us. It does not remove us from moral ambiguity . . . ." Yet, any nation *must* make decisions, *must* act in spite of moral ambiguity. The question, thus, is how Americans are trained to seek "God's will on earth" when nobody really "knows" God's will. Or, more accurately, when *everybody* can claim to know God's will, how are decisions made in conformity with that will? The answer is competition of ideas within the rules of the game. Ideologically, sovereignty belongs to God, but operationally His will is known through majority vote, fair play, or some such enabling rules. And here the structural importance of sport is apparent, for, at least during strategic periods of their lives, Americans learn that the highest rewards, the greatest glory, goes to those who have played hardest within the rules. As Caillois perceptively notes:

> It is not without significance that the Anglo-Saxon sport, par excellence, is golf, a game in which the player at any time has the opportunity to cheat at will, but in which the game loses all interest from that point on. It should not be surprising that this may be correlated with the attitude of the taxpayer to the treasury and the citizen to the state [2:83].

Caillois' comment is made in the context of an ingenious argument — that there is "a truly reciprocal relationship between a society and the games it likes to play. . . . Preferred and widely diffused games reflect, on the one hand, the tendencies, tastes, and ways of thought that are prevalent, while, at the same time, in educating and training the players in these very virtues or eccentricities, they subtly confirm them in their habits and preferences" [2:82–83]. *Agon,* or competition, is one of four styles of game he discusses. Significantly, along with chance (*alea*), it tends to replace vertigo (*ilinx*) and simulation (*mimicry*) styles as societies modernize, according to Caillois. Much that is magical or mysterious tends to be replaced by rationally conceived practices, in the sphere of play as well as elsewhere. "Regulated competition and the verdict of chance, implying both exact calculation and speculation intended to assign risks and rewards equitably . . . create law, i.e., a fixed, abstract, and coherent code, so profoundly modifying the social norms that the Roman adage *Ubi societas, ibi ius* . . . seems to affirm that society itself begins with this revolution" [2:126, also 87, 97, 101].

Competitive sports, student elections, and other "fair play" activities institutionalized in public schools may well be, then, crucial social structures for the transmission and maintenance of America's civil religion. This is the case not so much because "God" or "God's will" figures prominently in the participation, but because "habits and preferences" for rules enabling competi-

384

tion are "subtly confirmed" and given primacy over winning itself. This is not to assert that such inculcation is totally successful. Infidels abound in this civil, as in any, religion. It is significant, however, that persons in politically strategic positions appear more committed [10:361–382; 12].

Though free public education may be strategic for the inculcation of habits of fair play, other social structures obviously are also involved. Consider only the problem of higher level decision making. How are choices to be made? Bellah says, "The will of the people is not itself the criterion of right and wrong. There is a higher criterion in terms of which this will can be judged; . . ." How, then, does society know the higher criterion? The answer generally given is that we learn this through the Constitution and the court system which interprets it. Here, it is said, is the highest criterion by which the natural rights of man and the greatest societal goods are to be judged. Max Lerner [9:1290–1319] is probably the most famous of those observers who have, by derivation, reasoned that the U.S. Supreme Court and its members enjoy a sacred quality. The nation has a civil faith, so the argument goes, and its citizens regard the Constitution as the Holy Writ, the Court as the temple, and the Justices as high priests.

If this situation were true, the structural correspondence between "religion" as commonly understood and "civil religion" would be remarkable indeed. In fact, recent research indicates that the general public is woefully ignorant of their "temple" — what it decides, how many "priests" it has, and so forth [3]. It is quite incorrect to say simply that the Court plays a critical symbolic role for the civil religion's believers.

It is not incorrect to suppose, however, that the constitutional interpretative role of the Court is strategically related to America's civil religion. There still remains the problem of assessing and applying the higher criterion, and it is clear that, more than any other single agency, the Supreme Court is involved in that endeavor. It is no surprise, therefore, to find debate raging over the proper role of the Court and to find, moreover, that the debate is carried on in quasireligious terms.

The "natural law" position is a tenuous one, of course, because of the positivistic tradition in much of American jurisprudence. If, however, the central tenet of the national faith has it that man is endowed by his Creator with certain inalienable rights and if the judiciary's central task is to know and apply those rights, it is fairly obvious how jurisprudence is thrown into discussion of America's civil religion. One of the perceptive parties to this debate is Lon Fuller. In his recent Storrs Lectures at Yale, Professor Fuller elaborated a distinctive defense of natural law, and in the process he identified for courts a role very much in keeping with the civil religion [5].

The natural law to which courts are committed, says Fuller, is a "procedural" natural law [5:96 ff]. The morality it implies is an "internal morality," a "morality of aspiration," whereby the goodness of laws can be judged.

> Take, for example, the problems that may confront a judge in interpreting a statute. So far as the external aims of the statute are concerned, it is a part of the ethos of his office that the judge should remain, insofar as human capacity admits, neutral among the moral positions that may have been taken in the statute with regard to such questions as divorce, contraception, gambling, or the requisition of private property for public use.
>
> But the very same considerations that require an attitude of neutrality with regard to the external aims of the law demand a commitment by the judge to the law's internal morality [5: 131–132].

Fuller discerns eight criteria for judging the goodness or internal morality of laws, though he suggests also the provisional character of this number [5: chap 2]. However, the decisive points for the discussion here are twofold: (1) There inheres — naturally — in the law an ideal model which it is man's obligation to discover and emulate. The correspondence to "God's will on earth" in the civil religion is easily seen. And (2) the ideal is "procedural," not substantive; that is, it is meant to encompass negotiations between parties holding all manner of substantive ends. The relevance of this point for pluralistic America is also easily seen, for, as Baron noted about one "prophet" of the civil religion, "Jefferson conceded . . . that in their 'Metaphysical' aspects religious bodies might differ widely, but demanded that as social organizations they should all conform to the new political patterns of American democracy" [1:41].

Those "political patterns of American democracy," I submit, are the genesis of America's civil religion. If Protestant, Catholic, or Jewish "metaphysics" (narrowly conceived) has moved in the direction of the nation's faith, such change may be explicable on other grounds, but it has not been mandatory. Americans are still free to hold whatever cognitive ideologies they choose. But, precisely because they have that freedom, they have had to develop a new supernatural political ideology which can articulate their pluralism. The outcome has been a "civil religion" in America. Free public education has been vital in training citizens to this religion, and the judiciary is vital in orchestrating the inevitable conflicts.

There are gaps, of course. In a proposition which only future historians can assess, Bellah claims that foreign policy is the arena of our "third time of trial." Whether our civil religion can become "simply one part of a new civil religion of the world" is not at all certain. But, given the momentum of America's understanding of its own experience, perhaps there are grounds for hope.

REFERENCES

1. Baron, Salo: *Modern Nationalism and Religion* (Harper & Row, Publishers, New York, New York) 1947.
2. Caillois, Roger: *Man, Play, and Games*, Meyer Barash, translator, (Free Press, New York, New York) 1961.
3. Dolbeare, Kenneth M, and Hammond, Phillip E: The Political Party Basis of Attitudes toward the U.S. Supreme Court, *Public Opinion Quarterly*, Winter 1967.
4. Eckardt, A Roy: *The Surge of Piety in America* (Association Press, New York, New York) 1958.

5. Fuller, Lon: *The Morality of Law* (Yale University Press, New Haven, Connecticut) 1964.
6. Hammond, Phillip E: Religion and the "Informing" of Culture, *Journal for the Scientific Study of Religion*, vol 3, Fall 1963.
7. Herberg, Will: *Protestant-Catholic-Jew* (Anchor Books, Doubleday & Co, Inc, Garden City, New York) 1955.
8. Herberg, Will: Religion and Education in America in Smith, J W, and Jamison, A L: *Religious Perspectives in American Culture* (Princeton University Press, Princeton, New Jersey) 1961.
9. Lerner, Max: The Constitution and the Court as Symbols, *Yale Law Journal*, vol 46, 1937.
10. McClosky, Herbert: Consensus and Ideology in American Politics, *American Political Science Review*, vol 58, June 1964.
11. Marty, Martin E: *The New Shape of American Religion* (Harper & Row, Publishers, New York, New York) 1959.
12. Stouffer, S A: *Communism, Conformity, and Civil Liberties* (Doubleday & Co, Inc, Garden City, New York) 1955.
13. Vahanian, Gabriel: *The Death of God* (George Braziller, Inc, New York, New York) 1961.

RESPONSE

by Robert N. Bellah

I HAVE LEARNED from all of the above comments. I am happy to say that I share almost all the value positions of the various commentators. But I also see from these comments how difficult it is to get across an analytical interpretation of so controversial a subject. It is clear that what I mean by "civil religion in America" is not exactly what most of the commentators mean, nor do they agree one with another. The notion needs further clarification, and I will concern myself with that task in these brief notes.

388

Much as I appreciate the rigor of his position and the values for which he stands, I must strongly disagree with Leo Pfeffer. What I mean by civil religion is certainly not what Dean Weigle meant by a "common core." The civil religion is not merely a least common denominator of the "three major faiths." Such "religion in general" certainly does exist in America and stands in ambiguous relation to both civil religion and church religions. But what I mean by civil religion is a set of religious beliefs, symbols, and rituals growing out of the American historical experience interpreted in the dimension of transcendence. Neither the Constitution nor the Supreme Court nor anyone else can legislate that a people shall not interpret its own experience religiously. It is my conviction that any community of people with a strong sense of its own identity will so interpret its experience.

Criticism of the form which that common religious understanding takes is most appropriate and relevant. I certainly share much of the critique of Pfeffer, Brogan, and some of the others. But when Brogan implies that Englishmen, with their casual attitude toward flag ritual, are free from this curious American aberration of a civil religion, then he is indulging in nonsense. A religious self-interpretation of English history goes back at least to Shakespeare and Milton. There is scarcely a single perversion of the American civil religion which lacks its parallel in nineteenth or twentieth century Britain.

Pfeffer's polemic stance leads him to take the "cookie prayer" as somehow typical of American civil religion but not to mention, for example, the Lincoln Memorial in Washington, D.C. It is not helpful to include in one's analysis only the ridiculous end of the spectrum. If it be argued that I did the opposite, I think it is clear from my original article that I did so deliberately because so much of the analysis in this area has concentrated on the banal.

But the difference between Pfeffer's and my analyses comes out most clearly with respect to the "use" of religion as an instrumentality for the attainment of national goals. It is a deep misunderstanding of my position to imagine that I "warmly endorse" the use of religion when the ends are commendable. Religion deals with the realm of ends. When religion is "used" as a means, there is always a perversion, no matter how noble the ends. Yet there is a relation between ends and means and between religious ends and national goals. Pfeffer seems to argue that the danger of "unhallowed perversion" is so great that any connection whatever between these two realms must be avoided. This would be to say that religion, civil or otherwise, must never have anything relevant to say about the most pressing concerns of men. Such a position is, in my opinion, entirely untenable. It is also utterly "idealistic" since it has never been and is not likely to be the case.

Again it is not a question of whether or not there will be a connection between religious commitments and political goals, but what kind of connection. A situation in which religion becomes a "handmaiden of national purposes" (and I am glad to see that Pfeffer recognizes that not only civil religion is vulnerable to such a use) is a perversion. A proper relation, in my opinion, is one in which national purposes are the handmaiden of the fundamental value commitments of the civil religion. I tried to differentiate some situations in which this proper relation was achieved and some in which it was not. I may be mistaken in my instances. Self-delusion in these matters is remarkably easy. But to abdicate every effort to relate national purposes to the fundamental value commitments which give our nation meaning is surely a misguided way to avoid falling into error. We are not so easily spared responsibility for moral decision.

The assumption that civil religion must necessarily be a perversion or a form of idolatry seems to be shared by Brogan and Whitney as well as by Pfeffer, although Whitney's position is considerably more nuanced than the other two. It is interesting that Brogan and Whitney emphasize rather different origins for the American civil religion. Brogan finds the chief source in Protestantism and Whitney in the Enlightenment. It is my conviction that these are indeed the two principal traditions behind civil religion. The question becomes, then, why did two positions neither of which is intrinsically idolatrous produce an idolatrous civil religion? The Protestant position places God and the Enlightenment places Reason above any merely national loyalty; both traditions subject national loyalties to judgment in terms of these higher principles. It is my contention that the core of the American civil religion is in essential continuity with its two chief sources in this respect, that it is a way of relating national loyalty and identity to principles which transcend them, rather than an assertion of the eternality or ultimacy of the nation itself.

Whitney's position is curious in another respect, namely the sharp distinction he makes between "civil" and "transcivil" religion. Whatever the case may be with Christianity, and it is a complicated one, it is clear that both Judaism and Islam over most of their history and in several forms have been civil religions. What Christians call the Old Testament is precisely the religious interpretation of the history of Israel. Is it so clear that American analogizing from the Old (or New) Testament is necessarily religiously illegitimate? Why should the history of a people living two or three thousand years ago be religiously meaningful but the history of a people living in the last two or three hundred years be religiously meaningless? Again it is a case of how it is done, not whether it is done. The notion of Providence by no means necessarily implies the sempiternality of the nation, even though it may sometimes have been used that way.

Whitney is of course right to see the civil and the "transcivil" religions as potentially giving rise to conflicting loyalties. But I would suggest that he is wrong in implying that they must necessarily do so. Nor is the only way of avoiding conflict to insist on the total privatization of noncivil religions. Here Rousseau's is not the final statement when it comes to American civil religion, even though tendencies in that direction are found, as Whitney suggests, in our own Enlightenment background. But the other source of our civil religion, activistic Protestantism, has never wholly accepted this solution, nor has it had to break fundamentally with the civil religion when it took a socially relevant position.

The question, and it is the most delicate issue of all, is how the civil and noncivil religions are to be related. The polemic critique

391

of the civil religion seems to imply that there is necessarily a deadly struggle between them unless general perversion is to ensue. I have argued that there is at least one central strand of the American civil religion which does not make the nation ultimate and is genuinely consonant with a transcendental religious tradition, partly, of course, because it is a development out of it.

Hammond's comment is a refreshing turn in the direction of sociological reality. The educational system, competitive sports, and the legal system may be, if Hammond is correct, more useful references than cookie prayers to the civil religion in action. Insistence on fair play, enabling rules, the search for truth wherever it may lead — all are inherently antiidolatrous. Here we have a model of a self-revising society which is not ultimate in any finite form but always subject to higher demands and considerations. If Hammond's analysis is valid, and I find it extremely attractive, then the nonidolatrous strand of the civil religion which I documented chiefly in the words of a few thinkers and statesmen, notably Lincoln, is also deeply embedded at the homely level of everyday institutions. But I suspect that Hammond's analysis will not easily be understood by some of the critics. It crosscuts the usual definitions of the "religious" and brings out considerations that some may find irrelevant. Perhaps because I am also a sociologist, I find this just the strong point of Hammond's remarks. His analysis allows us to outflank the usual definitional hassles and get a glimpse of functioning social reality.

With the exception of Hammond's and to some extent Whitney's, the comments are much more evaluative than analytical. The issues involved are not neutral ones, and it is easy to see why strong feelings are aroused. While I feel that my original paper was a contribution toward analytical clarity, it was also strongly evaluative, as some of the critics point out. Nor does that seem to me inappropriate. Hammond is right in seeing education as a central institution of the civil religion. And yet the American university community is probably more divorced from the noncivil religions than is any other significant group of Americans. It seems to me legitimate for the university community to bear some of the burdens of the civil religion. Critical self-consciousness may be the best antidote for the kinds of perversions which the commentators are so quick to point out. My paper, then, has partly a constructive intent. It is meant as a contribution toward the reformation as well as the understanding of the American civil religion.

9. REPORT FROM SOUTH INDIA

by John B. Carman

WHAT is the present religious situation in India? This is in principle an outsider's question, even though in fact a growing number of Indians are asking this and similar questions and even though in Europe and North America a very large number of people find it a matter of course to inquire about a religious situation in which they themselves are involved. The concept of a "religious situation" is, I believe, peculiar to the modern West; its closest analogues in past epochs and in other cultures are the occasional descriptions by travelers of the customs of an alien people. The religious man involved in a premodern tradition, whether in East or West, may ask many questions: "What is the nature of ultimate reality?" "What is the present state of my soul?" "How shall I attain the state of eternal bliss?" or such questions as "What forms of worship are appropriate in our present age?" "What is wrong with our religious community?" or "What is the condition of those outside our community?" but he would either confuse the question about the "religious situation" with one of these questions or he would find it meaningless.

A question about the religious situation is a question of a modern westerner who, frequently without realizing it, has learned to look at his entire world, even the world that is "inside" him, the world in which he shares, as if it were an external object. It is in this sense an "outsider's" question, even if the man asking it is an "insider," a participant in the religious situation he seeks to understand. This is not to say that it is not a significant and valuable question, not only for social scientists or historians who are deliberately "external" in their approach, but also for those who, in understanding themselves as religious men,

395

try to include a conception of their relations with the culture in which they participate.

"The religious situation" is a deliberately nonspecific concept. It includes the total world of religious people in their variegated contact and interconnection with aspects of life that are not specifically religious. It includes religious institutions as well as religious feelings. While it is something wider than the believer's self-understanding, it is not simply the understanding of one or more outside observers. It is rather the comprehensive but always elusive object that the observer seeks to grasp and to understand.

To ask about the religious situation in India today is to ask a significant question, but one that confronts sizable obstacles in the way of an answer. Some of these obstacles are rather obvious. Indeed, it may seem impertinent for one outside observer of the Hindu religious situation to attempt an answer at all. Yet the obvious difficulties facing a relatively inexperienced student in generalizing validly on a vast subject do not worry me so much as the less obvious difficulties. This essay is intended only as an initial and very tentative exploration. It is clear that the many specific aspects of the Indian religious situation ought to be treated in separate essays by those most qualified to discuss them.

No, what worries me, what lies somewhat heavily on my academic conscience, is the question of whether I personally should agree to try to describe the religious situation in India. I have heretofore attempted to minimize the distance between myself and the Hindus whom I am trying to understand by limiting myself to that meaning of religious phenomena that is more or less apparent to them. To try to understand the total Hindu situation means perforce to seek to grasp quite different attitudes among Hindus towards both the Divine Object of religious activity and the means employed in such activity. More than that, however, while attempting to see the relation between these diverse approaches to religious life, one discovers factors of which some or all of these various kinds of Hindus are unaware — sometimes even factors that would seem repugnant to them.

No doubt this is true also in looking at the religious situation in North America, but we are far more used to the outside critic's dissection of our religious motivations and his explanations of our religious behavior. More important still, in spite of all our objectivity, we are seeking to understand a religious situation in which we ourselves participate, and this participation prevents us from too external an understanding. The American Christian observer of the Hindu religious situation has no such built-in safeguard against the hazards of an objectivity that misses what is most important to the Hindu. If, then, he insists on a kind of understanding that is other than and even contrary to the Hindu's own understanding of his religious and social environment, he should do so with full awareness of the stance that he is taking, and he should be willing to recognize the possibility that his understanding of the religious situation may be *less* rather than *more* profound than the self-understanding of many Hindus.

THE DIFFERENCE BETWEEN THE SOUTH AND THE NORTH

I shall limit myself to some comments on the Hindu situation in South India. While this may seem a considerable limitation, it still leaves as the object of our inquiry the situation of more than a hundred million Hindus in India's four southern states. The boundaries of the Hindu community in South India are even more difficult for the outsider to discover. The difficulty is due not so much to the fact that the religious situation is fluid as that the labels attached to it mean different things to different persons. "South India" is usually taken to include the four southern states speaking Dravidian languages: Madras (Tamil), Kerala (Malayalam), Andhra Pradesh (Telugu), and Mysore (Kannada) with a total population of about one hundred and thirty millions. The Dravidian languages contain a great many Sanskirt words, as well as words from North Indian languages, but their basic linguistic structure and vocabulary indicate that they belong to a separate family of languages, not part of the vast Indo-European language family. For over two thousand years they have been influenced by Sanskrit and its vernacular derivatives (first the Prakrits, and later the present languages of the rest of India), and in the case of three of them the prestige of the Sanskrit tradition has sometimes obscured the fact of their non-

Sanskrit origin from the Brahmin literati. In the case of Tamil, however, there is an ancient literature in classical Tamil preceding the medieval Sanskritized Tamil, and for the last several centuries there has also been a distinct non-Brahmin tradition of Tamil religious literature among the Śaivites.

It is not surprising, therefore, that the contemporary separatist movement in South India has flourished in and is largely confined to the "Tamil Land." In all four southern states the other castes have gradually succeeded in ousting the Brahmins from their previous near monopoly in government and the professions, but only in Tamil Nad has this movement been given a strong ideological base, in which both the religious authority and the cultural authority of Brahmins have been sharply challenged. We shall return to this point at greater length presently, but it is well to note from the start that the remarkable success of the Progressive Dravidian Party (Dravida Munnetra Kazhagam) in Madras State in the February 1967 elections has laid bare the conflict between two cultures that has shaped so much of South Indian life for the past two thousand years.

Much of the contemporary religious situation in South India, as in much of Asia, can be seen as a still intensifying encounter between "East" and "West" or, in more general terms, between traditional agrarian cultures and modern technocracy. It is important to keep in mind, however, that this encounter between East and West is added to — and sometimes superimposed upon — an ancient encounter between "North" and "South," between Aryans and Dravidians. This encounter has gone through a number of stages in different parts of India since the Aryans first entered India more than 3,500 years ago. Each stage has developed certain forms — whether compromise or synthesis — which have been hallowed by tradition and have given the impression of an unchanging culture and a static society. This impression is not only that of outsiders but of the members of the society as well. But, as in western history each crisis has revealed the seams in the fabric of its Graeco-Roman, Hebrew, and Celto-Germanic culture and sometimes rent that fabric afresh, so each crisis in South Indian history has brought into question the previously accepted relationship between the Sanskritic and Dravidian elements in South Indian culture. To me, living here in the midst of the present transition, it appears that the superimposition of the East-West encounter on that between North Indian and South Indian cultures is producing a more profound upheaval than any previous one. So it appears to many observers, but by no means to all, and many of those involved in the present situation would deny that there was any radical change, any crisis, any threat, to established Hindu institutions. Many more would be unable to affirm or deny a "crisis of faith"; they simply have no idea what such a crisis might be.

In the present Hindu situation in South India there is both structure and tension, and with respect to both there are different perspectives, among Hindus as well as between most Hindus and most outside observers. To the orthodox Hindu, the structure of society is copermanent with the vast duration of the present evil age (*the Kaliyuga*), the last of the four ages, in which the cow of righteousness (*dharma*) tries to stand on only one leg. The presently accepted dharma is not only copermanent with this age but is a kind of pale reflection of the pattern of the more righteous ages in the distant past. The hierarchy of castes is an essential part of the pattern of this noneternal but basically permanent order. The classical Hindu law books (*dharma-śāstras*) prescribe both duties between and duties within castes. There is no suggestion that any of the main castes have ever been elsewhere than within this social fabric, certainly no suggestion that the leaders of Hindu society, the Brahmins, should have entered India less than four thousand years ago and South India more recently than that. Yet this quite different view of Hindu social structure is held by almost all western observers and by a growing number of Indians who are prepared to accept the conclusions of western and westernized historians.

THE BRAHMINS

According to this modern historical view, the Brahmins entered India between 2000 and 1500 B.C. as the hereditary priests of a group of tribes that called themselves the *Aryas*, the "noble" people. These seminomadic tribes were related in language and social structure to other tribes to the Northwest, some of whom at about the same time were invading western Asia, Asia Minor, and Europe. Within a few centuries, tribes speaking Indo-European languages stretched from North India to Ireland (where the Celts also named themselves the "noble" people). In many countries these new invaders entered with a much lower level of material civilization than that enjoyed by the previous inhabitants, and nowhere was this more true than in North India, where the invading Aryas encountered the remarkable civilization that was unearthed a generation ago on the banks of the Indus, at Mohenjo-Daro and Harappa. It seems likely that this civilization was already declining when the Aryas first appeared, and it is, moreover, uncertain how much the local inhabitants whom they first fought and conquered had been affected by the great city centers of this civilization. There is much that is still unknown about the Indus Valley civilization, due in part to the failure of all attempts to decipher its script, but these archaeological discoveries have in any case effected a revolution in our understanding of Indian history. Like the Hellenes invading the Minoan Empire, the Aryas were not moving into the lands of primitive peoples, but invading the land of a civilized people or peoples. So much is almost certainly true, but the contemporary enthusiasts for Dravidian culture go beyond that fact to identify the Indus Valley civilization as Dravidian, indeed as continuous with ancient Tamil culture. Such identification is possible and indeed more likely than the insistence of some Brahmin scholars that the inhabitants of the Indus Valley cities were Aryans, but it is by no means proved. Whether proved or not, this "history" has become a powerful instrument in the hands of the Tamil critics of the Brahmin cultural domination, for it reverses the roles that Brahmins and non-Brahmins have played in South Indian history during the last two thousand years and makes it appear that originally it was the Brahmins themselves who were the uncouth barbarians.

Barbarians or no, these Aryan invaders were a vigorous people who gradually extended their sway to the East and South, conquering the earlier inhabitants as well as pushing them back. Within the Aryan community were the same three classes of nobles, priests, and commoners that existed in kindred Indo-European tribes in Europe. Those earlier inhabitants who were admitted into Aryan society as servants or slaves (dāsas or dasyus) were called Śūdras, "those who have been purified," and were thus distinguished from groups that did not accept Brahmin priestly authority at all and thus remained outside or below the Aryan community. The Śūdras did not enter fully into the religious privilege of Aryans; their young men did not share the initiation ceremony of "sacred birth" and therefore Śūdras were distinguished from the three Aryan classes or castes (varnas) who were called "the twice-born" (dvijas). As the Aryans moved south and east, the proportion of Śūdras they incorporated in their society grew higher and higher, and among the Śūdras there were hereditary endogamous occupational groups (kūla or jāti) between whom there already was or gradually developed a hierarchy comparable to, and possibly modeled upon, the hierarchy of the three Aryan varnas.

Over a period of many centuries the Brahmin priestly class established its claims to be superior to the warrior class (the Kshatriyas) and to be the chief religious functionaries for the Śūdras. Neither development, however, occurred without resistance or was altogether completed. There are a few echoes in the Upanishads of efforts by members of this warrior class to show that they are qualified to instruct the Brahmins, and in the movements of Jainism and Buddhism we see not only the revival of a pre-Aryan ascetic tradition (Yoga) but also a severe challenge to Brahmin supremacy. The Jain and Buddhist leadership was originally drawn from the Kshatriya varna, later from the Vaishyas (Aryan commoners), and Jain and Buddhist monks enjoyed the patronage of many princes as well as at least partial support from the Śūdras.

During the same centuries the religion of the Aryas was gradually changing, and much of the change seems to have been an adjustment to and borrowing from the pre-Aryan religion (or religions) of India. Thus by the time of Aśoka (300 B.C.), not

401

only had Brahmin priestly leadership been severely challenged, but the actual contents of the worship conducted by the Brahmins differed more and more from the ritual of the Vedas. New gods became more prominent than the old Aryan gods praised in the Vedic hymns, and the new gods were also differently worshiped. Instead of sacrifices in the open air, worship was now conducted before images of the deities housed in an elaborate temple. Moreover, animal sacrifices were no longer offered to the new high gods (Vishnu and Śiva, and originally also Brahmā), though the goddesses of the land continued to be propitiated with animal sacrifices — some of them conducted by non-Brahmin Śūdra or Outcaste priests. Perhaps as a result of Jain and Buddhist influence on general moral sensibilities, or as a result of diminished patronage from the princes, the Brahmins conducted fewer and fewer of the elaborate animal sacrifices. A few Brahmin families retained and retain to this day the right to perform Vedic animal sacrifices, a right that they validate by performing one such sacrifice every three generations.

The Aryan "conquest" of the Dravidian South was not primarily military, but cultural and religious. It is true that Aśoka's armies came into part of South India and that there were other military adventurers, but on the whole South India remained under the rule of non-Aryan gentry right down to the time of the sporadic Muslim conquests and the coming of western trading companies.

The non-Aryan rulers were attracted by North Indian culture and religion (all of which by this time was an amalgam of Aryan and pre-Aryan culture). The princes and wealthy landowners would grant their patronage to and require the clerical assistance of the ascetic Jain or Buddhist monks or the married Brahmin priests. During the early centuries A.D., the Brahmin communities in South India were often in a more precarious social position and enjoyed less royal patronage than the Buddhist and Jain monks, but gradually the balance tilted in their favor. First the Buddhists declined in numbers and influence; later the Jains lost their remaining royal patronage. It was not until about A.D. 1100, however, that the Brahmins acquired a monopoly of court favor, and this not as a united group but as the respective proponents of a number of antagonistic sects.

The result of this history is that for the last thousand years South Indian society has been officially under Brahmin intellectual and cultic leadership, but the official pattern for the society is one that was worked out in North India a thousand years earlier under very different circumstances. In theory, the same "caste system" operates in the South as in the North, and indeed it can rightly be said that this Hindu system has been much less weakened or liberalized by the Muslim presence in the South than in the North. However, in North India the Brahmins are only one of the three higher or "twice-born" castes, which together constitute as much as a third of the population, whereas in South India, the Brahmins are almost the only representatives of the original Aryan community to have become an integral part of the South Indian social structure, for there are very few Kshatriyas, and most of the few who claim to be Vaishyas are merchants who retain their North Indian connections. The Brahmins are then in practice the major and in some areas the only "higher caste." The majority of the population belongs to the various Śūdras castes, among whom there is also a definite rank, and below the Śūdras there is about one fifth of the population in the various "Outcaste" or "Harijan" groups. Hindu society in South India thus consists of three main divisions, Brahmins, Śūdras, and Outcastes. But the relatively small number of Brahmins (four percent of the population and in the villages much less) are the only ones to be full participants in the classical Hindu or "Aryan" religious community. Between them and even the highest Śūdras, who may be economically better situated than they, lies a cultic gulf as great as or even greater than that between the lowest Śūdra kūlams and the "Outcaste" kūlams. For more than a thousand years, this relatively small group of Brahmins in South India has maintained and even extended its religious functions and consolidated its economic privileges. As we shall see in the following section, the Brahmins are not the only priests, or perhaps even the most important priests, in much of South Indian village society, but, even in villages where the Dravidian cult is

403

very significant and only one of a hundred families is Brahmin, the Brahmins have enjoyed an immense prestige and in many areas a near monopoly on all learned professions. The prestige in most areas remains, but the privileges are increasingly questioned, and the spread of education has ended their monopoly of learning.

RELIGION OF THE SOUTH INDIAN VILLAGES

South Indian society is traditionally a society of both village and city. Most of the people live in the villages; the many towns and small cities are not large, but they play an important cultural role, not only in politics and commerce, but also in religious observance. Most of the large temples are in or near the old cities and towns, though a few temples are connected with monastic establishments deliberately set away from the towns. The towns are centers of Brahmin population, not only because of the temples, but also because town economy gives scope for the intellectual talents of Brahmins. The presence of temples in which Brahmins are the officiating priests (*gurukkals* or *archakas*), as well as the presence of the socially more elevated Brahmins who are religious teachers and the mainstay of the intellectual occupations, give to religion in the town a more Brahminized or "Sanskritic" flavor than is to be found in many South Indian villages. Yet it would be an oversimplification to describe town religion as Brahminical and village religion as Dravidian, for the culture of the town is in the village, and some of the cultic practices of the villages also take place in large cities. The following account of specifically village religion attempts to distinguish the Dravidian from the Sanskritic factors as an aid to understanding. It is too abstract and schematic to ring true to the experience of any particular Hindu somewhere on the spectrum that it attempts to describe, but hopefully it does not involve a gross distortion of that experience.

The religion of South Indian villages is a complex of beliefs and rites serving to relate men to those powers that are thought to underlie both the various patterns of order in society and cosmos and the numerous threats or actual events of disorder. In general, villagers consider the all-Indian or "Sanskritic" deities as the ones that support the patterns of order, whereas they tend to blame the "Dravidian" goddesses and demonic spirits for all difficulties and disasters.

"Sanskritic" or Brahminical Hinduism had a number of conponents, some of which are scarcely to be found in the more remote villages, especially if there are only a few Brahmins. Thus some limited portions of the ancient Vedic rites are present in the household worship of orthodox Brahmins and of North Indian merchants, but nowhere else in the village. Study of the orthodox philosophies, especially of one of the subschools of the Vedānta, is likely to take place only in those villages with a relatively large Brahmin community or with a family that faithfully upholds a family tradition of scholarship. Sectarian worship is more common in the village, but exclusive loyalty to one sect or another is generally confined to Brahmin families and a few of the higher Śūdra families, except in areas where one of the Śaiva sects is strong.

There are, however, other more popular features of Sanskritic Hinduism that do affect even remote villages in South India. Many of them are features of popular Hinduism in North India. This is most obviously the case with the annual cycle of festivals and fasts, which shows clear influence of the more northerly change of seasons. The worship of the images of deities in temples or household shrines and pilgrimages to the more famous temples, sacred rivers, and other holy places are also important features of all-India Hinduism to be found in South Indian villages.

The villager is familiar with the notion of a single Supreme Being far transcending the lower deities. Unless he is a strict sectarian, he will use either the names of Vishnu or the names of Śiva to refer to the Supreme Being. Except for Smārta Brahmins and a few others who follow Śankara's Advaita philosophy, village Hindus do not conceive of the Supreme Being as the impersonal Ultimate, Brahman, but as the transcendent form of one or other of the two chief gods: Vishnu or Śiva. Not much importance is given to the idea of the Supreme Being as a combination of the chief gods, either as the *Trimūrti* (Brahmā, the Creator, Vishnu, the Preserver, and Śiva, the Destroyer) or as Harihara (Śankaranarayana) a composite figure, half Vishnu and half Śiva. A much more important idea to villagers is that the Supreme Deity, whether conceived as Vishnu or Śiva, includes His Divine Consort, who is His own Divine energy Śakti.

The same high gods, Vishnu and Śiva, in various incarnations (Vishnu) or forms (Śiva), are also conceived, along with Brahmā, as a plurality of coequal gods, called *devas*. On a slightly lower level in the popular mind are the consorts of the great gods, the goddess Sarasvati (of Brahmā), Lakshmi (of Vishnu), and Pārvati or Durga (of Śiva), as well as the associate of the great gods, especially the two sons of Śiva: Ganesh, the elephant-headed god who removes obstacles, grants small boons, and protects the home, and Skandha or Murugan, especially popular in the Tamil country. Sometimes villagers also consider in this category: Hanuman, the monkey king who helped Vishnu in his incarnation as Rama to win back his wife Sita, and Nagendra, the cobra god who enhances fertility, who is worshiped at simple shrines under trees or at those anthills thought to be inhabited by cobras. With the partial exception of Murugan, all these deities are revered by Hindus all over India, though there are distinct regional preferences and even more distinct regional modes of worship.

The village deities are quite local; most of them are goddesses whose power does not extend beyond the village boundaries. They are sometimes identified with the consort of Śiva, and their cult has some resemblance to the cult of Kali in Bengal, but this cult is different in several respects from the worship of Vishnu, Śiva, and the other devas. The village goddesses are associated with the well being of the village as a whole, but they are believed to cause the epidemic diseases and other village disasters when they are angered. Similar in character to the goddesses are the ghosts and spirits, especially the spirits of persons in the village who have recently met with a violent death, and villagers use similar rites to placate them and/or keep them away. There

406

are also less personal powers; strange powers that are believed to pervade certain objects are greatly prized as "amulets" or "fetishes," and then there is the magical power that everyone believes can be acquired and manipulated by knowing certain secret techniques. A few people in the villages are recognized as expert magicians; in addition, some women are suspected of being witches and of casting an "evil eye." The North Indian belief in the sacredness of certain trees and of certain animals, especially the cow, is shared especially by the Brahmins and the higher Śūdra castes, but the "dogma" of the sacred cow, so enthusiastically promoted at present in North India, does not seem to evoke such an emotional response among South Indian Hindus. The almost complete lack of support in the South for the recent anticow slaughter agitation in North India is a clear indication of this, even though there are large areas in South India, especially in Mysore State, where cows may not be slaughtered according to State law or local ordinance.

In general, the Sanskritic gods are regarded as favorable or gracious, whereas the Dravidian goddesses and demonic spirits are considered as capricious in their favors, or even as positively malevolent. Śiva stands in this as in other respects somewhat in between. He is the Lord of fertility as well as the Great Destroyer, and His devotees consider both His governance of the material universe and His rescuing the soul from this universe as acts of grace. Moreover, the Sanskritic Śiva, worshiped with fruits and flowers, is often considered to be wedded to one of the local Dravidian goddesses, to whom animal sacrifices must be offered.

The two types of Sanskritic worship are in principle quite distinct, though in practice there may be some mixture. The ancient Vedic sacrifice consists of offering into a sacred fire accompanied by hymns, spells, and gestures. The worship of the major Hindu gods on the other hand, centers round an image of the deity, either a carving representing the god in one of the recognized forms or a traditional symbol such as the *lingam* of Śiva. After the god has been requested to dwell in the image through the special ceremony of "giving life" to the image, the image is regarded as his body, and much of the daily activity of the priests consists in

407

feeding and clothing the god and otherwise attending to his needs as would the personal servants of a king. The lay worshiper brings his offerings — fruits, flowers, money, or water ceremonially carried from the temple reservoir — and stands within or before the shrine to say his personal prayer and get *darshan* ("sight," "view," or "vision") of the god.

The shrines of the village goddesses usually consist of low "sheds" of stone slabs or bricks, only a few feet high, enclosing the idol of the goddess, often a crude stone slab with some marking upon it, but uncarved. Except where the cult of the goddess has become part of a temple complex, there is no regular care of the deity. The animal sacrifices sometimes take place before the shrine, but these occur infrequently, at most in an annual ceremony, but often only at more distant intervals when some disaster has occurred. A Brahmin priest, who otherwise has no connection with this type of deity, is brought to utter the efficacious Sanskrit verse (mantra) that will instill the life breath (prāna) of the goddess in the image, but the presence of the goddess is by no means localized in the image. She pervades the territory of the village. When she wishes to make her will known, at the time of a sacrifice, she takes possession of a woman — often in the family of her Outcaste priests — and this woman goes into a hysterical trance, uttering words that, if not intelligible, are interpreted by the priest.

Many Hindus would protest that this entire cult of the village goddesses is not Hindu; not only does it contravene Hindu norms and offend Hindu sensibilities, but it is led by priests from groups who are completely outside the Hindu community, the Outcastes. Two generations ago this would certainly have been the view of all the Brahmin intelligentsia of South India, and it would still be voiced by many. However, there are two objections to leaving this cult of the village goddesses outside the scope of the present Hindu situation. The first is that within the last two generations most Hindu leaders in all parts of India have not only consented to but insisted upon regarding the "scheduled castes and tribes" as part of the Hindu community. In part this has been because of a moral reformation: the recognition that this section of the Indian population should no longer be forced to live in such degradation. Mahatma Gandhi gave the Outcastes a new name, *Harijans*, "children of God" (literally, "offspring of Vishnu"). This name has now been officially adopted; Harijans are allowed in all Hindu temples, and various compensatory advantages are offered to Harijans, including the reservation of some jobs, reservation of a proportion of the seats in schools and colleges, etc. In most cases, this aid is given only if the Harijans declare themselves to be Hindus. Converts to Christianity are excluded. This reveals the other motive behind the inclusion of Outcastes in the Hindu community: the desire to prevent their conversion to Christianity or Islam or even – in the case of Ambedkar and his followers – to Buddhism. In the case of the Arya Samaj, this includes a movement to reconvert such people to Hinduism, through a ceremony of purification (śuddhi). This work of the Arya Samaj is largely confined to Northern and Central India, but the recent elections have shown that that Hindu communalism of the North Indian type has gained some followers in the southern states. However, there have been Hindu reformers in South India who have also sought to recognize the Outcastes as full members of the Hindu community. One of the most influential of these was Śri Nārāyana Guru, a nineteenth century Advaita ascetic from the very large Ezhava Outcaste community in Kerala. He preached the doctrine of "one caste (kūla), one religion (dharma), one God (Iśvara)." His memory is so greatly revered in Kerala that the State observes both his birthday and his death anniversary as holidays. Whether reluctantly or enthusiastically, contemporary Hindu leadership in South India accepts Outcastes and tribals, and sometimes Jains, Buddhists, and Sikhs as well, as belonging to the Hindu community. Hindu doctrine recognizes a variety of types and levels of religious practice, depending upon the spiritual maturity of the persons concerned (*adhikārabhedavāda*), so the religious practices of Outcastes are recognized to be a part of the total Hindu "religious situation."

The second objection to omitting this cult from our survey is that the worship of the village goddesses is by no means confined to the Outcaste groups. It is true that the hereditary officiants at the sacrifice come from the Outcaste and lower Śūdra castes, but most of the castes in the village take some part in the ceremonies. All but the Brahmins and merchants (Vaishyas) come to witness the ceremonies and share in the consecrated food, and even the Brahmins share the general belief in the reality of the village goddesses and demonic powers and sometimes have sacrifices made in their behalf. Even though this Dravidian cult may not come within a Hindu intellectual's own understanding of what it means to be a Hindu, it is part of the total Hindu religious situation. Moreover, it is a part of it that reveals clearly its southern or Dravidian pole.

An objection of a different type to the inclusion of reference to this cult has come from a different quarter: from educated Harijans, both Hindus and Christians. They insist that these sacrifices are rapidly on the decline and that it is better to omit mention of gruesome ceremonies that must make those who take part in them appear ridiculous to the rest of the world. This is a subject of great sensitivity, and for that reason it is impossible to obtain reliable figures, but it does appear that the cult of animal sacrifice is on the decline. The orthodox Hindu criticism of killing animals has had more effect as the village has moved closer in culture to the town. The increasing influence of modern urban culture on the village has weakened also the villagers' belief in the power of the goddesses. To some extent the small-pox vaccinator has taken over the function of the buffalo-sacrificing priest. Yet the wave of sacrifices occasioned by the recent drought and the occasional outbreaks of epidemic diseases indicates that it is still too early to consign the cult of village goddesses to the pages of the forgotten past.

Village religion, both Sanskritic and Dravidian, is closely bound up with rites performed on special occasions. The Sanskritic rites are in general connected with important events in the various rhythmic cycles of existence. These include: (1) the daily round, from arising in the morning to retiring at night, celebrated particularly in Brahmin families; (2) the yearly round of the seasons, punctuated by the annual festivals marking significant agricultural events or remembering the special days of various gods; and (3) the life cycle of each individual, from before birth until after death. A special form of the ritual of the daily round are the ceremonies performed in the larger temples, the services rendered to the deity present in the temple at all the significant times from his awakening in the morning to going to sleep at night.

All of these Sanskritic ceremonies mark significant times in the orderly cycles of existence, and they contrast sharply with most of the Dravidian ceremonies, which are performed when minor disorders or major disasters threaten or actually occur. Even the Sanskritic ceremonies, however, usually take place at the crisis points in the regular patterns of order. Both in the life of the individual and in the annual cycle of the seasons, there are crucial points of transition when it is not certain whether the process will continue normally. It is at such uncertain times that the protection and support of benevolent deities is most necessary and the malevolent influence of demonic spirits or wrathful deities is most to be feared. For this reason many Sanskritic rites have adjuncts of a somewhat different character, more like that of the Dravidian sacrifices; these are the rites to ward off or banish all demonic powers and untoward influences. The consultations with the astrologer that loom so large in Hindu life, in town as well as village, have the same double function of maximizing the possibility of an auspicious event and minimizing the danger that something inauspicious will spoil the occasion. In addition to the ceremonies to ward off evil influences that are ancillary to the Sanskritic rites themselves, there are additional precautions taken by the family through magic, which have a mixture of Sanskritic and Dravidian elements. In some places the farmers have an annual agricultural festival that involves animal sacrifice. It is significant that it is held just before the monsoon rains are supposed to begin, a time when the hope of great blessing is accompanied by the fear of disaster. Good rains will bring an abundant harvest, but the rains may not come at all, they may be too long delayed, or too much rain may fall at once.

411

Much Sanskritic ritual aims at ensuring ritual purity and eliminating or warding off impurity. States of impurity, whether caused by moral lapses or by certain bodily states, are considered dangerous, for in such an impure state one is especially susceptible to dangerous influences from demonic spirits. There are two "opposites" to the state of ritual impurity. One is the state of ritual purity required to carry out certain religious acts, and this same kind of purity is what is involved in the relatively greater purity of a higher caste, which makes it important for the members of that caste to avoid polluting contact with members of lower castes. There is also a second "opposite" to ritual impurity, however, that is even more significant in the lives of village Hindus and perhaps urban Hindus as well. This is the "auspicious" state. For the ascetic who has cut himself off from society, ritual purity is a normal state, but for others it is only an unusual and temporary condition. It is the auspicious state that is the quintessence of normal life in society. It is most fully contained in the state of marriage and is most clearly symbolized in the emblems of auspicious womanhood that the married woman is allowed and expected to wear. The concept of *samsāra*, fluctuating and transient worldly existence, is identified with the married state, but this does not indicate a basically negative view of marriage. Samsāra here does not have the primarily negative connotation that it does for Hindu ascetics and some philosophers. Here samsāra is conceived as a mixture of pleasure and pain; it is the mixed blessing of life in this world. The basis as well as the fulfillment of this worldly life is to be found in the auspicious state of marriage, in which both men and gods find a basic happiness that can spread over the whole of existence.

[This discussion of village religion owes much to the studies of M.N. Srinivas [5] and S.C. Dube [1]. More particularly, however, I am indebted to the Rev. P.Y. Luke for the information he gathered in 1959 in the course of studying some Protestant Christian congregation in villages forty-five miles north of Hyderabad. Mr. Luke and I are coauthors of a book reporting on the study, which I hope will soon be published, probably under the title, *A Rural Church in Andhra Pradesh*.]

THE HINDU SECTS

There is no clear line between rural and urban Hinduism in South India, but in general life in the towns has made it possible for some groups of Hindus to be involved but little, or not at all, in the Dravidian cult and to construct a community life that joins righteous living in the world to the quest for eternal salvation. These communities are the great Hindu sects. Textbooks on Hinduism usually mention the sects of Vishnu and of Śiva. Among the Vaishnavas, Vishnu is worshiped as the Supreme Lord; among the Śaivas, Śiva holds this supreme position. In each case the devotees consider all other gods to have only the status of exalted creatures. Besides the Vaishnavas and Śaivas, there are in some parts of India, notably Bengal, representatives of a third great sect, the Śāktas. For them Śiva has only a theoretical preeminence; the really significant Deity in this world is the great Mother Goddess, who is the consort of the somnolent Śiva. As far as I can ascertain, there is little evidence of a separate Śākta sect in South India, though some features of the faith and practices of Śāktas affect the religious life of members of other sects.

This familiar enumeration of sects has left out what may well be the largest and most influential sect in South India, the Smārtas. This is partly because the Smārtas do not consider themselves as a "sect" in the same sense as Vaishnavas and Śaivas. They worship five gods: in addition to Śiva and His consort Pārvati, Vishnu, Ganesh, the son of Śiva, and the Vedic sun god Sūrya. The name Smārta may have been originally an indication of their innovation; they follow the later Hindu scriptures considered as *Smriti*, as well as the Vedas and Upanishads that constitute sacred scripture proper (Śruti). "Smārta" also has a conservative connotation. In contrast to the sectarian Vaishnavas and Śaivas, the Smārtas continue to give equal honor to the five most important deities. Smārtas are by no means popular polytheists, however, for in South India they are followers of the Advaita philosophy of Śankara. The ultimate reality, Brahman,

413

is beyond personality, but Brahman may be approached by devotees through any one of the chief gods considered as the One Supreme Lord.

Many Smārtas attach importance to the conception of the *Trimūrti*. The ultimate Brahman when seen at the level of the world has the "three forms" of Brahmā, the Creator; Vishnu, the Preserver; and Śiva, the Destroyer of the Universe. Probably the majority of Smārtas bestow most of their devotion on Śiva. The Smārta community includes the largest single proportion of the Brahmin caste in South India and is almost exclusively Brahmin. It is therefore sometimes considered as the Brahmin section of the Śaivite sect, but this is rather inaccurate. The Smārtas are not exclusive worshipers of Śiva, as are the sectarian Śaivites, and their Advaitic philosophy is very different from the theism of the Śaiva Siddhānta in Tamil Nad and somewhat different from that of the Vira Śaivas (Lingayats) in Karnātaka (Mysore State). There are very few sectarian Śaivites among the Brahmins; most of them are either Smārtas or Vaishnavas. As a consequence, the religious literature of the Smārtas is preeminently in Sanskrit, that of the sectarian Śaivites in Tamil or Kannada.

It is partly the very preeminence of the Smārtas in South India that has concealed their separate sectarian existence, for they are not only the largest single Brahmin group but the one that has taken most to western education and that has the majority of positions in government offices and in the professions. When the Smārta Brahmins express their faith, they claim to speak for all educated Hindus, or even for all Hindus. Along with the Ramakrishna Movement, which shares the same Advaitic philosophy, Smārtas are the spokesmen for Hinduism in the modern world. They continue to support the classical Advaita of Śankara in monastic houses and in Sanskrit schools, but they also express themselves well in English and have expounded a number of modernized versions of the Vedānta, the most famous of which is that of the recently retired President of India, Dr. Radhakrishnan. Smārtas are in some ways the most catholic, in others the most exclusive, section of Hindus. They are free to worship in both Vaishnava and Śaiva temples or to confine their worship to their homes, but among them there continue strict traditions of Vedic ritualism and classical Hindu asceticism. Their philosophical doctrine of māyā does not lead to any indifference to worldly affairs, nor does their monism lead them to advocate a wiping out of caste distinctions. This world has some kind of provisional reality, and, as long as it continues to have that reality for any individual, he must continue to observe all its built-in distinctions and rules. Yet the consciousness of the relativity of the world and of all human notions of transcendent reality does give Smārtas a certain freedom in adjusting to changing conditions in society and changing conceptions of the universe. They believe in the nameless and formless One that is paradoxically both the basis and the contradiction of the reality we know in this world, and, for the few individuals who are willing to pay the price of the complete abandonment of worldly life, there is the possibility of realizing that One Reality, even in this life. The breach between worldly life and the life of renunciation is both intellectual and moral, but it does not lead to a lack of contact between the ascetics and the rest of the Smārta community. Smārtas do not have to be formally initiated into the Smārta community in addition to their initiation as Brahmins, but Smārta families do often have a pastoral relation to some ascetic teacher. Two of the monastic houses (maths) tracing their lineage back to Śankara are in South India, one at Śringeri in Mysore State and one at Kanchipuram, near Madras City. The heads of these maths are called the *Jagadguru* (the teacher of the universe) and bear the name of the founder. The Śankaracharya of Kānchi, is this year celebrating the Diamond Jubilee of his accession (He was chosen for the office while still a boy). He occupies a position of immense respect in South India that goes far beyond the Smārta Brahmin community, but it is for that community, at least near Madras City, that he fulfills the role of supreme pastor. While he performs no initiations, he receives the many who go simply for the blessing of being able to see him (getting darshan); some send him questions concerning interpretations of the religious law that affect their personal lives. The Śankaracharya spends much of his discussions speaking of the importance of continuing the observance of ritual duties. His pessimism about the consequence of Hindus' abandoning their traditional rituals distinguishes him in mood, though not in philosophy, from the many English-educated spokesmen for Hinduism among the Smārtas, who present a picture of Hindu resurgence, of confident adjustment to the modern world.

VAISHNAVA COMMUNITIES AND SAIVITE GROUPS

There are two major Vaishnava *sampradayas* (denominations) in South India and two main Śaivite groups. Both the Vaishnava groups are composed largely of Brahmins, whereas the Śaivite sects are almost entirely non-Brahmin. When one approaches the subject of one's own study, as I do in this section, he is all the more aware of the inadequacy of this brief sketch of the "religious situation" in conveying the faith of the religious persons he is trying to describe.

The Sad-Vaishnavas ("True Vaishnavas"), as they call themselves, are the followers of the thirteenth century Brahmin philosopher, Mādhva, whose system of *Dvaita* is the sharpest attack on Śankara's Advaita within the Vedānta, i.e., within the scope of those systems of thought that claim to be based on the Upanishads. Mādhva's home was in Udipi, on the west coast of India in what is now Mysore State, and the center of his sect continues to be there. The philosophy of Mādhva is reminiscent of the Semitic religions in its sharp separation between Creator and creature. This fact, and certain other features, have led some western scholars to suppose that Mādhva was influenced by Christianity. Since the Syrian Christian community of Kerala lived only a few hundred miles to the south along the coast, such influence is clearly possible, but there are philosophical antecedents of Mādhva's position in the pluralistic logic-metaphysics of Nyāya and in the popular philosophy of much Vaishnava devotion, which finds expression in some of the Purānas and sectarian Vaishnava works. In its emphasis on the performance of

Vedic ritual, the Mādhva community is scrupulously orthodox. As with some of the Vaishnava groups in North India, devotion is directed largely to the incarnation of Vishnu as Krishna, but unlike the North Indian Krishna-worshipers, the followers of Mādhva do not emphasize Krishna's love play with the *gopis* (cowherd-girls). Their devotion to Krishna is that of servants to their infinitely exalted Lord. The poet saints of Karnātaka spread some of the doctrines of Mādhva among other castes, in addition to a less exclusively sectarian devotion to Vishnu, but the followers of Mādhva are confined to the Brahmin community, especially in Mysore State. One of their distinctive customs is a communal meal, restricted to members of the sect, the giving of which is regarded as an especially meritorious act (a "complete offering") on the part of the donor.

The Śaiva sect of Karnātaka dates back in its present form to the twelfth century reformer Basaveśwara, who tried to realize *within* society the casteless community of Śaiva ascetics. The members of this sect call themselves Vīra Śaivas, the heroic or advanced devotees of Śiva, but they are popularly known as "Lingayats," because each one carries on his body a tiny silver *lingam*, the sacred symbol of Śiva. Each devotee has therefore an individual shrine. Basaveśwara gathered followers from a number of Śūdra castes and insisted that there should be no caste distinctions between them. Though living as householders, they claimed the possibility of realizing Śiva open to Śaiva ascetics. Like ascetics, they are buried rather than cremated when they die, for in entering the sect they have already severed the attachments that bind them to this world. In course of time the Lingayats became themselves a caste, considered to be among the higher Śūdra castes. They are exclusive Śaivites, and they maintain their own temples manned by their own priests. They have a number of followers in Andhra Pradesh, but their numerical strength is greatest in certain sections of Karnātaka (Mysore State). In recent years they have played an active part in the politics of Mysore State and have led in the movement of the Śūdra castes to wrest political control from the Brahmins.

The Śaivites of Madras State have a less cohesive communal

order than the Lingayats but a much more fully developed and well defined system of doctrine, known as the Śaiva Siddhānta. ("Siddhānta" means the correct and definitive philosophical position stated at the end of a debate.) They are largely drawn from two of the upper and land-owning castes among the Śūdras, the Mudaliars and Vellalas, but membership neither cancels nor reinforces a particular caste status. Neither do the Śaivites of Madras State claim the status of ascetics; they maintain monastic houses of considerable size and wealth, but they have a much more crucial relationship to their ascetics than do the Smārtas. They become the disciples of some ascetic teacher and treat their guru almost as Śiva incarnate; it is their guru who mediates the grace of Śiva accomplishing their salvation. It is not necessary to become an ascetic to enter into the path of salvation, but it is necessary to enter into a binding personal relationship with an ascetic who has abandoned society. The Tamil Śaivite doctrine is based on the Tamil hymns of the ancient poet saints, called the Nayanmars (probably A.D. fourth to eighth centuries, though tradition puts them much earlier), and upon a tradition of Śaivite works in Sanskrit. The brief summary of doctrines, the *Sivajnānabotham*, was written in Tamil by Meykanda Devar in the thirteenth century, and the authoritative commentaries on this work are also in Tamil. Their doctrinal position is a theism not too different from that of the Tamil Vaishnavas; there is equal emphasis upon reliance on the Lord's grace and more emphasis upon a confession of one's sin and helplessness. The Smārta term "advaita" is used to indicate, not oneness of being, but inseparable closeness in the relationship between the Lord and the soul who has been released from the bonds of matter, selfishness, and ignorance that kept him separated from His Lord. Because most Śaivas have been a part of the Śūdra population and use Tamil, they may well have had a greater influence on the rest of the non-Brahmins than have the largely Brahmin sects of the Vaishnavas and Smārtas. One possible indication of this is that in Tamil śaiva also means "vegetarian." The Brahmins were perhaps presumed to be vegetarian because of their caste, while the non-Brahmin Śaivas were vegetarians because of their faith.

The Tamil Vaishnavas, many of whom live in the other three southern states, are called Śri Vaishnavas: "those who worship Vishnu in conjunction with His consort Śri." They are split into two subsects, the Vadagalais (Northerners) and Tengalais (Southerners), over a host of what seem to outsiders as minor doctrinal points. Most of these points, and certainly the respective names of these subsects, make clear the presence in this sect of the underlying tension between the Brahmin and non-Brahmin poles in the South Indian religious situation. The sect appears to have been organized by Nāthamuni in the tenth century A.D., when he reformed the worship and administration of the ancient Vaishnava temple on the sacred island of Śri Rangam in the river Kaveri, near modern Tiruchirapalli. Though a Brahmin, he collected the hymns of the predominantly non-Brahmin Azhvārs and introduced them into temple worship. His grandson Yāmuna gave the doctrines of the sect their distinctive form, and Yāmuna's successor Rāmānuja elaborated those doctrines and attempted to demonstrate that they constituted the correct understanding of the Sanskrit tradition of wisdom coming down from the Upanishads. There are some indications in Rāmānuja's Sanskrit writings that salvation is open to all, not only to learned Brahmins. A favorite story told of him in the Tamil biography is that, when he had been taught one of the secret formulae (mantras) leading to salvation and pledged to secrecy on pain of condemnation to hell, he went back to the temple, climbed the tower, and shouted the secret for all to hear, since he considered his being sent to hell a small price to pay for bringing salvation to so many people. It is one of the great ironies of South Indian religious history that the Tamil hymns by both Brahmin and non-Brahmin devotees of the Lord who offers free and universal grace should be daily chanted by Brahmin priests in temples from which Outcastes were for centuries excluded. It seems to me that if this synthesis between Brahmin and Dravidian religious traditions had succeeded, the history of South India would have been significantly different, and the present cultural isolation and political rejection of Brahmins in Madras State would not be taking place. In any case, it did not succeed, and we can gain some understanding of why it did not from the present nature of the Śri Vaishnava community.

The majority of Śri Vaishnavas are Brahmins, and the leadership of the community is entirely in Brahmin hands, but Śri Vaishnavas have always recognized that caste privileges and membership in the community of Vishnu's devotees are not the same thing. In principle, the latter always take precedence. Śri Vaishnavas must be initiated into the community by the *āchāryas* assigned to their family by tradition; they receive a brand on the shoulders, are taught a special mantra, and formally make their act of surrender to the Lord. Their teaching in the faith is formally begun by their āchārya, and, even though they may receive most of their religious instruction from other teachers, they continue to recognize their āchārya for the rest of their lives and to revere him as one through whom the Lord and His Gracious Consort, Śri, have mediated salvation to them.

Since salvation is already accomplished by God's grace, all the activities of religious life are conceived, not as efforts to win meritorious karmas, or even the favor of the Lord, but simply as the joyful duty of one who knows that he is fulfilling his eternal destiny to be a *sésha* (servant) of the Lord. For most Śri Vaishnavas, their duty, for Brahmins, consists in performing the prescribed daily and occasional worship. Non-Brahmins are similarly bound to perform their caste duties, and they must cultivate the kind of purity in their eating, bathing, and all the care of their bodies that is appropriate to the servants of the Lord, who is "infinitely auspicious and utterly opposed to anything defiling," as Rāmānuja so often says. Śri Vaishnavas believe that God is not beyond personality and not beyond virtues; He is the source of all the virtues and excellences in creaturely existence. In Him the virtues that men know are not dissolved, but purified and infinitely exalted. The devotee is expected to emulate His Lord, who dwells within him as his Inner Controller, the soul of his soul. This is why a sect that considers the words, "Giving up

420

all *dharmas*, resort to Me!" as the climax of the Lord's teaching in the *Bhagavadgītā* (18.66) should, far from being antinomian, tend to a ritualistic moralism. It may be that it is this emphasis on ritual purity in every aspect of daily life that has effectively discouraged the growth of the sect among non-Brahmins. It is also true that the sect has been subject to continuous criticism by more socially conservative Smārta Brahmins because it has been willing to accept non-Brahmins within the community of devotees, and this criticism has over the centuries led to the stiffening of caste rigidity. The position of the non-Brahmin Vaishnavas has not been enviable. In order to belong to this predominantly Brahmin community with its emphasis on ritual purity, they have had to adopt a style of life that makes other non-Brahmins look upon them as pseudo-Brahmins, yet they are often not fully accepted by Brahmin Śri Vaishnavas.

The most celebrated doctrinal difference between the northern and southern schools of Śri Vaishnava concerns the doctrine of divine grace. The northern school accepts the analogy of the monkey: the baby is dependent on its mother, but it must still take the action of hanging on. The southern school accepts the analogy of the cat: the mother picks up the kitten without the kitten's having to do anything but cry out. It is significant that these very analogies are used in one of the Śaivite hymns, written several centuries before the Vaishnava dispute began in the thirteenth century, and that the poet takes the position of the southern school. The names "northern" and "southern" refer not only to the early geographical centers of the two schools, but to the relative emphasis given to Sanskrit and Tamil. Both schools accept a temple ritual based on sectarian Vaishnava manuals and employing both Sanskrit verses from the Vedas and selections from the Tamil Vaishnava hymns of the Azhvars, but for their personal devotions members of the northern school tend to prefer the Sanskrit scriptures while members of the southern school tend to prefer the Tamil hymns. At one stage in the doctrinal controversy, the leading theologian of the southern school, Pillai Lokāchārya, vowed to write no more works in Sanskrit, but to restrict himself to Tamil so that women and Śadras could study the *meaning* of the saving teaching of the Upanishads. On almost all the points at issue, the differences between the two schools are questions of degree, and their significance lies partly in their evidence to the struggle in both groups to hold together the Sanskritic and Dravidian strands in their heritage.

The "Dravidian strand" of theistic realism found in both Śaivism and Vaishnavism in South India is a far cry from the cult of the village goddesses. Indeed, the only point of connection would seem to be that the deity in South India has never been fully domesticated in any sacerdotal or gnostic system. He or She remains sovereign; sovereign if capricious; still more sovereign when most gracious. The important reason for using the same name, however, is not to isolate some pure Dravidian doctrine or mode of worship; it is simply to indicate that this was also a religious cult developed and supported by the pre-Aryan inhabitants of South India. It is almost certain that the devotional movements in South India owe much to influences from the North, as does also the Tamil ethical wisdom of the earlier *Tirukkural*. Just as the Sanskritic tradition under Brahmin control developed under the influence of the pre-Aryan culture of North India, so the Tamil civilization of the South greatly enriched its religious heritage after the coming of the three North Indian religions of the Buddhists, Jains, and Brahmins.

The Śrī Vaishnava movement represents a distinctive new phase in South India's religious and cultural development; for it was an attempt at a fusion, not only of two intellectual and cultic traditions, but of two sharply distinguished social communities. It is an attempt which has partially failed, but the failure should not blind us to the partial success, nor to the magnificence of the attempt itself. It was daring for a group of Brahmins to appropriate a tradition of Tamil hymns, daring to argue the agreement of these hymns with the Sanskrit scriptures, still more daring to allow Śūdras and Outcastes to become fellow members of the community of devotees, and perhaps most daring of all to insist that the venerable Sanskritic tradition did not help a Brahmin one whit in attaining salvation. All must surrender not only their wealth, but their privileges and even their caste virtues (their dharmas) at the feet of the Lord, to receive them back at His pleasure and to use them in His service.

One further aspect of Śri Vaishnava life deserves comment. Rāmānuja himself was an ascetic, but he became an ascetic, not because he had to do so in order to enter the path to salvation, but because his wife could not overcome her caste prejudices. Ascetism is permissible for those Śri Vaishnavas who feel that they cannot be faithful devotees in the conditions of life in society, but it is not considered essential, even for the āchāryas who must initiate others into the community. Of the seventy-four descendents of the men whom Rāmānuja is said to have appointed to the office, only ten or twelve are ascetics. Even they do not completely break their connection with the social order; if they are Brahmins, they continue to wear the sacred thread. As for Smārtas the doctrine of māyā relativizes their worldly concerns, so for Śri Vaishnavas the doctrine of Divine grace does not negate but relativizes the various paths to salvation. You may perform your daily ritual as a member of society or you may live in detachment from the world in order better to remember the Lord, but your salvation does not depend on either activity, on either mode of life, but solely on the gracious will of the Lord, a Lord who wills not only the salvation of the individual, but the maintenance of right order in society.

SOUTH INDIA'S ENCOUNTER WITH THE WEST

South India has been under increasing influence from the West ever since the Portuguese landed on the west coast in 1498. Long before that, there had been trading contacts between South India and the Roman Empire, and small numbers of Christians and Jews came to India. Later a Muslim community developed in Kerala, and, with the spread of Islam in North India and the establishment of some Muslim kingdoms in the South, there developed sizable groups of Muslims, especially in the cities and towns. The Muslim influence on religion and social structure was not nearly so great as it has been in North India. The encounter of South Indian Hindus has been largely with the Christian and secularized West.

We must distinguish between the effects of this encounter on the three main groups in South Indian Hindu society: the Brahmins, the Śūdras, and the Outcastes. The Brahmins have been in respect to their occupations the most affected, with respect to their religion the least. Except for the Syrian Christians in Kerala, the Brahmins were the only group with a high rate of literacy, and as a group they took earlier and more thoroughly to the English education that became available in the nineteenth century. The initial effect of this modern education was to consolidate and extend their economic and political power, especially of the group of Brahmins in the more favorable position when this period began, the Smārtas. Modern education introduced some change in the ideas and mode of life of Brahmins, but it did not fundamentally change their beliefs or their practices. There were some who were attracted to the Hindu reform movements of North India and a relatively few who became completely westernized.

The effect of the encounter with the West on the Śūdras and Outcastes of South India was more profound. More and more young people from the Śūdra castes received some western education, and this encourages them to seek new kinds of work in the towns and cities, in occupations previously monopolized by the Brahmins. With increased education and greater mobility, members of the Śūdra castes increasingly challenged the static social hierarchy of South India, developed ways of improving their family and caste fortunes, and challenged the Brahmins' prerogatives. Except in Madras State, it is only the political and economic power of Brahmins that has been gradually taken over by the wealthier and more highly placed Śūdra castes. The greater educational opportunity and social mobility among the Śūdras have two apparently opposite effects. On the one hand, these tendencies have led to some imitation of Brahmin habits and modes of life, but, on the other hand, they have made the Śūdras open to new ideas and practices from western sources, both Christian and secular. We shall return in a moment to the

424

most significant instance of this new freedom of thought and action among the Śūdras: the Dravidian Separatist Movement in Madras State. Here it should be noted that, while a relatively large number of Śūdras received education in Christian schools, only a few became Christians. Thus far almost all the Śūdra converts to Christianity have become Roman Catholics.

British rule, Christian missions, and the beginning of industrial society have all had a profound effect on the Outcaste groups in South India. To these three factors must be added a fourth: the awakening Hindu consciousness to the century-long injustice to which Outcastes had been subjected and, as a consequence of this awakening, a variety of measures to remedy past wrongs, improve both the economic fortunes and the social position of the Outcastes, and make them full members of the wider Hindu community. It is quite probable that in previous centuries a number of the converts to Islam in India came from Outcaste groups. Certainly from the beginning of western Christian missions, a large majority of converts to Christianity have been Outcastes. This was not due, in the first place, to any deliberate policy on the part of the early Christian missionaries. Quite the reverse. They had hoped to convert the leaders of Indian society, the Brahmins, following the historical precedent of Christianizing the Celtic, Germanic, and Slavic tribes in Europe. However, though the Brahmins and Śūdras avidly took to the western education offered by Christian missionaries and some of them showed considerable interest in learning about Christianity, very few were at all interested in joining the Christian Church. For the few who did become Christians, conversion meant a sharp break with the past, both because of the attitudes of their own families and castes and because of the view of Church membership held by most missionaries. Only in a few cases did several families from the same caste in the same village make a collective decision to become Christians. Among the Outcastes, however, this practice of group decision to join the Christian Church became very common and led in some areas of South India to circumstances that are somewhat misleadingly called "mass movements." Many of those Outcastes who did not become Christians were nevertheless greatly affected by education in Christian schools and by countereffforts of sections of the Hindu community to retain their allegiance to the Hindu tradition. Because of the large proportion of Outcaste groups in all four southern states, this change in their social position and outlook on life has already had considerable consequences for the present Hindu situation, though in some respects the full effects of this revolution are yet to be felt by most other Hindus.

In Kerala, the religious situation is rather different, for the long established Christian and Muslim groups have a considerable economic footing and are accorded a relatively high social status by the higher caste Hindus. During the nineteenth and early twentieth centuries, a number of Outcastes in Kerala joined various Christian churches, Syrian, Roman Catholic, and Protestant. Yet all these Christian missionary efforts and the Hindu movement of Śri Narayana Guru together touched only a fraction of Kerala's large Outcaste population. For this reason, perhaps, the newest "missionaries" in Kerala have found a ready hearing among the Outcastes. These new missionaries are the Communists. The intermittent Communist rule in Kerala in the last decade has curbed the economic privileges of higher caste Hindus. I do not know what effect Communism is having on the "religious situation" of Hindus, apart from those, like the Chief Minister, E.M.S. Nambudripad, who have broken decisively with the Hindu community and joined the Communist Party.

It is only in the Tamil-speaking part of South India that the present movement of the other castes to advance themselves at the expense of Brahmin privileges has received a distinctive ideological base. The most important ground for this unique Tamil movement lies in the nature of the Tamil literary tradition and the attitude of Tamilians toward their own language. The "language issue" often seems to outsiders to be too trivial a matter to generate such bursts of oratory and even outbursts of violence as have occurred in Tamil Nad in recent years. Indeed, far more than language is at stake, yet the language itself is crucial. Tamil is the only non-Sanskritic language with an independent literary tradition and the only modern language in

426

India that has literature going back at least two thousand years. That classical Tamil and modern Tamil are the same language is partly a matter of literary convention, for modern spoken Tamil diverges widely in pronunciation and vocabulary from classical Tamil. It is a convention, however, that is accepted unthinkingly by all Tamil speakers. An important role is played even by the Tamil script in strengthening the link of the present language with classical Tamil. The Tamil script is designed to represent the relatively few sounds in classical Tamil words and it does even that with much less accuracy than do the other, almost perfectly phonetic, Indian scripts. Certain Grantha letters are added to represent distinctive Sanskrit sounds not present in classical Tamil, but their presence betrays a "foreign" word. Other sounds must be approximated with the nearest equivalent in the Tamil alphabet. During the medieval period, Tamil, like the other Dravidian languages, was heavily Sanskritized, but, unlike the other languages, Tamil retained a distinction between this Sanskritized language and the classical form of the language. The modern reformers of Tamil, who seek to rid Tamil of all the "foreign" words acquired from Sanskrit and other languages in the course of the last two thousand years, simply have to invoke this distinction and relentlessly work out its consequences.

The nineteenth century literary renascence had its parallel in the case of other modern Indian languages, but it had the support of the ancient Tamil tradition and the distinctive Tamil feeling about that tradition just referred to. This literary renascence was associated with an expanding interest in ancient Tamil history, and the discovery of the Indus Valley civilization made it possible for some historians to advance the view that classical Tamil culture was the heir of that lost civilization, otherwise destroyed by the Aryan invaders.

In 1920 a political dimension was added to the non-Brahmin movement, when a group of wealthy Śūdra landowners formed the Justice Party, won the first provincial elections held by the British, and assumed the government of Madras Presidency. In 1925 a more popular development was initiated by E.V. Rama-swami Naicker, known as the Self-Respect Movement. Naicker's

427

long career has been dominated by his passionate hatred of caste, especially of Brahmin caste privileges, and he has made it his mission in life to expose what he considers the strategy by which Brahmins brought all of Indian life under their control. Naicker's attitude towards religion was greatly influenced by the writings of Robert Ingersoll, an American rationalist of the late nineteenth century. Naicker adapted Ingersoll's attack on Christianity for his own critique of Hinduism, especially ridiculing the stories in the Purānas, the caste system, and the pretension of the Brahmins.

In 1937 the Congress Party won the election, and a ministry composed entirely of Brahmins made Hindi a compulsory subject in the high schools. Naicker led a successful popular protest and went on to propose that South Indians could escape North Indian domination only by creating a separate independent State. In 1949 the movement split, the younger leaders under C.N. Annadurai, and the majority of members established the *Dravida Munnetra Kazhagam*, the Progressive Dravidian Party. In the years since the split, Annadurai has gradually minimized three features of Naicker's program that had brought him much criticism. First of all, Annadurai insisted that it was the principle of caste superiority that should be opposed, not individual Brahmins. Secondly, he dropped his demand for an independent Dravidian State. Finally, while continuing his criticism of the caste system, he stopped attacking the personal beliefs and devotional practices of Hindus. This last change in policy brought him much more support from the Śaivites, and the first change gradually affected the attitude of Brahmins towards the D.M.K. Many of them supported the Party in the last elections. A study in one suburb of Madras indicated that the D.M.K. obtained more votes than the Congress Party from all castes except the Brahmins, but, even among the Brahmins, the D.M.K. candidates received almost as many votes: 44%, as against 47% for the Congress [3].

The ideology of the D.M.K. is secular, but it does not advocate simply a rejection of the past; indeed, it is very proud of the Tamil heritage and harks back to a "golden age" before the cultural subjugation by North Indians. Its patron saint is Tiruvalluvar, the author of the *Tirukkural*. Just in the last few weeks the D.M.K.-led Madras Government has directed that a picture of Tiruvalluvar should replace the picture of one of the Hindu gods that frequently is placed inside the front windshield in the State Transport buses. (I have even been told that bus conductors will soon be expected to be able to recite at least a hundred stanzas from the *Tirukkural!*). The *Tirukkural* is a book of proverbs from the period of early Tamil literature, before the development of sectarian Śaivism and Vaishnavism. While the *Kural* is not areligious, it is not committed to any particular religious system; some have thought that the author was a Jain. In its relatively nontheological practical concern, it resembles the wisdom literature of the ancient Near East present in the biblical books of Proverbs and Ecclesiastes, and it may similarly reflect an age or a circle that had grown tired or skeptical of conflicting metaphysical systems and turned to a predominantly this-worldly morality. Yet there is a vast difference between the moral wisdom of Tiruvalluvar and the rationalistic anticlericalism of Ingersoll. From which source is inspiration really to come, or will still another patron saint be found, perhaps even Karl Marx? This last possibility is by no means farfetched. The D.M.K. as a whole has had no doctrinaire economic theory, but it has a left wing that has worked closely with the Communists, especially in this last victorious campaign, where the D.M.K. led a coalition including both the free-enterprising Swatantra Party and the left-wing Communists to a smashing victory of unexpected proportions over the Congress Party. The D.M.K. has formed a Ministry without its partners in the election campaign, but the left-wing Communists continue to be actively cultivating one of the main sources of D.M.K. strength, college students.

[The new graduates of the Madras University who received their degrees on August 31, 1967, were presented with a pocket edition of the *Tirukkural*. Reporting this the Madras daily, the *Hindu*, said, "This is the first time that *Tirukural* is being distributed among new graduates. The copies have been brought out by the Deiviga Peravai, sponsored by the Hindu Religious and Charitable Endowments Board at the instance of the Education Minister, Mr. V.R. Nedunchezhian." An accompanying photograph shows a monk of the Dharmapuram Adheenam presenting a copy to a new graduate clad in academic robes. The D.M.K. Minister of Education is clearly willing to utilize not only the funds but also the prestige of the Hindu temples and maths to spread the philosophy of the *Tirukkural*. Characteristically, however, it is an ascetic from a Śaiva (non-Brahmin) monastery who presents the book to the student. Perhaps this partial *rapprochement* between the D.M.K. and Hindu religious bodies in approaching students is not unrelated to the Communist activities among students referred to above [2].]

Though the D.M.K. has dropped its explicit critique of religion, such incidents as removing the gods' pictures from the buses indicate that the D.M.K. government will not actively support any Hindu institutions. On the matter of caste, the government is more aggressive; it is now offering prizes for intercaste marriages. Perhaps more important in changing popular Hindu opinion than official government policies are the many popular propaganda techniques that the D.M.K. has so successfully employed for the last two decades: stories, songs, and films. Many of these are not explicitly political propaganda; they are good entertainment, and all the more effective propaganda for that reason. What is their effect on the "Hindu situation"? No one yet knows. It is clear that the leaders of the party do not go to temples to worship but that many active party workers still do. It is also known that many non-Brahmin politicians who rail against Brahmin priestcraft in their public speeches continue to call in Brahmin priests to perform various ceremonies. The students are often very much caught up in the general cultural movement that the D.M.K. spearheads, as well as in its specific political programs. Many are very much estranged from the religion in their own family background, often an estrangement connected with their personal revolt against the authority of their parents and uncles. It is perhaps too early to say what pattern of religious life they will adopt when they become the heads of families. South Indian women of all castes have in practice a higher social status than the North Indian Hindu lawbooks sanction, and they have traditionally had a major role in family worship. Although the number of women going to schools has vastly increased, they have in general received less education than their husbands, and they are less inclined to revolt against the traditions of the past. In many families, therefore, worship is left largely or entirely to women; the men are more or less passively involved in religious activities at home and more or less indifferent to religious matters outside. There is, however, another very recent development that points to another reaction on the part of some groups in Tamil Nad: this is the move to replace the Sanskrit verses used in the ritual, in both Śaiva and Vaishnava temples, with Tamil verses. The Hindu Religious and Charitable Endowments Board is encouraging this change. Since this Board operates under the supervision of the Education Minister of the present D.M.K. government, it is not too difficult to guess its motives, but what are the motives of the devotees themselves?

How have Brahmins reacted to the various aspects of the non-Brahmin movements? When the Justice Party was in power in Madras Presidency (1920–1937), a number of Brahmins went to the cities of North India to seek employment because the reservation of a high proportion of jobs in government offices deprived them of their expected livelihood. Some of this emigration might have taken place in any case, like that of Syrian Christians to all parts of India, simply because the number of college graduates and high school graduates, respectively, was much higher in Madras Presidency than in North India. Whatever the reasons, this emigration of educated Brahmins from South India is a fact. One of the reasons for the North Indians' desire to have Hindi as the language of administration in the Central Government is to recover for North Indians the large proportion of positions in Central Government bureaus now held by South Indian Brahmins. This may be one important reason why so many Tamil Brahmins make common cause with the Tamil non-Brahmins in opposing the introduction of Hindi as the one national language and in its positive corollary, the retention of English as the language of the Central Government. Deprived of their traditional monopoly of the "civil service" level of Government positions, Brahmins have also turned more and more to private business, which was formerly regarded with some disdain. It is possible that the general economic strength of the Brahmin community has actually been increased by the forced diversification in their modes of employment.

During the height of Ramaswami Naicker's virulent anti-Brahmin campaign, non-Brahmins would sometimes insult and ridicule Brahmins when they passed them on the street. Later Annadurai and other younger leaders of the Dravidian Movement protested to Naicker that it was the principle of caste superiority that should be attacked, not individual Brahmins, or even the Brahmin community. Naicker refused to abandon his campaign of hatred, insisting that it was impossible to destroy the snake's poison without killing the snake. This difference was one of the points that led Annadurai to break from Naicker and his Dravidian Party (Dravida Kazhagam) and establish the Progressive Dravidian Party. In Annadurai's speeches and writings, there has been an increasing mellowing in his attitude towards the Brahmins. One cause of this moderation was the discovery by those who had received a modern education that the Brahmins were not so racially distinct from the other castes of Tamil Nad as the Brahmins themselves had maintained. There is no longer, if indeed there ever was, a *pure* Aryan or *pure* Dravidian race. Annadurai's new attitude has removed Brahmins' fear of the D.M.K. and has helped some Brahmins to support it as a political party. Even as a cultural program, many Brahmins are sympathetic to the glorification of Tamil culture. They, after all, had much to do with the preservation of the separate Tamil tradition for the past two thousand years, and a few of them were leaders in the Tamil literary revival of the nineteenth century.

The effect of modern life on Brahmins has been less on their traditional beliefs than on the performance of the many rituals that have in the past formed such a distinctive part of their life. Such apparently small matters as a modern haircut instead of the traditional shaving of the head represent an adjustment to modern life and to the non-Brahmins that would have been unthinkable even a generation ago. On the whole, Brahmin men tend to minimize their separate Brahmin status outside of the home. Even when they are visiting temples, they often dress like other Hindus. They are also much less punctilious in eating outside the home, though they generally remain vegetarians. Even within the home, a fairly large proportion of the men (no one knows what percentage) no longer perform even the *Sandhya Vandanam* (morning worship) regularly. In many homes, the more elaborate worship is left to the women.

Neither the effects of the non-Brahmin movements nor the reduction in ritual observance seem to have fundamentally shaken the faith of Brahmins. Their faith is given intellectual expression in many different forms, and some Brahmins have engaged in an extensive revision of their traditional beliefs, but they do not seem to suffer from the sort of "crisis of faith" that has affected so many religious people in the West and, perhaps to a lesser extent, in Japan. Whatever their conception of ultimate reality, they seem to have few doubts about it, and they seem equally confident about their membership in the Hindu community and in the narrower Brahmin community or some particular section of that. For some, indeed, their confidence about their faith and their mode of religious life seem even to be enhanced by the more universal vista that has come to India in the modern age. Certainly there are areas of concern, and there are some devout Hindus who are pessimistic about the future. Brahmin scholars who see all their sons go into sciences or engineering have to face the fact that in their particular family, an ancient tradition of intellectual devotion is coming to an end. Since this is happening in so many families, it is a matter of some concern. There are also some who share the views of the Śankaracharya of Kanchi, who maintains that Hinduism cannot survive as a religion without its distinctive rituals. It may be, of course, that there are crucial concerns that have remained hidden to this outside observer. At any rate, the face that the South Indian Brahmins turn to the world, in spite of their ready admission of national problems and their more cautious confession of personal problems, is one, not of despair, but of confidence, in the ancient and everlasting Hindu way of life, the *Sanātana dharma*.

Acknowledgment: This kind of article is obviously dependent on a great many sources, which cannot all be named. I should like, however, to mention my general indebtedness for

433

my understanding of Hinduism to Professor Norvin Hein, my teacher at Yale Divinity School, and to Professor Jan Gonda of the University of Utrecht. My understanding of the South Indian religious situation has been greatly aided by Mr. Charles Ryerson, now a graduate student in the Religion Department of Columbia University, and Sri K.K.A. Venkatachari, my present pandit in Madras. I should also like to say how much I have profited from the advice given by the "commentators" and from their written comments. The approach in this article owes much to the approach taken by my friend and senior colleague at the Harvard Center for the Study of World Religions, Professor Wilfred Cantwell Smith, in his book, *Islam in Modern History* [4].

REFERENCES

1. Dube, S C: *Indian Village* (Routledge, Kegan Paul, London, England) 1955.
2. *The Hindu*, Fri, Sept 1, 1967.
3. Madras Christian College, Department of Politics and Public Administration: study conducted in Tambaram, reported in the *College Magazine*.
4. Smith, Wilfred Cantwell: *Islam in Modern History* (Princeton University Press, Princeton, New Jersey) c 1957; paper back in Mentor Books (New American Library, Inc, New York, New York).
5. Srinivas, M N: *Religion and Society among the Coorgs of South India* (Clarendon Press, Oxford, England) 1952; reprinted by the Asia Printing House, 1965.

COMMENTARY

by Hasan Askari

DR. CARMAN'S paper is exclusively concerned with the Hindu religious situation. Though he is aware of other religious traditions in the area, his paper might give the impression that the

Hindu component is the only significant strand in the web of the South Indian religious situation. This impression, it seems to me, would blind one to the fact that Muslims and Christians, too, are crucial to the nature and the dynamics of the South Indian religious situation.

I cannot agree that there were only a few Muslim Kingdoms in the South and that their impact upon Hindu society, in comparison with that of the North, was negligible. Firstly, they were not *just* kingdoms, but highly dynamic processes, not in terms of Islam versus Hinduism, but of an intermingling of Islamic culture with the Hindu culture processes, and *more* profound than the Muslim-Hindu encounter in the North. Secondly, the Muslims in South India do not constitute one monolithic group but are divisible into a few diverse and highly divergent societies and cultures, say, the early Muslim settlers along the Southern West Coast, the Muslim Royalty of Persian origin having preeminence over the upper Deccan Plateau, and the later nobility and soldiery of Turkish origin coming from the North.

Each group had a complex urban organization that reacted differently towards the native challenge. The Bahmani mode of reaction was categorically different from that of the late Moghuls. It is difficult to generalize under one head the entire Muslim complex of the South and say that it did not exert any influence upon the Hindu institutions. Finally, it is not correct to suggest that the Muslim influence upon the Hindu culture was great in the North. There were periods when one tradition had a preponderant influence over another. There is no evidence that the Muslim impact in the North was decisive. It was always an encounter swinging from hostility and rejection to adjustment and tolerance, whereas in the South, especially under the five Muslim Kingdoms that sprang up after the disintegration of the Bahmani Empire, the mode of Hindu-Muslim interaction was of assimilation, exchange, and mutual enrichment. However, the movement was reversed by the orthodoxy that characterized the late Moghul period of influence and power in the South. If we start to read the cultural history of India only from the middle of the eighteenth century, we are often led to exclude from our analysis the role of the Muslim influence as a cultural process,

435

since by that time the Muslim culture was disintegrating and suffering most severe political setbacks.

Even about the Christian and the Western secular influence, which Dr. Carman acknowledges as of more crucial significance, the paper does not give any analysis. This makes the account of the religious situation less dynamic and related only to the structure of caste and subcaste situations and to the different philosophical and religious schools present in the South. The picture of the Hindu religious situation is therefore only static. I have no competence to judge this description, but what impresses me is the lucidity with which the picture is drawn. It is the first bold attempt to portray the Hindu religious situation with real understanding of the religion and with a wider perspective than that of any particular Hindu, who sees the situation from the vantage point of his particular caste and sect.

What makes the paper a valuable document is the reference it makes to an almost total absence among Hindus of awareness of any crisis of faith: "they simply have no idea what such a crisis might be." This is something crucial in itself. In our opinion this fact has such great implications for the entire Hindu society that it deserved more elaboration and analysis in the paper, not a mere reference. It is difficult to say that the Hindu mind has lacked this "crisis of faith" during all periods. It is probable that it has undergone real crises of faith at different times whenever there was a severe challenge from within or without. It is not difficult to recall at least three such challenges: the early Aryan encounter with the advanced cultural tradition of the country, the Buddhist challenge, and Islam.

To meet these challenges and many more, the Hindu mind has evolved the new intellectual and social tools reflected in its philosophical career and in the varying modes in which social stratification was brought about. "Arjuna" in the *Bhagavadgita* is a symbol par excellence of crisis in faith. But I would agree with Dr. Carman that such a crisis in Hindu faith does not obtain in contemporary India. Neither in casual dialogue nor in formal speech nor in literature do we find the signs of awareness of crisis. At least for an "outsider," the threat *to* Hindu religion seems

436

maximum in the present century, incomparably vaster than at any other time. The threat flows from modernity. But paradoxically, modernity is an occasion for the birth of the Hindu community. Let me explain.

The Hindu mind, throughout its long historical career, has been disposed to conceive any threat whatsoever in terms either of challenge to its dogmas or to its caste privileges. To the former it was able to respond by reformulating its philosophical position, while a threat of the latter kind it was able to meet by rearranging its caste structure. The Hindu mind, I believe, was thus able to respond to the challenges of Buddhism and Islam. Modernity, however, cannot be conceived as a challenge in either of the two traditional modes. It is not a point-to-point encounter with Hindu dogma or social structure. Modernity is a total environment, total and quite new; it is therefore a quite different kind of challenge.

This new force, I believe, entered the Indian scene with the British influence in the subcontinent. Even the nineteenth century Hindu response to British influence, however, was not based on a grasping of its real import. The challenge was immediately translated into political terms, and the threat was looked upon as something external. But the real fact was that modern institutions were becoming internalized in the Hindu environment. The greatest threat was to the Hindu social structure. The growth of a highly urbanized complex shattered caste barriers and created an "openness" in Hindu society, which was a totally new phenomenon. The cleavage between traditional Hindu society and the new urban order could not be closed either by a fresh philosophical formulation or by a reorganization of the traditional social structure. The efforts of Hindu intellectuals and seers in the nineteenth and twentieth centuries, however, have been almost entirely turned to the reconstruction of their religious doctrines and rituals. They have not seemed to realize that it is not only the religion that is being threatened, but that the entire fate of Hindu society is at stake.

Modernity, with its complex of technology and new sociopolitical institutions, bypassed the old religious and philosophical

437

doctrines, created a new openness and a cleavage in the Hindu social order, and thereby forged a totally new consciousness among Hindus, a consciousness of being *one community* beside and above the caste structure. This process was aided by the new communication system brought about by modern technology. It was within this system of communication that the Hindu community was born. This community disregarded the dangers that each new technological and social institution posed for the specific content of its religious tradition and went ahead to exploit modernity in order to create the Hindu nation. It is this utilization of modernity to develop a unitary Hindu community that prevents the Hindu mind from noticing the real danger that modernity holds for the entire Hindu heritage. The Hindu's awareness of crisis is blocked by his recognition of modernity as an opportunity for conceiving Hindu society as one integrated community. He does not realize that this new Hindu community lacks an authentic center because it is evolving outside the traditional Hindu heritage of religion and philosophy. Hindus who are attached to this traditional heritage and who take a highly complacent attitude towards their contemporary modern environment may well be incapable of affecting the future structure of the Hindu community. They may be powerless to prevent it from organizing itself around quasifascist ideals.

COMMENTARY

by M. Yamunacharya

THE RELIGIOUS SITUATION in South India is highly complex. Dr. John B. Carman has threaded through this complexity and is able to present clearly the different strands in this web. It is a very accurate portrayal of what has happened and what is happening in this complex situation. With my own inside knowledge of the situation in which I and many of my educated contemporaries are involved, I am in a position to vouch for the factual fidelity of the account and a remarkable insight into the processes of change that are subtly permeating the religiosocial complex in South India.

A word must be said regarding the Hindu intellectual in the modern world with respect to his traditional beliefs and his performance of traditional rites. The Hindu intellectual has had opportunities to come directly under the influence of modern currents of thought, especially those regarding traditional beliefs and traditional rites. He is gradually turning away not merely from Hindu traditional beliefs and traditional rites but from every traditional belief and traditional rite. Ritualism in religion is especially his *bête noir*. He is as much against Hindu ritualism as against ritualism in all religion. Many educated young men profess atheism, but their atheism has been mild and non-aggressive. In an average modern Hindu household today we find on the one side persons who are deeply religious and orthodox and on the other very sceptical minded members living together in harmony and peace. A kind of loose coexistence has become a workable proposition. No sceptical member of the household tries to impose his scepticism on other members of the family who cling to old traditional ways. Similarly the orthodox do not care to impose their orthodox ways on the nonbelieving members of the family. The domestic regime is no longer so rigid as it once was. The scepticism of the educated Hindu young man, and less frequently of the Hindu young woman, is not taken seriously by the members of the family treading traditional ways. An interesting thing about this is that one may remain a Hindu living in a Hindu household without at the some time believing in many of the traditional beliefs or practising the rituals.

An intriguing attitude sometimes expresses itself in a religious situation like this. When there is a rite to be performed at home, the performance is a must and the unbelieving young man also acquiesces in it without any conviction about the need for performing the ritual or its efficacy.

I had recently an experience which is a pointer to this religious situation. The father of a family had just died, leaving behind him his wife and a number of sons and daughters. Priests had to be called in to officiate at the obsequies. The sons performed the ritual punctiliously without demur but at the same time with a good deal of mental reservation. The rituals were performed as they should be. The tradition-bound members of the household and other relations were quite happy and congratulated the sons on observing a sacred religious duty and responsibility. But off and on there were discussions among the younger nonbelieving members as to the validity and meaning of these rites. They did not have the audacity to defy the entire traditional ritualistic routine. It was not due to the fact that they had no faith in the efficacy of the ritual but because some of them at least wanted their religion to be entirely free from ritualism. Some of them were fond of saying, "We need religion but we do not like the way in which it comes to us."

There was one evident factor responsible for this attitude. None of these halfhearted critics of ritualism knew Sanskirt in which the Mantras are recited. Their lack of familiarity with Sanskrit was so pronounced that they really did not have the opportunity, nor did they seek one, to understand the meaning of the ritual. The priest was merely looked upon as a professional man who did a required service for a fee that was grudgingly paid to him.

In this religious situation revealed in the South Indian setting, a few features emerged prominently. One is the gradual loosening of faith in the teachings of religion mainly due to indifference or ignorance of one's own faith and deliberate indifference to its teachings, its practice, its literature, and so on. The second is the somewhat loose and tenuous hold that religious practices in the home have on modern educated youth. The third is the grudging concession youth makes to the need for religion but a corroding dissatisfaction that it does not come to them in the way in which they want it to come to them.

A fourth factor which ensues from this is the seeking of some substitute for one's own specific family religious tradition. This has made some new cults popular even among educated people and has brought to them a new type of orthodoxy, or even a new form of superstition, in place of the old. There is a certain sporadic revival of orthodoxy among the modern educated Hindu youth, especially among those who have long been in the West but who, on coming home, try to recapture a tradition from which they had been temporarily lost.

A fifth and last factor is the gleaming hope in all this that desperate efforts are being made by knowledgeable persons towards the reconstruction of religious thought in such a way that something of value in the traditional ways is eagerly preserved at the same time that the door to innovation is opened in a way which does not corrode the vitals of a traditional religious faith. And one wonderingly observes that in all this process of change no serious strains and stresses are visible on the surface which might lead to a radical rupture from the past. The same spirit of gradual assimilation, accommodation, and synthesis of diverse and fresh elements seems to be at work in modern Hinduism as it has been at work down the centuries. As to the shape of things to come, one can only hazard the guess that Hinduism will yet emerge strong and free, shedding some of its excrescences for which it will be none the worse.

COMMENTARY

by Eugene F. Irschick

ONE of the important contributions of this paper is the concept that "each crisis in South Indian history has brought into question the previously accepted relationship between the Sanskritic and Dravidian elements in South Indian culture." The culture of South India over the past two thousand years has largely been the result of the historical, social, and literary relationship between Brahmans and non-Brahmans (Sudras). When the religious and social positions of either Brahmans or non-Brahmans are threatened and a crisis in the political and cultural life of the area occurs, the accepted relationship between Brahmans and non-Brahmans is also challenged. What has made this dichotomy between Brahmans and non-Brahman and between Sanskritic and Dravidian elements so enduring in the Tamil country over a period of two thousand years has been the fact that in language, in religious practice, and in social interaction the difference has always been maintained. Whether in the ways Brahmans or non-Brahmans live apart from each other in the villages, whether in the kind of speech employed by each or in the religious tradition fostered by each, division is made plain daily.

Professor Carman argues that the effect of modernization on the "Dravidian-Sanskritic" encounter has provoked a more serious dislocation of religious and social loyalties than even before. He suggests that at various times in the South Indian past attempts have been made to integrate the two cultures, non-Brahman/Brahman, Dravidian/Sanskritic, but that these attempts have largely failed. This failure has had much to do with the enduring quality of the segmented nature of South Indian society and religious practice.

Recent research on the growth of separatism in the Tamil area during the twentieth century bears out Professor Carman's assertion. One facet of the dislocation of the accepted relationship between Brahman and non-Brahman in South India has been the demand by non-Brahmans that they have the majority of government positions and educational places. This has meant that the traditional position of the Brahman as the holder of power in the secular world has been destroyed. More important, the achievement of these demands has permitted non-Brahmans to take advantage of the role of "inheritors of Dravidian culture" which they claim for themselves. The effects of the challenge to the Brahman sacerdotal position and Sanskritic religion have had even more radical effects in South India. There is little question but that the repositioning of religious and cultural loyalties which is an essential ingredient of the movement to oust South Indian Brahmans is the most dramatic confrontation that Brahmans and Sanskritic culture have had to face in the long history of South India.

10. URBAN RIOTS, GUERRILLA WARS, AND "JUST WAR" ETHICS

by Richard Shelly Hartigan

WHEN many large cities across the United States erupted last summer in spontaneous and seemingly unreasoned violence, the blame was often laid upon "criminal elements" and malcontents who would seize any opportunity to make trouble. Yet for many public officials, Negro spokesmen, and objective observers, the 1967 riots seemed markedly different from isolated, racially charged incidents of the recent past. Some Negro leaders spoke of the riots as being a kind of guerrilla war; Senator Robert Kennedy linked our nation's willingness to kill thousands in Vietnam to a growing disposition towards violent change at home; and the very term "ghetto riots" stirred faint but unmistakable recollections of a despairing people rushing towards a self-imposed Armageddon in Warsaw, 1943.

As simplistic and sometimes strained as these analogies might be, it is nevertheless true that urban riots and guerrilla wars are two shapes of the same genre, two types of modern intergroup conflict which have more in common with each other than either has with traditional, formalized warfare. Indeed, further scrutiny may even reveal that in certain important respects urban insurrections and guerrilla wars are more similar to nuclear war, that other form of modern conflict, than to conventional war.

The Christian ethical tradition has, for almost two thousand years, maintained a somewhat ambivalent position regarding war. Though the mainstream of this tradition has satisfactorily accounted for and accommodated itself to war, it has done so with a certain uneasiness which now and then has been marked by the reemergence of various sects committed to doctrinal pacifism.

Nevertheless, over the course of a thousand years (roughly

443

from St. Augustine to Francisco de Vitoria), the labor of numerous Christian philosophers and theologians did produce a body of norms designed to confine and control warfare among Christian peoples. In its formalized, modern version this tradition is known as the Christian doctrine of just war. Though sovereigns often ignored its rules or bent them to suit their purposes, the just war doctrine did represent a conscientious attempt to harmonize the Christian imperative of love with the inevitably recurring destruction and violence of war.

Since the advent of nuclear weapons, many social scientists and philosophers have returned to the doctrine in an effort to discover if its rules are still applicable, at least to some degree. Not surprisingly, the doctrine has not fared well when its rather rigid, legalistic, and sometimes anachronistic dicta are confronted by the complexities and fluidity of the nuclear context. The major reason for this is, of course, the fact that too much has been required of the doctrine by those who have sought to apply it. Francisco de Vitoria could address his contemporaries with convincing clarity as to the requirements incumbent upon them for the just initiation and prosecution of sixteenth century war, but he could do so precisely because his normative exposition was developed in terms of sixteenth century political reality. In short, it is unfair to expect that rules which were formulated four hundred years ago will apply with the same authority today.

Because the just war doctrine may not be applicable *in toto* to a potential conflict situation dominated by sophisticated weapons systems, it does not follow that this tradition is completely sterile of response today. It may be that this rich tradition, which has contributed so much to the development of the international positive law of war, may yet provide valuable insights for dealing with modern conflict situations, not only of the nuclear variety but also of the guerrilla type as well. At a moment when so few guidelines exist, the investigation is surely worth the effort.

Before proceeding further, it should be pointed out that no claim to immutability is made for the norms which will be discussed. Norms (values, standards) evolve from many sources within a culture and the political philosopher need not assume

444

the burden of defending their validity. One task which he cannot abandon, however, is the necessity to regularly reevaluate the community's value system in terms of that community's current practice. It will often be discovered that a community no longer follows in practice the norms to which it ostensibly subscribes, in which case the inconsistency may be resolved by adjusting practice to conform to traditional values or by more closely defining the cultural consensus so as to indicate new norms. The following discussion assumes that the American political community as an heir to the Judeo-Christian ethical and political tradition still adheres to the norms which will be cited and that, if inconsistency is revealed, the indicated course will be readjustment of policy or practice rather than abandonment of these norms.

THE DOCTRINE OF THE JUST WAR

St. Augustine, the properly acknowledged father of the just-war doctrine, attempted to make peace with war, that is, he sought to reconcile the necessity of violent conflict with the principle of Christian forbearance. The degree to which he succeeded is evidenced by the fact that his arguments were considered authoritative by all major later writers on the subject. It is interesting to note that Augustine was not just synthesizing the thought of his predecessors but was in many instances in disagreement with them and the pacifistic interpretation which they gave to the Gospels. Origen, Tertullian, and Lactantius, for instance, were the most prominent early Christian writers who inveighed against killing and who asserted unconditional pacifism as the only proper Christian stance [1]. As has often been noted, the *City of God* was intended as a defense against pagan critics who accused the Christian faith of sapping the martial energies of Rome, thereby exposing the empire to the barbarian attacks which it was suffering at Augustine's time. But the work was also a polemic, aimed against a view of Christian pacifism which, if accepted, tended to corroborate the pagan charges. The first important

445

feature which should be noted about the Augustinian just-war doctrine is that it represented a justification for war and for Christian participation in the armed services, while at the same time limiting the kinds of conflict that might be considered justified.

What this position clearly implies is that war, and the Christian's involvement in it, must be accepted as a "stern necessity." With this implied acceptance of public violence as a requirement for the maintenance of public peace, the main thrust of Christian social theory was destined to be concerned with the *control* of warfare rather than its eradication. Early Christian pacifism denied the justifiability of any form of violence, public or private. As such it sought to provide an alternative to violence, thereby eliminating killing altogether. Therefore, Christian pacifism (and its later historical counterparts) aimed at eliminating the *causes* of war and killing. The Augustinian position on the other hand, and the tradition which has dominated Christian ethical thought on war since Augustine's time, represented an acceptance of war and its concomitant destruction as an evil, but as a necessary evil which, under certain circumstances, could become a relative, justified good. This represents a turning point of no mean dimension, for it set the tone of further speculation by philosophers and theologians. In effect it conceded the inevitability of intergroup conflict and consigned the role of Christian moral teaching on war to the position of a control factor, largely dependent for its efficacy upon the willingness of adherents to the Christian faith to abide by the Church's teaching.

This effect is not immediately apparent from the statements of Augustine himself. His expressed concern is with the conditions under which aggressive war may be waged. According to Augustine, war is just if it is declared by the public authority and if there exists unmistakable necessity to recover goods unjustly confiscated and/or to avenge another "real" injury [9; 3]. Augustine's concern is therefore with what is today called in international law the *jus ad bellum* or the justified conditions for initiating a conflict. So abhorrent were the evils of war and so certain must one be of the justness of his cause that in the schema of

446

St. Augustine few wars could be justified. A fitting theoretical control of war was seemingly achieved.

The society of the medieval period which followed was considerably different, however, from that within which Augustine had dwelt. War for the peasant or feudal lord was not conducted in terms of imperial boundaries or transgressed rights, and there hardly existed a public authority in any meaningful sense. In response to the predominant conflict form of the age, the "private" feudal war, there arose an almost spontaneous reaction from the endangered populace. Originating in Catalonia and spreading through France and Germany, a true peace movement asserted its influence in a concerted effort to limit petty warfare. Springing from the peasants and lower clergy, spreading rapidly to include Church synods, the lay-inspired peace effort finally won papal approval at the Council of Clermont in 1095. Henceforth, the Peace of God was for two centuries to stand as a set of regulations, immunizing certain categories of the population from attack, which no knight or baron could violate with impunity from popular and ecclesiastical censure. What had been added to the Augustinian notion of *jus ad bellum* was a custom of *jus in bello* or the proper means by which a just war should be conducted.

[The *Peace of God* must be distinguished from its later companion, the *Truce of God*. The former was a set of rules which stipulated that certain individuals should not be attacked in wartime. Through gradual elaboration those immunized from attack included pilgrims, merchants, clerics, women, children, and serfs. The *Truce*, on the other hand, stipulated certain times of the week, month, or year as periods during which no conflict should occur. The available literature on these two important medieval phenomena is sparse and inaccurate. The best study is that by Dolorosa Kennelly, C.S.J., *The Peace and Truce of God* [7].]

Though the dicta of the Peace of God were appropriate to a feudal society where warriors were easily distinguishable from the rest of the population and wherein the Church wielded tremendous social influence, they were poorly constructed to

447

cope with the conflict situations of the fifteenth and sixteenth centuries. By then the Reformation had occurred and the Church's authority in political as well as spiritual matters was greatly diminished; the Renaissance produced not only great art but also a revolution in weapons and military tactics which rendered the feudal levy obsolete; and, finally, the contestants in military struggles were now well-defined, politically homogeneous, and centrally controlled units, the nation-states.

Against this background, a Dominican theologian at the University of Salamanca sought to integrate the Church's moral teaching on war with the customs and practices of his time. Francisco de Vitoria (died 1586), in his *De Indis et de Jure Belli Relectiones* [13] combined not only the theoretical contributions of his philosopher predecessors with the laws and traditions governing warfare which had sprung from the medieval peace movements and codes of chivalry, but also applied this synthesis to the prevalent conflict forms of his day. The net result was a compendium to which the founder of positive international law, Hugo Grotius, turned when he wrote his own famous treatise on war and peace, *De Jure Belli ac Pacis*, in 1625. Vitoria skillfully blended the two categories of *jus ad bellum* and *jus in bello* in such a way that no substantial additions since his time have been made to the doctrine of just war. With certain refinements, it is stated today virtually unchanged since the sixteenth century and may be summarized as follows: (1) the war must be declared by the legitimate public authority; (2) a real injury must have been suffered; (3) the damage likely to be incurred by the war may not be disproportionate to the injury suffered; (4) there must be reasonable hope of success; (5) all possible means of peaceful settlements must have failed; (6) those prosecuting the war must have the right intention; and (7) only legitimate and moral means may be employed in prosecuting the war [8].

One very important portion of Vitoria's presentation should be cited here because of the relevance which it has to the contemporary discussion of the moral use of nuclear weapons. Since Augustine, all writers on moral philosophy had maintained the principle of innocent immunity, that is, that innocent life may not be taken intentionally. Contemporaneous with this principle

448

was the custom, derived from the Peace of God, that those who did not actively engage in warfare should be left unmolested. Vitoria united principle and practice to declare that civilians or noncombatants should be spared in war not just because it was usually done but because they were "innocent" in the sense in which the moral philosophers had used the term. In judging the legitimate and moral means which were proper to employ in a just war, the principle of noncombatant immunity was to become one of the most important norms.

Though the development of international positive law does not, strictly speaking, fall under a discussion of the Christian just-war doctrine there is sufficient connection at some points to warrant brief comment. The substantial reliance of Grotius on his Scholastic predecessors has been noted already. Through him and other writers in the school of secular natural rights the spirit and often the letter of the Christian doctrine survived but, as one recent commentator has observed, with sometimes questionable advantage [11]. The Scholastic or Christian just war doctrine was developed as a normative guide for the statesman or "Prince." Its suasive power had ultimately only moral sanction. When its dicta were incorporated into a legal system which possessed no substantial tangible power of sanction, its inability to control conflict effectively was made patently obvious. Such was the result when in the nineteenth century international positive law recognized the right of a sovereign to be judge of the justice of his own cause. The inevitable result of the flagrant hypocrisy with which rulers proclaimed the justness of their position was that the whole apparatus of natural law, just war, and its associated international law prescriptions fell into disrepute and were consigned as medieval anachronisms to the intellectual bone yard.

The nineteenth century witnessed the assertion of legal positivism as the only properly "scientific" approach to jurisprudence. The penultimate sterility of this "value free" legal philosophy was not finally demonstrated until the Hitler era, though the struggle for a normative anchor was presaged by the League of Nations and various antiwar pacts signed by the western powers after World War I. Confronted by a conflict which no one desired, which wrought destruction heretofore undreamed of and which concluded in no meaningful political gain for any of the participants, a kind of malaise affected the victorious allies so that, despairing of being able to control future wars, they conceived as their task the final eradication of all war. Naïve as their expectation may appear in retrospect, it is understandable that this alternative would be compelling, since virtually all normative control factors on the waging of justified violence seemed to have disappeared. The major leadership of the western political community was therefore embarking on an attempt, abandoned fifteen hundred years before, to eliminate the causes of war since it no longer seemed possible to control organized public violence.

Yet through this period, the old just-war principles had been surreptitiously insinuating themselves into that very body of international law which had proved inadequate. In 1899 and again in 1907 conventions of the major European powers met at the Hague to adopt rules of land warfare [2], in some measure reminiscent of the United States Military Code of Francis Lieber, enacted after the Civil War. These conventions, still in force today, deal with the obligations which belligerents must assume not only with regard to prisoners of war and occupied populations but towards civilians in time of war as well. Since the League of Nations', and thus far the United Nations', commitment to the illegality of all war (save "police actions" and "defenses against aggression") has not proved satisfactory for the elimination of worldwide international conflict, it is not surprising that theorists and jurists are once again turning to the old just-war doctrine as a possible normative system which would offer some guide to the control of that violence which seems so much a permanent part of our political condition.

THE MODERN DILEMMA

Contemporary efforts by a variety of scholars to resurrect the just-war doctrine have been commendable for their sincerity and thoroughness; unfortunately the results have been less than satis-

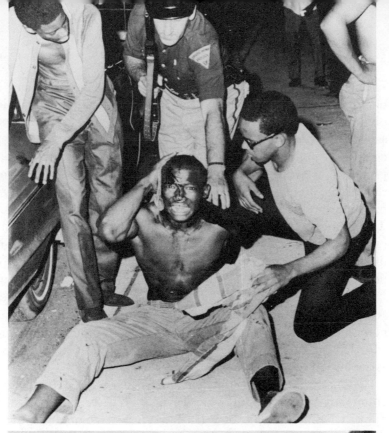

factory. An arbitrary starting point of this renascence may be chosen as 1944, when John C. Ford, S.J., condemned the Allied obliteration bombing strategy of World War II [4]. Father Ford argued that no moral or legal justification could be discovered to condone a policy which so callously destroyed civilian life and property in the name of military necessity. Ford's position, though preatomic or prenuclear, is important because his analysis has been applied by so many later writers to the nuclear situation. The main emphasis of his reasoning, a concentration on the morality of means, has also been followed, thereby subordinating discussion of just cause to the prior consideration of whether or not the means are proper which would be employed in warfare.

Ford concluded then, and also later in a discussion of nuclear attacks on cities, that the principle of innocent noncombatant immunity was necessarily violated by an all-out attack on a city and that no attempt to justify the inevitable deaths of civilians as accidental or unintended could be accepted.

By 1960 there was sufficient unrest within the intellectual community over the Dulles policy of massive retaliation against Soviet cities in the event of war between the two nuclear powers that articles and books began to appear which explored the ethical ramifications of this stance in particular and of the nuclear stalemate in general. The list of authors, representative of numerous disciplines and professions, who have contributed to the growing literature concerned with the ethical or normative implications of nuclear conflict is too extensive to review here [10; 11; 5]. A number of important studies of the past seven years should be mentioned, however.

William Nagle's book, appearing in 1960 [10], is noteworthy primarily because it brought together for the first time an impressive group of theologians, social scientists and humanists, and public officials to discuss, each from the vantage of his own expertise, the morality of modern war, with "modern war" conceived in nuclear terms. Though none of the presentations provided definitive conclusions, the work did live up to its subtitle in presenting an excellent introduction to "the state of the question." Shortly thereafter, in 1961, Professor Paul Ramsey published his provocative study [12] in which he offered the analysis of a Protestant theologian, conversant with the jargon and reference frames of the social and military scientists, on the contemporary relevance of the Christian doctrine of just war. While making distinctions and pointing out obsolescences in the just-war doctrine, Ramsey contributed constructively to the delineation of the moral problem. He concluded persuasively that "counter people" warfare could never be condoned within the Christian value system, yet he was not pessimistic about the fact that certain types of nuclear conflict would be permissible within the strictures of the traditional formula. One of the most recent and able studies of the problem is by an international law professor, William V. O'Brien [11]. Going beyond the question of the morality of engaging in nuclear war, O'Brien has subjected the concept of nuclear deterrence to critical examination, along with other current defense policies. His conclusion is that only to a limited degree can the just-war doctrine in its traditional formulation be applied today.

The literature pertaining to the normative limitation of nuclear weaponry has undergone a most rapid evolution in the last decade as indicated by the representative works just cited. From a hesitant, exploratory examination of the problem to be considered, to an in-depth analysis and attempted accommodation, to a full-fledged critique, the relevance of traditional norms to contemporary policy and practice has been examined. Yet it is interesting to note that, thus far, theorists have been so legitimately preoccupied with the possibility of nuclear conflict that they have virtually ignored, or are only now turning to, the moral implications of the real and present conflict types with which we are engaged, most notably guerrilla warfare.

Of the conditions and principles which together comprise the Christian doctrine of just war, most seem anachronistic today: princes are no longer the actors in international politics; causes are far more complex than in previous centuries; and the means available for carrying on conflict are radically different. Finally, the very nature of even the most limited war is such that the human and material resources of the contestants are almost in-

453

evitably totally mobilized and involved. Given these conditions, is there anything of relevance which the just-war doctrine can contribute?

In all the discussions of whether or not the United States could morally embark upon a nuclear conflict, a single issue inevitably intrudes itself as a stumbling block. The crux of the problem has been the physical inability of modern weapons systems to discriminate sufficiently between "legitimate" military targets and noncombatant, civilian centers. This fact has forced most writers to conclude that either noncombatant immunity as a norm must be denied, and with it the principle of innocent inviolability from which it is derived, or adherence to the norm must be maintained, even at the cost of refusing to use certain weapons in such a way that the principle would be violated. The contemporary school of just-war theorists has wrestled with this dilemma for some time now, unwilling to deny the legitimate use of defensive force to the political community, but equally unwilling to sanction the use of weapons in that defense which would necessarily abrogate a most cherished limitation on the use of force.

TWO VIABLE NORMS OF THE JUST-WAR DOCTRINE

A very persuasive argument can be made in favor of the continued viability of two principles contained in the just-war doctrine. The first is the principle of innocent immunity and the second is that of proportionality of likely damage to real injury. With regard to the former principle it has already been noted that it has received a great deal of attention from writers who have generally despaired of its applicability in a total war situation. What these writers have failed to take into account is the fact that a norm or principle can be extrapolated from its temporary formulation or concrete expression, thereby permitting it to be applied in a new form within a different context. If the principle of noncombatant civilian immunity is viewed in the light of its historical development, a very significant distinction

454

appears. The legal formulation of immune civilians, considered expressive since the time of Vitoria of the Christian norm of "innocent" immunity, must in reality be distinguished from that norm as representing merely a traditional, practical expression of the principle that innocent persons should not be slain intentionally. If this distinction is made, the dilemma which has vexed modern just-war theorists substantially vanishes [6]. The problem has been that the changed nature of modern warfare, in both its aims and means, has tended to obliterate the distinction between civilian and noncivilian, since nearly everyone, it is contented, is involved in the "war effort." However, though the old category of "civilian" may be obsolete, given the nature of possible nuclear war between complex, industrial societies or of actual conflict of the guerrilla type, it does not necessarily follow that the underlying principle of "innocent" immunity must also be abandoned. It is still quite reasonable to assert that there exist individuals and groups within any society who should be considered innocent, that is, not responsible, and that steps ought to be taken by a belligerent to protect these persons. There are degrees of responsibility for belligerent action, a fact recognized by the medievals when they enjoined that clerics, pilgrims, women, and children should not be subjected to attack. These same degrees of responsibility obtain today though they are far less capable of easy discernment. Nevertheless, in each real or potential conflict situation certain persons can with accuracy be perceived as so obviously removed from responsibility that application of the norm of innocent immunity would require their protection. The innocent may differ from one situation to another but there will always be some who are innocent, and these must be regarded as immune from intentional attack.

But, it is argued, this is precisely the sticking point, for regardless of the distinction made here between civilian and innocent, the fact remains that adherence to the norm of innocent immunity requires the prohibition of, or refusal to use, certain weapons, strategies, and tactics which would violate the norm. This is true, but the distinction is no mere quibble for it undercuts the contention that "there really are not any civilians anymore, there-

455

fore any means may be used," and it forces a confrontation between avowed norms and present practice.

Before turning to concrete examples, the second norm described above must be explained. In the just-war doctrine, the principle of "proportionality" simply means that the employment of force may not be disproportionate to the injury which has been suffered. Hence, no nation would be justified in declaring war on another state merely to avenge a trivial breach of diplomatic courtesy; nor would it be permissible to use tanks and flamethrowers to reduce an unruly mob which could be dispersed with firehoses. Obviously, application of this principle would mean eschewing any attempt to "crush" or annihilate one's antagonist.

When these two principles are applied to actual or potential contemporary conflict situations what is the indicated course of action? Applying first the principle of innocent immunity, it is obvious that the line of thought must run as follows: in the Soviet or Chinese societies, in a Vietnamese village, or in an urban slum there either are or are not individuals who by any criterion of responsibility for hostile action should be considered innocent. If it is judged that there are such persons (and it can hardly be denied that there will be some) then commitment to the norm of innocent immunity requires that measures be taken to protect those innocent from direct or intentional attack; if, because of the nature of the weapons available or the tactics indicated for military success this immunization is not possible, then those weapons and tactics may not be used. Such is the required course of action *if* the norm is to be retained and concretely applied.

The principle of proportionality would tend to reenforce this line of reasoning in a somewhat oblique manner. Along with the requirement that disproportionate force ought not to be employed in seeking a military victory, there is also implicit in the principle the stricture that means be proportioned to ends and that competing values in a community's value system be considered in terms of their circumstantial priority. For example, hypothesizing an extraordinary situation, it would be disproportionate and hence not permissible to take political or military action which would almost certainly result in the mutual extinction of a number of political communities merely to preserve those communities' "way of life." The point is that unless a community is presumed to be suicidal it will give greater priority to its continued existence than to the form of that existence. The possibility of such a choice, though remote, is not impossible. The "either Red or Dead" discussions of a decade ago strike us now as fatuous in the extreme, but the options provided then were considered for a time at least as real. The idea that a political community would choose obliteration and extinction rather than temporary subjugation to a foreign power suggests the near limits of lunacy. Yet there were serious writers who contended that nothing would be worse than that the United States should have to live under Communist hegemony. Indeed, at least one thing can be deemed worse than such an unfortunate occurrence and that is the extinction of the political community and along with it the political form which that community cherished so much that it would suffer destruction rather than permit the slightest alteration. The principle of proportionality would most certainly forswear such dogmatic reasoning and actions as would the weight of the tradition from which the principle has sprung.

If these two principles are to be taken seriously and if their implications are to be conjured with, then it is possible that a reevaluation of the United States' "conflict-policy" might be in order. What has been only hinted at thus far is the necessity to view the various modern conflict situations as being essentially related, at least in terms of the application of these principles. In the case of innocent immunity, for example, though application of the principle to possible nuclear conflict would demand some change in planned military policy, it would not necessitate the complete abandonment of nuclear weaponry or defense, for there still remain conceivable circumstances under which some nuclear weapons might be used. However, the very same conditions which have vexed theorists concerned with the massive use of nuclear weapons are compounded by the situation of guerrilla war. The wholesale destruction of lives and property, singularly exemplified by the obliteration bombing of World War II and the atomic blasts of Hiroshima and Nagasaki, has pointed to the need for the reinstatement of suitable controls on the use of force. But what has not been sufficiently noted is the fact that a guerrilla war involves the participants in the same kind of "indiscriminate" slaughter usually associated with whole-sale destruction of cities and civilian populations. The attitude and tactic are the same whether they result in the obliteration of a Russian city, the destruction of a village in the Mekong Delta which harbors suspected Viet Cong, or the "accidental" death of women and children, caught in a cross fire in a rioting slum. In none of these instances are the principles of innocent immunity or proportionality sufficiently employed as normative guides for action.

The obvious retort is that guerrilla warfare is a different "kind" of conflict because it involves an entire population in such a way that discrimination of the kind required to conform to the norm of innocent immunity is impossible. But the charge of impossibility applies logically only with respect to the weapons used, the tactics employed, and the goals envisaged. There is no impossibility involved in determining that there are innocent women, children, and aged who could not possibly be involved in the most minimal "war efforts." What is implied by such an assertion is that it is not possible to discriminate between the innocent parties and the legitimate aggressor when we use the means by which one country is able and prepared to wage war with an enemy when the enemy is so intimately involved with the people as are guerrilla warriors. If this is correct, then a reassessment of our nation's military role in Vietnam is required.

Leaving aside the entire question of the justice of the United States' involvement in Vietnam, the means which this nation's armies are compelled to use may be subjected to critical evaluation against the criteria of the two norms which have been described. Though without doubt United States ground forces have made great efforts to spare noncombatants, these efforts have been largely nullified by the continued aerial bombardment of North Vietnam, in which many "innocent" persons have been slain. Perhaps it is true, as military leaders urge, that bombardment is necessary to achieve military success. If such is the case, then the choice becomes either one of military victory by the use of means which violate a highly esteemed norm in America's value system or the sacrificing of military victory in order that this community may remain consistent with its avowed norm. Finally, and this may represent the hardest fact to face, it is conceivable that there are certain types of subconventional conflicts which the United States, precisely because of its sophisticated weapons arsenal, cannot prosecute morally, that is, in conformance with its expressed values.

The aim of this discussion has not been to offer a definitive solution to a pressing problem. Rather more modestly conceived, the intent has been to demonstrate that certain principles, derivable from the Christian ethical tradition and its formulations pertaining to the limitation of force, are not quite so obsolete as some have concluded. The real challenge posed by modern forms of conflict is not the possible obsolescence of traditional norms. Rather, the challenge is in the decision which this political community must make. Is it to continue to abide by these norms to which it has long subscribed and therefore accept the task of adjusting military and even political practice, if necessary, to conform to them? Or will the community take the fateful step and abandon these standards, thereby implicitly rebuking fifteen centuries of accumulated ethical reasoning and with it forfeiting at least a modicum of control on the unrestrained use of force?

REFERENCES

1. Bainton, Roland H: *Christian Attitudes toward War and Peace* (Abingdon Press, Nashville, Tennessee) 1960.
2. Carnegie Endowment for International Peace: *The Hague Conventions of 1899 and 1907 Respecting the Laws and Customs of War on Land* (Carnegie Endowment for International Peace, Washington, D.C.) 1915.

459

3. Eppstein, John: *The Catholic Tradition of the Law of Nations* (Washington, D.C.) 1935.

4. Ford, John C, S.J.: The Morality of Obliteration Bombing, *Theological Studies*, vol 5, September 1944.

5. Hartigan, Richard Shelly: Noncombatant Immunity: Its Scope and Development, *Continuum*, vol 3, Autumn 1965. See bibliography.

6. Hartigan, Richard Shelly: Noncombatant Immunity: Reflections on Its Origins and Present Status, *Review of Politics*, April 1967.

7. Kennelly, Dolorosa, C.S.J: *The Peace and Truce of God* (unpublished Ph.D. dissertation, University of California, Berkeley, California) 1963.

8. McKenna, Joseph C: Ethics and War: A Catholic View, *American Political Science Review*, vol 54, September 1960.

9. Migne, J P: *Patrologiae Cursus Completus*, series latina, vol 34, no 781. Contains Saint Augustine, Questiones in Heptatuchum, VI, 10.

10. Nagle, William J, ed: *Morality and Modern Warfare* (Helicon Press, Inc, Baltimore, Maryland) 1960. See bibliography.

11. O'Brien, William V: *Nuclear War, Deterrence and Morality* (The Newman Press, Westminster, Maryland) 1967.

12. Ramsey, Paul: *War and the Christian Conscience* (Duke University Press, Durham, North Carolina) 1961.

13. Vitoria, Francisco de: DeIndis et de Jure Belli Relectiones, translated by John Pawley Bate in *The Spanish Origin of International Law* (Clarendon Press, Oxford, England) 1934.

11. JAPANESE PEACE MOVEMENTS

by Robert T. Bobilin

IT MAY BE impossible, certainly exceedingly difficult, for religious faith and the faithful to provide the energy and motivation needed for peace between nations. The "dilemma of the churches" between interests of a universal or international nature and those of a very particular or national character is not merely a Christian and western dilemma but a human one. As Reinhold Niebuhr suggests, "Since the absolute must always be symbolized in terms of the relative it leads naturally to the absolutizing of the relative, so that devotion to God comes to mean loyalty to 'holy Russia' or obedience to the Jewish law, or acceptance of the prejudices of western civilization, or conformity to puritan moral standards or maintenance of a capitalistic civilization" [41:183–184]. Nevertheless, some would agree with the hopes of W.C. Smith, "that the task of constructing even that minimum degree of world fellowship that will be necessary for man to survive at all is far too great to be accomplished on any other than a religious basis" [54:116].

We have had too many demonstrations of how religious institutions can become part of the thrust of nationalism — how at times religious faith may be used to heighten provincial prejudices, add to divisiveness, and even incite group conflict — to expect that there is a simple or single formula that will resolve the dilemma. The decisions of our mass societies are more complex than those of the provincial societies in which the ethics of most of the world's faiths were incubated [33:122]. The increased power that man has for both creation and destruction has enormously enlarged the consequences of decisions and, to the extent that there is a conflict in the use of this new power, complicated the process of decision making itself. When great religions become "mass organizations governed by religious bu-reaucracy" [16:85], religious institutions will participate in the power struggle and adopt some of the political methods of their cultures. Nor should one forget that we are just beginning to work out the ways in which we can communicate something meaningful between the various religious traditions [55:196]. The purpose of this paper is to sketch some of the relationships between Buddhist, Christian, and Shinto groups in Japan as they have struggled with the relationship of their religious faith to the problems of war and peace and with some "peace move-ments" that have resulted.

A study of antiwar protests and peace movements as social phenomena may be guided by Katz' statement that peace move-ments by their very nature exist outside the central influence structure in a nation state [27:356–390]. The identification of the actual central power structure in a time of social crisis may present some difficulties. The consciousness and evaluation of effective means to political influence certainly would differ in traditional and hierarchical societies from what we would find in more recently democratizing and less hierarchical states. Baum-gartel suggests that "participation in peace movements is so over-determined, in a dynamic sense, that the foundation for effective action is weak" [3]. Persons with a sense of alienation may tend to be participants in these movements opposed to a society and its methods. Therefore, the interest may be weak in rational problem solving or in the rationalization process that is part of accommodation and assimilation.

Yinger has demonstrated the tendency toward accommodation to the society of "church" type of peace movements in the United States [63]. Despite the apparent universal compromise of religious groups with culture as Yinger, Durkheim, and Lanternari have shown, there is an "explosive element" coming from the power of ideals at the religious level which "seems never to be completely bottled up" [63:226; 31]. Yinger has indicated that sect protests — which in their inception stress particular sociopolitical goals — are more likely to remain sec-tarian than to develop into accommodated church type move-ments.

462

The source of socioreligious protest may also be analyzed according to whether it emerges from within what Redfield terms the "little tradition" or the "great tradition" [49:12–16]. The great tradition is the literate or scholarly stream in which the classical or orthodox sources of religious tradition are interpreted. The little tradition is more the popular, mass, or folk religious expression. In periods of social crisis the effectiveness of protest may be enhanced or determined by the desertion of the intellectuals from the establishment and their joining forces with popular or mass religion.

The peace movements of each nation reflect the particular history, culture, and social conditions of the environment. Peace movements in the United States, for example, reflect the struggle of western Christianity with the application of such items of faith as "the Kingdom of God," "turning the other cheek," and "just war." Not only are these phrases that may have a general meaning in their Christian setting; at times they have had rather specific historical or biblical reference.

The historic "peace churches" of the West — the Society of Friends, the Mennonites, and the Brethren, all of them in a sense sectarian witnesses of the peace ideal — find no real counterpart in the traditional religions of Japan. Not only must westerners not expect to find a Japanese idiomatic equivalent of their own doctrines or religious concerns, but they cannot assume that Japanese organizational patterns or methods of social or political expression will necessarily be similar or comparable to western ways.

Central to any consideration of social forces in Japan is recognition of the preeminence of political values in Japanese life. Loyalty to leaders and to community or nation, as symbolized in hierarchical authority, is a chief feature of thought and religion in both Tokugawa and Meiji Japan [4:1–26]. Nakamura makes the point that Japanese Buddhism and Confucianism, in yielding to and supporting the morality of nation and emperor as primary in the hierarchy of values, depart markedly from the interpretation in other Buddhist nations and in Chinese Confucianism [40:386 ff]. The Japanese Buddhists, unlike the rest of the Mahayana Buddhists, have emphasized responsibility to the ruler and state [40:474–476]. The counterpart of this idea that the state and nation constitute a moral entity is that prior to 1945 Buddhism and Confucianism were not thought to be ideologies or transcendent standards by which life or the social order might be evaluated. Rather they were thought of as common sense elements necessary for the social order, but practical and within and inherent in the order itself [48:6].

Morality and ethics, in the Japanese case, are not grounded in a religious sense or interiorized in the individual; they are more dependent on roots outside the individual, in group, community, and "national polity" (Kokutai). "In the last analysis . . . the real locus of Japanese morality was not in the conscience of the individual but in the affairs of the nation" [34:10]. Japan has had a shorter history of modernization than the West. That may partly account for her "historical failure to develop a tradition of individual opposition on grounds of conscience" [21:86].

In what follows, "movements" are sometimes discussed in terms of certain individuals who are leaders of religious groups. It is important also to recognize that those whom Mannheim called the "socially unattached intellectuals" are a social force. In both cases there are degrees in which they may represent or indicate social movements or trends. Given the emphasis on national unity and destiny that an increasingly restrictive and militaristic Japanese government had as its policy in the period before World War II, it is surprising perhaps to find some of the movements and individuals we shall discuss. What opposition or protest is to be found perhaps should be considered much more significant than that opposing nationalism and militarism in countries having traditions of greater freedom, where loyalty to central authority was less the national ethos.

It might be expected that a gap would exist in most countries between the intellectuals and the average citizen. It has been suggested that in Japan in the era following World War II this gap is particularly wide in matters dealing with international problems and foreign policy [53:5]. It could be assumed, then, that those intellectuals and leaders who protested against government policy in the years preceding the war, particularly in the 1930s, had a much wider gulf between themselves, on the one hand, and the people or the government, on the other.

Among the intellectuals and political parties before the war, Scalapino and Masumi tell us that "controversies took place at a level of theoretical abstraction that had little direct relation to the political realities of the Japanese world. The adherents of Marx, Kautsky, Bernstein, Lenin, and the Fabians joined battle, but the participants and the audience were few" [52:17]. After the War, the intellectuals were left without traditions of criticism. "The outstanding characteristic of postwar intellectual developments," writes Edwin Reischauer, "has been their diversity and lack of cohesion" [50:309]. The appeal of Marxism to some Japanese intellectuals can be better understood, since it did provide a comprehensive ideology that apparently was lacking in both prewar and postwar Japan. To those who looked to the western world for new insights, Marxism contained an important and dynamic universalism that could be used as a tool for intellectual criticism of Japanese nationalism [17:13]. It can be maintained that not until Khrushchev's denunciation of Stalin in 1956 did Marxism yield its pivotal place in Japanese intellectual circles, although after 1951 it had begun to give way to a mixture of pacifism and Marxism, the unity of which lay only in opposition to the regime and its ratification of a mutual security pact with the United States [18:81–90].

The frequent cry of Japanese intellectuals is that they have little political impact on the nation. This may be true not only because of the separation between those who operate at an abstract or theoretical level and the average man of practical affairs, but also because many intellectuals do not know how to convert western theories into practical Japanese political currency [20:115–117]. It has been characteristic of many peace movements, both east and west, to play the role of naysayer rather than to be the proponents of specific live options in foreign affairs [63: passim]. In Japan, peace movements in the sense of well organized, national movements with international peace as their goal are to be found chiefly in the period following World War II. Care must be taken, however, not to impose western concepts of organization and mass movements on a quite different Japanese situation.

Neither in Asia nor in North America have we yet found a way to enduring world peace, nor have any of the methods of voluntary organizations found ways to act effectively in providing moral or political leadership toward that goal. One of the chief means that the American public has had for influencing American foreign policy is through its political parties. The votes for or against a candidate are likely to be quite important to him, whereas he can take more lightly public outcries after an election [32:176]. Religious leaders, religiously motivated peace movements, and the general memberships of American churches have been and are reluctant to come to terms with the political structures and power that are necessary to put principles into practice. It is important to notice in the case of Japan that, for the most part, "the prewar two-party system was essentially an artificiality, sustained by the strong feudalistic flavor that still permeated modern Japan, especially in the rural areas, and by the stunted development of organized labor [52:17]. In the postwar period the conservative party, known since 1955 as the Liberal Democrats, has been in power with only a very brief interruption. The opposition parties have been deeply split. The achievement of national power has not been a live option to opposition parties, and this has added to the frustration of opponents of the government in foreign policy matters.

EARLY PROTESTS

The modernization and economic development of Japan is a remarkable achievement. Opened forcibly to the western world in 1853 by Admiral Perry, Japan learned quickly and, through defeating her in 1895, helped to open China to western interests. She established herself among the powers by defeating Russia in 1905. Before the coming of the "black ships" of the American navy, Japan had been officially closed to outside contacts even though there had been a persistent interest in "Dutch learning."

In a sense, then, her international relations and foreign policy began in the late 1800s. Before that, of course, foreign affairs were not a concern of Japanese people. Since that time there have been only brief periods when international relations involved popular participation.

Masao Takenaka has made a useful distinction between "democratic nationalism" and "absolute nationalism" in Japan [58:59 ff]. He suggests that the first term can be used in the case of middle-class liberals who in the early period of the Meiji restoration advocated a parliamentary system and opposed the foreign domination of Japan through unbalanced tariffs and extraterritorial rights. An early example of democratic nationalism is Hiromichi Kozaki's *A New Theory of Politics and Religion* written in 1886, in which he is severely critical of the feudalistic and hierarchical social system of Japan and the absolute power of the emperor. Absolute nationalism on the other hand "was concerned with the expansion of the rights of the state at the expense of the rights of citizens" [58:58].

The war with China was the first experience of a modernizing Japan engaging in international war. The war increased nationalist feeling and the power of militarism. Organizations of Christians and Buddhists officially gave their support to the war [42:349–350]. Christians collected funds, enlisted nurses, and distributed handbills to support the war, according to newspaper reports [42]. Buddhist priests let the army use temples for temporary barracks and sent chaplains into the army. The chief abbot of the Nishi Honganji received recognition from the Emperor for helping to maintain morale during the war [28:231]. While the majority of the Japanese exulted in the success of the Japanese army, more than a few went to China before and after the war to work for the reconstruction of China. Miyazaki Toten, for example, became a friend and associate of Sun Yat-sen [29:67–68].

The Sino-Japanese War did provide a goad to the conscience of some Japanese. Kanzo Uchimura, a patriotic Christian who had written with ardor of his devotion to the two "Js," Jesus and Japan, is an example. During the war he wrote, "We face the

467

battleground as the saviors of Asia. We have already half guaranteed Korean independence. But it is only a beginning. Our
mission will not end until we save Manchuria, China, Annam,
Burma, and finally India, that holy land of Buddhism, from the
yoke of the west" [29:67]. The purpose of Japan in China he
saw as an "awakening," the rescuing of China from foreign domination, rather than military conquest. After the war, however,
he saw the tragic nature of the conflict and the arrogance that it
was evoking among nationalist elements in Japan. Uchimura became a pacifist and repented his advocacy of the war.

A meeting of liberal Buddhists and Christians (and one Shinto-
ist) in September 1896 resulted in the organization of a movement known as the Teiyu Ethical Society. Part of their purpose
was to oppose nationalism and the growth of sectarianism in
religion. The group was discontent with orthodoxy and chau-
vinism, especially because the two factors tended to combine
forces at that time. Anesaki tells us the group had among its
leaders Yoki, a former disciple of Niijima, and Takayama, who
had turned from nationalism to individualism [1:369–370].
Takayama later was to have marked influence on a revival of
Nichiren Buddhism. He wrote with a blend of romanticism,
individualism, and patriotism. The group continued to exist at
least until 1928, but by that time "had entirely changed its
constitution" [1].

In 1901 Uchimura, Isoo Abe, and Naoe Kinoshita, all Christian humanists, joined with a number of Marxian socialists to organize a society to propagate pacifism — The Society of Idealists.
All of these men were associated with the *Yorodzu Choho*, an
influential newspaper of national importance, and were friends
of its publisher, Ruiko Kuroiwa. Kuroiwa's newspaper took a
liberal, antigovernment position. The paper shifted its position
just before the war with Russia. At this point Uchimura and the
other two left the *Yorodzu*. The *Heimin Shimbun* (the *Commoners' Newspaper*) was then established by Sakai Kosen to
carry on the pacifist cause from a Marxist point of view. The
Christians contributed to the paper, although they did not take
part directly in its publication. On its first anniversary, when a

468

decision was made to publish the *Communist Manifesto*, the Christian Socialists broke with the paper and started a monthly which published for a year [43:306–307].

During the Meiji era and especially in its early years, the Japanese probably were fairly united in their sense of having to prove their nationhood, their own identity against the intrusion of danger from the outside. The goal was to achieve *fukoku kyohei* a "wealthy state with a strong army" [26:425]. Shuichi Kato tells us that the time between the Sino-Russian War and the Russo-Japanese War may "be characterized by definite split between the protagonists of *kokken* and those of *minken*." These were the protagonists of "the rights of the people" and the partisans of "the rights of the state." During the period between the two wars, when no crisis pressured the intellectuals and others in their adherence to nationalistic purposes, the common ground between the state and its critics diminished. "An authoritarian bureaucracy developed while the liberal intellectuals (and also the early anarchists and socialists) became more conscious of the miseries of the people in mines, factories, and villages" [26:426–427]. The war had been won at the expense of the welfare of the common people, yet the popular sacrifice was not recompensed by the much acclaimed military success.

Main bodies of all religious groups, including the Christian, supported the War of 1904–1905. Feeling ran high that the nation had been deprived, by the Treaty of Shimonoseki, of its fairly won position on the mainland [19]. There were five sources of opposition. First, the Marxist criticisms by writers in the *Heimin Shimbun*. Second, Uchimura and a small group of Christians opposed the war on the basis of a pacifism that opposed all war as morally wrong, both for the state and for the individual. Uchimura resigned as columnist for the *Mainichi* and a little later turned his attention from social protest to biblical studies [19:117]. Third, antiwar sentiment was expressed by independent writers. Two novels of Naoe Kinoshita that appeared about this time were protests against war. Kinoshita was a Christian convert but increasingly turned to the Socialist movement as a stimulus. Akiko Yosano expressed her peace sentiments

469

in poetry [26:429; 34:147, 154–155]. Criticism generally was concerned with the injustice and immorality of the war and its ineffectiveness in achieving a sense of nationhood; it did not deal with political alternatives faced by the government internationally [28:232].

It should be mentioned that Tolstoi's writings had an appeal about this time to Christian socialists such as Uchimura as well as to non-Christian intellectuals. Tolstoi is an interesting example of a peace writer outside both Marxism and organized Christianity who had an impact on Japanese thought [1:374].

Fourth, another movement should be mentioned in connection with the Russian war. Oomoto, describing itself in terms of religious universalism, but having a neo-Shinto style in some of its rituals and thought, has had a tradition of peace activity going back to this time. One of the founders of Oomoto, Master Wanisaburo Deguchi, strenuously insisted in 1904 on the fact that "human desires arise, and wars break out, because military forces exist in the world" and pointed out that "nothing on earth is so evil as war or useless as armament." Later the movement came in for considerable persecution. In its early days Oomoto is interesting in that it probably represented rural and farmer resentment against the central government [46:3–4]. Perhaps of all the so-called "new religions" Oomoto had the earliest and most persistent relation to peace activities. Fifth, some "outstanding Buddhist laymen were also openly critical of the government's policies during the Russo-Japanese war" [28].

The period that followed the war of 1904–1905 was a more serious and somber time than that which followed the war with China; it was one in which the military penetrated into educational institutions, and this led to some "turbulence of ideas, and often a spirit of revolt" [1:385]. Marius Jansen writes, "Imperial Japan sought to affect and fix attitudes at the beginning, by developing standardized public school textbooks, which were first introduced in 1903. Thereafter, generations of lower school students received the mythology as truth, and scholars were advised to turn their critical approach to other areas of inquiry. 'Kokutai' gradually became a subject for serious and devout

470

investigation . . ." [21:82]. Soho Tokutomi, a journalist of the period, described the apathetic attitude toward the war among the youth as a "non-war attitude," which he distinguished from the "anti-war attitude" of socialists and Christians [34:512].

1905–1945

The Selfless Love Movement (Muga no Ai), founded early in 1905 by Shoshin Ito, a former priest of the Jodo Shinshu sect, attracted numbers of persons looking for a more satisfactory personal expression for their lives than the growing nationalism. In 1906 Hajime Kawakami, a well known literary figure and university professor, who was later to become a leading exponent of Marxism, joined this movement. He had read the New Testament and Tolstoi's *My Religion*. He gave up his teaching position at the University of Tokyo and renounced everything to devote himself to this movement. Later he turned to Zen and eventually returned to teaching. The Selfless Love Movement had devotees and importance as a national movement at least until the Second World War. Many of its adherents came from the Jodo sect; it was a communal, social service expression of Buddhism [7; 28:235; 60:820].

A movement directly interested in international problems was the Japan Peace Society founded in 1906 by Japanese liberals and some Christian laymen. From the inception, one of the moving forces in this group was Gilbert Bowles of the Friends Mission. Count Okuma served as Chairman and Count Itagaki wrote a statement for the organization calling attention to national aggression and national exclusion as evils to be combated. The organization was thus critical of both the Japanese and the United States governments [19:130].

In 1911 the Kotoku incident had repercussions for the religious, radical, and intellectual community, Shusui Kotoku, who had associated with Christians and was an anarchist, one of the group opposed to the war of 1904–1905, was accused and executed for a plot on the Emperor's life. Kotoku had been inspired by revolutionary syndicalism which he learned from the Industrial Workers of the World on a trip to San Francisco. Although he was most likely not involved in the plot, he and hundreds of radicals were arrested, twenty brought to trial and eleven, including Kotoku, executed [15:550]. Defense witnesses were not given ample hearing and the ruthlessness of the dealing with dissent broke opposition and liberal groups apart. Iglehart puts it vividly: "Sen Katayama fled to America, and later moved on to Moscow where he died. Sakae Osugi left the Christian church and became a Communist, for years led a hunted life, and finally was strangled to death by a prison guard. The few remaining Christian advocates of gradual social change lapsed into silence. Even a suspicion of left-wing sympathies meant unemployment, recurring arrests, and possible conviction of crime" [19:156]. The gulf between the government and the intellectuals and others politically critical widened greatly after the death of Kotoku [26:430].

In an interesting sequel to the Kotoku affair, the government called a meeting of religious leaders to obtain unity in the fight against the radicals. The immediate occasion for the meeting was the return of the Vice Minister of Home Affairs from a visit to America where he had been impressed with the importance of Christianity. Seven Christians thus were invited to this meeting as well as thirteen Shinto and fifty Buddhist representatives. Top government officials appealed for them to take part in leading the people toward a greater morality, which was interpreted in terms of respect for authority and loyalty to the government. Religious leaders were divided as to the value of the meeting. Many Christians were relieved that they were not blamed for the Kotoku affair, and indeed were granted some recognition in being invited to the conference. Masahisa Uemura and Kanzo Uchimura would have nothing to do with the meeting. It is interesting that Anesaki writing in the late twenties omits any direct reference to the Kotoku incident, although he obviously implies reference to it [1:388–389] and tells us that there were repeated attempts by succeeding cabinets to involve religious leaders in ways similar to the 1911 meeting. But these, he judges, "bore little fruit" [1].

The momentum gained in two wars carried both public opinion and the government to further use of arms to develop the beginning of the Empire. The war with Russia had brought considerable economic strain. The exploitation of trade with Korea and use of its resources was an attempt to deal with this problem. The expansion of arms and industry and increase in the military budgets of establishment led both to heavier taxation and to the growth of numbers of new rich, *narikin* as they were called. Anesaki explains that the one-sided growth of wealth and the rise of a comparatively poor industrial worker group as a development of World War I led to restlessness and to growth of unions and socialist groups [1:393–394]. "The uneasiness of the educated class rose in high tide . . . and finally the rice riots of August 1915 made everyone realize the seriousness of the situation" [1]. The annexing of Korea in 1910 strengthened militarism. The path of empire was cleared in 1911 by the renewal of Great Britain's alliance with Japan and the extending of a trade treaty with the United States.

World War I apparently seemed remote enough not to involve the objections of many religious groups or intellectuals. Japan's participation in the military aspect of the war was relatively slight, and economically she benefited by producing for the allies munitions and other goods formerly supplied by European sources. Her merchant marine doubled in tonnage, and income from shipping soared. The number of factory workers increased greatly. During and immediately following the war period the problems of industrialism and urbanization were actually the greatest challenge to the consciences of those religious leaders who spoke out on social issues. Japan's tremendous expansion industrially together with her foreign trade developments meant that she was now subject to the problems of the business cycle.

On the other hand, with the security of Japan not at stake, with prosperity mounting, there was some criticism of the imperialist possibilities of the war and particularly of the army's attack on the Germans in the Shantung area. Some political parties used the phrase "Japan's Monroe Doctrine" and supported Japan's keeping Asia for the Asians [15:566–567].

473

The main bodies of Buddhism, Christianity, and Shinto supported the war actions of the government. In 1916 the Bukkyo Gokokudan (Buddhist Association for the Protection of the State), representing schools with Buddhist affiliation, set forth its aim to encourage the protection of the Imperial family and the state [38:235]. The Christian churches issued a manifesto to celebrate the victory. In this statement the importance of "the promotion of the national mission" was recognized as well as more general and usual Christian statements about peace, good will, the Fatherhood of God, and the Brotherhood of Man [19:152–153].

The twenties was a period of cross currents of great hopes in international affairs, an economic depression, increasing organization of labor, expansion of the Empire finally into Manchuria, and reaction to western exclusion.

Japan joined the League of Nations. The pressure from the international community, plus the failure of the army, despite tremendous expenditures, to accomplish much in the difficult war-lord ridden China conflict were two factors that made for a more liberal and international foreign policy in the twenties. Interest in developing international trade was also an important factor during this time [15:568–573]. Disarmament policies had some effect, and in 1922 the army was ordered to reduce its numbers by four divisions. In the same year at an Imperial Poem Convocation the poem published as the Emperor's read:

> The bright sun rising o'er the tranquil sea
> Appears to us a cheering sign of peace
> Now coming to the nations of the earth [19:170].

The worldwide disillusionment about World War I was, however, reflected in the thought of some religious leaders in Japan. The abbot of the influential Shin sect, referring to the war, wrote in the *Eastern Buddhist* in 1921: "We now fully realize how wrong we have been in the choice of our pathway to civilization" [14:253]. In the same article the abbot defended Japan against charges of militarism on the basis that "the enlightened and influential elements of her people loathe any kind of military demonstration" and that her recent "abnormal expenditure" on military preparations was in part Japan's following after modern commercialism and industrialism. He was convinced that peaceful idealism had begun to assert itself in the period following the war [14].

An interesting editorial written by D.T. Suzuki in the same issue of the *Eastern Buddhist* states:

> The world is ready now for the plainest and loudest announcement that . . . all our religions are united in demanding peace on earth and glory in Heaven. And by peace we mean the prevalence of justice, fair deal, and humanness all over the world, not only among individuals but among nations; and by glory we mean the triumphant march of spirit over matter, of light over darkness, of love over selfishness [56:292–293].

Dr. Suzuki went on to urge a League or Conference of Religions "in which practical men of affairs will be helped to climb the ladder of peace and disarmament" [56].

The writers of the above articles in the *Eastern Buddhist* base their religious concern on the principle *paccaya* or *anataman*. This is the Buddhist teaching as to the nature of the self, or ego and selflessness. As Suzuki puts it, "To assert the ego beyond the legitimate limits of the interrelationship of things means violence" [56:271]. As Suzuki interprets this teaching, it should apply to nations as well as individuals, in the sense that national pride, arrogance, greed, imperialism, and self-aggrandizement stem basically from ignorance and self-assertion, which cause suffering. The law of mutuality or interdependence of all life (based on the *sunyata* or *mu* concept) implies the karmic principle of moral causation. It is possible to build behavior and attitudes with good will (*karuna* of *jihi*) and peaceful results in mind, as well as to recognize anxiety and suffering. The oneness of all things finds its unity in the Buddha nature. The individual ego gains its significance only when it relates or looses itself in the greater unity [1:67].

It is interesting to note that a second issue of the *Eastern Buddhist* in 1921 and another number in 1924 contained articles on peace but that no subsequent articles on the subject of world peace appeared.

Earlier, Oomoto was discussed in connection with the Russian war. It is in the 1920s that it comes to the fore as a popular movement. Although its influence and activity have come down to the present, in terms of numbers of devotees its boom was in the twenties when it claimed between two and three million adherents. Undoubtedly its popularity was due in great measure to the charismatic personality of its cofounder Onisaburo Deguchi. At the age of twenty-seven he was led by "Divine inspiration" to meditate in the mountains near Kameoka. During a week of meditation and asceticism in one of the caves on the mountain "his soul soared into the Spiritual world and learned by personal observation the innumerable mysteries of heaven and hell." During this time he gained also "knowledge of the Universe and for the first time had consciousness of his mission as the Savior of Mankind" [46:6]. According to Harry Thomsen, he began using characters in writing his name that have been used only by the Imperial family and he came to believe that he must "take over the throne to reverse the social order of the country and re-establish Japan as the Kingdom of God" [59:130]. These events led to his arrest and the destruction of the buildings where a headquarters had been established. After his release from a brief prison term in 1921 he dictated a revelation of eighty-one volumes of four hundred pages each, at the rate of a volume every three days [46:6–7]. The international interests of the movement soon took form. In 1923 Esperanto was introduced as an important feature of the movement. An impressive stone plaque near their headquarters building reads, "One world, one language, one God." The interest in Esperanto has been maintained to the present. In 1965 an international Esperanto convention was held at their headquarters. While his main following at home was rural and farmer, Deguchi established close contacts with the Taoists, the Red Swastika Society of China, and the Bahais. In 1924 he visited Mongolia where, after getting himself in trouble with the local war lord by announcing that he was the "Saviour of the World," he was saved from a firing squad at the last moment by the Japanese consul [59:131].

476

In 1925 he wrote further inspired scripture, *Michi no Shiori*, in which he states that "both war and quarrels are acts of wickedness. They never occur where people live in the Heart of God and work for the sake of mankind as a whole. . . . Because of the maintenance of their military might, the nations of the world are easily spurred on by greed to start a war" [13:8–9]. In the same year he established a League of Religions with headquarters in Peking and the Universal Love and Brotherhood Association with headquarters in Kameoka, Japan. The object of these organizations was "to bring about a true friendship among peoples on earth and establish a one-world family system irrespective of creed, race and nationality" [46:8]. They claimed to have more than one hundred branches and federations all over the world, and according to their report "developed as a great international peace movement organization in concert with peace organizations of other countries" [46]. In 1935 the government arrested Deguchi, his wife, and more than fifty followers. Not only the buildings, but the trees and religious shrines of the Headquarters were destroyed. The *Japan Times* explained, "It goes without saying that the authorities must interfere with a religious sect whose teachings are incompatible with the foundation of the country, or whose believers fail in their duties to the state" [24]. During this period the government also arrested leaders and banned a number of other religious movements. Oomoto revived soon after the termination of World War II. Deguchi died in 1948, but the movement has stayed alive.

Another movement that had significant teachings about peace is Itto En, founded as a communal, Tolstoyan, service movement near Yamashina in 1928 by Tenko Nishida. Tenko had given away all his possessions in order to live a life freed from attachments and completely devoted to altruistic service, placing his trust in "the Light." The movement has been influenced religiously by Shinran, Zen, Tolstoi, and Jesus and has leaders and members of various religious backgrounds [59:230]. One is free to hold religious beliefs of his own as a participant in the community.

The drama group of Itto En, known as Swa Raj, has consistently used materials that stress a peace theme. In the Itto En community of several hundred persons there are school teachers who have had drama as one of their major interests. They have developed the Swa Raj as part of their school activities as well as a function of the community as a whole. The drama troup has toured extensively, into villages, slums, and prisons and has had an influence that more sophisticated groups might not be able to effect. It is also one reason for the reputation of the community.

After the Second World War Tenko Nishida was elected to a term in the upper house of the Diet. He introduced a bill for "national repentance," but it was not passed. During most of his term he was silent, and he was not reelected [12].

In the 1920s and 1930s the main bodies of Japanese Buddhism went along with government policies. When students and others participated in political protests, they generally renounced Buddhism [5:117–118]. It is interesting that, among socialist groups, a number of leaders such as Seido Takazu came from families of Buddhist priests but renounced their tradition. One of the leading theoreticians of the Japanese Communist Party, founded in 1922, was Manabu Sano, who also turned from his Buddhist background and appealed to those receiving charity from the Higashi Honganji Temple to join in the struggle for Communism. Later Sano returned to Buddhism and urged Buddhists to develop a more active social program [5]. The anti-Buddhistic criticisms of Japanese Marxists in the early thirties led some Buddhists to consider Marxist thought. Jiro Seo was one of the leaders and founders of the Youth League for the Renewal of Buddhism (Sinko Bukkyo Seinen Domei) that took an active part in antiwar and in labor demonstrations in the early thirties. At the time of the war with China in 1937 the government suppressed this group.

The history of efforts of the government to regiment religion and to use it "as a means of the spiritual mobilization for the Pacific phase of the World War II" has not been written [62:99–100]. The government's effort affected all religious groups, and, as in all countries, religion generally came to heel and dutifully followed Caesar. There were exceptions to this in Japan as elsewhere: Kagawa and some Christians, the neo-Shinto

Oomoto, and some Nichiren leaders. Here, of course, there are degrees of protest and conformity for a variety of reasons. In the case of the investigations and imprisonment of the Nichiren-ites, the cases against them generally involved a refusal to subordinate Buddha, the Lotus Sutra, or Nichiren principles to the worship of Amaterasu Omikami [62:112-115]. A similar matter came to the fore in the case of Christians. Under pressure from the government's Indoctrination Bureau, the general secretary of the National Christian Council wrote a pamphlet which likened "the fatherly beneficence" of the Emperor in Asia toward the family life of mankind to its heavenly counterpart in God the Father and his Kingdom. Another pamphlet issued by the National Christian Council looked upon the China conflict as an effort to correct an erring people: "with tears in our hearts we have raised aloft the whips of love" [19:252]. In a somewhat revised version of the Apostles' Creed, God was not described as "the Father Almighty, Maker of Heaven and Earth," but, in order not to conflict with the Shinto of the time, as "the Father of Jesus Christ" [19:253]. During the war years, sixteen thousand individuals were imprisoned by the government for disloyalty of one kind or another. Probably only a small percentage of that group were imprisoned for a religious disloyalty.

There were some individuals of prominence who objected to the militarism of the government. Masaharu Anesaki, Professor of Buddhist Studies at the University of Tokyo, during the early thirties spoke out in the Diet and at other places, criticizing the increased militarism [8]. The year after *Kokutai no Hongi* (Cardinal Principles of the National Entity of Japan) was published as official doctrine to be used in schools as the source of Japanese thought, Kyoto Imperial University sponsored a lecture series for the general public which was intended to "check the growing anti-intellectualism of the times and give people a sounder understanding of Japan and the world" [60:858]. Kitaro Nishida, a leading professor of philosophy and lifelong student of Buddhist and western thought, was requested to deliver the first lectures. In 1939, a year later, one of his colleagues, Teiyu Amano, was attacked by the nationalists. Nishida was advised by some of his colleagues not to publish his lectures, but despite possible danger he went ahead. He was later criticized as being pro-western [60]. With the pressure to conform and with a police state enforcing unity for the national war effort, the period immediately before and during the war was undoubtedly a time of agony, anxiety, and uncertainty for many thoughtful persons, Buddhist, Christian, and Shinto.

A man who combined social passion and pacifism was Toyohiko Kagawa. Although he had been living and working among the dwellers of the slums in Kobe since 1909, he first came to public notice in 1921 during the time of a shipyard strike in that city. He had become one of the organizers of an infant labor movement. Later he was to become a leader in socialist and cooperative movements. In an autobiographical novel *Beyond the Death Line*, the hero states Kagawa's convictions:

> I am a Christian Socialist, but at the same time an advocate
> of the principle of nonresistance. I am living in the slum for
> the saving and inspiring of the poor. Yet, please be not worried.
> . . . I respect the workman as well as all human beings, and
> therefore I shall never attempt to kill anybody.

In the thirties Kagawa was increasingly concerned about the threat of war and the action of Japan in China. He apologized to the Chinese for the action of the Japanese government. In 1940 he was arrested and held for a short period for engaging in peace propaganda. Kagawa represents no movement or organization but is one of the great individuals who was a prophet for his times, much of the time a lonely prophet [2: passim]. Toward the end of the war he publicly criticized the saturation bombings of the Allies.

PEACE MOVEMENTS SINCE WORLD WAR II

On September 2, 1945, the representatives of the Japanese government came aboard the U.S.S. *Missouri* and signed papers of unconditional surrender. During the war neither peace nor defeat or surrender had been spoken or written about, as required by law. Yet probably the section of the Constitution of 1947 that met with most approval was Article Nine in which "the Japanese people forever renounce war as a sovereign right of the nation and the threat or use of force as a means of settling international disputes" [19:258–277]. The powerful symbol of the national cause, the Divinity of the Emperor, was radically changed by his own edict. Shinto was disestablished by Allied edict. With the loss of the old traditions there prevailed a state of aimlessness, lack of identity, and purposelessness for many, perhaps confusion for most. *The Stranger* by Albert Camus became a best seller. With political prisoners freed and freedom of expression gradually returning, Marxism asserted itself. Russia, after all, was one of the victorious powers, giving an air of respectability to the Marxist cause. As Shunsuke Tsurumi has indicated in his *Contemporary Japanese Thought* (Gendai Nihon no Shiso) "at a time when all other groups were moving from right to left adjusting to the times, only the Japanese Communist Party, from the time of its establishment, stood immovable like the north star. In this sense the Communist Party provided an index by which the Japanese intellectual could determine the degree to which he himself had fluctuated with the times from 1926 to 1945" [30:10]. Craig brilliantly sums up many of the currents in postwar Japanese consciousness, "Marxism, Nihilism, and the Soka Gakkai have been among the most highly visible phenomena of the post-war era, but the era itself was generally characterized by a new receptivity toward all recent Western ideas and by the strong re-emergence of universalistic tendencies of Japan's own modern tradition" [15:833].

Certainly this was another time of great collective shock. The traditional religions had not provided success or succor. The tremendous ethical and spiritual need that came with the rapid changes of defeat, occupation, rebuilding, and various forms of democratization led, in religion, to many messianic, prophetic, and syncretic groups in the "new religions." As H. Neill McFarland has pointed out, these were "crisis religions" in the face of threats to "traditional existence at times when radical transition had already begun" [36:259]. They may come about from what

Margaret Mead calls the "ferment of the half-abandoned old and the half-understood new" [37:214–215].

Many of these religious movements had actually been organized much earlier, but this was a time of their revival, division, and proliferation. Many championed world peace, sometimes merely to adhere to popular opinion and sometimes out of long-standing conviction.

In 1946 Oomoto got off to a new start, but the possibilities of this movement were frustrated for the time being when Onisaburo Deguchi died early in 1948. Kagawa was called in by Prince Higashikuni and given a private office in the government mansion so that he might be on hand to advise the government. On Kagawa's suggestion, September 1945 was declared to be a Month of Penitence [19:269]. Kagawa was able soon to return to his work with city dwellers in the work of reconstruction.

Before considering further the role of religion in postwar peace activities, we need to sketch some of the developments on the international scene and the response to them in Japan. By 1947 the occupation had accomplished most of its reforms and in 1947 the Japanese Constitution was enacted with renunciation of war as part of the constitutional provisions. During 1948 it became apparent that the Chinese civil war was going to eventuate in victory for the Communists. Because of this, the United States tended to look to Japan as a potential ally and military base in the Far East. By this time Japan's conservative government and the occupation powers were having some embarrassing second thoughts about Article Nine. In 1950, with the invasion of South Korea, Japan became an important base of operations and source of supply. Japan regained her independence in 1951, but on the same day signed a controversial security treaty with the United States that allowed the Americans to continue to operate military bases on Japanese soil. Japan lost former colonies and the status of Okinawa was left somewhat unclear, but the United States continued the use of the island for military purposes.

The left wing of the peace movement in Japan was particularly affected by the 1951 Soviet testing of atomic bombs and by the 1953 test of hydrogen weapons. Even greater was the impact of the denunciation of Stalin by Khrushchev and of the Hungarian revolt in 1956. Public discussions on the renewal of the mutual security pact started in 1958. On one controversial night in May of 1960, the revised pact was extended by a vote of the Diet. Protest over this incident has had much to do with the method of the Kishi government in maneuvering the vote. More recently, Marxist and Socialist groups have been torn by the Sino-Russian split [15: chap 10; 52: chap 2].

The postwar period has been characterized by the political dominance of the conservative party in all but one year. The Liberal Democratic party has maintained about 55% to 65% of the popular vote, and the Socialists have been gradually increasing their vote from 25% to 35%. The Communist Party has only gained about 4% of the vote since 1951. Its postwar high was about 10% in 1949. The Soka Gakkai, the Nichiren Buddhist sect, has been playing an increasingly prominent political role.

Pacifism has been a popular slogan in the postwar period, and groups meaning very different things have used it for their own purposes. However, it is to be noted that "Pacifism and Marxism both have had a deep influence on the Japanese Socialist movement. Each of these now lends its weight to the neutralist cause" [52:131–132]. While to American ears there are certain themes that make the Japanese Socialist sound quite Marxist, particularly on some economic issues, the Socialists accept no dictation from Moscow or any other foreign capital. On the contrary, the Socialist position has given them a sense of unity with Asian, Indian, and Afro-Asian neutralists. Recall that such outstanding Christian leaders as Uchimura and Kagawa were also at once committed pacifists and Socialists. In prewar times Marxism and the Communists had provided a comprehensive and universal perspective that was attractive to many intellectuals. It also was attractive to some because it was western and seemed to be relevant to the worldwide development of science and technology.

There are three prominent organizations or movements in Japan that have had international peace as their prime concern. They have competed sometimes with bitterness for public support. The oldest and for a long time the largest group is the

Japan Council against Atomic and Hydrogen Bombs (Gensuikyo), whose national meetings sometimes (in 1962 and 1963) have ended in chaos. The February 28th meeting in 1963 resulted in the entire executive committee's resigning en bloc [44:16; 51:21]. The Gensuikyo meetings have been picketed with vehemence by the members of the Zengakuren (the National Federation of Student Self Government Associations). This is a militant student group that at one time cooperated with the Gensuikyo but now is very active in its opposition. A third group is the Kakkin Kaigi (The National Council for Peace and against Nuclear Weapons) under the leadership of Dr. Masatoshi Matsushita, president of Rikkyo University (St. Paul's). In general this group is the most moderate of the three mentioned and has among its supporters a number of religious groups.

Gensuikyo started as a neighborhood protest by housewives in Tokyo's Suganami ward. A number of Japanese fishermen were in the fallout area when the United States was testing bombs near Eniwetok. Great public indignation supported the movement in protest to this threat to the sailors of the "Lucky Dragon." There were hints that the Communists had altered the original intent of the protest from that of a humanitarian protest to an anti-American movement. Conflict between Socialists and Communists within the Gensuikyo broke out into the open, and when the Soviets began testing in 1961 there was further division. This pattern prevailed in 1962 and in 1963 with the Socialists and other groups unable to gain control of the movement. Oomoto and some Buddhists were members of the movement, but after 1963 Oomoto began greater cooperation with Kakkin Kaigai.

A religious group that has stayed with the Gensuikyo is the Nichiren movement, Nipponzan Myohoji, a smaller movement in terms of devotees than some of the other Nichiren new religions, but one of the most active and interesting groups. Founded by Nittatsu Fujii, its present chief abbot and once a priest of the Nichiren sect, it has as one of its missions to assist Buddhism in India. This is on the basis of an interpretation of the Lotus Sutra that, in the days of trouble and crisis (Mappo), Buddhism will come back to its homeland. The priests of the order wear robes similar to those of southern Buddhism, even though they are not recognized as being related to any orthodox southern group. Before the Second World War there was some cooperation by Myohoji with the militarists. Priests of this sect were treated as high-ranking military officers during the war. They were stationed in Manchuria, India, Ceylon, Burma, and other Asian countries [39]. They have maintained a Buddhist temple in Bombay, India, for at least twenty years. For a time after the Second World War, Nittatsu Fujii was a friend and follower of Gandhi [10].

In the period after World War II, there has been a metamorphosis to a leftist and pacifist stance. In 1961 this sect spearheaded a World Religionists Peace Conference in Kyoto. This meeting, as did another in 1964, brought clergymen and laymen from many countries to Japan. Although it appeared that the conference was used for cold war propaganda by pro-Russian groups in 1961, the leaders of the movement are dedicated, energetic, and devout Buddhists. One of their prime leaders is Gyotsu Sato, a graduate of the Japanese military academy who was converted to Nichirenism after the war. A former colonel, he was one of a number of officers who were disciplined because of their opposition to Tojo. Sato explains that this stemmed from criticism of army action in China [11].

Nipponzan Myohoji has been active and articulate in the drive against A and H bombs, the movement against U.S. bases, and in many other activities all over Japan. With the Japan Christian Association for Guarding Democracy, Oomoto, and other groups, they collected several million signatures on a petition against the Security Pact and presented it to the Speaker of the Diet [44]. As part of their activities with Gensuikyo, they have organized peace marches, pilgrimages, and demonstrations. Earlier, they had the support of religious groups such as the Japan Council of Religionists for Peace, Oomoto and Konko Kyo. In general they are more interested in organizing religious and other groups in peace efforts than they are in proselytizing for members. Indeed, it would appear that their chief purpose is to be a peace movement.

The second major group, the Zengakuren, a student movement, was expelled from the Gensuikyo because it was "too violent." Zengakuren maintains that it wanted to protest the 1961 atomic bomb testing by the Soviet Union. It has proven a vociferous opponent of its parent group. Numbers of students at some Christian universities have participated in the group and been part of its demonstrations. The movement is badly split into a number of factions. They have had a bad press because of their clashes with the police and for their efforts in the 1960 Tokyo riots which led to President Eisenhower's staying home. However, it should be mentioned also that on August 5, 1962, three Zengakuren students were arrested in Moscow's Red Square for protesting Russia's new nuclear tests [51:23].

Kakkin Kaigi, by comparison with the preceding two groups, is the least volatile. Dr. Matsushita, president of this group founded in 1961, explains that he is more interested in truth than in propaganda [9]. "We are impartial, although we are not exactly 'neutral.' Gensuikyo is violent against America but very lenient toward the Soviet Union. It classifies America and other Western countries as 'war powers'; the Soviet Union and Communist China as 'peace powers.' We do not agree with this view. We believe rather that such an attitude would promote war. Further, we believe that opposition to using, possessing, and testing of nuclear weapons should be above our political opinions. We are not affiliated with any political party. We are determined and serious, but we are not radical" [9]. Kakkin has the support of the Democratic-Socialist Party, at least unofficially, and the labor union Zenro, the rival of Sohyo, and of Tenro, the Japan Coal Miners' Union [51:23]. In addition to many Christians and Buddhists, Dr. Matsushita lists Rissho Kosei Kai and Perfect Liberty Kyodan among the new religions that support Kakkin Kaigi. Rissho Kosei Kai is an important Nichiren group that claims over two million members in Japan and has been very active in interfaith and international religious meetings. Their founder, Nikkyo Niwano, was the only Buddhist from Japan present at Vatican II. This involvement by Kakkin Kaigi is one of their first political or near political ventures. Since they have been involved with competition with Soka Gakkai, they may be forced into more overt political activity.

On March 8, 1963, the Japan Buddhist Council for World Federation was founded. This organization includes an impressive cross section of Buddhist leaders and is part of the World Federalist movement. The Japanese Delegation to the Twelfth World Congress of the World Association of World Federalists, held in San Francisco in June 1965, was the largest delegation from any nation. This was due in good measure to the Buddhists. Oomoto had sixteen delegates. The Buddhists included the Rev. Sogen Asahina of Engakuji Temple and the Rev. Nichijo Fujii of Minobusan Kuonji — nationally known leaders of the Soto and Nichiren sects. There were twenty-two priests in the delegation from eight different sects. The Nichiren sect was represented by nine priests. Perhaps World Federalism is safe politically and relatively noncontroversial and thus provides an outlet for liberal Buddhists. The Japanese delegates were somewhat disappointed to find other countries not represented so well as Japan at the world meeting. This group had sent two priests to South Vietnam in October of 1963 to submit an appeal to President Diem, and the coup took place in Saigon while they were there. They have submitted several appeals to the United States government and North Vietnam urging a cease fire [22].

The Nichiren sect since the early 1950s has had a Peace Committee. Their main efforts have been of an educational nature against the use of atomic weapons. It has felt some difficulty in participating in the larger peace movements because of political overtones and controversies. Members of the Nichiren Peace Committee have been interested in the peace activities of other countries, and, when they have visited the United States on the occasion of the World Federalist Conference and for other meetings, they have visited peace organizations in the United States.

The National Christian Council has looked with alarm at the dangers from the use of Japan for military bases, especially when

Okinawan bases were to be enlarged, and has protested. In 1954 they issued a statement appealing to Christians in America to cease the testing of atomic bombs in the Pacific. Again, when the new weapon "Honest John" was put in the hands of Japanese self-defense forces, they spoke up in protest. The delegates to the World Council of Churches in 1954 requested a repudiation of the cold war by Christians. The Christian Peace Council was formed in 1951 with the impetus of the Korean War and at the beginning had both pacifist and nonpacifist members. The members of the Japanese Fellowship of Reconciliation were instrumental in setting up the organization. Professor Inoyue of Tokyo Union Theological Seminary, himself a nonpacifist, was chairman of the group but later decided that he should relinquish his position when political controversy seemed to be important to the group's decisions. The Christians are now split into two ideological camps and groups reflecting the break in the pacifist movement as a whole. One group sent a delegation to the Prague Peace Conference in 1963, and at this conference, too, the delegation apparently was divided as to how impartial their criticism of the major powers should be. The other group sent representatives to China. The Japan Christian Council for Peace in Vietnam last year sent a delegation to the United States to appeal to leaders and churches in this country to bring an end to the war in Vietnam. Five delegates were received warmly by the National Council of Churches of Christ in the United States. Nevertheless, the Japanese Council noted with some dissatisfaction the concrete proposals later put forth by the American group. The differences seemed to center on the recognition of the Geneva agreements and the settlement of who should be involved in the peace negotiations. The Japanese Christians took the position that the Liberation Front should be recognized as a legitimate party to the talks [23:430].

Is pacifist Japan going to rearm? Apparently there is a gradual shift in the public sympathies in this direction. Neutralism has had an appeal for at least a third of the Japanese public for many years [52:130]. Over 200,000 Japanese still suffer from radioactive diseases due to the Hiroshima and Nagasaki bombings.

Japan would be one of the most vulnerable nations in a nuclear war. She has great urban concentrations of population only a short distance from Russia and China.

Nevertheless, an effort to achieve the capacity to defend herself has appeal for many. Further, there is a desire to get rid of foreign control and to establish herself in the international community.

The chief point at issue is revision of the Constitution. This revision is being studied and debated within the religious groups and peace movements of the nation [6:275 ff].

Many evidently agree with former Premier Kishi's statement, "Japan cannot be said to have found itself as a nation just because everyone has a TV set, plenty to eat and a higher income" [25:11]. Kishi is advocating eliminating Article Nine.

CONCLUSION

Generally government pressure before World War II did not allow for the free development of voluntary associations interested in international peace. Criticism and opposition in the Sino-Japanese War, Russian-Japanese War, and the First and Second World Wars came mainly from a few outstanding individuals, messianic religions, small groups of Marxists, liberal Christians, and Buddhists without any national base. The only national aspect of criticism came through some journalists and writers in the popular press. Most of the movements were quite short lived, and the leadership was forced to compromise.

Marxism provided the chief comprehensive critical perspective in political matters that was consistently attractive to intellectuals. The importance of political values and hierarchical authority gave strength to a central government as it developed an expansionist and militarist program.

The protest of the intellectuals with Buddhist backgrounds such as Anesaki, Nishida, Kawakami, and Suzuki were not intended to involve them in sustained political action and present a picture of relatively isolated action. It might be questioned as

490

to whether Buddhism was the major factor in their protests. However, the stringent controls of the government in preparing for war, make it difficult if not impossible to evaluate Buddhism's role. The wartime history of Japanese religions has not been written.

More significant perhaps is that Japanese Buddhist thought did not provide any transcendental or transcultural frame of reference for criticism of society or the government. Hajime Nakamura concludes that while universal religions, including Mahayana Buddhism, generally "advocate the transcending of limited human relationships," this "fact of religion . . . is scarcely seen in Japanese religion" [40:415]. The exceptions to this generalization might prove illuminating, but the Japanese case seems to be an illustration of the assimilation of the "great tradition" of classical Buddhism to the "little tradition" of popular religion as it syncretized with Japanese culture. The Japanese focus on a "limited social nexus" has proved to be dominant over the more universal ethic in Buddhist thought. Political conservatism has more often than not had the reenforcement of the Buddhist as well as the Shinto religious community [5:117]. However, the persistence in a religious tradition of a transcendent frame of reference is no indication that either the scholars or the popular devotees will challenge the power structure. As Max Weber has pointed out, Protestantism with its ethical system normally has "legimated the state as a divine institution and hence violence as a means" [61:124].

As in the case of the labor movement and socialism, so in the case of aspects of the peace movement, ideological incentive tended to come from sources other than Japanese. This is particularly true, of course, in the case of Christian and Marxist intellectuals. The movements with more of a Japanese base and popular support, Muga no Ai, Itto En, Omoto Kyo, Shin Bukkyo Doshikai, perhaps are all the more significant for being exceptions to the general status quo of religion. They, too, are syncretic types of religions. They demonstrate that there are "explosive" aspects to religious phenomena that are difficult to put down, even in a tightly controlled social order.

After the Second World War, pacifism in various forms has proved popular. But, as Japan moves toward full independence, pacifism seems to be less and less a real choice.

Substantial peace movements have risen and played a role in shaping public opinion in postwar Japan. At least three such movements are of national significance. Religious groups, Buddhist, Christian, and Shinto, have participated in these movements or formed councils, committees, or conferences on their own.

The ideological divisions within and the separation from the intellectuals without have limited the effectiveness of postwar movements. The peace or antiwar efforts of some of the new religions, Nipponzan Myohoji, Omoto Kyo, Konko Kyo, as well as the Christian groups, have persisted despite the limitations of the political situation and the difficulty they have had in finding live options to support. It is yet to be seen whether the peace efforts of these groups will provide further evidence for Weber's statement that the "pacifist interests of petty bourgeois and proletarian strata very often and very easily fail" [61:171].

The ranks of the pacifists and those in the peace movements have since the war generally been divided between Communist or Marxist pacifists with loyalties to either the Russian or the Chinese view of international issues on the one hand and idealistic pacifists on the other. The pacifism of the Marxists or Communists holds that the causes of war are economic and political and that the "social struggle to solve such conflicts is the way to achieve peace" [57:86].

The general political frustration has been that no critical opposition party with live alternatives has yet been able to seriously challenge the conservative forces that have maintained their power for many years. This has meant that peace movements and opposition groups in general have had to find outlets outside of party structure for making their point known. Dramatic demonstrations, peace marches, petitions, and international conferences are ways of accomplishing this. Soka Gakkai recently has represented a rightest challenge of serious proportions. It remains an open question as to whether Christians, Buddhists, or Shintoists will be able to find the means to successfully influence public opinion and government policy on issues of war and peace. The answer is by no means clear.

REFERENCES

1. Anesaki, Masaharu: *History of Japanese Religion* (Kegan Paul, Trench and Truber, now Routledge & Kegan Paul, London, England) 1930.
2. Axling, William: *Kagawa* (Harper & Row, Publishers, New York, New York) 1946.
3. Baumgartel, Howard: *Psychology and World Affairs* (Mimeographed paper presented at the Psychology Colloquium, University of Kansas) Dec 7, 1966.
4. Bellah, Robert N: *Tokugawa Religion* (The Free Press, Glencoe, Illinois, now The Free Press, New York, New York) 1956.
5. Benz, Ernst: *Buddhism or Communism: Which Holds the Future of Asia?* (Doubleday & Company, Inc, Garden City, New York) 1965.
6. *Contemporary Religions of Japan*, vol 4, no 3, Sept 1963. See "Chronology" in this and later issues.
7. Conversations with Buddhist leaders at Otani and Kyoto Universities.
8. Conversations with Dr. Anesaki's son-in-law, Dr. Hideo Kishimoto, July 1961.
9. Conversations with Dr. Matsushita, Aug 1965.
10. Conversations with leaders of Nipponzan Myohoji, July 1965.
11. Conversations with Gyotsu Sato, Aug 1965.
12. Conversations with Tenko Nishida and religious leaders in Kyoto, Aug 1961.
13. Deguchi, Onisaburo. *A Guide to God's Way* (Oomoto Central Office, Kameoka, Japan) 1957.
14. *The Eastern Buddhist*, Nov–Dec 1921.
15. Fairbank, John K; Reischauer, Edwin O; and Craig, Albert

M: *East Asia, The Modern Transformation* (Houghton Mifflin Company, Boston, Massachusetts) 1965.

16. Fromm, Erich: *Psychoanalysis and Religion* (Yale University Press, New Haven, Connecticut) 1950.

17. Hall, John Whitney: *Changing Conceptions of the Modernization of Japan* (Princeton University Press, Princeton, New Jersey) 1956.

18. Hayashi, Kentaro: How to Approach Postwar Japanese History, *Chuo Koron*, Sept 1964. Reprinted in *Journal of Social and Political Ideas in Japan*, vol 3, no 2, Aug 1965, pp 67–71.

19. Iglehart, Charles W: *A Century of Protestant Christianity in Japan* (Charles Tuttle Co, Ltd, Tokyo, Japan) 1959.

20. Ike, Nobutake: The Political Role of the Japanese Intellectuals, *The Transactions of the Asiatic Society of Japan*, third series, vol 5, Tokyo, Japan, 1957.

21. Jansen, Marius B: *Changing Attitudes Toward Modernization* (Princeton University Press, Princeton, New Jersey) 1965.

22. Japan Buddhist Council of World Federation: *World Federation and Japanese Buddhism*, Aug 1965, Tokyo. Also, conversations with Buddhist members of the delegation, July and Aug 1965.

23. Japan Christian Council for Peace in Vietnam: Open letter to the NCC, *The Christian Century*, Apr 6, 1966.

24. *Japan Times*, Oct 2, 1936.

25. *Kansas City Times*, Oct 4, 1965.

26. Kato, Shuichi: *Japanese Writers and Modernization* in Jansen, Marius B, reference 21.

27. Katz, Daniel: Nationalism and Strategies of International Conflict, in Kelman, Herbert C: *International Behavior* (Holt, Rinehart & Winston, Inc, New York, New York) 1965.

28. Kitagawa, Joseph: *Religion in Japanese History* (Columbia University Press, New York, New York) 1966.

29. Kosaka, Masaaki: The World and Meiji Japan in *Philosophical Studies of Japan* (Japanese National Commission for

Unesco, Tokyo, 1962, Japan Society for the Promotion of Science). See also Kosaka, Masaaki: *Japanese Thought in the Meiji Era* (Pan-Pacific Press, Tokyo) 1958, pp. 332–374.

30. Kuyama, Yasushi: The Structure of the Contemporary Japanese Mentality, *Japan Studies* (Nishinomia, International Institute for Japan Studies) vol 1, no 5.

31. Lanternari, Vittorio: *The Religions of the Oppressed* (The New American Library, Inc, New York, New York).

32. Lefever, Ernest: *Ethics and United States Foreign Policy* (Meridian Books, The World Publishing Company, Cleveland, Ohio) 1957.

33. Mannheim, Karl: *Diagnosis of Our Time* (Oxford University Press, Inc, New York, New York) 1944.

34. Maruyama, Masao: Patterns of Individuation and the Case of Japan: A Conceptual Scheme, in Jansen, Marius B, reference 21.

35. Maruyama, Masao: *Thought and Behaviour in Modern Japanese Politics* (Oxford University Press, Inc, New York, New York) 1963.

36. McFarland, Neill: Religion and Social Change in Japan, *France-Asia*, May–June 1962.

37. Mead, Margaret: *New Lives for Old* (William Morrow & Co, Inc, New York, New York) 1956, quoted in McFarland, Neill, reference 36.

38. Metraux, Guy S, and Crouzet, Francois: *Religions and the Promise of the Twentieth Century* (The New American Library, Inc, New York, New York) 1965.

39. Murano, Senchu: editor of the *Young East*, in a letter dated July 2, 1962.

40. Nakamura, Hajime: *The Ways of Thinking of Eastern Peoples* (Japanese National Commission for Unesco, Toyko, Japan) 1960.

41. Niebuhr, Reinhold: *Reflections on the End of an Era* (Charles Scribner's Sons, New York, New York) 1934.

42. Oguchi, Iichi, and Takagi, Hiroo: Religion and Social Development, in Kishimoto, Hideo: *Japanese Religion in the Meiji Era* (Obunsha, Tokyo, Japan) 1956.

495

43. Ohata, Kiyoshi, and Ikado, Fujio: Christianity, in Kishi-moto, Hideo: *Japanese Religion in the Meiji Era* (Obunsha, Tokyo, Japan) 1956.

44. *Oomoto*, vol 6, no 3–4, Oct 1961.

45. *Oomoto*, vol 8, no 5–6, July–Aug 1963.

46. Oomoto Central Office: *Brief Sketch of Oomoto* (Kameoka, Japan).

47. Oomoto Central Office: *Oomoto, Ever Living Up to Peace Doctrine* (Oomoto Central Office, Kameoka, Japan) 1962.

48. Oshima, Yasumasa: *Reflections on the Philosophy Behind Traditional Political Thinking* (The Gotham Foundation Research Center, Tokyo, Japan) 1961.

49. Redfield, Robert: The Folk Society, *American Journal of Sociology*, vol 52, Jan 1947.

50. Reischauer, Edwin O: *The United States and Japan* (The Viking Press, Inc, New York, New York) 1965.

51. Reynolds, Earle: To Our Great Regret, *Liberation*, Oct 1962.

52. Scalapino, Robert A, and Masami, Junnosuke: *Parties and Politics in Contemporary Japan* (Berkley Publishing Corporation, New York, New York) 1962.

53. Seki, Yoshiko: Introduction, *Journal of Social and Political Ideas in Japan*, vol 1, no 1, Apr 1963.

54. Smith, W C: *The Faith of Other Men* (The New American Library, Inc, New York, New York).

55. Smith, W C: *The Meaning and End of Religion* (The Macmillan Company, New York, New York).

56. Suzuki, D T: *The Eastern Buddhist*, Nov–Dec 1921.

57. Takeda, Kiyoko: The Ideological Spectrum in Asia, in De Vries, Egbert: *Man in Community* (Association Press, New York, New York) 1966.

58. Takenaka, Masao: *Reconciliation and Renewal in Japan* (Friendship Press, New York, New York) 1957.

59. Thomsen, Harry: *The New Religions of Japan* (Charles Tuttle Co, Ltd, Tokyo, Japan) 1963.

60. Tsunoda, Ryusaku, et al: *Sources of Japanese Tradition* (Columbia University Press, New York, New York) 1959.

496

61. Weber, Max: Politics as a Vocation, in Gerth, Hans H, and Mills, C Wright, ed: *Essays in Sociology* (Oxford University Press, New York, New York).
62. Woodward, William P: The Wartime Persecution of Nichiren Buddhism, *The Transactions of the Asiatic Society of Japan*, third series, vol 7 (Tokyo, Japan) 1959.
63. Yinger, Milton: *Religion in the Struggle for Power* (Duke University Press, Durham, North Carolina) 1946.

12. CHRISTIANS AND THE STRUGGLE FOR A NEW SOCIAL ORDER IN LATIN AMERICA

by Gonzalo Castillo-Cardenas

IN MEXICO CITY, that great Latin American metropolis of more than six million inhabitants, there is an unusual square called Plaza de las Tres Culturas (Square of the Three Cultures). It occupies the center of an impressive group of tall apartment buildings constructed by the government specially for public service employees. The Plaza is built on two levels. On the first are the remains of Aztec pyramids, perhaps temples, with prehispanic ceramics and murals. They belong to the first culture, that admirable civilization of the ancient past, of which the country is justly proud. Some stairs lead up to the second level of the Plaza. There the prominent feature is a typically colonial Catholic Church with its adjoining convent. It is built on top of the ruins of the Aztec temples, with materials taken from the pyramids. That church represents the second culture, characterized by the dominance of the Church and the imposition of Christian religion on the Indians by the Spanish conquerors. When one is through with the visit a question remains in the mind: "And where is the *third* culture?" If one asks this question of any tourist guide, he will smile with delight and, pointing to the ultramodern buildings which surround the Plaza, will say with great pride: "The third culture is Mexico of today!" As you walk between these buildings you see schools, child care centers, sports stadiums, swimming pools, consumer cooperatives, parks, and so on. If you mention the absence of church buildings, the guide explains that the government cannot allow these as a part of a public project because Mexico is a secular state that cannot promote any religion.

This Plaza illustrates the two strongest factors which are to determine the future both of the Church and of Latin America as a whole: *first*, the gradual emancipation of society from religious criteria and, *second*, the concern for the building of a new social order oriented towards the solution of the fundamental material problems of the masses. These two factors maintain an intimate relation of cause and effect, and both are signs of a slow and painful process of human liberation which, although considered irreversible, is as yet far from being definitive. Powerful forces of inertia, the accumulated weight of sacralized traditions and of vested interests, both national and international, and the psychological impact of an amazingly durable social order based on privilege and authority, these are the retarding forces which are as yet far from being subdued. The concern for building a new social order and the preoccupation with the material welfare of the masses, for example, do not necessarily lead to a better human situation. They may bring about, as is now the case in most of the continent, new forms of paternalism and human exploitation, together with the reinforcement of the old structures of power and privilege.

Similarly, the secularization of culture, which has already taken place in urban centers and among the educated elites, is as yet a precarious and contradictory phenomenon. In Mexico, for example, as well as in other countries, the emancipation from religious tutelage has been attained more rapidly in political institutions than in the minds of the people. Uruguay is probably the only country where "laicization" as an attitude toward life has penetrated deeply into social institutions as well as into the mentality of the masses. There are, however, other countries where the influence of dogmas and religious criteria, the attachment to tradition, and the ecclesiastical influence and even control over the nation and its institutions are still very tenacious. Such is the case in Colombia, where the peasants still show a superstitious reverence towards the priest as well as towards other religious symbols [3:220 ff] and where the National Congress would not take any important measure in the field of education, or in matters touching "public morality," without having the consent of the Church's hierarchy. In the same country, according to a recent study, attempts to pass laws granting married women the right to hold property, or introducing the possibility of divorce, could not even be considered by the Congress because of the opposition of the Cardinal [4: 102 ff].

Important phenomena can be observed also in many countries which seem to contradict the process of secularization, indicating not only a persistence of religious control over the minds of the people but also an increment. One is impressed by the numerical strength in Brazil of "Spiritism," whose adherents already number over twelve million; by the persistence of rituals such as *Candomblé* and *Macumba*, especially among that Negro Latin America whose existence is often forgotten; by the survival of Voodooism in Haiti; by the many syncretistic forms of popular Catholicism among the Indian and Mestizo Latin Americans; and last, but not least, by the dramatic growth of the Pentecostal Movements chiefly in Brazil, Chile, Mexico, and Puerto Rico, a religious phenomenon which takes place in every racial segment of the population. Should one see in all this religious exuberance a fresh manifestation of the profound need of human nature for transcendental securities and the signs of a divine answer to such human need? Or should one rather consider it as a hopeless refuge before the irresistible advance of secularization? Are such religious phenomena other unconscious forms of social protest and rebellion, the temporary "religious and communal response to the social disorganization of large segments of the people, a phenomenon produced by the situation of social *anomie* characteristic of every society in transition" [2:2]? No matter what interpretation we give to the persistence and increment of popular religiosity, it is a fact that must be reckoned with both in the traditional churches and in any social study dealing with the factors which retard social development. Among social scientists there is a growing conviction that the possibility of securing extensive popular backing and commitment to the building of a new social order depends largely on the emancipation of the popular mind from religious and supranatural controls.

For the churches, this is a difficult truth to accept. The fact is well known that the Christian churches in Latin America, particularly the Roman Catholic, have been in the past bound to a prescientific mentality, accompanied by social sequels such as fatalism, resignation, lack of incentive for economic development, and social passivism. The lack of social solidarity, which is probably the greatest internal obstacle to social development, seems also to be related to an oversimplified universality of religious origin, consisting in a leap from family loyalty to a transcendental identification with humanity as a whole, bypassing any true solidarity with intermediate communities such as the town, the city, the province, and the nation. Because of all this, many young theologians believe that the Christian churches will have to stop being agencies for the promotion of more religious devotion, more rites, and in general more religiosity among the people and that, on the contrary, precisely because of the churches' share of responsibility in the historical process that has led to the present impasse, they should today recognize as part of their legitimate task the eradication from the popular mind of all irrational beliefs, fears, and inhibitions that are cultural barriers to social change. When committed Christians attempt to integrate themselves into the process of emancipation from the past in search of a new social order, they find that they are required to make the irrevocable decision to give up the advantages and the apparent security of traditionalism, oversimplified universalism, and ecclesiastical privilege, a renunciation which is the price for radical social change. The significant fact today is the existence of Christian minorities of growing influence, in all churches and in all countries, that are willing to submit to this renunciation with all its consequences.

CULTURAL AMBIVALENCE OF LATIN AMERICA

It would be impossible to understand the internal tensions that Latin American Christians and the churches are experiencing today, and even less the options that some Christian segments are taking, without realizing the cultural ambivalence which characterizes the reality known vaguely by names such as *"Latin America," "Ibero-*America," *"Indo-*America," or simply "America South of the Rio Grande." The countries covered by these names, especially those that have had a relatively high Indian or Mestizo population, face the problem of the coexistence of two cultures within one nationality. One culture is typically western, the patrimony of a privileged minority of descendents from early colonizers; the other culture is a syncretistic type, where the Indian element is mixed with western or African elements, in proportions which vary from country to country.

A material acculturation has been imposed on the Indian or syncretistic segments of the people, while the nonmaterial aspects of the imported culture have been limited to outer forms without their content. We have received, for example, economic, political, juridical, and religious (both Catholic and Protestant) institutions without having assimilated in our values and patterns of conduct (at least in so far as the popular masses are concerned) the true meaning of the same institutions. It is the case of countries whose authenticity has been hindered because of persistent ideological colonialism. In this regard Latin America's distinctive contradiction is that, while it definitely belongs to the "Christian West" in all its outer forms and with respect to its ruling classes which are racially and culturally of European origin, its countries nevertheless share in all the structural and ideological problems of the noneuropean countries colonized by the West. Thus it is not surprising that, while the ruling classes are identified more and more with European and North American colonialism, the masses are in fact closer to Asia and Africa and, together with these continents, consider themselves to be part of the "Third World." This ambivalence has become today extremely radical due to the rapid growth of the popular class and its increasing awareness of itself as an oppressed and marginated majority, while on the other side a narrowing privileged minority increases its identification with economic, political, and ideological colonialism from abroad.

It is not difficult to see the problem which most Christian churches and Christians in general encounter in this situation. In what measure have their forms of life, mission, organization, and patterns of the ministry been simply one more aspect of the imposition of alien institutions without the application or assimilation of their content? This question becomes increasingly valid with respect to those ecclesiastical traditions that we might call "classic," i.e., belonging to traditional Christianity. Presbyterians, Methodists, Baptists, Lutherans, Episcopalians — all of them — imported wholesale their sacralized traditions, their systems of "doctrine and government," their books of "common worship," their architectonic styles, and their predilect emphases — in doctrine, organization, and program. This corpulent ecclesiastical heritage, the result of each denomination's confrontation and adjustment to historical situations completely alien to Latin America, was handed down to the new converts in equivocal association with the preaching of the Gospel. Two features, however, common to all these imported religious systems had an immediate relevance to the Latin American situation: one, their common emphasis on spiritual liberation, which in the long run has contributed to the secularization of the continent through its influence upon great numbers of people who never became "converts," but who were nevertheless emancipated from religious fanaticism; and, two, their common bent against Roman Catholicism, which found an immediate response in many segments of the population because of the well known counter-reformation type of Catholicism which had prevailed for centuries all over the continent. Today, when the banner of liberation has passed to very different hands and when the reformation movement is almost everywhere on the march *inside* Catholicism, classic Protestantism in Latin America finds itself in desperate need of renewal.

Growing minorities of ministers and laymen are increasingly conscious of this need. However, the problems they confront are baffling. Renewal is either too difficult, because of the tenaciousness of "the old ways" which were introduced hand in hand with "the truth of the Gospel," or else renewal is too easy, because the specialists on church renewal from the "mother churches" have already achieved a number of "new approaches, new patterns, and new structures" which are ready made, free for the asking, or without asking. The first problem leads to desperation; the second, to further alienation by the perpetuation of the essentially imitative character of Latin American Protestantism. In fact, we may ask whether it is possible to initiate the renewal of the Church in Latin America on the basis of a "renewed orientation" from New York, Geneva, or Germany, without having such "renewal" become a simple prolongation of the same old ideological colonialism which has characterized the past.

CHURCH RENEWAL AND THE SOCIAL ORDER

This question leads to a more basic one about the very possibility of "Church renewal." Theologians agree that the renewal of the Church is not a human achievement but a gift of God to a people that is loyal to Jesus Christ in a concrete human situation. This means that renewal is linked with Christian engagement in a specific human context. The question, therefore, as to whether the renewal of the Church is possible at all, apart from the renewal of society in general, becomes the crucial question for Latin American Christians. To a minority of avant-garde Christians within all denominations, it becomes increasingly clear that the struggle for a new social order takes precedence, as a Christian task, over the task of "renewing the churches." This appears to be precisely what the Cuban experience is teaching the rest of the continent, because as far as I know, the Church in Cuba is now passing through a most promising process of renewal that was not possible before the revolution. This process is described as follows by a Presbyterian pastor who is currently fulfilling his ministry in Cuba "in the midst of revolution":

> In the past we had lived in a situation of comfortableness. Everything had been relatively easy, and even though we had not been particularly successful in increasing the number of church members (Protestants were about 2% of the total pop-

504

ulation), we were, however, respectable people, and to some extent we enjoyed of extraordinary influence and privileges. This is not so any longer, and it will probably never be so again in the future.

The rapidity of the social and economic changes which take place in Cuba, coupled with a permanent process of Marxist indoctrination, place the Church in a situation that she did not desire for herself: that of being required to assess the revolutionary achievements, and at the same time to revise her own program of action; that of finding new evangelistic methods, while engaged in the task of self-examination and self-purification. All this in the moment when the Church is decimated in her membership, and when she has to be able to inspire trust and hope in the midst of so much defeatism and disillusionment [1:6].

It sounds like a superhuman task, but according to the same reporter — and the testimony of many others — the Church in Cuba is living up to her momentous responsibility. Christians are learning to discern the autonomy of the Gospel with regard to every form of social and political organization of society; the churches are realizing that their complete dependence on finances, patterns, and organizations from abroad, which characterized the past, must be followed by a situation of *independence*, if they are going to be able to enter into a genuine relationship of *interdependence* with the sister churches from all over the world; church members are showing a greater sense of responsibility and commitment, not only to the humanistic endeavour of the revolution, but also to the specific tasks of the Church as an organization. As a consequence, "there is a *lay thrust* in the Church that is expressed in the desire of the Church's people to train themselves to be able to share in tasks which in the past were reserved only to the clergy: laymen are taking over the posts left vacant by pastors who have abandoned their congregations" [1:17]. As a response to the nationalization of all church schools in Cuba on May 1, 1961, every congregation became engaged in a most intensive program of Christian education, which has greatly dynamized the life of the parish.

The Cuban experience seems to indicate, therefore, that in

certain historical situations nothing short of a revolutionary change in the structures of society will be able to break up the old structures of the Church, making her receptive to the gift of renewal, which comes from God! This priority of the struggle for a new social order was perfectly understood by Father Camilo Torres, that great Christian who was assassinated in February 1966, when he decided to devote himself fully to the revolutionary cause in Colombia. At that time he wrote a "Message to the Christians," saying:

> I have left the privileges and duties of the clergy, but I have not left the priesthood. I believe that I have devoted myself to the revolution out of love for my neighbour. I will not say the Mass, but I will realize this love to my neighbour in the temporal, economic, and social realms. When my neighbour has nothing against me, when I have realized the revolution, I will then say the holy Mass again. Thus, I believe that I will be able to obey Christ's command, "if you are offering your gift to the altar, and there remember that your neighbor has something against you, leave your gift before the altar and go, first be reconciled to your brother, and then come and offer your gift" [6:35].

TENSIONS IN LATIN AMERICAN CHRISTIANITY OVER THE SOCIAL QUESTION

An awakening to these problems on the part of a growing minority of Christians — awakening that coincides with a consciousness of the true nature of their problems by Latin American societies — has produced in recent years a series of strong tensions that are at the same time a danger and a hope for the future of the Church:

(1) There is a tension between those who see the future of the Christian mission inextricably linked with the safety, prestige, and survival of the existing religious institutions, such as dogmas, "principles," and organizations (which are threatened by the advance of secularization) on the one hand and, on the other hand, those who are convinced that such institutions must

radically change, or even disappear, and that Christians, both clergy and laymen, must be in a relation of full freedom with respect to such institutions in order for them to be able to participate responsibly *as Christians* in the secular processes that are determining the future of their own countries. This tension is particularly acute because present-day Protestantism in Latin America is passing through an institutional hardening which in the past had been attributed only to Roman Catholicism. The churches seem predisposed to chastise, persecute, expel, and openly condemn, "casting into outer darkness," the elements that for reasons of conscience take positions in social and political matters that do not harmonize with religious and ecclesiastical interests. Cases are multiplied throughout the continent in almost all denominations. The list is already an impressive one of Protestant pastors who have lost their charges or been forced to leave the country due to the withdrawal of the backing of their churches.

Documentation of this new crisis of the freedom of conscience, within churches that were in the past the main claimants of it, is difficult to gather, partly because — contrary to the case with Catholicism — Protestant problems in most cases do not yet reach the public press and they are seldom put into writing at all. The documentation that does exist remains dispersed in churches' minutes, private correspondence, and small religious pamphlets. Some of the "cases" referred to above, which are of the personal knowledge of the author, have to do mainly with church ministers. For example: the first Venezuelan convert of the classic denominations to achieve high quality theological training found it impossible, upon return from seminary, to continue with the Church, and in 1956 he joined the communist party. Later he entered other forms of revolutionary action. In Brazil, a number of Presbyterian pastors and professors of theology have been harassed and threatened by the authorities of their own Church, some of them expelled from their posts, particularly after April 1964, because of their convictions about the implications of the Gospel for social and political questions. In 1965, a Lutheran pastor in Ecuador, because of pressures within his Church, was

508

forced to leave the country and is now working elsewhere in Latin America. The young and poor Evangelical Church of Ecuador has had to fight for her life since the moment of her foundation because of the pressures put on her by the U.S. missionaries in the field. Similar instances have taken place in Colombia.

In Catholicism the most symbolic case was that of Father Camilo Torres, mentioned above. Tension with the Colombian hierarchy first put him on the margin of the institutional Church, then on the margin of civil institutions, and finally, totally abandoned by his own Church, resulted in his violent death. Similar cases, without having led yet to the supreme sacrifice, but involving persecution and jail, have taken place in Brazil, Peru, and other countries.

(2) There is tension between individualism, firmly rooted in the ideological colonialism of Iberian origin, which in the past had a determinative influence on the continent, on the one hand, and the claims of social solidarity and national integration which are indispensable for economic development and social justice, on the other. Latin American Protestantism, for example, has appropriated for its own, without deliberation or theological formulation, but — up to now — by general consensus, the "doctrine" that individual self-promotion socially and economically is a natural consequence of the regeneration of the inner man through faith in Christ. This dogmatic position conflicts with those groups of Christians who have become aware of the complex structural aspects, national and international, that make possible or impede the social and economic betterment of a country. These groups of Christians have come to understand that the social solidarity of all the members and segments of a country that attempts to achieve economic development is the condition *sine qua non* to attain the desired goal within social justice. On their side they have the evangelical teaching of the indissoluble solidarity of every man and his neighbour. The minority of Christians that think thus also understand the mission of the Church in a different way. For them the Church is not only concerned with a congregation of believers, separated from the

rest of society, whose temporal and eternal well-being would be the purpose of Christianity to achieve. Rather, it is the Church's task to work together with all the segments of society, with all men, even with seeming adversaries, who are in search of a social and economic order that benefits everyone, lifts all to a higher level, and attains national development within a framework of social justice. This understanding assigns to the Church a humanist mission with a Christian inspiration. The confrontation is, therefore, between two conceptions of the mission of the Church, one which concentrates on the Christian believer and his social and economic ascent as an individual and the other which puts the emphasis on solidarity with society as a whole. The groups that embody these two tendencies tend to assume radical positions within the churches, making denominational unity increasingly precarious.

(3) There is tension between those, on the one hand, who still believe in the possibility of gradual evolutionary change, counting on the rational cooperation of the dominant classes, and those, on the other hand, who are convinced of the need for and justification of active resistance to the established "order," even to the point of subversion, for the sake of the majority. Behind these two positions there is a *theological* conflict. There are those who believe that God's interest is concentrated on the Church and on her freedom to fulfill what she considers her mission. For them, as long as this freedom is not threatened, there exists a social order that, without being perfect, is at least tolerable. But there are also those pastors and laymen who are convinced that God's interest is concentrated on man's well-being in actual situations and that the established order in many countries is an affront to God because it is precisely an affront to man. The latter segments of Christians believe that active resistance to this "order" so as to force the inauguration of a new social order, rationally planned economically, based on social justice in its internal relations and on national dignity in its external commitments, should be considered a Christian task. "When an authority exists contrary to the people," wrote Father Camilo

Torres, "that authority is not legitimate and is called tyranny. We Christians can and must fight against tyranny."

It is within this context that we encounter the problem of recourse to force as a revolutionary instrument. It is a matter of effectiveness. The question is whether Christians, convinced that the present "order" is an "affront to God and man" and conscious of the multiple forms of violence that the established order exercises against the weak, the deprived, the poor, the marginated people — who are the majority — are going to resist this situation *effectively* until they attain the goal of a new social order based on justice or if, on the contrary, they are simply going to be content with a permanent rebellious attitude that achieves nothing or with certain isolated reforms equivalent to social anesthesia. Christians who understand the necessity for carrying the struggle to the end reason this way: The most important thing in Christianity is love for one's neighbor because "he who loves his neighbor fulfills the law." This love, to be genuine, must search for efficacy. If benevolence, alms, a few free schools, a few housing projects — what has been called "charity," be it individual, national or international — does not solve the problems of underdevelopment, then we have to look for efficacious means to do so. The privileged minorities that have the political power are not going to apply these means, because generally effective means force minorities to give up their privileges. It is then necessary to take power away from the privileged minorities and give it to the poor majorities. This revolution can be peaceful if the privileged minorities do not resist violently. Revolution is therefore the form of attaining a social orientation that allows the practice of love for one's neighbor, not only in an occasional and transitory way, nor only for a few, but permanently and for the majority of our neighbors. Therefore, revolution is not only permitted, but is obligatory, for those Christians who see it as the only effective way of fulfilling love to one's neighbor.

The conclusion of the El Tabo Consultation on Church and Society (Chile, January 10–20, 1966) in this respect is basically the same, although greater emphasis is laid on "private decision" by individual Christians. The pertinent paragraph says:

> Within this context [of permanent social violence exercised by the established order] the immediate Christian task would be: to uncover and point to those forms of permanent social violence; detect their causes and possible remedies; put the latter into practice with the least use possible of direct violence; when finally he should decide for one way or the other, remember that he might never be in absolute certainty about his course of action, and hence he should keep as close as possible to his brothers who might have decided differently from him. As Luther, the Christian of today, after taking his position on the use of force, should submit himself to God's judgment and forgiveness: "This is my decision, God help me" [5:14 ff].

For those who favour a gradual, peaceful change, the reasoning and the position that we have just given constitute the clearest and more justifiable cause for rejection or expulsion from the bosom of the Church. In fact, the churches are already divided in this respect, even though the two positions go on wearing the same Christian or denominational label.

By careful analysis of these two positions, in the light of recent developments in such countries as Brazil, Argentina, the Dominican Republic, Colombia, and Peru, we are led to ask if we Christians in Latin America are not in danger of falling victims of a conflict between two myths. On the one hand, the myth of peaceful, painless change that aspires to social transformation without basic alteration of the system or great political modifications or even without touching the centers of power; and, on the other hand, the myth of rural guerrilla warfare that has its inspiration and example in the Cuban success, without distinguishing between the situations in Latin America before and after the Cuban revolution. Consequently, in the search for possible alternatives to the myths we have mentioned, Christians who are committed to the struggle for a new social order are beginning to understand the necessity for constant dialogue with technicians and experts in social development.

Summing up, we can affirm that the tensions which we have

analyzed concerning the level of beliefs and positions within the Church reveal a deeper tension between two theologies: one, centered in a rather abstract God, the other centered in man; one, integrist and separatist in relation to society in general, the other based on solidarity and commitment to society as a whole; one, attached to dogmas, principles, and structures of traditional Christianity, the other committed only to man as he is found in particular situations. In the words of Teilhard de Chardin: "Around us the real struggle doesn't take place between believers and non-believers, but between two kinds of believers, two ideals, two concepts of God. A religion of the earth is being formed against the Religion of Heaven."

ECUMENICAL PROJECTIONS

(1) The Christian minorities to which I have been referring, committed to the struggle for radical change, are a phenomenon of extraordinary significance if we take into account the traditional conditions of Christianity, both Protestant and Roman Catholic, in Latin America. Some years ago, the Christians who were most aware of the social problems, not finding an authentic revolutionary movement based on a Christian-inspired humanism, felt themselves forced to resort to communism as the only agent of social revolution. This is not the case today. Chile is an example, even though the results attained so far do not justify any hope for a genuine revolution to take place under the so-called "Christian Democracy." In Brazil, Peru, and Colombia, the leaders who have become symbols of the revolutionary cause and who have made the greatest popular impact in recent years have been Christian-inspired revolutionaries. Within Protestantism today, in every country, both in classic denominations and in more recent ones, even among Pentecostals and Fundamentalists, there exist leftist Christian minorities who attract attention for their renewed thinking and their social vocation. Thanks to the Latin American *Junta of Church and Society*, these Protestant groups, scattered over the continent, are gaining a sense of

513

continental unity and acquiring coherence of thought and action. This is a new fact of the greatest ecumenical import in the history of the continent.

(2) The Movement of Church and Society within Protestantism and the revolutionary movements of Roman Catholic extraction are coming closer together. In situations of misery, margination, and exploitation, social commitment is providing a solid meeting ground that never would have been possible through ecclesiastical dialogue. In the present Latin American situation, mere ecclesiastical ecumenism is insufficient and even dangerous because of its easy tendency to become one more separatist activity that takes place *intra muros*, having as its goal that which, according to the New Testament, is the starting point: the unity of the Church. We find insufficient also that kind of religious ecumenism which, taking as its basis a common theism and often motivated by defensive considerations (anticommunism), ignores God's commitment to man in His incarnation and lacks, therefore, the basis for an authentic historic involvement on behalf of men in specific situations.

The experience of unity in the cause of social revolution, however, is opening up a new, deeper, and more dynamic concept of ecumenism. It is a Christian ecumenism whose distinctive feature is efficacious love (pro-existence) without discrimination and having Jesus Christ for its example. It is the expression of human social solidarity based on the presence of Jesus Christ in all men, even in those who are seemingly dangerous and adverse, such as the prisoners and the marginated of the parable according to St. Matthew 25:31–46, which could be called the parable of social solidarity. The ecumenism which Christ creates, according to the thinking of the Apostle Paul, is expressed in the "new creature," for whom "neither circumcision counts for anything, nor uncircumcision." Or, as we would say today, the new creature overcomes the division between religion and nonreligion, between theism and atheism, breaking down the absolute rigidity between these opposites, because the "new creature" takes place in Christ, who is *agape* (Galatians 5:6). In the words of a young theologian, closely identified with the Latin American situation: "The new man, without denying the differences that exist in this world, overcomes them because they are relative. When love is put into practice then ecumenism (or, simply, Christianity) takes place, even unconsciously, because there are men who live as the Lord wills, even though they do not know it themselves; for they ask, 'when did we see you in jail and visit you?'" (Karl Lenkersdorf).

(3) The experience of unity that is beginning to appear among Christians committed to social change in Latin America is revealing new aspects of the division of world Christianity and, at the same time, is opening new possibilities for the expression of a genuine ecumenical unity. The real Christian scandal, for instance, is not so much the lack of unity that makes it impossible for all Christians to take part in the same religious rites and practices or that hinders living together within a single ecclesiastical organization. The most scandalous aspect of Christian division is what is revealed in unjust international relations which perpetuate underdevelopment, with Christians participating on both sides. When this happens between so-called "Christian nations," the scandal is even greater. However, the realization that the struggle for the social redemption of man is universal, present in all countries, both in the developed ones and in those of the Third World, is opening up new possibilities for approximation, new points of contact, new incentives for identification, and solidarity between countries that would otherwise maintain irreconcilable political and economic positions. In Latin America, for example, there are those of us who might feel infinitely separated mentally and psychologically from the United States for very justifiable reasons; we are, however, discovering how near we are in fact to the valiant fighters for civil rights who are giving their lives and possessions for the cause of justice in complete identification with the ideals of the revolutionary movements of Latin America. This has led us to ask ourselves whether we really are as distant as we thought we were and to discover the human link that goes beyond ideologies, myths, and the unjust structures that separate us.

(4) Finally, I think that the revolutionary, Christian-inspired

515

vocation that is appearing in Latin America — a kind of evangelical charisma with social and political content — promises to give the revolutionary movement in general some of the attitudes which are indispensable for the success of the cause. The strong sense of "brotherhood" which has been characteristic of evangelical congregations in Latin America can be widened and converted into cement that is essential for the cohesion of all those who seek social renewal. Up to the present, evidence of this promise is as yet slight, but noteworthy, such as the attempt of Father Camilo Torres to create a "United Peoples' Front" in Colombia. Upon gathering strength, this tendency could overcome the worst of the problems of all the opposition movements in Latin America, which is their division into small units surrounding a leader.

Furthermore, one observes a certain morale, without fear of sacrifice, based on transcendent convictions that recall those examples of tenacity and valor recorded in the first centuries of Christianity. Like the early Christians, the new revolutionaries feel "Blessed to suffer persecution for righteousness' sake," knowing that afflictions and poverty are all they can expect from the order of injustice that prevails on the continent. It is impossible to miss this spirit in the following paragraph of a message of Camilo Torres to Colombian political prisoners:

> From jail the revolutionary should give an example to the people of valor and decision, a spirit of sacrifice and loyalty to the revolution. His time there should be spent in studying to prepare himself to better understand the justice of revolutionary ideals, to be ready for the day when he regains his freedom. The political prisoner should demonstrate to the guards and to the other prisoners that there is a great difference between him and a common delinquent. By his conduct the revolutionary should exact from the jailkeepers the treatment that his rank as a fighter for the people deserves. Rather than feel ashamed for being a prisoner, the revolutionary should feel proud to suffer persecution for righteousness' sake [6:81].

Whether Christianity manages to impress this morale on the movement of social redemption or not will greatly depend on the growth of the revolutionary vocation among Latin American Christians.

REFERENCES

1. Cepeda, Rev Rafael: Iglesia en Revolución (mimeographed paper presented to the Student Christian Movement, La Habana, Cuba) August 27, 1962. A summary of this paper has been published in English under the title "The Church in Cuba," *Student World* (Geneva, Switzerland) no 1, 1964, pp 77 ff.
2. D'Epinay, Christian Lalive: Changements sociaux et développement d'une secte, le Pentecôtisme au Chili, 1909–1960 (mimeographed paper, summary of a doctoral thesis to be presented to the University of Geneva, Switzerland).
3. Fals-Borda, Orlando, *Peasant Society in the Colombian Andes* (The University of Florida Press, Gainesville, Florida) 1955.
4. Haddox, Benjamin E: *Sociedad y Religión en Colombia* (Co-edición de Ediciones Tercer Mundo y Facultad de Sociología de la Universidad Nacional, Bogotá, Colombia) 1965.
5. El Tabo Consultation on Church and Society, Report of Group 3: *Crisis and Revolution in Latin American Political Structures* (Montevideo, Uruguay).
6. Torres, Camilo: *Camilo Torres, Biografía, Plataforma, Mensajes* (Ediciones Carpel-Antorcha, Medillin, Colombia).

13. THE MORMONS

by David L. Brewer

THE CHURCH of Jesus Christ of Latter-day Saints, or Mormon church, has been known to the American public largely through peculiarities which have become political issues. Polygamy became such an issue about 1850; it remained a popular identifying symbol long after its formal abrogation in 1890. Another peculiarity, the church's Negro policy, is receiving national attention today and is bidding fair to replace polygamy as the principal identifying peculiarity. If the civil rights movement has made Mormon Negro policy a significant issue, the presidential aspirations of George Romney have made it a dramatically prominent issue. [The parts of this essay which deal with the Negro question are based largely upon research conducted in 1964, including interviews with prominent Utah leaders, in religious, economic, academic, medical, legal, and governmental institutions. See reference 5.]

George Romney has come to symbolize this recent encounter between Morman values and the national conscience for several reasons. He is a prominent Republican aspirant to the United States presidency; he is also a "good" Mormon, having held a number of important church offices, including stake president (administrator over several congregations). Mr. Romney has been a successful governor in a forward looking state with a complex social structure, an imposing industry, and its share of racial problems. In his governorship Mr. Romney has been progressive on the racial issue, instituting civil rights laws that are the envy of leaders in other states and in the nation.

A further consideration is especially impressive to Republicans and Mormons: George Romney has lived the American dream, having risen from farm boy to become one of America's most

518

successful industrialists before becoming a prominent political leader. George Romney is just one of the Mormon leaders who has to face the Mormon Negro question, but he may be the most significant one for years to come.

The problem at issue is generated by the fact that the Mormon church ordains all "worthy" males, aged twelve and over, to the priesthood; but Negroes are absolutely barred. Although they may join the church, even membership is discouraged. When they do join, exclusion from the priesthood limits their fellowship and activity. The sacred higher ordinances of the temple, including the much celebrated eternal marriage, are not accessible under any conditions.

This priesthood restriction is justified by Mormons on the basis that Negroes were less righteous than whites in a premortal state, and are therefore less worthy in mortality. Although church leaders vigorously assert this policy and belief concerning Negroes has nothing to do with civil matters, there is a growing feeling that a policy which defines black skinned people as less than worthy in the eyes of God does affect the personal attitudes of its adherents.

The church's Negro policy is not its only problem in coming to terms with modernity; it is its most distinctive problem, however, because this policy is most in contrast with values which are coming to constitute the core of the American social conscience — in a land where increasing affluence is making the fulfillment of the ideals of freedom and equality seem more and more possible of achievement.

Mormonism began with a vision of a new and different American continent, the chosen land, spoken of by the prophets. It began with revelations of God and the *Book of Mormon*, translated from golden plates. It began with a priesthood of all worthy males and a doctrine of eternal progress. In its early history, in Missouri, the church first acquired a negative viewpoint toward Negroes when it compromised in order to throw off the accusation of abolitionism which had been leveled at its members. In Illinois there developed a belief in eternal marriage and family life, combined with the doctrine of polygamy. When the church gave up polygamy in 1890, it seemed that the way was open for an easy adjustment to American society. The separated holy community, blessed with a belief in progress through hard work and the pursuit of knowledge, could overcome its separatism and fit into American life.

In large measure a victory over separatism has happened. Although the church was seriously damaged by the polygamy crisis it gradually achieved a new adjustment. The old way of economic cooperation was gone. In its place there were competitive agrarian individualism and an ecclesiastical institution deeply involved in money-making business ventures. (Interestingly, a church welfare program, initiated during the depression, did not alter this individualist temper. This program was conceived in rugged individualist, antigovernment terms.)

In the transition, however, the community came so completely to terms with American middle-class mores that it is frozen there. The economic overadaptation now combines in various ways with separatist tendencies of the community and with revelatory literalism to make the modern adjustment difficult.

To understand the structure of this institutional resistance to modernizing secularism it is necessary to examine specifically some of Mormonism's distinctive beliefs.

PRIESTHOOD AND WORTHINESS

Since the Mormon church has no professional ministry, the work of the church is accomplished solely by its active members. The staffing of the many positions in the church's complex system of offices is largely a function of its priesthood, which is a hierarchical system of authority organized into the higher and the lower priesthoods, each with three subdivisions. For each sublevel there is outlined a range of authority and potential functions which becomes progressively broader as the member advances from bottom to top.

All Mormon males may be ordained to the priesthood if they are "worthy." To evaluate their worthiness, potential priesthood bearers are interviewed concerning their habits and beliefs. If the decision is positive, they are ordained by the laying on of hands and recitation of a simple prayer which includes certain key words and phrases. Interviews and the ordination ceremony are conducted by men holding the higher priesthood.

There may be some ambiguity about what being worthy means in specific cases, since the church sometimes uses involvement to encourage conformity. Nevertheless, its major referents are well known. Minimally, worthiness is assumed to require accepting the church authorities as prophets, being an active church goer, abstaining from alcohol, tobacco, tea, and coffee, tithing, and being sexually moral. It also includes not being a Negro.

Negroes are not considered worthy to hold the priesthood under any condition. The church teaches that every human existed as an independent spirit, with free agency, in a premortal world. Putting this belief in a context of traditional rugged individualism, Mormons defend the restriction of Negroes as a punishment for their lack of obedience and righteousness in premortality. Each individual Negro must have been less obedient than non-Negroes in the spirit world; bearing the responsibility for this, he deserves to be born a Negro and denied the priesthood. In contrast, each non-Negro, especially if privileged with birth into a good L.D.S. home, must have been particularly righteous in the spirit world, which explains his worthiness to be born into such a fortunate environment.

The Negro policy was anticipated in 1830 by the *Book of Mormon*'s doctrine of the curse. The Lamanites, ancestors of the American Indians, were cursed with a dark skin when they rebelled against God. Following publication of the *Book of Mormon*, Joseph Smith published the first part of the *Book of Moses*, which declared that "a blackness came upon all the children of Canaan, that they were despised among all people."

Still later, the "Mormon Missouri Compromise" occurred, as a result of persecution by proslavery settlers. The Mormon newcomers were identified as tactless zealots who favored the abolition of slavery. To prevent conflict, a Mormon newspaper published in 1833 an article suggesting that members avoid controversy over the slavery issue — a reasonable request since most of the Saints were Yankees and Yorkers. But the article angered Missourians, apparently because it also mentioned the possible abolition of slavery. To further placate the non-Mormons, the editor wrote another article, insisting his original intent had been to keep Negroes from coming to Missouri *and* from becoming Mormons. Although the editorial retreat didn't prevent trouble, it did have a significant effect upon the Mormon racial mentality.

The compromise was complete when Joseph Smith began to defend slavery. He also began translating the "Book of Abraham," used later to justify excluding Negroes from the priesthood. In this document Pharaoh is identified as a descendant of the Canaanites through Ham. Interestingly, Mormons also identify the Canaanites with Cain, and thus consider the curse of Cain as the apparatus through which a lineage was provided for rebellious spirits.

Joseph Smith subsequently opposed slavery but his later views were not sacralized in scripture. It is possible that this is because, after Joseph became more liberal, an event occurred which may have involved an attempt to deal with the Negro question. The Kinderhook plates, made of brass, were uncovered in a mound near Nauvoo. "I have translated a portion of them," he said, "and find they contain the history of the person with whom they were found. He was a descendant of Ham, through the loins of Pharaoh, king of Egypt, and that he received his kingdom from the Ruler of heaven and earth." Joseph did not publish a translation before his death, a year later. The origin of the Kinderhook plates is a matter of controversy [13:372].

Since Smith's views opposing slavery were not sacralized in scripture, after his martyrdom in 1844 and the arduous migration to Utah, slavery was defended by Brigham Young, who had some slaves. Apparently it was in Utah that Negroes were first denied the priesthood.

This policy caused very little trouble for the church until World War II, partly because Utah remained relatively isolated and partly because other issues than race were at the center of national politics. In the 1940s, the integration of the armed forces and a new experience with racism in Germany, plus the growing realization that rugged individualism was not solving the world's problems, began to stir the national conscience. Other changes began to emerge, including more affluence, a blossoming intellectualism and a new civil rights movement — each pressing hard upon beliefs and doctrines which favored the maintenance of special privilege.

Although Mormon leaders continually reaffirm that the church's Negro policy has nothing to do with civil rights, the importance of priesthood and the worthiness it implies — a high evaluation in the eyes of God as well as man — cannot be entirely isolated from deep personal feelings about people and behavior relative to them. Although Mormons are prone to personalize relationships with others, even with the "unworthy," they still feel Negroes to be something less than whites in the eyes of God.

Probably no other characteristic of the church is more blatantly out of tune with America's emerging social conscience. As racial tensions grow, as riots in the cities continue, as Mormon political leaders are confronted with questions about civil rights and especially about their deeper feelings about Negroes, the church becomes more threatened by modernity.

For a number of reasons it appears that the church's policy is unlikely to change in the near future. The peculiar origin of the church encourages leaders to assert that change cannot come without a specific revelation. The only publication of the Utah period thought to be a revelation is the Manifesto — a brief announcement rescinding polygamy. The fact that this "revelation" came only when the church was about to be dismantled by the government holds a lesson for the Negro issue. The age and conservative mind of leaders dispose them to defend traditional beliefs, both secular and sacred. The failure of the church to involve intellectuals in its power structure makes a rapprochement with modernity at this level extremely difficult.

Also relevant to this matter is the resurgence of belief in rugged individualism and economic individualism within the church. This viewpoint, more influential in recent years, sug-

523

gests that secular policy should not give special privilege to minorities, but that equality should and will evolve naturally when Negroes deserve it; it cannot or should not be accomplished by policy change.

Another reason for resistance is the fear of intermarriage, already deeply embedded in American culture and thought by some social scientists to be the central meaning in most opposition to racial equality. In Mormondom this dread both reinforces and is reinforced by the priesthood concept of worthiness and the doctrine of the curse. Mormons are likely to feel that admitting Negroes to the temple would encourage intermarriage.

As these resistances to change combine and support each other in various ways, there is an interesting possibility that the central element in the church's institutionalized defense system may be its racial policy and doctrine — because it is here that the anti-modern stance is most shocking and apparent.

A MORMON SYNDROME

The restriction of Negroes from the priesthood has significance partly because the priesthood is so fundamental in members' lives. (The basic direction of this discussion owes much to stimulating ideas presented by Clyde Tidwell.) It is not a function merely of a few leaders but of worthy males in every family in relation to the temple where family life originates. In fact, the power of priesthood upon the Latter-day Saint conscience is profoundly influenced by the function of the temple. Only worthy Mormons are allowed to enter the temples to participate in certain celestial ordinances. If the priesthood requires worthiness, the standards for temple activity are even more exacting. For the higher ordinances men must be priesthood holders and good ones. The standards of worthiness for women are no less exacting, even without the priesthood. Negroes are absolutely barred from these higher ordinances.

The most celebrated higher ordinance is celestial marriage. Worthy members are married for time and eternity, and children are sealed to them in eternal bonds. The result is a kind of eternal familism, with endless ties reaching back to Adam and Eve.

Celestial marriage is more than a mere function of priesthood —it is the essence of the highest order of priesthood. Latter-day Saints believe that almost all mankind will be saved, but the highest glory in the Celestial Kingdom, where God dwells, is reserved for those united in eternal family ties, according to the celestial order. Those who attain this glory may become gods and have spiritual children. God himself is the literal Father of every human spirit; and therefore he has a wife, our Mother in Heaven.

Eliza R. Snow, a wife of Joseph Smith, and later of Brigham Young, celebrated this belief in words of a song much loved by Latter-day Saints.

I had learned to call thee Father, Through thy Spirit from on high;
But until the key of knowledge was restored, I knew not why.
In the heavens are parents single? No; the thought makes reason stare!
Truth is reason, truth eternal Tells me I've a mother there [9:139].

The ascendancy of the family concept is apparent here. In a fundamental sense, the family is a central part of the church as an institution, perhaps the most central part; Mormons go to church to hear about the wonders of eternal family and eternal belongingness.

Another higher ordinance of the temple, and a necessary prelude to celestial marriage, is the "endowment." The endowment is a ceremonial blessing and dramatic learning experience which is supposed to communicate to the participant the meaning of existence — from premortality to postmortality. In this learning experience, including the revealing of certain sacred symbols and the taking of sacred vows, the individual is helped to prepare for celestial marriage and the celestial kingdom.

Partly because of the impersonal orientation "necessary" to objective observation, and partly because the taboos of the

525

temple can be overwhelming, the centrality of eternal marriage, and the endowment which prepares for it, have been somewhat neglected in discussions of Mormonism. Nowhere is this neglect more interesting than in the lack of discussion of a certain intimate artifact, the "garment of the holy priesthood." All "worthy" members who have been endowed are supposed to wear this garment at all times. It is first worn in the temple after participants in separate chambers, have undergone a ritual bath. The uniqueness of this garment, the standard underwear of Latter-day Saints, resides in certain markings in the cloth which stand for ideals such as health, honesty, virtue, justice, and obedience.

As symbols of the holy priesthood, these garments are believed by members to give protection against physical and moral danger. This belief, taken quite literally, is sometimes celebrated in archetypal stories about faithful members who miraculously escaped fatal injury, or, more interestingly, who didn't escape entirely but were left unscathed in those areas covered by the garment.

As symbols of the holy priesthood and of the sacredness of the eternal relationship between husband and wife, the garments have overwhelming significance for the Mormon conscience. They are ever present reminders of sacred vows made in the temple. Mormons are probably the only religious group on earth who are intimidated by their underwear.

This priesthood-worthiness-eternal-belongingness complex is further complicated by the Mormon emphasis on happiness. It is the essence of Mormon thought that worthiness is sought and found *in relationships*. There is no Faustian strain in the Mormon religious experience, no contemplative search for individual mystical experience. Happy comradeship is the order of heaven as well as of Zion on earth. The power of this belief lies in the belief that happiness is not merely an opportunity, but a mandate. It is one Mormon evidence of worthiness. A favorite passage in the *Book of Mormon* states that "Adam fell that men might be; and men are that they might have joy" [4]. This makes happiness an end, an ultimate toward which life and the gospel are directed. Man must learn to be happy in this life, since "that same spirit which doth possess your bodies at the time that ye go out of this life, that same spirit will have power to possess your body in that eternal world" [3].

The essence of Mormon this-worldly happiness, even in the face of suffering, is portrayed in the words of a song written as the Saints crossed the plains on their way west.

Come, come, ye Saints, no toil nor labor fear;
But with joy wend your way.
Though hard to you this journey may appear,
Grace shall be as your day.
'Tis better far for us to strive
Our useless cares from us to drive;
Do this, and joy your hearts will swell —
All is well! all is well! [7:13]

It is especially within the family relationship, the togetherness eternally established, that worthiness and happiness are linked to interpersonal goodness. The following words come from another church hymn, the sentimental theme song of the King Family's recent television show, itself an interesting public performance of what might be called a Latter-day Saint family togetherness ceremony.

There is beauty all around When there's love at home;
There is joy in every sound When there's love at home.
Peace and plenty here abide, Smiling sweet on every side.
Time doth softly, sweetly glide When there's love at home;
Love at home; love at home;
Time doth softly, sweetly glide When there's love at home
[8:169].

Value is placed upon harmonious relationships. Since belongingness is sacralized and eternalized, as a condition for the highest glory, peacefulness is also valued. This exaggeration of the positive thinker's viewpoint found in middle-class mores, this outwardly friendly, placid, personalizing of life, finds hostility, antagonism, and negativism in general to be very threatening. In the Latter-day Saint community even *formal* relationships take on an engaging kind of bland openness which tends to suppress self-consciousness of the basic instrumental character of those formal relationships. The strong Mormon preference for apparent friendliness and harmony also has roots in the approved use of priesthood authority. Although authority is beyond question, its exercise is supposed to be benevolent and gentle, as revealed in this passage from the *Doctrine and Covenants:*

> No power or influence can or ought to be maintained by virtue of the priesthood, only by persuasion, by long-suffering, by gentleness and meekness, and by love unfeigned; By kindness, and pure knowledge, which shall greatly enlarge the soul without hypocrisy, and without guile — Reproving betimes with sharpness, when moved upon by the Holy Ghost; and then showing forth afterwards an increase of love toward him whom thou hast reproved, lest he esteem thee to be his enemy . . . [6].

The benign exercise of priesthood is supported by a parallel belief in complete obedience to authority. Since church leaders, especially general authorities, are guided by revelation, members are supposed to accept authority without question. Criticism of general authorities is especially abhorred and is normally looked upon as evidence of apostasy. "Bitterness" about the church, its leaders, or life in general is distinctly out of place; the Mormon tends to associate it with rejection of the gospel. This Mormon syndrome of worthiness, eternal togetherness, and happiness, with an emphasis upon explicit friendliness, kindliness, and harmoniousness is encountering strange new forces in the modern world. To the extent that worldly influences seem to oppose fundamental values in the Mormon syndrome, and to the extent that they are potent influences, they may of course be expected to threaten and menace the institution.

Because the modern Negro problem symbolizes for Mormons a dangerous and powerful worldly influence having precisely these negative elements, it has come to stand for the whole breaking through of the outside world upon the holy community.

Three major dimensions of the Mormon community especially need to be discussed in relation to the encounter with worldly influences. In each instance the Negro question will be highlighted [11:488].

LITERALISM

Mormons believe in the Christian *Bible* "as far as it is translated correctly," but they also have other scriptures. Through their belief in modern-day revelation, three other books have been given full status as scriptures.

The *Book of Mormon* is believed to be a translation of some golden plates, a record of God's dealings with ancestors of the American Indians, Israelites who migrated to the American continent centuries before Christ. The *Doctrine and Covenants* is a record of modern revelations given to the church during its organization. The *Pearl of Great Price* is a small book containing miscellaneous inspired writings, including those of "The Book of Moses" and "The Book of Abraham."

Latter-day Saints tend to be quite literal in their interpretation of scripture, especially of those writings revealed to Joseph Smith. These peculiarly Mormon scriptures are considered virtually perfect renditions of God's holy word since they have been directly revealed or else translated under divine inspiration. The immediacy of the revelations gives them a sacred aura that is not easily challenged. This literalism is qualified, of course, by the community of opinion current among general authorities. The belief that present church leaders are divinely inspired makes it possible for them, within limits, to choose the view of scripture which is to be taken as literal. Although leaders' interpretations don't always agree, the institution has had remarkable success in limiting open disagreement. And the orthodox member is likely to see even greater harmony than actually exists. It may be that the Mormon literalism is more limiting than a literalism based on exegesis or proof text methods alone. The question of meaning cannot, in the final analysis, be settled by consulting scriptural language but only by consulting inspired statements of Mormon general authorities.

The fact that no new revelations have been published in the Utah period also fosters literalism. (The Manifesto, a brief statement which rescinded polygamy in 1890, is a possible exception.) General authorities, defensive of the principle of modern revelation, now concentrate upon legitimizing Joseph Smith's revelations rather than upon publishing new ones. The tendency is to accent Smith's authenticity and perfection.

In addition there has so far been little scholarly work on the social context of Mormon revelations, oriented either to the 19th century milieu in which they appeared or, in the case of the *Book of Mormon* and *Pearl of Great Price*, to the world in which they supposedly originated. Such a "higher criticism," though it has seen some beginnings, is not likely to develop soon; since the church's ministry consists entirely of unpaid volunteers, religious training is limited to a few professionals in the church's education system. There is almost no consistent religious scholarship.

Another characteristic of the church which contributes to literalism is its authority structure. The most important church leaders are the president, his counselors, and the twelve apostles. These leaders, appointed for life, now have an average age of seventy years. Naturally their perspectives tend to be anchored in an earlier and simpler religious world view. Increasing age and the ravages of office have increased their drift toward conservatism. Also, the lack of philosophical and theological training, even at this topmost level, means that antiintellectualism is a convenient, even an attractive, response to many questions, including questions of doctrine and scripture.

Mormon literalism thus has a number of mutually reinforcing dimensions. In many ways, the institution encourages simple literalist reactions to things that are threatening and perplexing. Perplexing problems, on the other hand, are *characteristic* of modernity. The heterogeneity of an urban society confronts its members with a complex daily life that often cannot be adequately handled within a simple, traditional viewpoint. The intellectualism which seems to be an established dimension of the modern world finds narrow, simplistic answers, including some aspects of Mormon literalism, to be abhorrent, dangerous, and trite. Steeped in a literalism that has to some extent narrowed in recent years, Mormonism cannot entirely avoid the impact of a modern generation which is looking for modern answers.

THE CURSE

When the orthodox Mormon defends the doctrine of the curse, based upon passages in the *Bible, Book of Mormon,* and *Pearl of Great Price,* he is defending his belief that God specifically placed a dark skin upon certain races of man as a punishment for unrighteousness. Because of his beliefs in revelation and in interpretations by general authorities he is unlikely to imagine that scripture could contain fallible attempts by humans to explain racial characteristics. When a Mormon explains his church's Negro policy he does so with passages from the *Pearl of Great Price* that are vague in meaning and which have dubious significance for priesthood in the modern time. Because of the peculiar quality of Mormon literalism, however, he considers these passages adequate support for the church's position.

Beginning in the late 1930s and continuing into the 1950s, the L.D.S. Department of Education, at that time independent of Brigham Young University, was administered by leaders inclined toward scholarship and intellectualism. A new generation of institute teachers (providing college-level religion classes) and seminary teachers (high-school level) were employed. Many had impressive religious and philosophical training, often from non-Mormon universities. There was a growing commitment to intellectual and liberal interpretations of the Mormon institution and its doctrine. For a time, religious liberalism flourished at Brigham Young University. This was an especially attractive enterprise, since Mormon doctrine, even in its literal context, embodies a positive view of man's nature, an emphasis upon worldly accomplishments, a doctrine of eternal progress, and a belief that knowledge and learning are a necessary part of achieving the highest glory.

A higher criticism was beginning to take shape as scholars studied Mormon scripture in historical context. The extensive documentary holdings of the church, including many from the early history, came under scrutiny of skilled researchers. New philosophical and religious interpretations were taught in the institutes and seminaries, producing a level of intellectual excitement which has never since been approximated in Mormondom.

Several perceptive and objective writings were published during this period. In contrast to earlier superficial anti-Mormon writings, some of these new critiques were systematic challenges to the very foundations of Mormonism.

Central to the challenge, in the institute and seminary teaching as well as in scholarly writing, was the concern with Mormonism's Negro policy. This policy was challenged on the basis of its antihumanitarian consequence. It was considered in terms of the social milieu in which Joseph Smith translated the *Book of Abraham* — proslavery Missouri. The scriptural foundation was challenged on the basis that the curse of the priesthood is nowhere explicitly identified in connection with a *racial* curse. The viewpoint developed that, even assuming a scriptural justification, the priesthood restriction occurred in the days of Abraham at a time when the priesthood was apparently controlled by only one tribe of Israelites, the Levites. Questions were raised regarding early Mormon history, since Joseph Smith had ordained a Negro to the priesthood in Nauvoo. It was pointed out that the first restriction of Negroes had apparently occurred in Utah, when Brigham Young was prophet, seer, and slaveholder.

Reaction to the new criticism began in 1953 with the appointment of a new, unusually conservative administration. A new unified educational system was established, combining Brigham Young University and the institute and seminary system, and introducing other centralizing structures. Many church educators were dismissed or transferred to Brigham Young University where control was more effective. In this purge, which continued for several years, the quality of the educational system was seriously altered. At about the same time, accessibility to church library facilities, especially those dealing with the institution's origins, was seriously curtailed. During this period leaders became more defensive concerning doctrinal legitimacy and began to emphasize more vigorously the infallibility of authoritative revelations. In the heat of the purge and the reeducation campaign, the Negro question often became a subject of excited secretive debate. According to one prominent sociologist, a Mormon underground was developing around the Negro problem [11].

The Negro problem has attained even greater centrality today. In the church's encounter with modernity and its many ramifications, including the political significance of the race issue, church members and non-church members alike are more aware of the Negro policy and the various viewpoints that surround it than ever before. From an insignificant remnant of Southern Protestantism picked up in Missouri, there had developed a church policy. It remained relatively insignificant and unnoticed for many years, then became an issue that caused people to choose sides and work out elaborate doctrinal and intellectual justifications, pro and con. Partly because the policy is deeply embedded in the Mormon syndrome, change is unlikely — literalism in the Mormon world always has the final word.

The literalist approach to the church's Negro policy may be illustrated with interview data taken from the author's 1964 research. Following are the responses of three different general authorities to the question, "To what extent will the civil rights movement affect L.D.S. church policy?"

"Not at all. This is the Lord's decision to make."

"Well, I don't know about that. No one that knows his limitations will try to answer that, till you get up to the top."

"No, definitely not. Christ was crucified because he wouldn't change his policy. That's something we have no right to change, just as members of the church" [5].

It is important to note that these respondents are prominent church leaders. Their sense of absolute dependence upon decisions from a higher authority underlines the difficulty with which the church institutes any major change.

SEPARATISM

Separatism is a defense mechanism employed by religious institutions to avoid the disturbances and dangers of a threatening world. The Mormon church, the holy Mormon community, has gone through several periods in its relationship to the world. Before the Saints came to the Salt Lake Valley in 1847, the most severe threats to the holy community and its sacred beliefs came from other groups. At first, in Ohio and Missouri, the community lacked the size and organization to defend itself, and so persecution was met with an inward turning of responsibility. Revelations blamed the Saints for their own troubles with the gentiles.

By the time the Saints had migrated to Illinois in 1839, the missionary system had brought rapid growth, and the accumulation of revelations in Ohio and Missouri had resulted in a complex, effective organization. The new Illinois situation offered certain other advantages, including the semiisolated condition of Nauvoo and a favorable political-social climate. As a result, the community resorted to an outward turning of responsibility and a semiseparatist posture. The Saints engaged in persistent, organized attempts to gain legal compensation for injustices experienced in Missouri. They also organized a large city militia to serve as a military deterrent.

When the Saints migrated to Utah, in 1847, the first major problem in community survival was the severity of the physical environment. Freed from social conflict for a time, Mormons began to practice polygamy openly. This brought the community once more into conflict with the world. Another migration would not help — there was nowhere else to go to escape the eastern establishment. The holy community tried every available means, short of open warfare, to protect its sacred values from the gentiles. The separatist reaction, already built into the Mormon mentality by earlier persecution, began to take more definite shape. As the government prepared to use force against the holy community, separatism reached its zenith.

Polygamy was finally relinquished in 1890. In the aftermath, the church also began to surrender control of major economic structures, including the holy community's cooperativist system. The community began to move toward economic individualism; in the process of reintegration, the church itself became involved in profit-making ventures.

The new integration, based upon agrarian individualism, has

535

turned out to be overly stable, partly because of a rapprochement of certain doctrinal and organizational aspects of the church and partly because of the antigovernment posture inherited from the polygamy crisis.

As agrarian individualism has become old fashioned in the modern world, another kind of separatism has developed to defend it. The Mormon family has become central in the defense of individualism, and traditional moral values. It is to the family, more and more, that the church directs its attention, in the attempt to keep its young people "unspotted from the world." It is in the home that the holy community "lives, breathes, and has its being."

SEPARATISM AND THE NEGRO

Mormons, with their traditional material optimism and belief in worldly success, are becoming more and more affluent. At the same time, growing industrialization and urbanization create a more complex society in which more education and sophistication are necessary. As more leisure becomes available, people develop more sophisticated tastes, and more interest in personal enjoyment. Related to this is the development of an impressive entertainment technology which caters to those forbidden symbols that sell products, and brings Hollywood into the living room. These forces are disturbing to the Mormon concern with morality and worthiness. Mormon emphasis on friendliness, happiness, belongingness, and harmoniousness also runs into problems in modern society. Urban society is itself the locus of alienative, social structures which can be threatening to a need for peace and harmony.

Accompanying the urban tendency toward increasing affluence and an expanding communications technology is a new revolution of rising expectations. Minorities which have been experiencing severe deprivation are becoming more hostile and demanding. Negro violence in American cities is especially disturbing to middle-class Americans. Strident demands for freedom now, and development of an angry black power movement are threatening to the desire for peacefulness in the family.

The prototypical threat to moral values is often experienced as interracial. Negroes are thought by many to be immoral and undisciplined, with loose sexual standards and unusual sexual capacity. It is thought by many social scientists that the basic fear behind most racial discrimination and segregation is related to attitudes about Negro sexuality and the sexual mixing of the races. This concern with defilement is central to the Mormon fear of intermarriage that would threaten the celestial worthiness of the entire family.

The concepts of righteousness and goodness are deeply associated with "whiteness" in Mormonism. In Joseph Smith's visions, heavenly beings and resurrected angels always appeared in celestial white. Celestial marriages and other temple ceremonies occur in surroundings furnished in white. Such meanings further reinforce the tendency to associate Negro blackness with sin, immorality, and unworthiness, the qualities which the family most vigorously opposes in the development of "good" Mormon character.

Interview statements may be used to illustrate the intensity of this concern with the family institution, and the threat to the holy community's peace and harmony [5]. One general authority was asked "To what extent does church policy with regard to the Negro affect race relations in civil life?" He replied that there would be

> "little effect on employment or public accommodations. But it will affect relations such as courting. No faithful Latter-day Saint wants his children to lose the priesthood. Would you want your children to lose the priesthood?"

Another general authority responded to the same question as follows.

> "I think it involves intermarriage, and we've got to fight that to the bitter end. The civil rights leaders want to have intermarriage."

537

This same leader was asked what he thought would result from the Negro civil rights movement in the U.S.

"I think Negroes are foolish to cause all this trouble. They should give it a little time. They have the law now. It has to ripen."

Still another general authority, commenting upon the civil rights movement and racial problems in general, stated,

"I love all people — the Mexicans, the Indians, and all races. But these riots show that civil rights isn't the real concern of Negroes. Some of these communist agitators have taken over, and this is the real basis of the movement."

AGRARIAN INDIVIDUALISM

The cooperativist orientation which characterized the early Mormon farming community gradually gave way to agrarian individualism during the Utah period. This transition, which was becoming apparent after the polygamy capitulation has continued until the present despite the challenge of modernizing forces. The major characteristic of agrarian individualism is the belief that individualistic hard work is virtuous and leads to success. This perspective had obvious significance on the soil, in pioneer days, but its relevance for modern urban life is ambiguous, since technology is taking the labor out of many occupations. Nevertheless, the characteristic persists in the urban situation, especially in small businesses and in middle class occupations where many migrants from rural areas are situated. In these urban occupations, agrarian individualism is confronted with structures which seem very formal and impersonal, but which offer greater opportunity for economic advancement. There results an overly competitive, somewhat alienated kind of individualism — a search for personal improvement, combined with a yearning for the traditional and the simple that characterized life on the soil [12:250–253].

The transition to individualism occurred largely because the church was forced to give up its theocratic control of the cooperative community in the aftermath of the polygamy crisis. Later, to recover from severe economic strain, the institution itself became involved in money-making business ventures. The business involvement, and the small business mentality that accompanied it, have deepened until the present time.

If this turning to competitive economic individualism was strongly encouraged by the government's dissolution of the church's theocratic control, it was related also to the traditional success of the Mormons in mastering their material environment. Mormons are optimistic about the material world, and about the nature of man (with the exception of the Negro belief). They believe that humans lived before mortality as spirits, but chose mortal birth because the materiality of this sphere would offer greater opportunity for achievement and learning, and for testing their moral fiber. After the resurrection, they will live in a material existence of purer quality; that is the next step in the eternal progress of man.

In the rapprochement with economic individualism, an individualistic interpretation of Mormon doctrine emerged. Each spirit was believed to have attained that birth which he deserved, based on past performance. Negroes, because they couldn't hold the priesthood and were otherwise deprived, must have been especially unrighteous, while caucasians, especially those born to good Mormon environments, must have been especially righteous. This combination of economic individualism and belief in eternal progress, which characterizes institutional belief and practice today, is a potent combination.

As the church has grown in size and complexity, the rapprochement with the business ethic has served the Mormon institution well. Banking on the deep moral commitment of its members, the church has had unusual success in obtaining tithing and other donations. An incentive system for promoting church attendance and activity has been organized around an elaborate system of church offices. Statistics on church attendance and other activities are collected and computed. The results are reported in church meetings to spur the membership onward in their competition among congregations. Numerous personal and group awards are given in church meetings to ceremonialize the value of competitive achievement. Since Mormonism has no professional ministry, leaders tend to be successful men in the community, often businessmen or organizational men. With the church's involvement in money-making business ventures, and the use of businesslike techniques to motivate members, the frequent recruitment of businessmen is probably unavoidable.

Thus economic individualism has strong roots in the Mormon community, due to its anchorage in certain theological interpretations, plus the elaboration of church organization around the need for business success and efficiency and the ideal of competitive achievement. It is further reinforced by the antigovernment posture which was inherited from the polygamy crisis.

Modern society is bringing changes which threaten the secular roots of economic individualism. With the development of a welfare oriented society, the worth of the individual is less and less dependent upon his individualistic accomplishments. At the same time, technological developments bring changes in the occupational structure, requiring more skill and knowledge, and less labor. New social movements are arising which argue for changes in the socioeconomic structure, favoring those who have traditionally resisted middle class individualism.

AGRARIAN INDIVIDUALISM AND THE NEGRO

The use of federal power to solve Negroes' problems, as in the civil rights legislation, is highly suspect among Mormons. This is partly because the federal government itself is regarded with distrust. In Missouri the government had denied civil protection to the Saints while, in the early Utah period, the government had protected the morals of America by prosecuting the Mormons.

As civil rights has become an interest of government, Latter-day Saints have responded with a ready made defensive posture; although Mormons claim to favor civil equality, support for civil rights programs is rare among the orthodox. It is interesting that among church writers apparently no apologist for the church's Negro policy has also defended civil rights legislation.

540

The agrarian individualist viewpoint considers economic independence a most fundamental kind of freedom. An expression of this is found in the views of a prominent church authority, expressed in interview [5].

"Negroes have their freedom, and they ought to be free, under the constitution — Free to enter into business if they want to, or be farmers, or anything."

In this context, the turmoil going on in American cities is seen as an attempt by Negroes to get what they don't deserve. Negroes are identified by many as opposed to traditional business values, to the dignity of hard work, and to independent striving as means to success. Another general authority made the following remarks, when asked to give his views on the racial issue.

"No race should be given special privileges. The Negroes are making many enemies in the way they're acting. Civil rights isn't the real question. No one should be given anything he hasn't earned."

The belief that Negroes are asking for special privileges, is undoubtedly reinforced by recent race riots and the destruction of property and lives. Negroes are perceived as out of harmony with traditional agrarian values which are so much a part of the Utah scene. The emphasis upon hard work as a route to success seems diametrically opposed to the strident demands for "freedom now." The black power movement and the elaboration of government programs seem out of harmony with the anticollectivist attitudes of rural and recently rural people. Thus, although many modern trends continue to threaten the individualistic ethic, an early or easy adaptation to the modern world seems unlikely.

THREAT AND RESPONSE

How does a religious institution respond when confronted by influences which threaten its most fundamental values? What is the nature of Mormonism's reaction to the problems which are introduced by modernizing secularism? How can the Mormon institution maintain its equanimity?

Successful adaptation of established religions is often very difficult because of their anchorage in sacred traditions. If uncertainty and danger associated with threats are great, institutional defense mechanisms are likely to be desperate, or even magical. Bronislaw Malinowski has suggested that magic emerges in precisely those situations where uncertainty and danger are most intense [10:25–36].

Modernizing secularism is experienced as an intense *danger* because it contains elements which conflict with a number of Mormonism's basic values. It challenges the belief in God, the relevance of traditional moral values, the appropriateness of a centralized authority structure with absolutist control, and a host of specific beliefs concerning man and his universe.

Modernizing secularism is also an intense *uncertainty* in that the traditional Mormon mentality cannot comprehend all of the things happening in today's world. Traditional concepts are inadequate to deal with the meanings of the cybernetics revolution, the hip generation, the civil rights movement, or international politics. The traditionalist's bewilderment is enhanced by the belief that important things should be simple and easily understood.

One way to avoid being endangered by uncertainties that are deeply threatening is to be very involved in other things. Activity and busy-ness are especially effective devices for achieving insulation from thoughts, feelings, and experiences which might be disturbing. If this results in the deepening of inner uncertainty, it nevertheless may give individuals an outer sense of equanimity and confidence.

Mormons have always believed in being active. In early church history, the priesthood of all worthy males, a complex office structure, and a doctrine of eternal progress were developed to encourage the activism necessary to build the Kingdom of God on earth. The need to master an environment under settlement conditions, to build homes, churches, schools, and temples, and to maintain cooperative farming made the emphasis upon activism especially functional. But that modernism which is disturbing the equilibrium of religious belief is also freeing man — giving him more leisure to think and doubt.

Within Mormonism, however, activism has not lost its moral significance. The word "active" is very important. It is the word most often used to describe the "good" member. Church activity is necessary, since it is an essential condition of worthiness.

Interestingly, church "activity" has come to refer almost exclusively to those kinds of church involvement which can be easily categorized or measured, to be used as evidence of worthiness when members are interviewed. Included are frequency of attendance at church meetings and at the temple, payment of tithes and donations, and keeping the Word of Wisdom.

Activity is further encouraged by the elaborate system of offices of the church, with positions always waiting to be filled. It is encouraged by a complex system of secretarial and clerical duties. Records are kept, statistics are compiled, reports are prepared, comparisons are announced.

All of this takes place in numerous meetings of various types and for all ages. A strong religious orientation exists in all of these activities; members believe that their "testimony of the gospel" is strengthened in church activities, including parties and dances. They gain a knowledge of truth by "doing." Testimony is itself a form of activism. Members are expected to stand up spontaneously at certain meetings and declare that they know the gospel is true. They are encouraged to do this especially when they experience doubt, because the very act is likely to bring inspired knowledge of the truth. The emphasis upon knowledge is significant, since knowledge replaces faith when one receives the inspiration of the Holy Ghost.

Activism has thus taken on ritualistic meanings of a quasi-magical intensity. Members stay involved and keep busy to avoid the doubt and uncertainty of a threatening world. They become deeply involved in inventing new ways to get and keep others active and to improve the statistical indicators. Activity for activity's sake becomes the mode. The expression of testimony, one kind of activism, often becomes a magical formula, a way of ending thought and discussion about controversial issues such as the Negro question which are so threatening to most Mormons.

Thus, one response of an institution threatened by "dangerous uncertainty" is to make outdated structures perform a magical defensive function. Another response, however, is to form alliances with institutions which are already performing magical defense functions. This latter possibility seems to attract certain elements in the church today.

Ezra Taft Benson, an apostle who was Secretary of Agriculture under President Eisenhower, epitomizes the interest in alliance with political ultraconservatism. In an address to the Latter-day Saint General Conference in 1965, Elder Benson stated,

> Before I left for Europe, I warned how the Communists were using the civil rights movement to promote revolution and eventual takeover of this country. When are we going to wake up? What do you know about the dangerous civil rights agitation in Mississippi? Do you fear the destruction of all vestiges of state government?
>
> Now Brethren, the Lord never promised there would not be traitors in the church. We have the ignorant, the sleepy and the deceived who provide temptations and avenues of apostasy for the unwary and the unfaithful, but we have a prophet at our head and he has spoken. Now what are we going to do about it? [14:255]

These words betray an intense concern with threats to faith, harmony, stability, and security in the civil rights movement, promulgated in part by traitors within the church.

This alliance of political and religious fundamentalism, an interesting nativist reaction, bears a compelling similarity to values developed in relation to the Ghost Dance of the Plains Indians. The Ghost Dance became important in the late nineteenth century when certain Plains Indian tribes were threatened by secularizing influences which had begun to transform their culture. The Ghost Dance was performed to bring back ancestors of the golden age. According to Ghost Dance doctrine, the buffalo would return, and the white man would be destroyed by a great wind.

544

The modern nativist reaction, increasingly popular in Mormon circles, seeks to bring back traditional mores, and to get rid of those traitors and evil elements who bring disturbance into the Mormon community. The willingness to employ such radical dogma, especially considering its nonreligious basis and its quasi-magical quality, suggests that the failure of nerve, the disturbance of faith, is profound.

In Europe, in the nineteenth century, the Roman Catholic church often found itself aligned with political conservatism, in what it saw as efforts at self-defense. Such alignments, however, cost the church heavy losses among the middle and working classes. When a church tries to defend itself by joining the intransigent stand for lost causes, it runs the risk of rendering itself a lost cause.

Believing their church to be divinely founded, Latter-day Saints tend to accept the unwarranted theological conclusion that it is thereby immune to the normal processes of historical causation. Even liberal, intelligent Mormons often do not see the great danger of their repeating costly errors made by other religious groups. They may also fail to observe the predicament of religious groups around them, not realizing that the confrontation with modernizing secularism is a worldwide phenomenon.

In an eloquent portrayal of the dilemma which faces traditional societies confronted by secularizing influences, Ruth Benedict cites the words of a Digger Indian chief [2:19].

> "God gave to every people a cup, a cup of clay, and from this cup they drank their life. . . . Our cup is broken now. It has passed away."

What will happen to the cup of the Mormons, from which they drink their life, under the complex stresses of modern society? One serious possibility is that separatist tendencies may increase, falling into place around the church's Negro policy and racial doctrine. When religious beliefs defend themselves, they often do so by incorporating or elaborating defense structures. In the process, they tend to become more central to the institution. Thus, when polygamy came under attack in early Utah history, it became more and more dominant and sacred, until many members came to view it as the most important church doctrine of all [1:239].

As the Negro policy runs into difficulty, it too may become more dominant. This would alter the church's structure to an extraordinary degree. The likelihood of such a denouement is conditioned by several other possibilities. What is the future of the church's intellectuals? Will the institution find a way to use their talent within its structure? Now that civil rights laws have been passed in Utah, as well as in the nation, will the legalistic temper of Mormon thought create for members an increased strain with regard to the Negro policy? If so, how many decades will pass before the strain has significant impact in decision making positions?

REFERENCES

1. Arrington, Leonard J: *Great Basin Kingdom* (Harvard University Press, Cambridge, Massachusetts) 1958.
2. Benedict, Ruth: *Patterns of Culture* (Houghton Mifflin Company, Boston, Massachusetts) 1956.
3. *Book of Mormon*, Book of Alma, chap 34, v 34.
4. *Book of Mormon*, Second Nephi, chap 2, v 25.
5. Brewer, David L: *Utah Elites and Utah Racial Norms* (doctoral dissertation, University of Utah, Modern Microfilm Co, Salt Lake City, Utah) 1966.
6. *Doctrine and Covenants*, sec 121, v 41–43.
7. *Hymns: Church of Jesus Christ of Latter-day Saints* (Church of Jesus Christ of Latter-day Saints, Salt Lake City, Utah) 1950. Come, Come, Ye Saints.
8. *Hymns: Church of Jesus Christ of Latter-day Saints* (Church of Jesus Christ of Latter-day Saints, Salt Lake City, Utah) 1950. Love at Home.
9. *Hymns: Church of Jesus Christ of Latter-day Saints* (Church of Jesus Christ of Latter-day Saints, Salt Lake City, Utah) 1950. O My Father.
10. Malinowski, Bronislaw: *Magic, Science, and Religion* (Doubleday & Company, Inc, Garden City, New York) 1948.

11. Nelson, Lowry: Mormons and the Negro, *The Nation*, vol 174, no 21, May 24, 1952.
12. O'Dea, Thomas F: *The Mormons* (University of Chicago Press, Chicago, Illinois) 1964.
13. Smith, Joseph: *History of the Church of Jesus Christ of Latter-day Saints*, vol 5, B H Roberts, ed (*Deseret News*, Salt Lake City, Utah) 1949.
14. Turner, Wallace: *The Mormon Establishment* (Houghton Mifflin Company, Boston, Massachusetts) 1966.

COMMENTARY

by Lowell Bennion

DAVID BREWER's essay on Mormonism contains insights and emphases that one might expect from someone who is looking at the movement both from within and as a sociologist. His paper points up the problems that organized religions, perhaps others as well as Mormonism, have in making themselves relevant in modern society.

This commentary will take issue with Professor Brewer on several points and then call attention to other aspects of contemporary Mormon culture.

Dr. Brewer has limited his perspective on the Mormon scene by centering his analysis largely on the Negro issue. This is said, admitting that the Negro issue is the most pressing social problem facing the LDS Church today and realizing too that Brewer is using the subject as a means of illustrating basic social processes. Nevertheless, there are many interesting things going on in the Mormon movement today quite unrelated to this issue.

Brewer tends also to identify the whole of Mormon culture with his particular emphases, which belies the complexity and diversity of Mormon society. Some of his characterizations are dominant; others represent a minor element, but they all give the impression of being pervasive. The reader who is not a Mormon might well come away from Brewer's essay thinking that all

547

Mormons are literalists, separatists, agrarian individualists, arch conservatists, that the general authorities are all old men of one mind, and that intellectuals play no role in the Church whatever. The Mormons are not single minded. A study of the voting patterns of Utah since 1932, for instance, will show that, with one or two exceptions, Utah has followed national trends regardless of the conservative influence of some church leaders. One has the feeling that Brewer is fitting reality into a model for which there is a substantial but insufficient basis. A few illustrations may justify this criticism.

In several places Dr. Brewer speaks of the holy Mormon community. This may be justified in a place or two, but it is a descriptive phrase foreign to contemporary Mormons, who are far too realistic and pragmatic to think of themselves in such sacred terms. Their priesthood, temples, and the Bible are called holy, but their community, never.

When Joseph Smith first recounted his visions of Deity and resurrected beings, he made God, Christ, and personal immortality so real and vivid in contrast to the abstract language of Christian creeds that Mormon writers and preachers made the most of the contrast by making man and mortality the prototype for God and eternity. This extreme anthropomorphism, represented by Brewer's reference to God's wife, is rarely mentioned in *contemporary* Mormonism.

Likewise his reference to the garments providing physical protection is a hark back to an earlier age. The many car accidents in recent decades have undermined this simple faith once held by some. Garments are symbolic and have spiritual meaning for those who find meaning in them.

Dr. Brewer gives the impression that economic individualism is a new mode of life developed in postpolygamy days after 1890. He writes, "the cooperativist orientation which characterized the early Mormon farming community gradually gave way to agrarian individualism, during the Utah period." This is misleading. Strong individualism has been present among the Mormons from the beginning, both in doctrine and in economic enterprise. Efforts to develop communitarianism both in Missouri and in

548

Utah were halfhearted, mostly short lived, and ended in failure. Brigham Young who introduced the cooperative mercantile business (ZCMI) and the Second United Order was a first-rate capitalist himself throughout his thirty years in Utah. The truth is that individualism and cooperation have existed side by side in Mormon society from the beginning until this day, but they express themselves in different ways from decade to decade. O'Dea has illustrated this dualism in a contemporary Mormon community [5]. The Mormons inherited the Protestant Ethic, which was strengthened by Mormon theology, and the impact of technology on Mormon society may not be greatly different from its impact on American society at large [4].

It is not clear to this reviewer what Brewer means when he says that agrarian individualism "has continued until the present" and speaks of it as part of Mormon society today. Mormonism is not an agrarian society any more than America is. Mormons are caught up in the maelstrom of business and professional life. Not a single general authority now serving has ever made a living on a farm. They are largely lawyers and businessmen, though they may entertain some nostalgia for a simpler age.

THE NEGRO PROBLEM

The Negro problem is the most critical social issue facing the Mormon Church today. Brewer is right in indicating that the fact that Negroes are barred from holding the priesthood in the Church is related to the failure of Mormons as a people to be in the forefront of any civil rights movement. This situation, as he clearly presents, has increased racial prejudice among Mormons. Individual Mormons, notably George Romney, have worked hard and effectively to promote civil rights despite the lethargy of the people as a whole.

That Mormons should be found discriminating against a minority group in America is ironic since they themselves suffered persecution for sixty years and more. Moreover, they believe the constitution is divinely inspired. Basic Mormon theology and the

549

Mormon ethic give no justification whatever for racial discrimination.

This last assertion may surprise both Mormons and those who are not Mormons, but withholding the priesthood from the Negro is not a doctrine of the Church; it is church practice, which needs to be justified by church doctrine. Nowhere in Mormon scripture is it stated that a Negro cannot hold the priesthood. Nowhere is this practice justified on the basis of fundamental doctrine pertaining to God, man, or Christ. No new *revelation* is needed to change doctrine; there need only be a change of *practice*.

There are of course passages in the Old Testament, *Book of Mormon*, and even a few in the New Testament which can be used to justify ethnocentrism, but the overall consensus is weighted heavily on the side of God's impartiality, the brotherhood of man, and equal access to all the gifts of the Gospel by all men [1].

If this be true, why do the Mormons deny the Negro the priesthood? No Mormon really knows. The practice apparently began in the early 1850s under the leadership of Brigham Young in a day when slavery, though disputed, was still part of the natural order and the American scene. Once established, it has been explained and rationalized in various ways, all based on the assumption that the Negro was either neutral or less valiant for Christ in his premortal existence — a theory for which there is not a scrap of evidence either in scripture or logic.

This Negro issue illustrates the diversity of feeling and opinion among Mormons on social issues today. Not only academicians and liberal "intellectuals" are disturbed by the practice but orthodox and nonacademicians as well. Even general authorities are not of one mind on this problem and struggle over it as does the body of the Church.

Institutional factors stand in the way of change. Authority is vested in the prophet-president of the Church. He alone is authoritative in matters of doctrinal interpretation and Church policy. Mormons are loyal to their prophet, believing him to be spokesman for God. In their basic moral conviction, many would like to see the Negro have all the gifts and privileges of life which they themselves enjoy. But many Mormons do not agitate for this change because their tradition is to believe in prophetic leadership. To question this is to question the validity of their faith. Most Mormons would adjust quickly, many happily, to a prophetic announcement that the time has come for all men to enjoy the gifts of God on the same impartial basis.

LITERALISM

Dr. Brewer characterizes the Mormons as literalists, though he admits that general authorities have been selective in their literalism. This point merits underlining. Mormonism began with a flood of new revelations which clearly established the Bible as a good but incomplete guide to religion. It was to be supplemented by continuous revelation from God but given to his "servants *in their weakness, after the manner of their language that they might come to an understanding.*" Revelation was to be adapted to the needs of the time and to the thinking of men as well.

Mormon leaders have been quite free and diversified in their interpretation of scripture. Leading scriptorians such as James E. Talmage and Joseph Fielding Smith have agreed on repentance and baptism but have been far apart in relating the Gospel to life in some areas. Mormon leaders are not scripture bound; they talk of practical matters in the present. They are not sheep in one fold, but independent and divergent in attitude and viewpoint. Some of the oldest are most liberal. Ezra Taft Benson, friendly to the John Birch movement, speaks for himself on political issues, not for his colleagues and not for the Church.

This commentary will be concluded by looking at the direction in which the Church is going and by raising some questions relating to possibilities.

A most basic question is whether an institution as it grows in number, in age, in tradition, in complexity of organization can be true to its original idea and purpose. Of great interest too is the definition of its purpose in the ongoing historical process.

In the pioneer stage of Mormon history, living one's religion and meeting the demands of daily existence by building communities, conquering the desert, gathering to Zion, preaching the Gospel were one and the same. Today, a Mormon can, if he will, separate his business or professional life from his religious living. Some do and some do not.

Much effort is expended by the Church in missionary service, temple work for the living and dead, extensive church building programs, and in Church organizational work — teaching, recreation, education. Efforts are made to help young and old to keep the faith of their fathers, to marry in the Church, to be unspotted from tobacco, alcohol, and unchastity, to promote good marriages, prevent divorce, and to qualify youth for vocational life.

The Mormons try to take care of their own. Vast holdings in cooperatively owned and operated farms and minor industries provide for the material wants of members in need. Home teachers, priesthood quorums, and women of relief societies move in to help any member in time of illness, accident, or other crisis.

The increasingly impersonal, urbanized society of today which leads to much loneliness and alienation among men is counteracted in Mormon society by an elaborate system of primary relationships fostered by the Church. From early childhood to the grave, an active Mormon is a participant in an intimate fellowship; he belongs to his group; he calls fellow members brothers and sisters and greets them by name with a handshake.

Lacking in the contemporary Mormon movement is an examination of social issues from a social point of view. The curricula of the Church and sermons from the pulpit deal almost exclusively with theological beliefs, religious history, scriptural understanding, and the application of Gospel principles to personal and family life. Public issues of the day — civil rights, the United Nations, war in Vietnam, trade with communist nations, urban renewal, the etiology of crime and its treatment — are never examined in the light of Christ's teachings or of the theology of the Church. The social morality of the Hebrew prophets has not been revived in this century.

One international, world issue is talked of in the Church, namely communism and, to a lesser extent, socialism. Beginning with the influence of that able Mormon prophet-statesman, J. Ruben Clark, Jr., in the 1930s, a number of leaders, including Elder Benson, have been outspoken critics of these two movements because they are seen as destructive of freedom and individual development. But attacks on communism have been, in the main, quite general in character, with emotional overtones, and have not examined carefully the underlying political, economic, and social causes [2; 3].

In some Protestant and Catholic circles in contemporary theology, there seems to be a trend away from the concept of God as Absolute with an emphasis on man's becoming an active partner with God, who needs man to help fight his battles. This is an old theme in Mormon theology, which has limited God's power by the coeternal existence of matter, time, space, law, and other uncreated aspects of the Universe, relieving God of responsibility for both natural and moral evil, and making freedom, not God-given but, inherent in the eternal intelligence of man [6]. This radical kind of Mormon-Christian theology is little known either by Mormons or by those who are not Mormons, but its practical implications are a significant part of the Mormon ethos.

Mormonism has been called humanism in a context of faith. One of its presidents said, "a religion which cannot save a man temporally, cannot save him spiritually." Whether the humanistic, this-worldly values in the Mormon tradition will receive emphasis, and in what direction, in modern society will be of great interest. Can the Church reject modernity and yet help people to self-realization through the added knowledge and resources available in this century?

These are a few of the concerns and issues Mormons entertain as they live in the twentieth century.

REFERENCES

1. Book of Mormon: II Nephi 26:23–33.
2. McMurrin, Sterling M: *The Philosophical Foundations of Mormonism* (The University of Utah Press, Salt Lake City, Utah) 1959.

3. McMurrin, Sterling M: *The Theological Foundations of Mormonism* (The University of Utah Press, Salt Lake City, Utah) 1965.

4. Nelson, Lowry: *The Mormon Village* (The University of Utah Press, Salt Lake City, Utah) 1952.

5. O'Dea, Thomas: A Comparative Study of the Role of Values in Social Action in Two Southwestern Communities, *American Sociological Review*, vol 18, no 6, Dec 1953.

6. White, Owen Kendall, jr: *Mormon New-Orthodoxy* (master's thesis at the University of Utah, Salt Lake, Utah) 1967, gives an excellent review of Mormon theological trends.

14. MARSHALL McLUHAN, PLAYFUL PROPHET

by Allen Lacy

IT'S PROBABLY BEST at the outset to admit the worst about Marshall McLuhan and his recent "book," *The Medium is the Massage*. McLuhan is, among other things, something of a fad. Just as academic year 1965–1966 was the year of death-of-God theology, 1967–1968 is the year of McLuhan. He has become a celebrity, a recording star, a popular oracle. He has even become an extraordinarily well-paid college professor, if the newspaper accounts are correct. And he shows clear evidence of enjoying himself very much indeed amidst affluence and popularity. "All that remains for McLuhan," one of my colleagues sighed recently, "is to have an abridged version of *Understanding Media* in *Reader's Digest* – unless he can somehow manage to get quoted by Twiggy." It is abundantly clear that for some persons McLuhan lacks the requisite seriousness to be taken seriously.

For such persons, *The Medium is the Massage* is little apt to create confidence in McLuhan's credentials. It is, again admitting the worst, a cute book, from the title page on. It has a multiple author (McLuhan and his friend Quentin Fiore, who designed the graphics, plus a rather puzzling functionary — Jerome Agel described as a "coordinator," whatever that is). Furthermore, it frustrates, by obvious design, the usual expectations a reader has of a book: that the editor will have imposed an inconspicuously consistent style on typography and pagination; that the text will be reasonably well-ordered, beginning at the beginning, continuing through the middle, and proceeding to the end; and that text and illustrations will have a close and immediately obvious mutual relation. In no respect does *The Medium is the Massage* con-

555

form. Typography is extremely erratic, shifting inexplicably from boldface to regular to italic type, and from one type size to another. Occasionally the text is printed in quite singular ways: upside-down, slanted across the page, even backwards. (Pages 54–55 must be read in a mirror!) Pagination is equally curious and unconventional: page numbers sometimes appear at the top of pages, sometimes at the bottom, and there are several long stretches with no numbers at all. Furthermore, it matters little where the reader begins. To work from the middle toward both ends would be as sensible as beginning on page 1. And the book could easily be shorter, or longer, with very little difference. The illustrations are disparate, to say the least: Grant Wood's "American Gothic," a female cellist clad only in a transparent raincoat, the Fairmount Water Works in Philadelphia, a giant walk-in vagina of wire and papier-mâché, children of the past century attending looms, Amherst seniors walking out on Secretary McNamara, Marilyn Monroe applauding Khrushchev, the procession of world rulers at the Kennedy funeral – images united only by their common appearance in the same jittery scrapbook. Nor is the text any less fragmented and incoherent than the illustrations. It is composed largely of quotations from such divergent sources as A. N. Whitehead and W. C. Fields, William Wordsworth and John Dewey, Michael Faraday and Lao-Tze, J. Robert Oppenheimer and *Variety*, John Cage and Bob Dylan – and a great number of quotations from McLuhan's own previous writings.

The Medium is the Massage, then, is clearly a very odd book, and all the more so when one considers the paradoxical relation of the author to his product. McLuhan is widely understood to believe that the dominance of print over other media has reached its end. The book, in short, is obsolete . . . yet McLuhan himself has added four books to the world's libraries. Perhaps this irony is inconclusive, since he has recently produced a long-playing record of a "happening" also called *The Medium is the Massage*, a production in which crucial parts of his doctrine are uttered by a parrot. There is, however, the more embarrassing matter of his rejection of copyright on pp. 122–123. Copyright

556

laws are obsolete, outmoded by such technical developments as xerography. But *The Medium is the Massage* is itself copyrighted, and it is doubtful whether either Bantam Books or Random House, the publishers of the paper- and hard-bound versions respectively, would look kindly toward the kind of "instant publishing" by xerography that McLuhan describes on p. 123. Concerning this matter, one of my book-oriented friends (himself a man of sizable royalties protected by copyright laws) announced that he thought McLuhan to be somewhat disingenuous at best, and not to be taken seriously until he turns the royalties from *The Medium is the Massage* over to a relief fund for unemployed typesetters!

McLuhan's typographical games with his readers aside, his interest in popular culture (which many persons take, mistakenly, to be entire approval), marks him for some as an intellectual clown, unworthy of serious attention. I submit, however, that McLuhan is a deadly serious man, but utterly free of sentimentality and moralism, who for perfectly good reasons of strategy adopts increasingly "non-serious" means of communication — and that he therefore *incarnates* the problem he would seduce his reader into seeing. To argue this thesis necessitates the somewhat thankless task of explaining parables, exegeting jokes, analyzing play, and so on. Nevertheless, despite McLuhan's own strategy, his doctrine is capable of more solemn statement than he gives it in *The Medium is the Massage*.

McLuhan's central point, that the medium is in some sense the message (that is, his understanding of the creative, rather than passive or neutral, function of media in human perception), is nothing really new, though it is so far from being a part of contemporary common sense as to be startling. Since the late eighteenth century, beginning perhaps with G. C. Lichtenberg, more and more thinkers have begun to suspect that the traditional Western understanding of the relations between thought, language, and reality is incorrect. Ingrained in Western thinking is the notion that words, language, concepts, judgments, syntax, propositions, and so on, are simply neutral tools. According to this common model, reality is "out there," but available *immedi-*

557

ately (without the intervention of media) for our perception, thought, understanding, and manipulation. There comes a time, however, when we want also to *talk about* our perceptions of reality — and thus, the birth of speech. Language is simply a vehicle of communication, a convenient medium whereby men transfer among themselves their already-existing judgments, thoughts, truths, perceptions. Truth is simply the conformity of language to objective reality. In short, the medium is *not* the message. (One corollary of this view is the cultural imperialism so deeply ingrained in Western thinking. Faced with the perfectly coherent and consistent alternative systems of belief of non-European peoples, the European can only conclude that such thought is "primitive." Most anthropologists have learned better, but it would be overstating the case to conclude therefore that cultural imperialism is dead.)

Increasingly, however, philosophers and anthropologists have departed from such linguistic absolutism. Kant made a start in pointing out that such basic forms of intuition as time and space, and such categories of thought as causality and substance, cannot be ascribed to things-in-themselves. He failed, however, to recognize the possibility that these categories are not universal structures of human consciousness by virtue of physiology. They belong to the knowing mind . . . but the knowing mind differs quite a bit in structure from culture to culture. In short, perception is learned in language-systems which are themselves contingent and culturally-variable. Furthermore, we can never be aware of our own language-system, which is the basis of our perception, unless something intervenes — perhaps an anthropologist or someone else who has learned a structural awareness of the role of language-systems in knowledge and perception, via his deliberate encounter with other cultures, or via his accidental dissatisfaction with his own. Increasingly, there is an awareness of the creative relation between "word" and "world," between language and reality. Language is not simply a vehicle for transporting objective facts and information. It enters into our perception of reality at the outset. Facts and information are inescapably shaped by the language in which they are conveyed. In short. the medium *is* the message.

But the doctrine is larger. Information is transmitted in non-verbal ways, too. Other transactions, not necessarily verbal in any explicit way, also shape our world by shaping our perception. Systems of kinship and inheritance, rituals and myths, patterns of marriage and child-raising, methods of using space in constructing dwellings and arranging clusters of buildings — all embody the same invisible creative force in societies that language does. In a certain extended sense, these things are themselves languages, for they pattern perception even as they convey information. Here again, perception is learned without being explicitly taught, and without the process becoming perceptible or conscious. "Media" thus enable us to grasp reality, to perceive, to conceive, to manipulate much of our environment. But media also become part of our environment — the invisible part. Their invisibility comes from our participation in them, that is to say, from their very function.

This, then, is part of McLuhan's message — a commitment to the theorem that "languages," or, better, "media" (which of course vary historically and culturally) give us our "world." The corollary is that a very large part of our environment — its structure, its very architecture — is systematically invisible and must remain so unless something intervenes. McLuhan is not moving on virgin territory here by any means, but he does make a large contribution to a general theory of communications with enormous implications for philosophy, anthropology, historiography, and politics, not to mention history of religions and systematic theology, and he advances substantially an ongoing dialogue among such persons as G. C. Lichtenberg, Wilhelm von Humboldt, Miguel de Unamuno, Benjamin Whorf, Ludwig Wittgenstein, Weston LaBarre, Kenneth Boulding, and Claude Lévi-Strauss, to name only a few.

A second serious point implicit in *The Medium is the Massage* is that we live in difficult, possibly even apocalyptic, times. Despite his often exuberant optimism, McLuhan's world is a distressful place in which hope is far from easy or automatic: a world of "wars, revolutions, civil uprisings," dominated by a pervasive cold war fought with "subtle electronic informational media" and by sporadic hot wars, "tragic games," fought in "the backyards of the world with the old technologies"; a world in which the old arrangements, "the old civic, state, and national groupings have become unworkable"; a world of I.C.B.M.'s and thermonuclear weapons (pp. 9, 138, 18). Easily the most distressful feature of McLuhan's world, however, is that at present human beings don't seem to be coping very well with its problems. The traditional methods of coping (schools, political parties, the organization of expertise in bureaucratic structures) fail so disastrously in perceiving the structure of the present age that they are worse than useless. "We look at the present through a rear-view mirror" (p. 75). Our educational systems are modeled on outmoded nineteenth-century patterns of assembly-lines and inventories. Furthermore, the functions they serve — the production of specialists to perform fragmented jobs, and the classification of relatively scarce information — are anachronistic in a world where electric circuitry is rapidly abolishing the fragmentation of work into specialized jobs and where information has exploded into superabundance. Our educational establishment is trying to instruct, when it should be "probing," "exploring," and teaching "recognition of the language of forms." The end result of the perceptual failure of education in its present organization is that it manages to "suppress all the natural direct experience of youth," the drop-out being its natural product. The meaning of the widespread unrest among students today is that, programmed by the pervasive media of our time to want "total involvement," they cannot accept the goals implicit in nineteenth-century forms of education: "the young today reject goals. They want roles" (pp. 18, 19, 100, 101 *passim*). But not only education — politics is similarly involved in anachronistic gestures, outmoded responses to a new environment. The old politics, based on what McLuhan calls "a great consensus of separate and distinct viewpoints" (what C. Wright Mills frequently called "a community of publics"), is no longer possible, given the new kinds of human mutual involvement brought about by electric technology. "Politics offers yesterday's answers to today's questions" (p. 22). Thought itself — and certainly rhetoric — shares in the deterioration of education and politics as effective

instruments of coping with environment. "Our most impressive words and thoughts betray us — they refer us only to the past, not to the present." (p. 63). For example: *honor, glory, free world, commitment*, and (very curious, perhaps an example of the orientalization of the West of which McLuhan speaks?) *"face."*

McLuhan's sobriety about our time is far from unique, of course. He shares it with Barry Goldwater, among others. The uncommon thing is that McLuhan sees the turmoil of the present as essentially a conflict between the media and technologies of the past and those of the present, a conflict between perceptual responses appropriate to past media and responses necessitated by new media. Ours is an "Age of Anxiety" largely because it is a transitional period from one technology to another. We are everywhere "trying to do yesterday's jobs with today's concepts" [p. 8]. "In the name of 'progress' our official culture is trying to force the new media to do the work of the old" [p. 81]. To get McLuhan's point fully, it is helpful to recognize that the V-2's over London and the *Enola Gay* over Hiroshima constitute "information" of vast and dire import. McLuhan writes in *The Medium is the Massage* [p. 138], "It is no longer convenient, or suitable, to use the latest technologies for fighting our wars, because the latest technologies have rendered war meaningless. The hydrogen bomb is history's exclamation point. It ends an age-long sentence of manifest violence!" It is to be hoped that he is correct, that the meaninglessness of these technologies will in fact preclude their use. It should be pointed out, however, that the *rhetoric* which went along with the old technologies of printing, gunpowder, and nationalism is still in daily use. (Most Americans, when they think of foreign relations, adopt unconsciously a conceptual political analysis originating with John Locke: "state of nature," "state of war," "state of civil government," "act of aggression," and so on. The danger here is that Locke's model is almost entirely mechanistic, and thus appropriate only to a world which has long since vanished under the impact of the enormous speeds and energies of modern technology. There is *no* answer in *Of Civil Government* to the problems of anti-colonial movements, guerilla warfare, nuclear weaponry, or cold war.)

Despite his underlying sobriety in *The Medium is the Massage*, McLuhan is no pessimist. "There is absolutely no inevitability as long as there is a willingness to contemplate what is happening" (p. 25). But how, precisely, *is* one to contemplate what is happening, if what is happening is the result of active, but invisible, environmental processes and structures? "The ground rules, pervasive structure, and over-all patterns of environment," McLuhan tells us, "elude easy perception" (p. 68). But if we are to contemplate what is happening, and then act on our contemplation, the invisible must become visible. This is more than a structural necessity; it is also a unique historical necessity of our time, because of the enormous power and speed of our new technology, compared with previous technologies. McLuhan argues that writing (information at a distance) created armies and the conditions of warfare. The computer, the I.C.B.M., the nuclear warhead — all alter the political and military equation drastically. Mistakes are instantaneous in their consequences today. We simply can afford no longer to live with an invisible environment, nor with the old fragmented geopolitical patterns of perception. But the question remains, how do we "see" the media, the modes of perception in which we dwell?

McLuhan's answer lies in his notion of "anti-environments." If we are to see what is structurally invisible, a counter-structure is required, which confers visibility. McLuhan suggests several possibilities. First, there are artists, poets, and other kinds of sleuths. "Anti-environments, or countersituations made by artists, provide means of direct attention and enable us to see and understand more clearly" (p. 68). One thinks of Picasso's *Guernica*, which conveys better than any newsreel the horrors of bombing civilian populations — or of Andy Warhol's soup cans and Brillo pads, which lay bare the gay banality of the supermarket. His antisocial character confers on the artist a clear vision of the world and an ability to make the invisible plainly visible to others. "The poet, the artist, the sleuth — whoever sharpens our perception tends to be antisocial; rarely 'well-adjusted,' he cannot go along with currents and trends" (p. 88). Another prime source of the anti-environmental vision is what McLuhan calls *amateurism*, which is anti-environmental because it "seeks the development of the total awareness of the individual and the critical awareness of the groundrules of society." Amateurism is successful because "the amateur can afford to lose," and thus can afford to venture what the professional, who "tends to accept uncritically the groundrules of his environment," cannot (p. 93). McLuhan himself is an amateur in the very areas where he makes the greatest contributions. A professor of English, he is unusually wide-read in such esoterica as anthropology and history of technology. And his remarks on professionalism versus amateurism are worth further exploration. Certainly many of the major intellectual forces in our civilization are the work of gifted and insightful amateurs. One thinks of the highly unprofessional philosophers Marx, Nietzsche, and Unamuno, whose work is considerably more vital and interesting today than the work of their more professional competitors. Sören Kierkegaard would apparently qualify neither as professional theologian nor churchman nor philosopher. McLuhan mentions Michael Faraday as a scientific example of the creative amateur: one could certainly add the names of Darwin and Mendel. Inasmuch as the founder of a profession is by logical necessity an amateur, Sigmund Freud would qualify, though most of his disciples would not. One thinks further of the often-depressing silence of our own experts in matters concerning the public welfare. With a few exceptions such as J. Robert Oppenheimer — whose experience was untypical in many ways — scientific advisors and technical experts are often so imprisoned by their professionalism that they fail to see the larger issues posed for society by their own work. It is no accident that many of the full-page ads in *The New York Times*, open letters on political and moral questions of warfare, pollution, unemployment, and so on, are signed not by qualified experts, but by amateurs: clergymen, theologians, historians, musicians, artists, playwrights, and so on. At present, our government is richly blessed with councils of experts. Perhaps it should also have its councils of amateurs: in matters of social policy, as in matters of love, the amateur very often has an advantage over the professional.

To contemplate what is happening, then, it is useful to consider the concurrent anti-environments of artists and amateurs, whose common witness is clear enough. In the last age of transition, at the end of the Middle Ages, artists and amateurs responded to the new medium of print with a common enthusiasm for detachment, lineality, sequentiality, fragmentation, thus clearly revealing what the new age would be like. In our time, artists are urging simultaneity on us. *Our* new age demands "retribalization," abandonment of the fragmented and fixed viewpoint, and discovery of the "technique of suspended judgment" (p. 69). We must explore the use of "not single but multiple models for exploration." The old rationality of analysis and classification must be replaced by "probing" of all sensory fronts simultaneously, and by the tentative use of multiple models of explanation.

*   *   *

McLuhan, I think, is really in the business of *transcendence* — of getting above our immediate situation, or, to use his own metaphor, "probing" about in it to find out what it's like, and then communicating something of what he finds. But even more than communicating the conclusions of his own probes, he is, on his own account, interested in getting his readers to make their own probes. "I want observations, not agreement," he tells Gerald Stearn in an interview recently published in *Encounter* (June 1967). Again and again in lectures and published interviews he characterizes his work as descriptive rather than prescriptive. Similarly, he rejects completely the moralistic standpoint. Moralism gets in the way of observation, for "the moralist typically substitutes anger for perception," hoping that "many people will mistake his irritation for insight" (*Encounter*). But it would be mistaken to think McLuhan an uncommitted, neutral, or aesthetic spectator after the Kierkegaardian model. It is abundantly clear in his writings that he wants the world changed. Indeed, it must be changed, for it's changing already.

"The medium, or process, of our time — electronic technology —
is reshaping and restructuring . . . every aspect of our personal
life . . . forcing us to reconsider practically every thought,
every action, and every institution formerly taken for granted"
(p. 8). Even should human beings remain completely passive,
there is still a great force making for change: popular culture,
transmitted electrically, an "active" and "not necessarily benign"
force (p. 100). The question is not, will there be change? It is
rather, what kind of change: haphazard, drifting, and blind . . .
or deliberate, based on accurate observation and programmed
with the genuine best interests of human beings in mind? If
change is to be deliberate and benign, it must be based on understanding: understanding of the effects of the new media and
technologies; and understanding that the new technologies themselves are capable of being programmed. "If you want to change
the world," McLuhan tells Gerald Stearn, "you must understand
it." As it is, we are shaped by a largely-invisible environment.
But properly understood — made visible — the environment is
susceptible of "formulation, patterning, shaping" (*Encounter*).
"We have already reached a point," he writes, "where remedial
control, born out of knowledge of media and their total effects
on all of us, must be exerted. How shall the new environment be
programmed now that we have become so involved with each
other?" (p. 12). There are two disjunctive possibilities: either
haphazard change — almost certainly disastrous and Orwellian,
given the enormously efficient speed and energy of modern technology — or deliberate artifice, conscious change, directed
toward building a more livable world through the new technologies. "We have become aware of the possibility of arranging the
entire human environment as a work of art, as a teaching machine designed to maximize perception and to make everyday
learning a process of discovery" (p. 68).

It is abundantly clear, I think, that McLuhan belongs to the
best intellectual traditions of the West, among the great emanci-
pators — among those persons who have sought to enlarge human
freedom by making us aware of forces, situations, structures, or
things, previously unperceived, which nevertheless have power

to shape — often to distort — human existence. It would not be farfetched to draw at least a structural comparison between Freud and McLuhan. For Freud, human life was often warped by deep unconscious forces restricting the range of choice. And through a process of mapping out these forces, fundamentally a descriptive process, Freud sought to increase the therapeutic possibilities of rationality, consciousness, choice, and freedom. "Where id was, there shall ego be." Similarly, for McLuhan, where invisible media are, there is potentially a genuinely human environment — a corporate world of persons, rather than a fragmented world of isolated individuals, or an all-too-tribalized commune of media-slaves.

Why, though, *The Medium is the Massage* — a playful scrapbook, full of games and puns and frivolity, albeit mixed with darker images and premonitions? If McLuhan has serious things to say, shouldn't he say them seriously, rather than upside-down, backwards, and hindpart to? Shouldn't serious things be said with decorum, or at least with footnotes and bibliography?

The answer to this question lies partly in McLuhan's understanding of the functional and strategic importance of anti-environments, partly in his analysis of our media-imprisoned world. It is extraordinarily difficult for a serious message to make itself heard. There are many more people in our world than there used to be, and most of them are talking, delivering serious messages of one sort or another. Simply stating something seriously is no guarantee it will be heard. The soapbox is universal. Serious statement and moralistic rhetoric are daily bread for our spirits. In our world, *everything* is said seriously: from the merchandising of stomach pills to the dissemination of military and political advice leading only to Armageddon, the most suspicious enterprises are clothed in the highest rhetoric. Furthermore, if McLuhan is correct, the traditionally serious institutions of society — education, science, politics, and very often the pulpit — are compromised by their failure to understand the effects of media and the nature of the transitional period from the old, print-dominated technology to the new electric environment. Seriousness? That's the business of the experts, the professionals. Expertise, however, has an odd way of being counterproductive, of adopting the most dangerous sort of narrow utilitarianism: as Herbert Marcuse has pointed out, the rationality of expertise often turns out to be in the service of shockingly irrational goals. How, then, is a serious amateur to make his voice heard?

McLuhan's own answer to this question is the use of humor. "Humor — as a probe of our environment — of what's really going on — affords us our most appealing anti-environmental tool" (p. 92). Humor is McLuhan's key stratagem in his ultimate purpose of making people see their world clearly enough to act on it. Early in his book, he writes, "When two seemingly disparate elements are imaginatively posed, put in apposition in new and unique ways, startling discoveries often result" (p. 10). And humor is based precisely upon such juxtaposition. Perhaps the comic vision is part of the salvation of our time. If McLuhan is right, it may be that Jules Feiffer and Russell Baker, Art Buchwald and Dick Gregory, are ultimately more effective in building a livable and humane world than Walter Lippmann or James Reston. And if the comedy of *The Medium is the Massage* is at all effective, it may be among the major therapies of our time.

* * *

McLuhan's analysis of the structural effects of media on perception is of enormous suggestive value, I believe, for understanding the religious situation of our time. Himself a practicing Roman Catholic, McLuhan makes little attempt to draw out the implications of his system for religious matters (see, however, the interview in *Encounter*, p. 50). Nevertheless, his "probes" bristle with exciting possibilities in this regard. In what follows, I will attempt only to mark out a few main areas of possible exploration, restricting myself largely to Protestantism.

1. McLuhan's writings, especially *The Gutenberg Galaxy*, open a new path for exploring the constellation of events and personalities surrounding the Reformation of the sixteenth century. Historically, the connections between print and Protestantism have long been known. Any reasonably well-informed college sophomore knows that the printing press made it possible for Luther's Ninety-five Theses to gain very rapid and wide

dissemination, turning what was the isolated questioning of one university teacher into a turbulent historical movement in very short order. The printing of Bibles made every Protestant his own priest — often to the chagrin of conservatives like Luther — and had enormous effect in stimulating education towards universal literacy, in promoting nationalism and national literatures, in dissolving traditional authorities and systems and producing new ones.

McLuhan, however, opens an entirely new line of inquiry. The medium of print is not just a vehicle: it has its own message. The theological revolution of the sixteenth century is a conceptual revolution resting on a technological foundation. The historian has seen the Reformation as essentially the outbreak of effective religious differences (schism, parties, acrid disputes, violent pamphlet warfare on every side, and finally open and actual bloodshed). Obviously, there is abundant evidence of difference: Lutherans, Roman Catholics, Anabaptists and other radicals, Calvinists, Anglicans, and so on to the scores of denominations produced by Christians in early modern times. The things that divide Christians intellectually from the sixteenth to the twentieth centuries are obvious. But McLuhan opens a new avenue into the things that unite them, even when the process of fragmentation first gets underway. A church historian with a firm grasp on McLuhan's understanding of the effects of print on perception may well be able to do a great deal with the thesis that all of the various theological parties of the sixteenth century were coping with perceptual problems brought about by the introduction of the new media of print. Particularly worth exploring are the violent contrasts between Luther and the Anabaptists of the 1520's. Luther was an extraordinarily complex man, caught in many ways between the old and the new: between the authority of the corporate Church and the claims of individual conscience; between the old unity of the *corpus christianum* and the emerging religious nationalisms. Luther was deeply conservative in many ways. Much of his thought points into the past rather than toward the modern. He was unbothered by sequential necessities in his writing of theology: his concept of time was richly non-lineal, productive of much paradox. And he was a man of staggering anxieties and self-doubting. In comparison with Luther, the Anabaptists were much more confident, much more modern men. Their theology, while it lacks the richness of Luther's, is much more consistent, simple, and direct . . . and much more individualistic. In Anabaptist theology, the prime emphasis is on the individual believer. The Church is a community of individual believers; consider, in this connection, the weight given in Anabaptist theology to *believer's* baptism, *believer's* personal confession, *believer's* sanctification, and the *believer's* shunning of non-believers. The theological conflict between Luther and the Anabaptists comes largely over the issue of infant baptism, but the larger perceptual issue would seem to concern the nature of the Christian's life in *time*. For Luther, time is rich and simultaneous. In the life of the Christian, there is great temporal depth. Each moment of his life refers to the Incarnation, Crucifixion, and Resurrection of Christ. Each moment in his life refers, further, to his own baptism. Baptism takes place in infancy, but it is never completed until a man dies. The entire life of a Christian is an act of baptism. Such thinking seemed only devious to the Anabaptists. Baptism takes place in a single moment, and it brings about a before-and-after change in the believer. Baptism involves a freely-willed decision, and it therefore makes very little sense to baptize newborn infants. Most of the differences between Luther and the left-wing sectarians would seem to flow from underlying differences on the question of the nature of temporality.

2. Using McLuhan's analysis, a variety of Protestant popular theology, especially common in America, makes a new kind of sense. I refer to what might be called "segregationalist Protestantism," but with the caveat that the reference includes more than racial views. Segregationalist Protestantism comprises a cluster of beliefs, apprehensions, vague and not-so-vague feelings: that Sunday is a holy day, but the rest of the week is for business as usual; that life on earth is followed by a kind of spatially-located week-long Sunday; that ministers are better than other people, or at least holier; that the business of the

clergy is tending to religious matters (the specialization of labor in the spiritual realm!), and that they had best leave political, economic, and social issues strictly alone; that the church is a building, archaic in architecture and occupied only on Sundays, except for minor weekday functions such as choir practice and except for the labors of the church mice who mimeograph the Sunday bulletins; and that Christianity is terribly important, except that it doesn't have to do with anything very much except itself. After one reads McLuhan, all of these things make a certain kind of sense, not as theology but as perceptual patterns created by the media of a preceding age. Can it be suggested that the man in whom the visual sense, strengthened by the repeatability of the process of printing, dominates is a man who is likely to see religion as separated from everything else, and that he will build religious "community" in the image of his own fragmented point of view?

3. As McLuhan describes the present time, a new sensory ratio of total involvement of all the senses is now emerging, creating new sorts of sensibility, but amidst the remainder of the old perceptual patterns created by the technology of print. If he is correct here, we can expect to see new kinds of perceptual patterns in religion, new notions, new departures, all tending in the direction of involvement — and also new kinds of conflict in religious communities as the new technologies suggest patterns of innovation in religious responsibility and action, meeting resistance from adherents of the older patterns. There would seem to be abundant evidence of just such a thing. Protestant churches are, at some echelons, in a highly innovational mood. There is significant experimentation with new kinds of campus ministry. Some local churches are undertaking coffee houses as exploratory projects. The ministers of some urban churches, located adjacent to racial ghettoes, hope to involve their congregations, made up largely of commuting "parishioners," with the problems and possibilities of the geographical parish. Beginning in the late 'fifties, chaplains and pastors began to engage in sit-ins and bus rides to far distant trouble spots. There is some cooperation between secular and ecclesiastical agencies in dealing with the difficult

problems of urbanization and suburbanization. There is in contemporary Protestantism (as well as Roman Catholicism) an adventurous, experimental spirit. But the total truth is that it is quite spiritedly resisted in a great many quarters. Protestantism in our time is a creature of internal conflict, very often conflict between clergy and congregations. Not a few seminary students have found that a theological education, combined with a deep concern for the problems of our time, actually *unfits* them for "success" in their ministries! McLuhan's analysis goes a long way, I think, toward contributing a measure of charity to our judgment of such tragicomedy.

4. Finally, if McLuhan is correct about the future, there is much to hope for. One of the incidental effects of the retribalization of man through a new sensory ratio is that many presently almost-incomprehensible things in our distant religious past will become fresh again. The visual dominance of the recent past obscures much of the richness of the Biblical narrative. It may well be that Christianity is moving toward major new forms of community, and toward new kinds of action (corporate action especially) based on new structures of perception. If so, Marshall McLuhan's writings will be indispensable guidebooks.

15. IS IT A REVOLUTION?

by Robert G. Hoyt

I⊤ SEEMS to me difficult for the amateur Christian to form a properly nuanced attitude, an attitude neither romantic nor cynical, toward the phenomenon of ecumenism. My Christian amateur, let it be clear, is not "the average churchgoer," if such a creature exists; he is rather a believer seriously interested in religion but not as an academic or professional calling. I think John Cogley had men and women of this sort in mind when he said in a symposium a few years ago that many rank-and-file pewholders in this country anticipated by decades some of the views about church unity only now being put forward, often rather timorously, by their clerical leaders. As Mr. Cogley pointed out, such laymen knew one another as human beings first, and only secondly as Presbyterians, Anglicans, Baptists, Roman Catholics, Methodists. And, in the ordinary encounters guaranteed by life in a hopelessly heterogeneous society, the believer was likely also to know atheists and agnostics, some of them not merely decent fellows but principled and heroic far above the run of Christians. Such experiences were denied all but unusually adventurous clergymen.

In the circumstances of the layman's life, then, it had become difficult for anyone except the diehard fundamentalist not to question, at least interiorly, the solidity of the walls marking off confessional boundaries, and this despite the best efforts of wall-tenders. Hence, when ecumenism — particularly the Protestant-Catholic variety — went public and became respectable, it found a prepared audience. I remember, for example, the delight I felt in reading the prefatory remarks given at an early "tri-faith" symposium by the chairman, a Catholic priest and college president. What delighted me was his suggestion that the moment had arrived for religionists to take public account of one of the most obvious sociological facts: most of us profess a given faith because we are born into it. The thought itself was hardly novel; it dawns on most of us in early adolescence, inserting into our religious consciousness at least a certain tentativeness, preparing the way, in many, for skepticism or disbelief. Yet, however obvious the fact and however universal its realization, it was the first time I as a Catholic could remember its being treated by a responsible Catholic spokesman as a *significant* truth, a truth with possible theological meaning, therefore a datum to be examined rather than fobbed off. I'm pretty sure that as an adolescent I was made to feel guilty (as though I must be shallow or impious) for suggesting that my own faith could be seen as an accident of circumstance rather than as a proof of God's special favor for me; and guilty for the related suggestion that the sincerity of Protestants might carry some other message besides imposing on me a duty to feel sorry for them in their benightedness. I'm also sure that as an adult, as teacher and parent, I have met the same queries from youth with the same techniques. But the techniques don't work any longer, even within those who use them.

For a very long period the divisions among Christians were not only self-perpetuating but self-intensifying; it was largely through rejecting the errors of others that we specified and deepened our own confessional loyalty, which we identified with faith. For multitudinous reasons beyond the scope of this essay, and beyond my competence to examine, the situation has changed. Instead of tempting us to righteous polemics, the fact of disunity — even aside from the fat target it offers to the non-believing satirist — makes us feel vulnerable. In this new situation there are several possible responses to disunity. One has been noted: a drift toward one or another stage of disbelief. Another, not systematic or even consciously intended, is a blurring or dilution of confessional particularities, the creation of a bland American religious soup in three great flavors. The third is the movement which is the subject of Robert McAfee Brown's excellent book, *The Ecumenical Revolution*.

574

In a way I have already suggested the only serious negative criticisms I shall have to offer of the book. Among clergymen-professors, Stanford's Dr. Brown is assuredly the least clerical and the least pedantic, and I am sure he would dislike being labeled a professional Christian. Inevitably, however, he writes as a professional theologian with an added pastoral-institutional bias, and he therefore misses something of the existential situation in which my amateur Christian, the "consumer" of religion, finds himself. Those lay Christians most likely to read *The Ecumenical Revolution* are not going to find their own eagerness recognized or any nod given to the degree of sophistication they have achieved about inherited, battle-bred rituals of denominational distinctiveness. I don't mean that they will feel slighted; rather, that they will not be alerted to the possibility that they have a contribution to offer the ecumenical enterprise.

Secondly, Dr. Brown does not, in my view, make adequate provision to include in the ecumenical consciousness an element critical of ecumenism, as a basis for dialogue with those Christians who are hostile to the movement. Insofar as such hostility stems from hyperorthodox rigidities, not much in the way of dialogue is achievable. But some "evangelical" criticism of the unity movement is based on the suspicion that it is really a cuddling together for comfort, a sign not of vitality but of a loss of courage and conviction; a product of the belated but profound realization among churchmen that religion no longer counts for much in the conduct of life or the councils of nations — so that something, anything, must be done. That is to say, ecumenism is identified by its enemies with indifferentism.

In my judgment there is no more than, say, a tittle and a half of truth in this reading of ecumenism. But it is part of the ecumenists' basic charter that dialogue is to be sought with practically everybody, specifically and emphatically including the fundamentalists; and dialogue begins when one evidences a readiness to see some part of what the other man sees. It is patent that there *are* in fact sociological and psychological factors at work in promoting ecumenism; there are other and less obviously noble reasons for falling in with it besides a sudden, Spirit-born insight into Christ's prayer for unity in the seventeenth chapter of St. John. These background or contextual factors are not bad but neutral; they promote *both* indifferentism *and* ecumenism. Had *The Ecumenical Revolution* acknowledged this more clearly, Dr. Brown would have shared some common ground with churchmen who resist the movement; and he would have been better situated also to make clear to Christian amateurs the difference between the movement toward organic Church unity and the drift toward an anti-doctrinal or undoctrinal Christianity.

Bringing home this latter distinction is at least as important as enticing fundamentalists into the work of unity. I have already suggested that the time is long past when intelligent lay persons had to be persuaded of the human and Christian worth of persons wearing the wrong dog tags. For example, when the Second Vatican Council recognized the "ecclesial reality" of other Churches, for many lay Catholics it merely certified a pre-existing inchoate conviction. Insofar as the advanced views of laymen derive from common sense and reflect the experience of life in a pluralistic nation on a pluralistic planet, they are valuable; they generate impatience with the slow pace of the movement. From this perspective ecumenism is seen as an increasingly complacent new Establishment, a new craft union for specialized researchers rather than a movement ardently in pursuit of reconciling truth. I'm told that college students are not much excited about ecumenical activity, and — again from this perspective — it is easy to see why. There is a great deal more obvious relevancy and liveliness in the question whether the New Left will be able to come to terms with Black Nationalism than there is in the issue of whether intercommunion may perhaps come to be permitted on specific well-defined occasions some time in the next decade. The ecumenical movement, if it is to move, badly needs the push supplied by amateurs who feel they have heard, more than once too often, the saw that "you can't eliminate the problems of 400 years in a couple of months," and who think the Churches have to risk a bit of drama if what Dr. Brown labels a revolution is not to become an exercise in paper-shuffling, an

The consecration of Bishop Mark J. Hurley in San Francisco January 4, 1968, attended by Rabbi Alvin Fine, Episcopalian Rt. Rev. Richard Millard, Most Rev. John Shahovskoy, Russian Orthodox archbishop of San Francisco, and Mar Eshai Shimum XXIII, Catholic patriarch of the Church of the East, seated at the lower left.

end in itself, providing churchmen with one more distraction from what is happening in a world of hunger and heartache.

The trouble with impatience, however, is that it translates readily into "enthusiasm," in the sense of simplistic, anti-intellectual illuminism or pietism. And it is at this point (I thought I would reach it much sooner) that one can begin to celebrate Dr. Brown's book instead of nitpicking at its partial and minor failures. If it is true that the book does not seem to notice the favorable predispositions of amateurs toward the general notion of unity, it is much more true that Dr. Brown provides everything necessary to convert a vague bias into a principled conviction. If the amateur's impatience is a Good Thing when it is primarily a reaction against ecclesiastical fuddy-duddyism, it is bad to the degree that it merely registers an amiable prejudice in favor of Christian togetherness, or when it is a byproduct of ignorance about the problems of unity, or when it denies that ideas have consequences.

The Ecumenical Revolution is a successful antidote against these forms of impatience because it is very serious indeed without being in the least solemn or pedantic, and because it conveys mounds of information in compact, organized, readable fashion. Because the approach is almost wholly historical, the book produces another counterweight against fretfulness over the matter of pace — one comes to realize again how very far we (including the official bodies) have come and in how short a time. In unlabeled response to the notion that ecumenism represents a decay or a loss of religious energy, the book demonstrates rather than says that ecumenically oriented religion provides surprises, the best mark of life: corporate repentance, ecclesiastical statesmanship, the figure of Angelo Roncalli dangling his legs on the throne of Peter, the vision of Protestants, Orthodox, and Jews listening to a secret Roman Catholic conclave, the world press badgering, pressuring, influencing the world's bishops, white northern clergy eagerly responding to the call of a black Baptist prophet . . . this is not decadence.

Nor is the proper ecumenical stance toward confessional differences in any way reminiscent of indifferentism. The approach, demonstrated by Dr. Brown on a hundred different pages, does indeed put the most sacred formulations up for re-examination, but the effort as depicted here is one of penetration, of mutual, gradual, correction and refinement, careful reordering of doctrinal priorities, common turning toward the sources.

Not everything in the record, it should be noted, is uniformly attractive. When churchmen decide to express group repentance they are inclined to make a production of it, with the result, not consciously intended, that their contrition gets more attention than their sin. When they issue statements about their negotiations they do so at more than adequate length; and they can be just as inclined as any worldly diplomats to word-play disguising a lack of progress as progress.

No single volume attempting to condense the history and judge the current status of the ecumenical revolution could hope to deal subtly or fully with every aspect. Nor could it adequately relate what is happening between the Churches to what is happening within them. One of the many problems complicating the life of an ecumenist is that while the Churches approach one another they are intramurally undergoing profound transformations, the final results of which are much in doubt. Dr. Brown does not always convey a sense of the uncertainty of this process or of the suffering attending it. But who could? This is for the most part a private agony. It may be a more serious criticism — or it may reveal a newspaperman's bias — to say that he does not bring the reader inside the movement, to experience it as the persons who energize it do.

To return to my beginning. My "amateur Christian" will gain from this volume some sense of the massiveness of the ecumenical movement, and a conviction of its irreversible character. But, though I think Dr. Brown is both naturally optimistic and religiously hopeful, his reader will not be likely to conclude that unity is just around the next corner; the problems are not scanted. The layman who has previously experienced the movement from a distance, who has grown weary of committees and interim statements, who wants the professionals to get where everyone knows they're going, may regain some of his sense of wonder

579

that anything can happen at all, and may acquire a greater sympathy with the experts who must endlessly reassess their own traditions and those of others, the mood of their people and of their administrative or hierarchical superiors, the effects of an agreement with this congregational body on negotiations with that episcopal one. But I hope he will read between the lines as well, because I think Dr. Brown has left something there to feed one's impatience along with one's sense of achievement and gratitude.

PART TWO

Defining the Religious Dimension

Members of the Haight-Ashbury district in San Francisco gathered at a three-day wake staged to mourn the "Death of the Hippie" October 10, 1967.

16. SECULARIZATION AND THE SACRED: THE CONTEMPORARY SCENE

by Huston Smith

RELIGION has lost ground startlingly in the last decade, at least in the eyes of the general public in the United States. In 1957, 14% of a Gallup national sample was of the opinion that "religion is losing its influence." By 1962 the figure had risen to 31%, by 1965 to 45%, and by 1967 it stood at 57% [9:820]. In ten short years the proportion of Americans who see religion as in retreat has quadrupled, jumping from one seventh to over half the population. Yet squarely within this decade of seeming collapse, an astute sociologist has observed "in the United States . . . at the moment something of a religious revival" [1:36].

The cognitive dissonance occasioned by Gallup's evidence and Robert Bellah's perception sets the problem for this paper. Is one of the two mistaken, or are sacred and secular related in ways complex and subtle enough to allow both to be correct?

"Secular" characterizes regions of life that man understands and controls, not necessarily completely but (as the saying goes, and here it is precisely accurate) "for all practical purposes."

Thus defined, secularization has increased steadily with the advance of civilization. Primitive man obviously managed or we wouldn't be around, but there was little in his life that he understood sufficiently to effect clean control over it. As a consequence his society was whole, compacted in the sense — among others — that the sacred encompassed almost everything; economics and medicine, for example. Among tribal peoples hunting, and husbandry have sacred sides to them: Toda priests are occupied with their sacred buffalos, and totemic rites bind Arunta hunters to their prey in ties that both expedite and legitimize their kills. Likewise with healing: medicine men are simultaneously physicians and priests.

583

In *civilizations* the situation is, as we know, otherwise. Whether we read "In God We Trust" on our currency as vestigial or as a precise index of the degree to which the almighty dollar has become in fact our god, western economies have become completely secular. This is not to claim that we understand or control the economic order completely, but it does say that we believe that what happens in the economic order is due either to planned human intervention or to chance and that what we don't understand of it is due to our (provisional) ignorance rather than to its (in-built) mystery. Similarly with modern medicine. Priests now enter the picture with the approach of the inexorable — death. Healing itself, even psychiatric healing, has become a secular art.

Politics is a third sphere of civilized activity that has become secularized. In China the process is currently passing through a decisive phase as Mao's theologically oriented cultural revolution goes to the mat against the practical pragmatisms of nation building. But in the West the battle is over. The splice between politics and religion (the priest-king) has gone the way of the splice between medicine and religion (the medicine man). To see Lyndon Baines Johnson as having been even once upon a time a holy man requires the spiritual clairvoyance of a Hindu. (The reference is to Goswamy's surprising astrological discovery during the heat of the 1964 presidential campaign that the Democratic candidate had spent his preceding incarnation as a sannyasin practicing austerities along the banks of the Ganges [7:191].)

It might seem natural to suppose that with man's progressive mastery of domains of his existence and the attendant fissiparous emancipation of these from the custody of religion, the sacred is shrinking, becoming residual. We shall do well, however, to resist jumping to this conclusion hastily. The family, too, once held sway over activities that have progressively moved away from it — activities like manufacturing, education, entertainment, and religious instruction — but it doesn't necessarily follow that the family dimension has declined in importance. It could continue to be important but in different ways; as the locus of intimacy, for example, which in our impersonal society has become more problematically important than ever before.

How is it with the sacred? Does it stand in inverse ratio to the secular, in which case advancing secularization simply decreases it, as ladling from a bucket lowers its waterline? Or is the sacred something of a constant in human experience, changing not so much in quantity as in the region where it appears and in the forms of its manifestations?

I suspect that the truth lies somewhere in between. The sacred is less evident in contemporary life than it was in the past, but to this perception three others, less obvious, should be added. (1) More of the sacred persists than meets the eye. (2) What remains of the sacred is durable, sufficiently so that it is not likely to decline much further. (3) On the contrary, the sacred is likely to make a comeback; there are already signs of it. Thus the current low water mark of the sacred represents not so much a transition point in a long-range, irreversible trend as a temporary dip caused by a spiritual drought that another century could easily reverse. These are major claims, and, as they are not altogether supported by majority opinion, they call for justification. I shall begin with some theoretical considerations, then proceed to ones that are a bit more empirical.

THEORETICAL CONSIDERATIONS

If "the secular" defines regions of life that man *controls*, the view that the secular is displacing the sacred entails the corollary that life is becoming more manageable and (if one goes all the way down this road) will eventually become completely manageable. In actuality, however, it is far from clear that man's control over his life is increasing. *Parts* of life are coming under control — disease and the death rate, for example, or physical drudgery and plumbing. But several knotty considerations lie between this incontestable premise and the conclusion that life *as a whole* is becoming more manageable.

One: As often as not, human problems behave like quicksilver.

Just when we think we have gotten one under our thumb, it scoots off, free, wild, and on the loose. Thus we get control of the death rate only to find ourselves confronted with a population explosion. Or we master the power of the atom to find ourselves handed, precisely at that moment, the problem of nuclear destruction. We used to regard technology as our servant; it did our bidding. Now there is fear that technology is becoming master: weaving a swiftly accelerating mechanical complex which, like a conveyer belt, is carrying us who knows where and without anyone's — certainly not ourselves' — having set its direction. (See S. Giedion, *Mechanization Takes Command*.) To the extent that this fear is justified, technology merely dethrones *deus ex machina* in order to enstool itself as *deus in machina*. In the latter instance, as in the former, man remains creature. We are back to the same general problem we faced when we asked the relation of secularization to the sacred. There the form of the problem was: does increasing secularization diminish the sacred? Here the question takes the form: does solving problems encountered in human life reduce the total number of problems or simply replace some old problems with new or other problems? Another way to word the question is: Are human problems finite in number?

Two: If the preceding point was that it is far from clear that man's life is in fact coming more under his control, this second point is that the notion of complete control doesn't even make sense; it can't take coherent shape even as an ideal. Man is by nature a social being and as such lives, necessarily, inexorably, as one independent will among many. No one of these wills can be omnipotent without (per impossible) ceasing to be social, for social existence necessarily involves give *and take*. "Omnipotent" and "social" are logical alternatives. Charles Hartshorne argues that this precludes even God's being omnipotent.

Three: Not only is total control impossible — logically inconsistent with the human condition — it isn't even attractive. To enter a friendship, to say nothing of marriage, with intent to control is to soil the relationship from the start. Life requires that benefits accruing from control be balanced by benefits latent in openness and surrender. The more resolved we are to have things our own way, the less open we grow to possible virtues in alternative ways. Unless we see a great and vital capacity in the capacity to surrender to another in love or to surrender to obligation in the sense of feeling its claims upon us, cynicism and nihilism will result.

That parts of life have come under our control is, then, no indication that all of it will. The latter vision can't be realized or even consistently conceived. It shouldn't be realized, and there is question whether we are moving in its direction at all. The relevance of this to our inquiry is as follows: The sacred is not synonymous with what exceeds man's control, but, assuming that it lies somewhere therein, there is no reason to suppose that it has less scope today than in the past. Life continues to dangle over seventy thousand fathoms; only the region of the deeps has altered.

Where, within the uncontrolled, might we expect the sacred to show itself now that it has withdrawn from areas like medicine, economics, and politics? To economize our search we should recall that the sacred exceeds not only our control but our comprehension. The weather remains unmanageable, but it has ceased to be religious: before meteorology, the nature gods have fallen. In looking for the divine we should look not only to what we don't control but also to what we don't understand.

One thing that meets these two conditions is the unconscious. By definition, we don't know what goes on there, for if we did it would be conscious. And we don't control it. "Where id was, let ego be," Freud counseled; he would have been the first to insist how far we are from completing the program if, indeed, we ever can. To these two features of the unconscious, exceeding our comprehension and exceeding our control, we should add a third condition of the sacred which the unconscious also satisfies: vital importance. Recent experimental studies of sleep are reported to reveal that a surprising proportion of the time male subjects are dreaming they have erections, something like eighty per cent of the time. If the report is accurate, it provides experimental support for what I believe to be true in any case: the unconscious houses the springs of our vitality.

Incomprehensible, indomitable, and important — these are

authentic marks of the sacred, and the unconscious possesses them all. As an example, Dr. Ronald D. Laing, Director of the Langham Clinic for Psychotherapy in London, argues that in certain instances psychosis provides a state of mind in which religious resources of the unconscious can surface with unusual freedom [4; 3]. The unconscious holds over us the power of life and death — psychic health and insanity. We stand in relation to it as creature, a sufficient reason being that (as remarked) it is unfathomable: its thoughts are not our thoughts nor its ways our ways, "our" referring here to what we possess consciously. Man isn't noticeably open to the divine from any quarter today, but, angle for angle, the unconscious provides a better angle than most from which the divine may appear. This partly explains the striking impact that Hinduism and Buddhism are having on the West, especially on western youth. Asian religious symbolism — "Atman is Brahman," "each of us possesses the Buddha-mind already" — accommodates epiphanies through the unconscious more readily than does Judeo-Christian symbolism in which tradition the fact that God is as present in the depths of our being as "out there" could come to a contemporary bishop (John A.T. Robinson) as *news* [6].

This point about Asia, however, is in passing. I want to extend discussion of the unconscious only one paragraph further to note some recent discoveries that may throw light on *how* the sacred gains access to the unconscious. The empirical evidence undergirding the following paragraph may be found in Michael S. Gassaniga's "The Split Brain in Man" [2:24 – 29].

It has been known for some time that the human brain consists of two hemispheres, each of which controls, substantially, the opposite side of the body. To this familiar fact are now added two new ones. After the age of four, speech faculties become concentrated in the brain's left hemisphere, leaving the right hemisphere almost completely nonverbal but — this is the companion discovery — not unintelligent. For example, epileptics whose brain hemispheres have been divided surgically can with their right-hemisphere-controlled left hands match cigarettes to ashtrays instead of to less related objects while they remain unable to *name* any of the objects they are handling. Another example: when a subject's left eye only was shown a picture of a nude woman inserted in a sequence of more conventional pictures, a sly smile spread over the subject's face and she began to chuckle, despite the fact that she was unable to name or describe what she had seen. Asked what amused her, she answered: "I don't know . . . nothing . . . oh — that funny machine." This discovery that half of our brain is nonverbally intelligent bears on the present discussion by advancing our understanding of one way in which the unconscious figures in our lives. Half our lives — the half governed by our right hemispheres — floats and swims in media and ways which, not provisionally but in principle, defy comprehension because it bypasses speech, the prerequisite of reflective, self-conscious awareness. The finding helps us to understand experiences that impress themselves on us as noetic while remaining ineffable, a class of experiences with which religion (through mysticism) has been involved from its inception to LSD.

In addition to the unconscious, there is another border on which the sacred retains its rights in the face of continuing secularization; namely, life's evolutionary frontier.

Man is a creature who, because he is still evolving, is in transition, in passage. In evolutionary perspective he walks backward into the future, able to look retrospectively over the road he has traveled but not forward to what lies ahead. Thus he lives always on the verge, always on the brink of a "something more." His outreach for this "more" effervesces as a restlessness built into his very nature. Like the expanding universe itself, man is bent on pouring over endless horizons. The intimation of "something waiting, go and find it" belongs to the very essence of his humanity.

Every day brings *something* new and unpredictable, but for the most part this new isn't new in kind; it's more of the same — minor variations on familiar themes. We move closer to what I wish to point to when we think of new *stages* in life's development: when a person moves for the first time into sexual love, for example; or senses with excitement the endless possibilities of

589

human thought; or confronts existentially not death in general but his own death. At such times we encounter not just new experiences but new *kinds* of experience. The evolutionarily new that I wish to identify is like this and at the same time different. It resembles life's new stages in heralding experiences that are new in kind, but differs from them in that they cannot be expected to appear at roughly predictable points in the natural unfolding of a normal life. Instead of being predictable, they are unexpected; instead of typical, they are atypical; instead of natural, they seem to be in ways quite unnatural. They have the feel of opposing our lives, not perhaps in their inclusive possibilities but at least in their present, standard, common-to-everyone conditions. Thus cognitively the experiences present themselves as mysterious: they don't just introduce information of which we were heretofore ignorant; their disclosures are in an unusually precise sense an affront to intelligence because they seem true — truer, à la Plato's Myth of the Cave, than what we ordinarily know — while refusing to fit not only into our standard frames of reference but into our normal modes of knowing. Similarly affectively. The experiences feel simultaneously threatening and promising, like that (we may imagine) of the amphibians when they first flapped their way onto mudbanks wondering if they could survive in their new medium while sensing at some level the larger life that would be theirs if they did. And just as mystery defies (in ways) knowledge, so too this larger life, when it glimmers, has the feel of countermanding in important ways our natural existence. The "better" which it intimates, for example, is as discontinuous with our normal value experiences as so-called spiritual values differ from values that are purely physical. Just as mystery isn't information in overload, "the peace that passeth understanding" isn't an orgy of pleasure. It is value of a distinctive kind — blessedness? — which has the character of in-spite-of. It is symbolized by the Indian doctrine of *lila* which holds that, despite the fact that things are in just about the worst state imaginable, *nevertheless* all is well. It is the experience reported by a New York housewife who, in the midst of a deep depression caused by her sister's suicide which left three children motherless, found her depression suddenly lifted and replaced by an inexplicable serenity that embraced rather than eclipsed clear-eyed cognizance of all that had happened. It appears again in the terminal cancer patients who, as reported by Sidney Cohen in "LSD and the Anguish of Dying," *Harper's*, Sept 1965, continue under LSD to feel their pain but in a way which no longer matters, so completely is it set in cosmic perspective.

I am suggesting that philogony recapitulates ontogony; that experiences of radical novelty, signaling the advent of amplier being, that come to all of us as individuals when we move into a new life stage are paralleled on a different level in certain individuals who represent, as it were, the human species moving into a new stage of *its* existence.

If I were asked to name a third life domain available to the sacred in our time, I would name interpersonal relations, that treacherous, sublime, highly elusive, unmeasurable terrain where two or more persons meet and exchange words and feelings.

The importance of these relations needs no documenting. They create and sustain us. But importance alone, as we have seen, doesn't make something sacred. Personal relations have always been important, but in the past they have provided less of an aperture for the divine because they were less problematical. In traditional societies most men and women lived their entire lives in a single primary group whose members knew one another intimately and for life. Such ever present communities didn't prevent unhappiness, but they did spare their members the deeper disturbances that appear when communication breaks down seriously: acute anxiety, loneliness, withdrawal, and identity confusion.

Today, thanks to the fact that our society has become impersonal, these maladies are with us. American families now change residence across state lines on the average of once every five years. And wherever they live, they usually work elsewhere. As a consequence they know one another only (a) in stages of life and (b) in aspects of self: in roles, such as husband, professional, customer, voter, client.

These developments have produced in industrial societies a

kind of crisis in communication; personal relations, while continuing to be essential, have become precarious as never before. This combination of importance and fragility provides a clearing for the divine, particularly when, to these two attributes are added the mystery — unpredictability, unfathomability — that attend deep encounters between persons as self-aware as contemporary men and women have become. A perceptive soul like Buber sensed this and wrote a tract for our time, *I and Thou*, which argues that God lives precisely in the intersection of lives at depth level. Encounter Groups (T-Groups, Sensitivity Training Groups) provide another evidence that the interpersonal has become an area where the sacred can enter man's life today. Last summer I directed in India a seminar composed of sixteen American and sixteen Indian university women. The Americans found encounter group exercises both more threatening and more significant than did the Indians, who (still nurtured by relatively tight and stable primary associations) chattered merrily along as if this were their normal fare. Westerners may like or feel threatened by encounter groups, but almost invariably they find the experience to be different. It also tends to be *important*, for some the most important experience of their lives. With a dozen or so independent and emotionally charged souls affecting the course of the group, it is unpredictable and *uncontrolled*. And the course of the group *defies comprehension;* there come points when so much is going on at so many levels interpreted so divergently by everyone present that one looks out upon the group with eyes of insanity, so totally lacking is anything that approaches an objective grasp of what's happening. All three prerequisites of the sacred are present. It is, therefore, no surprise to find coming from the pen of one of the most practiced leaders of sensitivity training (encounter) groups an article titled "Sensitivity Training as Religious Experience." When, writes James Clark,

> for forty or fifty hours one is confronted in a complex and deeply human way by nearly a dozen other people in a circle with no imposed task to fly into, no hierarchy to bind, contain and ritualize, more often than not one expands. A person

experiences the limits he and his environment have imposed on him, and expands beyond them. Knowing what one cannot give, one is able to offer what one can give. And knowing what one can give leads to a sense of where one is in the universe and a genuine experience of interdependence, the prizing of all men, the mystical, deep, religious, expansive experience of knowing that "no man is an island."

Of an encounter group at Tavistock Institute, Margaret Rioch writes: "Everyone, I think, suffered a sea change into something rich and strange" — which is to say, something bordering, at least, on the sacred.

In arguing the continuation of the sacred in history, I have deliberately scanned for places in which the sacred is appearing with greater force now that former apertures such as economics, medicine, and politics have closed to it. But in attending thus to the new I do not wish to suggest that all the former apertures are contracting. "As it was in the days of Noah," so today: the sacred comes to man in ultimate situations where his helplessness glares. In the realization that he dominates nature and finds it reliable only in part; in death, chance, guilt, and the total uncertainty of the world, man faces failure. Such ultimate situations bring either total darkness or night-sight glimmerings of a sacred that exists through and in spite of the transcience of worldly existence.

EMPIRICAL IMPRESSIONS

Thus far, in arguing that the sacred is not so much declining as shifting its locus, I have been guided by theoretical considerations stemming from my reflections on man's nature and his current condition. I turn now to considerations that are a bit more empirical. Granted that the evidence I cite is more impressionistic than statistical, I see it nevertheless as counting for something.

Item: Last year while teaching for a quarter at Santa Barbara, I was invited to the home of a family I had chanced to know in

Mexico. In the course of the evening it developed that a visiting sister was completely wrapped up in the Los Angeles chapter of Maharishi Yogi's International Meditation Society, while the sophomore high school daughter was a moving spirit of the local chapter of the Sokagakai Chanting Sect. Driving home I stopped for gasoline and found the filling station attendant completing Suzuki's *Zen Buddhism.* In a single chance evening I had met six persons, and three of them were involved — two very deeply — with religion in forms that elude the usual church statistics.

Item: Lest the preceding episode be discounted on grounds that it is precisely what one might expect from Southern California, I choose my next one from more staid New England. Two years ago a group of eight MIT upperclassmen formed a preceptoral group and asked me to be their instructor. It was to be an independent study project which the students were to conduct themselves; my role was to be that of adviser and consultant. Ostensibly on Asian thought, it began respectably enough with standard texts from the Chinese and Indian traditions, but, as the weeks moved on and the students' true interests surfaced, the original syllabus began to lurch and reel until I found myself holding onto my mortar board wondering whether to continue the role of sober professor or turn anthropologist, sit back, and observe the ways of the natives. For natives in thought-patterns they were; far closer to Hottentots than to positivists. In the end the anthropologist in me triumphed over the academician, for I found the window to this strange and (in the technical, anthropological sense) quite archaic and primitive mentality irresistible. I cannot recall the exact progression of topics, but it went something like this: Beginning with Asian philosophy, it moved on to meditation, then yoga, then Zen, then Tibet, then successively to the *Bardo Thodol,* tantra, the kundalini, the chakras, the *I Ching,* karati and aikido, the yang-yin macrobiotic (brown rice) diet, Gurdjieff, Maher Baba, astrology, astral bodies, auras, UFO's, Torot cards, parapsychology, witchcraft, and magic. And, underlying everything, of course, the psychedelic drugs. Nor were the students dallying with these subjects. They were *on* the drugs; they were eating brown rice; they were meditating hours on end; they were making their decisions by *I Ching* divination, which one student designated the most important discovery of his life; they were constructing complicated electronic experiments to prove that their thoughts, via psychokinesis, could affect matter directly.

And they weren't plebeians. Intellectually they were aristocrats with the highest average math scores in the land, Ivy League verbal scores, and two-to-three years of saturation in MIT science. What *they* learned in the course of the semester I don't know. What ·I learned was that the human mind stands ready to believe anything — absolutely anything — as long as it provides an alternative to the totally desacralized mechanomorphic outlook of objective science. Some may see the lesson as teaching no more than the extent of human credulity. I read it otherwise. If mechanomorphism is the truth, then indeed the students' behavior reveals no more than man's unwillingness to accept it. But if being *is* sacred, or potentially sacred, the students' phrenetic thrusts suggest something different. In things of the spirit, subject and object mesh exceptionally. No faith, no God; without response, revelation doesn't exist. It follows that the sacred depends, not entirely but in part, on man's nose for it. Given noses as keen for the chase as were those students', if the sacred lurks anywhere in the marshes of contemporary life, it is going to be flushed out. Or better — because it goes further in bridging the subject-object dichotomy — drives which are this strong help to *generate* the sacred.

Item: While on the subject of science, let us remember that the fact that Japan is the most literate nation in the world and the most industrialized and scientifically knowledgeable nation in Asia has not prevented over 500 new religions from springing up there since World War II. As in the case of the MIT students, this suggests that the sacred isn't necessarily related to science as alternative or even rival. Progress in one need not spell decline of the other. On a recent flight from Chicago to Boston I found myself seated by a physics professor. She discussed physics with interest, but flying saucers with passion — passionate belief. UFO's are not, to be sure, ideal exemplars of the sacred, but they impinge on it by virtue of awakening numinous feelings. For, if they exist, they are probably manned by creatures more advanced than we. So they do more than puzzle. They are strange.

Item: In his psychological investigations of "peak experiences," Professor Abraham Maslow has found both that such experiences are virtually universal — almost all his subjects reported having had them — and that, to an extent that surprised him as investigator, they tend to be religious in character and feel.

Item: Science fiction is booming. Only in part is this due to impetus derived from space exploration; we can as readily turn the matter around and say that the desire to transcend the earth springs in part (symbolically, unconsciously) from the motive that produces science fiction: the desire to transcend earth-bound experience. In the past this desire, working on the imagination, produced the "Gothic" novel with its supernatural divine and demonic interferences in the natural processes of life. It produced also the spiritualistic novel with its ambiguous psychic phenomena which were neither clearly natural nor clearly supernatural. Today science fiction, especially as attached to space exploration as in *Stranger in a Strange Land*, accomplishes the same imaginative transcendence by envisioning encounters with natural but transterrestrial beings. "Mythological as well as psychic supranaturalism are replaced by a transterrestrial naturalism: the earth is transcended, not through something qualitatively other, but through a strange section of something qualitatively the same — the natural universe" [8:44].

Interest in science fiction, I am not the first to suggest, is evidence of man's continuing fascination with at least the prospect of domains that transcend the ordinary.

Item: In the Youth Revolution, particularly as it focuses at the moment in the Hippies, the sacred appears to be coming into something of a renaissance.

596

With their beads and bells, their tambourines and capes, their bows and arrows, their wild hair and beards, their flutes and their flowers, the Hippies present a bizarre spectacle. In many respects they also present a confused spectacle: sad-eyed, hungry, diseased kids in Haight-Ashbury bumming for dimes, like sheep without a shepherd. Certainly they present a confusing spectacle.

I am not echoing Pope Innocent III on the Children's Crusade: "While we sleep they go forth to conquer the Holy Land" [5]. But I am saying that clear-eyed or confused, divine or demonic, the Hippies evidence a lively sense of the sacred.

Asked on a nationwide television program to capsule the difference between themselves and their parents, a teen-aged girl said, "We come right out and say 'God.' "

In "Each one do his own thing; whatever your thing is, do it," they reach out to recapture a sense of vocation.

With the Diggers, they recover the "culture of poverty" and work to give instead of get — free meals, free clothes, free mattresses, free transport, free medical and legal aid.

Confronting police with "flower power," they resurrect Gandhi's faith that might arises from right and that truth and love can overcome anything.

With their Be-ins (not Do-ins), their going where the action isn't, they evidence what Tillich called ontological as against prophetic faith, celebrating the holiness of the "is" rather than the "ought," the present rather than the future. For the first time since the Renaissance and the Reformation, western society is hearing, through them, the suggestion that perhaps the contemplative life is the equal of the active one. With tribalism and Strawberry Fields Forever they seek the recovery of community. Turning on, they seek by their own lights the inner light. Tuning in, they approach the natural order sacramentally. Dropping out, they assert by splitting the scene the rights of the private life against the public life and announce that their kingdom is not of this world. Throughout, theological supernaturalism is replaced by psychological supernaturalism defined as saving truths available only through altered, turned-on, states of consciousness whether induced by drugs or otherwise. Leslie Fiedler may exaggerate in writing that "our students are living on the edge of one of the greatest religious revivals that will ever have struck civilization," but I cannot read words like the following without sensing that the sacred in some guise is at work on their source:

> It came down to me that what we were about out there at that community [Strawberry Fields Forever] is what religion is about. I decided to try and put it into a word form so that it would be a point of departure for people to look at themselves and to look at what was going on there. I wrote up the basis for the religion. Once on a trip I flashed that LSD should be re-named "trust." Because that's kind of where I get to on it. It's the same thing that prophets or religious teachers are on to when they talk about faith and belief and acceptance, too. Then out of another acid trip I took one time when I was all crippled up with muscle spasms in my back, I got into a thing where to be honest is to be God. And the idea that in God there is no deception . . . with reality, with what is. There is only WHAT IS. And that if I'm honest with you, then I am treat-ing you as God. I'm God and I'm as God with you and you are as God with me. And that's what God is. God is everything here, whether it's known or not, but when you're honest, it CAN be known. Because of the feelings we have, especially when we're just super-open. And that, that's what the brotherhood of man and mystical union is all about. That kind of unity, a unity where we are without veils or deceptions or games be-tween us, with only pure truth in life [10:3].

In the first, theoretical, half of this paper I said that I did not want my preoccupation with new places where the sacred is showing itself to cast doubt on its continuance in some of the old places. I want to make the same point in this empirical half. All the spots where I have reported encountering flashes of the sacred are outside church and synagogue, but this doesn't mean that the sacred is not continuing to show itself there too. It is; in what proportion relative to previous generations, I have no way of estimating.

598

CONCLUSION

In this statement I have characterized as sacred that which is vitally and problematically important to us and exceeds our comprehension and control. I am not confident, however, that this is the only or perhaps even the most valuable approach to the subject. What conclusion would have emerged, for example, if we had approached the sacred as designating, primarily, wholeness?

I have not wanted here to press the accuracy of my view of the sacred but rather to gauge the sacred's vitality and prospects. The polarity of the sacred and the secular continues to hold its place among the mighty opposites that streak life's *coincidentia oppositorum:* yang and yin, systole and diastole, action and repose, freedom and form, centrifugal and centripetal. Notwithstanding Bonhoeffer's vision of an approaching age in which man is not religious at all, man remains *homo religiosus,* not in the eighteenth century reading of the phrase to be sure, but in the sense of being by nature vulnerable to transcendence and the sacred. When, in this year of our Lord 1967, 57% of the American public said "religion is losing its influence," they should have said (if given the opportunity to be precise), "institutionalized religion is losing its influence in certain areas of life where its presence used to be more evident." But institutionalized religion isn't all of religion, and the fact that the sacred is withdrawing from certain spheres doesn't mean it isn't moving into others. Robert Bellah could be right in detecting "in the United States . . . at the moment something of a religious revival."

REFERENCES

1. Bellah, Robert: Religious Evolution, *American Sociological Review,* vol 29, no 3, June 1964.
2. Gassaniga, Michael S: The Split Brain in Man, *The Scientific American,* vol 217, no 2, August 1967.

599

3. Liang, Ronald D: *The Politics of Experience* (Pantheon Books, Inc, New York, New York) 1967.
4. Liang, Ronald D: Transcendental Experience in Relation to Religion and Psychosis, *Psychedelic Review*, no 6, 1965.
5. Mayer, Milton: The Young: Their Cause and Cure, *The Progressive*, vol 31, no 9, Sept 1967.
6. Robinson, John A T: *Honest to God* (The Westminster Press, Philadelphia, Pennsylvania) 1963 and (SCM Press, London, England) 1964.
7. 10,000 Red-Gilt Envelopes, *The Nation*, vol 200, no 8, Feb 22, 1965.
8. Tillich, Paul: *The Future of Religion* (Harper & Row, Publishers, New York, New York) 1966.
9. Wiener, Jack: Mental Health Highlights, *American Journal of Orthopsychiatry*, vol 37, no 4, July 1967.
10. Wright, Gridley: Strawberry Fields Forever . . . ? *Southern California Oracle*, no date.

17. THE SECULARIZATION OF THE SACRED

by Joseph Campbell

As I understand the phrase "the secularization of the sacred," it suggests an opening of the sense of religious awe to some sphere of profane experience or, more marvelously, to the whole wonder of this world and oneself within it. The Indian saint and sage Śri Ramakrishna said, for example,

> One day, it was suddenly revealed to me that everything is Pure Spirit. The utensils of worship, the altar, the door frame — all Pure Spirit. Men, animals, and other living beings — all Pure Spirit. Then like a madman I began to shower flowers in all directions. Whatever I saw, I worshiped.
>
> One day, while worshiping Siva, I was about to offer a bel-leaf on the head of the image, when it was revealed to me that this Virat, this Universe, itself is Śiva. . . . Another day I had been plucking flowers, when it was revealed to me that each plant was a bouquet adorning the universal form of God. That was the end of my plucking flowers. I look on man in just the same way. When I see a man, I see that it is God Himself who walks on earth, as it were, rocking to and fro, like a pillow floating on the waves [23:396].

Another time, when he was approaching an image of the goddess Kāli to pay it worship, someone said to him, "I have heard that it was made by the sculptor Nabin."

"Yes, I know," he answered. "But to me She is the embodiment of Spirit" [23:487].

Actually, this order of experience is basic, not only to Indian religiosity, but to the entire range of the high religions of the Orient eastward of Iran. We have it in the Buddhist aspiration: OM MANI PADME HUM: "The Jewel in the Lotus": The Jewel of Absolute Reality is in the Lotus of the Universe; likewise in the Chinese concept of the Tao:

> The Valley Spirit never dies:
> It is the base from which heaven sprang and earth.
> It is here within us all the while [39].

The ultimate goal of Oriental worship is, accordingly, the realization of one's own identity with this reality and recognition of its presence in all things — not, as in our western religions, to worship a god distinct from his creation, of a different order of being — apart — "out there." A telling statement to this point appears in the Brhadāranyaka Upanisad (circa ?700 B.C.):

> This that people say: "Worship this god! Worship that god!" — one god after another — this whole universe itself is His creation! And He Himself is all the gods. . . .
> Whoever worships one or another of those, knows not: He is incomplete as worshiped in one or another. One should worship with the thought that He is one's own essential Self, for therein all these become one.
> Whoever thus knows, "I am brahman!" becomes this All; not even the gods have the power to prevent his becoming thus, for he then becomes their Self. So whoever worships a divinity other than this Self, thinking, "He is one and I another," knows not. He is like a sacrificial animal for the gods. And as many animals would be of service to a man, even so is each single person of service to the gods. But if even one animal is taken away it is not pleasant. What, then, if many? It is not pleasing to the gods, therefore, that people should know this [6: 1.4.6].

Compare with this, the Book of Genesis:

> Then the Lord God said, "Behold, the man has become like one of us, knowing good and evil; and now, lest he put forth his hand and take also of the tree of life, and eat, and live for ever" — therefore the Lord God sent him forth from the garden of Eden, to till the ground from which he was taken. He drove out the man; and at the east of the garden of Eden he placed the cherubin, and a flaming sword which turned every way, to guard the way to the tree of life [Genesis 3:22–24].

But this Way to the Tree of Life is exactly the *mārga*, the "path," of the Indian disciplines, the *tao* of the Chinese, the "Gateless Gate" of Zen. And the cherubim at the entrance to the Garden of the Knowledge of Immortality, guarding it with a flaming sword, correspond exactly to the temple guardians at the entrance to any Oriental sanctuary.

Never shall I forget a picture that I saw in a New York newspaper during our recent war with Japan. It showed one of the two giant temple guardians at the gate to the Tōdaiji temple in Nara: fierce figures with lifted swords. There was no picture of the temple itself, or of the Buddha within, beneath the Tree of Enlightenment, hand lifted in the "fear-not" gesture, but only that one threatening cherub in his frightening attitude and beneath the picture, the legend: "The Japanese worship gods like this."

The only thought that crossed my mind, and is with me still, was the obvious one: "Not they, but we!" For it is *we* whose god would keep men out of the Garden. The Buddhist idea, on the contrary, is to go past the guardian cherubim and to pluck the fruit of the Tree of Immortal Life — ourselves — right now — while here on earth.

RELIGIONS OF IDENTITY

Such an aim and such a realization I am going to call "mythic identification." Briefly, the underlying idea is that the ultimate truth, substance, support, energy, or reality of the universe transcends all definition, all imaging, all categories, and all thought. It is beyond the reach of the mind, i.e., transcendent. Consequently, to ask, as our theologians do: "Is the Godhead just? merciful? wrathful?" "Does it favor this people or that: the Jew, the Christian, or Mohammedan?" is ridiculous. That is simply to project human sentiments and concerns beyond their temporal sphere, and so, to short circuit the problem altogether. It is a kind of anthropomorphism, hardly more appropriate to a developed religion than the attribution of gender to the source-mystery of being — which is another of the pompous absurdities, however, of our own curious tradition. But now, on the other hand (and here is the great point): that which is thus ultimately transcendent of all definition, categories, names, and forms is the very substance, energy, being, and support of all things, including ourselves: the reality of each and all of us. Transcendent of definition, transcendent of enclosure, it is yet immanent in each. OM MANI PADME HUM.

Take, for example, a pencil, ashtray, anything, and, holding it before you in both hands, regard it for a while. Forgetting its use and name, yet continuing to regard it, ask yourself seriously: "What is it?" As James Joyce states in *Ulysses* (and here is the touchstone of his art): "Any object, intensely regarded, may be a gate of access to the incorruptible eon of the gods" [18]. Cut off from use, relieved of nomenclature, its dimension of wonder opens; for the mystery of the *being* of that thing is identical with the mystery of the being of the universe — and of yourself. Schopenhauer, somewhere in his great work *The World as Will and Representation*, has summarized the leading theme of his philosophy in a single memorable sentence: "Every thing is the entire world as Will in its own way." And in the Indian Chāndogya Upanisad there is the famous phrase addressed by the charming sage Aruni to his son, Śvetaketu: *tat tvam asi:* "You are It!" "You, Śvetaketu, my son, are yourself that immortal life" [9].

The Oriental sages and their texts are unanimous in insisting, however, that the "you" referred to in teachings of this kind is not exactly the "you" you think yourself to be, individuated in space and time, a temporary member of this world of passing forms, named, loved, and separate from your neighbor. *Neti neti,* "not this, not this," is the meditation properly applied to everything so known, so named and numbered: all those facets of the jewel of reality that present themselves to the mind. "I am not my body, my feelings, my thoughts, but the consciousness of which these are the manifestations." For we are all, in every particle of our being, precipitations of consciousness; as are likewise, the animals and plants, metals cleaving to a magnet and waters tiding to the moon. And as the physicist, Erwin Schrödinger, states in his book, *My View of the World:*

To divide or multiply consciousness is something meaningless. In all the world, there is no kind of framework within which we can find consciousness in the plural; this is simply something we construct because of the spatio-temporal plurality of individuals, but it is a false conception [36:3].

. . . What justifies you in obstinately discovering this difference — the difference between you and someone else — when objectively what is there is *the same?* . . . This life of yours which you are living is not merely a piece of the entire existence, but is in a certain sense the *whole;* only this whole is not so constituted that it can be surveyed in one single glance. And this, as we know, is what the Brahmins express in that sacred, mystic formula which is really so simple and so clear: *Tat tvam asi*, this is you. Or, again, in such words as "I am in the east and in the west, I am below and above, I am this whole world [36:21–22].

Letting *a* signify oneself and *x*, ultimate reality, we might represent this manner of self-identification, as follows:

$$a \neq\, = x.$$

As known phenomenologically, *a* is not *x;* yet, in truth, is indeed *x*.

The oxymoron, self-contradictory, the paradox, the transcendent symbol, pointing beyond itself, is the gateless gate, the sun door, the passage beyond categories. Gods and Buddhas in the Orient are, accordingly, not final terms — like Yahweh, the Trinity, or Allah in the West — but point beyond themselves to that ineffable being, consciousness, and rapture that is the All in all of us. And in their worship, the ultimate aim is to effect in the devotee a psychological transfiguration through a shift of his plane of vision from the passing to the enduring, through which he may come finally to realize in experience (not simply as an article of faith) that he is identical with that before which he bows. These are, then, *religions of identity*. Their mythologies and associated rites, philosophies, sciences, and arts are addressed, in the end, not to the honor of any god "out there" but to the recognition of divinity within.

605

Returning to our text, "The Great Forest Book" or *Bṛhadā-ranyaka Upaniṣad*:

He has entered into all this, even to the fingernail tips, like a razor in the razor case, like fire in firewood. Him they see not; for as seen, he is incomplete.

When breathing, He is named breath, when speaking voice, when seeing the eye, when hearing the ear, when thinking mind: these are just the names of His acts. Whoever worships one or another of these, knows not; for He is incomplete in one or another of these. One should worship with the idea that He is just one's self (*ātman*), for therein all these become one.

That same thing, namely, this Self, is the footprint of this All, for just as one finds cattle by a footprint, so one finds this All by its footprint, the Self [6:4.1.7].

Something similar appears to have been implied in the following quotations from the earliest religious writings known: the *Pyramid Texts* of the Fifth and Sixth Dynasties of Old-Kingdom Egypt (circa 2350–2175 B.C.) where the spirit of the deceased takes back into itself the manifold powers of the various gods that during his lifetime had been regarded as without.

It is he who eats their magic and swallows their spirits. Their Great Ones are for his morning meal, their middle-sized ones are for his evening meal, their little ones are for his night meal, their old men and old women are for his fire [22:93–94, Text 404].

. . . Behold, their soul is in his belly. . . . Their shadows are taken away from the hand of those to whom they belong. He is as that which dawns, which endures [22:95, Text 413].

And again, a millennium or so later, more explicitly, from *The Book of the Dead:*

My hair is the hair of Nu. My face is the face of the Disk. My eyes are the eyes of Hathor. My ears are the ears of Ap-uat. . . . My feet are the feet of Ptah. There is no member of my body that is not the member of some god. . . .

I am Yesterday, Today, and Tomorrow, and I have the power to be born a second time. I am the divine hidden Soul who creates the gods. . . .

Hail, lord of the shrine that stands in the middle of the earth. He is I and I am he, and Ptah has covered his sky with crystal [7:190–191, 196–197].

Essentially the same, or at least a like, idea is suggested in certain early Mesopotamian seals, some of which are of about the date of the *Pyramid Texts*. Figure 1, for instance, shows a

devotee approaching the altar of the Lord of the Tree of Life, with his right hand lifted in worship and on his left arm a goat, his offering. The gracious god, in return, proffers the cup of ambrosial drink, drawn from the fruit or sap of the tree, which bestows the gift of immortality that, centuries later, was to be denied to Adam and Eve. The god is horned, like the moon above his cup; for the moon is the sign celestial of the ever enduring resurrection. As Lord of the Tides of the Womb, forever waxing and waning, it carries — like life — its own death within it; yet, also, its victory over death. In Figure 2 we see its

crescent again. However, the tree, this time, is attended by the dual apparition of a goddess known as Gula-Bau, whose later classical counterparts, Demeter and Persephone, were the goddesses, without peer, of both the Orphic and the Eleusinian mysteries. In this ancient Babylonian seal of circa 1750–1550 B.C. (approximately one millennium earlier than the Garden text of the Bible), the dual goddess of the plains of life and of death is passing the fruit of deathlessness to a mortal woman approaching from the left. Figure 3, from an early Sumerian seal, circa

2500 B.C., presents the god and goddess together, Lord and Lady of the Tree, in the company, however, of the Serpent, not the moon: for as the moon sheds death in the figure of its shadow, so the serpent its slough, to be born again of itself. They are equivalent symbols, heavenly and earthly, of the ever dying, ever living Being of beings that is life in the garden of this world [41].

In India, Śiva is the counterpart — worshiped to this hour — of the god at the foot of the Tree, dispensing the moon-elixir of life; and in the sixth century B.C., when the prince Siddhārtha in his meditations arrived at the foot of that same World Tree, he there achieved the boon of Illumination, which he then dispensed to the world, in the place and role of the god. Likewise, in the classical mystery cults, the aim of the quest of the initiate was to realize in himself divinity. "Happy and Blessed One," we read on a golden Orphic tablet of circa 300 B.C., "thou shalt be God instead of mortal" [15:585]. And Apuleius, A.D., second century, at the end of the ordeal of *The Golden Ass* was, through the bounty of the goddess Isis, transformed into the likeness of a god: "In my right hand I carried a lighted torch and a garland of flowers was on my head, with white palm leaves sprouting out on every side like rays. Thus I was adorned, like to the sun and made in fashion of an image, when the curtains were drawn aside and all the people crowded to behold me" [1:294].

Among the North European Celts and Germans, also, the wonderful drink of "Deathlessness" (Sanskrit *amrta*, Greek ἀμβροσία) was known under many guises. Odin (Wotan) gave an eye for a sip from the Well of Wisdom at the foot of the

World Ash, Yggdrasil, where it was guarded by Mimir, the dwarf; and aloft in Valhall, his hero hall, the warrior dead drank of a mead served by the Valkyries that restored them to life and joy. The Celtic sea god Manannan served in his dwelling under waves an ale that bestowed immortality on all his guests; and, for a taste of the sort of knowledge gained by initiates of the Celtic race, we have the famous charm of Amairgen the magician, from the Irish *Lebor Gabala* ("Book of Invasions"). Compare the words of the Upanisad, above cited by Erwin Schrödinger:

I am the wind that blows o'er the sea;
I am the wave of the deep;
I am the bull of seven battles;
I am the eagle on the rock;
I am a tear of the sun;
I am the fairest of plants;
I am a boar for courage;
I am a salmon in the water;
I am a lake on the plain;
I am the word of knowledge;
I am the head of the battle-dealing spear;
I am the god who fashions thought in the mind [26:91–92].

RELIGIONS OF RELATIONSHIP

But now, in irreconcilable contrast to this ancient, practically universal, mode of experience of the world's and one's own dimension of divinity, which I have termed "mythic identification," there is the order of beliefs derived from the biblical tradition, where Yahweh, as we know (arriving very late on the scene), cursed the serpent of the Garden (Figure 3) and with it the whole earth, which he seems to have thought he had created. Here God creates the World and the two are *not* the same: Creator and Creature, ontologically distinct, are *not* to be identified with each other in any way. In fact, an experience of identity is the prime heresy of these systems and punishable by death. Their formula, therefore, is not, as in the earlier and more general order, $a \neq = x$, but a is related to x:

$$a \text{ R } x.$$

And what is the medium of relationship? The local social group. For example, in the Hebrew context: God ordained a Covenant with a certain Semitic people. Birth as a member of that holy race, and observance of its rituals of the Covenant, are the means of achieving a relationship with God. No other means are known or admitted to exist.

Comparably, in the Christian view: Christ, the only son of God, is at once True God and True Man. This, throughout the Christian world, is regarded as a miracle, whereas, in keeping with the earlier formula of $a \neq = x$, we are *all* true god and true man: "All things are buddha things"; "Brahman sleeps in the stone": what is required is only that one should waken to that truth and thereafter live, *buddha*, "illuminated" (from the root *budh*, to know, to notice, to wake, to revive, to come to one's senses). According to the Christian view, no one except Christ can declare: "I and the Father are one" (John 10:30); hence, also: "No one comes to the Father, but by me" (John 14:6). Through Christ's humanity, we are related to him; through his Godhood, he relates us to divinity. Thus he, and he alone, is the pivot. Apart from him, we are apart from God, who, though just and merciful, is wrathful too, and was sorely offended by Adam's sin, the guilt of which we have all somehow inherited. God, in Christ, became Man. Accepting death on the Cross, he atoned mankind with the Father. No individual, however, can participate in that reconciliation but by membership in his Church, which he founded on the Rock of Peter, some time around A.D. 30.

Mythologized, the Cross of Christ was equated early in the Middle Ages with the Tree of Immortal Life, the tree forbidden in the Garden, and Christ crucified was its fruit; his blood, the ambrosial drink. The sacrifice of the Mass, furthermore, was interpreted as "a renewal of the Sacrifice on Calvary," through which the Redeemer imparts to the faithful of his Church the grace gained for them on the Cross. In terms of the imagery of the closed garden gate with the cherubim and the turning sword, Christ, as a kind of Prometheus, had broken past the frightening guard and gained access for mankind to immortal life, as sung in the hymn, *O Salutaris Hostia*, sung at the Benediction of the Blessed Sacrament:

> O Salutaris Hostia,
> Quae caeli pandis ostium. . . .
>
> O saving Victim,
> Who hast opened wide heaven's gates. . . .

However, in contrast to the Oriental, Buddhist, and Vedāntic ways of interpreting the symbolism of the guarded gate and passage to the tree — as referring, namely, to an inward, psychological barrier and crisis of transcendence — the authorized Christian reading has been of an actual, concrete, historic event of atonement with an angry god, who for centuries had withheld his boon of paradise from mankind, until strangely reconciled by this curious self-giving of his only son to a criminal's death on the Cross. The fact of the crucifixion has been read as the central fact of all history, and along with it certain other associated "facts" are accepted, such as in other mythological traditions would be interpreted psychologically (or, as theologians say, "spiritually") as symbols; such as: (1) the Virgin Birth, (2) the Resurrection, (3) the Ascension, (4) the existence of a heaven to which a physical body might ascend, and, of course, (5) that Fall in the garden of Eden, circa 4004 B.C., from the guilt of which the crucifixion has redeemed us.

God in this system is a kind of fact somewhere, an actual personality to whom prayers can be addressed with expectation of a result. He is apart from and different from the world: in no sense *identical* with it, but *related*, as cause to effect. I call this kind of religious thinking, "mythic dissociation." The sense of an experience of the sacred is dissociated from life, from nature, from the world, and transferred or projected somewhere else — an imagined somewhere else — while man, mere man, is accursed. "In the sweat of your face you shall eat bread till you return to the ground, for out of it you were taken; you are dust, and to dust you shall return" (Genesis 3:19).

The sacred is now not secular, of this world of mere dead dust, but canonical, supernaturally revealed and authoritatively preserved; that is to say: God, from "out there," has condescended graciously to accord special revelations: (1) to the Hebrews, historically, on Sinai, via Moses; (2) to mankind, historically, in Bethlehem, via Jesus; but then also, apparently, (3) to mankind, once again, historically, in a cave near Mecca, via Mohamet. All, it will be noted, Semites! No other revelations of this desert god are admitted to exist, and *Extra ecclesiam nulla salus.*

To the formula of mythic dissociation, therefore, there must now be added that of "social identification": identification with Israel, with the Church as the Living Body of Christ, or with the Sunna of Islam — each body overinterpreted by its membership as the one and only holy thing in this world. And the focal center and source of all this holiness is concentrated in each case in a completely unique and special fetish; not a symbol, but a fetish: (1) the Ark of the Covenant in the Temple; (2) the Torah in the synagogue; (3) the transubstantiated host of the Roman Catholic Church; (4) the Bible of the Reformation; (5) the Koran, and (6) the Ka'aba of Islam.

In India and the Far East, such revered supports of the religious life would be known, finally, to point beyond themselves and their anthropomorphic god: beyond names, forms, and all scriptural personification, to that immanent transcendent mystery of being which defies thought, feeling, and figuration. For, whereas the attitude of focused piety is there recognized as appropriate for those not yet prepared to live in the realization of their own identity with "That" (*tat tvam asi*), for anyone ready for an actual religious experience of his own, such canonized props are impediments. "Where is Self-knowledge for him whose knowledge depends on the object?" we read in a Vedāntic text. "The wise do not see a this and a that, but the Self (*ātman*) Immutable" [24:175]. "You have your own treasure house," said the eighth-century Chinese sage Ma-tsu, "why do you search outside?" [32:30].

However, as another sage, Wei-kuan, once declared to a monk in quest of enlightenment: "As long as there is 'I and thou,' this complicates the situation and there is no seeing Tao."

"When there is neither 'I' nor 'thou,' is it seen?" the monk then asked.

"When there is neither 'I' nor 'thou,'" came the paradoxical answer, "who is here to see it?" [38:90–91]. Or, to quote, again, Ramakrishna:

> The essence of Vedānta is: *brahman* alone is real and the world illusory; I have no separate existence; I am that *brahman* alone. . . . But for those who lead a worldly life, and for those who identify themselves with the body, this attitude of "I am He" is not good. It is not good for householders to read the Vedānta. It is very harmful for them to read these books. Householders should look on God as Master and on themselves as His servants. They should think, "O God, You are the Master and the Lord, and I am Your servant." People who identify themselves with the body should not have the attitude of "I am He" [23:593].

The point is simply that the meditation "Not this, not this" (*neti neti*) must be accomplished before "I am brahman" (*brahmāsmi*) and "it is here, it is here" (*iti iti*). However, when the latter is begun, the fetish, the idol, is left behind, as it was when Ramakrishna flung his flowers all about. And there is a parallel here to Socrates' doctrine of Beauty in the *Symposium* when he states (quoting the wise woman Diotima) that when the lover has learned to appreciate the beauty of one individual body,

> . . . he must consider how nearly related the beauty of any one body is to the beauty of any other, when he will see that if he is to devote himself to loveliness of form, it will be absurd to deny that the beauty of each and every body is the same. Having reached this point, he must set himself to be the lover of every lovely body, and bring his passion for the one into due

proportion by deeming it of little or of no importance [31: 561–562].

No such whoring after alien gods, however, for the lover of that jealous god in the Bible! Nor is there any allowance, there, for the following of one's own light: the leadership and guidance of one's own expanding, deepening, enriched experience of the nature of the world and oneself. All life, all thought, all meditation, is to be governed by the authority of the shepherds of the group; and there can be no doubt, from what we know of the history of this tradition, that this authority was imposed and maintained by force.

But any religious symbol, so interpreted that it refers, not to a thought-transcending mystery, but to a thought-enveloping social order, misappropriates to the lower principle the values of the higher and so (to use a theological turn of phrase) sets Satan in the seat of God.

THE EUROPEAN GRAFT

And is it not one of the strangest anomalies of history that a religion of this overbearing kind — exclusive, authoritative, collective, and fanatic — should have been carried intact from its Levantine hearth to be grafted onto the living stock of Europe? In the light of what can be seen today in the so-called Christian world, the graft would appear not to have taken hold. And in earlier centuries, also: the outstanding characteristic of the history of the Church in Europe has been its agony in a constant battle against heresies of all kinds, on every side, in every age — and heresy now has won. Already in the fifth century, the Irish heresy of Pelagius posed a challenge that the African Augustine was supposed to have put down. But Pelagianism today is the only brand of Christianity with any possibility of an Occidental future. For who, outside of a convent, actually believes today, in his heart, that every child born of woman, throughout the world, will be sent to an everlasting hell, unless somebody of Christian faith splashes water on its head, to the accompaniment

614

of a prayer in the name of the Father, Son, and Holy Ghost? Furthermore, since there was no garden of Eden c 4004 B.C. — nor even c 1,800,000 B.C. in the period of Zinjanthropus — no Adam and no Eve back there, no serpent speaking Hebrew and, consequently, no Fall — no guilt — then what is all this talk about a general atonement? Unless Fall and Redemption, Disobedience and Atonement are poetic names for the same psychological states of ignorance and illumination that the Hindus and the Buddhists also are talking about! In which case, what happens to the doctrine of the unique historical importance of the Incarnation and Crucifixion of Christ?

Meister Eckhart surely understood this when he preached to his congregation: "It is more worth to God his being brought forth spiritually in the individual good soul than that he was born of Mary bodily" [29: no 88, p 221]. And again: "God is in all things as being, as activity, as power" [29: no 2, p 10]. Such teachings were condemned by John XXII; and Eckhart fortunately died before responding to the summons to Rome — or the Church might now have him on its record as well.

The great period of the breakthrough of the native European spirit against the imposed authority of decisions made by a lot of Levantine bishops at the Councils of Nicaea, Constantinople, Ephesus, and Chalcedon (A.D., fourth to eighth centuries) occurred in the twelfth and thirteenth centuries, in the period, precisely, of the rise of the great cathedrals: the period marked by Henry Adams as that of the greatest Christian unity — whereas actually it was a period of heresy bursting everywhere: Waldensians, Albigensians, and multitudes of others, the establishment of the Inquisition, and the Albigensian crusade.

As I see it, this breakthrough followed as the consequence of the courage of an increasing number of people of great stature to credit their own experience and to live by it against the dictates of authority. And I see the evidences of this courage in the spheres, successively, of feeling, thinking, and observation: love, philosophy, and science. I shall here deal only with the first, which marked the dawn, the first fair light, of the world we know today. It was eloquently and bravely announced at the very start of the twelfth century in the life and letters of Abelard's Heloise; defined psychologically in the poetry of the Troubadours and Minnesingers; celebrated with exquisite art in the Tristan romance of the great German poet, Gottfried von Strassburg; and brought to its culminating statement in the unsurpassed Grail romance of the greatest poet of the Middle Ages, Wolfram von Eschenbach.

The beautiful though ugly story of Heloise and Abelard is known to all: of how he, in his middle thirties, the most brilliant intellectual of the schools of Paris, deliberately seduced her, a girl of seventeen; and, when she was about to bear their child, sent her for protection to his sister in Brittany, then, conscience stricken, urged her to a secret marriage. She argued strongly against this, declaring, firstly, that domestic life would be beneath his dignity as a philosopher and, secondly, that she would rather be his mistress than bind him with a matrimonial chain. But he insisted, and, as the world knows, following the marriage, her uncle, the brutal canon Fulbert, sent a gang of thugs who castrated him, and he, in turn, sent Heloise to a convent. Then, after years of silence, not another word from him to her, she wrote to him:

> When little more than a girl, I took the hard vows of a nun, not from piety but at your command. If I now merit nothing from you, how vain I deem my labor! I can expect no reward from God, as I have done nothing from love of him. . . . God knows, at your command I would have followed or preceded you to fiery places. For my heart is not with me but with thee . . . [40:29–54].

Essentially the same sentiment is expressed in Gottfried's poem, a century later, in the words of his hero Tristan, where he states that for Isolt's love he would accept an "eternal death" in hell [14:157]. And again, seven centuries later — today, in the twentieth century — James Joyce's hero, Stephen Dedalus, in *A Portrait of the Artist as a Young Man*, declares to a Catholic schoolmate: "I will not serve that in which I no longer believe, whether it call itself my home, my fatherland, or my church.

. . . And I am not afraid to make a mistake, even a great mistake, a lifelong mistake, and perhaps as long as eternity too" [17:281].

EROS, AGAPE, AMOR

Now in theological sermons we are used to hearing of a great distinction between fleshly and spiritual love, *eros* and *agapē*. The contrast and conflict were already recognized and argued by the early Christian Fathers and have been argued ever since. An important point to be recognized, however, is that the ideal of love, *Amor*, of the lovers and poets of the Middle Ages, corresponded to neither of these. In the words, for example, of the troubadour Giraut de Borneil, *Love is born of the eyes and the heart* (*Tam cum los oills el cor ama parvenza*): the eyes recommend a specific image to the heart, and the heart, "the noble heart," responds [34:34], that is to say, this love is specific, discriminative, personal, and elite. *Eros*, on the other hand, is indiscriminate, biological, the urge, one might say, of the organs. And *agapē*, too, is indiscriminate: Love thy neighbor (whoever he may be) as thyself. Whereas, here, in the sentiment and experience of *Amor*, we have something altogether new — European — individual. And I know of nothing like it, earlier, anywhere in the world.

In Sufism and the Indian "left-hand path," with which this concept and experience of *Amor* has often been compared, the woman is treated rather as a vessel or symbol of divine import than as a person, individual in character and charm. She is commonly of lower caste, and the consortium is undertaken as a programmed spiritual discipline. Whereas here, on the contrary, the woman was almost always of equal or superior rank and honored for and as herself. In an essay in *The Dance of Siva* on the disciplines of a Hindu-Buddhist "left-hand" cult called "Sahaja" (root meaning "cognate, innate," hence, "spontaneous"), the late Dr. Ananda K. Coomaraswamy has described their aim as a mystic realization of

617

the self-oblivion of earthly lovers locked in each other's arms, where "each is both." . . . Each as individual has now no more significance for the other than the gates of heaven for one who stands within. . . . The beloved may be in every ethical sense of the word unworthy. . . . The eye of love perceives her divine perfection and infinity, and is not deceived. . . . The same perfection and infinity are present in every grain of sand and in the raindrop as much as in the sea [11:103].

In the Oriental literature, the great principle of this erotic discipline is described as the transformation of *kāma* into *prema* through "self-elimination." *Kāma*, "desire, lust," is exactly *eros*. *Prema*, "divine love," which is described as "the fulfillment of divine desires in and through our whole being" [12:145], may not correspond to *agapē*, as today understood in the Christian fold; however, in the orgiastic "love feast" (*agapē*) of such early Gnostic sects as the Alexandrian-Syrian Phibionites of the first five Christian centuries — described with horror, yet in detail, by Saint Epiphanius [c A.D. 315–402; see ref 13] — essentially the same ideal may be recognized of a conscientiously unmoral, depersonalized "love-in." And there can be no doubt that in twelfth and thirteenth century Europe, the period of the Troubadours, there developed in certain quarters of the rampant Albigensian heresy, a formidable resurgence of this type of religious thought and practice. Denis de Rougemont, in his learned volume *Love in the Western World* [33], has even argued that the cult and potery of *Amor* was a byproduct of this "Church of Love."

It seems to me essential to remark, however, that the aim in the troubadour "cult" (if we may call it that) of *Amor* was not in any sense ego extinction in a realization of nonduality, but the opposite: ego ennoblement and enrichment, through an altogether personal experience of love's poignant pain — "love's sweet bitterness and bitter sweetness," to quote Gottfried — in willing affirmation of the irremediable yearning that animates all relationships in this passing world of ephemeral individuation. It is true that in the doctrine of love represented by the Troubadours, marriage was not only of no interest, but actually contrary to the whole feeling, and that, likewise in India, the highest type of love, from the point of view of the Sahajiyā cult, was not of husband and wife, but (to quote one authority), "the love that exists most privately between couples, who are absolutely free in their love from any consideration of loss and gain, who defy society and transgress the law and make love the be-all of life" [12:144]. It is almost certainly not by mere coincidence that the greatest Indian poetic celebration of this ideal of adulterous (*parakiya*) love — namely the *Gita Govinda* ("Song of the Cowherd") of the young poet Jayadeva — is of a date exactly contemporary with the flowering in Europe of the Tristan romance [c A.D. 1175; see ref 16:352–358]. A moment's comparison of the two romances, however, immediately sets apart the two worlds of spiritual life. The Indian lover, Krishna, is a god; the European, Tristan, a man. The Indian work is allegorical of the yearning of flesh (symbolized in Radhā) for the spirit and of spirit (symbolized in Krishna) for the flesh, or, in Coomaraswamy's terms, symbolic of "the 'mystic union' of the finite with its infinite ambient" [11:103]; whereas the European poets, Thomas of Britain (c 1185), Eilhart von Oberge (c 1190), Béroul (c 1200), and Gottfried von Strassburg (c 1210), the four leading masters of the Tristan cycle, have represented the lovers as human, all too human — overwhelmed by a daemonic power greater than themselves. In the poems of the first three, the power of the potion, the releaser of the passion, is treated simply as of magic. In Gottfried's work, on the other hand, a religious dimension opens — heretical and dangerous — when he states, and states again, that the power is of the goddess Minne (Love). And then, moreover, to ensure his point, when the lovers flee to the forest, he brings them to a secret grotto of the goddess, described explicitly as an ancient heathen chapel of love's purity and with a bed — a wondrous crystalline bed — in the place of the Christian altar.

Now Saint Augustine had already compared Christ's death on the Cross to a marriage: "Like a bridegroom," he wrote, "Christ went forth from his chamber, he went out with a presage of his nuptials into the field of the world. He ran like a giant exulting on his way and came to the marriage bed of the cross, and there in mounting it he consummated his marriage. And when he perceived the sighs of the creature, he lovingly gave himself up to the torment in place of his bride, and he joined himself to the woman forever" [3:428].

Saint Bernard (1091–1153) in his passionate "Sermons on the Song of Songs" had provided further inspiration for Gottfried's radical secularization of the sacred in an area of life utterly rejected and condemned by the authorities of Rome, whose very name, ROMA, was the contrary, the reverse spelling, of AMOR. Marriage in the Middle Ages was little better (from the point of view of the Troubadours) than sacramentalized rape: an affair exclusively of family, political, and social concerns, whereby the woman (or rather, teen-age girl) was used for the ends of others, and into which the accident of love could fall only as a calamity, perilous to the social order as well as to the lives — both eternal and earthly — of its victims. Woman, with her power both to experience and to inspire love, was — like Eve, her prototype — the "Door of the Devil" (*janua diaboli*). And Bernard, in his sermons on the Song of Songs, assigning to the passion of love a yonder-worldly, virginal, nonexistent object, had striven with every ounce of his zeal to turn this energy of the glory of life to the ends ordained by the Church.

> I think [he preached] that the chief reason why the Invisible God wished to become visible in the flesh, and to live as a Man among men, was manifestly this — that He might first win back the affectations of fleshly creatures who could not love otherwise than in the flesh, to the salutary love of Himself in the Flesh, and thus step by step lead them finally to a love that is purely spiritual. Was it not, ultimately, in this degree of love that they were standing who said: *Behold, we have left all things, and have followed Thee* — Matthew 19:27 [4:113]?
>
> By desire, not by reason, am I impelled. A sense of modesty protests, it is true: love, however, conquers. . . .
>
> I am not unmindful of the fact that the *king's honor loveth judgment* — Psalm 99:4. But intense love does not wait upon judgment. It is not restrained by counsel; it is not checked by a

sense of false modesty; it is not subject to reason. — I ask, I implore, I entreat with all my heart: *Let him kiss me with the kiss of his mouth* — Canticles (Song of Solomon) 1:2 . . . [4:82–83].

Thus, therefore, even in this body of ours the joy of the Bridegroom's presence is frequently felt, but not the fullness of it; for although His visitation gladdens the heart, the alternation of His absence makes it sad. And this the beloved must of necessity endure until she has once laid down the burden of the body of flesh, when she too will fly aloft borne up on the wings of her desires, freely making her way through the realms of contemplation and with unimpeded mind following her Beloved *whithersoever He goeth* — Apocalypse (Revelation to John) 14:4 [4:141].

Essentially, Bernard was doing with the name and figure of Christ exactly what the Indian Jayadeva, half a century later, was to do with the name and figure of Krishna, the Incarnation of Vishnu, lover and seducer of the buxom matron Radhā and the other married Gopis, luring them with his flute from their husbands' earthly beds to the rapture of divine love in the forest of Vrindavan. But the Hebrew Song of Songs itself — a composite of scraps of erotic Levantine poetry, such as abounds, for example, throughout the *Arabian Nights* — had already been reinterpreted, before admission to the Canon, as metaphoric in this same way of the love between Yahweh and Israel.

> How graceful are your feet in sandals,
>   O queenly maiden!
> Your rounded thighs are like jewels,
>   the work of a master hand.
> Your navel is a rounded bowl
>   that never lacks mixed wine.
> Your belly is a heap of wheat
>   encircled with lilies [37].

Whether as Krishna, Yahweh, or Christ — and the Bride as Radhā, the Holy Jewish Race, Holy Mother Church, or the individual soul: the lover in all of these devotional traditions is an agent of spiritual transformation, converting *eros* into *agapē*,

kāma into *prema;* whereas in the Tristan legend the two lovers
are equally of this world. In India the ultimate union is registered as the realization of *identity*, an experience of nonduality,
where "each is both." In Israel and the Catholic Church, the
union is a *relationship*, where the two terms, God and Creature,
though united, remain distinct. Yet in both contexts, the tide of
thought is away from the marriages of *this* world to *that*.
Saint Paul's announcement that "the desires of the flesh are
against the Spirit, and the desires of the Spirit are against the
flesh" (Galatians 5:17) and Coomaraswamy's statement that
when "lovers locked in each other's arms" realize self-oblivion,
"each as individual has now no more significance for the other
than the gates of heaven for one who stands within," amount,
in the end, to much the same: namely, a spitting out of this
world. That is not the mood of the Tristan romance, or of anything that has ever been really great and typical of Europe, from
the period of Homer to *Finnegans Wake*.

If $a \neq\, = x$ be taken as the formula of the Oriental, Buddhist-
Vedāntic order of experience, and $a \,R\, x$ the Levantine, Hebrew-
Christian-Islamic, then $a \,R\, b$ will represent the European, where
b is not an assumed being or personality transcendent of temporality, but another phenomenal entity, like a: as were both Tristan and Isolt. The Greeks and Romans, Celtic and Germanic
peoples have generally tended to maintain a decent respect for
the interests and value judgments of the empirical sphere of experience. And yet their perceptions have not been confined to
this foreground view. There is more to $a \,R\, b$ than meets the eye.

In Gottfried's representation, for example, of the mystery of
love, as symbolized particularly in the grotto chapel of the goddess Minne, something not a little like the Indian sahaja concept
appears, when he writes that the young lovers, when they had
drunk of the potion, "realized that there was between them just
one mind, one heart, and one will. . . . The sense of a difference between them was gone" [14:151]. Through the influence
of the potion of love, that is to say, a dimension had opened
beyond the plane of time and space, wherein the two experienced themselves as one, though in the field of space and time

they remained two — and not only two, but each as an individual irreplaceable, not at all (as in Coomaraswamy's formula) of no more significance for each other "than the gates of heaven for one who stands within." For according to the principle of *Amor*, as opposed to both *agapē* and *eros*, the particular person, the form and character of the individuation of perfection, continues to be of great moment, even of central concern, and "in every ethical sense" respected. An appropriate formula for *this* mode of experience of the Love dimension, then, would be, where *a* is Tristan and *b* Isolt:

$$a \neq = x = \neq b$$

while in the field of space and time, which is where that dimension is experienced,

$$a \, \mathrm{R} \, b,$$

the experience of the *x* dimension being a function of R.

In Gottfried's poem, tragedy follows the inability of the characters to reconcile love (*minne*), on the one hand, and honor (*ere*), on the other. Gottfried himself and his century were torn between the two [42]. The Love Grotto in the dangerous forest represents the dimension of the depth experience (*x*) and King Mark's court, the world in which that experience has to be borne. Holiness, the ideal, and intimations of eternity are focused in the cave, which, though described as if in Cornwall, is not a historical place, but a shared psychological condition: "I have known that cave," states the poet, "since I was eleven years old, yet have never set foot in Cornwall" [14:215]. The lore and rituals of the Christian religion, on the other hand, are associated with the world, as part and parcel of the temporal sociopolitical order. Though himself probably a cleric, and certainly learned in theology, Gottfried is openly disdainful of current Christian doctrines. (See especially the poet's comment on the favorable outcome of Isolt's dishonesty in her trial by ordeal for adultery: "There it was revealed and confirmed for all the world that the very virtuous Christ is as yielding as a windblown sleeve: he adapts himself and goes along whatever way he is pressed, as readily and easily as anyone could ask" — lines 15733–15740.) He prays for inspiration, not to the Trinity and the saints, but to Apollo and the Muses; shows the destiny of his characters to have been governed neither by their own free will nor by God, but by the goddess of the Grotto, Minne, "Love," and employs the very language of Saint Bernard in celebration of the eucharist to recommend to his readers the lovers in adultery on their blessed crystalline bed.

> We read their life, we read their death,
> And to us it is sweet as bread.
> Their life, their death, are our bread.
> So lives their life, so lives their death,
> So live they still and yet are dead
> And their death is the bread of the living [14:3].

Chiefly, Gottfried's inspiration had sprung from his recognition in the Celtic legend, compounded of Pictish, Irish, Welsh, Cornish, and Breton elements, an order of poetic imagery congenial to his own mode of experience. It was a legend rooted, like all Arthurian romance, in the most ancient, native European mythological tradition — that of the old Megalithic, Bronze-Age goddess of many names, mother of the gods and the immanent power of all nature: the earth, not as dust, but as the source, the living body out of which all things proceed and to which they return at peace. Moreover, that Gottfried knew of whom he was speaking when he wrote of the goddess Minne is evident in his statement (among others) that her chapel, the grotto, *la fossiure a la gent amant* [14:209], had been designed and built for lovers by giants in prechristian times. The Grail legend, also, had sprung from that pagan base. Whereas in the Tristan legend the tragical theme is of a dissociation between the spheres of nature and society, sincerity and religion, the timeless forest and the timely court, love and life, in the Grail legend the leading theme is of the healing of that breach: a renewal of the Waste Land of the Christian social order through a miracle of uncorrupted nature, the integrity of a noble, resolute heart.

The earliest extant version of this most profound European

legends is the *Perceval, Li Contes del Graal* (c 1174–1180), of Chrétien de Troyes, the court poet of the Countess Marie de Champagne. Chrétien was apparently a clergyman, a canon of the Abbey of Saint-Loup [25:282]. The story had been assigned to him, he declares, by Count Philip of Flanders, who had presented him with a "book" in which the legend was contained [10]. But he left his poem unfinished. Like all his work, it is fluent and charming. However he here shows little sense for the import of the symbols and may have felt that they went against his grain.

The best known version of the legend is the one that inspired Tennyson — a late version translated by Malory from the work of a Cistercian monk, *La Queste del Saint Graal* (c 1215–1230) — in which the Grail is identified with the chalice of the Last Supper, and its quest is achieved by the saintly youth Galahad, who is not, like, Perceval, a married man, but a knightly monk, absolutely chaste, and whose achievement consists not in service to this world but in leaving it for heaven together with the Grail [27:20].

The primary source of the Grail symbol, on the other hand, was the vessel of ambrosial drink of the Celtic seagod, Manannan — compare p 609 and the cup in Figure 1 [21]. A second sphere of association was with the sacramental bowls of the late Classical Orphic sects that were brought into northern Europe during the Gallo-Roman period [19:194–260; 20] and, though indeed equivalent, in a way, to the Christian chalice of the Redeemer's blood, referred to a mystery rather of inward illumination than of reconciliation with an angry god. And one of the most impressive things about the great *Parzival* of the master poet Wolfram von Eschenbach (an exact contemporary of Gottfried) is the way in which the author linked his central symbol to both of these early contexts, the Celtic and the Classical, while at the same time suggesting the relevance of its legend to the cure of the malaise of his time. The Grail is not a vessel at all, but stone, "The Wish of Paradise," named "lapsit exillis" (*lapis exilis:* "little, feeble, or uncomely stone"), which, as we read in a late alchemical work, the *Rosarium philosophorum*, was a name of the Philosophers' Stone [2:171, note 117]. This alchemical Grail, Wolfram declares, furthermore, was carried from heaven to earth by those angels who had remained neutral when Satan turned against God and the war in heaven ensued. They were those, so to say, "in the middle," 'twixt black and white. And such a stone, brought down by angels, suggests the Ka'aba of Islam. Thus Wolfram makes an explicit effort to assimilate to his symbol Islamic as well as Christian themes. The Grail, for him, was a cult-transcending talisman of crosscultural associations, pointing to an image of man ("The Wish of Paradise") released from ecclesiastical authority, perfected in his nature through his own personal adventure, serving the world not through servitude but through mastery and love fulfilled, not ravaged and destroyed.

For, in connection with the Grail Quest, the obvious question arises as to why anyone in the Middle Ages should have thought it necessary to embark on such a lonely, dangerous enterprise when the Holy Mass, with Christ himself on the altar, was being celebrated, right next door, every day. The answer — simply and plainly — is that the Mass was an ecclesiastical sacrament associated with a doctrine of vicarious salvation, administered in those centuries, furthermore, by a clergy notoriously corrupt and protected by Augustine's antidonatist argument, the dogma, namely, of the incorruptibility of the sacrament on which salvation hung, no matter what the moral character of the clergy by which it was administered. In contrast: the Grail is housed, not in a church, but in a castle; its guardian is not a priest, but a king. It is carried, not by an assortment of questionable males, but by twenty-five young women, whose virtue must be unsullied, and the knight who achieves the quest, and so restores the Waste Land to bounty, succeeds through integrity of character, in the service of a singly focused love, *Amor*.

In Wolfram's work, furthermore, a number of additional points are made, among which, the following:

(1) The knight, on his first visit to the Castle of the Grail, fails to achieve the aim of the quest because he acts as he has been taught to act, not on the impulse of his nature.

626

(2) He is told, subsequently, that no one who has failed on the first visit will ever have a second chance, yet he resolves to succeed notwithstanding, and, when he has done so, he is told that he has accomplished a miracle, since, through his integrity of character and persistence in resolve, he has caused the Trinity to change its rules.

(3) Following his first failure and the shame that falls upon him as a consequence, he renounces God and wanders for some five years in a Waste Land. And when he finally returns in his heart to God, it is *not* to the churchly sacramental theology of his mother and her clergy, but to a view of God as a cosmic principle corresponding and responding to the movements — whether of love or of hate — of the individual heart.

(4) Parzival is striving to repair his failure through holding one-pointedly to his quest; yet what gains for him his victory is *not* directly his quest, but the fervor and the loyalty of his love — not for God, but for a woman, whose very name, Condwiramurs (*Conduire amour* — in Old French, the nominative singular ends in -s) reveals her role as the guide and vessel of the energy of his life.

(5) Wolfram's ideal of love is neither that of the Church nor exactly that of the Troubadours' *Amor*. The idea of marriage without love (the Church's view) he rejects, but he rejects also love in adultery. Love, for him, is absolute, singlefold, and for life. It makes no difference, furthermore, whether it is ritually sacramentalized. It is fulfilled in a union that amounts, in effect, to the only type of marriage worthy of the name.

(6) Parzival's half-brother is a Muslim, as noble as himself. "One might speak of them as two," states the author when they come together on a battlefield, "but they are actually one: the one substance, through loyalty doing itself much harm."

(7) Man's life is neither all black nor all white, nor can it ever be: but through integrity to oneself, to one's nature, the poet states, one trends toward the white, whereas irresolution augments the black. His hero's name he interprets, through the French, as *per-ce-val*, "through the middle."

(8) And finally, when the hero arrives the second time at the

627

Castle of the Grail, he is accompanied by his Muslim brother, Feirefiz, so that a noble heathen might attain to this goal inaccessible to most Christians. However, an amusing and most remarkable scene then takes place. For, when the Grail is brought in, the Muslim prince cannot see it. All he can see are the beautiful form and eyes of the lovely maiden queen, Repanse de Schoye (*Repense de Joie*), by whom it is carried. The Grail company becomes gradually aware of this alarming fact, and presently word arrives from the ancient, ageless Grail King Titurel, reposing on a couch in the next hall (an Arthurian counterpart, he was, of the old sea god, Manannan), that the reason the heathen cannot see the Grail is that he has not yet been baptized. An old priest thereupon enters who has baptized many heathen and he instructs Feirefiz in the doctrine of the Trinity. "Is that her god?" the Muslim asks. "If I accept that god, can I marry her?" Told "Yes!" he consents willingly and the sacrament is administered. But what a strange baptism it is! For the empty font is first tilted toward the Grail, whereupon it fills with water from the boon-bestowing stone; so that, although the form of the rite is ecclesiastical, its content is of another order, namely, of the so-called *aqua permanens*, the water of life of the alchemists and of the ancient prechristian world (see again, Figure 1).

Moreover, when the heathen, so baptized, beholds the Grail with his own eyes, there appears written upon it the following statement — which, I believe, is for the date A.D. 1210 absolutely unique; to wit, as Feirefiz reads: IF ANY MEMBER OF THE GRAIL COMPANY SHOULD, BY THE GRACE OF GOD, BE GIVEN MASTERY OVER A FOREIGN FOLK, HE MUST NOT SPEAK TO THEM OF HIS RACE OR OF HIS NAME, AND MUST SEE TO IT THAT THEY GAIN THEIR RIGHTS.

It is my belief and argument, in conclusion, then, that:

(A) in these twelfth and thirteenth century works and words of Heloise, the Troubadours, Gottfried and Wolfram, a noble, serious, profoundly significant secularization of the sense of the sacred is to be recognized, wherein the courage of love is the revealing power, opening, as it were, a dimension of union, won-

628

der, and sweet mystery in the world of separate beings, not quenching all thereby in a yonder sea, but augmenting each in its own form and right to regard;

(B) that, in rejecting absolutely the authority of the Church, these lovers and poets returned consciously and conscientiously to an earlier, prechristian, native European order of conscience, wherein the immanence of divinity was recognized in nature and its productions;

(C) but, then, also that, in this return, there was nevertheless a new factor, namely, a dissociation of the individual from the body of the group, as one unique in himself, who, if he is to realize his own potentialities, *must not* follow the paths or ways of any other, but discover himself his own. In fact, even in the monastic version of the legend, the Cistercian *Queste del Saint Graal*, it is declared that, when the knights of Arthur's court rode forth to adventure, they thought it would be disgraceful to start out in a group, but each entered the forest alone at a point that he had chosen, "there where he saw it most dark, and he found no way or path" [28:26].

THE WESTERN INDIVIDUAL

It is my thought, that the wealth and glory of the western world, and of the modern world as well (in so far as it is still in spirit, western) is a function of this respect for the individual, not as a member of some sanctified consensus through which he is given worth,

$$a \, R \, x$$

nor as an indifferent name and form of that "same perfection and infinity . . . present in every grain of sand, and in the raindrop as much as in the sea,"

$$a \neq \, = x,$$

but as an end and value in himself, unique in his *im*perfection, i.e., in his yearning, in his process of becoming not what he "ought" to be but what he is, actually and potentially: such a one as was never seen before.

This way of appreciating life was known already to the Greeks, in the Homeric epics, in Aeschylus and in Pindar. Nietzsche, in *The Birth of Tragedy*, writes of the perfect union in Classical art of the Apollonian and Dionysian principles: delight in the dreamlike wonder of individuated forms together with a poignant — even rapturous — recognition of their impermanence, not as a refutation but as a heightening of the wonder of their moment in the sun. "Short," wrote Pindar, in celebration of the young winner of a wrestling match, "Short is the space of time in which the happiness of mortal men groweth up, and even so, doth it fall to the ground when striken down by adverse doom. Creatures of a day, what is any one? what is he not? Man is but a dream of a shadow; yet, when a gleam of sunshine cometh as a gift of heaven, a radiant light resteth on men, aye and a gentle life" [30: lines 92–97]. It was in this mode that Greek science developed, Greek science as well as Greek art: through a recognition and search for general archetypes or principles in individual instances, yet with a recognition also of the value of the instance in itself, and particularly of the exception as revelatory of principles and powers yet unknown, which is precisely the opposite view to that of Archaic, Oriental, and Orthodox life, where anyone who picked up sticks on the sabbath was to be "stoned to death with stones by the congregation" (Numbers 15:32–36).

The coming of the Church to Europe reversed, for a time, the order of precedence in native European thought, placing the group before the individual, its fetishes above the quest for truth, and idiocy above genius (see I Corinthians 1:21: "For since, in the wisdom of God, the world did not know God through wisdom, it pleased God through the folly of what we preach to save those who believe"). The confessional, the heretic's death, and eternal hell were established, like the cherubim and turning sword at the gate of Paradise, to keep men out of the garden of an individual life. However, as the poet Blake found out when he was walking, as he declares, "among the fires of hell, delighted with the enjoyments of Genius, which to Angels look like torment and insanity":

> A fool sees not the same tree that a wise man sees;

and again,

> The apple tree never asks the beech how he shall grow; nor the lion, the horse, how he shall take his prey [5].

If it was in the kingdom of the courageous heart, as in that of Heloise, that the first portents appeared of the new age dawning for the West, it was through those of the mind and the observant eye (philosophy and science) that the promise was fulfilled. Heloise in her life was mangled and the country of the Troubadours turned into an eloquent waste; yet the ideal of heterosexual love that prevails in the world today was originally hers and theirs. Moreover, the history of the poetry and song of the modern West commences with the works of the Troubadours.

And likewise, in philosophy: though the bold Scholastic effort to bring reason to bear on religion was summarily crushed with the publication of the authoritative Condemnations of 1277 — where a catalogue of 219 philosophical propositions was condemned as contrary to Faith — what has triumphed in the modern world has been, obviously, not canonical, but individual thought; so that, although as late as 1864, Pope Pius IX could state in a Syllabus of Errors, condemning rationalism, socialism, communism, naturalism, the separation of Church and State, freedom of the press and of religion, that "The Roman pontiff cannot and should not be reconciled and come to terms with progress, liberalism, and modern civilization," a century later, John XXIII, found it prudent, rather, to relent and to do just that — with what result, however, the Church itself is yet to learn. The Protestant theologian, Rudolf Bultmann, who has been suggesting, meanwhile, what he calls a "demythologization," or rationalization, of the Christian religion, has found it necessary to hold — if there is to be any specifically "Christian" religion at all — to the Resurrection of Jesus from the grave, not as a mythic image, but as a fact — which is, of course, what has been the problem here, all along: the concretization of myth. Compare the so-called Second Letter of Peter which is actually not of Peter but of some later hand): "For we did not follow cleverly devised myths when we made known to you the power and coming of our Lord Jesus Christ, but we were eye-witnesses of his majesty" (II Peter 1:16).

One can only suggest to these stubborn gentlemen that if, instead of insisting that their own mythology is history, they would work the other way and dehistoricize their mythology, they might recover contact with the spiritual possibilities of this century and salvage from what must otherwise be inevitable discard whatever may still be of truth to life in their religion.

For it is simply an incontrovertible fact that, with the rise of modern science, the entire cosmological structure of the Bible and the Church has been destroyed and not the cosmological only, but the historical as well. The gradual, irresistible, steady development of this new realization of the wonder of the world and of man's place and possibilities within it, against every instrument of resistance of the Church — resistance even to the present hour — has been, and continues to be, the fruit of the labors of a remarkably small number of men with the wit and courage to oppose authority with accurate observation. Their work began inconspicuously in the period for Adelard of Bath (a contemporary of Heloise and Abelard), coming to two great moments of climax, first with the publication of Copernicus' *De revolutionibus orbium coelestium* (1543) and then of Darwin's *Origin of Species* (1859). The number of creative minds was few; yet the magnitude of the crisis brought about for the entire world by their probings of the wells of truth can hardly be overstated. For, in the broadest view of the history of mankind, it can be said without exaggeration that, with the rise of the modern scientific method of research in the sixteenth and seventeenth centuries and the development in the eighteenth, nineteenth, and twentieth of the power-driven machine, the human race was brought across a culture threshold of no less magnitude and import than that of the invention of agriculture in the eighth millennium B.C. and the rise of the earliest cities and city states in the fourth. Futhermore, just as the mythologies and rituals of the primitive hunting and root-gathering tribes of the earlier million-or-so years of human life had then to give place to those that soon arose of the high Bronze and Iron Age civilizations, so also, now, must those of our own outdated Bronze and Iron Age heritages give place to forms not yet imagined. And that they are already giving place surely is clear. For, firstly, in so far as the Waste-Land condition recognized by the poets of the Middle Ages persists within the Christian fold — where the sense of the sacred is still officially dissociated from this earth and its life (mythic dissociation) and the possibility of establishing a *relationship* with ultimate ends is still supposed to be achievable only through participation in the faith and rites of Christ's church (social identification) — the situation has worsened, not improved, since, for many, not only is the earth (as taught) mere dust, but the claims of the Church and its book to supernatural authorship have been destroyed absolutely and forever. And the resultant sense of alienation from value (variously interpreted in Marxian, Freudian, and Existentialist terms) is one of the most discussed spiritual phenomena of our time. "Man is condemned," as Sartre says, "to be free." However, not all, even today, are of that supine sort that must have their life values given them, cried at them from the pulpits and other mass media of the day. For there is, in fact, in quiet places, a great deal of deep spiritual quest and finding now in progress in this world, outside the sanctified social centers, beyond their purview and control: in small groups, here and there, and more often, more typically (as anyone who looks about may learn), by ones and twos, there entering the forest where they see it to be most dark and there is no beaten way or path.

REFERENCES

1. Apuleius, Lucius: *The Golden Ass*, W Adlington (1566), translator (Modern Library, Inc, Random House, Inc, New York, New York).
2. *Artis Auriferae*, vol 1 (Basel, Switzerland) 1593, p 210, as

cited by Jung, C G: *Psychology and Alchemy*, Bollingen Series XX, vol 12 (Pantheon Books, Randon House, Inc, New York, New York) 1953.

3. Augustine of Hippo: *Natali Domini IV, Sermo suppositus* 120:8. Translation from Marie-Louise von Franz: *Aurora Consurgens*, Bollingen Series LXXVII (Pantheon Books, Random House, Inc, New York, New York) 1966.

4. Bernard of Clairvaux, *Sermones in Canta Canticorum* XX.6, translation by Connolly, Terence L, S.J.: *Saint Bernard on the Love of God* (Spiritual Book Associates, New York, New York) 1937.

5. Blake, William: *The Marriage of Heaven and Hell*, 1793, "A Memorable Fancy" and "Proverbs of Hell."

6. *Brhadāranyaka Upanisad*.

7. Budge, E A W, translator: *The Papyrus of Ani*, reprinted in Horne, Charles F, ed: *The Sacred Books and Early Literature of the East*, vol 2 (Parke, Austin, and Lipscomb, New York, New York, and London, England) 1917, chap on "Abolishing the Slaughterings" and "On Coming Forth by Day in the Underworld."

8. Campbell, Joseph: *The Masks of God*, vol 4 (The Viking Press, New York, New York) chap 7 and 8.

9. *Chāndogya Upanisad*, 6.9.4.

10. Chrétien de Troyes: *Perceval (Li Contes del Graal)* A Hilke, ed (Halle) 1932, lines 63 ff.

11. Coomaraswamy, Ananda K: *The Dance of Śiva* (The Sunwise Turn, New York, New York) 1918.

12. Dasgupta, Shashibhusan: *Obscure Religious Cults as Background of Bengali Literature* (The University of Calcutta, Calcutta, India) 1946.

13. Epiphanius: *Panarion* 26.4.1, cited in Campbell, Joseph: *The Masks of God*, vol 4, *Creative Mythology* (The Viking Press, New York, New York) forthcoming, chap 3, sec 5, "The Gnostics."

14. Gottfried von Strassburg: *Tristan und Isold*, Friedrich Ranke, ed (Weidmannsche Verlagsbuchhandlung, Berlin,

Germany) 1959, lines 12499–12502, 12029–12037, 17136–17138, 235–240, 16700.

15. Harrison, Jane: *Prolegomena to the Study of Greek Religion* (Cambridge University Press, London, England) ed 3, 1922, Compagno Tablet, c 4th or 3d century B.C.

16. Jayadeva: Song of the Cowherd, in Campbell, Joseph: *The Masks of God*, vol 2, *Oriental Mythology* (The Viking Press, New York, New York) 1962.

17. Joyce, James: *A Portrait of the Artist as a Young Man* (Jonathan Cape, Ltd, London, England) 1916.

18. Joyce, James: *Ulysses* (Shakespeare and Company, Paris, France) 9th printing, 1927, p 396 (Random House, Inc, New York, New York) 1934, 409.

19. Leisegang, Hans: The Mystery of the Serpent, in Campbell, Joseph, ed: *The Mysteries*, Bollingen Series XXX, vol 2 (Pantheon Books, Inc, Random House, Inc, New York, New York) 1955.

20. Locke, Frederick W: *The Quest for the Holy Grail* (Stanford University Press, Stanford, California) 1960.

21. Loomis, Roger Sherman: *The Grail, from Celtic Myth to Christian Symbol* (Columbia University Press, New York, New York) 1963.

22. Mercer, Samuel A B: *The Pyramid Texts*, vol 1 (Longmans, Green & Co, Ltd, London, England) 1952.

23. Nikhilananda, Swami: *The Gospel of Śri Ramakrishna* (Ramakrishna-Vivekananda Center, New York, New York) 1942.

24. *Astavakrasamhitā* 18:38, Swami Nityaswarupananda, translator (Advaita Ashrama, Mayavati) 1940.

25. Nitze William A: Perceval and the Holy Grail, in *University of California Publications in Modern Philology*, vol 28, no 5 (University of California Press, Berkeley, California) 1949.

26. Nutt, Alfred, translator: *The Voyage of Bran, the Celtic Doctrine of Rebirth*, vol 2, Grimm Library, no 4 (David Nutt, London, England) 1897.

27. Pauphilet, Albert, ed: *La Queste del Saint Graal* (Edouard

Champion, Paris, France) 1949, contains the Old French text. Malory: *Le Morte d'Arthur*, renders the English translation in books 13–18.

28. Pauphilet, Albert, ed: *La Queste del Saint Graal* (Edouard Champion, Paris, France) 1949, p 26, lines 7–19.

29. Pfeiffer, Franz, ed: *Meister Eckhart*, vol 1, *Sermons and Collations*, C de B Evans, translator (John M Watson, London, England) 1947.

30. Pindar: *Pythian Ode VIII*, lines 92–97, for Aristomenes of Aegina, winner of the wrestling match, 446 B.C., translation by Sir John Sandys (Loeb Classical Library, Harvard University Press, Cambridge, Massachusetts) 1915.

31. Plato: *Symposium 210 b*, Michael Joyce, translator, in Hamilton, Edith, and Cairns, Huntington, ed: *The Collected Dialogues of Plato*, Bollingen Series, LXXI (Pantheon Books, Random House, Inc, New York, New York) 1961.

32. 101 Zen Stories, no 28, in Reps, Paul: *Zen Flesh, Zen Bones* (Anchor Books, Doubleday & Co, Inc, Garden City, New York) 1961.

33. Rougemont, Denis de: *Love in the Western World*, Montgomery Belgion, translator (Pantheon Books, Random House, Inc, New York, New York) rev ed, 1956.

34. Rutherford, John: *The Troubadours* (Smith, Elder, and Co, London, England) 1873.

35. Sartre, Jean-Paul: *Existentialism*, in Kaufman, Walter, translator: *Existentialism from Dostoyevski to Sartre* (Meridian Books, The World Pub Co, Cleveland, Ohio) 1957.

36. Shrödinger, Erwin: *My View of the World* (Cambridge University Press, London, England) 1964.

37. Song of Solomon: Canticles 7:1–2, *The Bible* Revised Standard Version (Thomas Nelson and Sons, New York, New York) 1953.

38. Suzuki, Daisetz Teitaro: *The Zen Doctrine of No-Mind* (Rider and Company, London, England) 1949.

39. *Tao Tê Ching*, VI.

40. Taylor, Henry Osborn: *The Mediaeval Mind*, vol 2 (Harvard University Press, Cambridge, Massachusetts) ed 4,

1925. The entire story is well retold here; the source texts are in Migne, PL clxxviii.

41. Ward, W H: *The Seal Cylinders of Western Asia* (Carnegie Institution, Washington, D.C.) 1910, publication no 100, figures 302, 389, and 388.

42. Weber, Gottfried: *Gottfrieds von Strassburg Tristan und die Krise des hochmittelalterlichen Weltbildes um 1200*, 2 vol (J B Metzlersche Verlagsbuchhandlung, Stuttgart, Germany) 1953.

18. RELIGION AS A CULTURAL SYSTEM

by Clifford Geertz

Any attempt to speak without speaking any particular language is not more hopeless than the attempt to have a religion that shall be no religion in particular. . . . Thus every living and healthy religion has a marked idiosyncrasy. Its power consists in its special and surprising message and in the bias which that revelation gives to life. The vistas it opens and the mysteries it propounds are another world to live in; and another world to live in — whether we expect ever to pass wholly over into it or no — is what we mean by having a religion — Santayana: *Reason in Religion* (1905 – 1906).

Two characteristics of anthropological work on religion that has been accomplished since the second world war strike me as curious when such work is placed against that carried out just before and just after the first world war. One is that it has made no theoretical advances of major importance. It is living off the conceptual capital of its ancestors, adding very little, save a certain empirical enrichment, to it. The second is that anthropological work draws what concepts it does use from a very narrowly defined intellectual tradition.

There are Durkheim, Weber, Freud, or Malinowski, and in any particular work the approach of one or two of these transcendent figures is followed, with but a few marginal corrections necessitated by the natural tendency to excess of seminal minds or by the expanded body of reliable descriptive data. But virtually no one even thinks of looking elsewhere — to philosophy, history, law, literature, or the "harder" sciences — as these men themselves looked — for analytical ideas. It occurs to me, also, that these two curious characteristics are not unrelated.

If the anthropological study of religion is in fact in a state of

639

general stagnation, I doubt that it will be set going again by producing more minor variations on classical theoretical themes. Yet one more meticulous case in point for such well established propositions as that ancestor worship supports the jural authority of elders, that initiation rites are means for the establishment of sexual identity and adult status, that ritual groupings reflect political oppositions, or that myths provide charters for social institutions and rationalizations of social privilege, may well finally convince a great many people, both inside the profession and out, that anthropologists are, like theologians, firmly dedicated to proving the indubitable.

In art, this solemn reduplication of the achievements of accepted masters is called academicism; and I think this is the proper name for our malady also. If we abandon, in a phrase of Leo Steinberg's, that sweet sense of accomplishment which comes from parading habitual skills and address ourselves to problems sufficiently unclarified as to make discovery possible, only then can we hope to achieve work which will not just reincarnate that of the great men of the first quarter of this century, but match it.

The way to do this is not to abandon the established traditions of social anthropology in this field, but to widen them. It seems to me that there are inevitable starting points for any useful anthropological theory of religion in at least four of the contributions of the men who, as I say, dominate our thought to the point of parochializing it — Durkheim's discussion of the nature of the sacred, Weber's *Verstehenden* methodology, Freud's parallel between personal rituals and collective ones, and Malinowski's exploration of the distinction between religion and common sense. But they are starting points only. To move beyond them, we must place them in a much broader context of contemporary thought than they, in and of themselves, encompass. The dangers of such a procedure are obvious: arbitrary eclecticism, superficial theory mongering, and sheer intellectual confusion. But I, at least, can see no other road of escape from what, referring to anthropology more generally, Janowitz [23:151] has called the dead hand of competence.

In working toward such an expansion of the conceptual envelope in which our studies take place, one can, of course, move in a great number of directions. Perhaps the most important initial problem is to avoid setting out, like Stephen Leacock's mounted policeman, in all of them at once. For my part, I shall confine my effort to developing what, following Parsons and Shils [38], I refer to as the cultural dimension of religious analysis.

The term "culture" has by now acquired a certain aura of ill repute in social anthropological circles because of the multiplicity of its referents and the studied vagueness with which it has all too often been invoked. (Though why it should suffer more for these reasons than "social structure" or "personality" is something I do not entirely understand.) In any case, the culture concept to which I adhere has neither multiple referents nor, so far as I can see, any unusual ambiguity: it denotes an historically transmitted pattern of meanings embodied in symbols, a system of inherited conceptions expressed in symbolic forms by means of which men communicate, perpetuate, and develop their knowledge about and attitudes toward life.

Of course, terms such as "meaning," "symbol," and "conception" cry out for explication. But that is precisely where the widening, the broadening, and the expanding come in. If Langer | 29:55] is right that "the concept of meaning, in all its varieties, is the dominant philosophical concept of our time," that "sign, symbol, denotation, signification, communication . . . are our [intellectual] stock in trade," it is perhaps time that social anthropology, and particularly that part of it concerned with the study of religion, became aware of the fact.

THE CULTURAL DIMENSION OF RELIGIOUS ANALYSIS

As we are to deal with meaning, let us begin with a paradigm: viz, that sacred symbol function to synthesize a people's ethos — the tone, character, and quality of their life, its moral and aesthetic style and mood — and their world view, the picture they have of the way things in sheer actuality are, their most comprehensive ideas of order [15]. In religious belief and practice, a group's ethos is rendered intellectually reasonable by being shown to represent a way of life ideally adapted to the actual state of affairs that the world view describes, while the world view is rendered emotionally convincing by being presented as an image of an actual state of affairs peculiarly well arranged to accommodate such a way of life.

This confrontation and mutual confirmation have two fundamental effects. On the one hand, they objectivize moral and aesthetic preferences by depicting them as the imposed conditions of life implicit in a world with a particular structure, a mere common sense that has been given the unalterable shape of reality. On the other, this confrontation and mutual confirmation support these received beliefs about the world's body by invoking deeply felt moral and aesthetic sentiments as experiential evidence for their truth. Religious symbols formulate a basic congruence between a particular style of life and a specific (if, most often, implicit) metaphysic. This congruence that religious symbols lend to a style of life and a metaphysic means that each is sustained with the borrowed authority of the other.

Phrasing aside, this much may perhaps be granted. The notion that religion tunes human actions to an envisaged cosmic order and projects images of cosmic order onto the plane of human experience is hardly novel. It is hardly investigated either. We have very little idea of how, in empirical terms, this particular miracle is accomplished. We just know that it is done, annually, weekly, daily, for some people almost hourly; and we have an enormous ethnographic literature to demonstrate it. But the theoretical framework does not exist which would enable us to provide an analytic account of it, an account of the sort we can provide for lineage segmentation, political succession, labor exchange, or the socialization of the child.

Let us, therefore, reduce our paradigm to a definition. Although it is notorious that definitions establish nothing, in themselves they do, if they are carefully enough constructed, provide a useful orientation, or reorientation, of thought, such that an extended unpacking of them can be an effective way of developing and controlling a novel line of inquiry. They have the useful virtue of explicitness. In this field especially, discursive prose is always likely to substitute rhetoric for argument. Definitions, then, commit themselves in a way that discursive prose does not.

Without further ado, then, a *religion* is:

(1) a system of symbols which acts to

(2) establish powerful, pervasive, and long-lasting moods and motivations in men by

(3) formulating conceptions of a general order of existence and

(4) clothing these conceptions with such an aura of factuality that

(5) the moods and motivations seem uniquely realistic.

(1) *A system of symbols which acts to.* . . . Such a tremendous weight is being put on the term "symbol" here that our first move must be to decide with some precision what we are going to mean by it. This is no easy task, for, rather like "culture," "symbol" has been used to refer to a great variety of things, often a number of them at the same time.

In some hands, symbol is used for anything which signifies something else to someone: dark clouds are the symbolic precursors of an oncoming rain. In others, it is used only for explicitly conventional signs of one sort or another: a red flag is a symbol of danger, a white of surrender. In others, it is confined to something which expresses in an oblique and figurative manner that which cannot be stated in a direct and literal one, so that there are symbols in poetry but not in science, and symbolic logic is misnamed.

In the work of yet others, however [27, 28, 29], the work symbol is used for any object, act, event, quality, or relation which serves as a vehicle for a conception. The conception is the symbol's "meaning," and that is the approach I shall follow here. The number 6, written, imagined, laid out as a row of stones, or even punched into the program tapes of a computer, is a symbol. But so also is the Cross, talked about, visualized, shaped worriedly in air or fondly fingered at the neck, the expanse of painted canvas called "Guernica" or the bit of painted stone called a churinga, the word "reality," or even the morpheme "-ing." They are all symbols, or at least symbolic elements, because they are tangible formulations of notions, abstractions from experience fixed in perceptible forms, concrete embodiments of ideas, attitudes, judgments, longings, or beliefs.

To undertake the study of cultural activity — activity in which symbolism forms the positive content — is thus not to abandon social analysis for a Platonic cave of shadows, to enter into a mentalistic world of introspective psychology or, worse, speculative philosophy, and wander there forever in a haze of "cognitions," "affections," "conations," and other elusive entities. Cultural acts, the construction, apprehension, and utilization of symbolic forms, are social events like any others; they are as public as marriage and as observable as agriculture.

They are not, however, exactly the same thing; or, more precisely, the symbolic dimension of social events is, like the psychological, itself theoretically abstractable from those events as empirical totalities. There is still, to paraphrase a remark of Kenneth Burke [6:9], a difference between building a house and drawing up a plan for building a house, and reading a poem about having children by marriage is not quite the same thing as having children by marriage. Even though the building of the house may proceed under the guidance of the plan or — a less likely occurrence — the having of children may be motivated by a reading of the poem, there is something to be said for not confusing our traffic with symbols with our traffic with objects or human beings, for these latter are not in themselves symbols, however often they may function as such. The reverse mistake, especially common among neokantians such as Cassirer (1953–1957), of taking symbols to be identical with, or "constitutive of," their referents is equally pernicious. "One can point to the moon with one's finger," some, probably well invented, Zen Master is supposed to have said, "but to take one's finger for the moon is to be a fool."

No matter how deeply interfused the cultural, the social, and the psychological may be in the everyday life of houses, farms, poems, and marriages, it is useful to distinguish them in analysis, and, so doing, to isolate the generic traits of each against the normalized background of the other two [38].

So far as culture patterns, i.e., systems or complexes of symbols, are concerned, the generic trait which is of first importance for us here is that they are extrinsic sources of information [18]. By "extrinsic," I mean only that — unlike genes, for example — the culture patterns lie outside the boundaries of the individual organism as such in that intersubjective world of common understandings into which all human individuals are born and in which they pursue their separate careers. Furthermore, culture patterns are extrinsic in that they persist after the human organism has died [46].

By "sources of information," I mean only that — like genes — culture patterns provide a blueprint or template in terms of which processes external to themselves can be given a definite form [21]. As the order of bases in a strand of DNA forms a coded program, a set of instructions, or a recipe, for the synthesization of the structurally complex proteins which shape organic functioning, so culture patterns provide such programs for the institution of the social and psychological processes which shape public behavior. Though the sort of information and the mode of its transmission are vastly different in the two cases, this comparison of gene and symbol is more than a strained analogy of the familiar "social heredity" sort. It is actually a substantial relationship, for it is precisely the fact that genetically programmed processes are so highly generalized in men, as compared with lower animals, that culturally programmed ones are so important, only because human behavior is so loosely determined by intrinsic sources of information that extrinsic sources are so vital [17].

To build a dam, a beaver needs only an appropriate site and the proper materials — his mode of procedure is shaped by his physiology. But man, whose genes are silent on the building trades, needs also a conception of what it is to build a dam, a conception he can get only from some symbolic source — a blueprint, a textbook, or a string of speech by someone who already knows how dams are built, or, of course, from manipulating graphic or linguistic elements in such a way as to attain for himself a conception of what dams are and how they are built.

This point is sometimes put in the form of an argument that cultural patterns are "models," that they are sets of symbols whose relations to one another "model" relations among entities, processes or what-have-you in physical, organic, social, or psychological systems by "paralleling," "imitating," or "simulating" them [10].

The term "model" has, however, two senses — an "of" sense and a "for" sense — and, though these are but aspects of the same basic concept, they are very much worth distinguishing for analytic purposes. In the first, what is stressed is the manipulation of symbol structures so as to bring them, more or less closely, into parallel with the preestablished nonsymbolic system, as when we grasp how dams work by developing a theory of hydraulics or constructing a flow chart. The theory or chart models physical relationships in such a way — i.e., by expressing their structure in synoptic form — as to render them apprehensible: it is a model *of* "reality." In the second, what is stressed is the manipulation of the nonsymbolic systems in terms of the relationships expressed in the symbolic, as when we construct a dam according to the specifications implied in an hydraulic theory or the conclusions drawn from a flow chart. Here, the theory is a model under whose guidance physical relationships are organized: it is a model *for* "reality."

For psychological and social systems and for cultural models that we would not ordinarily refer to as "theories," but rather as "doctrines," "melodies," or "rites," the case is in no way different. Unlike genes, and other nonsymbolic information sources, which are only models *for*, not models *of*, culture patterns have an intrinsic double aspect: they give meaning, i.e., objective conceptual form, to social and psychological reality both by shaping themselves to it and by shaping it to themselves.

It is, in fact, this double aspect which sets true symbols off from other sorts of significative forms. Models *for* are found, as the gene example suggests, through the whole order of nature, for, wherever there is a communication of pattern, such programs are, in simple logic, required.

Among animals, imprint learning is perhaps the most striking example, because what such learning involves is the automatic presentation of an appropriate sequence of behavior by a model animal in the presence of a learning animal. This sequence of behavior serves, equally automatically, to call out and stabilize a certain set of responses genetically built into the learning animal [33]. The communicative dance of two bees, one of which has found nectar and the other of which seeks it, is another, somewhat different, more complexly coded, example [14]. Craik [10] has even suggested that the thin trickle of water which first finds its way down from a mountain spring to the sea and smooths a little channel for the greater volume of water that follows after it plays a sort of model *for* function.

Much rarer are models *of* — linguistic, graphic, mechanical, natural, etc, processes which function, not to provide sources of information in terms of which other processes can be patterned, but to represent those patterned processes as such, to express their structure in an alternative medium. Perhaps models *of* may be confined, among living animals, to man. The essence of human thought is the perception of the structural congruence between one set of processes, activities, relations, entities, etc, and another set for which it acts as a program, so that the program can be taken as a representation, or conception — a symbol — of the programmed. The transposability of models *for* and models *of* which symbolic formulation makes possible is the distinctive characteristic of our mentality.

(2) . . . *to establish powerful, pervasive, and long-lasting moods and motivations in men by* . . . . So far as religious symbols and symbol systems are concerned this transposability is clear. The endurance, courage, independence, perseverance, and passionate willfulness in which the vision quest drills are seen in the Plains Indian are the same flamboyant virtues by which he attempts to live: while achieving a sense of revelation, he stabilizes a sense of direction [34]. The consciousness of defaulted obligation, secreted guilt, and, when a confession is

647

obtained, public shame in which Manus' seance rehearses him are the same sentiments that underlie the sort of duty ethic by which his property-conscious society is maintained: the gaining of an absolution involves the forging of a conscience [13]. And the same self-discipline which rewards a Javanese mystic staring fixedly into the flame of a lamp with what he takes to be an intimation of divinity drills him in that rigorous control of emotional expression which is necessary to a man who would follow a quietistic style of life [16].

It seems largely arbitrary whether one sees the conception of a personal guardian spirit, a family tutelary, or an immanent God as synoptic formulations of the character of reality or as templates for producing reality with such a character. Perhaps it is merely a matter of which aspect, the model *of* or model *for*, one wants for the moment to bring into focus. The concrete symbols involved – one or another mythological figure materializing in the wilderness, the skull of the deceased head of the household hanging censoriously in the rafters, or a disembodied "voice in the stillness" soundlessly chanting enigmatic classical poetry – point in either direction. They both express the world's climate and shape it.

They shape it by inducing in the worshiper a certain distinctive set of dispositions (tendencies, capacities, propensities, skills, habits, liabilities, pronenesses) which lend a chronic character to the flow of his activity and the quality of his experience. A disposition describes, not an activity or an occurrence, but a probability that an activity will be performed or that an event will occur in certain circumstances: "When a cow is said to be a ruminant, or a man is said to be a cigarette-smoker, it is not being said that the cow is ruminating now or that the man is smoking a cigarette now. To be a ruminant is to tend to ruminate from time to time, and to be a cigarette-smoker is to be in the habit of smoking cigarettes" [44:117]. Similarly, to be pious is not to be performing something we would call an act of piety, but to be liable to perform such acts. So, too, with the Plains Indian's bravura, the Manus' compunctiousness, or the Javanese's quietism which, in their contexts, form the substance of piety.

648

The virtue of this sort of view of what are usually called "mental traits" or, if the Cartesianism is unavowed, "psychological forces" (both unobjectionable enough terms in themselves) is that it gets them out of any dim and inaccessible realm of private sensation into that same well lit world of observables in which reside the brittleness of glass, the inflammability of paper, and, to return to the metaphor, the dampness of England.

So far as religious activities are concerned (and learning a myth by heart is as much a religious activity as detaching one's finger at the knuckle), two somewhat different sorts of disposition are induced by them: moods and motivations.

A motivation is a persisting tendency, a chronic inclination to perform certain sorts of act and experience certain sorts of feeling in certain sorts of situation, the "sorts" being commonly very heterogenous and rather ill defined classes in all three cases:

> . . . on hearing that a man is vain [i.e., motivated by vanity] we expect him to behave in certain ways, namely to talk a lot about himself, to cleave to the society of the eminent, to reject criticisms, to seek the footlights and to disengage himself from conversations about the merits of others. We expect him to indulge in roseate daydreams about his own successes, to avoid recalling past failures and to plan for his own advancement. To be vain is to tend to act in these and innumerable other kindred ways. Certainly we also expect the vain man to feel certain pangs and flutters in certain situations; we expect him to have an acute sinking feeling when an eminent person forgets his name, and to feel buoyant of heart and light of toe on hearing of the misfortunes of his rivals. But feelings of pique and buoyancy are not more directly indicative of vanity than are public acts of boasting or private acts of daydreaming . . . [44:86].

Similarly for any motivations. As a motive, "flamboyant courage" consists in such enduring propensities as to fast in the wilderness, to conduct solitary raids on enemy camps, and to thrill to the thought of counting coup. "Moral circumspection" consists in such ingrained tendencies as to honor onerous promises, to confess secret sins in the face of severe public disapproval, and to feel guilty when vague and generalized accusations are made

649

at seances. And "dispassionate tranquility" consists in such persistent inclinations as to maintain one's poise come hell or high water, to experience distaste in the presence of even moderate emotional displays, and to indulge in contentless contemplations of featureless objects. Motives are thus neither acts (i.e., intentional behaviors) nor feelings, but liabilities to perform particular classes of act or have particular classes of feeling. And when we say that a man is religious, i.e., motivated by religion, this is at least part — though only part — of what we mean.

Another part of what we mean is that he has, when properly stimulated, a susceptibility to fall into certain moods, moods we sometimes lump together under such covering terms as "reverential," "solemn," or "worshipful." Such generalized rubrics actually conceal, however, the enormous empirical variousness of the dispositions involved and, in fact, tend to assimilate them to the unusually grave tone of most of our own religious life. The moods that sacred symbols induce, at different times and in different places, range from exultation to melancholy, from self-confidence to self-pity, from an incorrigible playfulness to a bland listlessness — to say nothing of the erogenous power of so many of the world's myths and rituals. No more than there is a single sort of motivation that one can call piety, is there a single sort of mood that one can call worshipful.

The major difference between moods and motivations is that where the latter are, so to speak, vectorial qualities, the former are merely scalar. Motives have a directional cast, they describe a certain overall course, gravitate toward certain, usually temporary, consummations. But moods vary only as to intensity: they go nowhere. They spring from certain circumstances, but they are responsive to no ends. Like fogs, they just settle and lift; like scents, suffuse and evaporate. When present, they are totalistic: if one is sad, everything and everybody seems dreary; if one is gay, everything and everybody seems splendid. Thus, though a man can be vain, brave, willful and independent at the same time, he can't very well be playful and listless, or exultant and melancholy, at the same time [44:99]. Further, where motives persist

650

for more or less extended periods of time, moods merely recur with greater or lesser frequency, coming and going for what are often quite unfathomable reasons.

Perhaps the most important difference, so far as we are concerned, between moods and motivations is that motivations are "made meaningful" with reference to the ends toward which they are conceived to conduce, whereas moods are "made meaningful" with reference to the conditions from which they are conceived to spring. We interpret motives in terms of their consummations, but we interpret moods in terms of their sources. We say that a person is industrious because he wishes to succeed; we say that a person is worried because he is conscious of the hanging threat of nuclear holocaust. This is no less the case when the interpretations invoked are ultimate. Charity becomes Christian charity when it is enclosed in a conception of God's purposes; optimism is Christian optimism when it is grounded in a particular conception of God's nature. The assiduity of the Navaho finds its rationale in a belief that, since "reality" operates mechanically, it is coercible; their chronic fearfulness finds its rationale in a conviction that, however "reality" operates, it is both enormously powerful and terribly dangerous [24].

(3) . . . *by formulating conceptions of a general order of existence and* . . . . It ought to occasion no surprise that the symbols or symbol systems which induce and define those dispositions that we set off as religious are the same symbols as those which place those dispositions in a cosmic framework. What else do we mean by saying that a particular mood of awe is religious and not secular except that it springs from entertaining a conception of all-pervading vitality like mana and not from a visit to the Grand Canyon? Or that a particular case of asceticism is an example of a religious motivation except that it is directed toward the achievement of an unconditioned end like nirvana and not a conditioned one like weight reduction?

If sacred symbols did not at one and the same time induce dispositions in human beings and formulate, however obliquely, inarticulately, or unsystematically, general ideas of order, then

651

the empirical differentia of religious activity or religious experience would not exist.

A man can indeed be said to be "religious" about golf, but not merely if he pursues it with passion and plays it on Sundays: he must also see it as symbolic of some transcendent truths. And the pubescent boy gazing soulfully into the eyes of the pubescent girl in a William Steig cartoon and murmuring, "There is something about you, Ethel, which gives me a sort of religious feeling," is, like most adolescents, confused. What any particular religion affirms about the fundamental nature of reality may be obscure, shallow, or, all too often, perverse, but it must affirm something if it is not to consist of the mere collection of received practices and conventional sentiments that we usually refer to as moralism.

If one were to essay a minimal definition of religion today, it would perhaps not be Tylor's famous "belief in spiritual beings," to which Goody [20], wearied of theoretical subtleties, has lately urged us to return, but rather what Salvador de Madariaga has called "the relatively modest dogma that God is not mad."

Usually, of course, religions affirm very much more than this: we believe, as James [22:299] remarked, all that we can and would believe everything if we only could. The thing we seem least able to tolerate is a threat to our powers of conception, a suggestion that our ability to create, grasp, and use symbols may fail us, for were this to happen we would be more helpless, as I have already pointed out, than the beavers. The extreme generality, diffuseness, and variability of man's innate (i.e., genetically programmed) response capacities means that, without the assistance of cultural patterns, he would be functionally incomplete, not merely a talented ape who had, like some underprivileged child, unfortunately been prevented from realizing his full potentialities, but a kind of formless monster with neither sense of direction nor power of self-control, a chaos of spasmodic impulses and vague emotions [17].

Man depends upon symbols and symbol systems with a dependence so great as to be decisive for his creatural viability, and, as a result, his sensitivity to even the remotest indication that they may prove unable to cope with one or another aspect of experience raises within him the gravest sort of anxiety:

> [Man] can adapt himself somehow to anything his imagination can cope with; but he cannot deal with Chaos. Because his characteristic function and highest asset is conception, his greatest fright is to meet what he cannot construe — the "uncanny," as it is popularly called. It need not be a new object; we do meet new things, and "understand" them promptly, if tentatively, by the nearest analogy, when our minds are functioning freely; but under mental stress even perfectly familiar things may become suddenly disorganized and give us the horrors. Therefore our most important assets are always the symbols of our general *orientation* in nature, on the earth, in society, and in what we are doing: the symbols of our *Weltanschauung* and *Lebensanschauung*. Consequently, in a primitive society, a daily ritual is incorporated in common activities, in eating, washing, fire-making, etc., as well as in pure ceremonial; because the need of reasserting the tribal morale and recognizing its cosmic conditions is constantly felt. In Christian Europe the Church brought men daily (in some orders even hourly) to their knees, to enact if not to contemplate their assent to the ultimate concepts [28:287, italics original].

There are at least three points where chaos — a tumult of events which lack, not just interpretations, but *interpretability* — threatens to break in upon man: at the limits of his analytic capacities, at the limits of his powers of endurance, and at the limits of his moral insight. If they become intense enough or are sustained long enough, bafflement, suffering, and a sense of intractable ethical paradox are all radical challenges to the proposition that life is comprehensible and that we can, by taking thought, orient ourselves effectively within it. Any religion, however "primitive," which hopes to persist must attempt somehow to cope with these challenges.

Of the three issues, it is the first which has been least investigated by modern social anthropologists (though Evans-Pritchard's [11] classic discussion of why granaries fall on some Azande and not on others, is a notable exception). Even to consider people's religious beliefs as attempts to bring anomalous events or experiences — death, dreams, mental fugues, volcanic eruptions, or marital infidelity — within the circle of the at least potentially explicable seems to smack of Tyloreanism or worse.

But it does appear to be a fact that at least some men — in all probability, most men — are unable to leave unclarified problems of analysis merely unclarified, just to look at the stranger features of the world's landscape in dumb astonishment or bland apathy without trying to develop, however fantastic, inconsistent, or simple-minded, some notions as to how such features might be reconciled with the more ordinary deliverances of experience. To explain those things which cry out for explanation, man has an explanatory apparatus — the complex of received culture patterns (common sense, science, philosophical speculation, myth) that one has for mapping the empirical world. Any chronic failure of one's explanatory apparatus tends to lead to a deep disquiet. This tendency has been rather more widespread and the disquiet rather deeper than we have sometimes supposed since the pseudoscience view of religious belief was, quite rightfully, deposed. After all, even that high priest of heroic atheism, Lord Russell, once remarked that, although the problem of the existence of God had never bothered him, the ambiguity of certain mathematical axioms had threatened to unhinge his mind. And Einstein's profound dissatisfaction with quantum mechanics was based on a — surely religious — inability to believe that, as he put it, God plays dice with the universe.

But this quest for lucidity and the rush of metaphysical anxiety that occurs when empirical phenomena threaten to remain intransigently opaque is found on much humbler intellectual levels. Certainly, I was struck in my own work, much more than I had at all expected to be, by the degree to which my more animistically inclined informants behaved like true Tyloreans. They seemed to be constantly using their beliefs to "explain" phenomena, or, more accurately, to convince themselves that the phenomena were explainable within the accepted scheme of things, for they commonly had only a minimal attachment to the particular soul possession, emotional disequilibrium, taboo infringement, or bewitchment hypothesis that they advanced and were all too ready to abandon it for some other, in the same genre, which struck them as more plausible, given the facts of the case.

What they were *not* ready to do was abandon it for no other hypothesis at all; to leave events to themselves. And what is more, they adopted this nervous cognitive stance with respect to phenomena which had no immediate practical bearing on their own lives, or for that matter on anyone's.

When a peculiarly shaped, rather large toadstool grew up in a carpenter's house in the short space of a few days (or, some said, a few hours), people came from miles around to see it, and everyone had some sort of explanation — some animist, some animatist, some not quite either — for it. Yet it would be hard to argue that the toadstool had any social value in Radcliffe-Brown's sense [41] or that it was connected in any way with anything which did and for which it could have been standing proxy, like the Andaman cicada. Toadstools play about the same role in Javanese life that they do in ours, and in the ordinary course of things Javanese have about as much interest in them as we do. It was just that this one was "odd," "strange," "uncanny" — *aneh*. And the odd, strange, and uncanny simply must be accounted for. Or, again, the conviction must be sustained that it *could be accounted* for. One does not shrug off a toadstool which grows five times as fast as a toadstool has any right to grow. In the broadest sense, the "strange" toadstool did have implications, and critical ones, for those who heard about it. It threatened their most general ability to understand the world, raised the uncomfortable question of whether the beliefs which they held about nature were workable, the standards of truth that they used were valid.

Nor is this to argue that it is only, or even mainly, sudden eruptions of extraordinary events which engender in man the disquieting sense that his cognitive resources may prove unavailing or that this intuition appears only in its acute form. More commonly, man is possessed by a chronic unease because of a

655

persistent, constantly reexperienced difficulty in grasping certain aspects of nature, self, and society and in bringing certain elusive phenomena within the sphere of culturally formulable fact. Toward these solutions a more equable flow of diagnostic symbols is consequently directed.

What lies beyond a relatively fixed frontier of accredited knowledge looms as a constant background to the daily round of practical life. This unknown sets ordinary human experience in a permanent context of metaphysical concern and raises the dim, back-of-the-mind suspicion that one may be adrift in an absurd world:

> Another subject which is matter for this characteristic intellectual enquiry [among the Iatmul] is the nature of ripples and waves on the surface of water. It is said secretly that men, pigs, trees, grass — all the objects in the world — are only patterns of waves. Indeed there seems to be some agreement about this, although it perhaps conflicts with the theory of reincarnation, according to which the ghost of the dead is blown as a mist by the East Wind up the river and into the womb of the deceased's son's wife. Be that as it may — there is still the question of how ripples and waves are caused. The clan which claims the East Wind as a totem is clear enough about this: the Wind with her mosquito fan causes the waves. But other clans have personified the waves and say that they are a person (Kontummali) independent of the wind. Other clans, again, have other theories. On one occasion I took some Iatmul natives down to the coast and found one of them sitting by himself gazing with rapt attention at the sea. It was a windless day, but a slow swell was breaking on the beach. Among the totemic ancestors of his clan he counted a personified slit gong who had floated down the river to the sea and who was believed to cause the waves. He was gazing at the waves which were heaving and breaking when no wind was blowing, demonstrating the truth of his clan myth [1:130–131].

From Bateson's description, it is also clear that the chronic and acute forms of this sort of cognitive concern are closely interrelated and that responses to the more unusual occasions of it are

656

patterned on responses established in coping with the more usual. Bateson goes on to say:

> On another occasion I invited one of my informants to witness the development of photographic plates. I first desensitised the plates and then developed them in an open dish in moderate light, so that my informant was able to see the gradual appearance of the images. He was much interested, and some days later made me promise never to show this process to members of other clans. Kontum-mali was one of his ancestors, and he saw in the process of photographic development the actual embodiment of ripples into images, and regarded this as a demonstration of the clan's secret [1].

The second experiential challenge in whose face the meaningfulness of a particular pattern of life threatens to dissolve into a chaos of thingless names and nameless things — the problem of suffering — has been rather more investigated, or at least described, mainly because of the great amount of attention given in works on tribal religion to what are perhaps its two main loci: illness and mourning. Yet, for all the fascinated interest in the emotional aura that surrounds these extreme situations, there has been, with a few exceptions such as Lienhardt's recent [32:151 ff], discussion of Dinka divining little conceptual advance over the sort of crude confidence type of theory set forth by Malinowski; viz, that religion helps one to endure "situations of emotional stress" by "open[ing] up escapes from such situations and such impasses as offer no empirical way out except by ritual and belief into the domain of the supernatural" [36:67]. The inadequacy of this "theology of optimism," as Nadel [37] rather drily called it, is, of course, radical. Over its career, religion has probably disturbed men as much as it has cheered them, forced them into a head-on, unblinking confrontation of the fact that they are born to trouble as often as it has enabled them to avoid such a confrontation by projecting them into a sort of infantile fairytale world where — Malinowski again [36:67] — "hope cannot fail nor desire deceive."

With the possible exception of Christian Science, there are few if any religious traditions, "great" or "little," in which the proposition that life hurts is not strenuously affirmed, and in some it is virtually glorified:

> She was an old [Ba-Ila] woman of a family with a long genealogy. Leza, "the Besetting-One," stretched out his hand against the family. He slew her mother and father while she was yet a child, and in the course of years all connected with her perished. She said to herself, "Surely I shall keep those who sit on my thighs." But no, even they, the children of her children, were taken from her. . . . Then came into her heart a desperate resolution to find God and to ask the meaning of it all. . . . So she began to travel, going through country after country, always with the thought in her mind: "I shall come to where the earth ends and there I shall find a road to God and I shall ask him: 'What have I done to thee that thou afflictist me in this manner?'" She never found where the earth ends, but though disappointed she did not give up her search, and as she passed through the different countries they asked her, "What have you come for, old woman?" And the answer would be, "I am seeking Leza." "Seeking Leza! For what?" "My brothers, you ask me! Here in the nations is there one who suffers as I have suffered?" And they would ask again, "How have you suffered?" "In this way. I am alone. As you see me, a solitary old woman; that is how I am!" And they answered, "Yes, we see. That is how you are! Bereaved of friends and husband? In what do you differ from others? The Besetting-One sits on the back of every one of us and we cannot shake him off." She never obtained her desire: she died of a broken heart [49:197 ff, quoted in 42:100–101].

As a religious problem, the problem of suffering is, paradoxically, not how to avoid suffering but how to suffer, how to make of physical pain, personal loss, worldly defeat, or the helpless contemplation of other people's agony something bearable, supportable — something, as we say, sufferable. It was in this effort that the Ba-Ila woman — perhaps necessarily, perhaps not — failed and, literally not knowing how to feel what had happened to her, how to suffer, perished in confusion and despair.

Where the more intellective aspects of what Weber called the

"Problem of Meaning" are a matter affirming the ultimate explicability of experience, the more affective aspects are a matter of affirming its ultimate sufferableness. As religion on one side anchors the power of our symbolic resources for formulating analytic ideas in an authoritative conception of the overall shape of reality, so on another side it anchors the power of our, also symbolic, resources for expressing emotions — moods, sentiments, passions, affections, feelings — in a similar conception of reality's pervasive tenor, its inherent tone and temper. For those able to embrace them and for so long as they are able to embrace them, religious symbols provide a cosmic guarantee not only for their ability to comprehend the world, but also, comprehending it, to give a precision to their feeling, a definition to their emotions which enables them, morosely or joyfully, grimly or cavalierly, to endure the world.

Consider in this light the well-known Navaho curing rites usually referred to as "sings" [26 and 43]. The Navaho have about sixty different sings for different purposes, but virtually all of them are dedicated to removing some sort of physical or mental illness. The sing is a kind of religious psychodrama in which there are three main actors: the "singer" or curer, the patient, and, as a kind of antiphonal chorus, the patient's family and friends.

The structure of all the sings, the drama's plot, is quite similar. There are three main acts: a purification of the patient and audience; a statement, by means of repetitive chants and ritual manipulations, of the wish to restore well being ("harmony") in the patient; an identification of the patient with the Holy People and his consequent "cure." The purification rites involved forced sweating, induced vomiting, etc, to expel the sickness from the patient physically. The chants, which are numberless, consist mainly of simple optative phrases ("may the patient be well," "I am getting better all over," etc). Finally, the identification of the patient with the Holy People, and thus with cosmic order generally, is accomplished through the agency of a sand painting depicting the Holy People in one or another appropriate mythic setting. The singer places the patient on the painting, touching the feet, hands, knees, shoulders, breast, back, and head of the divine figures and then the corresponding parts of the patient, performing thus what is essentially a communion rite between the patient and the Holy People, a bodily identification of the human and the divine [43].

This is the climax of the sing: the whole curing process may be likened, Reichard says, to a spiritual osmosis in which the illness in man and the power of the deity penetrate the ceremonial membrane in both directions, the former being neutralized by the latter. Sickness seeps out in the sweat, vomit, and other purification rites; health seeps in as the Navaho patient touches, through the medium of the singer, the sacred sand painting.

Clearly, the symbolism of the sing focuses upon the problem of human suffering and attempts to cope with it by placing it in a meaningful context, providing a mode of action through which it can be expressed, being expressed understood, and, being understood, endured.

The sustaining effect of the sing (and since the commonest disease is tuberculosis, it can in most cases be only sustaining), rests ultimately on its ability to give the stricken person a vocabulary in terms of which to grasp the nature of his distress and relate it to the wider world. Like a calvary, a recitation of Buddha's emergence from his father's palace, or a performance of *Oedipus Tyrannos* in other religious traditions, a sing is mainly concerned with presenting a specific and concrete image of truly human, and so endurable, suffering, an image of suffering that is powerful enough to resist the challenge of emotional meaninglessness raised by the existence of intense and unremovable brute pain.

The problem of suffering passes easily into the problem of evil, for if suffering is severe enough it usually, though not always, seems morally undeserved as well, at least to the sufferer. Evil and suffering are not, however, exactly the same thing. This fact was not, I think, fully recognized by Weber in his generalization of the dilemmas of Christian theodicy Eastward. He seems to have been too much influenced by the biases of a monotheistic tradition in which man's pain reflects directly on God's goodness, since the various aspects of human experience must be conceived to proceed from a single, voluntaristic source.

For, where the problem of suffering is concerned with threats to our ability to put our "undisciplined squads of emotion" into some sort of soldierly order, the problem of evil is concerned with threats to our ability to make sound moral judgments. What is involved in the problem of evil is not the adequacy of our symbolic resources to govern our affective life, but the adequacy of those resources to provide a workable set of ethical criteria, normative guides to govern our action.

The vexation here is the gap between things as they are and as they ought to be if our conceptions of right and wrong make sense, the gap between what we deem that various individuals deserve and what we see that they get — a phenomenon summed up in that profound quatrain:

> The rain falls on the just
> And on the unjust fella;
> But mainly upon the just,
> Because the unjust has the just's umbrella.

Or if this seems too flippant an expression of an issue that, in somewhat different form, animates the Book of Job and the *Baghavad Gita*, the following classical Javanese poem puts the point rather more elegantly. This poem about the discrepancy between moral prescriptions and material rewards, the seeming inconsistency between "is" and "ought," is known, sung, and repeatedly quoted in Java by virtually everyone over the age of six.

> We have lived to see a time without order
> In which everyone is confused in his mind.
> One cannot bear to join in the madness,
> But if he does not do so
> He will not share in the spoils,
> And will starve as a result.
> Yes, God; wrong is wrong:
> Happy are those who forget,
> Happier yet those who remember and have deep insight.

661

Nor is it necessary to be theologically self-conscious to be religiously sophisticated. The concern with intractable ethical paradox, the disquieting sense that one's moral insight is inadequate to one's moral experience, is as alive on the level of so-called "primitive" religion as it is on that of the so-called "civilized."

The set of notions about "division in the world" that Lienhardt describes for the Dinka [32:28–55] is a useful case in point. Like so many peoples, the Dinka believe that the sky, where "Divinity" is located, and earth, where man dwells, were at one time contiguous, the sky lying just above the earth and being connected to it by a rope, so that men could move at will between the two realms. There was no death, and the first man and woman were permitted but a single grain of millet a day, which was all that they at that time required. One day, the woman — of course — decided, out of greed, to plant more than the permitted grain of millet and, in her avid haste and industry, accidentally struck Divinity with the handle of the hoe. Offended, he severed the rope, withdrew into the distant sky of today, and left man to labor for his food, to suffer sickness and death, and to experience separation from the source of his being, his Creator.

Yet the meaning of this strangely familiar story to the Dinka is, as indeed is Genesis to Jews and Christians, not homiletic but descriptive:

> Those [Dinka] who have commented on these stories have sometimes made it clear that their sympathies lie with Man in his plight, and draw attention to the smallness of the fault for which Divinity withdrew the benefits of his closeness. The image of striking Divinity with a hoe . . . often evokes a certain amusement, almost as though the story were indulgently being treated as too childish to explain the consequences attributed to the event. But it is clear that the point of the story of Divinity's withdrawal from men is not to suggest an improving moral judgement on human behaviour. It is to represent a total situation known to the Dinka today. Men now are — as the first man and woman then became — active, self-assertive, inquiring, acquisitive. Yet they are also subject to suffering and death, ineffective, ignorant and poor. Life is insecure; human calculations often prove erroneous, and men

must often learn by experience that the consequences of their acts are quite other than they may have anticipated or consider equitable. Divinity's withdrawal from Man as the result of a comparatively trifling offence, by human standards, presents the contrast between equitable human judgements and the action of the Power which are held ultimately to control what happens in Dinka life. . . . To the Dinka, the moral order is ultimately constituted according to principles which often elude men, which experience and tradition in part reveal, and which human action cannot change. . . . The myth of Divinity's withdrawal then reflects the facts of existence as they are known. The Dinka are in a universe which is largely beyond their control, and where events may contradict the most reasonable human expectations [32:53−54].

Thus the problem of evil, or perhaps one should say the problem *about* evil, is in essence the same sort of problem of or about bafflement and the problem of or about suffering. The strange opacity of certain empirical events, the dumb senselessness of intense or inexorable pain, and the enigmatic unaccountability of gross iniquity all raise the uncomfortable suspicion that perhaps the world, and hence man's life in the world, has no genuine order at all — no empirical regularity, no emotional form, no moral coherence. And the religious response to this suspicion is in each case the same: the formulation, by means of symbols, of an image of such a genuine order of the world which will account for, and even celebrate, the perceived ambiguities, puzzles, and paradoxes in human experience. The effort is not to deny the undeniable — that there are unexplained events, that life hurts, or that rain falls upon the just — but to deny that there are inexplicable events, that life is unendurable, and that justice is a mirage. The principles which constitute the moral order may indeed often elude men, as Lienhardt puts it, in the same way as fully satisfactory explanations of anomalous events or effective forms for the expression of feeling often elude them.

What is important, to a religious man at least, is that this elusiveness be accounted for, that it be not the result of the fact that there are no such principles, explanations, or forms or that life is absurd and that the attempt to make moral, intellectual or emotional sense out of experience is bootless. The Dinka can admit, in fact insist upon, the moral ambiguities and contradictions of life as they live it because these ambiguities and contradictions are seen not as ultimate. Rather, they are seen as the "rational," "natural," "logical" (one may choose one's own adjective here, for none of them is truly adequate) outcome of the moral structure of reality which the myth of the withdrawn "Divinity" depicts or, as Lienhardt says, "images."

It seems to me that one of the outstanding and, except for the work of Weber, untouched problems for comparative research in this whole field is how these aspects of the Problem of Meaning in fact intergrade in each particular case, what sort of interplay there is between the sense of analytic, emotional, and moral impotence. The Problem of Meaning in each of its intergrading aspects is a matter of affirming, or at least recognizing, the inescapability of ignorance, pain, and injustice on the human plane while simultaneously denying that these irrationalities are characteristic of the world as a whole. And it is in terms of religious symbolism, a symbolism relating man's sphere of existence to a wider sphere within which it is conceived to rest, that both the affirmation and the denial are made.

This is *not*, however, to say that everyone in every society does this, for, as the immortal Don Marquis once remarked, you don't have to have a soul unless you really want one. The oft-heard generalization [25, e.g.] that religion is a human universal embodies a confusion. It is probably true (though on present evidence unprovable) that there is no human society which totally lacks cultural patterns that we can call religious under the present definition or one like it. It is surely untrue that all men in all societies are, in any meaningful sense of the term, religious. But, if the anthropological study of religious commitment is underdeveloped, the anthropological study of religious noncommitment is nonexistent. The anthropology of religion will have come of age when some more subtle Malinowski writes a book called *Belief and Unbelief* (or even *Faith and Hypocrisy*) *in a Savage Society*.

(4) . . . *and clothing those conceptions with such an aura of*

664

factuality that . . . . There arises here, however, a profounder question: How is it that people believe this denial that evil, though inescapable, is a characteristic of the world as a whole? How is it that the religious man moves from a troubled perception of experienced disorder to a more or less settled conviction of fundamental order? Just what does "belief" mean in a religious context?

Of all the problems surrounding attempts to conduct anthropological analysis of religion, this is the one that has perhaps been most troublesome and therefore the most often avoided, usually by relegating it to psychology, that raffish outcast discipline to which social anthropologists are forever consigning phenomena they are unable to deal with within the framework of a denatured Durkheimianism.

But the problem will not go away. It is not "merely" psychological (nothing social is), and no anthropological theory of religion which fails to attack it is worthy of the name. We have been trying to stage Hamlet without the Prince quite long enough.

It seems to me that it is best to begin any approach to this issue with frank recognition that religious belief involves not a Baconian induction from everyday experience — for then we should all be agnostics — but rather a prior acceptance of authority which transforms that experience. The existence of bafflement, pain, and moral paradox — of The Problem of Meaning — is one of the things that drive men toward belief in gods, devils, spirits, totemic principles, or the spiritual efficacy of cannibalism. (An enfolding sense of beauty or a dazzling perception of power are others.)

The Problem of Meaning is not the basis upon which those beliefs rest, but rather their most important field of application:

> We point to the state of the world as illustrative of doctrine, but never as evidence for it. So Belsen illustrates a world of original sin, but original sin is not an hypothesis to account for happenings like Belsen. We justify a particular religious belief by showing its place in the total religious conception; we justify a religious belief as a whole by referring to authority. We accept authority because we discover it at some

point in the world at which we worship, at which we accept the lordship of something not ourselves. We do not worship authority, but we accept authority as defining the worshipful. So someone may discover the possibility of worship in the life of the Reformed Churches and accept the Bible as authoritative; or in the Roman Church and accept papal authority [35:201–202].

This is, of course, a Christian statement of the matter; but it is not to be despised on that account. In tribal religions, authority lies in the persuasive power of traditional imagery; in mystical ones in the apodictic force of supersensible experience; in charismatic ones in the hypnotic attraction of an extraordinary personality. But the priority of the acceptance of an authoritative criterion in religious matters over the revelation which is conceived to flow from that acceptance is not less complete in tribal religions than in scriptural or hieratic ones. The basic axiom underlying what we may perhaps call "the religious perspective" is everywhere the same: he who would know must first believe.

But to speak of "the religious perspective" is, by implication, to speak of one perspective among others. A perspective is a mode of seeing, in that extended sense of "see" in which it means "discern," "apprehend," "understand," or "grasp." It is a particular way of looking at life, a particular manner of construing the world, as when we speak of an historical perspective, a scientific perspective, an aesthetic perspective, a common sense perspective, or even the bizarre perspective embodied in dreams and in hallucinations.

The term "attitude" as in "aesthetic attitude" [3] or "natural attitude" [46; the phrase is originally Husserl's] is another, perhaps more common, term for what I have here called "perspective." But I have avoided "attitude" because of its strong subjectivist connotations, its tendency to place the stress upon a supposed inner state of an actor rather than on a certain sort of relation — a symbolically mediated one — between an actor and a situation. This is not to say, of course, that a phenomenological analysis of religious experience, if cast in intersubjective, non-transcendental, genuinely scientific terms [39] is not essential to a full understanding of religious belief, but merely that that is not the focus of my concern here. "Outlook," "frame of reference," "frame of mind," "orientation," "stance," "mental set," etc, are other terms sometimes employed, depending upon whether the analyst wishes to stress the social, psychological, or cultural aspects of the matter.

The question then comes down to, first, what is "the religious perspective" generically considered, as differentiated from other perspectives, and, second, how do men come to adopt it?

If we place the religious perspective against the background of three of the other major perspectives in terms of which men construe the world — the commonsensical, the scientific, and the aesthetic — its special character emerges more sharply.

What distinguishes common sense as a mode of "seeing" is, as Schutz [46] has pointed out, a simple acceptance of the world, its objects, and its processes as being just what they seem to be — what is sometimes called naïve realism — and the pragmatic motive, the wish to act upon that world so as to bend it to one's practical purposes, to master it, or, so far as that proves impossible, to adjust to it. The world of everyday life is itself, of course, a cultural product, for it is framed in terms of the symbolic conceptions of "stubborn fact" handed down from generation to generation. This everyday world is the established scene and given object of our actions. Like Mt. Everest, it is just there, and the thing to do with it, if one feels the need to do anything with it at all, is to climb it.

In the scientific perspective, it is precisely this givenness which disappears [46]. Deliberate doubt and systematic inquiry, the suspension of the pragmatic motive in favor of disinterested observation, the attempt to analyze the world in terms of formal concepts whose relationship to the informal conceptions of common sense become increasingly problematic — these are the hallmarks of the attempt to grasp the world scientifically.

As for the aesthetic perspective, which under the rubric of "the aesthetic attitude" has been perhaps most exquisitely exam-

667

ined, it involves a different sort of suspension of naïve realism and practical interest. Instead of questioning the credentials of everyday experience, that experience is merely ignored in favor of an eager dwelling upon appearances, an engrossment in surfaces, an absorption in things, as we say, "in themselves."

> The function of artistic illusion is not "make-believe" . . . but the very opposite, disengagement from belief — the contemplation of sensory qualities without their usual meanings of "here's that chair," "That's my telephone" . . . etc. The knowledge that what is before us has no practical significance in the world is what enables us to give attention to its appearance as such [27:49].

Like the commonsensical and the scientific (or the historical, the philosophical, and the autistic), this perspective, this "way of seeing," is not the product of some mysterious Cartesian chemistry but is induced, mediated, and in fact created by means of symbols. It is the artist's skill which can produce those curious quasiobjects — poems, dramas, sculptures, symphonies — which, dissociating themselves from the solid world of common sense, take on the special sort of eloquence that only sheer appearances can achieve.

The religious perspective differs from the commonsensical in that, as already pointed out, it moves beyond the realities of everyday life to wider ones which correct and complete them. Its defining concern, moreover, is not action upon those wider realities but acceptance of them, faith in them. It differs from the scientific perspective in that it questions the realities of everyday life, not out of an institutionalized scepticism which dissolves the world's givenness into a swirl of probabilistic hypotheses, but in terms of what it considers wider, nonhypothetical truths.

Rather than detachment, its watchword is commitment; rather than analysis, encounter. And it differs from art in that, instead of effecting a disengagement from the whole question of factuality, deliberately manufacturing an air of semblance and illusion, it deepens the concern with fact and seeks to create an aura of utter actuality.

668

It is this sense of the "really real" upon which the religious perspective rests and which the symbolic activities of religion as a cultural system are devoted to producing, intensifying, and, so far as possible, rendering inviolable by the discordant revelations of secular experience. From an analytic point of view, the essence of religious action is the imbuing with persuasive authority of a certain specific complex of symbols — symbols of the metaphysic that they formulate and of the style of life that they recommend.

Which brings us, at length, to ritual. For it is in ritual — i.e., consecrated behavior — that somehow this conviction is generated that religious conceptions are veridical and that religious directives are sound. It is in some sort of ceremonial form — even if that form be hardly more than the recitation of a myth, the consultation of an oracle, or the decoration of a grave — that the moods and motivations which sacred symbols induce in men and the general conceptions of the order of existence which they formulate for men meet and reinforce one another. In a ritual, the world as lived and the world as imagined, fused under the agency of a single set of symbolic forms, turn out to be the same world, producing thus that idiosyncratic transformation in one's sense of reality to which Santayana refers in my epigraph. Whatever role divine intervention may or may not play in the creation of faith — and it is not the business of the scientist to pronounce upon such matters one way or the other — it is, primarily at least, out of the context of concrete acts of religious observance that religious conviction emerges on the human plane.

This symbolic fusion of ethos and world view is involved in any religious ritual, no matter how apparently automatic or conventional. If the ritual is truly automatic or merely conventional, of course, it is not religious. It is mainly, however, certain more elaborate and usually more public religious rituals which catch up a broad range of moods and motivations on the one hand and of metaphysical conceptions on the other hand and which can thus shape the spiritual consciousness of a people. Employing a useful term introduced by Singer [47], we may call these full-blown ceremonies "cultural performances" and note that they represent not only the point at which the dispositional and conceptual aspects of religious life converge for the believer, but also the point at which the interaction between them can be most readily examined by the detached observer:

> Whenever Madrasi Brahmans (and non-Brahmans, too, for that matter) wished to exhibit to me some feature of Hinduism, they always referred to, or invited me to see, a particular rite or ceremony in the life cycle, in a temple festival, or in the general sphere of religious and cultural performances. Reflecting on this in the course of my interviews and observations I found that the more abstract generalizations about Hinduism (my own as well as those I heard) could generally be checked, directly or indirectly, against these observable performances [48].

Of course, all cultural performances are not religious performances, and the line between those that are religious and those that are artistic, or even political, is often not so easy to draw in practice, for, like social forms, symbolic forms can serve multiple purposes. But the point is that, paraphrasing slightly, Indians — "and perhaps all peoples" — seem to think of their religion "as encapsulated in these discrete performances which they [can] exhibit to visitors and to themselves" [47]. The mode of exhibition is, however, radically different for the two sorts of witness, a fact seemingly overlooked by those who would argue that "religion is a form of human art" [12:250]. For "visitors," religious performances can, in the nature of the case, be only presentations of a particular religious perspective, and thus can be only aesthetically appreciated or scientifically dissected. For participants, however, religious rituals are in addition enactments, materializations, realizations of the religious perspective — not only models *of* what they believe, but also models *for* the believing of it. In these plastic dramas men attain their faith as they portray it.

As a case in point, let me take a spectacularly theatrical cultural performance from Bali — that in which a terrible witch called Rangda engages in a ritual combat with an endearing monster called Barong. The Rangda-Barong complex has been extensively described and analyzed by a series of unusually gifted ethnographers [4, 5, 50, 2, 9]. I will make no attempt to present it here in more than schematic form. Much of my interpretation of the complex rests on personal observations made in Bali during 1957–1958 [19:282–302].

This ritual combat between the witch Rangda and the monster Barong is usually, but not inevitably, presented on the occasion of a death-temple celebration. The drama consists of a masked dance in which the witch – depicted as a wasted old widow, prostitute, and eater of infants – comes to spread plague and death upon the land and is opposed by the monster – depicted as a kind of cross between a clumsy bear, a silly puppy, and a strutting Chinese dragon.

Rangda, danced by a single male, is a hideous figure. Her eyes bulge from her forehead like swollen boils. Her teeth become tusks curving up over her cheeks and fangs protruding down over her chin. Her yellowed hair falls down around her in a matted tangle. Her breasts are dry and pendulous dugs edged with hair, between which hang, like so many sausages, strings of colored entrails. Her long red tongue is a stream of fire. And as she dances she splays, out in front of her, her dead-white hands, from which protrude ten-inch clawlike fingernails, and she utters unnerving shrieks of metallic laughter.

Barong, danced by two men, fore and aft in vaudeville horse fashion, is another matter. His shaggy sheepdog coat is hung with gold and mica ornaments that glitter in the half-light. He is adorned with flowers, sashes, feathers, mirrors, and a comical beard made from human hair. A demon too, his eyes also pop, and he snaps his fanged jaws with seemly fierceness when faced with Rangda or other affronts to his dignity, but the cluster of tinkling bells which hangs from his absurdly arching tail somehow contrives to take most of the edge off his fearfulness. If Rangda is a satanic image, Barong is a farcical one, and their clash is a clash (an inconclusive one) between the malignant and the ludicrous.

This odd counterpoint of implacable malice and low comedy pervades the whole performance. Rangda, clutching her magical white cloth, moves around in a slow stagger, now pausing immobile in thought or uncertainty, now lurching suddenly forward. The moment of her entry (one sees those terrible long-nailed hands first as she emerges through the split gateway at the top of a short flight of stone stairs) is one of terrific tension when it seems, to a "visitor" at least, that everyone is about to break and run in panic.

She herself seems insane with fear and hated as she screams deprecations at Barong amid the wild clanging of the gamelan. She may, in fact, go amok. I have myself seen Rangdas hurl themselves headlong into the gamelan or run frantically about in total confusion, being subdued and reoriented only by the combined force of a half-dozen spectators. One hears many tales of amok Rangdas holding a whole village in terror for hours and of impersonators becoming permanently deranged by their experiences.

But Barong, though he is charged with the same manalike sacred power (*sakti* in Balinese) as Rangda and though his impersonators are also entranced, seems to have very great difficulty in being serious. He frolics with his retinue of demons (who add to the gaiety by indelicate pranks of their own), lies down on a metallaphone while it is being played or beats on a drum with his legs, moves in one direction in his front half and another in his rear or bends his segmented body into foolish contortions, brushes flies from his body or sniffs aromas in the air, and generally prances about in paroxysms of narcissistic vanity.

The contrast is not absolute, for Rangda is sometimes momentarily comic as when she pretends to polish the mirrors on Barong's coat, and Barong becomes rather more serious after Rangda appears, nervously clacking his jaws at her and ultimately attacking her directly. Nor are the humorous and the horrible always kept rigidly separated, as in that strange scene in one section of the cycle in which several minor witches (disciples of Rangda) toss the corpse of a stillborn child around to the wild amusement of the audience; or another, no less strange, in which the sight of a pregnant woman alternately hysterically between tears and laughter while being knocked about by a group of gravediggers, seems for some reason excruciatingly funny. The twin themes of horror and hilarity find their purest expression in the two protagonists and their endless, indecisive struggle for dominance, but they are woven with deliberate intricacy through the whole texture of the drama. They — or rather the relations between them — are what it is about.

It is unnecessary to attempt a thoroughgoing description of a Rangda-Barong performance here. Such performances vary widely in detail, consist of several not too closely integrated parts, and in any case are so complex in structure as to defy easy summary. For our purposes, the main point to be stressed is that the drama is, for the Balinese, not merely a spectacle to be watched but a ritual to be enacted.

There is no aesthetic distance here that separates actors from audience and that places the depicted events in an unenterable world of illusion. By the time a full-scale Rangda-Barong encounter has been concluded, a majority (often nearly all) of the members of the group sponsoring it will have become caught up in it, not just imaginatively, but bodily. In one of Belo's examples [5:159–168] I count upwards of seventy-five people — men, women, and children — taking part in the activity at some point or other, and thirty to forty participants is in no way unusual. As a performance, the drama is like a high mass, not like a presentation of *Murder in the Cathedral;* it is a drawing near, not a standing back.

In part, this entry into the body of the ritual takes place through the agency of the various supporting roles contained in it — minor witches, demons, various sorts of legendary and mythical figures — which selected villagers enact. But mostly it takes place through the agency of an extraordinarily developed capacity for psychological dissociation on the part of a very large segment of the population. A Rangda-Barong struggle is inevitably marked by anywhere from three or four to several dozen spectators becoming possessed by one or another demon, falling into violent trances "like firecrackers going off one after the other" [5], and, snatching up krisses, rushing to join the fray. Mass trance, spreading like a panic, projects the individual Balinese out of the commonplace world in which he usually lives

673

into that most uncommonplace one in which Rangda and Barong live. To become entranced is, for the Balinese, to cross a threshold into another order of existence — the word for trance is *nadi*, from *dadi*, often translated "to become" but which might be even more simply rendered as "to be." And even those are caught up in the proceedings who, for whatever reasons, do not make this spiritual crossing, for it is they who must keep the frenzied activities of the entranced from getting out of hand by the application of physical restraint, if they are ordinary men, by the sprinkling of holy water and the chanting of spells, if they are priests. At its height a Rangda-Barong rite hovers, or at least seems to hover, on the brink of mass amok with the diminishing band of the unentranced striving desperately (and, it seems, almost always successfully) to control the growing band of the entranced.

In its standard form — if it can be said to have a standard form — the performance begins with an appearance of Barong, prancing and preening, as a general prophylactic against what is to follow. Then may come various mythic scenes relating the story — not always precisely the same one — upon which the performance is based, until finally Barong and then Rangda appear. Their battle begins. Barong drives Rangda back toward the gate of the death temple. But he has not the power to expel her completely, and he is in turn driven back toward the village. At length, when it seems as though Rangda will finally prevail, a number of entranced men rise, krisses in hand, and rush to support Barong. But as they approach Rangda (who has turned her back in meditation), she wheels upon them and, waving her *sakti* white cloth, leaves them comatose on the ground. Rangda then hastily retires (or is carried) to the temple, where she herself collapses, hidden from the aroused crowd which, my informants said, would kill her were it to see her in a helpless state. The Barong moves among the kris dancers and wakens them by snapping his jaws at them or nuzzling them with his beard. As they return, still entranced, to "consciousness," they are enraged by the disappearance of Rangda, and, unable to attack her, they turn their krisses (harmlessly because they are entranced) against their own chests in frustration. Usually sheer pandemonium breaks out at this point with members of the crowd, of both sexes, falling into trance all around the courtyard and rushing out to stab themselves, wrestle with one another, devour live chicks or excrement, wallow convulsively in the mud, and so on, while the non-entranced attempt to relieve them of their krisses and keep them at least minimally in order. In time, the trancers sink, one by one, into coma from which they are aroused by the priests' holy water, and the great battle is over — once more a complete standoff. Rangda has not been conquered, but neither has she conquered.

One place to search for the meaning of this ritual is in the collection of myths, tales, and explicit beliefs which it supposedly enacts. However, these are various and variable — for some people Rangda is an incarnation of Durga, Siva's malignant consort, for others she is Queen Mahendradatta, a figure from a court legend set in eleventh-century Java, for yet others, the spiritual leader of witches as the Brahmana Priest is the spiritual leader of men. Notions of who (or "what") Barong is are equally diverse and even vaguer, but they seem to play only a secondary role in the Balinese preception of the drama. It is in the direct encounter with the two figures in the context of the actual performance that the villager comes to know them as, so far as he is concerned, genuine realities. They are, then, not representations of anything, but presences. And when the villagers go into trance they become — *nadi* — themselves part of the realm in which those presences exist. To ask, as I once did, a man who has *been* Rangda whether he thinks she is real is to leave oneself open to the suspicion of idiocy.

The acceptance of authority that underlies the religious perspective that the ritual embodies thus flows from the enactment of the ritual itself. By inducing a set of moods and motivations — an ethos — and by defining an image of cosmic order — a world view — by means of a single set of symbols, the performance makes the model *for* and model *of* aspects of religious belief mere transpositions of one another.

Rangda evokes fear (as well as hatred, disgust, cruelty, horror, and, though I have not been able to treat the sexual aspects of the performance here, lust); but she also depicts it:

> The fascination which the figure of the Witch holds for the Balinese imagination can only be explained when it is recognized that the Witch is not only a fear inspiring figure, but that she is Fear. Her hands with their long menacing finger-nails do not clutch and claw at her victims, although children who play at being witches do curl their hands in such gestures. But the Witch herself spreads her arms with palms out and her finger flexed backward, in the gesture the Balinese call *kapar*, a term which they apply to the sudden startled reaction of a man who falls from a tree. . . . Only when we see the Witch as herself afraid, as well as frightening, is it possible to explain her appeal, and the pathos which surrounds her as she dances, hairy, forbidding, tusked and alone, giving her occasional high eerie laugh [2:36].

On his side Barong not only induces laughter, he incarnates the Balinese version of the comic spirit — a distinctive combination of playfulness, exhibitionism, and extravagant love of elegance which, along with fear, is perhaps the dominant motive in their life. The constantly recurring struggle of Rangda and Barong to an inevitable draw is thus — for the believing Balinese — both the formulation of a general religious conception and the authoritative experience which justifies, even compels, its acceptance.

(5) . . . *that the moods and motivations seem uniquely realistic.* . . . But no one, not even a saint, lives all of the time in the world that religious symbols formulate, and most men live in it only at moments. The everyday world of commonsense objects and practical acts is, as Schutz [46:226 ff] says, the paramount reality in human experience — paramount in the sense that it is the world in which we are most solidly rooted, whose inherent actuality we can hardly question (however much we may question certain portions of it) and from whose pressures and requirements we can least escape. A man (even large groups of men) may be aesthetically insensitive, religiously unconcerned, and unequipped to pursue formal scientific analysis, but he cannot be completely lacking in common sense if he is to survive.

676

The dispositions which religious rituals induce thus have their most important impact — from a human point of view — outside the boundaries of the ritual itself as they reflect back to color the individual's conception of the established world of bare fact. The peculiar tone that marks the Plains vision quest, the Manus confession, or the Javanese mystical exercise pervades areas of the life of these peoples far beyond the immediately religious, impressing upon them a distinctive style in the sense both of a dominant mood and a characteristic movement. The interweaving of the malignant and the comic, which the Rangda-Barong cambat depicts, animates a very wide range of everyday Balinese behavior, much of which, like the ritual itself, has an air of candid fear narrowly contained by obsessive playfulness. Religion is sociologically interesting, not because, as vulgar positivism would have it [30:10 ff], it describes the social order. In so far as religion does describe the social order, it does so very obliquely and very incompletely. Religion is interesting sociologically, rather, because, like environment, political power, wealth, jural obligation, personal affection, and a sense of beauty, religion shapes the social order.

The movement back and forth between the religious perspective and the commonsense perspective is actually one of the more obvious empirical occurrences on the social scene, though, again, one of the most neglected by social anthropologists, virtually all of whom have seen it happen countless times. Religious belief has usually been presented as an homogeneous characteristic of an individual, like his place of residence, his occupational role, his kinship position, and so on.

But religious belief in the midst of ritual, where it engulfs the total person, transporting him, so far as he is concerned, into another mode of existence, and religious belief as the pale, remembered reflection of that experience in the midst of everyday life are not precisely the same thing, and the failure to realize this has led to some confusion, especially in connection with the so-called "primitive mentality" problem.

Much of the difficulty between Lévy-Bruhl [31] and Malinowski [36] on the nature of "native thought," for example, arises from a lack of full recognition of this distinction. Where

677

the French philosopher was concerned with the view of reality
that savages adopted when taking a specifically religious perspective, the Polish-English ethnographer was concerned with that
which they adopted when taking a strictly commonsense perspective. Both perhaps vaguely sensed that they were not talking
about exactly the same thing, but, where they went astray, was
in failing to give a specific accounting of the way in which these
two forms of "thought" — or, as I would rather say, these two
modes of symbolic formulation — interacted, so that where Lévy-
Bruhl's savages tended to live, despite his postludial disclaimers,
in a world composed entirely of mystical encounters, Malinowski's tended to live, despite his stress on the functional importance of religion, in a world composed entirely of practical
actions.

They became reductionists (an idealist is as much of a reductionist as a materialist) in spite of themselves because they failed
to see man as moving more or less easily, and very frequently,
between radically contrasting ways of looking at the world,
ways which are not continuous with one another but separated
by cultural gaps across which Kierkegaardian leaps must be made
in both directions:

> There are as many innumerable kinds of different shock
> experiences as there are different finite provinces of meaning
> upon which I may bestow the accent of reality. Some instances
> are: the shock of falling asleep as the leap into the world of
> dreams; the inner transformation we endure if the curtain in
> the theatre rises as the transition to the world of the stageplay;
> the radical change in our attitude if, before a painting, we
> permit our visual field to be limited by what is within the
> frame as the passage into the pictorial world; our quandary
> relaxing into laughter, if, in listening to a joke, we are for a
> short time ready to accept the fictitious world of the jest as a
> reality in relation to which the world of our daily life takes
> on the character of foolishness; the child's turning toward his
> toy as the transition into the play-world; and so on. But also
> the religious experiences in all their varieties — for instance,
> Kierkegaard's experience of the "instant" as the leap into the
> religious sphere — are examples of such a shock, as well as the

decision of the scientist to replace all passionate participation in the affairs of "this world" by a disinterested [analytical] attitude [46:231].

The recognition and exploration of the qualitative difference — an empirical, not a transcendental, difference — between religion pure and religion applied, between an encounter with the supposedly "really real" and a viewing of ordinary experience in light of what that encounter seems to reveal, will, therefore, take us toward an understanding of what a Bororo means when he says "I am a parakeet," or a Christian when he says "I am a sinner." Such an understanding of the qualitative difference between pure religion and applied religion will take us further toward understanding the Bororo or the Christian than we will get from either a theory of primitive mysticism in which the commonplace world disappears into a cloud of curious ideas or from a primitive pragmatism in which religion disintegrates into a collection of useful fictions.

The parakeet example, which I take from Percy [40] is a good one. For, as he points out, it is unsatisfactory to say either that the Bororo thinks he is literally a parakeet (for he does not try to mate with other parakeets), that his statement is false or nonsense (for, clearly, he is not offering — or at least not only offering — the sort of class-membership argument which can be confirmed or refuted as, say, "I am a Bororo" can be confirmed or refuted), or yet again that it is false scientifically but true mythically (because that leads immediately to the pragmatic fiction notion which, as it denies the accolade of truth to "myth" in the very act of bestowing it, is internally self-contradictory). Speaking more coherently, it would seem to be necessary to see the sentence as having a different sense in the context of the "finite province of meaning" which makes up the religious perspective than it has in the context which makes up the commonsensical perspective. In the religious, our Bororo is "really" a "parakeet" and, given the proper ritual context, might well "mate" with other "parakeets" — with metaphysical ones like himself not commonplace ones such as those which fly bodily about in ordinary trees. In the commonsensical perspective he is

679

a parakeet in the sense — I assume — that he belongs to a clan whose members regard the parakeet as their totem, a membership from which, given the fundamental nature of reality as the religious perspective reveals it, certain moral and practical consequences flow. A man who says he is a parakeet is, if he says it in normal conversation, saying that, as myth and ritual demonstrate, he is shot through with parakeetness and that this religious fact has some crucial social implications — we parakeets must stick together, not marry one another, not eat mundane parakeets, and so on, for to do otherwise is to act against the grain of the whole universe.

It is this placing of proximate acts in ultimate contexts that makes religion, frequently at least, socially so powerful. It alters, often radically, the whole landscape presented to common sense, alters it in such a way that the moods and motivations induced by religious practice seem themselves supremely practical, the only sensible ones to adopt given the way things "really" are.

Having ritually "leaped" (the image is perhaps a bit too athletic for the actual facts: "slipped" might be more accurate) into the framework of meaning which religious conceptions define and, the ritual ended, returned again to the commonsense world, a man is — unless, as sometimes happens, the experience fails to register — changed. And, as he is changed, so also is the commonsense world, for it is now seen as but the partial form of a wider reality which corrects and completes it.

But this correction and completion is not, as some students of "comparative religion," e.g. [7:236–237], would have it, everywhere the same in content. The nature of the bias that religion gives to ordinary life varies with the religion involved, with the particular dispositions induced in the believer by the specific conceptions of cosmic order he has come to accept. On the level of the "great" religions, organic distinctiveness is usually recognized, at times insisted upon to the point of zealotry. At the levels of the simplest folk and tribal religions the individuality of religious traditions has so often been dissolved into such desiccated types as "animism," "animatism," "totemism," "shamanism," "ancestor worship," and all the other insipid categories by means of which ethnographers of religion devitalize their data. Even at these "simple" levels, however, the idiosyncratic character is clear of how various groups of men behave because of what they believe they have experienced.

A tranquil Javanese would be no more at home in guilt-ridden Manus than an activist Crow would be in passionless Java. And, for all the witches and ritual clowns in the world, Rangda and Barong are not generalized but are thoroughly singular figurations of fear and gaiety. What men believe is as various as what they are — a proposition that holds with equal force when it is inverted.

It is this particularity of the impact of religious systems upon social systems (and upon personality systems) which renders impossible general assessments of the value of religion in either moral or functional terms. The sorts of moods and motivations which characterize a man who has just come from an Aztec human sacrifice are rather different from those of one who has just put off his Kachina mask. Even within the same society, what one "learns" about the essential pattern of life from a sorcery rite and from a commensual meal will have rather diverse effects on social and psychological functioning.

One of the main methodological problems in writing about religion scientifically is to put aside at once the tone of the village atheist and that of the village preacher, as well as their more sophisticated equivalents, so that the social and psychological implications of particular religious beliefs can emerge in a clear and neutral light. And when that is done, overall questions about whether religion is "good" or "bad," "functional" or "dysfunctional," "ego strengthening" or "anxiety producing" disappear like the chimeras they are, and one is left with particular evaluations, assessments, and diagnoses in particular cases. There remain, of course, the hardly unimportant questions of whether this or that religious assertion is true, this or that religious experience genuine, or whether true religious assertions and genuine religious experiences are possible at all. But such questions cannot even be asked, much less answered, within the self-imposed limitations of the scientific perspective.

681

THE ANTHROPOLOGICAL STUDY OF RELIGION

For an anthropologist, the importance of religion is twofold. It has a capacity to serve, for an individual or for a group, as a source of general, yet distinctive, conceptions of the world, the self, and the relations between them, on the one hand — its model *of* aspect. On the other hand religion serves as the source of rooted, no less distinctive, "mental" dispositions — its model *for* aspect. From these cultural functions flow, in turn, its social and psychological ones.

Religious concepts spread beyond their specifically metaphysical contexts to provide a framework of general ideas in terms of which a wide range of experience — intellectual, emotional, moral — can be given meaningful form. The Christian sees the Nazi movement against the background of The Fall which, though it does not, in a causal sense, explain it, places it in a moral, a cognitive, even an affective sense. An Azande sees the collapse of a granary upon a friend or relative against the background of a concrete and rather special notion of witchcraft and thus avoids the philosophical dilemmas as well as the psychological stress of indeterminism. A Javanese finds in the borrowed and reworked concept of *rasa* ("sense-taste-feeling-meaning") a means by which to "see" choreographic, gustatory, emotional, and political phenomena in a new light. A synopsis of cosmic order, a set of religious beliefs, is also a gloss upon the mundane world of social relationships and psychological events. It renders them graspable.

But, more than gloss, such beliefs are also a template. They do not merely interpret social and psychological processes in cosmic terms — in which case they would be philosophical, not religious — but they also shape them. In the doctrine of original sin is embedded also a recommended attitude toward life, a recurring mood, and a persisting set of motivations. The Zande learns from witchcraft conceptions, not just to understand apparent "accidents" as not accidents at all, but to react to these spurious accidents with hatred for the agent who caused them and to proceed against him with appropriate resolution. *Rasa*, in addition to being a concept of truth, beauty, and goodness, is also a preferred mode of experiencing, a kind of affectless detachment, a variety of bland aloofness, an unshakable calm. The moods and motivations that a religious orientation produces cast a derivative, lunar light over the solid features of a people's secular life.

The tracing of the social and psychological role of religion is thus not so much a matter of finding correlations between specific ritual acts and specific secular social ties — though these correlations do, of course, exist and are very much worth continued investigation, especially if we can contrive something novel to say about them. More, it is a matter of understanding how men's sense of the reasonable, the practical, the humane, and the moral is colored by men's notions, however implicit, of the "really real" and the dispositions these notions induce in men. How far they do so (for in many societies religion's effects seem quite circumscribed, in others completely pervasive); how deeply they do so (for some men, and groups of men, seem to wear their religion lightly so far as the secular world goes, while others seem to apply their faith to each occasion, no matter how trivial); and how effectively they do so (for the width of the gap between what religion recommends and what people actually do is most variable cross culturally) — all these are crucial issues in the comparative sociology and psychology of religion.

Even the degree to which religious systems themselves are developed seems to vary extremely widely and not merely on a simple evolutionary basis. In one society, the level of elaboration of symbolic formulations of ultimate actuality may reach extraordinary degrees of complexity and systematic articulation; in another, no less developed socially, such formulations may remain primitive in the true sense, hardly more than congeries of fragmentary by-beliefs and isolated images, of sacred reflexes and spiritual pictographs. One need only think of the Australians and the Bushmen, the Toradja and the Alorese, the Hopi and the Apache, the Hindus and the Romans, or even the Italians and the Poles, to see that degree of religious articulateness is not a constant even as between societies of similar complexity.

The anthropological study of religion is therefore a two-stage

683

operation: first, an analysis of the system of meanings embodied in the symbols which make up the religion proper and, second, the relating of these systems to social structural and psychological processes.

My dissatisfaction with so much of contemporary social anthropological work in religion is not that it concerns itself with the second stage, but that it neglects the first and in so doing takes for granted what most needs to be elucidated. To discuss the role of ancestor worship in regulating political succession, of sacrificial feasts in defining kinship obligations, of spirit worship in scheduling agricultural practices, of divination in reinforcing social control, or of initiation rites in propelling personality maturation are in no sense unimportant endeavors, and I am not recommending they be abandoned for the kind of jejune cabalism into which symbolic analysis of exotic faiths can so easily fall.

It seems to me not particularly promising to attempt these discussions with but the most general, commonsense view of what ancestor worship, animal sacrifice, spirit worship, divination, or initiation rites are as religious patterns. Only when we have a theoretical analysis of symbolic action comparable in sophistication to that we now have for social and psychological action, only then will we be able to cope effectively with those aspects of social and psychological life in which religion (or art, or science, or ideology) plays a determinant role.

REFERENCES

1. Bateson, G: *Naven*, ed 2 (Stanford University Press, Stanford, California) 1958.
2. Bateson, G, and Mead, M: *Balinese Character* (New York Academy of Sciences, New York, New York) 1942.
3. Bell, C: *Art* (Chatto and Windus, London, England) 1914.
4. Belo, J: *Bali: Rangda and Barong* (J J Augustin, Inc, Locust Valley, New York) 1949.

5. Belo, J: *Trance in Bali* (Columbia University Press, New York, New York) 1960.
6. Burke, K: *The Philosophy of Literary Form* (Louisiana State University Press, Baton Rouge, Louisiana) 1941.
7. Campbell, J: *The Hero with a Thousand Faces* (Pantheon Books, Inc, New York, New York) 1949.
8. Cassirir, E: *The Philosophy of Symbolic Forms*, R Mannheim, translator (Yale University Press, New Haven, Connecticut) 1953–1957, 3 vol.
9. Covarrubias, M: *The Island of Bali* (Alfred A Knopf, Inc, New York, New York) 1937.
10. Craik, K: *The Nature of Explanation* (Cambridge University Press, Cambridge, England) 1952.
11. Evans-Pritchard, E E: *Witchcraft, Oracles and Magic Among the Azande* (Clarendon Press, Oxford, England) 1937.
12. Firth, R: *Elements of Social Organization* (Watts, London, England; Philosophical Library, New York, New York) 1951.
13. Fortune, R F: *Manus Religion* (American Philosophical Society, Philadelphia, Pennsylvania) 1935.
14. Frisch, K von: Dialects in the Language of the Bees, *Scientific American*, Aug 1962.
15. Geertz, C: Ethos, World-View and the Analysis of Sacred Symbols, *Antioch Review*, Winter 1957–1958, pp 421–437.
16. Geertz, C: *The Religion of Java* (The Free Press, formerly of Glencoe, Illinois, now of New York, New York) 1960.
17. Geertz, C: The Growth of Culture and the Evolution of Mind, in J Scher, ed, *Theories of the Mind* (The Free Press, New York, New York) 1962, pp 713–740.
18. Geertz, C: Ideology as a Cultural System, in D Apter, ed, *Ideology of Discontent* (The Free Press, New York, New York) 1964.
19. Geertz, C: "Internal Conversion" in Contemporary Bali, in J Bastin and R Roolvink, ed, *Malayan and Indonesian*

Studies (Oxford University Press, Oxford, England) 1964, pp 282–302.

20. Goody, J: Religion and Ritual: The Definition Problem, *British Journal of Sociology*, 1961, vol 12, pp 143–164.

21. Horowitz, N H: The Gene, *Scientific American*, Feb 1956.

22. James, William: *The Principles of Psychology* (Henry Holt, now Holt, Rinehart & Winston, Inc, New York, New York) 1904, vol 2.

23. Janowitz, M: Anthropology and the Social Sciences, *Current Anthropology*, 1963, vol 4, pp 139, 146–154.

24. Kluckhohn, C: The Philosophy of the Navaho Indians, in F S C Northrop, ed, *Ideological Differences and World Order* (Yale University Press, New Haven, Connecticut) 1949, pp 356–384.

25. Kluckhohn, C: Universal Categories of Culture, in A L Kroeber, ed, *Anthropology Today* (University of Chicago Press, Chicago, Illinois) 1953, pp 507–523.

26. Kluckhohn, C, and Leighton, D: *The Navaho* (Harvard University Press, Cambridge, Massachusetts) 1946.

27. Langer, S: *Feeling and Form* (Charles Scribner's Sons, New York, New York) 1953.

28. Langer, S: *Philosophy in a New Key*, ed 4 (Harvard University Press, Cambridge, Massachusetts) 1960.

29. Langer, S: *Philosophical Sketches* (The Johns Hopkins Press, Baltimore, Maryland) 1962.

30. Leach, E R: *Political Systems of Highland Burma* (Bell, London, England; Harvard University Press, Cambridge, Massachusetts) 1954.

31. Lévy-Bruhl, L: *How Natives Think* (Alfred A Knopf, Inc, New York, New York) 1926.

32. Lienhardt, G: *Divinity and Experience* (Clarendon Press, Oxford, England) 1961.

33. Lorenz, K: *King Solomon's Ring* (Methuen, London, England) 1952.

34. Lowie, R H: *Primitive Religion* (Boni and Liveright, New York, New York) 1924.

686

35. MacIntyre, A: The Logical Status of Religious Belief, in A MacIntyre, ed, *Metaphysical Beliefs* (SCM Press, London, England) 1957, pp 167–211.

36. Malinowski, B: *Magic, Science and Religion* (Beacon Press, Boston, Massachusetts) 1948.

37. Nadel, S F: Malinowski on Magic and Religion, in R Firth, ed, *Man and Culture* (Routledge & Kegan Paul, London, England) 1957, pp 189–208.

38. Parsons, T, and Shils, E: *Toward a General Theory of Action* (Harvard University Press, Cambridge, Massachusetts) 1951.

39. Percy, W: Symbol, Consciousness and Intersubjectivity, *Journal of Philosophy*, 1958, vol 15, pp 631–641.

40. Percy, W: The Symbolic Structure of Interpersonal Process, *Psychiatry*, 1961, vol 24, pp 39–52.

41. Radcliffe-Brown, A R: *Structure and Function in Primitive Society* (The Free Press, formerly of Glencoe, Illinois, now of New York, New York) 1952.

42. Radin, P: *Primitive Man as a Philosopher* (Dover Publications, Inc, New York, New York) 1957.

43. Reichard, G: *Navaho Religion* (Pantheon Books, Inc, New York, New York) 1950, 2 vol.

44. Ryle, G: *The Concept of Mind* (Hutchinson, London, England; Barnes & Noble, Inc, New York, New York) 1949.

45. Santayana, G: *Reason in Religion*, vol 2 of *The Life of Reason, or The Phases of Human Progress* (Constable, London, England; Charles Scribner's Sons, New York, New York) 1905–1906.

46. Schutz, A: *The Problem of Social Reality*, vol 1 of *Collected Papers* (Martinus Nijhoff, The Hague, Netherlands) 1962.

47. Singer, M: The Cultural Pattern of Indian Civilization, *Far Eastern Quarterly*, 1955, vol 15, pp 23–36.

48. Singer, M: The Great Tradition in a Metropolitan Center: Madras, in M Singer, ed, *Traditional India* (American Folklore Society, Philadelphia, Pennsylvania) 1958, pp 140–182.

49. Smith, C W, and Dale, A M: *The Ila-Speaking Peoples of*

Northern Rhodesia (Macmillan and Company, London, England) 1920, vol 2.

50. Zoete, B de, and Spies, W: *Dance and Drama in Bali* (Faber & Faber, London, England) 1938.

ACKNOWLEDGMENTS

Thanks are due to the individuals and publishers concerned for permission to quote passages from the following works: The Clarendon Press in respect to *Divinity and Experience* by G Lienhardt; Harvard University Press in respect to *Philosophy in a New Key* by S Langer; Hutchinson and Barnes & Noble in respect to *The Concept of Mind* by Gilbert Ryle; Macmillan in respect to *The Ila-Speaking Peoples of Northern Rhodesia* by G W Smith and A M Dale; The New York Academy of Science in respect to *Balinese Character* by Gregory Bateson and Margaret Mead; Martinus Nijhoff in respect to *The Problem of Social Reality* by A Schutz; The SCM Press in respect to *Metaphysical Beliefs* edited by A MacIntyre; Stanford University Press in respect to *Naven*, by Gregory Bateson.

COMMENTARY

by Talcott Parsons

CLIFFORD GEERTZ is certainly one of a very small number of social scientists of his age group who have been making genuinely creative theoretical contributions. His paper "Religion as a Cultural System" belongs in a rather short list of at all recent attempts anywhere close to this field. Perhaps the other most important one is Robert Bellah's "Religious Evolution" [1], which presents an especially important insight in the connection that he establishes between the extreme plasticity of the human

688

genetic constitution and the importance of symbolism in culture. Bellah's paper presents a considerable contrast with Geertz' work, and I shall comment on this later. Perhaps the major contribution of Geertz is to give a strong emphasis to the importance of the cultural aspect of religion and to bring treatment of that aspect into touch with a good many recent developments in the cultural field, with special reference to the analysis of symbolism and symbolic processes.

First, I think many of us would share with Geertz the conviction of the primacy of the cultural aspect of religion, still making allowance, as I think he does, for the fact that it is a general phenomenon of the "human condition" which clearly includes social and psychological aspects as well. Since probably in theoretical terms the cultural fields are less highly developed than are those of the social system and the personality, there is a special urgency about theoretical work in this area.

From my limited acquaintance with the literature I think it is probably fair to say that Geertz' paper is the most sophisticated brief outline of the culturally central components of *a* religious system which we have available. When I underline the "a," however, I wish to call attention to a few problems about his approach which concern me in the sense of "bothering." These are, I think, related to its stress as an anthropological conception and to the theme set by the quotation from Santayana — which Geertz uses as his motto — with its reference to the *marked idiosyncrasy* of "every living and healthy religion." My question, that is to say, is how far Geertz is bound to a conception of "cultural relativity" that is a drag on, rather than an asset to, the development of theory in social science.

Since I am a sociologist rather than an anthropologist, I hope I am not being invidious in calling attention to the fact that, of the four figures Geertz names to exemplify the "very narrow intellectual tradition" against which he is revolting, or at least which he thinks should be transcended, only one was primarily an anthropologist, Malinowski, and he certainly did not approach the stature of Durkheim, Weber, and Freud. Two are primarily identified as sociologists. Hence the fact that I am bothered by a suspicion of anthropological "ethnocentricism" may be merely a manifestation of my own sociological parochialism.

However that may be, there are two respects in which I think it is possible to build on the work of Durkheim and Weber which seem to me to be not merely neglected by Geertz but, at least possibly, impeded by his position. The first of these is comparative perspective on religion which, I have become increasingly convinced, must include an evolutionary dimension in a very central place. The second is the problem posed by the need for direct and specific theoretical articulation between the cultural aspect — not only of religion but of many other cultural phenomena, for example, ideology as dealt with by Geertz in a companion paper [2] — and the other aspects of a more comprehensive system of action (with respect to my own interests, in particular the social system aspects).

The two problems are clearly interrelated. Indeed it is my impression that Geertz does considerably greater justice to the articulation of the cultural system with the personality of the individual than with the social system. This may be related to his emphasis on idiosyncrasy at the cultural level. At a number of points he seems to maintain that a substratum of generalized psychological need is at least one of the principal factors making for the importance of idiosyncrasy. There is, that is to say, a generalized need to feel that the symbol system defines *our* particular conception of order and moods and motivations which can be shared and recreated ritually.

With their partially idiosyncratic symbol systems, religions have certainly encompassed almost wholly the most general conceptions of the general order of existence for populations of individuals but, beyond this, have had a great deal to do with the delineation of the boundaries of societies; indeed the relatively "primitive" type of society, which is still the favorite object of study for anthropologists, is usually nearly coextensive with a religious system.

I think we can say, however, that the "higher" religions (an evolutionist must not shy away from such terms) *always* transcend any particular society. Thus even Confucianism, the most "particularistic" of the religions associated with the general "philosophic breakthrough" of the first millennium BC, has become an essential constituent of the culture, not only of China, but also of Japan and Korea and much of Southeast Asia. Certainly Hinduism and Buddhism, and also Judaism, if not alone, then through its impact on Islam and still much greater impact on Christianity, have gone far beyond a role in any particular "ethnic" community. We all know that this means that there are still idiosyncratic elements in each society — and in many subdivisions thereof — in which a religion is institutionalized. This is true even within "branches" of what usually passes for the same principal subdivision of a religion; thus clearly Irish-American Catholicism is in many ways very different from Latin-American versions, and certainly New England Congregationalism from North German Lutheran Protestantism.

A view of the cultural nature of religion which does not make room for something more generalized and less idiosyncratic than the conception Geertz gives us cannot satisfy the sociologist who is concerned with comparative and eventually evolutionary problems and who takes seriously the very great importance of religion in defining and influencing the ranges of comparative variation among social systems and the temporal concatenations of their evolutionary change. There is a very important sense in which social systems, especially *societies*, are "caught in the middle" between on the one hand, cultural systems which in their more developed phases are *more* general in relevance in organizing human action than any society is, and, on the other hand, the personalities of individuals. It is for this reason that an attempt, such as Bellah's in his paper on Religious Evolution, to systematize these ranges of variation in religion is at least very much more useful to the comparative sociologist than is Geertz' formulation. However tentative and subject to revision and, in various respects, incomplete the Bellah scheme is, it represents a most important step beyond Weber, but very much by building on Weber's work, not by going outside the "narrow" Weberian framework.

The second problem mentioned above concerns theoretically specific articulation with the theory of the social system. Though a number of other examples, such as the very important relations between Confucianism and the patrilineal kinship system of classical China could be mentioned, I think Weber's conception of the economic ethic will serve better than any other single example.

As Weber worked this out in the essay on the Protestant Ethic, it was in many respects one sided and incomplete. It did, however, articulate the type of orientation to "worldly" activities to be expected in a distinctive type of religious culture on the part of people participating in what sociologically we call the "occupational structure" of developing western society (especially in the version called "business proprietorship" but also extensible to various types of employed status), so that the "aura of factuality" to which Geertz refers could help us to understand distinctive patterns of behavior and organization which most social scientists had conceived to be very remote from religion. A similar type of analysis was used by Weber in his discussions of the *legitimation* of authority, in a context which was not confined to government but included also private organizations. Work done since Weber's has greatly clarified the range of relevance of the "Protestant Ethic" concept cross culturally in analyzing comparable patterns of orientation in religious traditions other than Protestantism (cf Bellah, Elder's thesis, and Geertz himself). Further clarified is the range of the relevance of the Protestant Ethic within Western society, above all showing that this relevance is not confined to profit-making business but extends also to science (Merton) and law (Little); and, at least as important, organizationally it is perhaps even more relevant to the motivation of associational types of organization [3], e.g., in the professions, than to the bureaucratic type which Weber emphasized so strongly in his account of "rational bourgeois capitalism."

Propelled by his wish to break away from the "very narrow intellectual tradition" to which he refers, Geertz has placed emphasis on the idiosyncrasy of the particular religious system. This emphasis tends to put him in some danger of prematurely burning some very important bridges which Weber above all had, if not built, at least laid important foundations for and to which Durkheim had contributed, though more implicitly. The type of bridge which particularly concerns the *sociologist* of religion is precisely the one over which, however complex the relation, it is possible to follow lines of analysis from cultural to social system and vice versa. (A remarkable essay in the social-to-cultural direction is the section entitled *Stände, Klassen und Religion* in Weber's *Religionssoziologie*, which in the English translation was broken up into the two chapters entitled "Chapter VI. Castes, Estates, Classes, Religions; VII. Religion of Non-Privileged Classes.") When the problem is put in this way, I do not believe that Geertz would be insensitive to it. I do, however, think it fair to say that the tenor of his article is such as to discourage interest in this type of problem.

More directly internal to Geertz' analysis itself, I may make one further point. Besides the symbolic character of religion as a cultural system, the item in the definition of greatest concern to the macrosociologist is the third, "conceptions of a general order of existence." The point I wish to note is that in giving content to this category, instead of introducing something quite new, Geertz takes over with only minor change Weber's scheme for analyzing the "problems of meaning," the problems of "understanding" or "making sense" of one's experience, the problems of the moral balance of the human condition, i.e., the "problem of evil" and of "suffering." I heartily agree about the centrality of these problems, but Geertz does not, in giving them the position he does, break out of the "narrow intellectual tradition."

Finally I should just like to mention an important problem of perspective. Our generation has seen an immense increase of awareness of, sensitivity to, and study of nonwestern cultures by western scholars, as well as contact with their opposite numbers in other societies. This inevitably raises in an acute form the question of how far Weber was right, in his Introduction to his general series on the Sociology of Religion, reprinted in the English translation of *The Protestant Ethic* [4], that the social and cultural developments of the modern West were of *universal* significance in the development of human society and culture. Weber, and many social scientists who stand in his tradition, may in this context be accused of "ethnocentrism," and I have the impression that this problem seriously concerns Geertz. Quite clearly it is a crucial problem, but I very much doubt whether anything approaching a definitive position on it will be attainable in our time. At least I do not think the "Weberians," of whom in this sense I count myself one, can yet be ruled out of court on this issue.

REFERENCES

1. *American Sociological Review*, June 1964.
2. Apter, David, ed: *Ideology and Discontent* (The Free Press, New York, New York) 1964.
3. Loubser and Adams.
4. Weber, Max: *The Protestant Ethic and the Spirit of Capitalism* (Scribner, New York, New York) 1948.

19. RITUAL

[In June 1965 the Royal Society of London held a symposium on "Ritual Behaviour in Animals and Man" organized by Sir Julian Huxley, the proceedings of which were published in *The Philosophical Transactions of the Royal Society of London*, Series B, No. 772, Vol. 251, 25 December 1966. The officers of the society have generously permitted republication of the final paragraphs of a paper by K. Z. Lorenz, the part of Sir Julian Huxley's Introduction which discusses human ritual, and the full text of a paper by Erik H. Erikson. Edward Shils has contributed a slightly revised version of his paper presented at the symposium, only a greatly abbreviated version of which was published in No. 772 of *The Philosophical Transactions*.]

FOREWORD: RITUAL AND SURVIVAL

by K. Z. Lorenz

THE MORAL of the natural history of pseudospeciation is that we must learn to tolerate other cultures, to shed our own cultural and national arrogance, and to realize that the social norms and rites of other cultures, to which their members keep faith as we do to our own, have the same right to be respected and to be regarded as sacred. Without the tolerance born out of this realization it is all too easy for one man to see the personification of evil in the god of his neighbor, and the sacred inviolability of rites and social norms, which is one of their most important properties, can lead to the most terrible of all wars, to religious or pseudoreligious (ideological) war — which is exactly what is threatening us today.

We must also learn to tolerate and indeed welcome changes

695

in our own norms and rites, so long as they tend in the right direction — toward greater human fulfilment and fuller human integration.

Ritual in Human Societies
by Sir Julian Huxley

Although there is wide disagreement as to the use of terms like *ritual* in anthropological or psychological discussion, for simplicity's sake I shall use *ritualization* in a broad sense to denote the adaptive formalization and canalization of motivated human activities so as to secure more effective communicatory ("signalling") function, reduction of intra-group damage, or better intra-group bonding. *Ritual* (my italics throughout) as an adjective is defined by *The Shorter Oxford Dictionary* as "pertaining or relating to . . . rites; of the nature of . . . a rite or rites": and *rite* is defined as "a *formal* procedure in a *religious* or other *solemn* observance; a custom or practice of a *formal* kind (e.g., rites of hospitality); the general or normal *custom, habit* or *practice* of a country, now especially in relation to *religion* or *worship* (e.g., the Roman rite)." *Ritual* as a noun is defined as "a prescribed order of performing *religious* or other *devotional* service; a book containing the order to be observed in the celebration of religious or other *solemn* service . . . the performance of ritual acts."

I am not competent to discuss human ritualization in detail, but as an evolutionary biologist I would like to stress some general points. The first is the striking operational similarity between its results and those of ritualization in higher animals, which, as Lorenz has pointed out, clearly demonstrate the convergent evolution of functionally analogous but not genetically homologous behavior-organs. Second, there is the radical difference between biological evolution in animals, based on genetic transmission, and cultural evolution, based on non-genetic cultural transmission (tradition). In certain primates, e.g., the Japanese Macaque (*Macaca fuscata*), what may be called proto-tradition occurs, leading to each group having its own food tradition, with a particular range of acceptable foods. Now and again new foods may be incorporated in the traditional menu, and new rituals (e.g., special food-washing ceremonies) may develop in relation to them (see [27]). This depends largely on man's capacity for true (symbolic) language, which itself can properly be regarded as ritualized (adaptively formalized) behavior (see [131] and [24]). The only well-formalized animal language is that of bees [10].

Third, there is man's unique learning capacity, which promotes a much greater complexity and variety of ritualizations than is found in any type of animal. This, as Erikson [7, 8] has pointed out, coupled with the unique prolongation of man's learning period and his outstandingly slow post-natal development to maturity, necessitate a succession of behavioral ritualizations adapted to the successive stages of his psychosocial ontogeny. Accordingly, the process of human ritualization in psychosocial evolution has a primarily ontogenetic, not a phylogenetic basis; is directed mainly by psychosocial selection, not by the genetic mechanism of natural selection; and is relatively extremely rapid, operating in terms of decades instead of in millennial periods, and shows acceleration.

Fourth, the phenotypic variability of man's behavior has steadily increased during psychosocial evolution, owing to his unique learning capacity interacting with his increasing cultural complexity, and has led to a high degree of individuation. In man, individual variety is greater than in any other organism, and individuals can play a far more important role in influencing social activities and cultural evolution. This importance of the individual is enhanced by man's symbolizing activities, whereby outstanding individuals acquire large accretions of significance, and become social, political, or religious heroes. We need only think of the permanent enhancement of individuals like Jesus or Napoleon, Moses or George Washington, Virgil or Michelangelo, or the ephemeral enhancement of musical virtuosos or film stars. The same applies to single outstanding events, which may become occasions for repeated commemorative rituals and celebrations.

Fifth, man alone has crossed the threshold to full self-consciousness. This leads to the formation of a much more definite body-image, and also of a true self-image, both of which become important elements of many ritualizations.

Sixth, in man alone does infantile repression of guilt occur, with resultant formation of the Freudian Unconscious and Super-ego, and the further consequence of projective thinking, by which man projects elements of his own personality into natural objects and forces, thus personalizing them; and into or onto other persons, real or imaginary, slave or ruler, friend or foe, thus endowing them with qualities not inherently theirs.

Finally, many more human ritualized activities have a strong autesthetic or self-rewarding component. When wholly autesthetic (e.g., in ritualized or disciplined private meditation) they tend to lose their allaesthetic communicatory (signal) function.

As a result of these various distinctive properties of man's mental life and capacities, behavior, and development, the process of ritualization in man is far more complex, elastic, and various than that in animals, and leads to a much wider range of results.

In man, we find not only the adaptive canalization and ritualization of overt behavior, but also that of thought or "inner behavior," resulting in motivated idea-systems and in internal (psychological or mental) organizations concerned with guilt and conscience, anxiety and "oceanic" feelings. Secondly, every human being has to construct his private ritualizations, his own canalization systems, to guide the chaos and conflict of infantile thought and feeling into individually adaptive as well as socially acceptable channels. Third, ritualization in the broad sense may spread from the emotional into the intellectual sphere, there resulting in adaptive canalizations of thought, like concepts and formulae, ethical and legal principles, scientific laws and theological doctrines. Such extended ritualization is no longer directly comparable with ritualization in animals and should perhaps

698

be more strictly categorized as formalization, but both have similar functions, and both must be considered together in any general survey of the adaptive canalization of behavior.

The resultant organizations of thought and behavior can be almost infinitely more complex than anything seen in animals — e.g., kinship and caste systems, religions and cosmologies, with their symbolic expressions in rites and ceremonies, architecture and art.

The arts involve ritualization or adaptive canalization of the creative imagination, the sciences involve rational conceptualization based on a self-corrective exploration of experience, and logic and mathematics involve abstract reason.

Creative works of art and literature show ritualization in this extended sense, in being "adaptively" (functionally) organized so as to enhance their aesthetic stimulatory effect and their communicatory function. They differ from all other products of ritualization in that each is a unique creation (though they may share a common style, which of course is itself a ritualizing agency). As Heisenberg said when playing Beethoven's Opus 111 to a group of scientists, "If I had not existed, someone else would have discovered the Uncertainty Principle: but if Beethoven had never existed, we should not have had this great piece of music. That is the difference between science and art."

A successful work of art is an organized whole, of variety integrated in unity, involving diverse and sometimes conflicting elements of diverse quality, and operating at different levels of overt expression and on different levels of perceptual awareness: it acquires a significant form by transforming its content. This "structural situation" or aesthetically effective patterning by the artist on his work, can properly be regarded as a special kind of ritualization [11]. On this primary patterning, the secondary patternings we call *style, fashion*, and *taste* are superimposed.

As a result, the whole work (or single elements in it) exhibits the phenomenon of multivalence or multisignificance (including what Empson [6] calls ambiguity and aspects of Koestler's bisociation [20]), in carrying overtones and being supported by undertones, as well as in its overt expression. This is, perhaps, especially clear in poetry and oratory as against scientific description or logical argument. Obvious examples are Coleridge's *Kubla Khan* and Blake's *Tyger Tyger burning bright*, Churchill's "blood, sweat and tears," or Shakespeare's "The quality of mercy is not strained." (The multivalent potency of Blake's poem is so great that, on first hearing it recited, the young Bertrand Russell was overcome and had to lean against the wall to prevent himself falling.)

The proper development of personality involves a somewhat similar process of ritualization, *sensu lato*, in demanding the integration of diverse and sometimes conflicting elements or factors into an effectively organized and meaningful whole. Failure to incorporate certain elements, such as the proprioceptive factors involved in posture, or the aesthetic factors involved in the enjoyment or practice of the arts, leads to incomplete or faulty personality development.

This also applies to our perceptions, which we build out of the raw materials of direct sensation [4]. We normally impose on the process of perception a customary or "normal" framework derived from conscious or unconscious learning from experience.

The powerful formalizing effect of this ritualization of thought and feeling, even when unconscious, is revealed by our various escapes from it — into the fantasy-organized world of our dreams [14]; or the disturbing world induced by sensory deprivation (see [27]); or the ecstatic but profoundly significant world into which we are conveyed by what are appropriately termed the transports of sexual love at its highest and deepest; or the supernormal visionary world revealed by psychedelic drugs (see later); or, the abnormal world into which schizophrenics and other psychotics are driven (see later); or the new world of behavior imposed on the personality by hypnotically induced alterations of perception [9, 17:429]; the transcendent inner world discovered by the great painters, poets, and composers; or the transcendent inner world discovered by the disciplined and ritualized explorations of mediation, mysticism, and yoga [15: *passim*].

Both schizophrenia and psychedelic substances like LSD (lysergic acid diethylamide) seem to exert their effects by interfering with the "normal" ritualization of the perception-building process. In schizophrenia this is effected endogenously, by a genetic error of metabolism; the resultant lack of stable, adaptively formalized "standard" percepts and concepts leads to a progressive failure of communication with others, and this to eventual withdrawal into the abnormal "unrealistic" but sometimes rewarding private world which is all the schizophrenic has been able to construct (see [18]). This is a reversal of adaptive ritualization, as it increases ambiguity and impedes communication.

The administration of lysergic acid to spiders also has unadaptive results, paradoxically by causing them to construct webs of *greater* regularity than normal. They resemble schizophrenics in becoming "withdrawn" from exteroceptive stimuli; their perceptive awareness is thus reduced, and they do not adjust their webs to the irregularities of their sites [32, 33, 34, 35].

Psychedelic substances frequently enhance and distort visual perception of form and color, distort spatial perception, radically alter time-perception, and enhance the sense of significance (e.g., they can exert profound emotional and spiritual effects: they may induce an intensely rewarding state of well-being but in other subjects and other circumstances an appalling state of horror or despair) [15, 17:414 f].

The combined-effect of body tonus and perception is also an important factor in ritualizing behavior and may be experimentally altered to produce hallucinations.

Such facts seem to me to necessitate an ethological approach to human affairs in general, including human ritualization in the broadest sense. Ethological methodology includes (*a*) careful observation and description of ritualized behavior, followed by comparative study; and (*b*) its analysis, aimed at discovering the psychosocial mechanisms of its operation, and its relation to environmental and historical change [29, 30, 31: chap 9 and 11].

There are many fields in which such an approach should be profitable. One is the comparative study of various kinds of formalized expressive behavior in different cultures at different levels of development. Gestures are an obvious example: they

701

become ritualized into signals of threat or submission, greeting or desire [5: *passim*] and also may form the basis of social convention and group bonding. Another is the comparative study of rituals based on psychological projection — scapegoat rituals, from the Jews' expulsion of a single symbolic goat to the Nazis' scapegoating of the entire Jewish race; rituals of atonement for sin, from the Jewish Day of Atonement to the doctrine of Christ's vicarious atonement for the sins of mankind; and the multifarious rituals of sacrifice, including that of substitute sacrifice, like the killing of a substitute priest-king.

Then there are rituals involving masochism, like those of flagellants, and those involving sadism, like public executions and torture; military rituals — of discipline, from rigid rank-hierarchy to commando training, and of damage-reduction, from single combat and "gentlemanly war" to the Geneva convention; rituals of national prestige and bonding, like Russian May Day celebrations or British Coronation ceremonies (see [25]); medical rituals, from uroscopy and the Hippocratic oath to illegibility of prescriptions and the bedside manner; psychiatric rituals, greeting and hospitality rituals; legal rituals; appeasement rituals like hand-shaking; moral rituals, including their relation to tabu and to religion; and their fossilization in codes of purely external observances; mourning rituals (see [12]); liturgical rituals; parliamentary and committee rituals; oath-taking rituals (whose power was demonstrated by the Mau-Mau); and of course the universal *rites de passage* concerning birth and name-giving, initiation into adult life, marriage, death, and concern with ancestral spirits; and the equally universal seasonal rituals, like Christmas and Easter, together with long-period rituals, like anniversary and centenary ceremonies, and those concerned with calendrical cycles, as in Aztec and Maya culture.

Humor, except in rudimentary form, is peculiar to man. A study of the ritualization or canalizing of its expressions, from the licensed fooling of court jesters to comedy, farce, and satire, would be valuable.

Human displacement rituals merit further study — they obviously cover a wide range of activities, from scratching one's head when puzzled or lighting a cigarette when slightly frustrated to going off to play golf instead of sitting down to make a difficult decision.

Here I shall point out some of the general features of human rites and ceremonies.

First, although most human rituals and ceremonies are preponderantly symbolic and non-genetic, a few have an innate genetic basis and act as signals or automatic releasers of behavior in others. The classical example is the smile-signal operating between infant and mother ([28]). Starting as simple reflex behavior, it is elaborated by experience and is incorporated in the mother-infant bonding ritual [1, 2], and in later life becomes a flexible symbolic gesture of considerable importance in daily social life.

While some complex symbolic rituals, like those of solitary meditation and prayer, concern only the individual, most of them, like collective worship or tribal dancing, have a social function — to ensure individual participation in a group activity, and to canalize and intensify the group's mood.

All symbolic rituals and ceremonies are essentially magico religious in origin; during cultural evolution, extended ritualization tends to reduce their magical component, and often to secularize them. However, even the rituals of the higher religions still contain many magical elements.

Magic, in the strict anthropological sense, is based on the belief that both nature and man can be brought under compulsion and controlled by psychological means — through spells, incantations, prayer, sacrifice, and special personal or professional powers. Magical systems are logical, but not rational; they are based on the non-rational premises of primitive projective thinking and may continue to be believed in even where the rational-empirical approach has produced efficient new technological results: e.g., crop fertility rituals as necessary backing for neolithic agricultural techniques.

Magical belief-rituals survive and play a part even in the highest and most scientific cultures of today. They survive in our superstitions, our Polycrates complexes, our compulsion neuroses, in our reliance on the sacred force of oaths and on religious as against civil ceremonies for baptism and marriage, in our hero worship and our devotion to political and religious leaders, and in pilgrimage and petitionary prayer.

And when we say that we are "under the spell" of beauty or great music, or call a view of a work of art "magical," we are acknowledging the existence of magic, in the extended sense of non-rational, emotional, and often unconscious formalizing or patterning forces, which are essential for all transcendent experience. Instead of rejecting these forces or pretending that they do not exist, we must explore them and ritualize them to best advantage.

During psychosocial evolution, rituals evolve in various ways. They become ecologically adapted to different habitats and to different ways of life. Thus, after the neolithic revolution, hunting rituals had to be abandoned or relegated to a secondary position, and quite new rituals concerned with agriculture had to be evolved.

They also become politically adapted. The religiously tolerant Roman imperial system led to ritual syncretism; whereas societies which professed revealed dogmatic religions like Christianity and Islam were opposed to syncretism in principle and attempted to impose a single body of belief and ritual practice.

Human play differs from animal play in two important respects. First of all, children's play is not merely an expression of exploratory urges and enjoyment of the free exercise of motor expression; it also includes an acting out of various of their psychological problems — their relations with adults, with each other, with the environment. In all play involving catching and escape, fear as well as aggression is acted out (see, for example, [23]). Here, as in many other fields, psychoanalytic theory helps us to understand human ritualization (see [7]).

Secondly, it has partly been formalized into games — i.e., play subject to definite rules. Competitive games, especially team-games, are ritualized damage-reducing outlets for aggression, and can serve as substitutes for war, in William James's phrase.

The symbolic or ritually expressive "acting out" of personal

problems and conflicts through painting, writing, constructional play, or in actual dramatic form, is of psychiatric importance. The aim of magico-religious rituals like those of Haitian voodoo is to dissipate painful ideas and obsessive fears through symbolic and sometimes violent ritual expression [16]: conversion hysteria can be regarded as an unconscious attempt to achieve similar ends through a symbolic displacement activity.

An extension of one aspect of play is seen in *escape rituals* — organized activities in which man can escape briefly from the disciplined morality and monotony of everyday working life. They include carnivals and fairs, Dionysiac orgies, pharmaco-logico-religious rituals like the peyote ceremony of some Amer-indians, cup finals, and organized holidays *à la* Butlin. Theaters and cinemas and dance halls also provide an escape into the formalized other world of the stage-play, the film, and the dance.

Escape rituals are important social safety-valves: when traditional escape rituals have died out or been suppressed, safety-valve rituals spring up to take their place, sometimes ludicrously orgiastic like Beatlemania, sometimes socially anti-adaptive like teenage gang rivalry: one of the tasks of present-day industrialized societies is to provide adequate escape rituals for their members.

As in animals, stress situations readily lead to distortion of normally stabilized behavior in man, and may even produce total breakdown of the "inner ritualization" involved in personality patterning. Some human compulsive rituals are merely peculiar, like Dr. Johnson's obligatory touching of posts when out for a walk, or many people's semi-compulsive ritual of avoiding treading in the cracks between paving-stones. (A boy at my prep school invented an extraordinary private ritual, which I commend to the attention of my anthropological and psychological colleagues. Every morning at breakfast he would conceal some porridge, take it up to the urinal, and deposit it in the second compartment from the left.)

An ethological approach could clearly prove of great value in psychiatry. It could also prove of value in education. The ancient rituals of education *a posteriori* by flogging, or by other physical punishments, and the still existing ritual of education by a succession of quantitatively markable examinations involving the regurgitation of memorizable facts, are clearly inadequate. If education is not to consist in what Dorothy Parker scarifyingly described as "casting sham pearls before real swine," it must incorporate rituals, in the extended sense of organized integrative patterns, of explanatory adventure, enjoyment, and fulfillment, always free but always disciplined. Skinner [26] points out the value of scientifically formalized teaching methods.

Human ritualization resembles that seen in animals in showing the same pair of divergent trends — towards simplification and communication and immediate almost automatic action on the one hand, as in the mechanization of prayer into prayer-wheels or mere repetition of paternosters; and to complexification, delayed action, long continuances, and bonding function on the other, as in the Mass or the initiation rites of almost all cultures.

Finally I want to point out some peculiarities of human ritualization caused by the much greater speed of psychosocial than of biological evolution. This leads to a much higher frequency of non-adaptive or even mal-adaptive survival of rituals originating in relation to an earlier psychosocial environment.

A striking example concerns the Lisbon earthquake of 1755, where Pombal's rescue operations were gravely hindered by religious insistence on ceremonies of intercession [19]. Prayers for rain and ceremonies to avert divine wrath as manifested in pestilence or volcanic eruption, are non-adaptive in a scientific age.

On the other hand, adaptive time-binding and socially bonding traditional rituals in institutions are widespread. The smallest institution in which they can operate effectively seems to be the school [22]. The Old School Tie is a real bonding mechanism, as well as a piece of neckwear acting as a personal recognition signal.

There may also be survival of vestigial rituals, quite analogous to vestigial structures in lower organisms: e.g., the carrying of nosegays, originally to prevent catching contagious diseases, by English judges.

The converse effect is much more serious — the failure of existing human groups, including the human species as a whole, to ritualize their behavior adequately or effectively in relation to the radically new psychosocial situations of today. This applies to all three aspects of successful ritualization — its communicatory, its conflict-reducing, and its positive-bonding functions. Thus the discovery of simple and effective contraceptive methods, together with the growing menace of over-population, has rendered our traditional approach to sex obsolete: new ritualizations are needed to transcend promiscuity, male indulgence, and intemperate procreation, and build a true art of love with profound bonding effects, as well as a manageable world society.

Second, all religious, pseudo-religions and quasi-religions involve formalization or canalization: (*a*) of intellectual framework — a theology or ideology; (*b*) of ethics — a moral code; and (*c*) of expression — ritual in the restricted sense, liturgy, the cult of images, etc. With the weakening of traditional religious systems, better ritualization, of doctrine and moral practice as well as liturgy, is needed for their adaptation to modern conditions. It is still more urgently needed for emergent ideological systems. Attempts are being made to develop appropriate social and moral principles and marriage and funeral ceremonies of a quasi-religious nature for humanists, but much more must be done before a religiously and socially effective humanist system can emerge.

Third, as regards the world situation, the United Nations and its supra-national activities have been very poorly ritualized. Even its flag is a feeble symbol-stimulus compared with almost all national flags: it lacks both professional peace-keeping forces and anything comparable to the national development teams and service corps, like the U.S. Peace Corps and the British V.O.S. Professional ethologists and psychologists are needed to help remedy these deficiencies.

They are also needed to help in the most comprehensive task

before this generation — the achievement of a new and effective adaptive patterning of thought and belief about man's place and role in nature.

Intellectually satisfying patterns of thinking and emotionally satisfying patterns of expression and action are urgently needed to canalize successfully man's overriding world activities — the prevention of nuclear war, co-operative world development, the increase of quality rather than quantity, the building of fulfillment societies and of open-ended self-transforming psychosocial systems — in a phrase, the proper ritualization of human destiny on an evolutionary basis.

REFERENCES

1. Bowlby, J: An Ethological Approach to Research in Child Development, *British Journal of Medical Psychology*, 1957, vol 30, p 230.
2. Bowlby, J: The Nature of the Child's Tie to His Mother, *International Journal of Psychoanalysis*, 1958, vol 39, p 5.
3. Bowlby, J: Pathological Mourning and Childhood Mourning, *Journal of the American Psychoanalytic Association*, 1963, vol 11, p 3.
4. Cantril, H: *The Pattern of Human Concerns* (Rutgers University Press, New Brunswick, New Jersey) 1965.
5. Darwin, C: *The Expression of the Emotions in Man and Animals* (Murray, London, England) 1872 (2nd ed 1889).
6. Empson, W: *Seven Types of Ambiguity* (Chatto and Windus, London, England) 1930 (Peregrine Books, London, England) 1961.
7. Erikson, E: The Roots of Virtue, in J S Huxley, ed: *The Humanist Frame* (Allen and Unwin, London, England) 1961.
8. Erikson, E: *Insight and Responsibility* (Norton, New York, New York) 1964.
9. Fogel, S, and Hoffer, A: Perceptual Changes Induced by Hypnotic Suggestion . . . Effect on Personality, *Journal of Clinical Exp. Psychopath.*, 1962, vol 23, p 24.

709

10. Frisch, K von: *The Dancing Bees* (Methuen, London, England) 1954.

11. Gombrich, E H: *Art and Illusion: Meditations on a Hobby Horse* (Phaidon Press, London, England) 1960, 1963.

12. Gorer, G: *Death, Grief and Mourning in Contemporary Britain* (Cresset Press, London, England) 1965.

13. Haldane, J S: Animal Communication and the Origin of Human Language, *Scientific Progress*, 1955, no. 71, p 385.

14. Hartmann, E L: The Dream State. Review and Discussion of Studies of the Physiological State Concomitant with Dreaming, *New England Journal of Medicine*, 1965, vol 273, pp 30, 87.

15. Huxley, A L: *The Doors of Perception* (1954), *Heaven and Hell* (1956), 1 vol (Chatto and Windus, London, England) 1960.

16. Huxley, F J H: *The Invisibles* (Hart Davis, London, England) 1966.

17. Huxley, J S: Psychometabolism: General and Lorenzian, *Persp. Biol. Med.*, 1964, vol 7, p 399.

18. Huxley, J S; Mayr, E; Osmond, H; and Hoffer, A: Schizophrenia as a Genetic Morphism, *Nature* (London), 1964, vol 206, p 220.

19. Kendrick, T D: *The Lisbon Earthquake* (Methuen, London, England) 1956.

20. Koestler, A: *The Act of Creation* (Hutchinson, London, England) 1964.

21. Lilly, J C: Mental Effects of Reduction of Ordinary Levels of Physical Stimuli, etc, *Psychiatr Rep*, 1956, vol 5.

22. Lorenz, K: *The Natural History of Aggression*, translated from *Das Sogennante Böse* (Borotha-Schoeler, Vienna, 1963), 1965.

23. Opie, I, and Opie, P: *The Lore and Language of Schoolchildren* (Oxford University Press, Oxford, England) 1959.

24. Schenkel, R: Zur Ontogenese des Verhaltens bei Gorilla und Mensch, *Z Morph Anthrop*, 1964, vol 54, p. 233.

25. Shils, E and Young, M: The Meaning of the Coronation, *Social Rev.* (N.S.), 1953, vol 1, p 63.

26. Skinner, B F: The Technology of Teaching, *Proc Roy Soc,* 1964, vol B 162, p 427.

27. Southwick, C A (ed): *Primate Social Behavior* (Van Nostrand, London, England, and New York, New York) 1963. See K Imanishi (p 68) and J Itani (p 91) (Japanese macaque).

28. Spitz, R A and Wolf, K M: The Smiling Response: A Contribution to the Ontogenesis of Social Relations, *Genet Psychol Monogr,* 1946, vol 34, pp 57–125.

29. Tinbergen, N: Social Releasers and the Experimental Method Required for Their Study, *Wilson Bulletin,* 1948, vol 60, p 6.

30. Tinbergen, N: Behaviour and Natural Selection, in J A Moore, ed, *Ideas in Modern Biology, Proc XVI Int Congr Zool,* 1963, vol 6, p 521.

31. Tinbergen, N: *Social Behaviour in Animals* (Methuen, London, England and Wiley, New York, New York) 1965.

32. Witt, P N: Effect of Drugs on Spiders' Web-spinning, *Behaviour* (Leiden), 1952, vol 4, p 172.

33. Witt, P N: *Die Wirkung von Substanzen auf dem Netzbau der Spinne als biologischer Test* (Springer, Heidelberg, Germany) 1956.

34. Witt, P N: Do We Live in the Best of All Worlds? Spider-webs Suggest an Answer, *Persp Biol Med,* 1965, vol 8, p 475.

35. Witt, P N: Spider-web Building, *Science,* 1965, vol 149, p 1190.

THE DEVELOPMENT OF RITUALIZATION
by Erik H. Erikson

IN THIS zoological setting, I may consider it a sign of hospitality that the ontogeny of ritualization in man is to be discussed before that in animals. This permits me to give full consideration to man's complexity, and to dispense with the attempt to derive the human kind of ritualization from what has come to be called

711

ritualization in animals. Rather, I will try to show what in human life may be the equivalent of the ethologist's ritualization, and to present a developmental schedule for its ontogeny. (For a conception of the human life cycle underlying this attempt, see [1] and [3].) To do so, I must first set aside a number of now dominant connotations of the term. The oldest of these is the *anthropological* one which ties it to rites and rituals conducted by communities of adults (and sometimes witnessed by children or participated in by youths) for the purpose of marking such recurring events as the phases of the year or the stages of life. I will attempt to trace some of the ontogenetic roots of all ritual making but I will not deal explicitly with ritual as such.

A more recent connotation of "ritualization" is the *clinical* one. Here the term "private ritual" is used to conceptualize obsessional behavior consisting of repetitive solitary acts with highly idiosyncratic meanings. Such behavior is vaguely analogous to the aimless behavior of caged animals, and thus seems to provide a "natural" link with a possible phylogenetic origin of ritualization in its more stereotyped and driven forms. But it seems important to set aside this clinical connotation in order to take account of newer insights both in ethology and in psychoanalysis. There is now a trend in the ethological literature (recently summarized in Konrad Lorenz's *Das Sogenannte Boese*) [8] which follows the original suggestion of Sir Julian Huxley to use the word ritualization (and this explicitly without quotation marks) for certain phylogenetically performed ceremonial acts in the so-called social animals. The study of these acts clearly points away from pathology, in that it reveals the bond created by a reciprocal message of supreme adaptive importance. We should, therefore, begin by postulating that behavior to be called ritualization in man must consist of an agreed-upon interplay between at least two persons who repeat it at meaningful intervals and in recurring contexts; and that this interplay should have adaptive value for both participants. And, I would submit, these conditions are already fully met by the way in which a human mother and her baby greet each other in the morning.

Beginnings, however, are apt to be both dim in contour

and lasting in consequences. Ritualization in man seems to be grounded in the preverbal experience of infants while reaching its full elaboration in grand public ceremonies. No one field could encompass such a range of phenomena with solid observation. Rather, the theme of ritualization (as I have found in preparing this paper) can help us to see new connections between seemingly distant phenomena, such as human infancy and man's institutions, individual adaptation and the function of ritual. Here, I will not be able to avoid extensive speculation.

INFANCY AND THE NUMINOUS

Let me begin with the "greeting ceremonial" marking the beginning of an infant's day: for ritualization is to be treated here first as a special form of everyday behavior. In such matters it is best not to think at first of our own homes but of those of some neighbors, or of a tribe studied or a faraway country visited, while comparing it all — how could some of us do otherwise — with analogous phenomena among our favorite birds.

The awakening infant conveys to his mother the fact that he is awake and (as if with the signal of an alarm clock) awakens in her a whole repertoire of emotive, verbal, and manipulative behavior. She approaches him with smiling or worried concern, brightly or anxiously rendering a name, and goes into action: looking, feeling, sniffing, she ascertains possible sources of discomfort and initiates services to be rendered by rearranging the infant's condition, by picking him up, etc. If observed for several days it becomes clear that this daily event is highly ritualized, in that the mother seems to feel obliged, and not a little pleased, to repeat a performance which arouses in the infant predictable responses, encouraging her, in turn, to proceed. Such ritualization, however, is hard to describe. It is at the same time highly *individual* ("typical for the mother" and also tuned to the particular infant) and yet also *stereotyped* along traditional lines. The whole procedure is superimposed on the periodicity of physical needs close to the requirements of survival; but it is an

713

emotional as well as a *practical* necessity for both mother and infant. And, as we will see, this enhanced routine can be properly evaluated only as a small but tough link in the whole formidable sequence of generations.

Let us take the fact that the mother called the infant by a name. This may have been carefully selected and perhaps certified in some name-giving ritual, held to be indispensable by the parents and the community. Yet, whatever procedures have given meaning to the name, that meaning now exerts a certain effect on the way in which the name is repeated during the morning procedure — together with other emphases of caring attention which have a very special meaning for the mother and eventually for the child. Daily observations (confirmed by the special aura of Madonna-and-Child images) suggest that this mutual assignment of very special meaning is the ontogenetic source of one pervasive element in human ritualization, which is based on a *mutuality of recognition.*

There is much to suggest that man is born with the need for such regular and mutual affirmation and certification: we know, at any rate, that its absence can harm an infant radically, by diminishing or extinguishing his search for impressions which will verify his senses. But, once aroused, this need will reassert itself in every stage of life as a hunger for ever new, ever more formalized and more widely shared ritualizations and rituals which repeat such face-to-face "recognition" of the hoped-for. Such ritualizations range from the regular exchange of greetings affirming a strong emotional bond, to singular encounters of mutual fusion in love or inspiration, or in a leader's "charisma." I would suggest, therefore, that this first and dimmest affirmation, this sense of a *hallowed presence,* contributes to man's ritual making a pervasive element which we will call the "Numinous." This designation betrays my intention to follow the earliest into the last: and, indeed, we vaguely recognize the numinous as an indispensable aspect of periodical religious observances, where the believer, by appropriate gestures, confesses his dependence and his childlike faith and seeks, by appropriate offerings, to secure a sense of being lifted up to the very bosom of the supernatural which in the visible form of an image may graciously respond, with the faint smile of an inclined face. The result is a sense of *separateness transcended,* and yet also of *distinctiveness confirmed.*

I have now offered two sets of phenomena, namely, ritualization in the nursery (as an enhancement by playful formalization of the routine procedures which assure mere survival) and religious rituals (which provide a periodical reaffirmation for a multitude of men) as the first examples of an affinity of themes, which seem to "belong" to entirely different "fields" but are necessarily brought together as subject matter for this Symposium. By suggesting such a far-reaching connection, however, I do not mean to reduce formalized ritual to infantile elements; rather, I intend to sketch, for a number of such elements of ritualization, an ontogenetic beginning and a reintegration on ever higher levels of development. In adult ritual, to be sure, these infantile elements are both emotively and symbolically reevoked; but both infantile ritualization and adult ritual are parts of a functional whole, namely, of a cultural version of human existence.

I will now try to list those elements of ritualization which we can already recognize in the first, the numinous instance — emphasizing throughout the opposites which appear to be reconciled. Its mutuality is based on the *reciprocal needs* of two quite *unequal* organisms and minds. We have spoken of the *periodicity of developing needs* to which ritualization gives a *symbolic actuality.* We have recognized it as a highly *personal* matter, and yet as *group-bound,* providing a sense both of *oneness* and of *distinctiveness.* It is *playful,* and yet *formalized,* and this in *details* as well as in the *whole* procedure. Becoming *familiar* through repetition, it yet brings the *surprise* of recognition. And while the ethologists will tell us that ritualizations in the animal world must, above all, be *unambiguous* as sets of signals, we suspect that in man the *overcoming of ambivalence* as well as of ambiguity is one of the prime functions of ritualization. For as we love our children, we also find them unbearably demanding, even as they will soon find us arbitrary and possessive. What we love or admire is also threatening, awe becomes awfulness, and benevolence seems in danger of being consumed by wrath. Therefore, ritualized affirmation, once instituted, becomes *indispensable* as a periodical experience and must find new forms in the context of new developmental actualities.

This is a large order with which to burden an infant's daily awakening, and, indeed, only the whole sequence of stages of ritualization can make this list of opposites plausible. Yet, even at the beginning, psychopathology confirms this burdening. Of all psychological disturbances which we have learned to connect ontogenetically with the early stages of life, the deepest and most devastating are those in which the light of mutual recognition and of hope are forfeited in psychotic withdrawal and regression, and this, as Spitz and Bowlby have shown, can develop at the very beginning of life. For, the earliest affirmation is already reaffirmation in the face of the fact that the very experiences by which man derives a measure of security also expose him to a *series of estrangements* which we must try to specify as we deal with each developmental stage. In the first stage, I submit, it is a sense of *separation by abandonment* which must be prevented by the persistent, periodical reassurance of familiarity and mutuality. Such reassurance remains the function of the numinous and thus primarily of the religious ritual or of the numinous element in any ritual. Its perversion or absence, on the other hand, leaves a sense of dread, estrangement, or impoverishment.

In another context [3] I have suggested that the most basic quality of human life, *hope*, is the inner strength which emerges unbroken from early familiarity and mutuality and which provides for man a sense (or a promise) of a personal and universal continuum. It is grounded and fortified in the first stage of life, and subsequently nourished, as it were, by all those ritualizations and rituals which combat a sense of abandonment and hopelessness and promise instead a mutuality of recognition, face to face, all through life — until "we shall know even as also we are known."

716

THE PSEUDOSPECIES

In order to deal with the total setting which seems to give meaning to and to receive meaning from human ritualization, I must introduce three theoretical considerations of an incomplete and controversial nature.

Since ritualization in animals is for the most part an intra-specific phenomenon, it must be emphasized throughout that man has evolved (by whatever kind of evolution and for whatever adaptive reasons) in *pseudospecies*, i.e., tribes, clans, etc., which behave as if they were separate species created at the beginning of time by supernatural will, and each superimposing on the geographic and economic facts of its existence a cosmogeny, as well as a theocracy and an image of man, all its own. Thus each develops a distinct sense of identity, held to be *the* human identity and fortified against other pseudospecies by prejudices which mark them as extraspecific and, in fact, inimical to the only "genuine" human endeavor. Paradoxically, however, newly born man can fit into any number of such pseudospecies and must, therefore, become specialized during a prolonged childhood — certainly a basic fact in the ontogeny of familiarization by ritualization.

To speak of pseudospecies may be controversial enough. But I must now face a second conceptual dilemma in the form of Sigmund Freud's instinct theory. Whenever the noun "instinct" appears in psychoanalytic formulations it is helpful to ask whether the corresponding adjective would be "instinctive" or "instinctual," i.e., whether the emphasis is on an *instinctive pattern* of behavior, or an *instinctual drive or energy* more or less indifferent and divorced from prepared patterns of adaptiveness. As Freud put it in his *New Introductory Lectures:* "From the Pleasure Principle to the instinct of self-preservation is a long way; and the two tendencies are far from coinciding from the first." It will appear, then, that psychoanalysts usually mean instinctual drives, and this with the connotation of a quantitative excess devoid of instinctive quality in the sense of specific patterns of "fittedness" [6]. The evolutionary rationale for this free-floating quantity of instinctual energy lies, of course, in the very fact that man is, in Ernst Mayr's words, the "generalist animal," born to invest relatively nonspecific drives in such learning experiences and such social encounters as will assure, during a long childhood, a strengthening and widening of mutuality, competence, and identity — all, as I am endeavoring to show, supported most affirmatively by appropriate ritualizations.

I say "most affirmatively" because man's *moral prohibitions* and *inner inhibitions* are apt to be as excessive and maladaptive as the drives which they are meant to contain: in psychoanalysis we therefore speak of a "return of the repressed." Could it be, then, that true ritualization represents, in fact, a *creative formalization* which avoids both impulsive excess and overly compulsive self-restriction, both social anomie and moralistic coercion? If so, we could see at least three vital functions served by the simplest ritualization worthy of that designation:

(1) It binds instinctual energy into a pattern of mutuality, which bestows convincing simplicity on dangerously complex matters. As mother and infant meet in the first ritualization described so far, the infant brings to the constellation his vital needs, among them, oral, sensory, and tactile drives (subsumed as "orality" in Freud's libido theory), and the necessity to have disparate experiences made coherent by mothering. The mother in her postpartum state is also needful in a complex manner: for whatever instinctive mothering she may be endowed with, and whatever instinctual gratification she may seek in being a mother, she needs to be a *mother of a special kind* and *in a special way*. This she becomes by no means without an anxious avoidance (sometimes outright phobic, often deeply superstitious) of "other" kinds and ways typical for persons or groups whom she (sometimes unconsciously) dislikes, or despises, hates, or fears as godless or evil, unhygienic, or immoral.

(2) In permitting the mother to "be herself" and to be at the same time an obedient representative of a group ethos, ritualization protects her against the danger of instinctual excess and

arbitrariness and against the burden of having to systematize a thousand small decisions.

(3) In establishing mutuality in the immediacy of early needs, ritualization also does the groundwork for lasting mutual identifications between adult and child from generation to generation. For the mother is reaffirmed in her identification with those who mothered her well; while her own motherhood is reaffirmed as benevolent by the increasing responsiveness of the infant. The infant, in turn, develops a benevolent self-image (a certified narcissism, we may say) grounded in the recognition of an all-powerful and mostly benevolent (if sometimes strangely malevolent) "Other."

(4) Thus ritualization also provides the psychosocial foundation for that inner equilibrium which in psychoanalysis is attributed to a "strong ego"; and thus also a first step for the gradual development (to be sealed only in adolescence) of an independent identity [5] which — guided by various rituals of "confirmation" representing a "second birth" — will integrate all childhood identifications, while subordinating those wishes and images which have become undesirable and evil.

EARLY CHILDHOOD AND THE JUDICIOUS

Any ontological discourse suffers from the fact that it must begin to enumerate its guiding principles at the beginning, while only an account of their progression and differentiation as a whole can reveal their plausibility. The dimensions of ritualization suggested so far must now reappear on higher levels: mutuality between the child and that increasing number of adults with whom he is ready to interact, physically, mentally, and socially; the affirmation of such new mutuality by ritualization and this in the face of a new kind of estrangement; and the emergence of a new element of ritual.

A second basic element in human ritualization is one for which the best term would seem to be *judicial*, because it combines *jus* and *dicere*, "the law" and "the word." At any rate, the term

should encompass methods by which the *discrimination* between right and wrong is ontologically established. Eventually, this becomes an important aspect in all human ritual; for there is no ritual which does not imply a discrimination between the sanctioned and the out-of-bounds — up to the Last Judgment.

The ontological source of this second element is the second stage of life, that is, early childhood, which is characterized by a growing psychosocial autonomy and by rapid advances in development. As *locomotion* serves increased autonomy, it also leads to the boundaries of the permissible; as *discrimination* sharpens, it also serves the perception of conduct which "looks right" or "does not look right" in the eye of others; while *language development* (obviously one of the strongest bonds of a pseudo-species) distinguishes with finite emphasis what is conceptually integrated in the verbalized world, and what remains outside, nameless, unmeaningful, strange, *wrong*. All of this is given strong connotations by what Freud called "anality." It brings with it a new sense of estrangement: standing upright, the child realizes that he can lose face and suffer shame; giving himself away by blushing, he feels furiously isolated, not knowing whether to *doubt himself* or *his judges*. His elders, in turn, feel compelled to utilize and thus to aggravate this trend; and yet, is it not again in the ritualization of approval and disapproval (in recurring situations of high symbolic meaning) that the adult speaks as a mouthpiece of a supraindividual righteousness, damning the deed but not necessarily the doer?

I will never forget an experience which I am sure I share with all anthropologists (professional and amateur): I mean the astonishment with which we "in the field" encounter for the first time old people who will describe what is appropriate in their culture with a sense of moral and aesthetic rightness unquestionably sanctioned by the universe. Here is an example of what I was told among the Yurok Indians in Northern California, who depended on the salmon and its elusive ways (long hidden to science) of propagating and migrating.

Once upon a time, a Yurok meal was a veritable ceremony of self-restraint. A strict order of placement was maintained and

721

the child was taught to eat in prescribed ways; for example, to put only a little food on the spoon, to take the spoon up to his mouth slowly, to put the spoon down while chewing the food — and above all, to think of becoming rich during the whole process. There was silence during meals, so that everybody could keep his thoughts concentrated on money and salmon. This ritualization served to lift to the level of a kind of hallucination nostalgic oral needs which may have been evoked by very early weaning from the breast (quite extraordinary amoung American Indians). Later, in the "sweat house" the boy would learn the dual feat of thinking of money and *not* thinking of women; and the adult Yurok could make himself see money hanging from trees and salmon swimming in the river during the off season in the belief that this self-induced "hallucinatory" thought would bring action from the Providers [2:177].

This ceremonial style which undoubtedly impressed the small child and had precursors in less formal daily occasions invested similar ritualizations along the whole course of life, for cultures (so we may remind ourselves in passing) attempt to give *coherence* and *continuity* to the whole schedule of minute ritualizations.

This second element of ritualization is differentiated from the first primarily by an emphasis on the *child's free will*. In the ritualizations of infancy avoidances were the mother's responsibility; now the child himself is trained to "watch himself." To this end parents and other elders compare him (to his face) with what he *might* become if he and they did not watch out. Here, then, is the ontogenetic source of the "negative identity" which is so essential for the maintenance of a pseudospecies for it embodies everything one is not supposed to be or show — and what one yet potentially is. The negative identity furnishes explicit images of pseudospecies which one must *not* resemble in order to have a chance of acceptance in one's own. Behind the dreaded traits are often images of what the parents themselves are trying not to be and therefore doubly fear the child might become, and are thus *potential* traits which he must learn to imagine in order to be able to avoid them. The self-doubt and the hidden shame attached to the necessity of "eliminating" part of himself as well as the suppression of urges create in man a certain *righteous rage* which can turn parent against parent, parent against child — and the child against himself. I paint this matter darkly because here we meet the ontological origin of the divided species. Moral self-discrimination is sharpened by an indoctrination against evil others, on whom the small child can project what he must negate in himself, and against whom he can later turn that moralistic and sadistic prejudice which has become the greatest danger of the species man. His "prejudice against himself," on the other hand, is at the bottom of man's proclivity for compulsive, obsessive, and depressive disorders; while irrational prejudice against others, if joined with mass prejudice and armed with modern weapons, may yet mark the premature end of a species just on the verge of becoming one [5]. All of this, however, also underlines the importance of true ritualization as a supraindividual formalization transmitting rules of conduct in words and sounds which the child can comprehend, and in situations which he can manage.

In its full elaboration in a *judiciary ritual*, however, this judicious element is reaffirmed on a grand scale, making all-visible on the public stage what occurs in each individual as an inner process: the Law is untiringly watchful as is, alas, our conscience. It locates a suitable culprit who, once in the dock, serves as "an example," on which a multitude can project their inner shame. The unceasing inner rumination with which we watch ourselves is matched by the conflicting evidence which parades past the parental judge, the fraternal jury, and the chorus of the public. Judgment, finally, is pronounced as based on sanctified agreement rather than on passing outrage or personal revenge; and where repentance does not accept punishment, the verdict will impose it.

Both the ritualized establishment of boundaries of good and bad in childhood and the judiciary ritual in the adult world fulfill the criteria for ritualized procedures as suggested earlier: meaningful regularity; ceremonial attention to detail and to the total procedure; a sense of symbolic actuality surpassing the reality of each participant and of the deed itself; a mutual activation of all concerned (including, or so it is hoped, the confessing culprit); and a sense of indispensability so absolute that the need for the ritualization in question seems to be "instinctive" with man. And, indeed, the judicial element has become an indispensable part of man's phylogenetic adaptation as well as his ontogenetic development.

In seeing the judicial element at work, however, in public and in private, we can also perceive where this form of ritualization fails in its adaptive function, and this means in the convincing transmission of boundaries from generation to generation. Failure is indicated where fearful compulsion to conform replaces free assent to what feels right; where thus the obsessively formalistic becomes dominant over the convincingly ceremonial or where considered judgment is swamped by instinctual excess and becomes moralistic sadism or sensational voyeurism. All of this increases the hopeless isolation of the culprit and aggravates an impotent rage which can only make him more "shameless." Thus, the decay or perversion of ritual does not create an indifferent emptiness, but a void with explosive possibilities — to which fact this Symposium should pay careful attention. For it explains why "nice" people who have lost the gift of imparting values by meaningful ritualization can have children who become (or behave like) juvenile delinquents; and why nice "churchgoing" nations can so act as to arouse the impression of harboring pervasive murderous intent.

Here, again, the psychopathology attending individual misfunctioning and the social pathology characterizing the breakdown of institutions are closely related. They meet in the alternation of impulsivity and compulsivity, excess and self-restriction, anarchy and autocracy.

CHILDHOOD: THE DRAMATIC AND THE FORMAL

I have now attempted to isolate two elements in human rituals which seem clearly grounded in ontogenetic stages of development. In view of the "originology" which is apt to replace defunct teleology, it seems important to reiterate that I am not suggesting a simple causal relationship between the infantile stage and the adult institution, in the sense that adult rituals above all serve persisting infantile needs in disguise. The image of the Ancestor or of the God sought on a more mature level is (as we shall see) by no means "only" a replica of the mother's inclined face, nor the idea of Justice "only" an externalization of a childish bad conscience. Rather, man's epigenetic development in separate and protracted childhood stages assures that each of the major elements which constitute human institutions is rooted in a distinct childhood stage, but, once evolved, must be progressively reintegrated on each higher level. Thus the numinous element reappears in the judicial ritualizations as the aura adhering to all "authority" and later to a personified or highly abstract image of Justice, or to the concrete persons who as justices are invested with the symbolism and the power of that image. But this also means that neither the numinous nor the judicial elements, although they can dominate a particular stage or a particular institution, can "make up" a ritual all by themselves: other elements must join them. Of these, I will discuss in the following, the elements of *dramatic elaboration*, of *competence of performance*, and of *ideological commitment*. (See Table 1.)

First, then, the *dramatic* element. This I believe, is grounded in the maturational advances of the *play age* which permits the child to create with available objects (and then in games with cooperative adults and peers) a *coherent plot with dramatic turns* and some form of *climactic conclusion*.

While the second, the "judicial" stage was characterized by the internalization of the parental voice, this age offers the child a microreality in which he can escape adult ritualization and prepare his own, reliving, correcting, and recreating past experiences, and anticipating future roles and events with the spontaneity and repetitiveness which characterize all ritualization. His themes, however, are often dominated by usurpation and impersonation of adult roles; and I would nominate for the principal *inner estrangement* which finds expression, aggravation, or resolution in play, the *sense of guilt*. One might think that this sense should be subsumed under the judicial sphere; yet, guilt is an inescapable sense of self-condemnation which does not even wait for the fantasied deed to be actually committed; or, if committed, to be known to others; or, if known to others, to be punished by them.

This theme dominates the great tragedies, for the *theater* is adult man's "play." The play on the toy stage and the plays acted out in official drama and magic ceremonial have certain themes in common which may, in fact, have helped to induce Freud to give to the dominant "complex" of this stage the name of a tragic hero: Oedipus. That common theme is the conflict between hubris and guilt, between the usurpation of father-likeness and punishment, between freedom and sin. The appropriate institution for the aweful expression of the dramatic is the stage, which, however, cannot do without the numinous and the judicial, even as they, in any given ritual, rite, or ceremony, cannot dispense with the dramatic.

What is the form of psychopathology characterizing the play age and the neurotic trends emanating from it? It is the weight of excessive guilt which leads to repression in thought and to inhibition in action. It is no coincidence that this pathology is most dramatically expressed in *Hamlet*, the tragedy of the *actor* in every sense of the word, who tries to solve his inhibitive scruples by the invention of a *play within a play* and prepares his perdition in and by it. And yet, this perdition almost seems a salvation from something worse: that pervasive boredom in the midst of affluence and power, that malaise and inability to gain pleasure "from either man or woman" which characterizes the absence of the dramatic and the denial of the tragic.

The *school age* adds another element to ritualization: that of the *perfection of performance*. The elements mentioned so far would be without a binding discipline which holds them to a minute sequence and arrangement of performance. The mental and emotional capacity for such accuracy arises only in the school age; or rather, because it *can* arise then, children are sent to "schools." There, with varying abruptness, play is transformed into work, game into cooperation, and the freedom of imagination into the duty to perform with full attention to all the minute details which are necessary to complete a task and do it "right." Ritualization becomes truly cooperative in the whole arrangement called "school," that is, in the interplay between "teacher," "class," and individual child, and in the prescribed series of minute tasks which are structured according to the verbal, the mathematical, and the physical nature of the cultural universe. This, I submit, is the ontogenetic source of that *formal aspect* of rituals, provided by an order in space and time which is convincing to the sense as it becomes *order perceived* and yet also *participated in*. Adding this sense of detail, seriously attended to within a meaningful context, to the numinous, judicial, and dramatic elements, we feel closer to an understanding of the dimensions of any true ritual. But we also perceive the danger of overformalization, perfectionism, and empty ceremonialism, not to speak of the neurotic "ritual" marked by total isolation (and all too often considered the model of ritualization by my psychiatric colleagues).

ADOLESCENCE AND BEYOND:
THE IDEOLOGICAL AND THE GENERATIONAL

I have now concentrated on the ontogenetic and, as it were, unofficial sources of ritualizations in childhood. From here, one could continue in two directions: that is, one could discuss the always surprising and sometimes shocking spontaneous "rites" by which adolescents ritualize their relations to each other and demarcate their generation as (slightly or decidedly) different both from the adult haves and the infantile have-nots; or one could now turn to formal rites and rituals, for it is in the formal rites of confirmation, induction, etc., that adolescing man is enjoined for the first time to become a full member of his pseudospecies, and often of a special *élite* within it. For all the elements developed in the ontogenetic sequence already discussed now become part of formal rites which tie the infantile inventory into an ideological world image, provide a convincing coherence of ideas and ideals, and give youth the feeling of active participation in

727

the preservation or renewal of society. Only now can man be said to be adult in the sense that he can devote himself to ritual purposes and can visualize a future in which he will become the everyday ritualizer in his children's lives.

Our ontogenetic sketch has to include this stage because the reciprocal mechanisms by which adult and young animals complete the interplay of their respective inborn patterns can be said to be paralleled in man by no less than the *whole period of childhood and youth*. To be fully grown in the human sense means the readiness to join not only the *technology* but also certain *irreversible commitments* to one's pseudospecies; which also means to *exclude* (by moral repudiation, fanatic rebellion, or warfare) inimical identities and outworn or foreign ideologies. Elsewhere [5] I have undertaken to delineate the identity crisis which precedes the emergence in youth of a sense of *psychosocial identity* and the readiness for the ideological style pervading the ritualizations of his culture. Only an integration of these two processes prepares youth for the alignment of its new strength with the technological and historical trends of the day. I have called the corresponding estrangement *identity confusion*. Clinically (i.e., in those so predisposed), this expresses itself in withdrawal or in lone-wolf delinquency; while it is often a matter of psychiatric, political, and legal definition whether and where borderline psychosis, criminality, dangerous delinquency, or unwholesome fanaticism may be said to exist. Much of youthful "demonstration" in private is just that: a dramatization (sometimes mocking, sometimes riotous) of the estrangement of youth from the impersonality of mass production, the vagueness of confessed values, and the intangibility of the prospects for either an individualized or truly communal existence; but, above all, by the necessity to find entirely new forms of ritualization in a technology changing so rapidly that change becomes one of its main attributes. There are historical identity vacua when the identity crisis is aggravated on a large scale and met only by an ideological renewal which "catches up" with economic and technological changes [1].

We have also witnessed in our time totalitarian attempts at

involving new generations ideologically in staged mass rituals combining the numinous and the judicial, the dramatic and the precise in performance on the largest scale, which provide for masses of young individuals an ideological commitment encompassing perpetual change and, in fact, making all traditional (in the sense of prerevolutionary) values part of a decidedly negative identity.

I point to all this in the present context primarily because of problems concerning the ontogeny of ritualization. For what is in question is (1) the necessary coherence and continuity between early ritualization and overall technological and political trends, and (2) the role of youth in the rejuvenation of society and the integration of our humanist past with the technological age now emerging worldwide.

But before we come to the question of ritualization in the modern world we must mention a *dominant function of ritual in the life of the adult*. Parents are the earliest ritualizers in their children's lives; at the same time, they are participants of the instituted rituals in which the ritualizations of their childhoods find an echo and a reaffirmation. What, then, is the prime contribution of adult ritual to the ontogenesis of ritualization? I think ritual reaffirms the sanction needed by adults to be convincing ritualizers.

After the *rituals of graduation* from the apprenticeship of youth, *marriage ceremonies* provide for the young adult the "license" to enter those new associations which will transmit tradition to the coming generation. I am reminded here of a wedding ceremony which took place in a small town in the French Alps. The young Americans to be married faced the mayor; the tricolor was wound round his middle (which was soon to be regaled with ceremonial champagne). Above and behind him, *le Général* looked most distantly out of a framed picture into new greatness; and above him a bust of *l'Empéreur* stared white and vacant into the future, the brow wrapped in laurel; while even higher up, the afternoon sun streamed through a window, all the way down to the book out of which the mayor read phrases from a Code, to which a young bride from America could have agreed only with some reservations, had she fully understood them. Yet we few, in a foreign land, felt well taken care of, for the Western world shares many ceremonial values and procedures; and the couple accepted from the mayor a little booklet which provided for the entry of the names of the next generation.

Whether the ceremonies of the adult years call on personal ancestors in the beyond or on culture heroes, on spirits or gods, on kings or leaders, they sanction the adult; for his mature needs include the *need to be periodically reinforced in his role of ritualizer*, which means not more and not less than to be ready to become a numinous model in his children's minds, and to act as a judge and the transmitter of traditional ideals. This last element in the ontogenetic series I would call the *generational* which includes *parental* and *instructive, productive, creative*, and *curative* endeavors.

CONCLUSION

In the "freer" adult of the Western world we often observe an oppressive sense of responsibility in isolation, and this under the impact of two parallel developments, namely, the decrease of ritual reassurance from the ceremonial resources of a passing age, and the increase of a self-conscious awareness of the role of the individual, and especially of the parent and the teacher in the sequence of generations. Adults thus oppressed, however, are of little use to youth which prefers to gather around those who create new patterns of ritualization worthy (or seemingly worthy) of the energies of a new generation. The Symposium, having established the evolutionary significance of ritualization in man, may thus not be able to shirk the question whether fading rituals may or may not at this time be giving way to ritualizations of a new kind, dictated above all by new methods of communication and not always recognizable to the overtrained eye.

I hope, therefore, that this Symposium will come to discuss not only the question of the weakening of traditional ritual and of

730

"our" traditional sense of ritualization, but also the agencies which provide a reinforcement of ritualization in line with a new world image. This new cosmos is held together by the scientific ethos, the methods of mass communication, and the replacement of "ordained" authorities by an indefinite sequence of experts correcting and complementing each other. Pediatric advice, for example, offers knowledge and prudence as guides to parental conduct; modern technology attaches new ritualizations to technical necessities and opportunities in homes and at work; and worldwide communication creates new and more universal parliaments. We must review the accreditation of those who rush in to occupy places left vacant by vanishing ritualization, and who offer new "rituals" of mechanistic or autocratic, self-conscious, totally thoughtless, or all too intellectual kinds.

However, new sources of numinous and judicial affirmation as well as of dramatic and aesthetic representation can obviously come only from a new spirit embodying an identification of the

TABLE 1. Ontogeny of Ritualization

infancy	mutuality of recognition					
early childhood		discrimination of good and bad				
play age			dramatic elaboration			
school age				rules of performance		
adolescence					solidarity of conviction	
elements in adult rituals	NUMINOUS	JUDICIAL	DRAMATIC	FORMAL	IDEOLOGICAL	GENERATIONAL SANCTION

731

whole human species with itself. The transition will compound our estrangements; for could it not be that much of the ritualization discussed here owes its inescapability to a period in mankind's evolution when the pseudospecies was dominant? Will a more inclusive human identity do away with the necessity of reinforcing the identities and the prejudices of many pseudospecies — even as a new and more universal ethics may make old moralisms obsolete? If so, there seems to be a strong link between Huxley's Romanes lecture [7] and today's proceedings.

I am by no means certain that the elements of ritualization enumerated in this paper and charted with premature finality in Table 1 represent a complete inventory. I have outlined what I was able to discern, and what I believe the principles of further inquiry to be. At any rate, there can be no prescription for ritualization, for, far from being merely repetitive or familiar in the sense of habituation, any true ritualization is ontogenetically grounded and yet pervaded with the spontaneity of surprise: it is an unexpected renewal of a recognizable order in potential chaos. Ritualization thus depends on that blending of surprise and recognition which is the soul of creativity, reborn out of the abyss of instinctual disorder, confusion of identity, and social anomie.

One major example of creative ritualization in the modern era, namely Gandhi's technique of non-violent conflict (Satyagraha), has striking analogies to the pacific ritualization of animals as recently summarized by Lorenz [3]. For a preliminary report, see [4].

REFERENCES

1. Erikson, E H: *Young Man Luther* (W W Norton, New York, New York) 1958.
2. Erikson, E H: *Childhood and Society*, ed 2 (W W Norton, New York, New York) 1963.
3. Erikson, E H: *Insight and Responsibility* (W W Norton, New York, New York) 1964.
4. Erikson, E H: Psychoanalysis and Ongoing History, *American Journal of Psychiatry*, 1965, no 122, pp 241–250.

5. Erikson, E H: The Concept of Identity in Race Relations, in T Parsons and K B Clark, eds, *The Negro American* (Houghton Mifflin, Boston, Massachusetts) 1966.
6. Hartmann, H: *Ego Psychology and the Problem of Adaptation*, D Rapaport, translator (International Universities Press, New York, New York) 1958.
7. Huxley, J: *Evolutionary Ethics* (Oxford University Press, Oxford, England) 1943.
8. Lorenz, K: *Das Sogenannte Boese* (Borotha-Schoeler Verlag, Vienna, Austria) 1964.

RITUAL AND CRISIS
by Edward Shils

THE VICISSITUDES of human life are embedded in our very conception of its nature. Life is a perpetual struggle of the organism both to maintain its integrity, which requires safety, against the menacing intrusion of one part of the environment into the flow of sustenance of another part, and to maintain itself against the dangers of decay and wrongdoing within itself. Even if the environment were beneficent, the human being could not maintain a stable equilibrium; his growth brings with it difficulties for which he is unprepared.

The human being is not a passive recipient of sustenance and a passive object of deprivations. He is active; he has cognitive powers and curosity which reach outward into the universe and which seek an order as coherent and as comprehensive as possible. He is expansive in his desires. He seeks to acquire possession and control over his environment and he does so in a condition of ignorance and uncertainty as to whether he will be successful. Every new enterprise therefore courts the danger of defeat and destruction.

What is true of the individual organism is true of collectivities, of families and kinship groups, of armies and cities, of universities

733

and sects, of states and whole societies. Every collectivity lives in a changing environment; the changes in the environment sometimes bring advantages and sometimes deprivations. The avoidance of the deprivations brought by changes in the environment is a major task of every collectivity and above all of those who make themselves responsible for its maintenance. Complete success in avoidance of these exogenous deprivations for any extended period is practically impossible.

Every collectivity is in danger not only from changes outside itself but from changes within as well. The wants of its constituent members do not grow in harmonious articulation; relationships which were at one time mutually gratifying and thereby sustaining to the collectivity cease to develop in ways which permit reciprocity and consensus. In addition, external dangers generate internal dangers. Leaders who are effective at one stage in dealing with the external environment lose their legitimacy when the environment becomes unencompassable and their followers, subordinates, or dependents cease to be willing to accept them.

The frustration and defeat of new undertakings and the failure of old, once successful ones, the loss of honor and eminence, neglect, the defeat and decay of collectivities and the disappearance of particular relationships and persons, the dissolution of powers and possessions and the loss of territory, the dangers of hunger and of damages to the body, the failure of hopes and the falsification of beliefs, the awareness of wrongdoing and the risk of being in the wrong, chaos and the bewilderingness of the cosmos, civil disorder, and above all, death — the fear of death as much as its occurrence — these are the tribulations of man. The sufferings they cause embrace both the pain of what has already happened and been experienced, and the terror of what has not yet happened but is certain to happen — as death is certain — or, like the loss of honor, power, and possessions, might happen, but not inevitably.

Crises are situations in the lives of individuals, corporate groups, or societies in which the performance of established routines is rendered more difficult than ordinarily by the height-

734

ening of such tribulations, or situations in which anticipations of what is regarded as appropriate and legitimate are more frustrated or rendered more improbable than usual. Crises themselves can become predictable and efforts made to avert them or to render them less burdensome (e.g., by insurance or by planning). Because of the chronic incompatibility of many demands for the same scarce and much sought-after objects, because of the limitations of knowledge and foresight, and because aging and death are inevitable, individual men and their societies always live in a state of crisis. But there are crises and crises, and some are more severe than others. Let us look at some of the non-empirical defenses that are built to cope with crisis.

RITUAL, CEREMONIAL, ETIQUETTE

Ritual is a stereotyped, symbolically concentrated expression of beliefs and sentiments regarding ultimate things. It is a way of renewing contact with ultimate things, of bringing more vividly to the mind through symbolic performances certain centrally important processes and norms. Ultimate things are those which are beyond the ordinary, sensibly evident sequences of events; they govern or are thought to govern these events and offer guidance and imperatives to action. Ultimate things are sacred things.

Ordinary, sensibly evident sequences of events vary in the extent to which they arouse the need to be related to sacred things. Those events which are closest to the generation, reproduction, and cessation of the vitality of individuals and collectivities are among the most likely to arouse the need for connection with sacred things. Empirically observable events which contradict or infringe on those rules of life which designate the right relationship with sacred things also call forth the need to reaffirm (and reinterpret) that relationship.

Deprivations already experienced and dangers of future deprivations activate the need for contact with ultimate things, with higher powers.

735

It is said by some students of the subject that ritual is part of a system of beliefs and expressive actions which are espoused and performed in response to danger. Ritual is part of a complex act of self-protection from destructive, unintelligible, and immoral forces. By re-enacting contact with sacred things and reaffirming the rightness, ritual reinforces the beliefs which enable the actor to confront and deal with crises with some anticipation of effectiveness. Effectiveness might be thought of as a reduction in the probability of occurrence of deprivation, but it is more likely to be a fortification of a person's capacity to bear deprivations about to occur. Ritual sanctifies the participant by infusing into his self-consciousness, through contact with its symbolic manifestation, a tincture of sacredness. By renewing contact with the symbols or emblems of the norms and forces which are believed to be constitutive of the well-being of the collectivity and by re-establishing contact with essential principles and vital powers in the universe, those who practice the rituals feel themselves entitled to believe that they will walk along the right path and that danger will be avoided, but that if danger is realized, they will be able to interpret it correctly and behave appropriately.

Ritual and belief are intertwined with each other; yet they are separable. Beliefs and systems of beliefs could conceivably be accepted without adopting the practice of the rituals associated with them. When we speak of rituals in the sense we are discussing them here, we think of their cognitive or beliefful content. Logically, beliefs could exist without rituals; rituals, however, could not exist without beliefs.

Rituals stand on a continuum of kinds of stereotyped behavior running from ceremonial etiquette and usage on to habit and conditioned reflexes. An elaborate etiquette has much in common with ritual in its rigid stereotypical structure, in its specification of actions, and in its symbolization of differing appreciation of the charismatic qualities embodied in great authority, power, and eminence. But etiquette is at the periphery of the relation to sacred things while ritual is at the center.

"Ceremonial" belongs to the same family of rigidly stereo-

736

typed actions but is closer to ritual than to etiquette because it has more cognitive content; it is more likely to have some elements of belief associated with it and it is more likely to refer to vital features of collective life. Its occurrence is more concentrated than that of etiquette. It is performed in certain places and on certain occasions which are called "ceremonial occasions" — just as ritual is performed on specified occasions (in contrast with etiquette, which is performed continuously in interaction between persons of certain status positions).

RITUAL AND PREVAILING OPINION

Ritual — and much of what is said here applies to ceremonial too — has had a bad name for the past century among intellectuals raised, as so many of us have been in the past fifty years, in utilitarian traditions. Ritual is regarded as useless, as "mere ritual" on the same level as "incantation," which also has a bad name. Ritual is regarded as dangerous to adaptive action because it is "rigid." It is thought to be insincere; it is accused of failure to express actually experienced emotions or states of mind. In an age in which intellectuals, under Freudian influence, prize affective spontaneity, ritual is derogated as "compulsive." It is thought to be lacking in "genuineness"; it is charged with being "hollow," "external." Its traditional cognitive content is a burden; there is a certain embarrassment in its presence, even on the part of many who enjoy participation in ritual practices, because it is integral to particular beliefs which they either do not share or do not wish to acknowledge, or to a category of existence which they have been educated to disregard or dispute. It is thought that ritual is "out of touch with the times," that our time is inherently alien to ritual, and that rituals existing in this society are no more than survivals from the past, without value except as "spectacles."

Ritual, then, which in one form or another has been present in every epoch of human society has come in our own to be regarded as having no legitimate place in the economy of human life. Its name is blackened by its association with "magic," superstition, myth, religion, priestly ministrations, and submissiveness to divine authority. If ritual were only expressive, as Asian dances are thought to be, then it might have some chance of appreciation; but it instead has cognitive and moral contents of problematic associations, and on these accounts it is discredited. Cognitively, ritual speaks on behalf of cosmologies that are scientifically unacceptable; morally it involves conceptions of the sources of right and wrong that are repugnant to contemporary educated opinion.

The culture which is regarded by its most eminent figures as irreligious and wholly secular finds no place for ritual in its own society, even though it makes many steps forward in the study of rituals in other societies.

Nonetheless there is still a considerable amount of ritual performance in contemporary western societies. Much of it is of the traditional variety, associated with churches, but there is much else. The exercise of great authority which is constructed to maintain order, to protect and enhance life, and to deal therefore with great vicissitudes of individual and collective existence, continues to be surrounded by ritual. When a president is inaugurated, even in a country which believes that it has freed itself from the encrustations of aristocratic ceremonial and etiquette, the ritual is quite elaborate. There is a complex etiquette involved in approaching presidents and prime ministers. When a president or a prime minister dies and receives a "state funeral," a ritual performance which goes far beyond conventional or traditional religious requirements is enacted. National anniversaries like July 14 or July 4 or November 7 are republican rituals which cannot be accounted for if one views them as nothing more than survivals.

Judges in law courts are embedded in ritual, the higher the court, the richer the ritual. The practice of the legal profession is highly ritualized. Armies still insist on considerable ritual, particularly at the higher levels of authority. Many universities, and not just the ancient universities of the United Kingdom, have extensive ceremonials; many universities which do not have them seem, from time to time, to feel deficient for not having some. Still, is there any university which simply sends through the post a mimeographed notice to a former student attesting that he has

738

just completed his course of study, thereby eschewing convocation and degree-granting rituals? Even secondary schools think
they need such rituals to mark the passage from one stage of life
to the next.

Rituals do not exist only in institutions with a long and continuing tradition from a ritually more amply provided past.
They also come into existence in new institutions and in the personal relations of individuals. Rudimentary rituals which have
not been acquired through tradition certainly exist in families and
are asserted to confirm family identity and continuity. Christen-
ings and anniversaries seem to be reassurances against the often-
felt danger of dissolution about which senior members of families
are sometimes apprehensive. Crises of transition from one stage
to another in the course of the life of ordinary human beings
tend to be ritualized. The poverty of civil marriage ceremonies
is often felt acutely by those whose religious convictions are too
faint to allow them to be married in church. Even the deliberately anti-ritualist Soviet Union has decided to provide a Hall of
Marriages so that marriage rituals may be performed with appropriate seriousness. And what of funerals — and the desperate
improvisation of ritual-like performances among those who have
fallen away from the churches and who do not believe in immortality and the resurrection of the dead?

Modern "secular" society contains a great deal of newly generated ritual, quite apart from the religious and political ritual
"surviving" from an allegedly more ritualist past. It is very probable that there are fewer ritual acts per capita practiced nowadays than there were several centuries ago. Religious observances
in church and hearth, ritual in monarchical and aristocratic
institutions, and in emulatory non-monarchical regimes — all of
which were highly ritualized — have declined in frequency, both
within individual careers and among individuals in whole societies. There is less church-going nowadays in the sense that
smaller proportions of the population attend religious services
now than four centuries ago. Not many monarchies survive as
compared with a century ago; aristocracies and courts have gone,
too. Families appear to be more informal and more equalitarian —
and equalitarianism has in recent centuries been part of the re-

739

jection of authority and of the ritual in which it tends to become embedded.

Is it likely that this trend toward the further diminution of ritual practice will continue until ritual becomes extinct in our society?

DEATH, WAR, OTHER MISERIES

Crises are times of danger in the lives of societies, institutions, and individuals. Rituals are parts of systems of belief directed toward averting danger and fortifying the individual to face it by re-affirming connections with the most fundamental realities or norms, and by interpreting the danger in such a way as to make it coherent with the universe as understood in the body of beliefs of which the ritual is a part. Rituals are therefore parts of a systematic response to crises, actual and anticipated.

Let us begin with death, which preoccupies every system of belief about the position of man in the world and which enters into so many of the rituals that are parts of such systems of belief. Death is still a certainty for every living human being but is not as omnipresent a threat in present day advanced societies as it was before the relatively recent improvements in preventive medicine, nutrition, and obstetrics. I am inclined to think that this is one of the most important factors in the relative decline in religious belief and ritual observance which has occurred in the course of the past century. Scientism has probably contributed to the erosion of religious belief and ritual participation in the educated classes, but in the mass of the population science has influenced religious belief, not through direct confrontation but through its contribution to medical practice.

But as if to compensate for this, there is now the danger of nuclear war. The possibility of such war is the cause of the greatest crisis the human race has ever confronted, apart from death itself. Death is a permanent certainty, and the permanence and the certainty have, over a long time, permitted a development of beliefs and rituals to alleviate to some small extent the

740

terror that death inevitably inspires. Now that the belief in personal immortality and the ultimate resurrection of the dead no longer has the subscription of as large a proportion of the population as it once presumably did, one of the mechanisms which makes the thought of death a little more tolerable is belief in the survival of the collectivity and its culture. The danger of nuclear war destroys that consolation because it offers the prospect of death, individual and collective, simultaneously and certainly. Furthermore, the danger of nuclear war came upon mankind suddenly and dramatically, about twenty years ago. Measures which might be taken to reduce the losses inflicted in a nuclear war once it has occurred seem trivial. The techniques of its prevention, given the other attachments of human beings, are indeterminate. Thus in a sense, mankind, at least in the industrialized countries, faces a danger which, though not as certain as individual death, is by no means improbable and represents a far more comprehensive annihilation.

There are other crises, for example those resulting from the rapid growth of population, the expansion of the scale of society and corporate bodies, the automation of industry, and the prospect of a workless life for a large proportion of the members of a society, the strain of urban life in increasingly urbanized societies, the intensity of activity attendant on the growth of affluence and opportunity. These are crises to some people; we are already living in the midst of many of them and some people regard them as normal. Such crises grow gradually and imperceptibly. They are very unevenly effective and hence many people do not experience them at all as deprivations. Remedies or preventive measures, although not easy to imagine, seem at least to fall within human powers, so that even for those who see them as crises, there exists at least some possibility of rational action to avert them or at least to avert their worst consequences.

The other miseries which afflict the human race — accidental death and maiming, civil disorder, natural disasters, poverty, illness, unhappiness — have always existed. They are crises to those to whom they occur, but they are usually segregated. There are more specific actions which can be taken to avoid or to remedy

741

or compensate for some of them. They cannot in any sense be called modern crises, yet it is possible that heightened sensitivity and hedonism, and the more widespread expectation of a better human life over much of the earth's surface, have caused these ancient catastrophes and adumbrations of death to be experienced more painfully than used to be the case.

How have men reacted to these crises, particularly to those which are specifically modern? Have they engendered new patterns of belief and new ritual modes of defense?

The quantitative social survey evidence is not very decisive, in part because it does not go back far enough in time to enable us to compare different periods of time with respect to the frequency of ritual activity, and in part because the evidence deals with only one type of ritual practice, namely, formal religious observance. Impressions are equivocal. On the one hand, one is impressed by the expansion of church attendance in the United States in almost all sectors of society, by the major role played by Christian parties in the political life of Western Europe since the war, and by the extraordinarily diminished hostility of intellectuals towards religion in the period since the Second World War. On the other hand, one is struck also by the repeated observations, especially in Britain but also on the continent of Europe, concerning the meaninglessness of religious ritual, and by the extent to which some of the most important branches of Western Christianity have begun to acknowledge in one form or another the validity of these observations. There is no indication of an increase in church attendance in the United Kingdom or on the continent. Nonetheless the increased interest in religious matters seems significant. There seems to be, despite dissatisfaction or indifference toward inherited theologies and liturgies, a greater general appreciation of religion. It is difficult to say whether this sympathy extends more to unexpungeable religious needs of human beings or to the possible truth of some as yet unarticulated body of religious belief. A new ritual style or idiom, freed from associations with symbols that are no longer congenial, has not been created to correspond to the religious curiosity or sensitivity which is now being more widely and openly expressed. Yet I have an impression that many more or less "secular" persons regret the lack of an acceptable ritual.

Ritual continues to have a bad name in intellectual circles. But its total absence in grave situations strikes contemporaries as anomalous, even where they find the inherited ritual to be repugnant. Rational contrivance has not been able to devise rituals which, it is felt, possess the gravity of those having some substantive affinity with the very beliefs no longer regarded as credible.

THE EFFECTIVENESS OF RITUAL

Does this "ritual deficit" and the discomfiture about it make any important difference in the life of contemporary man? Numerous students have emphasized that ritual is not technological. It is not part of a chain of means and ends; it is not instrumental in any empirical sense. Even though rituals might be mechanisms of defense against dangers, the dangers they seek to mitigate have frequently had their way. The strength of ritual practice, which according to theory affirms and renews the solidarity of the community of participants, has not in the past proved sufficient to prevent the institutions within which they were practiced from foundering or falling into catastrophe. Armies have lost their solidarity and governments have often been indecisive even though their ritual practices were "adequate" according to the conceptions of the time and the experts of the ritual.

It is said that ritual, because it follows a prescribed pattern, tends to force conduct outside its own structure into a similar rigidity and thus has a stabilizing effect on the social order. The stability thus fostered allegedly contributes to adaptability to external necessities. There is unfortunately no worthwhile evidence on this important problem. Rigidity of conduct is certainly possible without ritual practice. The governments of the United States, China, and the Soviet Union, none of which is thought to

743

be highly ritualized in its procedures or conduct, have all shown considerably more rigidity than many outside judges regard as appropriate to the very dangerous situation in which they are participating. It is said of British society in the middle of the twentieth century, when it is certainly less ritualized than it was one or two hundred years ago, that it is unable to adapt itself to the new situation of Britain in the world. On the other hand, Japanese society, which is still one of the most ritualized in many spheres of life, has shown exceptional adaptability over the past century. Germany, too, which has been for a long time among the most ritualized of Western societies, has shown great vigor and skill in adaptation to the new circumstances of the past two decades. Unfortunately, in the present state of my knowledge, nothing much can be said, with respect to contemporary advanced societies, about the influence of ritual practices on the conduct of those who partake of them. It is difficult to say whether ritual participation does in fact fortify the participants against deprivations by strengthening their beliefs and their institutional attachments. Such influence as ritual practice might have on conduct is undoubtedly subtle and it is not massive or decisive. It probably does help to remind its participants of the gravity of some aspects of existence, and recalls to them some fundamental rules and symbols of a pattern of life. But in large-scale societies ritual is only one among many factors that activate fundamental normative orientations and images in human beings; and the maintenance of this state of activation requires constant support from authoritative institutions and environing opinion, quite independently of ritual practice. In smaller, less differentiated societies in which the religious community, the lineage, and the society are coterminous, participation in a religious ritual is also participation in a ritual of the whole society. In such a situation it is reasonable to think that ritual participation heightens directly the solidarity of the whole society. In large-scale, advanced societies of the present day, with their high degree of pluralism, of specialization of institutions and of segmentation of roles, participation in religious ritual probably cannot start a

744

U. S. 1st Infantry Division soldiers bow their heads during prayer services in entrenchments at Bu Dop Special Forces camp in Vietnam.

series of ripples which will run throughout all the individual roles and to all sectors of the societies. Still, even present-day societies are not so disaggregated that there is no connection among their various cultural and institutional centers. The affirmation of a connection with the center of the universe in a religious ritual within the framework of a church which belongs to the central institutional system might well have some reinforcing repercussions on the participants' relations with the center of the political system. But alone and unaided, in a society in which every other factor is hostile to the effectiveness of the central institutional system, ritual participation will not be a decisive factor.

Nonetheless, the importance of ritual in any large society lies in its expression of an intended commitment to the serious element of existence, to the vital powers and norms which it is thought should guide the understanding and conduct of life. It belongs to the category of actions like the creation of works of art, music, or literature. Ritual is an expressive act, but the forms of ritual expression are, for those who participate in them, prescribed by liturgical tradition. Their individuality must be fitted into the frame provided by tradition. Whereas works of art, literature, and music are produced in traditions which praise individual creativity and genius, ritual belongs to a tradition in which religion and art are fused. Those who practice established traditional rituals are reproducers and the experience of the ritual lacks the immediacy of feeling an expressive work gives to its creator. Yet despite this mediated character, it does express a form of cognitive contact with the serious core of reality.

Human beings are probably not much less impressed now by *la vie sérieuse,* as Durkheim called it, than they were in earlier stages of human history. They are, however, less continuously so, because as was pointed out earlier, until the emergence of nuclear weapons, the threat of death had become less continuously present. Further reasons for the decline in ritual practice may be seen in the diminished persuasiveness of the symbolic idiom which is used in our inherited rituals as well as in the

746

equalitarian hostility toward rituals connected with hieratic, monarchical, and aristocratic structures of authority.

THE SURVIVAL OF RITUAL

If ritual practice is nowadays relatively marginal and intermittent in its significance for conduct, and if so many of our rituals are connected to a theology and liturgy and systems of authority to which commitments are no longer so firm, it might be asked whether ritual will survive. I venture the opinion that, in a variety of ways, it will survive. As long as the category of the "serious" remains in human life, there will be a profound impulse to acknowledge and express an appreciation of the "seriousness" which puts the individual into contact with words and actions of symbolic import.

It is this sense of the "serious" which constitutes the religious impulse in man. This I regard as given in the constitution of man in the same way that cognitive powers are given or locomotive powers are given. Like those, they are unevenly given and unevenly cultivated, so that the sense of the "serious," the need for contact with the charismatic or sacred values, differs markedly among human beings within any society. Some persons, a minority, tend to have it to a pronounced degree and even relatively continuously; others, far more numerous, will experience it only intermittently and, except rarely, without great intensity. Finally there is a minority which is utterly opaque to the serious. (The matter is far more complicated than it is presented here. There is frivolity in its two senses of sacrilegiousness and "unseriousness"; there is deliberate and serious atheism and anti-clericalism and utterly "unserious" indifference toward the sacred. I think, however, that these are only variants of the rough classification previously described.)

To satisfy this universal need for contact with sacred values, for many persons the inheritance of religious beliefs with which our dominant rituals are associated will probably continue to

747

serve. They have already shown much greater tenacity than nineteenth-century positivists and utilitarians assumed. The need for order, and for meaning in order, are too fundamental in man for the human race as a whole to allow itself to be bereft of the rich and elaborate scheme of metaphorical interpretation of existence which is made available by the great world religions. The spread of education and of scientific knowledge, as well as the improved level of material well-being, will not eradicate them unless those who have these religions in their charge lose their self-confidence because of the distrust the highly educated hold toward the inherited metaphors.

The significance of authority is not going to diminish either, nor will the vicissitudes which endanger human life and which infringe on the foundations of morally meaningful order. As long as the biological organism of man passes through stages resembling those now known to us, there will be transitions from one stage to the next; each successive stage will require some sort of consecration to mark its seriousness. Nor will the spirits embodied in nuclear weapons ever allow themselves to be put back into Pandora's box. Mankind will never be able to forget the fact that the means for its very large-scale and almost instantaneous destruction exist and will continue to exist. And with this will be attendant a sense of need to reaffirm the moral standards through which mankind might be protected from this monstrous danger.

There will be a need for ritual because there is a need to re-affirm contact with the stratum of the "serious" in human existence. But the question is whether a new type of ritual which expresses the same persistent preoccupations in a new symbolic idiom will emerge. It is possible that the need for ritual will exist in varying degrees of intensity but that an acceptable ritual will not come into existence and become newly traditionalized, because, on the one hand, the system of beliefs that engendered the inherited ritual is no longer acceptable, and, on the other, the new beliefs about the "serious" will not find a widely acknowledged idiom or a custodianship intellectually, morally, and aesthetically capable of precipitating a new ritual.

748

COMMENTARY ON RITUAL AND LITURGY
by William F. Lynch, S.J.

RITUAL is an engrossing subject these days. The pro and con
of the events and discussions developing around it move to points
of strong interest and strong feeling.

I am especially interested in the strong-minded and inevitably
perceptive views of Julian Huxley. We can use the word inevitable in his case because it is hard to imagine a biologist and
anthropologist of his stature not being enormously conscious of
the eternal presence among us of all the forms of ritual and their
endless equivalents in human culture. And he is more conscious
than most that there are as many cultural as there are genetic
forms of rite. He has no hesitation, for example, in expecting or
calling for the emergence of a form of celebration that might
make mankind increasingly conscious of the evolutionary history
that opens before us. Surely this is a fine act of the imagination
which may relate to what Christian ritual, for example, has to
say about the emergence of a new man.

Let me mention a dimension of the discussion of ritual which
is very fascinating but may not be very clearly in our consciousness as the reality it is. If we take for granted that ritual may be
many things but that it is, in form, most clearly a *public* action,
then we can read and reread Professor Shils' sober analysis of
our situation, and will see, I propose, that one of the questions he
may really be asking is: do we believe in the validity, the honesty, and the authenticity of public acts in any direction? Is
there not a general distrust of public acts of the imagination?
Certainly there is a distrust of the political order. But — if I may
say something unfashionable — that is partly the result of the
collapse of the fantasies and false hopes and love of style that
had begun to develop in 1960, and partly the result of an inability to tolerate reality. We now see the political order in Manichaean terms. What I am thinking of, however, belongs to a
longer history than the events of the last few years; it belongs

749

to the long history among us of the private imagination, the flight of the arts from public life, and their refusal or inability to make *public* gestures. My own impression is that we are coming out of this period, and are a bit sated with alienation, but that the transition will take time.

Surely the status of public ritual has been affected by this modern history of the imagination. Here, too, a renaissance, if it is to occur, will take time. And it will not only be theorizing and speculations, it will probably be clusters of events that will continue to drive us into conflictual attitudes for and against participation in public gesture and action. These events, together with the sequences of reaction to them, obviously will have a large quality of unpredictability about them. The savage blow to the nation in the assassination of John Kennedy was coped with and given much healing by three most extraordinary days of public action and ritual, of such a kind as we could not have dreamed was in us. On the other hand there are still powerful reactions away from the present quality of much of our bureaucratic life and toward purely private revolt. But who has formalized and ritualized his life more than the hippie? Who, a few years ago, would have dreamed of the possible emergence of the be-in and the love-in!

There are clear voices, however, which also tell us the reverse of all this, voices which are saying that the movement in the transitional period ahead of us is away from ritual and common public gesture. Nowhere has this been more clearly said or accompanied by a more imposing theoretical structure than by Philip Rieff when he announces to us that "the spiritualizers," who have determined the shape of Western culture from the beginning, have given way now to "the psychologizers," and he refers to the latter as "inheritors of that dualist tradition which pits human nature against social order." He tells us that a new culture, centered in the well-being of the self, uncommitted to value forms in external reality, is making a revolutionary appearance, is indeed our real and central revolution. He puts this very large question: "In what does the self now try to find salvation, if not in the breaking of corporate identities and in an acute suspicion of all normative institutions?"

It is clear where this would lead any normal concept of ritual.

Rieff's descriptions of a new personality in the making in the West are so striking that he should be allowed to speak further. I give a number of brief quotations and would leave to the reader the obvious applications to our ritual and liturgical futures.

. . . the creation of a knowing rather than a believing person, able to enjoy life without erecting high symbolic hedges around it, distinguishes the emergent culture from its predecessor [3:23].

* * *

Dichotomies between an ultimately meaningful and meaningless existence belong to the eras of public philosophies and communal theologies. Ecologically, this transitional civilization is becoming one vast suburbia, something like the United States, populated by divided communities of two, with perhaps two junior members caught in the middle of a private and not always civil war; in relation to these intimate, though divided, communities of two, the public world is constituted as one vast stranger, who appears at inconvenient times and makes demands viewed as purely external and therefore without the power to elicit a genuine moral response [3:52].

* * *

In a highly differentiated democratic culture, truly and for the first time, there arose the possibility of every man standing for himself, each at last leading a truly private life, trained to understand rather than love (or hate) his neighbor [3:70].

* * *

The therapy of all therapies is not to attach oneself exclusively to any particular therapy, so that no illusion may survive of some end beyond an intensely private sense of well-being to be generated in the living of life itself. That a sense of well-being has become the end, rather than a by-product of striving after some superior communal end, announces a fundamental change of focus in the entire cast of our culture . . . [3:261].

These are some of the thoughts of Philip Rieff, analytic, thoughtful, a little too aphoristic, not knowing which way he himself should turn. If he is right and turns out to be a good prophet, shall we then say that most obviously this new form of personality in the West will turn the tide decisively against all ritual possibilities? We do not yet know. We must await many further manifestations of what can break out of the human psyche under the pressure of different sets of historical circumstance. It is not popular to sense a number of unusual possibilities: shall this private form of soul develop its own liturgies? Shall it go mad with the need of public gesture and go off into explosions of terrifying conformity? Is it possible that it will go fascistic (on the left or the right)? Western civilization has, before this, watched the development of the private soul and its romanticisms into mad public orders that mock the nature of more human rituals. I am speculating, therefore, that a complete suppression of the real thing in ritual can lead to what might be called pornographic forms of ritual. These suppressed forms have often been violent.

Philip Rieff is a skillful student of sociology and modern analysis. But he is not a historian, nor is he a historian of sociology after the manner of a man like Norman Cohn [1] who has been so competent at tracing the perennial bonds between the private mind and mad forms of social crusade.

It is doubtful if the private mind will lead us to the end of ritual. More likely it will lead us to the kind of conformity which is a corruption of real ritual. More probably our better chances lie always in the direction of *human* forms of public action and *reasonable* forms of ritual or liturgy. Our salvation may very well lie in seeing that we are caught in the two swings of a rejection of public ritual of the secular order and a drowning in many of its oppressive forms, especially in the forms of public conformity.

There is some reason to think that we may get hold of a human and reasonable understanding of ritual if we seek the help of the men of the imagination. Today they do not always

752

write directly about ritual matters; one has to look through paths of indirection for their kind of analysis and prediction.

It is they better than others who would see a curious paradox in the history of the word *ritual*. What has happened historically to this word needs no great or profound explanation. To ritualize something obviously means to formalize it to the point of the static; at its most awful pole of meaning it means to bring death to that which is living. This is what has happened to the word "ritual."

This is an ironic history for the word. Let us ask a few poets and a few imaginative people to help us reconstruct the other history of the meaning of rite and ritual.

The reconstruction would turn the recent static picture upside down. It would imagine *a static world* which needs a resurrection or coming to life; a ritual is *a living action* which brings such a dead situation to life. Among the imaginative essayists of 1967 on the subject there is Stanley Romaine Hopper's Introduction to *Interpretations: The Poetry of Meaning* [2]. Hopper is a good analyst of art-in-the-world. With the poet Wallace Stevens he imagines a dead world brought back from death by a poetic act of life; it is the world that is "ritualistic"; it is the rite that will restore life. Thus we may read the poem of Stevens with him:

> I placed a jar in Tennessee,
> And round it was, upon a hill.
> It made the slovenly wilderness
> Surround that hill.
> The wilderness rose up to it,
> And sprawled around, no longer wild.
> The jar was round upon the ground
> And tall and of a port in air.
>
> It took dominion everywhere.
> The jar was gray and bare.
> It did not give of bird or bush,
> Like nothing else in Tennessee [4].

To bring to light some hills of Tennessee is quite a task; at any rate the usual images begin to be reversed by the modern poet, who no longer blames the ritual act for our surrounding death, but sees it as entering like an active athlete onto the hopeless scene to restore it.

Francis Fergusson, one of our best contemporary analysts of dramatic form, suggests that Shakespeare himself could still think of the workmanship of bringing a world alive on the stage in basically ritualistic terms. The play within the play of *Hamlet* helps to bring the scene alive. An "action" describing the death of a king strikes in varying fashion into mind upon mind and conscience upon conscience. The play's the thing wherein we'll catch the conscience of the king — and all of us besides. It drives everybody into various acts of self-revelation.

This wish to be an action bringing a dead world alive, making it see, is one of the central wishes of the modern artist.

My suggestion is that if we follow this clue we may keep moving toward a human, reasonable, and creative ritual. And we may come to blame things a little more on the world and a little less on a static, straw-man image of the ritualistic.

Some such understanding as this of the role of ritual and liturgy may help the present liturgical revolution that is occurring at our precise moment in religious history. For where there is opposition and criticism — *cf.* the very strongly voiced criticism by Daniel Callahan in *The Commonweal* in August — it is still based on that cyclonic wave of protest against irrelevant religion that hit the churches a few years ago. The *Commonweal* article was a broad attack on those who play ritually while Rome is burning Such an attack will itself continue to be "relevant" only as long as many of those dedicated to the current renaissance in the liturgy will continue in their failure to appraise real ritual as that which can bring the rest of the world alive, or give the world focus or meaning. Certainly, religious ritual in our day, though vastly improved in form, cannot afford to become a corner of the world where pious and aesthetic feelings can be gratified in separation from the pain and trouble of all the other corners of the world.

It is this need of a related and creative role in history that is confronted by the July 1967 issue of *Christus*. The issue is dedicated to a study of Christianity as principle of newness (we would say *revolution!*) in the world. One of its best analyses is entitled the "Newness of the Liturgy," by the well-known musical innovator Joseph Gelineau, S.J. In Christianity, he reminds us, we have the declaration of the emergence of a new type of man who must rise from many forms of death. Correspondingly, the new liturgy reveals its own proper identity and character when it helps to draw man out of decadent forms of life and into a new way of life in Christ risen from the dead. Ritual repeats, reenacts, and reviews the historical moment which initiated the new era and the new spirit. But the other word that is important is *today*. "Truly it is right and it is good to give thanks at all times, O Lord, but especially today, when Christ our Pasch has been immolated." The whole mystery of the liturgy, says the writer, lies in this word *today*. There is no true newness if it is not actual.

Perhaps another form of speech would be to say that we go back in order to go forward.

The movement from the rite into life is most crucial, else the rite itself is in danger of being called dead. "That which you have done by way of mystery in communicating with the total Christ must be transposed and realized in all your relations with your brothers."

It would seem right and good, therefore, that this action which in mystery celebrates the historical birth of the new man should frequently be accompanied by a preaching which would look to the emergence of the undeveloped nations as new men, to the emergence of the Negro as a new man, to the emergence of hope in the whole of life.

The ritual and liturgical discussion that will move in this direction promises to be both lively and healthy in the few years immediately ahead of us.

As I close my own commentary I would like to give the following impression of where the liturgical movement stands at the end of 1967.

There has been a revolutionary change. "The people of God" have moved decisively into the picture. "The minister of God"

755

no longer holds a lonely control of the ritual situation. There is a welling up of large communal forces which begin to participate in the divine action. Only a minority are unhappy over the change. And there is no doubt that the popular changes will continue.

The hope is that this will prove to be only the first half of the revolution. The second half will occur when it becomes clear that *this* part of the people of God, now become a liturgical people, will turn in a creative way, as a new people, toward the rest of the world. It will be right and good that they should. The least they should do is behave as well as a jar in Tennessee.

It would require considerable space to discuss other possible changes in the structure of the Christian community that lie ahead of us as a result of the innovating liturgical period that we now enter upon.

There is no doubt that various small communities are beginning to form around a revolution within the revolution in ritual.

There is even considerable talk of the emergence of an "underground church." My own attempt at judgment would be that on the whole this is a melodramatic overinterpretation. Bad judgment and overreaction in a disciplinary direction could produce an ideological division over some new underground ritual events. But if a sense of humor is maintained and wins its own victory, if those administrators who could make mistakes have the good sense to realize that men simply must rebel at times and in degree against all the forms of the superego, then it is very doubtful that the disaster of disunity will strike the Christian community in the ironic form of a great struggle over the unifying sacrament of the liturgy. Some few bishops should think of this before they are tempted to precipitate anxiety.

One calculation is that there will always be some kind of struggle between the two meanings of liturgy and ritual we have been examining: between the image of ritual as a static, dead, formalizing thing and its image as that which gives life to a surrounding world. Intended though it be to conquer the static, it will always be in danger of succumbing to the thing it fights. It must always be ritualistic and disciplined, but it will always need reform and an occasional sense of humor, for which there is no substitute. The Middle Ages knew this. They had their feast of fools. And within the development of the solemn liturgical theater things could go so far as to add a not too mild touch of confusion to the rite, as, for example, when the ranting ministers of Herod ran madly through the choir beating bishops and canons and scholars with a bladder and then passed, according to the sober requirements of the Thirteenth-Century text of the Cathedral of Padua, to the more affectionate liturgical action of the day. Things with us will not go as far as with the medievalists. Undoubtedly there is and will be some kind of underground. But its own greatest danger is that it will get too tied to small, intimate groups, separated from the realities of the world.

REFERENCES

1. Cohn, Norman: *The Pursuit of the Millennium: Revolutionary Messianism in Medieval and Reformation Europe and Its Bearing on Modern Totalitarian Movements* (Harper Torchbooks, TB 1037).
2. Hopper, Stanley Romaine, and Miller, David L, eds: *Interpretations: The Poetry of Meaning* (Harcourt, Brace & World, Inc, New York, New York) 1967.
3. Reiff, Philip: *The Triumph of the Therapeutic* (Harper and Row, Publishers, New York, New York) 1966.
4. Stevens, Wallace: *Collected Poems of Wallace Stevens* (Alfred A Knopf, Inc, New York, New York) 1954.

PSEUDO-RELIGIOUS RITES IN THE USSR

by Nikita Struve

THE SOVIET PRESS has often discussed ways and means of ousting religious rites by the introduction of a special "communist" marriage ceremony, and holidays designed to replace the traditional ones of the Church calendar. This has always been part of the anti-religious campaign aimed at weaning the population away from the Church. The communist authorities have had to recognize that it is not enough to oppose such rites as baptism and the marriage ceremony; something had to be found to fill the void, and this has led to the introduction of civil ceremonies that, so it is hoped, will help to cut off the young generation still further from the Church and age-old traditions that lend an element of colorfulness and romance to everyday life.

Civil ceremonies were experimented with as early as the 1920s and met with very little success. In their revolutionary ardor, the communists tried to do away with the christening ceremony and even with Christian names, and, of course, some new civil holidays have become traditional in the Soviet Union since the Revolution. Before 1917 Russia was a theocratic state in which the religious and civil spheres were not separated. Church holidays were observed by all citizens, and even the celebrations, such as anniversaries, etc., of the temporal power had a religious flavor and were accompanied by religious ceremonies.

The October Revolution put an end to this, and such national holidays as May Day and the Anniversary of the October Revolution itself were introduced, all completely devoid of any religious content. This is not peculiar to the Soviet Union; revolutions invariably bring similar innovations in their train. In France, for instance, the greatest national holiday is of revolutionary origin and has nothing to do with religion. At the same time, however, the 14th of July does not set out to rival any Church holiday. The population regards the state and the Church holidays as wholly separated but not mutually exclusive. The same attitude is found in the Soviet Union, where the population considers national and Church holidays as belonging to entirely different spheres. The following extract from the *Derevensky Dnevnik* (Country Diary) by the Soviet writer Efim Dorosh illustrates this well. The author describes the celebration of the Church holiday of the Transfiguration in a small village where there is a collective farm. Not one of the farm workers went out to the fields that day, and the author records his conversation with one of the peasant women:

758

We had a talk about it with Natalya Kuzminichna; she told us: "I don't know really what holiday it is exactly; all I know is that it's an important one, and that it would be a sin to work." I said to her: "But you never go to church and goodness knows, it's probably ages since you've been to confession. What can this holiday mean to you? Just wait till the October Anniversary comes round, and then you can celebrate." But she only laughed at me, and of course I could not make her change her attitude [2:616].

This passage shows that the very idea of a national holiday replacing a religious ceremony does not even enter the head of an ordinary woman on a collective farm. She acknowledges that the things that are Caesar's must be rendered unto Caesar, but to God the things that are God's. And this strict separation of Church holidays from state ones in the minds of the people has made it clear to the anti-religious propagandists that it is absolutely essential to introduce new holidays and customs capable of supplanting religious rites. They want to establish communist traditions that can successfully rival the ancient ones. In the beginning, however, this decision caused dissent among the atheists, the majority of whom held that the invention of new rites would be tantamount to a return to religion in the shape of a surrogate for the latter. But these objections were overruled and after lively discussion in the press it was decided in 1964 to submit the plan for introduction of new holidays to the republican councils of ministers for approval. Now the USSR Supreme Soviet introduces a new national day of celebration almost every month. There is already "Woman's Day," "Miner's Day," "Fishermen's Day," "Railwaymen's Day," and "Militia Day," etc., and most sections of the working population are honored in this way. According to a recent study, which contains a detailed survey of pseudoreligious rites in the Soviet Union, there are twenty-two of these "Days" [4].

However, this plethora of new-fangled celebration days is more a propaganda stunt than a budding tradition. Persons who have visited the Soviet Union in recent years report that the new holidays and civil rites play little or no part in everyday life.

759

They do not appear to have taken root. There is a so-called "Palace of Happiness" in Leningrad, where the newly-invented civil marriage ceremony is performed in elaborate fashion, but there are not many of these palaces so far because they are expensive to put up. The *zvezdiny* rite (which is a revival of the *Oktyabriny* christening ceremony of the 1920s, with the only difference that babies are no longer given extraordinary, "revolutionary" names) is observed, for instance, in the Seredino-Budsky region of Kharkov Oblast, but is said to be entirely unknown anywhere else [3]. This artificial process of imposing new customs does not evoke much enthusiasm among the population, as official sources admit. The conversion of the carnival season into a "Russian Winter Festival" "has killed off this popular custom at the roots," [1:30] and a folk-lore specialist writes that "our new holidays and rites are threatened by a danger that has already started to make itself apparent. We have in mind the possibility that they will become rather desiccated and conventional, and turn into tedious bureaucratic measures" [6:23]. This waning of interest is demonstrated in a report from a correspondent in Grodno, who writes that the first few marriages were indeed performed with much pomp at the Grodno "Palace of Matrimony" but subsequently they became a pretty dull, routine affair. Elsewhere it is stated bluntly: "So far it is possible to name only one successful experiment in transplanting an old rite onto the soil of new social relations. That is the New Year Tree" [1:29].

Thus, there is recognition among the ideologists that efforts to introduce new customs usually meet with little success. "This gives us something to ponder on," says one expert in a survey of new rites [6:23]. Already the more intelligent among the propagandists seem to have come to the conclusion that artificially-concocted customs conceived by the bureaucracy are scarcely likely to flourish. For nearly half a century the Soviet authorities have been attempting the well-nigh impossible by introducing new customs to replace time-hallowed observances, and the extent of their failure to fill the void is reflected in the works of such contemporary Soviet authors as Yefim Dorosh, Vladimir Soloukhin, and A. I. Solzhenitsyn. There are Soviet specialists who are capable of analyzing the situation objectively and realistically, as is shown by the following extract from the leading atheist propaganda journal:

> A rite is the symbolic and aesthetic expression (and manifestation) of collective social relations, of the collective essence of man, and the bonds linking him not only with his contemporaries but also with his ancestors. A rite is the thread of time by holding on to which people form a nation. A rite is created as the expression of the spirit, traditions and way of life of a society [1:28].

This definition met with the disapproval of the editorial board of *Nauka i religiya*, and for good reason, because in the light of such an interpretation the present Soviet policy of introducing new customs appears hopeless and purposeless. Unfortunately, those with such a realistic approach remain "voices in the wilderness" in Soviet ideological circles.

The sterility of the new customs stems in no small degree from the fact that efforts are being undertaken to enforce them on the populace. A factory worker in Sumy Oblast writes:

> I would like to call to your attention that my wife, Kozyk, Varvara Petrovna, gave birth to a daughter on October 31, 1964, our third child, and that on November 18, I submitted the documents to the Seredino-Budsky *Zags* — both the notification of the birth and our marriage certificate. But they have not as yet issued a birth certificate for our daughter. Instead I am told, "the baby has to undergo *zvezdiny*, after which your daughter will be presented with a baby carriage and other gifts, in addition to the birth certificate." I categorically refused to have my daughter christened under such compulsion. At the *Zags*, however, they declared: "You will not get the birth certificate until you have the *zvezdiny* performed." And who thought up these *zvezdiny*, anyway? [3].

This case is the most striking example of objections to new, pseudoreligious rites. A rite without traditions, not grounded in history but imposed from above soon becomes a planned state "measure." Plans have to be fulfilled, and so coercion, softened by bribery, as in the case of the gifts at the *zvezdiny* ceremony, is resorted to. It goes without saying that such methods arouse suspicion toward the new rites, which seem to have sprung from nowhere. The whole problem represents a vicious circle from which the innovators can find no escape. To be sure, there are some Soviet social workers who realize the senselessness of artificially-created ceremonies. But what is the answer? To do without holidays or rites is impossible; life has to be made more colorful, especially as the time of noble sacrifice and heroic revolutionary deeds is over. One expert [1:29] has conceded that "nothing will come of inventing a marriage ceremony or any other custom," and suggests that the old, traditional ones be retained in a form suitable to Soviet society. This idea is less absurd than invention of totally new pseudoreligious rites, but is hardly likely to meet with much more success. According to this concept, a rite is only an incidental part of religious belief and is completely detachable from its original context. Its author may to some extent be right, but he nevertheless sees that traditional ceremonies such as christening and nuptial rites are indissolubly linked with Christianity. For this reason he does not propose that observances of Christian origin be adapted to communist requirements. Instead he clings to those observances that date back to pagan times. Why heathenism — itself a primitive form of religion — should be considered more suitable for a communist society than the Christian faith is not clear. Perhaps because paganism is long since dead and therefore no longer dangerous to Soviet ideology. Yet the Russian carnival survived into modern times not because it stood for the worship of the sun, as symbolized by the *blin* (pancake), but because it preceded Lent and was a psychologically necessary season of fun before parting with all the good things of this world during the ascetic period of the Church year. We have seen how transformation of the carnival into a "Russian Winter Festival" has failed in the Soviet Union. Balashov proposes that the old Slavonic *maslenitsa* period of revelry and pancake-making be converted into a modern observance lending some color to Soviet life. But he has no suggestion as to how this is to be done. If *maslenitsa* is divorced from Lent, then it is likely to die out or survive merely as a seasonal culinary occasion that will be in time forgotten. He points, it is true, to the successful experiment in "transplanting an old custom onto the soil of new social relations" in the shape of the New Year Tree festival. But the Christmas or New Year Tree is not such an old custom, nor is it specifically religious, and in Western countries it can easily be separated from the Church festival. Is it not possible, however, that the tree custom has become a Soviet tradition precisely because it is at least closely associated with the great Christmas festival and carries reminders of the latter? At any rate it is the only one that the Soviet regime has managed to introduce permanently.

The failure of the recent moves to conjure up new ceremonies devoid of all religious content for the Soviet citizen is bound up with the very meaning of a rite. Balashov has been previously quoted as referring to a "thread of time" by which nations are formed. This is true. A ceremonial observance links man to his fellows and to his ancestors; at Easter, for instance, Christians feel much closer to one another. They also feel close to those who are no longer with them, with those who once used to celebrate this festival. A religious rite is a thread that unwinds into the present from the depths of time. The Christian religious services can be traced back to the Jewish cult and beyond that all the way back to the ancient blood sacrifice to God. In the course of their historical evolution, Christian rites have accreted Greek culture and the individual stamp of each different country. And they are something else, too, which Balashov does not mention — a link with God. A rite unites mankind with a higher principle and a people senses this, even if it happens to forget the immediate meaning of some observance. In the Soviet Union Church rites survive not just because they are traditional or for aesthetic reasons. They exist primarily because they are felt, either vividly or vaguely, to be the visible, tangible expression of the higher meaning of life. If most Soviet parents have their babies baptized in church, it is because they desire consciously or unconsciously to impart some meaning to human life.

Faith, rites, and culture are links in the chain leading to unison with God. Without faith there is no rite; culture fades away, and the resulting void is filled with chaos and moral decay. If a rite is torn from this chain it becomes no more than a museum exhibit, and this is the quandary of the Soviet propagandists and ideologists.

REFERENCES

1. Balashov, D: The Traditional and the Modern, *Nauka i religiya*, 1965, no 12.
2. Dorosh, E: *Derevensky Dnevnik*, in *Literaturnaya Moskva*, 1956.
3. *Izvestia*, December 20, 1964.
4. Le nuove feste e i nuovi riti sovietici, in *Russia Cristiana* (Bergama) 1965, no 67–68.
5. Registry Office of Births, Marriages and Deaths.
6. *Sovetskaya etnografiya*, 1963, no 6.

20. RELIGIOUS PROCESSES IN THE TRAINING GROUP

by Philip E. Slater

. . . [meat] to those who eat it rarely has the effect of a mild intoxicant [11:139].

THE RELATIONSHIP of the group members to their leader is a major issue in any group. If the leader is in any way a source of deprivation for the other members (as in a therapy group, a "T-group," or a "basic encounter group," in which he refuses help, direction, and protection), the group's development will be strongly influenced by a fantasy involving a group revolt. In some instances this revolt receives direct, if symbolic, expression through events in the group. In other cases it is expressed more subtly, remaining in fantasy form but coloring the interpretation of, and feelings about, apparently innocent occurrences. In one sense it would be correct to say that the entire history of groups of this kind, which I shall lump under the term "training group," is an expression of this fantasy, involving the gradual rejection of, separation from, yet incorporation of the leader, his skills and his viewpoint. At a more microscopic level, one could say that every interaction between leader and group contains elements of this revolt.

THE REVOLT PATTERN

The usual form taken by the revolt is nowhere better described than by Bennis and Shepard:

The first section of this paper was presented at the annual meetings of the American Sociological Association in September, 1964, under the title "Rebellion and Evolution in Groups." The second section is based on Chapter V of my *Microcosm: Structural, Psychological, and Religious Evolution in Groups* [20].

765

A group member may openly express the opinion that the trainer's presence and comments are holding the group back, suggest that "as an experiment" the trainer leave the group "to see how things go without him." When the trainer is thus directly challenged, the whole atmosphere of the meeting changes. There is a sudden increase in alertness and tension. Previously, there had been much acting out of the wish that the trainer were absent, but at the same time a conviction that he was the *raison d'être* of the group's existence — that it would fall apart without him. Previously, absence of the trainer would have constituted desertion, or defeat, fulfilment of the members' worst fears as to their own inadequacy or the trainer's. But now leaving the group can have a different meaning. . . .

The event is always marked in group history as "a turning point," "the time we became a group," "when I first got involved," etc. The mounting tension, followed by sometimes uproarious euphoria, cannot be entirely explained by the surface events. It may be that the revolt represents a realization of important fantasies individuals hold in all organizations, that the emotions involved are undercurrents wherever rebellious and submissive tendencies toward existing authorities must be controlled [4].

Bennis and Shepard compare the event to Freud's myth of the primal horde.

The ubiquitousness of this phenomenon in groups of this kind suggests that it plays a significant role in group evolution — that an attack on the formal group leader is a necessary lever for the establishment of conscious bonds among the other group members [15; 16]. The revolt is not common to all groups, however, but primarily to those in which certain cultural aids to (a) differentiation, (b) interpersonal distancing, and (c) the satisfaction of dependency needs, have been stripped away. These are groups without formal procedures or rules of order (although the members bring with them knowledge of such procedures and make some effort to apply them). They are groups with no assigned formal task and no clearly defined group goals. They are groups in which candor, self-revelation, insight, and the expression of feeling are strongly and explicitly valued. They are groups in which the formal leader gives no directives.

With these props removed, fears which may well be intrinsic to group relationships become more manifest: first, fear of boundary-loss, for if feelings and impulses are to be permitted a role in the proceedings, and there is neither explicit agenda nor rules of order, your impulse can freely coalesce with mine even if I am unaware of the latter's existence, and my conscious controls can be swept away by forces coming both from within and without (as in the case of mob passion); second, fear of being overwhelmed, attacked, or excluded by a united group, for if there are no structural categories which differentiate people, and no formal procedures, there are no simple mechanisms for finding a safe niche in the group with the usual allies, enemies, superiors, and inferiors; finally, fear of being too close or too far away from others — of being too intimate or altogether abandoned.

The leader is a focal point for all these fears because he provides a potential solution. He is differentiated from other members by his position of authority. He has knowledge of the situation, and his role is traditionally one of structuring, of establishing proper distances, rules of behavior, and hierarchies. He is obviously the person who can remove much of this anxiety from the situation. Yet he does not. In fact he is typically viewed as doing nothing whatever.

Aside from this totally unrealized potential role of the leader, groups of this kind may be regarded as primitive — not that they resemble groups in contemporary nonliterate societies, which are not at all primitive in the way I mean — but because they approximate in a few respects what a group might be like in the absence of culture. This is of course a matter of degree — training groups are highly sophisticated pieces of civilization, but they are artificially impoverished with regard to certain crucial cultural products. They are thus interesting phenomena for the sociologist to study, for the same reason that *Lord of the Flies* [10] is an interesting sociological novel, or that sensory deprivation experiments and feral children are of interest to social scientists. Furthermore, there is an elemental quality to the principal concerns of training groups — why the group exists, what its purpose is, why the authority figure on which it depends is silent, and how it will all end.

It is not altogether surprising, therefore, that the first response to these sundry fears, and especially to the deprivation experienced at the hands of the leader is to "deify" the latter. Let us consider some examples of such deification.

(1) Ezriel describes the first meeting of a therapy group, in which the members are complaining about the silence of the therapist:

F4: I think we all agree that we have been rather left in the lurch, in the open.

M2: It may arise from the fact that Dr. Ezriel sits there and says nothing. As if we were all gathered in front of an altar [7:65].

This first example expresses the immediacy of the association between the feeling of abandonment and the fantasy of worship.

(2) Bion comments directly upon the worshipful attitude of a group of his patients and quotes one of them as saying, "I do not need to talk because I know that I only have to come here long enough and all my questions will be answered without my having to do anything" [5:445].

(3) Bennis discusses a group in which the members talk about "a sort of spontaneous fountain that will bring forth and all we have to do is sit and drink."

"I think you are referring to the rock pile" — the group leader [2].

This reference to the "rock pile" is followed by some comments about the importance of rocks in early religions, and it is worth noting that the "rock" theme is hardly less pervasive in training groups, whose members frequently make remarks about "the great stone face," or "holding the group at the foot of Mt. Rushmore," interspersed with ironic comments about Buddha and the Delphic Oracle.

768

One of the most common religious manifestations, however, is a fantasy which Theodore Mills and I have called the "experiment myth" — the notion that the group situation has been created for experimental rather than didactic or therapeutic purposes. For example:

"The course was an experiment in anxiety, similar to the conflicting Pavlov reflex experiments designed to make cats or white mice neurotic."

"The Department was . . . making a composite picture of each person, lifting his utterances out of context and splicing them on one after the other."

One group member after describing such a fantasy, to which, he said, he still clung, suggested that it provided a reason for the existence of the group, and then remarked that "it seemed better to think that there was a purpose, however hostile, behind the class than to remain in a group without any limits." Often, however, the myth takes the more benign form of utter confidence that the group leader knows exactly what he is doing and that everything that takes place in the group has meaning and purpose. (The kinds of comments made in these discussions always call to mind the conversation among the pots in the *Rubaiyat* of Omar.) The experiment myth thus announces that the apparent aimlessness and chaos of the group experience is really part of a master plan which will only be revealed at the latter day.

The religious fantasies, then, substitute permanence for abandonment, oral plenty for the frustration of dependency needs, and order for disorder. It is characteristic of training groups that they spend rather a lot of time in the passive enjoyment of such fantasies of the leader's omniscience, immortality, and ultimate nurturance. But as Jane Harrison points out, "mankind has always been apt to regard this attitude of serene and helpless dependence as peculiarly commendable" [11:108].

The revolt against the leader is directly connected both with the early sense of deprivation and abandonment at his hands and with these fantasies. It involves a shift from passivity to activity, and, since it can occur only when members have relinquished their desire to be favored over their peers, a sharp increase in group solidarity. But in the content of the discussion of revolt we see the recurrence of the same themes in different form: for the feeling that the leader has abandoned them (the "God is dead" theme) we find the fantasy that they are murdering him; for the feeling that he has deprived them we find the fantasy that they are eating him or wresting something from him; for the feeling that he knows the secret order that underlies the apparent confusion we find the notion that he is preventing order from emerging.

It is difficult to present a balanced thematic picture of the revolt because it always has a dual aspect. One can easily construct a violent "primal horde" image of the process by pointing to certain of its content, but at the same time one could say that nothing very dramatic or primitive actually takes place. There may be a sudden outburst of hostility toward the leader, with angry protestations, an exchange of sadistic fantasies about what they might do to him, perhaps some rather devastating ridicule or parody, but it is after all verbal. They may usurp his chair or grab some of his papers, but the mildest show of authority would quell these manifestations. Most interesting of all is the curious inconsistency of attitude around the leader's expulsion. Generally he is simply requested, sometimes very politely and without any visible hostility, to absent himself from the group for a session or so "as an experiment," and when the leader complies, it is presumably in response to this aspect of the revolt — i.e., the group's desire to "try its wings," to operate with more independence, to test what the effect of the leader really is and what their responses to him really are. Yet without any sense of inconsistency their prospective discussions of the efficacy of this device, and above all their retrospective accounts of it, are always sprinkled with references to "killing him," "throwing him out," "dethroning him," etc. — casual references to which no one seems to take any exception.

I would argue that both of these views of the situation are important, and if I seem to focus on the more dramatic and archaic aspects it is only because they are less fully understood.

This latter aspect is captured in a dream reported by a member of a group about a month after its inception:

> Everybody in the room was dancing around on the table. At the end of the room was an open casket. We danced around it, waving whirligigs and setting off firecrackers, but no voice came from the casket.

This dream fuses the early feeling of abandonment and loss with one of bloody celebration, leaving ambiguous the question as to whether the dream represents the desperate attempt of group members to get the leader to "take over," or their gleeful triumph at having got rid of him (i.e., of their dependence upon him). The group in question never in fact produced a successful revolt.

In other groups, however, the imagery leaves no doubt. The courting of silent members suggests to one of the more active participants that "it almost sounds as if we were recruiting for something." A question from the leader as to why a dance is being discussed yields the reply that they wish to dance around him at the stake. A group of business executives sets fire to the leader's name plate [3]. Another such group presents the leader with a 15-inch cigar, places his chair in the center of the table and suggests cutting the cigar into 15 pieces so each member can smoke one [14]. In another group a member explains his suggestion that the leader be expelled by saying:

> I don't want to get rid of him actually. Actually this is something rational. Not something I-ah-sat bolt upright in bed and said "Let's get him out of there." I was just thinking while driving along in the car what might give the group a little bit more latitude — more freedom.

The theme of eating is also salient in the context of revolt. Protestations of emptiness and cornucopia fantasies both give way to scenes of actual self-feeding. Thus in a session following Hallowe'en, in which a fantasy that the group would play "trick or treat" on the group leader was discussed, a member brought in a large supply of "Sugar Daddys" and passed them out to the group. A group with two formal leaders discussed expelling both, and the pro-expulsion faction later brought in cider and cupcakes for the group. In a graduate seminar engaged in *observing* a training group the instructor entered one day to find his chair usurped, while those who planned the coup passed a box of raisins around the room. On the day of the last meeting of another group the leader entered to find a paper figure with his name on it dangling from a hangman's noose attached to a ceiling microphone. The group members had brought in rolls and coffee, and insisted that every newcomer partake [13].

Other examples abound. The food may be crackerjack or wine, the talk may center around the agricultural surplus in the United States, an animal cracker, Easter eggs, Communion, the Seder and Elijah, or the Three Bears' porridge, but the theme is prevalent in any group which is either beginning, engaged in revolt, or about to end. In the beginning is the desire to be fed — later it becomes the desire to feed oneself.

Now to some extent these phenomena may be interpreted simply in terms of the resolution of dependency problems, and as a symbolic paradigm of the learning process: the members are at first passively receptive, then become actively involved and "take" from the leader the knowledge he will not give. That is to say, they relinquish the fantasy of passive learning and accept the fact that they can interpret group phenomena just as well as the leader.

Yet these fantasies also reflect a significant structural change in the group — the members shift from an "authoritarian" to a "democratic" definition of the situation — from trying to gain special favor from the leader and competing with peers (as in the traditional classroom setting) to uniting with peers in an effort to dispense with patriarchal authority. The murderous and cannibalistic fantasies express this change in terms of a kind of transfer — whether of *libido* or *mana* or whatever. Something which was formerly concentrated in the leader is now diffused among the members. A structure is killed, another born — a power is detached from the vehicle in which it resided and divided among many new vehicles.

I am using language here which is reminiscent of Frazer's discussion of the "sacred king" [8] and this is quite deliberate, for anyone who has been a group leader is probably quite conscious of the feeling of being treated sometimes as a sacred object and sometimes as a secular one. Even more interesting in this connection is Frazer's notion that if the vehicle of a sacred power (or more correctly, the object of a sacred attitude) decays, the power will also decay. (This is of course the basic principle of transference therapy, although it is seldom thought of in these terms). Now in a training group the fantasy of the leader's omniscience decays a little each time he opens his mouth, and particularly as the premises on which he operates become visible to all. As a result we find a curious difference in the attitude (not in the ability) of groups which have revolted, depending upon whether the revolt occurs early or late in the group's history. Groups which revolt early have an air of confidence and enthusiasm, as if they had miraculously slain a dragon and survived, while groups which revolt late seem more depressed and disappointed about how little difference the revolt makes. Once again, this is a matter of degree — all groups show some elation and some remorse. But the early-revolt groups seem to realize some emotional gain from having attacked an exaggerated and inflated leader image, before it had dwindled to reality. This was perhaps most succinctly expressed by a member in a group which revolted at almost the very end of the group's history, when, in questioning the utility of asking the leader to leave, he objected that the leader was "already dead."

Of the events which characteristically occur after a revolt has taken place, I will simply mention three. First, there is a sharp and immediate florescence of direct sexual interest between members, particularly on the part of females. Second, there is a sudden concern with the fact that the group will eventually end. Third, the revolt is occasionally used reminiscently as a device for strengthening group solidarity.

The first two occurrences lend themselves to multiple interpretation: the decay of transference, anxiety over the loss of authority, the acting out of oedipal fantasies, etc. But what con-

773

cerns us here is that they arise in part from the fact that the group is now invested with emotional importance *apart from* its connection with the leader. Prior to this time the leader *is* the group for the most part. The collection of peers does not exist as a significant emotional entity for most members. As we have seen, Bennis and Shepard quote members as saying that the revolt represents the moment at which the group became a group, and the moment when members became involved (an attitude which is shared, we might note, by the United States, the Soviet Union, and France), and this is corroborated by the sudden emergence of distress about the group's demise. Prior to this moment the death of the group is a meaningless concept since the member does not feel himself a part of it in a way that would make its nonexistence a threat to him.

The use of reminiscences about the revolt as a solidarity strengthening device also reflects this relationship. I have called these episodes "totemic feasts," and I will give an example of one. It took place about three months after the revolt, just prior to a spring vacation in a group which was run as a full year's academic course. The session in question terminated a period of group conflict, of somewhat hostile mutual analysis, of failure and regression, of anxiety and high absenteeism. The atmosphere was in general tense and depressed.

The session began with comments about the many absentees. Then one student suggested that the real question should not be, why were the absentees absent, but, why were the participants present? Someone then wondered what would happen if they all got up and left. Everyone laughed, and someone suggested that it would be even better if they all stayed and the instructor left. Everyone again laughed, the atmosphere suddenly livened, and amidst joking and laughter the group began to reminisce over the original revolt. After two or three minutes thus spent, they began to analyze the difficulties they had been having, and continued in a highly productive discussion for the rest of the hour. But this is perhaps merely what Durkheim's analysis of totemism would lead us to expect:

"There can be no society which does not feel the need of

774

upholding and reaffirming at regular intervals the collective sentiments and the collective ideas which make its unity and its personality" [6:427]. But "individual minds cannot come into contact and communicate with each other except by coming out of themselves; but they cannot do this except by movements. So it is the homogeneity of these movements that gives the group consciousness of itself and consequently makes it exist" [6:230–231]. Furthermore "collective sentiments can become conscious of themselves only by fixing themselves upon external objects" [6:419]. In other words, consciousness of the group as such originated in common action toward an external object, the leader, and whenever its collective self-awareness seemed to flag, it was necessary to relive this experience in order to strengthen itself.

As noted above, these "feasts" occur when the solidarity of the group seems to need renewal, or, in Durkheim's terms, "revivification." In the example given (and it is fairly typical), the group was about to separate for a period, academic requirements threatened to substitute a competitive struggle for cooperative endeavor, external forces tended to reactivate individual dependence on the instructor, and there was internal friction in the group. By the ritual act of collective recapitulation of its traditions, the group set these threats at naught.

THE EVOLUTION OF CONSCIOUS BONDS

> One reason why it is so hard to please the gods is that it is so hard to know beforehand at what moment they will have outgrown the sort of things which used to please them [11:244].

The significance of the revolt pattern is further illuminated by Bion's "basic assumption" paradigm. Bion suggests that groups often fall into one of three "basic assumptions" — that at times they act as if the group had met (1) "to fight something or to run away from it" (the Fight-Flight group), or (2) "to be sustained by a leader on whom it depends for nourishment . . .

775

and protection" (the Dependency group), or (3) to produce a Messiah through a *hieros gamos* (the Pairing group) [5:444–449]. These are static, timeless, unproductive states of mind in Bion's view, and are not viewed as belonging on any kind of continuum. A group may remain locked in one assumption for months or change several times in a single meeting.

Yet Bion shows some dissatisfaction with the completeness of this formulation. He observes certain common elements in the three assumptions — an instinctual quality, an underlying concern with leadership, an absence of any developmental process. He suggests that "they may not be fundamental phenomena, but rather expressions of or reactions against, some state more worthy of being regarded as primary" [5:449–456]. Bion hypothesizes the arousal of psychotic anxiety around extremely primitive infantile fantasies.

I would like to advance here a modification of Bion's theory — one which I do not regard as negating any of the statements just made, but rather as an extension of them. In the previous section I described the group revolt as separating two stages which bear considerable resemblance to the "dependency group" and the "pairing group," respectively. While I would agree with Bion that the assumptions themselves are static and nondevelopmental, it is my impression that they occur as defenses against feelings aroused at different stages of a developmental sequence.

This sequence I have called the continuum of boundary-awareness [20:167 ff]. It refers to the fact that groups typically evolve from a state in which the bonds which link the members and distinguish the group from other groups are vague and largely unconscious, to a state in which these bonds are conscious and discriminable. Since these bonds and boundaries are not all of a piece, but multiform and fluid, a group is at any moment held together by links some of which are conscious and some unconscious. Hence there is a great deal of what looks like (and may well be) backward and forward movement on this continuum, and the "basic assumptions" may thus occur at any time and in any order. Overall, however, one should be able to detect a tendency for the distribution of fight-flight responses to be skewed toward the earlier end of the group's life, and the distribution of pairing responses to be skewed to the later end. This is because the pairing group tends to occur when group self-consciousness has first been achieved and is in danger of being lost. The dependency group occurs when the only conscious bond binding group members together is their attachment to the leader, and there is danger of this link dissolving. The fight-flight response, which is the most primitive and elemental of all, occurs when unconscious bonds unite the group — when the only conscious unity is that of the individual ego, and even this is threatened with dissolution. All three mechanisms are like the "freezing" response of many animals in their anxious, automatic, and instinctual nature. Each tries to recapture magically some kind of conscious linkage which appears to be in danger of dissolving, and each is directed against what is experienced as a rising tide of unconsciousness. This *feeling* may arise at any time, but will tend to take a form appropriate to the developmental level of the group, relative to some specific group issue.

People who come together in a group initially interact almost entirely in terms of transference. Regardless of the sophistication of their task behavior, emotionally they are operating in terms of Piaget's motor stage of children's play ("seeking merely to satisfy . . . motor interests or symbolic fantasy") or his second stage, in which rules are imitated but the child "pays no attention to his neighbor" [19:42−43]. Ezriel remarks [7:68] that "when several people meet in a group, each member projects his unconscious phantasy-objects upon various other group members and then tries to manipulate them accordingly. Each member will stay in a role assigned to him by another only if it happens to coincide with his own unconscious phantasy. . . ." In other words, the group member tends to approach a new group setting by merely repeating old patterns of behavior with new materials. This also is true of neophyte marble players, as Piaget points out: "The child begins by incorporating the marbles into one or other of the schemas of assimilation already known to him, such as making a nest, hiding under earth, etc." But "then he adapts these schemas to the nature of the object," i.e., he is forced to

777

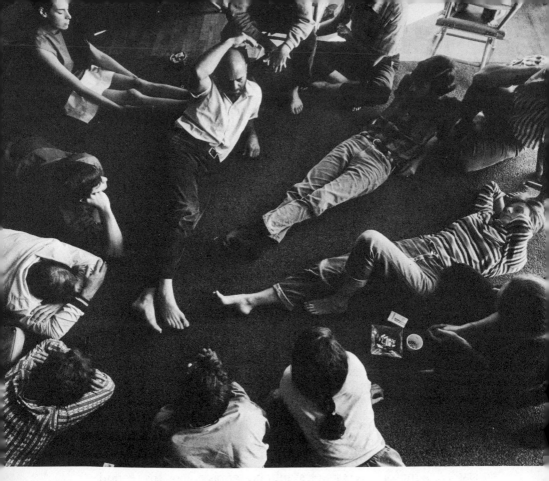

Participants at the Esalin Institute, Big Sur, California, hold a round-table discussion. Illustration courtesy Michael Alexander.

take into account the fact that the objects are round and small, will roll away, and so on [19:80-81].

A similar process occurs in the group setting, for while on the one hand, through trial and error, a culture evolves which maximizes the opportunity of most members to play their cherished private performances, on the other hand, as time goes by, more and more reality begins to intrude itself gratingly into their perceptions of one another.

The most dramatic change, however, is brought about through the leverage provided by having a common object for fantasy projection. The presence of an ambiguous authority figure allows the members to share a fantasy and as they become increasingly engrossed in this sharing they are gradually seduced into sharing a reality instead, and are thereby freed realistically to confront one another. That is, in order to realize the enjoyment of a shared fantasy they are led to invest it increasingly with group-relevant elements and decreasingly with personal familial elements, until it becomes dangerously susceptible to disconfirmation.

> Egocentrism in so far as it means confusion of the ego and the external world, and egocentrism in so far as it means lack of cooperation, constitute one and the same phenomenon. So long as the child does not dissociate his ego from the suggestions coming from the physical and from the social world he cannot cooperate, for in order to cooperate one must be conscious of one's ego and situate it in relation to thought in general. And in order to become conscious of one's ego, it is necessary to liberate oneself from the thought and will of others [19:87].

Piaget is saying here that cooperation is based on consciousness and separateness — that one must have an awareness of boundaries in order to communicate with others. If the ego and the social environment are not differentiated "the mind is unwittingly dominated by its own tendencies" — that is, by unconscious fantasies and reflexive interpersonal responses — and rational group effort is impossible. A dream reported in a group illustrates this point:

779

Andy: "I was in a big building — and it was a huge building: it wasn't just one movie theatre it was 10 or 12 movie theatres. And there were maybe 3 or 4 — maybe 2 or 3 movie houses on each floor, and there were about, oh, five or six floors. And I remember there wasn't any elevator and I had to keep climbing. And I'd walk into elevators — I mean I'd walk into movie places, and people would turn and look at me, very funny, and I'd feel very out of place, and I wouldn't have — this wasn't the movie I was looking for. So I'd go to another one, and I kept going up and up and up and up, and finally, I came to the last one, way up on the — really top floor, and I went in, and there were very strange-looking people in there — you know — it was really way out — beards and everything — and I walked in, and you know I really tried, I mean, after all this was the last one. I mean I really tried to fit in, and really tried to enjoy this movie, and I didn't even sit down. It wasn't what I was looking for, you know. So I went out, and I was really feeling kind of bad, you know, 'cause I'd already paid my money to get into this house. See you could take your choice of a movie but you had to pay when you came in the front door. And so I went out, and you know how often in an old building all the staircases will be nice staircases until the top floor, and there'll be sort of an attic floor up there, in which you go up sort of a stair ladder? It's not as nice as the other staircases. Well, I saw this thing and so I went up there, and it was really weird, 'cause there was this low-ceilinged place, dark, you know, and there was this guy sitting at this desk, and he was writing, or something, and when I came in, he went like that. He just pointed. He didn't say a word, and he didn't seem concerned with me. He noticed me and went like that and then he sort of dissolved — he went back to his work. He had no effect on me whatsoever. And I went up this very rickety ladder and there was a board across the rafters, and I had to follow this board across these rafters, and I was getting scared, you know, after all this was a strange place, and I didn't know what was happening. I kept getting cobwebs on me — it was really bad, really getting miserable up there. But I went on and I got over to this little place where he pointed at, and it was a little bitty room. And there wasn't anything there. There wasn't anything at all in this room. It was empty. So there I was."

780

Jack: "Did you wake up or what?"

Andy: "No. That was the end of the dream. I remember I sort of walked around confused for a while and looked back at him. And he was either gone, or he was paying no attention to me at all."

He added that it seemed related to the individual search for an ideal, that he felt better even at the end of the dream than after leaving the last movie where he couldn't fit in.

Ted suggested that it was related to the problem of trying to fit into a coherent group, and the group leader asked if they were saying that the ideal group was an empty room. They laughed, and Ted said, "Well, there's certainly the minimum of difficulty in interpersonal relations in it."

A long, still silence followed.

Maria: "So, let's be an empty room."

Shirley and Carol (overlapping): "We *are* being one."

An individual who enters a group for the first time perceives it as an undifferentiated mass. He may pick one or two individuals for special attention, but this will perforce be on the basis of unconscious fantasies — of transference. Thus insofar as he is discriminating he distorts, and insofar as he is empirical he is vague. Now, at the same time, all other group members are perceiving the group in a similar way, so that the first shared perception of the group members is that the group, with one exception (different in each case), is an undifferentiated mass. Furthermore, not only is this perception not in the forefront of consciousness, but also there is no awareness that it is shared.

This creates a rather tenuous state of affairs. If a member acts on his perception of specific individuals in the group, his distorted view of them will be likely to produce an abortive and confused interaction. If he acts on his perception of the group as an undifferentiated mass, however, he may suddenly find a rather overwhelming echo in the other members. This may be unnerving, since it blurs the boundary between himself and the group as a whole.

The sharing of fantasies about the leader tends to rescue the members from this horror, as previously noted, but initially it is a desperate remedy. The leader is differentiated out from the mass partly because it is perceptually easy to do so, but partly in order to counterbalance this mass — to create a hero warding off a devouring dragon. But the differentiation of the leader does not immediately produce clear differentiations among members and many groups do not progress far beyond this point. It is worth noting that a successful revolt usually involves a period in which the *differences* in members' attitudes toward the leader are brought forward. A group, in other words, cannot effectively revolt so long as it perceives itself as a mob or mass, but only when it can differentiate clearly between its members. This conflicts, of course, with the need for equality in and following the revolt, when a whole new set of anxieties emerges, touched off by the new awareness of the members' separateness from the leader.

Fundamentally, the group is attempting to substitute conscious bonds for unconscious ones. A conscious attachment is based upon an awareness of differences, whereas unconscious ones always entail mystical fusion. Group development is thus the gradual encroachment of light upon shadow, with the various "basic assumptions" being techniques applied at different points to defend against whichever shadows seem most fearsome at a given moment.

The blurring of boundaries between oneself and the group tends to occur when the group member experiences sudden reinforcement by the group of feelings, impulses, and fantasies of which he is not fully conscious. At such a time he will feel swept away by forces that seem to come both from within and from without. He will experience a sense of envelopment, which, unless he can somehow translate the unconscious material into something pleasant or at least familiar, will induce a feeling of incipient terror. "The awful, the uncanny, the unknown, is within man rather than without. In all excited states . . . man is conscious of a potency beyond himself, yet within himself. . . . The power within him he does not, cannot, at first clearly distinguish from the power without, and the fusion and confusion is naturally helped when the emotion is felt collectively in the group" [11:65].

782

Fight and flight are both mechanisms for warding off this state when it arises. Both serve to protect the boundaries that distinguish one individual from another. Fighting is a way of saying "this is me, I am different (in fact opposite) from you." It is like pinching oneself to be sure one is not dreaming, except that the members pinch one another, saying, as it were, "I hurt, therefore I am." The importance of fighting for individuation is best illustrated by Lorenz' observation that only species characterized by intraspecific aggression are capable of forming personal bonds [12:148 ff]. Flight, of course, simply removes the individual from the morass altogether. Instead of demonstrating separateness through contradiction, he does it through distance.

The feeling that one is dissolving is not merely frightening, however, but also pleasurable. The maintenance of boundaries by living organisms is enormously energy-consuming and tension-inducing. Indeed, it might not be altogether incorrect to say that boundaries *are* tension, that all tension is a function of the preservation of boundaries, and that all tension-release involves the reduction of boundary-maintenance, like water seeking its own level. In the most primitive layers of the unconscious this may even be the motive for joining a group. Like the mystic and the psychotomimetic drug cultist, the group member hopes to achieve ecstasy through the effusion of emotional energy and the release of tension which follows in the wake of a relinquishment of boundary armor and machinery.

There is always, in other words, a rather intense ambivalence about boundary maintenance, so that loss of individuality is at once a tempting yearning and an overwhelming terror. In most individuals emotional boundary loss seldom proceeds any great distance before anxiety sounds a warning bell, and the fight-flight mechanism goes into effect. The fight-flight *group* arises when mutual reinforcement of some unconscious fantasy seduces all or most members into moving farther in the direction of loss of individuality than they desired or anticipated. As students of mobs well know, groups elicit feelings of which people ordinarily manage to remain unaware. Confronted with his participation in some riot or other, a usually controlled individual will say, shamefacedly, "I don't know what got into me," thus revealing in a simple phrase the two most fundamental threats which group life poses to the individual: the loss of boundaries (". . . what got *into* me") and the submersion of conscious motives by unconscious ones ("I don't *know* what . . ."). Since consciousness is here equated with the boundary of the self, with unconscious impulses seen as coming from without, it may even be redundant to speak of these threats additively. The idiom itself, of course, is a survival from the medieval idea of demonic possession, and its persistence in popular speech is a grim reminder of the strength of unconscious motivation. Our culture has many patterns which normally protect us from such extreme manifestations of possession as the dancing manias of the middle ages, but mob reinforcement can hardly be said to have disappeared from modern life.

We might then think of Bion's mechanisms as attempts to maintain individual and group boundaries under conditions of constant flux: a flux produced on the one hand by increasing emotional involvement, and on the other by increasing secularity, consciousness, differentiation, and separateness. All are oriented toward maintaining a constant environment: the pairing group is an attempt to maintain the same balance between individual and group identity, under conditions of maximum consciousness and maximum involvement, that the fight-flight group is attempting to maintain under conditions of minimum consciousness and minimum involvement.

The preoccupations of a nascent group, or any group in an undifferentiated state and hence subject to fight-flight responses, bear a strong analogical relationship to some familiar mythological images. The seductive but frightening threat of ego-dissolution, for example, of merging with the group in terms of unconscious bonds, tends to assume maternal proportions [17; 18]. The unconscious attraction of the group offers on the one hand warmth, security, closeness, belonging, but on the other hand boundary destruction, loss of identity, loss of consciousness, psychic death. The imagery of group members at such times resembles schizophrenic fantasies of the mother as an enveloping or devouring monster with whom the child is now comfortably, now terrifyingly fused. Emergence from this state requires the development of consciousness, of differentiation: "the hero devoured by the monster cuts off a piece of its heart and so slays it. This symbolic process corresponds . . . to a conscious realization" [18:27].

In other words, the group is experienced as a maternal envelope so long as conscious awareness of its parts is not highly developed, and this enveloping mother threatens the conscious ego by its seductive appeal to the individual's own unconscious. The moment a piece of the undifferentiated mass is differentiated out, however, the "monster" is overcome, for now the ego experiences a sense of mastery over the group — it can be cognitively manipulated. The "earth-diver" myths, in which a god or animal dives into the endless waters of chaos and returns after a long time with a fragment of earth, from which the universe is fashioned, express this process. This experience of differentiation also provides the basis for much magical imagery: the formula, the key, the word, the lamp, all represent the experience of having obtained cognitive mastery over a threatening and inchoate social mass by differentiation and classification.

In a group setting the existence of an ascribed leader facilitates this process, and the leader tends quickly to become a role model for the ego and its kernel of conscious apprehension of the group. Neumann describes the phases in the development of consciousness as (1) embryonic containment in the mother, (2) childlike dependence on the mother, (3) adolescent lover of the mother, and (4) male hero struggling to overcome the mother [18:148; 17, passim]. This imagery is prominent in group fantasy, and the revolt against the leader cannot take place until it is felt that he is no longer needed as a hero to battle the dragon of chaos. The following examples will serve to illustrate group fears of deindividuation and ego submersion in unconscious bonds:

(a) In one group the fear of losing differentiating characteristics appeared in a series of meetings. It first took the form of a discussion of the anonymity of flocking birds, and of some individuals' experiences in losing their Southern and New York accents. The group was referred to as a single body, the presence of sexual differentiation was suddenly recognized with some surprise, experiences of mystical fusion with the world were discussed, the promiscuous use of the term "we" in the group aroused objections, and so on. It was argued that the group suffered from the absence of rules of order, which, in other groups, kept people from being "cut to pieces." After one silence a girl remarked that all she could think of was the science-fiction film *The Fly*, in which attempts were made to disperse and reassemble the atoms of a fly, a man, and a cat, with varying degrees of failure. She recalled particularly a scene in which a little insect with a man's head, which was caught in a spider-web, was crying "Help!" in a tiny voice, and one in which a mass of unassembled cat-atoms was crying "Meow!" Another discussion revolved around the loss of ego boundaries under drugs, still another around instances of blind conformity, such as lemmings marching into the sea.

(b) In a second group, these concerns took a more direct, less symbolic form. Several members reported an awareness of underlying emotions being aroused by the group setting — "a parallel stream . . . becoming more and more turbulent;" "there have been times when . . . my whole day has been terrible because there were things that started trains of thought I'm sure I'd prefer not to think about." One girl argued that even in a nudist colony one would feel less naked than "when these emotions sweep through you." Another reported her chagrin at a slip of the tongue: ". . . it's all right to keep it down to the subconscious level but in this class all of a sudden it erupts to the conscious level."

(c) In a third group the fear of such underground linkages — touched off by accounts of an incident of getting drunk and another of revealing too much in an interview — received rather literal symbolic expression. The group members first talked of the university dining hall system — a "central kitchen" connected to all the dining halls by "a vast network" of underground tunnels. They imagined food being carried through them, thought of the sewers of Paris, of rats, of collisions. This led to some extended comment on the discovery of alligators in New York sewers, on Venus' flytraps (alleged to be the true form of the group's observers), and thence to Kopit's *Oh Dad, Poor Dad.*

These images portray rather vividly the fear of being enveloped by emotional contagion — of being submerged in a group emotion the roots of which are not consciously perceived. The baby alligator flushed down the toilet prospers and grows in this underground world in which everyone is bound by unperceived links, until it is capable of devouring its former owner. On the surface the group members are comfortably separate and apart — what holds them together is rather primitive and anonymous: their food all comes from a common source and their excreta are also ultimately intermingled in one common cloaca.

These fears are mastered by substituting differentiated conscious linkages for unconscious bonds. Not that the latter ever disappear, but their proportionate role tends normally to diminish. As involvement in and commitment to a group increase, the pressure for some kind of bondedness grows correspondingly, almost by definition. If conscious bonds do not develop the pressure of the unconscious ones becomes overwhelming. One can always fall back on the communality of human emotion, of instinctual processes. But these are bonds which obliterate differences and one's feeling of a stable location in a known and mapped social context. Hence they tend to arouse panic, particularly in an individuated Western population. Part of the work of a group is therefore to establish a network of conscious linkages between individuals who have been explicitly differentiated from one another. The group must draw boundaries, identify locations, assign roles — in short, make a chart of Chaos — before it feels safe to draw close. Each member must be able to say, "I feel close to you because you are such-and-such, with these values and traits and this role in the group," rather than because they share a universal dread, or rage, or euphoria, or lust. Initially, groups tend to be rather brittle and extreme in this regard, fastening their members into narrowly specialized roles of almost stereotypic eccentricity, from which they often have great difficulty in extricating themselves. (This is very typical of adolescent friendship groups.) As a group progresses, however, more of their uniform humanity is often allowed to emerge.

Ordinary task groups are facilitated in this effort by a number of cultural devices: Robert's Rules, assigned roles, known extragroup statuses, and so on. The unusual amount of anxiety that appears almost immediately in therapy groups, sensitivity training groups, basic encounter groups, and the like, is due in part to the fact that they fly in the face of this process. They strip away most of the cultural aids, exert some pressure to confront feelings and ideas which are below conscious awareness, and force a recognition of the common humanity which members share beneath the camouflage of their individuated performances.

The threat of unconscious linkages is thus particularly intense in these groups, and they seem to be moving in two opposite directions at once. This is why such groups so invariably evolve the ossified pattern (the trainer's despair) of "taking turns on the griddle" — assigning a meeting or a portion of a meeting to a single individual and his "problem." While typically rather untherapeutic, this custom removes the threat of emotional communality to a considerable extent, by encouraging the pretense that all such problems are more or less unique to the individual under discussion. It is one of the most tenacious forms of resistance that a trainer encounters.

The process of translating unconscious bonds into conscious ones is expressed in mythology by the not uncommon theme of fashioning the cosmos out of a chaos-dragon. A typical example is the Babylonian creation epic, *Enuma Elish*, in which the god Marduk battles and destroys the goddess Tiamat and constructs the various parts of the universe from her corpse.

As noted before, the leader facilitates this process in the group, as does the father in the nuclear family (since he is the first important object recognized as existing independently of the mother), and he or she is initially experienced as a hero with whom the ego can identify. For a time the group members derive considerable pleasure from passively watching this hero defeat the chaos-dragon. He is unintimidated by the group, interprets its

788

process, exposes its follies, and so on. But after a time the leader, as he inherits the gravitational pull of the group on the dependency needs of individuals, also inherits its devouring image. In the early life of a group the leader is the only conscious symbol of the group's separate identity. The members have no "conscious" bond other than their identification with him. But this bond is not formed solely of conscious elements — much of their old fear of the group's power adheres to it. The ego must now differentiate itself from its savior, and the hero of the dragon-combat becomes the paternal ogre. Marduk becomes Cronus, the differentiated individuals must be once again disgorged from their sanctuary in the fantasy of an omnipotent, all-encompassing guardian. It is at this point — when the leader is perceived as more threatening to the individuated ego than the pull of group emotion — that the revolt typically occurs. The ego functions of the leader are incorporated and distributed, and the father who helped the children become independent of the mother is in turn overthrown. The group members are now freed to establish more intense bonds with one another, and the old mythical images, under more comfortable control, fall into balance and dwindle to benign symbols of unity. The old warfare between leader and mob, between tyranny and anarchy, between harsh god and hallucinogenic goddess, is transformed into a peaceful *hieros gamos* in which the principal roles can be assumed by any group member. (For a more extended discussion of the behavior and images that characterize the postrevolt group, the reader is referred to *Microcosm* [20].)

This rather hasty description of the evolution of boundary-awareness, the development of conscious bonds in groups, must suffice as a prelude to a correspondingly brief attempt to apply this frame of reference to religious evolution in general.

Such an effort must be undertaken with great caution, for while anyone but the most fanatical cultural relativist can perceive a vague evolutionary outline in comparisons of ancient, modern, and "primitive" religions, it is equally easy to dismember most of the conceptual schemes that have been proposed. Most of the difficulty comes, of course, from using empirical entities as units and then trying to prove that one or another is more "advanced." This is the sheerest folly, since every such entity, from world religion to primitive rite, is a complex agglomeration of compromises between several evolutionary levels. How could we compare, for example, a "dependency" religion like Judaism, which is relatively purged of magical ideas but also lacks a concern with immortality and rebirth (a "pairing group" emphasis), with Christianity, which fuses the two extremes of the boundary-awareness continuum? We cannot compare religions at this stage of our knowledge, but only the individual elements which are combined in various ways in empirical religious systems.

Classical magic, for example, in which a verbal or motor formula is seen as having an automatic effect on environmental forces, without these latter necessarily being personified, properly belongs to a stage in which the distinction between self and environment is not yet established, as Freud noted long ago [9:83 ff]. A subtle shift in emphasis appears, however, with those practices involving the control and placation of more or less personified forces, spirits, and bogies. There is an element of greater apartness and greater anxiety — a sense that one may be overwhelmed and destroyed unless proper measures are taken. This attitude corresponds to the beginning of boundary-awareness, for consciousness begins with a sense of its own weakness (so long as it is submerged no anxiety can exist). By imperceptible degrees this in turn shades into practices such as prayer, supplication, and sacrifice, which are appropriate objects for analysis in terms of a dependency orientation.

At the other end of the continuum we may put the concern with immortality, rebirth, and messianic fantasies found in the pairing group. These concerns arise from an awareness of personal or group individuality sufficient to generate the fear of personal extinction.

Other religious attitudes may similarly be located. The idea of *mana*, for example, in its most typical form, expresses the stage of awareness to which the fight-flight modality is most pertinent. Here a single force unites the universe, yet its unequal quantitative distribution establishes a primitive differentiation of objects;

it is "trembling on the verge of personality" [11:67]. Some of the concentrations, furthermore, are defined in terms of the social structure. Yet the idea of *mana* contains within itself the implicit fear of being overwhelmed and disintegrated by this generalized force. Its protuberances must be avoided by the average individual lest his puny ego be dissolved in its immenseness. Prominent persons are less subject to this danger by virtue of the greater support given to their individuality by the social structure.

This scheme also helps clarify shifting attitudes toward full-fledged deities. Over time we find a change from rituals of placation and sacrifice to those of praise. The former pertain to the fear of being swallowed up and absorbed. Rituals of praise involve a more sophisticated conception which presupposes some kind of narcissistic self-awareness on the part of the worshipper, projected onto the god. He now views the deity with a certain amount of detachment, as a separate being who has concerns which are independent of the worshipper's fears. He can therefore approach him with the same finesse that he would employ with a mortal leader — encouraging him to assume difficult responsibilities by flattering his narcissism. The narcissistic deity is most highly developed in the Judaeo-Christian and Islamic traditions, in which flattery becomes the principal offering.

Reform movements within religions in all parts of the world seem all to push in the same direction, seeking either to eliminate magical and "fight-flight" elements from the religion, or to emphasize immortality and rebirth at the expense of dependency attitudes. The decay of these movements similarly involves a reintroduction of the purged elements, so that what we see historically often appears not as evolution but as a series of shifting combinations, like cabinet coalitions in a multiparty system.

Consider also the many forms which may be taken by ancestor worship, which we would on the face of it place squarely at the "dependency" level of boundary-awareness along with the worship of major deities. This results from an image of the worship itself, of praying and paying homage to ancestors. But when we look at some of the associated beliefs and practices the picture becomes considerably more complicated. In many if not most societies with ancestor worship we find an associated fear of the dead returning, and a number of rituals and practices designed to ward off ghosts (the fight-flight group). These ideas pertain to a level at which individuation is minimal, problematic, and terrifyingly precarious. As the society becomes more sophisticated these ideas should drop out progressively, and give way to a focus on one's own immortality. It is at this point that the idea that the ancestors are dependent for their survival on the libations and homage of living descendants receives increasing emphasis, and usually takes the significant form of an absorbing preoccupation with producing male heirs (the pairing group). It is quite common to find all of these attitudes coexisting. Yet we should nonetheless be able to isolate the separate components — fear of the ego being swallowed up because of its inadequate separation from the dead, desire to perpetuate the nurturance and protection the dead provided while living, and desire to ensure one's own immortality by extending it to one's predecessors — and evaluate their relative importance to the members of the society [17:228]. (For a discussion of the problem of totemism, too complex to be discussed here, see *Microcosm* [20:223 ff].)

Modest support for this scheme can be found in Swanson's brilliant pioneer effort to establish empirical connections between religious patterns and social structure. Most encouraging in Swanson's data is the strong positive association between the presence of high gods, in particular *"active"* high gods (which provide the most meaningful expression of the dependent orientation), and a variety of social structural variables reflecting differentiation, specialization, and complexity in the society [21:55–81, 194–217]. It seems reasonable to interpret this relationship as expressing the increased awareness of individual and group boundaries which accompany such social complexity, the erosion of "fight-flight" attitudes brought about by the proliferation of conscious bonds, and the "fear of freedom" (in Fromm's sense) which results from individuation and provokes fantasies of more powerful supernatural beings.

An even closer correspondence may be found with the evolutionary scheme recently proposed by Bellah [1]. Bellah's five stages, while representing complex empirical amalgams rather than deductively derived segments of a single strand, still reveal a clear relationship with the continuum of boundary-awareness and its associated mechanisms. His first phase, *"primitive religion,"* is described in terms of weak and elastic distinctions between self and world, between mythical and empirical worlds, between religious and other roles. *"Archaic religion"* contains more characterization of mythical beings (their transformation into personified and motivated gods), an elaborated cosmology, priestly roles, a sharper distinction "between men as subjects and gods as objects," and the consequent emergence of communication systems such as worship and sacrifice, and of "a new degree of freedom as well, perhaps, as an increased burden of anxiety." *"Historic religion"* introduces a sharp dualism between the empirical cosmos, which is derogated, and life-after-death. Hierarchical ordering of mythical symbols is reflected in further social differentiations. Emphasis on salvation or enlightenment appears for the first time, as well as a new insistence on submission to divine will or understanding. *"Early modern religion"* is essentially equated with the Protestant Reformation, and evinces a return to worldly involvement, a collapsing of both symbolic and organizational hierarchies, a reversal of the separation between religious and nonreligious action, and a consequent tendency toward the development of a "voluntaristic and democratic society," despite some extreme initial authoritarianism. Bellah is a little vague about *"modern religion,"* but stresses its abandonment of dualism for an "infinitely multiplex" structure, the further detachment from religious specialists of religious symbolization and belief, the intensification of awareness of personal responsibility for such symbolization, and the fact that "culture and personality themselves have come to be viewed as endlessly revisable" [1:361–373].

Of particular interest in Bellah's scheme is the apparent alternation between differentiation and dedifferentiation of roles. This does not contradict our notion of increasing boundary-awareness, as one might initially assume. Role specialization is

793

really an intermediate form of individuation — when the ability to avoid losing oneself in the corpus of the collectivity is still problematic, the formation of specialized roles serves to fix an observably separate point of reference from which an individual can recognize both his connectedness and his separateness from the whole. This mechanism has the obvious disadvantage of rigidity, however, and typically disappears, both at the societal and at the small group level, when it is no longer required. In the training group, for example, as noted above, members often assume rather calcified roles early in the group's history, taking refuge from boundary-loss by becoming "characters," with a limited set of stereotyped responses. Later there is a desire to enrich the group's behavioral repertoire so that anyone can perform any role [20:162–166]. This represents the emergence of a degree of individuation which permits the abandonment of fixed roles — such a crude device being no longer necessary since fear of group envelopment has waned. It is as if a set of quintuplets, separated at birth, had been suddenly reunited in a jungle, and forced to wear brightly decorated and highly particularized masks for a time in order to tell one another apart, before becoming attuned to more subtle differentiating cues.

Thus we are faced with a familiar problem in evolutionary theory — at one level of conceptualization we observe a pendular movement, but another twist of the lens reveals a linearity. Specialized religious roles — absent in the "primitive" stage — are present in the next two, but tend to disappear in the two modern phases. On the other hand individuation itself tends consistently to increase. From the nondiscriminatory aspect of primitive religion we move to the personalization of mythical beings in archaic religion, to the elaboration of hierarchies in historic religion and to the complete individuation of belief in the modern phases, in which there is "increasing acceptance of the notion that each individual must work out his own ultimate solutions."

The central drama of each of Bellah's last three phases represents a partial overcoming of the dilemmas against which the three defensive modalities are directed. Bellah says of the world rejection of the historical phase that:

794

the world acceptance of the primitive and archaic levels is largely to be explained as the only possible response to a reality that invades the self to such an extent that the symbolizations of self and world are only very partially separate. . . . Only by withdrawing cathexis from the myriad objects of empirical reality could consciousness of a centered self in relation to an encompassing reality emerge. Early modern religion made it possible to maintain the centered self without denying the multifold empirical reality and so made world rejection in the classical sense unnecessary [1:374].

The central drama of the early modern phase is the resolution of dependency, and we are not surprised to find that revolt themes are prominent here. We note that it is preceded by a phase in which religious specialists "store up a fund of grace that could then be shared with the less worthy," and is itself a phase in which salvation (or enlightenment) is potentially available to everyone [1:368]. This recalls the cannibalistic themes surrounding the revolt and the importance of the timing of the revolt in relation to the trainer's perceived *mana*.

The central drama of the modern phase is, as in the post-revolt phase of the group, the crisis over the awareness of individual mortality and responsibility, and its working-through is similarly represented by the abandonment of dualism for "multiplexity," and of messianic hopes for individual enlightenment.

These examples will perhaps suffice to give some indication of the many parallels between religious evolution on a macrocosmic scale and the evolution of sacred attitudes in the training group. There are several possible explanations for such parallelism: psychological ones, such as Freud or Jung might offer, which would stress invariant psychic processes; or sociological ones — Durkheimian and Swansonian — which would stress the impact of common structural conditions on group ideation. It would require a considerable effort of mind, however, to hold either of these views in such a way as to force the exclusion of the other — an effort as fatuous as it would be strenuous. Perceptions and fantasies occur in individuals, but individuals do not exist unimbedded in a social structure. I have been discussing the kinds of changes

795

brought about in more or less shared fantasy systems by rearrangements of the bonds linking individuals together. These are social structural changes, but such changes cannot occur without also changing to some degree the psychic structure of the individual. Unfortunately, we live in an historical phase which has popularized the grotesque fantasy of the isolated individual organism (and its corollary, the independently pursued academic specialty), so that this obvious point is often disregarded. Some social theorists treat individuals as inanimate building blocks that can be combined in a variety of ways without affecting their internal structure. Others try to mask their acceptance of this error by calling the building blocks "roles," and persuading themselves that individuals can step in and out of these blocks without *this* having any effect on their psychic structure.

Complexities do not disappear by our ignoring them, however. An individual is born into a social system just as he is born into an atmosphere composed of various gases. If the proportion of oxygen in the atmosphere underwent a profound change, the structure of the individual organism would alter, and so with the social system. Individual balance is maintained by committing aspects of oneself in varying degrees to various groups and combinations of groups. These systems are fluid and changes in external bonds force internal rearrangements. The reason that groups spend so much of their time discussing — directly or indirectly — linkages, boundaries, distances, and commitments is that this is the most important business they have to transact, whatever their external goals. The religious themes that I have portrayed here as common to both the microcosmic and macrocosmic level merely reflect alternatives in the social circuitry of the species.

REFERENCES

1. Bellah, R N: Religious Evolution, *American Sociological Review*, vol 29, 1964.
2. Bennis, W G: Defenses against "Depressive Anxiety" in

Groups: The Case of the Absent Leader, *Merrill-Palmer Quarterly*, vol 7, 1961.

3. Bennis, W G: (personal communication) 1963.
4. Bennis, W G, and Shepard, Herbert A: A Theory of Group Development, *Human Relations*, vol 9, 1956.
5. Bion, W R: Group Dynamics: A Re-view, in M Klein, P Heimann, and R E Money-Kyrle, ed, *New Directions in Psycho-analysis* (Basic Books, Inc, Publishers, New York, New York) 1957.
6. Durkheim, E: *The Elementary Forms of the Religious Life* (Free Press, formerly of Glencoe, Illinois, now of New York, New York) no date.
7. Ezriel, H: A Psycho-analytic Approach to Group Treatment, *British Journal of Medical Psychology*, vol 23, 1950.
8. Frazer, J G: *The New Golden Bough.* Edited by T H Gaster (Criterion Books, Inc, New York, New York) 1959.
9. Freud, S: *Totem and Taboo* (Routledge & Kegan Paul Ltd, London, England) 1950.
10. Golding, W: *Lord of the Flies* (G P Putnam's Sons, New York, New York) 1955.
11. Harrison, Jane Ellen: *Themis* (Meridian Books, The World Publishing Company, Cleveland, Ohio) 1962.
12. Lorenz, K: *On Aggression* (Harcourt, Brace and World, Inc, New York, New York) 1966.
13. Mann, R D: (personal communication) 1963.
14. Miles, M: (personal communication) 1960.
15. Mills, T M: "A Sociological Interpretation of Freud's *Group Psychology and the Analysis of the Ego*" (unpublished manuscript) 1959.
16. Mills, T M: Authority and Group Emotion, in W G Bennis, et al, ed, *Interpersonal Dynamics* (Dorsey Press, Richard D Irwin, Inc, Homewood, Illinois) 1964.
17. Neumann, E: *The Origins and History of Consciousness* (Pantheon Books, Inc, New York, New York) 1954.
18. Neumann, E: *The Great Mother* (Pantheon Books, Inc, New York, New York) 1955.

797

19. Piaget, J: *The Moral Judgement of the Child* (Routledge & Kegan Paul Ltd, London, England) 1932.
20. Slater, P E: *Microcosm: Structural, Psychological, and Religious Evolution in Groups* (John Wiley & Sons, Inc, New York, New York) 1966.
21. Swanson, G E: *The Birth of the Gods* (The University of Michigan Press, Ann Arbor, Michigan) 1960.

PART THREE

Social Indicators
of the Religious Situation

60% of the American electorate votes in national elections; 68% attends religious services.

64% knows there are new editions of the Bible; 67% knows the President can override a Congressional veto.

51% can name the first book of the Bible; 50% can spell "cauliflower" correctly.

76% believes that churches are doing a good job; 80% believes that governments are doing well.

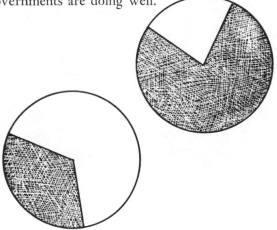

34% can correctly identify the Sermon on the Mount; 34% can name the United States Senators from their state.

21. MODERN SECULARITY: ITS MEANING, SOURCES, AND INTERPRETATION

by Guy E. Swanson

A INTRODUCTORY NOTE: The year 1966–1967 marked the sesquicentennial anniversary of the founding of Harvard's Divinity School, and conferences and colloquia were arranged in celebration. This paper was prepared for one of those conferences. All who attended received a preliminary paper by Thomas O'Dea, and I wove references to his paper into mine. I also tended to mention those points in his paper that I thought needed further examination and not to mention many of his points with which I fully agreed. Because I find a drastic redrafting of my paper impossible, I have let stand my references to his, and I must take this occasion to apologize to him for mistaken impressions that readers may form of his paper, which most of them will not have read.

* * *

Thomas O'Dea's interpretation deserves our further thought. It is one of the few comprehensive analyses of modern secularity. Among the significant earlier sociologists writing on this topic were Ferdinand Toennies, Emile Durkheim, Ernst Troeltsch, Georg Simmel, and Robert Park. O'Dea's is one of the very few accounts to be informed by important ideas and findings from the social sciences and also to be deepened by historical understanding. [See 52; 8; 10:221–227, 316–347, 627-629.] These very merits impel us to ask whether this interpretation is also faithful to the facts, whether other accounts are more faithful or at least equally plausible. And, in asking those questions, we must at once admit that existing knowledge permits no confident answers. It does, however, suggest the point from which to work: the distinction between secularism and secularization. O'Dea has much to say about the origin and consequences of these concepts. We must ourselves first consider their exact meaning.

Secularization is the great theme of Max Weber's comparative studies of religion [52, 53]. When Weber says that ancient Judaism involved a greater degree of secularization than did the religions of classical China or of India, and, when he declares that Protestantism represented a further development in the same direction, we see at once that secularization need not be the antithesis of vital religious impulse. Nor is it inherently a diremption of the secular order from the sacred or a stripping of sacred meaning from large ranges of human experience. Judaism and Protestantism incorporated a greater secularization than did other religions in just one specific sense: in them it was the general orientation and meaning of human behavior, not its detailed contents, which had sacred significance. Thus God desired not burnt offerings or the following of a particular formula in prayer, but a spirit attentive to him and a contrite heart; not intellectual assent to some list of his attributes but a commitment to his service wherever it might lead.

To say that secularization means attention to this world or to our era is correct, yet our saying that may involve us in a misplaced emphasis. The critical point is not that, under secularization, some acts are worldly and others sacred; the critical point is that some limited aspects of every act have sacred significance, the remaining aspects of any act gaining their meaning primarily from their relevance for life in this world and age. Thus, in Arminian Protestantism, the one aspect of every act that was taken to have sacred significance was the meaning of that act as a sign of obedience toward God; in contemporary Congregationalism the one crucial aspect of all our behavior is its import for our conduct and growth as whole persons — as living souls.

Weber provides us with another and still earlier example: purest Calvinism. On the one hand, Calvin denied that any earthly human activity had a bearing upon a man's salvation. In this way he gave such activity a purely secular relevance.

But to Calvin's first thesis was attached a second: the ardent, devoted pursuit of secular activities is an obligation man owes to God. Note that it was the ardor and the steadfastness of the pursuit, and the status of each act as an offering to God, that gave to secular activity this supernatural importance. In all their many other aspects, men's acts had secular status only.

From a sociological point of view, the process of secularization bears a striking resemblance to processes not inherently connected with religion but often accompanying growth in the complexity and abstractness of a society or of any other organization. I think especially of bureaucratization and professionalization. Indeed, it is our best and most common guess that secularization, like these counterpart processes, is an outgrowth of increased organizational complexity. Like secularization, the development of a bureaucratic system and of professionalization entails a partial separation of the technical and managerial functions from an organization's master goals and its underlying constitutional order. As in secularization, any immediate implementation of enduring objectives or of an enduring order is finally evaluated in terms of its effectiveness for promoting those objectives and that order. At the same time, the implementation is recognized as having its own imperatives and standards against which it must be judged.

As, under secularization, God is believed to be concerned with the generalized character of men's commitments and conduct, so, under growing complexity of organization and abstractness of objectives, a modern industry or government no longer tries to supervise employees' work at a refined level of detail. Rather than employing rules that govern the exact procedures by which work is carried out, the complex organization specifies the work to be accomplished, leaving to employees many decisions about how best to attain objectives. To repeat, what in the religious sphere we call secularization seems to be of the same order as professionalization and bureaucratization, and to have similar roots and consequences.

But we have yet to consider secularism. As O'Dea says, secularism is not secularization. Secularism is the denial that a sacred order exists, the conviction that the universe is in no meaningful sense an expression or embodiment of purpose, the belief that it is unreasonable, other than anthropomorphically, to have toward the universe or its "ground" a relationship mediated by communication or by any other interchange of meanings — to have toward it a relationship in any sense interpersonal. The clearest example is atheism. The more common approximation to secularism is intellectual agnosticism.

In considering the validity of O'Dea's scheme, it is convenient to begin with secularism, looking at observations that an account of secularism must put in order. Then we can take up secularization.

SECULARISM

True secularism is rare in human history and probably uncommon today. It is unfortunate that we have no satisfactory information about the prevalence of secularism in the Soviet Union or in any other state that has sought for some considerable time to stamp out religious faith [6:261; 49:424–428]. But we do know something about secularism in several other modern societies. Among them, and with the notable exception of France [14], there is little evidence that secularism is rampant [27:888–897, 24:145–157, 30:64–65, 3:18-A].

Information for the United States as tabulated by the public opinion polls has shown a consistent picture from 1941 to the present. In at least 7 investigations spread across that period of almost 25 years one finds 94% to 99% of American adults saying that they personally believe in God, between 1% and 3% saying they have no such belief, and the remainder undecided. The undecided people may be just that and may not be intellectual agnostics. A similar picture is obtained from studies in Brazil, Canada, and Australia [24:145–157]. Surveys in Scandinavia, Italy, the Low Countries, Czechoslovakia, and Great Britain report that between 80% and 85% of adults are believers, between 6% and 12% are undecided, and approximately 6% are atheists

[13:742–747 and 16: 8/11/57]. The figures for France, the major exception, show 66% of adults to be believers, 14% undecided, and 20% atheists [24:145–157]. A poll of the population of central and southern Sweden (published in 1957) records 27% of the respondents as saying that they believe in a God who intervenes in their lives. In this, 71% say that there is a God who governs the world. An additional 10% believe in a God whom they would not describe as governing the world [16].

The most recent report on religious belief was developed from surveys made in 1966 by the American Institute of Public Opinion (the Gallup Poll). This report provides us with responses according to degree of certainty: absolutely certain that there is a God, 81%; fairly sure, 12%; not quite sure, 3%; not at all sure, 1%; atheists, 2%; agnostics, 1% [3]. Collapsing categories, this produces a total of 3% of adults who reported themselves as atheists or agnostics and 4% who reported substantial doubts. The Institute also reported a breakdown of certainty of belief by denominational preference. From 3% to 6% of members of the major Protestant denominations are doubters as are 2% of the Roman Catholics. About 1% of the "Catholic" and "Protestant" respondents are atheists or agnostics. But among Jews the results are spectacularly different: 16% report themselves to be atheists or agnostics, 14% doubters, 31% fairly sure of God's existence, and 39% absolutely certain. (The comparable figures for absolute certainty are 88% for Roman Catholics and between 73% and 89% for the major Protestant denominations.) It is clear that secularism in the most explicit sense is more common in America among Jews than among Christians. (Unfortunately we lack the information about Christians and Jews in other countries that would be needed to judge whether this finding is peculiar to the American scene.) Dr. Gallup does suggest that the prevalence of secularism among Jews has increased rather recently. His survey in 1952 found that 88% of Jewish respondents were absolutely certain or fairly sure of God's existence. The total for 1966 is 70%. One might be tempted to attribute all his findings about Jewish-Christian differences to errors in sampling, the number of Jewish respondents in a national sample being relatively small. His essential result is consistent, however, with Lenski's report for a sample of adults taken in the Detroit metropolitan area in 1958, and with data of my own obtained in Detroit the following year [17; 51].

I do not want to minimize the frailties of information from opinion surveys, especially when the questions concern topics that might threaten respondents or make them feel that a conventional response is safest. But it would, likewise, be an error to think that there is evidence of more than a small minority of adults in the most advanced countries having adopted a clearly secularist position. (It is of course enormously important that we understand the sources and thrust of the secularist position when it does appear.)

Although these findings are slender, they are almost all that we have; and even they force us to ask searching questions about alternative interpretations, O'Dea's among them, of secularism. We must ask questions like these:

If modern interpreters are correct in saying that secularism is a product of urbanism, scientific advance, a money economy, education, and other features of social modernity, how shall we explain its greater strength in France than elsewhere in western Europe? In Europe as contrasted with the United States? Among American Jews as contrasted with American Christians, even as contrasted with Christians in major metropolitan areas?

If, as O'Dea states, great catastrophes — major wars, economic collapse, and the like — are of critical importance in encouraging secularism, why do the polls from countries for which we have data from the 1930s and also from the period after the Second World War show such stability in religious faith? Or why were the turbulent early Middle Ages what he describes them to be — an age of faith?

Is it only accidental that poll results from Canada, Australia, and the United States are similar? Is it that all

806

three are cultural backwaters, outside the main currents of modernity? That seems unlikely. May it not be that the distinctive social and political structure — Reformed Protestantism, egalitarian democracy — that Robert Alford and Seymour Lipset have shown to be present in all three countries is of critical importance, giving to the several aspects of modernity a meaning uncongenial to atheism or agnosticism [1; 37; 38]? May not the well known and distinctive features of French society encourage an opposite trend [37; 38; 36]?

No one presently knows the answers to these questions. I propose, however, that they underscore the importance of studying secularism separately from secularization, of asking why it is that secularism is a far more important issue in some countries than in others and more among Jews than among Christians in the United States. These differences are real. It seems unlikely that our research, our policies, and our discourse will advance an understanding of others or ourselves if we purposefully ignore these differences. Uncomfortable though it may at first be, we must find ways to face these truths together.

It will not do to leave the problem of secularism without asking whether observations of the general population may not obscure strong trends toward unbelief among those special sectors of a people that constitute its leading edge: the better educated, the more prosperous, the young, the better educated young, and the scientific, managerial, or political elites. Our information is again slight. In at least some countries of western Europe — Sweden is an example — firm belief in God is significantly but not dramatically associated with rural residence, lower income, the older age groups, and with being a woman [16]. In the United States no such regular trends appear: unbelief is distributed essentially at random with respect to age, education, and occupation. Roman Catholics are an exception: in America it is the more affluent and better educated Catholics (even when their education is not obtained in church schools)

807

who appear to believe with fewest reservations [17: for years 1958 and 1959]. From studies of sample populations in metropolitan Detroit we can say that first generation immigrants, whether Protestant or Roman Catholic, are more likely than the general population to be atheists, agnostics, or just doubters; that, among whites, men and women of either faith are more likely to be secularists if both they and their parents are or were unskilled laborers.

We can be fairly certain that unbelief is uncommon among political elites in the United States and that it probably is rare among businessmen and managers. Largely as a result of J. H. Leuba's studies in 1914 and 1933, it seemed that a majority of American scientists, perhaps more than 80% of the more eminent scientists [33; 34], were unbelievers. It was shown almost immediately, however, that Leuba's questions contained drastic imperfections. Thus, in a study of 1,321 students at Syracuse University in 1931, Daniel Katz and Floyd Allport found that only 21% exhibited a belief in God as that belief was defined by Leuba, despite the fact that at least 78% of these students had some meaningful belief in God [29:257–318; 28:192–195]. No one seems subsequently to have perfected and repeated the kind of research on scientists that Leuba began.

May it be that, although only a minority of the young are secularists, the trend in America is upward? There is no such evidence. The only three studies that I have found on this question show exactly the opposite trend [12; 26; 42]. All are studies of college students. All employ measures of interest in religion and of belief in God that had been administered to large samples of undergraduates in the same colleges several years earlier: at Dartmouth College in 1940 and 1955, at Northwestern University at seven different points in time from 1933 to 1949, at Ohio State and other universities at four points in time between 1929 and 1958. In each study the trend is toward significantly greater percentages of students expressing a strong interest in religion and/or significantly greater proportions believing in God. Once again, one regrets the absence of comparable data from other countries.

808

SECULARIZATION

Near the beginning of his paper, O'Dea states a major assumption of his analysis:

> Perhaps the most central and significant change in human awareness involved in the secularization of life has been the great diminution both in scope and in relevance, as well as in intensity and immediacy, of the experience of the sacred. This mode of apprehension has been progressively constricted and diluted for Western men and in very many instances has disappeared altogether.

From the data concerning atheism just examined we must immediately restrict his "very many instances" to 1% to 6% of the population of Western nations. If we add agnostics and the serious doubters, the range widens, bounded by 3% or 4% and, excluding France, by 25%. These last figures are substantial enough. "Western men," however, are almost too heterogeneous to permit easy generalization.

But surely O'Dea is right in thinking that there has been a "great diminution both in scope and in relevance, as well as in intensity and immediacy, of the experience of the sacred." The most obvious evidences of this in the United States are figures on belief in life after death (70% of the adult population claims a firm belief) and belief in supernatural punishments or rewards in the afterworld (the percentage of believers also being 70). Reports from some European countries show substantially lower percentages of adults holding these traditional doctrines, 40% to 60% being the range obtained [30; 24].

We can say from such findings that important traditional ties between man and God have dissolved. We do not know whether remaining ties have been strengthened or whether new ones are being developed. Perhaps we shall have reason to say of religion as we now say of the family: although it has lost many former functions and although many older doctrines have passed away, it seems an enduring institution, now founded upon more distinc-

809

tive bases than before and apparently indispensable for most people and for all societies. Perhaps we shall say no such thing.

We should, however, recall that, to take O'Dea's description at full value, we must overcome what seem to be contrary indicators. It is true that we have good evidence on these indicators exclusively from studies of American adults, but I have urged that we cannot ignore even our own population or assume that trends in other countries are necessarily the bellwethers of all that is to come. The findings I have in mind concern the religious participation of Americans. Some of these findings have to do with institutional participation, some with personal devotional activity or with informal attention to matters religious. In introducing them, I want first to provide an appropriate standard against which they can be appraised.

Walter Lippmann once demanded of his readers, in 1929, why people were not going to church as much as they once had. He gave his own answer:

> . . . they are not so certain that they are going to meet God when they go to church. If they had that certainty they would go. . . . The most worldly would be in the front pews . . . [35:48 – 49].

Lippmann's conclusion is logical but not compelling. It assumes that people do not meet God outside of a church. It assumes that their relations with God depend upon how often they meet him. It assumes that when they meet him, perhaps in church, they always or usually experience that meeting as one of great moment rather than often as a more routine contact. It assumes, finally, something that is by no means certain: that a larger proportion of American adults attended church before 1929 than attended in 1929 or, we could add, than attend church now.

We might think of a standard like Lippmann's as a normative standard. That kind of standard must be contrasted with realistic accounts of Western history since ancient times and with many ethnographic reports, all of them revealing a frequently casual observance of religious practices and doctrines. It may be that O'Dea leads us astray in the same respect that Lippmann does when he invokes by comparison with modern times the world of primitive and ancient man. "Primitive and archaic man," he declares:

> apprehended his world as infused and sustained by sacred powers and forces, which though invisible and outside the everyday world, nevertheless permeated it and rendered it actual.

One can agree that this describes primitive and archaic norms and yet not be surprised to find what the record often shows: a relaxed observance of rite and doctrine despite these norms.

Perhaps we can gain a better standard for judging religious participation if we compare it not with religious norms but with another presumably important form of social behavior: I have in mind a comparison with political participation.

The norms concerning political participation often make stringent demands. The American standard for conduct becoming to a good citizen requires that he inform himself about major issues before the public. He should make judicious assessments of candidates for public office. He should vote in all elections. He should test the truth of his beliefs by rational debate in the public forum.

When it is shown that the political participation of the American people falls far below this standard — and it has been shown beyond any doubt — the conclusion is inescapable. Or is it? Almost every informed student of the subject seems to believe that the American political system is vital and effective!

From the perspective provided by that conclusion, consider some comparisons of political participation with religious participation. All the findings I cite are taken from studies completed in the last 10 to 15 years. If we consider ours to be a vital political system, and if patterns of religious and political participation are similar, may we not, from existing evidence, have to rethink any proposal that religious institutions or interactions with a sacred order are on the wane? Here is a sample of the many comparisons now possible:

Item: Approximately 60% of the American electorate votes in national elections. Approximately 68% of the adult

811

population attends religious services in any given four-week period and 79% claims church membership. [36:181; 32: chap 4; 23:671–679].

Item: 76% believes that the churches are doing a good or excellent job in its area of the country; 80% believes that national or state governments are doing that well [25:326–337; 32: chap 11, 12, 18].

Item: 27% of the electorate reports it discussed politics with others prior to an election; 90% of the people in the Detroit area, the only geographic source of data on this point, reports discussing religion with others during the month just past [18 and 32:53].

Item: Fourteen out of every hundred Americans have written or wired a congressman or senator, 7 out of a 100 have done so more than once. 24% of the population has called on someone to invite his membership in a church. 88% of the population prays frequently or every day; 40% read from the Bible in the month just past and between 60% and 65% read from it during the past year. In metropolitan Detroit, 65% of all adults is self-exposed to religious programs on radio or television and 75% to reports of religion in the newspapers [32:68–69; 24:145–157; 25:326–337; 19: card 9 col 14, 15].

Item: Approximately 5 families in every 100 made a financial contribution to a political party or candidate in 1956. At least 40 in every 100 made a financial contribution to a religious body; 3 in every 100 tithe [32:60; 25:326–337; 5].

Item: The major Protestant denominations once again have an ample supply of ministers in service and also of candidates for the ministry, despite growth of church membership (and of numbers of local churches) far in excess of the rate of growth of the national population and despite sharply higher standards of training and ability required of students entering ministerial curricula. Positions in state and federal governmental service are going begging for lack of suitable applicants.

Item: Only 7% of all respondents says it has no strong feelings about its religious beliefs. Although there seem to be no dependable national estimates, the proportion of the electorate that declares itself indifferent to political positions and issues is always greater than 7% [24:149].

Item: 51% of the American people correctly name the first book of the Bible. That is about the proportion that knows the number of Senators from its own state — and that can spell "cauliflower" [22].

Item: 95% does not know what the initials IHS represent, just about the number which does not know that all members of the House of Representatives are elected every two years [22].

Item: 95% knows the name of the mother of Jesus. That is the proportion that can state the term of office of the President of the United States and correctly locate Texas or California on a blank map [22].

Item: Only 34% can correctly identify the Sermon on the Mount or can give the names of the current United States Senators from its state [22].

Item: About the same percentage of the population knows that there are new editions of the Bible as knows that the President can override a Congressional veto. The respective figures are 64% and 67% [22].

But there is no point in continuing. These comparisons can be multiplied at great length and with the same result. In the absence of good longitudinal information we cannot be certain of the meaning of the statistics on religion, but in the presence of comparable information from contemporary politics I believe that the religious data require our being cautious indeed concerning assertions of the present irrelevance of religion for the personal lives or institutional commitments of most Americans. The relative absence of serious discussion of religion in our public press may mirror indifference or it may reflect conformity to the standard of public tolerance. Tolerance may protect religious beliefs from searching examination or may produce the impression that they are of little consequence.

MODERN SECULARIZATION AND THE
EMERGING CONTENT OF RELIGIOUS DOCTRINES

For me, some of the most provocative things Thomas O'Dea has to tell us appear in his remarks about the social orientations and religious doctrines that seem to accompany secularization in the United States. There is a consistency in his picture, a consistency readily caught by his descriptions of the themes of many current movements of protest, including the student movements. Here are some representative phrases:

. . . the loss of the capacity for an I-Thou relation and its replacement by an I-It relation

. . . the loss of a sense of the sacred and the transcendent

. . . an uncanny nihilism lurking beneath the surface

. . . a loss of any ascendancy and leverage making critical rational choice possible with respect to the confusing array of human possibilities

. . . [the prevalence of youth with] placards in their hands, and aspirations in their hearts, but [a lack of] ideas and plans

. . . [the decline of] relation, celebration, and cultivation

I cannot say whether his description, or some other, will prove correct. On this subject, as on secularism and on the vitality of devotional institutional religion, my effort is to broaden our considerations by presenting alternatives. Unhappily I shall no longer be able to draw upon even fragmentary empirical studies in support of those alternatives. The portrait I draw of emerging religious doctrines has little basis other than casual observation and deep interest. It refers more largely to one population than to others: to laymen rather than to theologians, to Americans, to Christians, to Protestants and, among them, to the better educated.

I begin with a quotation from a recent paper of Robert Bellah's because it seems to catch an essential point about the difference between Christian doctrines under early secularization and the character of those doctrines under modern secularization. Of the period of early secularization he says:

> . . . the historic religions are all in some sense transcendental.
> . . . The discovery of an entirely different realm of religious reality seems to imply a derogation of the value of the given empirical cosmos: at any rate world rejection . . . is, in this stage for the first time, a general characteristic of the religious system.
> . . . in this sense the historic religions are all dualistic. The strong emphasis on hierarchical ordering characteristic of archaic religions continues to be stressed. . . . Not only is the supernatural realm "above" this world in terms of both value and control but both the supernatural and earthly worlds are themselves organized in terms of a religiously legitimated hierarchy. For the masses, at least, the new dualism is above all expressed in the difference between this world and the life after death. . . . Under these circumstances the religious goal of salvation (or enlightenment, release and so forth) is for the first time the central religious preoccupation.

And of doctrine under modern secularization he proposes:

> The central feature of the change is the collapse of the dualism that was so crucial to all the historic religions.
> . . . there is simply no room for a hierarchic dualistic religious symbol system of the classical historic type. . . . it is not that a single world has replaced a double one but that an infinitely multiplex one has replaced the simple duplex structure [11].

Bellah is properly hesitant to speculate about the doctrinal consequences of the collapse of a hierarchic dualism between the sacred realm and the secular. To provide an alternative to O'Dea's picture I must at this point be more rash. I must sketch with an assurance I do not feel. I must give some impressions, however tentative, of the experience men are coming to have of God subsequent to the decline of dualism, and I must offer some meaning for an image of Bellah's to which I subscribe, the image of the rise of a multiplex world.

There seems to me little evidence that the informally emerging theological formulations severely depersonalize men's experience of God: He is not the remote, indifferent divine draftsman or a watchmaker or a vague or abstract universal force. He is experienced, instead, as a collaborator with men in a functional division of labor, a division in which the acts of *all* collaborators are equally necessary for the attainment of the objectives of any in which *any* participant's action, being somewhat independent of the actions of others, sets new problems and opportunities for the work of his collaborators. This division of labor seems to me the multiplex situation of which Bellah speaks. There arise in this multiplex theological experiences having those properties that Harvey Cox has sensed. His words deserve quotation:

> . . . We speak of God in a secular fashion when we recognize man as His partner, as the one charged with the task of bestowing meaning and order in human history.
>
> . . . the hidden God . . . of biblical theology may be mistaken for the no-god-at-all of nontheism. Though He is very different from Godot in Samuel Beckett's play, like Godot He has the similar habit of not appearing at the times and places men appoint. . . .
>
> In the technopolitan culture, both horizontal kinship and vertical authority patterns are disappearing. What replaces them is a work team [15:256 – 257].

And, Cox continues:

> . . . we suggested designating this peculiarly urban phenomenon the I-You relationship. It describes very well the rewarding relationship one has with a fellow team member, with

whom one has worked on a research project or painted a house. It derives from work that is done together by two persons for whom the work is the key to their mutuality. . . . It may be that in addition to the I-Thou relationship with God, and the mystical experience which is already exceedingly rare, contemporary man could meet God as a "you."

. . . What seems at first sight irreverence may be closer to the heart of the self-humbling truth of God than we imagine [15:263 – 264].

As Cox would probably agree, his interpretation only accommodates to a further measure of secularization the conception essential to Calvin's statement of man's role: the secular life of man is "that activity . . . by which he fulfills the creation mandate to cultivate the earth, to have dominion over it and to subdue it." [50:7]. But there is a difference. For Calvin, man's secular activity was undertaken for the greater glory of God. For Cox, and for modern Protestants, secular activity is a share with God in a common task. In that undertaking, the special demands and standards of every specialized activity now have a more explicit, a more honorable status than Calvin might have appreciated, yet each is still judged, and all are integrated and given their final meaning, by their contributions to the overarching common task [20]. It is apparent that discipline is exercised in this as in all collaborative relationships. That discipline now proceeds from the imperatives of common involvement in a common undertaking – it is an instance of what Georg Simmel called "subordination under a principle." In an older view, man was thought subordinated to God's person and power, God being gloriously righteous but uncomfortably arbitrary [44:250–267]. To put the matter in still another fashion, the emerging Protestant position seems a kind of synthesis of the optimistic Arminianism of, let us say, a Henry Ward Beecher, and the searching neoorthodoxy of a Reinhold Neibuhr. The power and lordship of God reasserted by neoorthodoxy appear in the modern synthesis as sufficiently contained in God's independence and in his unavoidable involvement in human life. The encompassing love of God preached by Beecher now appears in the modern synthesis as

God's opening up a truly personal relationship between himself and men. God's love appears as his becoming a coworker with men, sharing responsibilities for their life together and bearing with them the heat of the day. In this kind of relationship and despite God's divinity, there emerges a significant equality with man because, as Simmel suggested, when all participants are subordinated to the exigencies of a common principle — a common undertaking — a hierarchical subordination of one collaborator to another is justified only by the technical requirements of their work, this leaving them equal as persons and equally necessary as fellow workers [44:263–264].

Perhaps we can more easily understand the spirit of this emerging interpretation if we see it in a setting not manifestly religious: in the restless stirring and critical stance of some college students which has come to have the collective label "The New Left." This movement has attracted some deeply alienated men and women who use the movement to legitimate personal problems and to elevate idiosyncratic difficulties to the level of cosmic truth. We should not take the more bizarre expressions at Berkeley as prototypical of events there or on other campuses. The themes of the New Left, in more moderate form, appear congenial, however, to a considerable proportion of college students. I see in these themes expressions of a new social relationship analogous to that just described between God and man and as having, in the student movements, a more accessible meaning. It is in the general properties of those movements that I want to find clues to what seems to me a formally similar relation of modern men to God, a relation strikingly similar in its ambiguities, in its ambivalence, in the prolixity of its forms, in its peculiar susceptibilities to passionate commitment and bleak distrust.

In both the theological movements and the student agitations, people seem to be working toward an understanding of a world in which a hierarchy of personal and institutional authority has decayed, and in which a new authority of principle and of common task is latent but not yet understood or articulated. There is a challenge to college administrators, as to God, to show their acceptance under the authority of a common enterprise of technical, rather than personal or institutional, prerogatives; to demonstrate through acknowledgment of student criticisms, often criticisms of a personalized sort, that they and the students are under a common discipline. The style of the student activists is not unlike that of children in a permissive home. They feel free to demand immediate attention and disrupt parental activities until attention is given. This might be taken to be childish behavior. I suppose that it sometimes is. But that appreciation fails to note an important difference: many student demands are couched in an essentially moral framework. College administrators are being challenged to demonstrate sincerity and depth of concern and to defend the validity or relevance of their standards and choices. The students further assert that authority given by a common participation in a community of learning is limited to that undertaking. It is therefore beyond the competence of a college administration to govern a student's outside activities: his political interests, sexual conduct, recreation, or living arrangements. Only a very few students have tried to gain administrative support for the proposition that whatever they do outside the university community is legitimate. A very large number take the position that their outside activities are a secular sphere having independent imperatives, a sphere in which university authority may not properly intrude.

For many students, I think, unpressed, purposefully unfashionable clothes, uncut hair, and even gross manners gain moral meaning in this same context. Students want to be valued for their share in the university community, not for irrelevant characteristics. If, they insist, one does academic work well, who has the right to ask that one wash hands or use a deodorant? And, they sometimes seem to say, if what we and the faculty are doing involves our joint growth as persons, is it not imperative that we be direct and personal with one another? That we all be free to be sometimes rude or brutally candid and so strip away the technical role differences and return us all to equality before the common task? Should we not all be holy fools — free to err and to vent impulse and to sulk and to love? To open ourselves to one another to the extent that we attain a greater confidence in our mutual acceptability, an appreciation of interdependence despite our differences, a discipline that flows directly from that interdependence [46:160–209]? Can anyone really believe he is deeply involved who does not sometimes lose his cool? Is any man at one with us who does not acknowledge his loneliness outside our dependencies? His need to be forgiven for his irrelevancies or errors or absurdities? Is it not respect we seek rather than mere respectability?

These new demands are evangelical. Intimate collaboration requires not mere accession to demands but an acceptance of their legitimacy and the taking as one's own of the standards upon which those demands are based. Students are asking their teachers and the administrators of their colleges for personal commitment, not qualified or judicious assent. If all are participants in a common enterprise, the need of any participant is its own justification for requiring the help of others. True conversion to these views must be sealed by public witness to past error and present commitment, by agreement to accept criticisms for one's own good and the common good, by enduring responsibility for others and toward others [7, 41]. It requires also that everyone acknowledge that his part and his vision of the common enterprise are partial, that the interpretation of responsibilities and meanings is consequently subject to debate and to persistent open disagreements, that there is, as a necessary consequence of those disagreements, the need for forgiving and for accepting forgiveness.

Of course there is much in these drifts of student opinion that will pass. Much may be laid to inexperience. More may be laid to a joyous testing for new limits when old disciplines have collapsed. There too often is no effort to find with faculty and administration some new common disciplines and to accept these as binding upon students, not just upon teachers. There is as yet little sense of the special rights that the technical role of faculty and administration carries. There is almost no appreciation of the costs and contradictions inherent in social intimacy, no sense of the destructive consequences of demands for final solutions. The current spirit is a breaking of the old, not a building of the new. But that must come. The new student spirit is not that of a modern Wandervogel: it is an effort to attain a depth of participation in the community commensurate with actual responsibilities in it; it is an attempt to deal with this age and this place, not to withdraw in search of a vanished golden age or a simpler world or an ideal so pure that it cannot be actualized [9]. It is, I think, more akin to radical politics than to anomie, egoism, or nihilism.

I have described this new student unrest because it may enable us better to appraise modern trends among Protestant laymen. I have already suggested that the experiences those laymen have of their relations with God have important similarities with the situation of students in relations with faculty and administrators. There are, to be sure, important differences. But the similarities may be sufficient to allow us to employ either situation to illumine the other. In that connection, we may listen again to Harvey Cox speaking of man and God wrestling with a common problem:

> . . . in secular society politics does what metaphysics once did. It brings unity and meaning to human life and thought. In today's world we unify the various scholarly and scientific specialties [not under some abstract principle but] by focusing them on specific human issues. . . . truth is not unified today in metaphysical systems. Rather it is functionally unified by bringing disparate specialties to bear on concrete political complexities [15:254].
>
> . . . Secular talk of God occurs only when we are away from the ghetto and out of costume, when we are participants in that political action by which He restores men to each other in mutual concern and responsibility [15:256].

And Cox' suggestion of the outcome of unity through a common undertaking may be indicative of the order that will emerge under analogous circumstances in the universities. God, he writes:

> . . . is teaching man to . . . become mature, free from infantile dependencies, fully human. . . . He will not perpetuate human adolescence, but insists on turning the world over to man as his responsibility.

821

. . . In a society marked by vertical authority . . . , man tends to experience God in the classic I-Thou encounter. God is seen as another who has authority over me. The relationship is a confrontation. We have suggested . . . that a new type of interhuman relationship seems to be emerging in urban society, one that is just as human as I-Thou but is qualitatively different. It occurs often in the kind of work team described above, a relationship one has in addition to I-Thou experiences in the family or with intimate friends. . . . Rather than participation or confrontation, it is a relationship of alongsideness.

Perhaps in the secular city God calls men to meet Him first of all as a "you." . . . Like his relationship to his work partner, man's relationship to God derives from the work they do together. Rather than shutting out the world to delve into each other's depths the way adolescent lovers do, God and man find joy together in doing a common task [15:258–259; 263–265].

I had a second reason for examining the recent student movements. It was to observe that they seem a response to exactly that growth in social complexity and in the division of labor — in professionalization, in formal organization, and in functional interdependence — of which O'Dea makes so much in interpreting secularity and which underlies Cox' suggestions for a reformulation of man's experience of God under secularity [39]. I propose that this common source of student ideology and modern theological trends helps to account for the qualities they share.

But I propose also that we may be wrong if we think that most or all of the new experiences of God arise from perspectives set by an urban existence. What Cox describes in an I-You relationship sounds appropriate to modern trends, but he derives it from the impersonality of urban life as enforced by the great size of urban populations and by the social heterogeneity embodied in a proliferating division of labor. Derived in this manner, the I-You relationship — however constant, however important, however equalitarian — takes on a formalistic character. It is a relationship between colleagues or coworkers or comrades. It may be close, but one would be unlikely to think it intimate or informal or passionate. What Cox may miss in making his derivation, and what some of the movements of protest among the young may better reflect, is the integration of an urban and highly democratized society not merely through political contests and the marketplace but also through great complex organizations, each confronting persistent requirements for fresh adaptations, each highly formalized and rationalized, each requiring ever more skill from its participants, each increasingly dependent on the commitment and conscience of those participants if the organization is to have the high quality of service that it needs. Chief among these are the organizations with the central function of defining the whole society's purposes and interests and choices; these organizations include especially the society's basic political and legal structure, the religious bodies, and the institutions of higher education.

What these great organizations and institutions increasingly require is not the passive devotion but the initiatives and creative contributions of highly skilled participants. In this they become interestingly like "voluntary" organizations. To obtain the kind of service they need from educated men who have and prize integrity of judgment, they must involve their participants in making choices and by that means obtain from them self-dedication. The society at large, and each major organization and institution within it then become ever more thoroughly a moral community [39: chap 2, 4, 8].

Consider why this is so. The more creative initiative, involvement, and skill that an organization requires of people, the more it must depend upon their discretion and their personal dedication to organizational interests. That dedication will arise only if the organization respects its participants as persons and if it nurtures them not merely as employees or citizens but as independent men and women: nurtures their personal growth and personal powers in their own interest. In a democratized society these requirements are even greater because it is more likely that people must be persuaded of the desirability of a program before they will mobilize behind it.

All of these developments are recent, becoming clearly established only in the last twenty years.

All point in a similar direction: more and more of the citizens or labor force of a modern society or organization must be committed to the discovery and advancement of the long-range interests of that society or organization. They must think not merely of the present situation but of the future; of the character that the collectivity can and should have at some later time; of enduring and generalized interests, not merely of present exigencies. Personal loyalty and devotion will be effectively mobilized only in pursuit of a vision of that sort. This makes a citizenry or a labor force the active trustees of a society and of its institutions. The development of this ideology is already obvious in the professions and among managerial and political elites. I suggest that it is being spread by education and new social demands to larger and larger sectors of the population.

But this is not the whole story. The remainder has similarities to Cox' analysis, but it contains also crucial differences. The first point of difference is that he writes of the relations between men in an urban setting, and I write of relations between men and their society and its major institutions. The second is his stress on social diversity as against mine on the overarching normative organization of even the most complex societies. The third is his focus on shifting ad hoc social relations whereas I am here focusing on enduring bases of a society's unity. I will mention a further difference a bit later.

When societies and institutions depend upon their members in the manner I have described, their members gain an additional relationship to the whole. They might previously have served as the beneficiaries, agents, or servants of their social order, both empowered by the social order and subordinated to it; the effect of these new developments is to make members in one crucial aspect normative equals. The relationship is now analogous to that between two close friends — one of them perhaps far wealthier or more knowledgeable or stronger than the other — who are made equal by the depth of their dependence upon one another for whatever has brought them together. Each becomes responsible for evaluating the other's needs and interests and, with independent judgment, for determining and acting upon what will best advance those interests. In this situation friends are under the authority of their mutual commitment to enhance each other as persons; they are mutually under what we have seen to be the "authority of principle." We find in professional codes the fullest expression of a relation of responsibility and authority found similarly between an employer and the professional employees who, while serving him, are also importantly independent of him and equal to him. I am suggesting that the experience of having an important normative equality with one's society and its institutions, of equality under the authority of principle, is a rapidly growing experience in the most advanced societies.

What does this mean for theological formulations? Sociologists have repeatedly suggested, and, on occasion, have shown that conceptions of God and of relations with him reflect men's experiences of their society and of major institutions within it [21; 40; 11; 45]. The historic "world" religions are understood by sociologists to reflect, in their doctrines concerning God's universality and transcendence, the newly developed realms of universal meaning and commitment embodied in the great political empires in which those religions first appeared. I have recently published evidence that the Protestant Reformation — with its emphasis on God's transcendence and on the belief that his powers as a personality (his knowledge, judgment, and wisdom) were never immanent in any finite person or institution — arose in just those societies in which the ultimate "constitution" of the political order was organizationally separated from day-to-day actions [47].

Both in the historic world religions and in Reformation Protestantism, men were identified as God's creatures or dependents or servants or worshipers. The most dignified role allotted them was as God's images or as children in his household. But men were in all cases God's subordinates. What I propose is that new trends in the relation of men to their society and institutions, although in no way expunging the earlier roles, make another role the chief one, namely, the role of man as equally dependent with God in a common task. This sounds like Cox' conclusion,

825

except that, in coming to it from the social facts that I have just sketched, we see that the proper name of the common task is love [46:160–209]. And whereas Cox stresses the diversity of specialized tasks that God and man may jointly undertake and whereas Bellah writes of the rise of a multiplex social world, the formulation I now advance stresses the generalized, unified character of relations between men and God. (What Cox and Bellah have to tell us may well be right. I think it is. I also think that it is subordinate to the broader context I am now describing.)

When all is said, the ultimate nature of a society, as of any organization, resides in social interdependence. It resides in the fact that each participant requires that others relate to him as person if his existence as a person is to be sustained. The essential legitimation of any organization, a *society* included, is that it nurtures men as persons, as distinctive human beings, as living souls. It is, I think, just to the extent that advanced societies *require* from each member an increasing exercise of his personal powers on his society's behalf and to the extent that societies *depend* upon their participants' self-commitments, that people are both enabled and impelled to require proof that they will, in return, be nurtured as persons.

We need not avoid the proper words. Nurturing men as persons is loving, and the nurturance obtained is love itself. The most advanced societies seem especially to need the responsible love of their members and appear in return to be required to nurture their members as persons. To the extent that men's experience of God is suggested by their experience of society, these new social developments will require fresh theological formulations.

The sense of equality in loving interdependence with society or with God leads to the grounding of participants' actions on the ultimate interests of their fellows, hence to illimitable pressures that every social standard be examined for its ultimate legitimacy.

This entails assessments of all standards and requirements and policies. Some students have stenciled on their sweatshirts, "Why not, dammit?" Behind that question seems to be an effort, and a

826

responsibility, to make not just this society but all human association an object to be judged and shaped and accepted only on its intrinsic merits. At least some students have taken arms against the rationalized demands that an advanced society makes upon them. The cry of Paul Goodman for "people, not personnel" catches exactly what is involved. The hippies' understanding of a "love-in" is limited, but it may in advanced societies be prophetic of a thoroughgoing institutionalization of the standard that social relations must be judged on what they do to men and for men as human persons.

My suggestion amounts to this. The newest phases of social evolution enable and impel the clarification — in terms of a "corporate actor" — of the very core of the society's normative character, of the society's very "identity," if you will; and a man, as an individual person, relates to that "identity" of his society as to a collective person; and all participants in the society are equal by virtue of the depth of their dependence on others for nurture as persons.

I do not foresee that a new theology correctly reflecting such social experiences, any more than a theology reflecting what Cox finds salient, will mask God's power or transcendence or justice or his pervasive goodness or love. These are ineluctable facts and they constitute a basis of separation between God and man. Nor do I think that such a theology will obliterate the obvious fact that men pursue their own ends which may significantly diverge from God's. This fact is a basis for the emphasis on sin in traditional Christianity. What I do think is that a theology correctly formulating the new social experiences will put in a new context the facts of separation and sin. They will be subordinated to the overriding fact of loving interdependence between human persons and the divine. In that context there is still judgment. Even from those people with whom we are most lovingly intimate we expect and need evaluations of a searching objectivity. The greater our intimacy, the more knowing and penetrating we expect such evaluations to be. Perhaps more than Cox, I anticipate that a new theology will have to deal with the jealousy, failure, responsibility, condemnation, deviance, repentance, reconciliation, and forgiveness that are inherent in any loving relationship. But under love neither friend nor God, however stern, acts primarily as an overseer or a recorder of imperfections. Nor does one become primarily the dependent, agent, or servant of either friend or God, although we will probably depend upon, represent, and serve both. The God with whom men may relate primarily through loving interdependence has lost neither power nor transcendence. He is still the Lord of History and the Creator and Father and Governor, and his works are acts of grace. But the chief soteriological fact becomes, in this new situation, not his dissimilarities from men but his loving interdependence with them. He and his world are seeking each other and they require each other for their fulfillment as persons.

I began this discussion of modern secularization with some quotations from O'Dea, especially his descriptions of current movements of protest including student movements. It is obvious that I too sense that these movements have something to tell us about a new theology, if what they reveal comes only through the features of those movements that are homologous with emerging theological discourse. Perhaps what O'Dea has stressed concerning those movements is more accurate than the meanings I have drawn from them. That remains to be determined. It also remains to be known whether the vigorous involvement in these movements of both Jewish and Christian students presages some growing affinities in the experiences both will have of social things.

My final comments concern the organized religious communities: the sects and denominations, the churches and the temples. In Bellah's words, these communities no longer, under secularization, perform as "the exclusive or perhaps even the primary interpreters of man's relation to the ultimate conditions of his existence" [11]. The clearly secular institutions now share significantly in that process, and they do so of right and under God. A maturing secularization should mean that each institution infuses the others, secular organizations being responsible not only for their special works but also for identifying their roles in a sacred order. This is a way of restating Philip Selznick's point that, to survive and function in modern society, secular organizations must become institutional. But the concomitant is that religious organizations may come to be more secular, to identify their structure and operations as but one of the necessary, specialized sectors of the division of labor, each sector having a different but equally legitimate role — a problem now confronting the Soviet state and mirrored in efforts there to define separate and limited spheres of legitimate activity for the secular "church" (the Communist party) and for the Soviet Government.

Among the first things that children are taught is that God is love. They learn only later, if at all, how arduous are the demands of a career in love. If there is merit to the sketch I have given of a new theological situation, then the religious bodies and their officers will have soon to confront the meaning for them of assisting men in this newly arduous career. Research has shown how inadequately the old conceptions express the role of the clergy: preacher, priest, parson, evangelist, missionary, cleric, pastor. Conceptions of the laity are even less adequate. One senses that, as Protestantism made every man equally a priest, the emerging society makes every man a minister. But even that label is too limited. The demand upon men from one another and from society will be that they do more than care for one another or provide support or oversight or service or aid. It will increasingly, I think, be that every man nurture the other as a person and that all derive their powers not primarily as Men of God or as Men for God but as men having, together, a community with God. If this is so, it will mean that men within the urban nexus must find new ways of coming together as persons even when not intimates — as I and thee — and must find their unity not simply in bonds of neighborhood or kinship or citizenship, but also as members of a community of living souls, human and Divine.

What, within that community, might be the role of specialized religious communities? Under secularization it is improbable that it will consist of sacramental functions, of being God to man. It is more probable that religious communities must serve

829

to remind all men and all organizations of their mutual incompleteness, to nurture mechanisms and an environment in which differences among them can be reconciled if not removed, to witness by their own faithfulness and inner life to the powers possessed by an embodied community, by objective justice, and by incarnate charity: the powers to nurture, to elevate, to revive, to renew.

REFERENCES

1. Alford, Robert R: *Party and Society* (Rand McNally & Co, Chicago, Illinois) 1965.
2. Allport, Gordon W; Gillespie, J M; and Young, J: The Religion of the Post-War College Student, *The Journal of Psychology*, vol 25, Jan 1948, pp 3–35.
3. American Institute of Public Opinion, 1952, 1966 surveys, reported in *The Detroit News*, vol 267, May 15, 1966, p 18-A.
4. American Institute of Public Opinion, *see also* Erskine, Hazel, particularly reference 24.
5. American Institute of Public Opinion (AIPO): News Service Release, Apr 4, 1953.
6. Bauer, Raymond A; Inkeles, Alex; and Kluckhohn, Clyde: *How the Soviet System Works: Cultural, Psychological, and Social Themes* (Harvard University Press, Cambridge, Massachusetts) 1959. Points to a sharp decline in theism.
7. Beauvoir, Simone de: *The Ethics of Ambiguity*, Bernard Frechtman, translator (Philosophical Library, Inc, New York, New York) 1948.
8. Becker, Howard: *Ionia and Athens*, unpublished doctoral dissertation (Department of Sociology, The University of Chicago, Chicago, Illinois) 1930.
9. Becker, Howard: *German Youth, Bond or Free* (K Paul, Trench Trubner, London, England) 1946.
10. Becker, Howard, and Wiese, Leopold von: *Systematic Sociology* (John Wiley & Sons, Inc, New York, New York) 1932.

11. Bellah, Robert N: Religious Evolution, *American-Sociological Review*, vol 29, June 1965, pp 366, 371.

12. Bender, Irving E: Changes in Religious Interest: A Retest after 15 Years, *Journal of Abnormal and Social Psychology*, vol 57, July 1948, pp 41–46.

13. Cantril, Hadley, ed: *Public Opinion, 1935–1946* (Princeton University Press, Princeton, New Jersey) 1951.

14. Charlton, Donald G: *Secular Religions in France, 1815–1870* (Oxford University Press, London, England) 1963.

15. Cox, Harvey: *The Secular City, Secularization and Urbanization in Theological Perspective* (The Macmillan Company, New York, New York) 1965.

16. *Dagens Nyketer* (Stockholm, Sweden), August 11, 1957. The survey was sponsored by and published in this newspaper. I am indebted to Dr. Börge Hansen of the University of Stockholm for a translation of the report.

17. Detroit Area Study, Code-Book Tabulations (Department of Sociology, The University of Michigan, Ann Arbor, Michigan).

18. Detroit Area Study (Department of Sociology, The University of Michigan, Ann Arbor, Michigan) tabulation for deck 11, column 9.

19. Detroit Area Study (Department of Sociology, The University of Michigan, Ann Arbor, Michigan) tabulation for card 9, columns 14, 15.

20. Durkheim, Emile: *The Division of Labor in Society*, George Simpson, translator (The Free Press, formerly of Glencoe, Illinois, now of New York, New York) 1947.

21. Durkheim, Emile: *The Elementary Forms of the Religious Life, a Study in Religious Sociology*, Joseph W Swain, translator (George Allen and Unwin, Ltd, London, England) no date.

22. Erskine, Hazel G: The Polls: Textbook Knowledge, *The Public Opinion Quarterly*, vol 27, Spring 1963, pp 133–141.

23. Erskine, Hazel G: The Polls: Church Attendance, *The Public Opinion Quarterly*, vol 28, Winter 1964, pp 671–679.

24. Erskine, Hazel G: report on American Institute of Public

Opinion (AIPO) surveys (1944, 1948, 1954) in The Polls: Personal Religion, *The Public Opinion Quarterly*, vol 29, Spring 1965, pp 145–157.

25. Erskine, Hazel G: The Polls: Organized Religion, *The Public Opinion Quarterly*, vol 29, Summer 1965, pp 326–337.

26. Gilliland, A R: Changes in Religious Beliefs of College Students, *Journal of Social Psychology*, vol 37, Feb 1953, pp 113–116.

27. Hart, Hornell: *Ladies Home Journal* 1941 survey reported in Religion, *American Journal of Sociology*, vol 47, May 1942, pp 888–897.

28. Johnson, Paul E: *Psychology of Religion* (Abingdon Press, Nashville, Tennessee) 1959.

29. Katz, Daniel, and Allport, Floyd H: *Student's Attitudes* (The Craftsman Press, Syracuse, New York) 1931.

30. *Ladies Home Journal* 1948 survey, reported in *Time Magazine*, vol 52, Nov 1, 1948, pp 64–65.

31. *Ladies Home Journal* 1941 survey, *see* reference 27.

32. Lane, Robert E: *Political Life, Why and How People Get Involved in Politics* (The Free Press, New York, New York) 1959.

33. Leuba, James H: *The Belief in God and Immortality* (Open Court Publishing Co, LaSalle, Illinois) 1921

34. Leuba, James H: Religious Beliefs of American Scientists, *Harper's Magazine*, vol 169, Aug 1934, pp 291–300.

35. Lippmann, Walter: *A Preface to Morals* (The Macmillan Company, New York, New York) 1929.

36. Lipset, Seymour: *Political Man, The Social Bases of Politics* (Doubleday & Company, Inc, Garden City, New York) 1960, notes on France.

37. Lipset, Seymour M: *The First New Nation, The United States in Historical and Comparative Perspective* (Basic Books, Inc, Publishers, New York, New York) 1963.

38. Lipset, Seymour M: The Value Patterns of Democracy: A Case Study in Comparative Analysis, *American Sociological Review*, vol 28, Aug 1963, pp 515–531.

39. Miller, Daniel R, and Swanson, Guy E: *The Changing*

American Parent (John Wiley & Sons, Inc, New York, New York) 1958.

40. Parsons, Talcott: *Societies: Comparative and Evolutionary Perspectives* (Prentice-Hall, Inc, Englewood Cliffs, New Jersey) 1966.

41. Patrick, Denzil G M: *Pascal and Kierkegaard, A Study in the Strategy of Evangelism*, 2 vol (Lutterworth Press, London, England) 1947.

42. Rettig, Salmon, and Pasamanick, Benjamin: Changes in Moral Values among College Students: A Factorial Study, *American Sociological Review*, vol 24, Dec 1959, pp 856–863.

43. Ross, Murray G: *Religious Beliefs of Youth* (Association Press, New York, New York) 1950.

44. Simmel, Georg: *The Sociology of Georg Simmel*, Kurt Wolff, translator (The Free Press, formerly of Glencoe, Illinois, now of New York, New York) 1950.

45. Swanson, Guy E: *The Birth of the Gods, The Origin of Primitive Beliefs* (The University of Michigan Press, Ann Arbor, Michigan) 1960.

46. Swanson, Guy E: The Routinization of Love, Structure and Process in Primary Relations, in Klausner, Samuel Z, ed, *The Quest for Self Control, Classical Philosophies and Scientific Research* (The Free Press, New York, New York) 1965.

47. Swanson, Guy E: *Religion and Regime, A Sociological Account of the Reformation* (The University of Michigan Press, Ann Arbor, Michigan) 1967.

48. Til, Henry R Van: *The Calvinistic Concept of Culture*. See reference 50.

49. Tucker, Robert C: Religious Revival in Russia? in Inkeles, Alex, and Geiger, Kent, ed, *Soviet Society, A Book of Readings* (Houghton Mifflin Company, Boston, Massachusetts) 1961. Points to a recrudescence of belief.

50. Van Til, Henry R: The Calvinistic Concept of Culture (Baker Book House, Grand Rapids, Michigan) 1959.

51. Vetter, G B, and Green, M: Personality and Group Factors

in the Making of Atheists, *Journal of Abnormal Social Psychology*, vol 27, July–Sept 1932, pp. 179–194.

52. Weber, Max: *The Sociology of Religion*, Ephraim Fischoff, translator (Beacon Press, Boston, Massachusetts) 1961.

53. Weber, Max: monographic studies on India, China, and Israel.

22. AMERICA'S INSTITUTIONS OF FAITH

by Edwin S. Gaustad

For many, to speak of *institutions* of faith is to speak of faith fossilized, frozen, hopelessly irrelevant. When talking about religion in America it is less embarrassing to pretend that this vague entity has little if anything to do with "Baptists" or "Lutherans" or "Catholics" or "Elijah Muhammed." Organized religion is what one apologizes for, not what one writes essays on.

Yet it is the institutions of faith in America which possess the traditions, resources, and personnel that ultimately make religion in America worth talking about at all. Understandably, many writers are loath to enter the denominational morass for fear of never finding their way out. Or they succumb to a more modern kind of fear that "equal time" will not be given. They read or remember that there are about 250 denominations in America, and clearly there's no time for equal attention to each – so they pass on. But pluralism need not mean pandemonium.

Pluralism is, of course, no new fact of American life, however much the cliché character of the word today would otherwise suggest. The seventeenth century provided variety enough: Huguenots in Charleston, Anglicans in Tidewater Virginia, Catholics in St. Mary's City, Swedish Lutherans along the Delaware River, Quakers and Presbyterians farther up the River, Dutch Reformed in Manhattan, Puritans in New England, Baptists, and Heaven-knows-what-else in Rhode Island. Current wide eyed comment about pluralism must therefore imply something more than mere variety.

Two additional implications, at least, are normally present. First, pluralism is more than a word for Protestantism's wondrous penchant for a seemingly endless spawning of new divisions. Despite Lord Baltimore's early colonizing adventures,

Protestantism pervaded the British colonies of North America from 1607 until well into the nineteenth century; and, notwithstanding its remarkable diversity, a working harmony was often achieved, especially in the decades of the early national period. From at least 1850 on, however, Protestantism faced — and generally feared — the swelling ranks of Catholics and Jews. Then, rather than calm discourse about pluralism, one heard strident cries about anarchy, popery, and shattered destiny. So pluralism today is a broad term including not only the varieties of Protestantism but also of Judaism and Catholicism, and indeed of secularism as well.

Secondly, the term pluralism today carries no pejorative tone, perhaps not even a neutral tone. Use of the word generally implies that this postprotestant or even postreligious era is not to be deplored and feared but embraced and preserved. Pluralism is good, variety is nice, diversity is our chief national asset. Though value judgments have all but disappeared from academic prose, it is still considered legitimate to extol the virtues of pluralism and the glories of diversity.

Even in America, nevertheless, pluralism has its limits. The institutions of religion are not scattered in hundreds of meaningless fragments. While the ecclesiastical patterns may bear some resemblance to a crazy quilt, the design is not totally devoid of meaning; moreover, some of the colors are beginning to run. Ten denominational families or traditions of Christendom account for 90% of all religious group membership in America. If the Jewish population is added, we account for 94% of the total number with religious affiliation (see Table 1). Already pluralism begins to be more manageable.

The ten major traditions are these: Roman Catholic, 46¼ millions; Baptist, 23½ millions; Methodist, 14¼ millions; Lutheran, 8¾ millions; Presbyterian, 4½ millions; Christian, 4¼ millions; Episcopal, 3½ millions; Eastern Orthodoxy, 3¼ millions; Latter Day Saints, 2 millions; and the United Church of Christ, 2 millions. The Jews belong in this list too, but, since membership figures present special problems, it is necessary to speak of Jewish population rather than Jewish religious affilia-

TABLE 1

MAJOR DENOMINATIONAL FAMILIES IN AMERICA

Family	Membership 1965	%, National population
1. Roman Catholic	46,246,000	23.8
2. Baptist	23,631,000	12.2
3. Methodist	14,280,000	7.4
4. Lutheran	8,793,000	4.5
5. Presbyterian	4,418,000	2.3
6. Christian	4,268,000	2.2
7. Episcopal	3,411,000	1.8
8. Eastern Orthodox	3,160,000	1.6
9. United Church	2,070,000	1.1
10. Latter Day Saints	1,969,000	1.0
Total	112,246,000	57.9
11. Jewish population	5,600,000	2.9
Total	117,846,000	60.8

Inclusive religious group membership, all groups in the United States, in 1965 was 124,682,000. The ten listed, together with the Jewish population, constitute 94% of all those having any religious affiliation. The source of these data is Jacquet [9], who presents them in another form.

tion. These 11 groups, then, encompass all but about 6% of institutional religious membership in America. In view of their magnitude, a word about each group is appropriate.

Since 1850, the Roman Catholic Church has been the largest institution of faith in America. Membership figures can be endlessly (and fruitlessly) debated. It should be noted only that Catholic parishes follow a broadly inclusive principle in reporting membership. (Orthodox synagogues, for example, report only adult males and Baptist churches only "believing," i.e., adult members.) But that the Roman Catholic Church is America's leading denomination cannot be doubted.

In addition to having an impressive total membership, Roman Catholics have the largest parochial school system in America: over 5 million pupils in elementary and secondary schools. More than 300 colleges and universities in the United States receive major support from this Church. Monastic establishments, less obvious on the American than on the European scene, are nevertheless a significant institution. There are more than 180,000 Catholic nuns in the nation — rather bewilderingly separated into about 500 orders. More than one third of the Catholic priests in America are also members of a religious order [11].

The Catholic family is about twice the size of the largest Protestant group, the Baptists. Yet the number of Baptist churches is about four times that of the Catholic churches. Why? First, one must recall the differences in membership accounting noted above. But, secondly, the nature and function of the local churches in the two traditions vary greatly. The Catholic edifice tends to serve hundreds many times per week; the Baptist structure often serves only a few dozen for an hour or two per week. In Catholic terms, many a Baptist church would be a mission or a chapel or, in Spanish days, an *asistencia*. Though Baptist membership data can also be endlessly debated, there can be no doubt that, in America, the Baptist family is Protestantism's largest. The Baptist "family," to be sure, includes some 29 groups, but four fifths of the total membership is in only 4 groups: the Southern Baptist Convention (10¾ millions), the National Baptist Convention, USA, Inc (5½ millions), the National Baptist Convention of America (2¾ millions), and the American Baptist Convention (1½ millions).

The member of the Baptist family chiefly responsible for the notable family size is white: the Southern Baptist Convention. Established in Georgia in 1845, this group, particularly in the twentieth century, has enjoyed phenomenal growth. Almost one half of all Baptists in America belong to this Convention. Still predominantly "southern" in outlook and geographic scope, the Convention has expanded beyond the boundaries of region and nation; its current growth rate (1.7%) is now only slightly higher than the growth rate of the national population (1.3%).

The size of the total Baptist family is due in part to the strong attraction that the Baptist tradition has had for the American Negro. Ironically, that denominational family which is most integrated in the whole (at least one third of the 23½ million Baptists are Negroes) is rarely integrated within its several divisions. The last Federal Census of religion (1936) showed that 67% of all Negro church members were Baptist. While mobility, disillusionment, the Black Muslims, and a growing secularity may have altered this percentage, Negro Baptist churches and Negro Baptist leaders — for example, Martin Luther King and Adam Clayton Powell — still occupy prominent positions in the contemporary scene.

Thanks to a 1939 merger, much of the Methodist family, a more closely united family than the Baptists, is organized under a single umbrella. "The Methodist Church" accounts for more than 10 million of the 14¼ million Methodist total, with 3 large Negro bodies contributing almost 3 millions more. A merger with the Evangelical United Brethren Church, now under way, will bring another ¾ million members into the family. (Only a predominantly German ethnic background has kept EUB from being within the Methodist household long before now.) After that merger, Methodism will still not be the largest Protestant body. It is, however, by far the largest group participating in the significant discussions relating to a new American church: the Consultation on Church Union (see Table 2 below). The Methodist Church is divided into five geographical regions or jurisdictions. It also has, by way of national organization, a "Central Jurisdiction" which is racial, not geographical, in its rationale; regarding it, quarrel has been continuous. As embarrassment over this 1939 compromise mounts, many Methodists consider this issue to have priority over all others related to organizational structure. Thus, in 1967, merger negotiations with the Evangelical United Brethren came close to being scuttled by the internal tension concerning the Central Jurisdiction.

Before proceeding with the denominational families, it is appropriate at this point to comment on the religious affiliation of the Negro — appropriate because that affiliation is concentrated in the three denominational families discussed above.

About two thirds of all Negro church members are Baptists, the vast majority of this number being found in one of two Conventions: the National Baptist Convention of America (approximately 2¾ million members) or the National Baptist Convention, USA, Inc (approximately 5½ million members).

There are 3 million Negro Methodists, divided among four major groups: African Methodist Episcopal (about 1¼ millions), African Methodist Episcopal Zion (over 1 million), Christian Methodist Episcopal (about ½ million), and the controversial "Central Jurisdiction" of The Methodist Church (over ⅓ million).

Baptists and Methodists together account for four fifths of the total Negro church membership. Roman Catholicism, having made great gains among American Negroes since World War II, is the only other denomination with a sizable Negro membership: about ¾ million. All other groups, including small Pentecostal sects, the Black Muslims, and predominantly "white" ecclesiastical bodies, probably would not exceed one million in total Negro membership (Figure 1). C. Eric Lincoln [1] estimated the membership of the Black Muslims as "more than 100,000" in 1960. But the vigor of that membership, which is mainly young and male, gives an impression of even greater size. The Protestant Episcopal Church has about 80,000 Negro members out of a total membership of about 3½ millions while the Congregationalists, or United Church, include about 40,000 Negro members in a membership of 2 millions [12].

America's nearly 9 million Lutherans have most dramatically reversed the rules of that all-American game of divide and disappear. From 24 separate organizations at the beginning of the present century, Lutheranism has reduced its diversity to 3 major entities: the American Lutheran Church (over 2½ millions), the Lutheran Church in America (over 3 millions), and the Lutheran Church, Missouri Synod (almost 2¾ millions). With one exception the other Lutheran bodies are quite small; the exception is the rigorously conservative Wisconsin Evangelical Lutheran Synod which in 1964 reported a membership of 358,000. Having conquered divisions due largely to varied ethnic origins and immigration patterns, Lutheranism stands ready to make a more powerful impact on American culture.

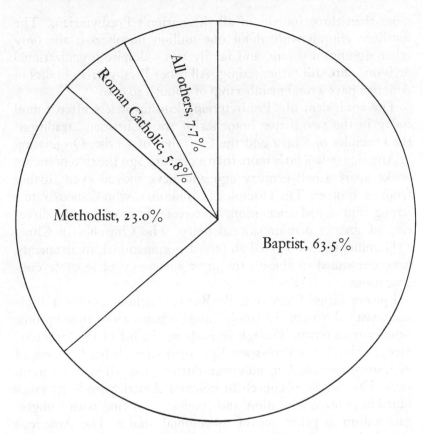

FIGURE 1. Negro church membership in America, 1965 [12 and 9].

Negro Baptists	7⅓ millions
Negro Methodists	2¾ millions
Negro Roman Catholics	¾ million
All others (estimated)	1 million

Presbyterians, like the Baptists and unlike the Methodists, remain divided, north and south, along lines that hardened just before the Civil War. Unlike the Baptists, however, the northern branch of Presbyterianism (USA) is far larger than the southern (US) branch is. Furthermore, in 1958, northern Presbyterians did consummate a merger with a small Scottish communion to form the United Presbyterian Church, USA, a body now comprising more than three fourths of all the nation's Presbyterians. The southern church with about one million members is the only other significant group, and family ties — despite organizational division — are still rather strong. All other Presbyterian bodies in America have a total membership of about 150,000.

The equivalent of "Presbyterian" kinship is less often found today in the two major branches of the "Christian" tradition: the Disciples of Christ and the Churches of Christ. Originating in America only a little more than a century ago the two branches broke apart a half-century ago and have moved even further from each other. The Disciples (2 millions), who demonstrate a strong ecumenical orientation, have recently moved in the direction of greater denominational unity. The Churches of Christ (2 ¼ millions), who avoid all interdenominational involvements, have continued to cherish the utter autonomy of separate congregations.

Episcopalians in America, like Roman Catholics, enjoy a single ecclesiastical structure; "family" and "organization" then become synonymous terms. Though seventh on the list of the "top ten" (see Table 1), the Protestant Episcopal Church has for most of its history exercised an influence out of proportion to its numbers. The Anglican church in colonial America made its voice heard in politics, education, and economy — vying with Congregationalism as prime mover in colonial affairs. The American Revolution temporarily tumbled Anglicans from their eminence, but by the middle of the nineteenth century the climb back to prominence had been made. Unlike most other groups cited in Table 1, the Episcopal Church does not numerically dominate any given area of the country; rather, its presence is felt via wealth and prestige in every region.

Eastern Orthodoxy has been beset, as has Lutheranism, by ethnic diversity and organizational division. Unlike Lutheranism, Orthodoxy has not yet reversed this proliferation. Still too new to a disestablished environment, still too attached to Old World politics, the Eastern churches confront an Americanization process already completed in most other ecclesiastical bodies. The Greek Archdiocese of North and South America (1 ¾ millions) is the largest unit within this family, but Russian, Syrian, Romanian, Bulgarian, Ukrainian, and Carpatho-Russian groups also have sizable memberships. Symbolic actions such as participation in Presidential inaugurations notwithstanding, Orthodoxy stands largely aloof from the political and cultural life of the nation — though its rich colors add brilliance to the crazy quilt pattern of American religion.

The United Church of Christ is the modern form in which traditional Congregationalism now appears. A colonial giant, Congregationalism was badly outdistanced in the nineteenth century by such front runners as the Baptists and the Methodists. In the present century, Congregationalists began to recoup their relative numerical losses by setting out on a deliberate ecumenical path. In 1931 Congregationalists merged with the "General Convention of the Christian Church" and in 1957 with the Evangelical and Reformed Church. In the decade since that last merger, the United Church — as its title hints — has actively sought and promoted church union of far broader compass than any yet attained.

The tenth largest family in Table 1, like the sixth largest, is a product of America's own religious fecundity. The Church of Jesus Christ of Latter Day Saints, though originating in the East (New York), is today primarily a phenomenon of the West. In the "Utah Church" (1 ¾ millions), as the principal member of the family is sometimes called, the geographical particularity that prevails is unrivalled by that of any other religious group in America.

Utah and contiguous counties of Nevada, Idaho, and Wyoming are indisputably "Mormon territory," often to the extent that entire counties are devoid of any other church or sect. Such regionalism may be compared with — but not equalled by — the Baptist concentration in the Southeast, the Lutheran majorities in the Midwest, the Catholic dominance in the Northeast and the Southwest [8]. There are only two major Mormon groups, the "Utah Church" having nine tenths of the total membership. The Reorganized Church of Jesus Christ of Latter Day Saints has fewer than 170,000 members, and three other tiny Mormon schisms account for a total of about 5,000 members.

Judaism, finally, constitutes one of the nation's major religious families, though the "family" designation is even more complex to define here. Not only do denominational differences exist (Orthodox, Conservative, Reform), but differences as well between Jews identified on religious grounds and Jews identified on other grounds. Statistical data are generally given in terms of Jewish population (note Table 1), not Jewish synagogue membership. The population figure is clearly too large for Judaism, but a membership figure of adult males (e.g., 205,000 Orthodox Jews in 1964) is just as obviously too small. The academic mind is happy to conclude that the truth "is somewhere in the middle"; greater precision is elusive.

The relative strengths of Orthodox, Conservative, and Reform sentiment in America may be partially gauged by consulting a three-city study reported by Alvin Chenkin [7:23]. One half to two thirds of those interrogated expressed a preference for Conservative Judaism over the two competing "denominations." In Camden, New Jersey (1964), the indications of preference were: 8% Orthodox, 66% Conservative, 22% Reform. In Detroit, Michigan (1963), this was the response: 17% Orthodox, 49% Conservative, and 26% Reform. In Providence, Rhode Island (1963), it was 16% Orthodox, 56% Conservative, and 24% Reform [7:145].

Judaism, like Mormonism, has a geographical concentration. In general it is urban; in particular it is in the Northeast. One half of the nation's Jews reside in five counties of New York and eight of New Jersey. One third of the American Jewish population lives in New York City alone. After New York (14.06%) and New Jersey (5.27%), the states with the greatest percentage of Jewish citizens are these: Massachusetts 4.54%, Maryland 4.22%, Pennsylvania 3.87%, Connecticut 3.68%, California 3.48%, Illinois 2.85%, Rhode Island 2.69%, and Florida 2.27%.

America's religious patterns can be understood largely in terms of these eleven families, all standing within the Judeo-Christian tradition (Figure 2). Buddhism (especially Zen), Hinduism (especially Vedanta), and Islam are present but are statistically insignificant — as are the cults that draw on or pervert these traditions. The Black Muslim movement may constitute an exception to the above, but its relationship to worldwide Islam is tenuous at best. It stands more as a rejection of Christianity as the white Man's religion than as an embrace of the "five pillars" of Islam.

Even the eleven major families may, a decade hence, be reduced in number. The most dramatic reduction on the horizon would result from discussions related to the Consultation on Church Union. Stemming from a suggestion offered in 1960 by Eugene Carson Blake (then Stated Clerk of the United Presbyterian Church, USA, now president of the World Council of

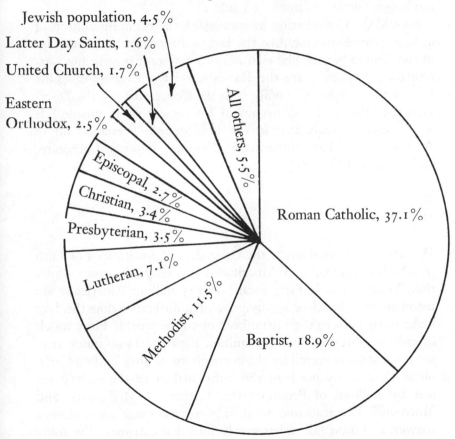

Jewish population, 4.5%

Latter Day Saints, 1.6%

United Church, 1.7%

Eastern Orthodox, 2.5%

Episcopal, 2.7%

Christian, 3.4%

Presbyterian, 3.5%

Lutheran, 7.1%

Methodist, 11.5%

All others, 5.5%

Roman Catholic, 37.1%

Baptist, 18.9%

FIGURE 2. Major denominational families in 1965. Total inclusive church membership (in 1965), 124,682,000 [9:198–210].

Churches), the Consultation has moved deliberately and perceptively ahead in its effort to create a church "truly catholic, truly evangelical, and truly reformed." With the publication of *Principles of Church Union* in 1966, the cooperating denominations attracted others to active participation. An annual *Digest* of the proceedings of the Consultation on Church Union [3] provides the best means for staying abreast of this rapidly changing movement. Basic reports and principles are published also [4, 5]. By the middle of 1967 the number of full participants had grown to ten denominations, including all or part of five of the ten largest Christian families (Table 2).

Should the Consultation be successful, the resulting church of at least 25 millions would be the largest Protestant denomination in the United States. The two major Protestant groups not participating at present are the Baptists and the Lutherans. (One half of the "Christian" family is in the Consultation — the Disciples; the other half — Churches of Christ — remains outside.) It is conceivable, then, that in the next decade Protestantism in America would have three major divisions: Baptists, Lutherans, and a "United Church."

THE MEANING OF THE DATA

We have been considering the basic data of institutions of faith to which belong 94% of Americans with religious group affiliation. What do these facts mean? If 125 million Americans are members of a church or synagogue, what difference does this fact make to them or to their neighbors or to the world? How much of culture is molded by 23½ million Baptists? How much personal behavior is altered by the convictions of 46¼ million Catholics? How many needs of the individual or of the society are met by millions of Presbyterians, Lutherans, Methodists, and Mormons? The academic mind likes to raise questions it cannot answer, and these fall rather neatly into that category. Yet some meaningfulness in the fact of membership can be suggested here.

The 125 million church members (64% of the total popula-

TABLE 2
PRINCIPAL MERGERS, 1939–1967

Constituent bodies	Resulting body	Date
Methodist Episcopal Church Methodist Episcopal Church, South Methodist Protestant Church	The Methodist Church	1939
Congregational Christian Churches Evangelical and Reformed Church	United Church of Christ	1957
Presbyterian Church, U.S.A. United Presbyterian Church of North America	United Presbyterian Church in the U.S.A.	1958
American Lutheran Church Evangelical Lutheran Church United Evangelical Lutheran Church	The American Lutheran Church	1960
United Lutheran Church Augustana Lutheran Church Finnish Evangelical, Suomi Synod American Evangelical Church	The Lutheran Church in America	1962

CONSULTATION ON CHURCH UNION, 1962–

United Presbyterian Church in the U.S.A. Presbyterian Church in the U.S. Episcopal Church United Church of Christ Christian Churches (Disciples of Christ) Methodist Church African Methodist Episcopal Church African Methodist Episcopal Zion Church Christian Methodist Episcopal Church Evangelical United Brethren	No name yet chosen	No date yet named

tion) may be that and nothing more: mere names on a roster. It is hardly surprising that much membership is nominal, whether the subject of discussion be church, club, or political party. What may be surprising is that even more than 64% of adult Americans identify themselves as attached in some way — if only by sentiment or preference — with a particular denominational tradition. Remarkably, more than 96% somehow, in some degree, relate themselves to the major religious traditions of Judaism or Christianity.

To some, it is equally remarkable that church membership in America has steadily increased, not declined, over the course of the last one hundred years — and even longer (Figure 3).

The United States Census Bureau [1] in 1957 asked a desig-

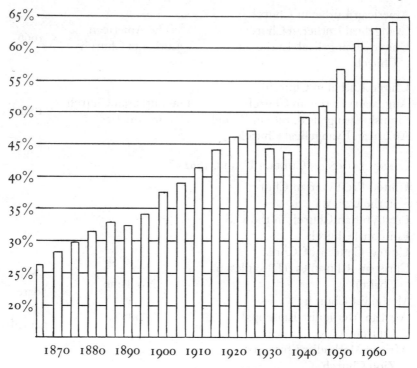

FIGURE 3. Percentage of national population with religious affiliation 1865 to 1965 — E. S. Gaustad, *Historical Atlas of Religion in America* (New York, New York) 1962, pp 110 – 111 and elsewhere.

848

nated sample of the nation's population (over 14 years of age), "What is your religion?" Responses, of course, do not imply membership or attendance, but they do imply at least a self-identification with some specific religious tradition. The sample included 638 counties and independent cities; responses were obtained from about 35,000 households. (See Table 3.)

TABLE 3

RELIGIOUS PREFERENCES IN AMERICA, 1957
Civilian population, 14 years old and over

Family	Number identifying themselves	%, Adult population
1. Roman Catholic	30,669,000	25.7
2. Baptist	23,525,000	19.7
3. Methodist	16,676,000	14.0
4. Lutheran	8,417,000	7.1
5. Presbyterian	6,656,000	5.8
6. "Other Protestant"	23,678,000	19.8
7. Jewish	3,868,000	3.2
8. "Other religion" (includes Eastern Orthodoxy)	1,545,000	1.3
9. No religion	3,195,000	2.7
10. Religion not reported	1,104,000	0.9
Total population, 14 years and over	119,333,000	100.0

A sizable degree of religious involvement is in part measurable. For example, church attendance is the pattern for nearly one half of the nation in any "typical" week. (In 1955 and 1958, the percentage was as high as 49%.) According to Gallup polls, average attendance in church or synagogue has in the past generation never fallen below one third of the total population of the country. Catholics are the best churchgoers at 68%, Protestants a poor second at 38%, and Jews poorest with 22%. Among major Protestant groups, Lutherans have the highest rate of attendance (43%), Episcopalians the lowest (31%). The higher the level of education, the greater the likelihood of church attendance.

849

And the secular city may not really be so secular, for the greatest level of church attendance is in the urban centers of one-half million or more inhabitants. Fewer citizens attend church in the West than in any other region of the nation, but even western America's record of attendance (33%) looks excellent when compared with the Anglicans of England (7%) or the Lutherans of Sweden (3%).

The voluntary principle has often been cited as the defining feature of American religion. Nowhere is that principle more severely tested than in the matter of financial support — and regularly the test is passed. In 1966 the principal Protestant groups collectively contributed about 3 billion dollars to local and other benevolent causes. (The highest per capita giving was by the Free Methodist Church of North America — $358 per member — as compared, for example, with that of the Methodist Church — $59 per member.) Another billion was expended for the construction of religious buildings in 1966. Jewish philanthropy flows through a myriad of federations, services, and appeals, an estimated 2 ½ billion dollars having been raised by this minority group in the quarter-century from 1940 to 1965. The contributions of America's Catholics have been such as not only to support their churches, schools, seminaries, and hospitals at home but to provide also, in the 1960s, approximately one half of Catholicism's total missionary budget around the world.

To be sure, commitment, relevance, and involvement cannot be established alone by data on church preferences, church attendance, and church support. Such evidence can only warn against accepting easy generalizations regarding "nominal" religion; the burden of proof begins to shift, and the defining of terms begins to be more refined.

The major question remains: what of the churches' influence in American society, what of their cultural leadership, what of their social pecking order? Again, much rests on subjective guesses and casual hunches. A folk humor, sometimes translated into humorless propositions, avers that as one moves up the economic scale, one automatically shifts religious affiliation from Baptist to Presbyterian to Episcopalian to Unitarian. The joke and the proposition require changed names from one part of the

850

country to another, from one period of time to another. Social status does vary according to time and place. In one region the power structure is Baptist; in another, Dutch Reformed; in another, Roman Catholic. In one era the intellectual leadership is Unitarian; in another, Presbyterian; in another, Jewish. The economic stratum served by the Salvation Army in one town may in another be served by Episcopalians. Pecking orders there may be, but the names and numbers constantly change: only the name of the game remains the same. Herbert W. Schneider has studied religion and the class structure [13]. Though the data he used are now twenty years old, they do reveal in the immediate postwar period relationships between religious affiliation, on the one hand, and economic class, education, political preference, and union membership on the other hand. Regarding economic status, Roman Catholics and Baptists manifest a similar distribution; each group has about two thirds of its membership in the lower economic stratum. However, "The Presbyterian, Episcopal, Jewish, Congregational, Christian Science, and Reformed groups exceed their 'upper-class' quotas" [13:264].

TABLE 4

POLITICAL LEADERSHIP IN AMERICA, 1967, BY DENOMINATIONAL FAMILY

Senate	*House*	*Governorships*
1. Methodist 24%	1. Roman Catholic 22%	1. Methodist 20%
2. Episcopal 15%	2. Presbyterian 17%	2. Roman Catholic 18%
3. Roman Catholic 13%	3. Methodist 16%	3. Episcopal 16%
4. Presbyterian 12%	4. Episcopal 12%	4. Baptist 12%
5. Baptist 12%	5. Baptist 10%	5. Presbyterian 10%
6. United Church 6%	6. United Church 5%	6. United Church 10%
7. LDS (Mormon) 4%	7. Jewish 4%	7. Lutheran 6%
8. Lutheran 3%	8. Christian 3%	8. Christian 4%
9. Unitarian-Universalist 3%	9. Lutheran 2%	9. LDS (Mormon) 4%
10. Jewish 2%	10. LDS (Mormon) 1%	10. ————
(all others 6%)	(all others 9%)	(no others)

851

One measure of cultural impact may be essayed in the political realm. Examining the religious affiliation of the members of the Ninetieth Congress and the current governors suggests some degree of cultural contribution on the part of the several denominations. Of course, there is an element of religion in America which regards increased cultural involvement as a sign of decreased spiritual integrity. But, without passing judgment on that thorny issue, it is still possible to measure the degree of political leadership provided by or offered to the major religious traditions. Table 4 is based on a poll conducted by the staff of *Christianity Today*, a fortnightly journal. For identification on the religious affiliation of individual congressmen, consult the journal [2].

Looking first at the United States Senate in 1967, one quickly notes that one fourth of the Senate is Methodist. Since Methodism represents only 6% of the national population, this denomination's political involvement is clear. Similarly, Episcopalians account for 15% of the Senate's membership but for only 2% of the national population. Similar disproportion prevails for the Presbyterians (12% of the Senate), for the United Church (4%), and for the Mormons (4%), all of whom have percentages of representation four times as great as their population ratio would warrant. The prize in this regard is held by the Unitarians who, though less than one tenth of 1% of the population, account for 3% of the Senate membership. Baptist and Jewish representation in the Senate (12% and 2%, respectively) is about equal to their population ratio. But Roman Catholics (13%) and Lutherans (3%) are underrepresented, while Eastern Orthodoxy is totally absent from the Senate list. This pattern of underrepresentation persists in the case of Eastern Orthodoxy and to a lesser extent in the case of Lutheranism.

In the 435-member House of Representatives, Roman Catholicism has the largest denominational bloc, 96 Catholic congressmen. This proportion (22%) is almost precisely the fraction of the national population which is Catholic. There are, however, 71 Presbyterian congressmen, five times as many as some sort of "religious reapportionment" would allow. The next largest group is Methodist (69 members), two and one-half times as many as their population ratio. Episcopalians (53 members) have six times as many representatives as sober statisticians should predict, and the United Church (23 members), five times as many. Again, Baptist (43) and Jewish (16) membership in the House, as in the Senate, is about what their ratio within the national population would suggest. The same is true of the Christian Churches (17) and of the Mormons (9). Lutheranism (10) has less than one half of its legitimate expectation, while Eastern Orthodoxy (2) is once more woefully deficient.

Among the fifty governors, only nine denominational families are represented — all from those listed in Table 1. The only missing denominational family from the Table is, as now may be expected, Eastern Orthodoxy. None of the fifty governors is Jewish. There are 10 Methodist governors, 9 Roman Catholic, 8 Episcopal, 6 Baptist, 5 each for the Presbyterians and Congregationalists (United Church), 3 Lutheran, and 2 each for the Disciples (Christian) and the Latter Day Saints (Mormons). From all these data, four observations may be made.

First, denominational size and political influence show no close correlation. The groups mentioned in Table 1 are surely and repeatedly represented in both houses of Congress and in the states' gubernatorial mansions as well. But the order and magnitude of their representation shows considerable variation. The highest group in the Senate is third in the country, while the Senate's second largest group is the country's seventh. Similarly, the group ranked second in the House ranks fifth in the nation while the fifth-ranking group in the House is the second ranking in the nation. And so the pattern — if pattern it be — goes.

Second, while 36% of the general population is not affiliated with any church or synagogue, that percentage drops sharply in the political world. In the House those who report no religious affiliation are less than 1%, in the Senate just 1%, and among the Governors it is 0%. In view of this situation, the 36% of America's nonaffiliated may argue that they are the most underrepresented minority in the country — even more neglected than Eastern Orthodoxy. The cynical aspiring politician, studying

Table 4, might argue that he should either be a Catholic or a Methodist, or, failing that, then a Unitarian — unless he were running for governor!

Third, while America's entry into the postprotestant era (or even a postchristian one) is widely acclaimed, the political stratum of American life does not appear to have entered that era. In the Senate, 80% are Protestants, among the governors 78%, and in the House of Representatives over 70%. (In all cases Mormons, who do not consider themselves Protestants, are not included in these totals.) This heavy Protestant dominance is due, as has been noted above, to the disproportionate representation enjoyed by certain Protestant groups: namely, Methodists, Presbyterians, Episcopalians, and Congregationalists (United Church).

Fourth, Lutheranism and Eastern Orthodoxy still suffer some degree of cultural isolation. The fourth largest religious family in America, Lutheranism lags far behind smaller Protestant groups. Its low representation in the House of Representatives is particularly surprising; of those states where Lutheran population is heavily concentrated, only Minnesota sent a significant delegation (3) of Lutherans to the House. The explanation lies, of course, in the ethnic, linguistic, and organizational diversity which has not only divided Lutherans from each other but has to some degree separated Lutherans from the surrounding culture. Since that complex of problems is now being resolved, Lutheran political participation is almost certain to rise sharply in the years just ahead.

Among the top ten, Eastern Orthodoxy alone is unrepresented either in the Senate or on the governors' roster. In the House it is, in 1967, represented for the first time. Ethnic differences among the Orthodox are often compounded by competing political and ecclesiastical loyalties, both at home and abroad. Also, the "Eastern" of Eastern Orthodoxy is more than a convenient title: it is a reminder that the later Roman and medieval periods as well as the Renaissance, the Reformation, the Enlightenment, etc, are not parts of the heritage of this group. Understandably, both Orthodox laity and clergy sometimes find dialogue with their "Western" neighbors frustrating and difficult. Until, in something like the pattern of Lutheranism, Orthodoxy begins to conquer its internal divisions, it is not likely to conquer its cultural insulation or its politically disenfranchised status.

The wave of rapidly growing Pentecostal and other "third force" movements has yet to leave its mark on the political shorelines. Seventh Day Adventists elected their first Representative in 1966, while Churches of God, the Church of God in Christ, Assemblies of God, Nazarenes, and Jehovah's Witnesses have yet to make even that modest debut. Many of these groups are, of course, small when compared with those listed in Table 1; together, however, the denominations named in the previous sentence had in 1965 a membership of about 2½ millions — placing them as a group ahead of both the Latter Day Saints and the United Church. While these third force movements share some common elements in purpose and approach, it is misleading to treat them as a single-minded entity. It is their many mindedness which directly affects their social responsibility and their cultural impact.

The same may be said, of course, of American religion as a whole and of Protestantism in particular. Cultural impact does appear to be related to unity of purpose if not to uniformity of organization. Today's ecumenical trend is therefore, among other things, an agonizing response to the impotence which fragmentation and incessant schism bring. Or, if not that, it is a counterthrust directed against a type of ecumenicity either feared or deplored. Within American Protestantism, three cooperative agencies endeavor to speak for more than a single ecclesiastical tradition. Of these three, the National Council of Churches of Christ is certainly the most significant. With a current membership of 42 millions, the National Council includes all or part of the seven Protestant families cited in Table 1. (Neither the Latter Day Saints nor, of course, the Roman Catholics is included among the Protestants, and neither group is within the Council; Eastern Orthodoxy, on the other hand, is in the Council, or at least about three fourths of its total membership is.) More Baptists and Lutherans are outside the

855

National Council than are inside; nevertheless, that ecumenical body can operate in the name of about two thirds of all American Protestants.

The National Association of Evangelicals, with a membership of about 2 millions, demonstrates a markedly conservative theological orientation. Among its affiliates are such groups as the Free Methodists, the Evangelical Mennonite Church, the Ohio Yearly Meeting of Friends, and — largest of all — the Assemblies of God (½ million members). The third cooperative agency, the American Council of Christian Churches, stands politically far to the right of the National Association of Evangelicals. This group also sets itself deliberately against the basic direction of the National Council. Its quite modest membership is drawn from about a dozen groups ranging in size from the General Association of Regular Baptist Churches (121,000 members in 1960) to the Fundamental Methodist Church (1,000 members) and ranging in ideology from fundamentalism to the Militant Fundamental Bible Churches — of which there were 13 in 1960. (See Figure 4.)

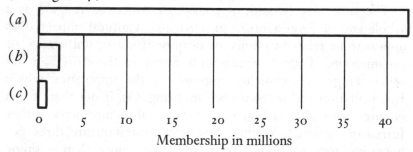

FIGURE 4. Protestant cooperative organizations in America, 1960. (a) National Council of Churches, 40 millions; (b) National Association of Evangelicals, 2 millions; (c) American Council of Christian Churches, ¼ million. For data on the National Council see Jacquet [9]. Data on the National Association of Evangelicals and on the American Council of Christian Churches were provided by those bodies.

Apart from politics, what other kinds of cultural force are exerted by America's denominations? Answers are neither easy nor uniform. The response will often depend, moreover, on the special aspect of culture under examination. Is it music? Consider the power of the Lutheran's tradition of great music or of the Negro Baptist's blend of jazz, hymn, and folksong. Is it art? Note the leadership manifest in Catholicism, both East and West, especially in the Benedictine direction of a liturgical renaissance. Is it education? Try to write American history without attention to the Presbyterian and Congregational stimulation and support in this area of national culture. Is it literature? Consider the remarkable flowering of Jewish letters, particularly in the last thirty years. None of these cultural catalysts bears much direct relationship to family size or to financial contribution, and none lends itself to unarguable measurement. But all of them — including the family size, the financial contributions, the stated preferences — show religion in America to be now, as in the past, intimately tied to what goes on in synagogue and church, in synod and in conference. One cannot, after all, ignore everything that transpires under parochial labels and family names even though these do, on occasion, appear as a stumbling block and an offense to all.

REFERENCES

1. Bureau of the Census: *Current Population Reports*, Series P-20, number 79 (Superintendent of Documents, Government Printing Office, Washington, DC 20402) Feb 2, 1958.
2. *Christianity Today* (Washington, DC) issue of Dec 9, 1966, pp 276-277.
3. Consultation on Church Union: *Digest*, issued annually from 1962 (Executive Secretary, Consultation on Church Union, Box 69, Fanwood, New Jersey).
4. Consultation on Church Union: *Principles of Church Union* (Forward Movement Publications, 412 Sycamore Street, Cincinnati, Ohio 45202) 1966.
5. Consultation on Church Union: *Consultation on Church Union: The Reports of Four Meetings* (Forward Move-

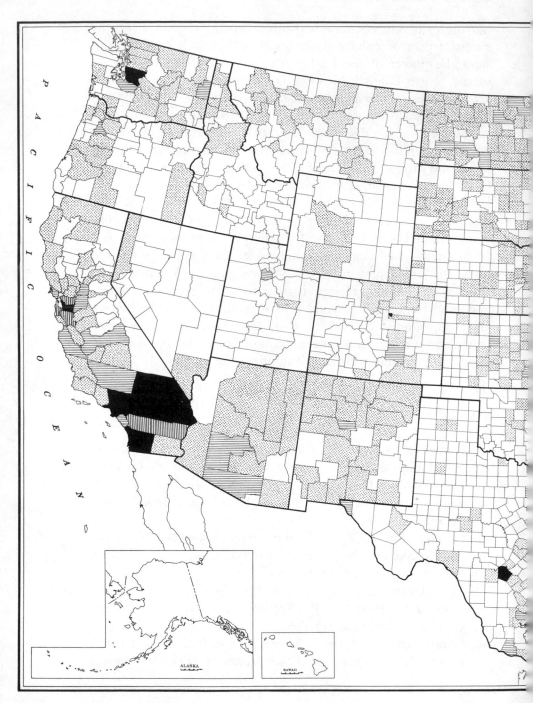

© 1968 *by Edwin S. Gaustad*

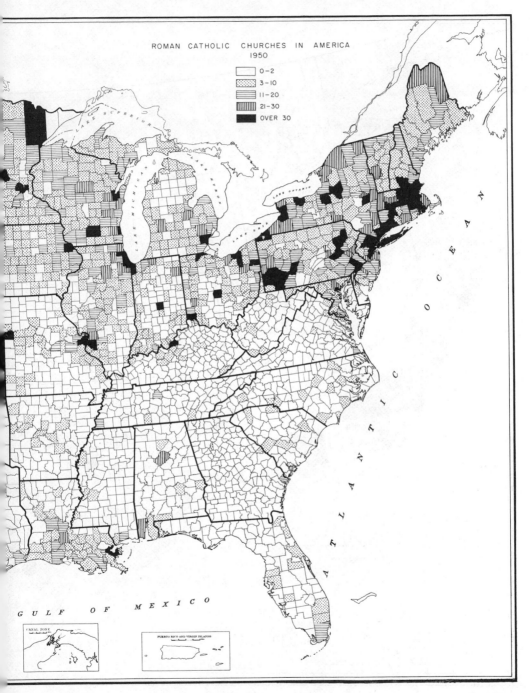

ROMAN CATHOLIC CHURCHES IN AMERICA
1950

0–2
3–10
11–20
21–30
OVER 30

859

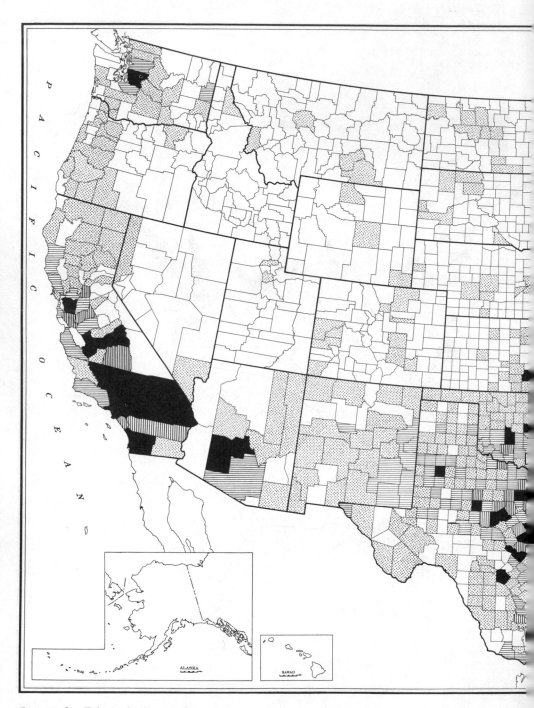

© 1968 by Edwin S. Gaustad

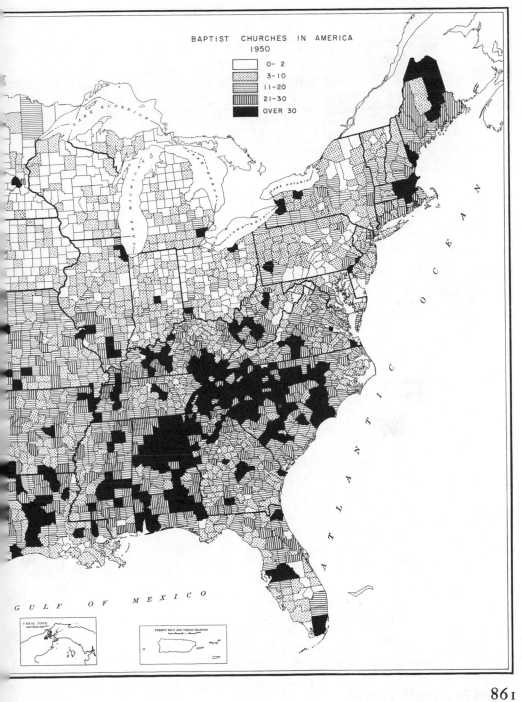

BAPTIST CHURCHES IN AMERICA
1950

	0- 2
	3-10
	11-20
	21-30
	OVER 30

LAKE SUPERIOR

LAKE MICHIGAN

LAKE ONTARIO

ATLANTIC OCEAN

GULF OF MEXICO

CANAL ZONE

PUERTO RICO AND VIRGIN ISLANDS

861

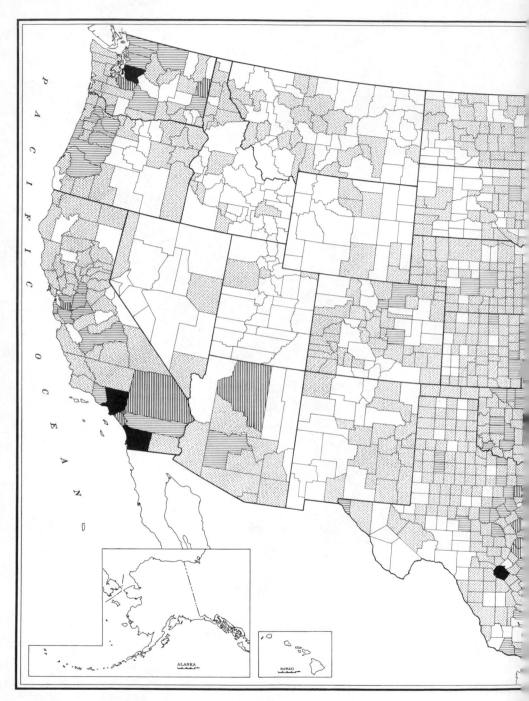

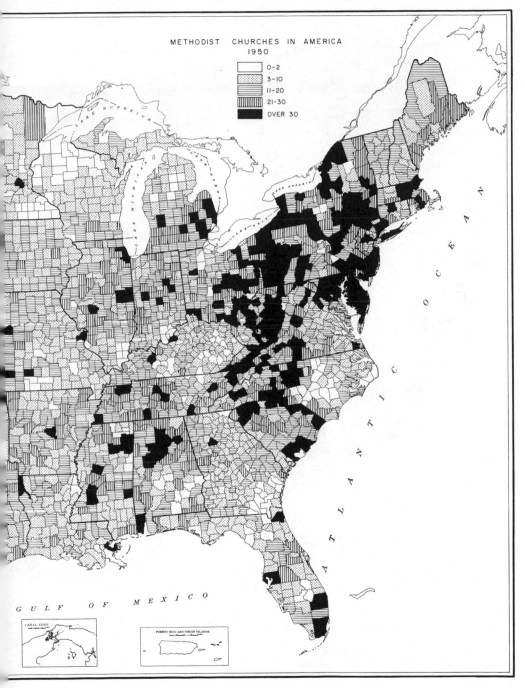

METHODIST CHURCHES IN AMERICA
1950

	0-2
	3-10
	11-20
	21-30
	OVER 30

863

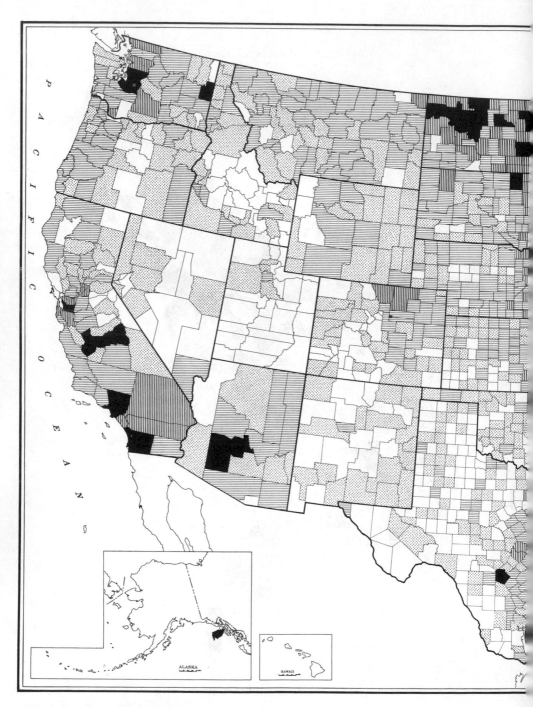

© 1968 by Edwin S. Gaustad

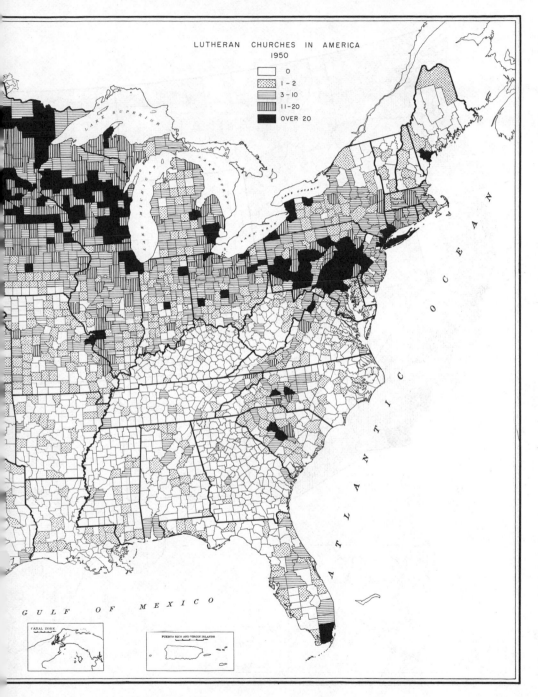

LUTHERAN CHURCHES IN AMERICA
1950

☐	0
▨	1 - 2
▤	3 - 10
▥	11 - 20
■	OVER 20

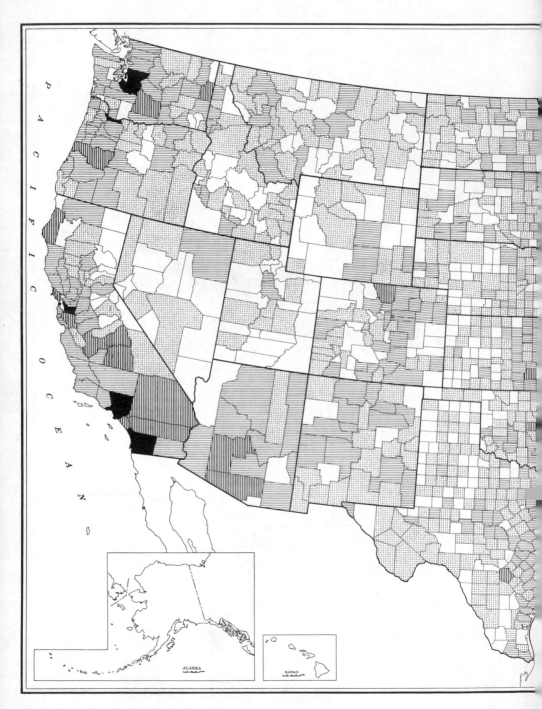

© 1968 by Edwin S. Gaustad

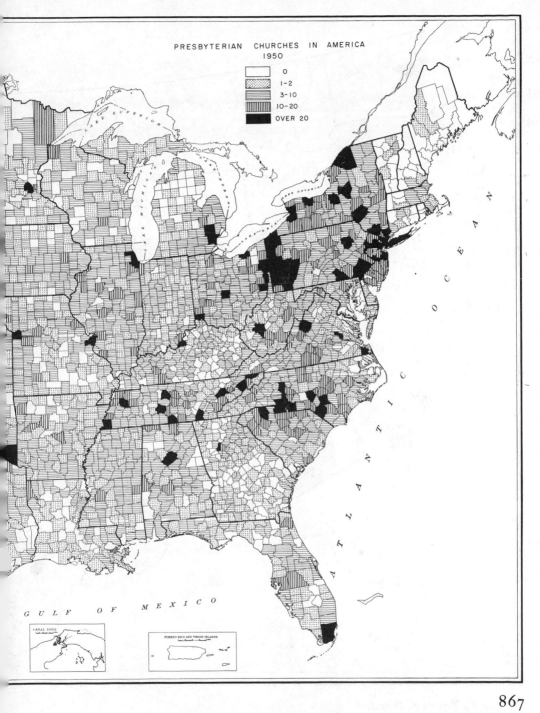

PRESBYTERIAN CHURCHES IN AMERICA
1950

- 0
- 1-2
- 3-10
- 10-20
- OVER 20

LAKE SUPERIOR

LAKE MICHIGAN

LAKE HURON

LAKE ERIE

LAKE ONTARIO

ATLANTIC OCEAN

GULF OF MEXICO

CANAL ZONE

PUERTO RICO AND VIRGIN ISLANDS

867

© 1968 *by Edwin S. Gaustad*

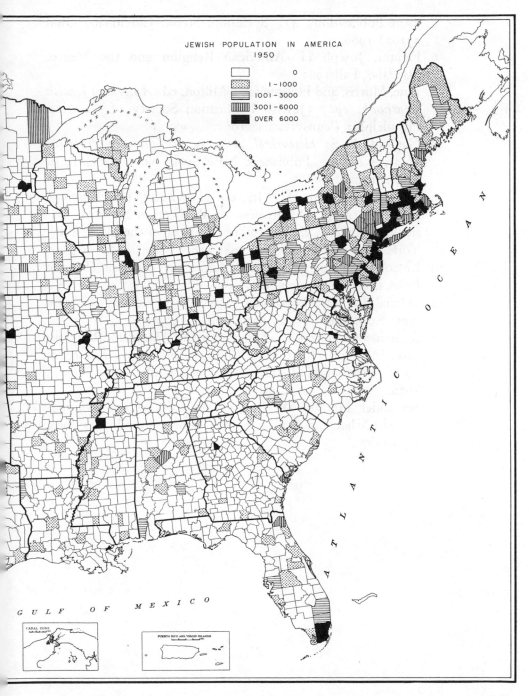

JEWISH POPULATION IN AMERICA
1950

	0
	1 – 1000
	1001 – 3000
	3001 – 6000
	OVER 6000

ment Publications, 412 Sycamore Street, Cincinnati, Ohio 45202) 1966.

6. Fichter, Joseph H: American Religion and the Negro, *Daedalus*, Fall 1965.

7. Fine, Morris, and Himmelfarb, Milton, ed: *American Jewish Yearbook, 1965* (Jewish Publication Society of America, Philadelphia, Pennsylvania) 1965.

8. Gaustad, E S: *Historical Atlas of Religion in America* (Harper & Row, Publishers, New York, New York) 1962, fold-out map.

9. Jacquet, Constant H, Jr, ed: *Yearbook of American Churches, 1967* (Department of Publication Services, National Council of the Churches of Christ in the USA, New York, New York) 1967, pp 198–210.

10. Lincoln, C Eric: *The Black Muslims in America* (Beacon Press, Boston, Massachusetts) 1961.

11. Official Catholic Directory, 1966 (P J Kenedy & Sons, New York, New York) 1966, fold-out chart.

12. Richardson, Harry V, The Negro in American Religious Life, in Davis, John P, ed: *American Negro Reference Book* (Prentice-Hall, Inc, Englewood Cliffs, New Jersey) 1966.

13. Schneider, Herbert W: *Religion in 20th Century America*, rev ed (Atheneum Publishers, New York, New York) 1964, Appendix A.

23. EASTERN EUROPE

ORTHODOXY AND THE
YOUNGER GENERATION IN THE USSR
by Dmitry Konstantinov

THE ORTHODOX CHURCH is a vital and profound source of the spiritual and intellectual ferment now occurring in the Soviet Union as part of the irreversible process of renewal taking place before our eyes. Despite the fundamental conflict between the dogmas of the Orthodox Church and the values of the Soviet regime, it is the inspiration from religion that pervades much of the urge to attain new spiritual horizons.

Orthodoxy has experienced many vicissitudes over the last half century and has been bent to the needs of the regime in the latter's religious policy. Yet, in the face of all the pressure and persecution at the hands of the communist authorities, for many decades, and especially under Stalin, the Church remained the only haven of spiritual freedom and the only antithesis to the official materialist philosophy. Christianity, embodied in the Church, is seeping into every strata of Soviet society and is affecting everyone who is not dead in spirit. In one form or another it is stimulating the spiritual awakening of the most disparate groups within this society. Here and there this process comes to a halt and peters out at differing stages of the individual's spiritual and mental development. But sometimes Christian values are transformed into philosophical or political ideas in which the principles of intellectual and political freedom predominate. Notwithstanding its apparently conservative nature, so often commented upon by foreign writers, Orthodoxy is imbued with a spirit of freedom. And, although the dogmatic and canonical stability of Orthodoxy protects it from all assaults on its wholeness, the creative spiritual freedom within it bears fruitful results both

871

within the Church and outside it. There is a need to stress this fact, because a widely held opinion asserts that the "conservatism" and "limitedness" of the Church are obstacles preventing Orthodoxy from influencing the Soviet young generation. This is not true; if any impediments do exist, they arise because the young sometimes find it hard to thoroughly understand Orthodoxy in its complexity and diversity.

What are the paths by which young people in the Soviet Union are approaching Orthodoxy? Dealing with the matter ten years ago, I arrived at the conclusion that one of the main ways is simply by becoming acquainted with the liturgy at Mass [13; 14]. This is still largely true today. Recently, however, new means of religious education have been made available in the shape of the Scriptures: nowadays religious literature in mimeographed or even printed form is passed from hand to hand, and the works of Russian and Western religious philosophers are being studied, now that access to them is becoming easier. Religious literature comes in from abroad, and even the Moscow Patriarchate manages to print some.

In a recent article on the present position of the Orthodox Church in the USSR, an American journalist compared Orthodoxy in the Soviet Union with an iceberg, only the tip of which shows above the surface [22]. The main part of the religious processes so far remains invisible and therefore only the results are apparent, not the impulse behind them. We have to judge these processes chiefly from what we read in the Soviet press, which almost daily sounds the alarm over religion. A reflection is also to be found in letters received in the West from religious believers, the accounts of those who have visited the Soviet Union, and in the illegal literature produced in the country itself, examples of which find their way abroad. The outside observer is faced with the hard task of analyzing this mosaic of information and of piecing together an accurate picture of the situation.

Any examination of the influence of the Orthodox Church over the young generation in the Soviet Union must deal with all the different degrees of commitment to religious faith, beginning with those who are wholehearted members of the Church and ending with those young people who, although perhaps not practicing Christians, are capable of expressing such sentiments as this:

> And the wind has borne away
> So much time.
> Yet Rus is still scattered with little churches
> Waiting for God [27].

One may next quote the most arresting examples of the way in which youth is being drawn to the Orthodox Church. Over the past few years the Soviet press has been reporting a succession of cases of young people who have fallen under religious influences. There was Valeri, the son of a high Party member, brought up in an antireligious atmosphere, who joined the Komsomol and studied at the Moscow Physical Culture Institute. Suddenly, however, he began losing interest in his studies, after a short while became completely indifferent to Komsomol activities and submitted two applications, one for permission to leave the Institute, the other to enter a seminary [2]. Unfortunately we cannot know the process which took place within Valeri to engender such a transformation.

"I am through with him," said the wife of a young collective farm worker, Melenti Romanenko, after he decided to enter the priesthood despite her desperate efforts to prevent him from doing so, in which she went as far as to denounce him to the local office of the state security committee. Yet none of the authorities with which Romanenko had to deal, in order to obtain the necessary papers allowing him to leave the farm, made any difficulties, although they could easily have done so. They simply completed the legal formalities without attempting to dissuade the young man from his purpose by means of any atheist arguments. This suggests that they may even have been tacitly in sympathy with or at least not antagonistic to his desire to devote his life to the Church, despite having themselves been brought up in a nonreligious atmosphere [3].

Then there is the case of Vasili Dyukov, a young bricklayer who had just married and settled down with his wife. The harmonious married life was not to last long. Vasili started meeting the local clergy and attending Mass at the local Orthodox Church and within a short time decided to enter a seminary. This was a heavy blow to his wife, who was completely indifferent to religion and did all in her power to prevent her husband from carrying out his intention. In the end he gave up the idea, but was soon drafted for military service, during which, it appears, he still clung to religion [29].

It had been a longstanding wish of G. Filippovich, a contributor to *Nauka i religiya*, the antireligious journal, to write a report about a Soviet village where religion has had its day and where, as a result of well organized propaganda, "religious survivals" had been overcome. In order to gather the necessary material, Filippovich travelled through the Mari ASSR and eventually came to the town of Volzhsk, where he went to see the head of the local branch of the atheist *Znaniye* organization. What ensued is worth quoting verbatim:

> I asked a man I met in the hall where the head of the atheist department was.
>
> "He is not in," the comrade answered briefly.
>
> "Will he be in today?"
>
> "No, nor tomorrow either, nor the day after tomorrow. He is studying for his exams."
>
> "What for?"
>
> "For admission to a seminary. He has already submitted his application."
>
> "You must be joking," I said. To be quite frank, I felt he must be insulting me. "I am asking you a serious question," I said.
>
> "Well, I'm answering you seriously. If you don't believe me, ask comrade Ponomarev, secretary of the town committee on ideology. His office is on the second floor."

Filippovich goes to see the secretary, who confirms what he has been told and says with some embarrassment that it is "a case that can hardly be said to flatter us," and this is the title Filippovich gives to his article [19:73].

The religious focus of the town of Orenburg is still the Nikol-

874

sky Cathedral, which is not far away from school No. 35. The Soviet press has something to complain about on this score:

> Peacefully they (the church and the school) stand almost side by side, but in reality, where the spheres of influence of these two focuses clash, a never ending struggle is taking place for the human soul. The teaching staff at the school is not bad, and our whole way of life aids it in this struggle. And yet it does not always emerge victorious. Inozemtsev, a pupil at this school, graduated and then went into a seminary. He returned to his home town as a priest. Now he officiates and helps to lure children into church [4].

Another pupil, Ilya Borodin, after graduating from school No. 34 in Orenburg also took holy orders, although he later left the church.

The fact that all these cases have been reported in the Soviet press is evidence enough that they are not isolated; otherwise so much publicity would not be given to them. To judge by the concern shown by the authorities, the people who cherish the desire to devote their lives to the Church come from all walks of life, belong to all age groups, and are clearly quite numerous. In the middle of the 1950's, for instance, there were eight seminaries and two ecclesiastical academies in the USSR, but the number of applicants for admission was far higher than the number of vacant places. Each seminary had an average of 2,000 students annually, not counting those taking evening courses. It is also reported that there was no lack of girls ready and willing to marry newly ordained priests [1:213–236].

The Soviet press has ceased to claim that only old people go to church, and that it is old women who predominate. It is true that women and the elderly of both sexes do form a large part of congregations in churches in the Soviet Union, but this is the case in the West as well, and even in prerevolutionary Russia there were usually few young people and men at services. One reason is that women the world over are much more punctilious in observance of religious rites than men. In the Soviet Union there is an additional factor accounting for the large number of women attending church: it is safer for a woman to perform religious devotions than for a man when the state is hostile to religious observance and victimization may result at a man's place of work, as happens in the Soviet Union if someone is found to be a regular church-goer. Some excuse may even be found for sacking such a person. Also, more indulgence is shown to women who display "ideological immaturity" by going to church.

In the last few years, however, the proportion of young people attending Mass has increased, and this is being admitted by the authorities. A photograph appeared in the press showing a group of believers during Easter Service, waiting for the consecration of cakes and *paskha* (a sweet cream cheese confection traditionally eaten at Easter) [21:2]. The congregation included children, teenagers, and young girls and women hardly over 30 years of age. Another photograph showed an 18-year-old pilgrim carrying a cross. The accompanying article displayed a frankness that marked a new departure in the official approach, which had hitherto tried to play down this participation by the young. The author is writing about the town of Tambov:

> I was told by local atheists: "Only old people go to church. We went to church during Lent in order to see for ourselves. And you too can go and see for yourself. . . ." The following Sunday I went and saw for myself. The Pokrovsky cathedral comprises two churches. . . . It has a long one-storey wing on one side where babies are christened and funeral services held, etc. All this is done by six priests.
>
> The cathedral priests deserve credit for working without bureaucracy or formalism. That Sunday morning they celebrated Mass three times, heard confessions, held a memorial service for the souls of the dead, administered the sacrament to those who had just adopted the Orthodox faith, and gave the Eucharist to those thirsting for the body and blood of Christ. The same morning one priest was christening babies in the side wing, another was holding funeral services in the cemetery, and still another was doing his rounds "on call" in his car.
>
> The church-yard was overcrowded. There were old men and women, as expected by the atheists. There were also persons who had not been foreseen. Against the background of fresh green foliage and the black garments of the pilgrims stood out

the whiteness of the babies' quilts. There was also a quiet, jostling crowd of small boys and girls with little multicoloured bows in their plaits, their mouths agape with wonder. These young boys and girls who had just been made "acquainted with Orthodoxy" had not been foreseen in any atheist plans either, nor had their godparents of Komsomol age or slightly older, but completely ignorant of church matters. They are kindly instructed by old women, but not by those backward grandmothers whom the atheists gave up as hopeless a long time ago.

. . . Between the early and late Mass a queue of people formed in front of the confessional, waiting to repent of their sins. There again we see old women as foreseen by the plan, including, however, pupils of the first few grades [21:32]–

There is, however, still a law on the Soviet statute book that forbids children and teenagers under 18 to attend Mass. An editorial to Kostyukov's article states mournfully: "Unfortunately, the facts cited above are not only typical of Tambov."

Another article describes church life in Georgia, and refers in particular to the Cathedral of Mtskheta:

The Mtskheta Cathedral. The marriage service of a young couple is being celebrated with great pomp. The groom, Merab Vasholomidze, a junior staff member in an important ideological establishment, namely, the Institute of Philosophy, had his civil marriage performed at a registry office, and then decided to consolidate it by means of a ceremony in church. . . .

. . . There were another one and a half hours to go before the all-night service, but the bells were already calling for service. An aged priest placed one child after the other into the font with a haste ill befitting his age, while a young priest of the Russian Orthodox Church, aged about 30, was celebrating mass in the right nave of the church. The relatively small space was crowded with devout worshippers. Here too, the number of young people was not small [18:71 – 72].

And another correspondent writes that "something is wrong" in the village of Ternov in Voronezh Oblast: "The clergymen have built a rather strong nest here. It happens that young people attend church service. A cunning, ingenious priest is doing his duty, christening babies, marrying young couples" [9]. The correspondent adds that the priest has started cooperating with the local Komsomol. A report on religious life in the town of Kentau in the Chimkent Oblast of Kazakhstan asks: "And who are these believers? They include grey-bearded, aged men, but also still very young people" [8]. Elsewhere in the press we find a description of the Pskovo-Pechersky Monastery just before the beginning of the evening service: "The janitor at the gate, our old friend Vasili, a lay-brother who had come to work at the holy cloister from Novgorod, is hardly capable of keeping off the masses of people" [31]. Reference is specifically made not to "masses of old women and children" but to "masses of people." A quotation from an article written by the Soviet writer Valeri Tarsis, who recently came to live in the West, is an apt commentary:

> Despite atheist propaganda, the number of believers has been growing like flowers after a good spring shower. Last year, on the eve of Easter, my friend and I took a cab and visited ten Moscow churches. This was on Good Friday, and I was happy to see in front of every church long queues of believers holding white bags with *kulich* and *paskha* which they had brought along for consecration. And it was even more delightful to see the faces of numerous young girls among the crowd of believers, amounting on the average to up to 5,000 people. The school-girls had put on their white Sunday aprons, and I noticed that the crowds were considerably larger than in 1963 when I also visited our churches [23].

However, the conditions under which the rising generation comes to join the Orthodox Church are still more interesting than the above evidence testifying to participation by young people in religious ceremonies. The following are excerpts from the numerous reports on the subject that have been appearing in Soviet antireligious literature. For example, in an article entitled "Encounters in Stavropol" M. G. Mikhailov writes:

> I asked Ye. R. Androsova about her education. "High school. Then I attended the Stavropol Pedagogical Institute," adding

with a smile, "They fired me from the institute — upon my own request" [20].

The article reveals that the reason why the girl was dismissed was that she had not made a secret of her religious feelings. And Androsova referred to her girl friends, who are also true believers:

I am not the only one. The same thing happened the year before last to Nina Ivleva at the agricultural institute, who is a Baptist. Valya Podgaiskaya had to leave the pedagogical institute. First we were grieved, but then we understood: everything God does is for the best [33:32].

The same periodical carries an article about a carpenter, Yevdokim Morgachev, whom the workers at the Urban Foodstuffs Organization had elected to their trade union committee but whom the management refused to approve as a member because he was a believer. One of the not infrequent cases is cited, too, of the dismissal of a gifted girl Komsomol member. She was expelled from the university because she had studied the Bible and become a believer [17]. Another girl, fifteen-year-old Lyudmilla L., a student at the Tyumen School of Commerce, started attending an Orthodox Church and eventually turned wholly to religion, which affected not so much her studies as her general conduct and attitude towards all kinds of social activities. After it was found out that she had joined the Church, Lyudmilla was deprived of her only means of existence, her scholarship, and forced to leave school. When faced with the alternative of choosing between the Church and her scholarship, Lyudmilla decided in favour of the former. The newspaper claims that now she stands on the steps of the church with hand outstretched for alms [30].

Viktor Lebedev, a young lorry driver from the town of Uren in the Urals, joined the Orthodox Church and wanted to enter a monastery but could not do so, since he was married. So he became a missionary and proved to be successful in his work, because he is reported as having "followers." The authorities intervened to put a stop to his activities. He was classed as a "parasite" and sentenced to exile in a "remote region of the republic." However, before the order could be carried out Viktor left the town of Uren and disappeared without trace [29].

It may be seen from the Soviet press that despite the antireligious propaganda conducted by the Party, Orthodoxy remains an "infectious threat" to youth in the eyes of the authorities. In addition to the cases cited above, publicity has been given to a lorry driver in Omsk Oblast named Sergei Kozodoyenko, who adopted the Orthodox faith at the age of 35, and to a girl who came to believe in God after attending Mass [26]. Many of these young believers startle the authorities by their readiness to make sacrifices, their heroic attitude, and extraordinary perseverance in their determination to cling to their faith. The case of young Anna Skorik, as reported in the press, showed an endless series of persecutions for the sole reason that she was a believer. Since her childhood Anna had been closely connected with the Church and had managed to remain faithful to it despite all the humiliations that the "young fanatic," as she is called, had to suffer at school. She still would not give way even when every employer refused to give her a job, when her sister was dismissed from her place of work, and when the order came for her to leave her home town, followed by legal proceedings against her for organizing "illegal prayer meetings."

Neither Anna Skorik nor any of the other youngsters whose cases have been quoted above, and many others like them, can count on any support from the Church in their efforts to resist pressure from the authorities. The Church is in no position to render such aid. Nevertheless, both the young generation and those of mature age are fearless in the face of repressions. A priest belonging to the catacomb church in Tekeli, Kazakhstan, who was discovered and sentenced to five years' imprisonment was only 34 years of age [6].

The open observance of such Church rites as marriage ceremonies, baptism, etc, over which the Soviet press has repeatedly expressed great concern, must also be mentioned. Marriage in church has become quite popular among Soviet young people and even among Komsomol members. Komsomol member Valentina Khvorova in the village of Selezni in Tambov Oblast and Aleksei

Mukin from the neighbouring village of Lysye Gory were married at an Orthodox church, and so was the Komsomol secretary, Masha Pudovkina, also from the same village. Both Khvorova and Pudovkina were expelled from the Komsomol shortly after. The correspondent reporting on this mentions that there are no churches functioning in this particular rural region, and so young couples wishing to get married travel to other areas where the churches have not been closed, especially to the town of Tambov [10]. In Volsk, for instance, 10 couples were married in church and 206 babies christened in 1961, and in 1962 the figures had risen to 59 and 1,795 respectively [16].

Any discussion of religious activities in the Soviet Union should include reference to the problem regarding children. As mentioned above, the Soviet government passed a law in 1962 forbidding minors to enter an Orthodox church. Christening and receiving the Eucharist is allowed only in the case of babies under 18 months and this only if the names of the parents, godparents, and other persons participating in the ceremony are registered with the authorities. These governmental measures were intended to prevent younger age groups from following in the footsteps of that part of the rising generation which has adopted Orthodoxy.

It was stated in the Soviet press in 1964 that approximately 500 miners in the town of Tekeli went to the Orthodox church of Taldy-Kurgan in order to have their children christened there, because apparently there was no longer a church in Tekeli. This was a rather dangerous venture in view of the compulsory registration of the parents, introduced in order that measures could be taken against the latter. According to the same press report: "the young wives of two lorry-drivers in Taldy-Kurgan had their babies christened in the customary way. . . . And after her husband divorced her, a certain Elvira Kim made haste to find consolation in church by having her daughter Galya baptised" [7]. But baptism is not confined to babes in arms: Lyda Sh., a trained nurse said to be an outstanding worker and Komsomol member, was christened at the age of 20 and then married in church [10]. These are only a few examples, but they all testify to the fact that the public as a whole is in favour of baptism [12:155–157].

Another effort to combat religious upbringing was the formation of numerous state-run boarding schools to which the children of parents with religious beliefs were sent. Over the last few years there has been a wave of legal proceedings in the Soviet Union against parents who bring up their children as Christians. The object of these measures has been to remove such children from the "unhealthy influence" of their homes and place them in state boarding schools.

Cases also occur in which one parent wishes the offspring to be reared in a religious atmosphere, while the other does not. When matters end up in the divorce court, it is the state that steps in to order the removal of a child from the care of a religiously inclined parent. These problems also find their reflection on the pages of the press. For example, the wife of Guards Captain Valentin Vasilyevich B. was awarded custody of their son Yura after her husband divorced her. She, in turn, passed him on to her parents in order to have him brought up as an Orthodox Christian. The grandmother started rearing the child according to strict religious rules and even held prayer meetings in her own flat because the local church had been closed. The captain tried to change matters by submitting a complaint to the newspapers. He also wrote two letters to his former wife about the religious education of his child. The answer to the first one was: "You shall not get the child. It is no business of yours where he is being brought up," and to the second, which mentioned the religious services held in grandmother's flat: "Do not oppose prayers at home. If you do not like them, clear out" [15].

Obviously, if the Soviet press is shocked by the fact that school children are wearing crosses and that thousands of them are sold annually in Orenburg and intended largely for children [5], then the religious issue can by no means be simply reduced to one involving just "grandmothers and grandfathers." The blame has to be laid at the door of the young or relatively young parents who cherish the wish to give their children a moral code grounded in religion.

It is evident that the number of divorces caused by quarrels over religion has been increasing in the USSR. The organ of the Soviet trade unions reports the divorce of Mariya and Petr Lukyanenko, who could not get along with each other because she was a believer and he an atheist. Then there is Aleksander and Nina Shuplenov, who have five children, and Dimitri and Lyudmila Ryazan, who were divorced on similar grounds. The same thing happened in the family of P. Kilmenkov, with the only difference, however, that the quarrel did not lead to divorce, although the family was split into two camps [28:16–17]. "Father and mother started to fight over their daughter. Father used to read fascinating fairy tales to Tanya, but mother dinned into her head: 'Hail Mary, full of grace. . . .' Father used to take the little girl to matinees, whereas mother dragged her by the hand to church" [24]. This is the account of what had been happening in the household of the young doctor, M. E. Muranova, and her husband, a Party member and teacher of history. The conflict assumed such proportions that the couple divorced one another, and the father received custody of his daughter. This shows that divorce on religious grounds is recognized in the Soviet Union.

The Soviet authorities are not only interested in cases in which a religious conflict has sprung up. They also interfere with the life of families in which both parents try to give their children a religious education. From its own atheist point of view, the Soviet press is absolutely right in proposing, on the basis of Article 227 of the RSFSR Penal Code, to bring to court the case of a bricklayer named I. Shevchenko who brought up all six of his children in a strictly Orthodox spirit and let his daughter marry a young student at a seminary [18:47]. The inhabitants of the town of Buguruslan also wanted to bring an action in court against the Old Believer, P. Samartsev, for bringing up his children according to religious precepts and who refused to let them wear Young Pioneer ties. Yet, no matter what the future of these children is going to be, a spark of religion has been kindled in their souls [11]. In the village of Rudakovo in Gorky Oblast there lives the Zauzolkov family. The children never go to the cinema, do not join in the social life of the pupils, and read only religious books. The family is said to belong to an underground religious organization [30].

Concerned over the large number of such families, the authorities have resorted to punishment by the arm of the law. Recalcitrant parents are brought to trial, and a most revealing case of this kind was that of forester Dimitri Sokhranyaev in Pskov Oblast, who brought up his children strictly according to the rules of the Orthodox Church, for which reason he was accused of "morally mutilating his children." The latter were taken away from their parents, who were still relatively young and had been brought up under the Soviet regime. The fact that Sokhranyaev had formerly been an activist and convinced atheist lent particular interest to the proceedings and made his "crime" all the more heinous in the eyes of the press [25].

Another development that is reported in Soviet newspapers is the appearance of illegal religious literature which young people help to distribute. It is said to be printed in the town of Maikop and to contain mainly religious excerpts from the Bible and Psalms. It is smuggled into the pockets and desks of pupils and teachers during classes [32].

Against this background of religious activity it does not seem strange that during a lesson devoted to Russian culture in the eighteenth century, a young Soviet teacher should let his pupils read a text dealing with the self-educated inventor, Kulibin, who built a clock with a small door from which angels emerge when the clock strikes the hour, remove the stone from God's tomb and sing "Christ has risen." It is obvious that there are enough forces among the young generation to wage a relentless fight for a new triumph of the Orthodox Church in the USSR [32].

As a final witness we may quote a correspondent of the Soviet army newspaper. What he says provides a clue to the present mood of young Soviet believers. The correspondent had a talk with a soldier who was a member of the Orthodox Church. The conversation lasted a long time and ended with the soldier saying to the major: "I am sorry for you, comrade major, you have learnt nothing in life" [15].

From the above it can be seen that those of the Soviet young generation who belong to the Orthodox Church are playing a decisive role in the country's spiritual renewal. There is some evidence, too, that this is not a sporadic phenomenon but a widespread movement that has been going on under the surface of Soviet life. It is too early to say whether it is already an organized movement, but at any rate it is an irreversible process that will triumph in the end.

REFERENCES

1. *Grani*, no 48, 1960, pp 213–236.
2. *Izvestia*, Oct 14, 1960.
3. *Izvestia*, May 20, 1961.
4. *Izvestia*, Nov 27, 1965.
5. *Izvestia*, Nov 28, 1965.
6. *Kazakhstanskaya pravda*, Feb 17, 1963.
7. *Kazakhstanskaya pravda*, Mar 12, 1965.
8. *Kazakhstanskaya pravda*, Nov 4, 1965.
9. *Komsomolskaya pravda*, Mar 26, 1963.
10. *Komsomolskaya pravda*, June 6, 1963.
11. *Komsomolskaya pravda*, July 3, 1963.
12. Konstantinov, D: The Atheist Howl, *Russko-Amerikansky pravoslavny vestnik*, New York, no 10, 1965, pp 155–157.
13. Konstantinov, D V: *Pravoslavnaya molodezh v borbe za Tserkov v SSSR* (Orthodox Youth in Its Fight for the Church in the USSR) Munich, 1965, Institute for the Study of the USSR.
14. Konstantinov, D V: Soviet Youth in Its Fight for the Church (1920–1930) *Vestnik Instituta po izucheniyu i kultury SSSR*, Munich, no 1 (14) 1955.
15. *Krasnaya zvezda*, Feb 14, 1965.
16. *Krokodil*, no 16, 1963.
17. *Literaturnaya gazeta*, Oct 20, 1962.
18. *Nauka i religiya*, no 5, 1963, pp 47, 71–72.
19. *Nauka i religiya*, no 5, 1964, p 73.

20. *Nauka i religiya*, no 4, 1965.
21. *Nauka i religiya*, no 12, 1965, pp 2, 32 – 34.
22. *The New York Times*, Mar 7, 1966
23. *Posev*, Frankfurt, Feb 25, 1966.
24. *Pravda*, Nov 2, 1962.
25. *Selskaya zhizn*, June 14, 1962.
26. *Selskaya zhizn*, June 28, 1962.
27. *Sfinksy*, no 1, reprinted in *Grani*, Moscow, no 59, 1965, p 24.
28. *Sovetskiye profsoyuzy*, no 8, 1963, pp 16 – 17.
29. *Sovetskaya Rossiya*, June 29, 1962.
30. *Sovetskaya Rossiya*, Sept 27, 1962.
31. *Sovetskaya Rossiya*, Nov 18, 1964.
32. *Uchitelskaya gazeta*, Feb 16, 1963.
33. *Vestnik russkogo studencheskogo khristianskogo dvizheniya* (Bulletin of the Russian Student Christian Movement) Paris and New York, no 78, 1965, p 32.

CHRISTIANITY AND THE
NEW EXODUS IN EAST EUROPE
by Max L. Stackhouse

SECULARIZATION is a term and a process that has had much attention in the West from theologians, social scientists, and ethicists. It has been portrayed as a major cultural trend that shows no sign of retarding. It has been celebrated, lamented, doubted, defied, encouraged, and debunked. It is an unavoidable subject in the analysis of the place of religion in contemporary cultures.

Understanding secularization trends in Eastern Europe is both intrinsically interesting and pertinent to discussions in the West. The characteristics of the process there pose four questions. First, are religious belief and practice actually on a rapid decline in Communist states, and is there no need for them in socialist societies? Contradictory reports from the East, suggest both that the churches are populated only by old women and also that

887

there is tremendous vigor in clandestine and especially sectarian, religious activity. This question also forces us to ask whether man has any fundamental religious need or drive or whether religion is merely the creation of a particular set of human artifacts.

Study of the secularization process in Eastern Europe, secondly, may reveal how successful the efforts at *intentional* secularization have been. What happens to religious beliefs and practices when they are systematically deprived of their relationship to social and cultural functions? Does the isolation of religion, its excision from public function purify religion and make it more significant — as advocates of "religionless Christianity" claim — or does isolation in fact deprive religion of whatever importance it pretends to possess?

Third, large numbers of Christians who have interpreted Marxism as a prophetic movement divorced from its religious roots more by historical accident than by necessity wonder whether Marxist categories are capable of dealing with religious phenomena in other than reductionist or polemical fashion. The mechanistic economism of some official Marxist theory seems never to touch the nerve of religious belief or theological insight. Can Marxism develop the means to a sensitive and realistic assessment of what is at stake in religious commitment and participation?

This question is of considerable import, especially because of the fact that social theorists, including Marxists, are in a very real sense the "secular theologians" of our day. The "death-of-God" theologians certainly do not represent the most important new directions of thought, but the social theorists may when they attempt to come to grips with the fundamental forces that shape man and his destiny. As in any theological dispute — that is, any dispute that concerns man's proper object of ultimate loyalty and his theoretical and practical interpretation of what is ultimately valuable and powerful — it is crucial that we find out whether the modes of expression and conceptualization are capable of bearing the weight of the task.

What possibilities, finally, are there now for serious discussions between Christians and Marxists on the role of religion in society? Dialogue between Marxist and Christian modes of thought is proceeding on several fronts. It is not a new discussion, being rooted in the very origins of Marxism itself. The Marxists have already forced the recovery and positive reassessment of eschatological (especially deriving from Joachim) trends in Catholicism and of the "Radical Reformation" in Protestantism. Christian Socialists in Europe and certain representatives of the Social Gospel and Christian Realist movements of the late nineteenth and early twentieth centuries in America have drawn heavily on the neglected or suppressed social dimensions of religious experience that are fundamental to man's sense of the meaning of life – dimensions accented by the Marxist tradition from which they drew. The flow of influence is not one-way. Reports from Europe indicate that there are several Marxist scholars reading Christian literature, not to get back to God, but to gain insight into human nature that fills gaps in Marxist theory. And Teilhard de Chardin and Paul Tillich are reputed to have numerous readers.

Several major efforts are being made to bring Christian-Marxist discussion into focus. The Paulus Gesellschaft has published a considerable amount of material on Christianity and Marxism today; Notre Dame Press has recently published a volume of papers from a conference on "Marx and the Western World"; and the World Council of Churches is sponsoring a major consultation on Christian-Marxist relations this year.

Both Marxists and Christians have complained, however, that far too much of the conversation has been focused on points of philosophical convergence or difference. Relatively little mutual effort has been made to examine the concrete relationship of religious belief and practice to the actual social life of the people. Still less has been done in the area of secularization from a sociological perspective. It may be possible to find a new ground for Christian-Marxist discussion through the social sciences if the discussions focus on topics of mutual concern.

Especially important pressure points at which to take the pulse of Marxist research on these issues are two "International Colloquia on the Sociology of Religion in Socialist Lands." The papers of the first, held in Jena in 1965, have recently become available in a volume edited by Olof Klohr [1]. The second, held in Prague in 1966, is as yet available only through secondary reports. Norman Birnbaum, who was invited to the second conference as a representative of the International Sociological Association, has written an insightful commentary on the proceedings and responses in Prague as a participant-observer. It is hoped that this review together with the report of Professor Birnbaum will give a glimpse of what is going on in the East. Furthermore, I hope to make available in English materials from the first conference in a way that will illuminate the four questions raised above.

A very large part of the material presented at the Jena Conference deals with the rates of defection from Christianity in socialist countries. Todor Stojtschew, of the Bulgarian Academy of Sciences' Institute for Philosophy, leads off the reports on the secularization process by citing the results of a 1962 survey of religiosity in Bulgaria, a study undertaken in order to facilitate overcoming the object of study! Although the desiderata for deciding whether one is religious or not religious are not specified, it appears that the principal criteria are participation in or willingness to defend church activities. The results indicate that 35.51% of the population are religious by these criteria and 64.44% are not, while .05% gave no indications.

Stojtschew is primarily concerned with analyzing the make-up of that 35% of the population. He shows that it consists of 12.68% of the men and 22.83% of the women; that it favors older persons (the rate is 78% among those over 69 but only 12% among those in the 18–23 age bracket); that it includes persons from farms, middle-sized businesses, and prosperous craft groups more frequently than it includes workers, officials, and small farmers. In short, he concludes that religion exists among those least affected by socialism. Religion, Stojtschew reports, will certainly be thrown off as society disposes of the fetters of the past. There are, it is true, more than one-third of the society who are still "religious," but when Stojtschew looks at "the intensity of religion" he finds religious decline more striking than expected. Only 5.76% are "religious in the first intensity"; these are sincere, spiritual persons or church dignitaries who attempt to extend their zeal and who give arguments for their faith. Another 14.39% are at the second level, which involves observing religious festivals, but also being quite tolerant of nonbelievers. More than 15% are disenchanted with religion even though they are not separated from all religious practices. Thus, of the 35% of the total population who are recorded as "religious," the overwhelming majority are already started along the path of secularization, even if they often are held to religion by various personal ties.

Stojtschew's reporting is representative of what one might expect of a rather narrow Marxism linked with a rather narrow view of statistical research. Nothing is out of line. He has proven to his own satisfaction that, in large measure, religion will automatically decline as socialization proceeds. Although every other paper points to similar if less dramatic trends, nearly all the other papers are more subtle, suggestive, and informative.

Wolfgang Masula of East Germany's Friedrich Schiller University points out that the secularization process is far progressed in three large cities of his country. The decline in religiosity is measured both by membership and participation in ordinary church activities and by the frequency of participation in the rites of passage such as baptisms, confirmations, marriages, and funerals. The exodus from the church, however, began at the turn of the century and thus is not so immediately bound to intentional socialization. Using previous studies, Masula shows that both the size and the rate of nonparticipation is growing rapidly. Active involvement has declined from highs of 97% to 18–20%. It is true, he points out, that the highest growth rate of nonbelievers has been since the founding of the East German government (D.D.R.), but he suggests that this phenomenon is deeply affected by the separation of church and state, as well as being an indication of realistic rather than illusionary ways of dealing with life. Separation allows a new freedom to leave the church without having to endure prejudice from one's superiors and peers.

891

Masula's careful presentation of the decline of religious activity points to several items on which he does not explicitly comment. For one thing, the figures show a surge of piety, or at least a recession in defection rates, from the years 1933 to 1946, especially among members of the Evangelical Church. And more recently, the exodus rate has been higher for that same group than for the Roman Catholics. One wishes for more analysis of this phenomenon.

In conjunction with his colleague Hans Lutter, a student of secularization in rural areas, Masula does take into consideration factors of age, education, degree of urban and industrial participation, and social class. While for the most part his data lead to the familiar conclusions that those groups closest to the typical economic, political, and cultural development of socialist society are clearly the furthest along the secularization process, his evaluation suggests some other issues. For one thing, he points to the decreasing difference in per cent of believers among men and women since the founding of the D.D.R., and takes the occasion to note that women are not by *nature* more religious than men, although nearly all studies show higher belief among women. They are more prone to religion where lack of equality with men prevails.

There are several "bliks" in his data that give him considerable concern. The white-collar workers are the least religious, lower by an almost negligible 2% than the blue-collar workers but considerably lower than the collectivized farmers (45.4%: 77.8%). Is the white-collar class the one most affected by socialization?

Further, there is a steady decline in religiosity according to age from those over 60 to those under 14. However, between the ages of 14 and 25 there is an unexpected surge of participation of nearly 10%. Masula recognizes that this is unexpected, but explains it in terms of the dependency of this group on their parents and the need for social interaction at a relatively intimate level. One can not help but wonder, however, how parental dependency affects youth at this age, especially in view of the fact that the religious participation rates for the parents of this age group are lower than for the youth. Further, one wonders whether a relatively independent youth culture is not in the process of formation, finding sanction — in the midst of an industrializing and urbanizing society — in the churches. The youth group movement, Y.M.C.A. and Sunday School movements played precisely such a role in the United States nearly two generations ago at a comparable moment of transition to an urban society.

Masula provides data to support his contention that the decline of church membership, great as it is, is not as great as the loss of belief. Responses to questions in anonymous questionnaires indicate that only 4.9% of the youth between 14 and 18 believe that in the final analysis the course of man's life and of world history is dependent on God. But this leads one to a very awkward possibility that Masula does not face: any rising rates of religious participation among the youth may derive from a need for relatively independent group formation outside the given social structure. Such a possibility has considerable sociological and theological import. Masula concludes that the tie to the church is merely formal and that adolescents will leave the form, as they have left the content, when they grow older.

A very interesting difficulty occurs here, however. If a wedge is driven between belief and participation, in what way is objective participation in religious activities indicative of the actuality of belief structure? How are comparative figures regarding earlier religious participation to be evaluated? Can we assume that everyone who went to church in 1900 was a "true believer" but that present churchgoers are not? That hardly corresponds with reports of pastors of that period who spoke of the woeful few who really believed. And, expecting that Marxist sociologists are no better and probably worse than a good number of Western sociologists in framing questionnaires about people's beliefs, what evidence do we have that youth are not rejecting formulations that few serious and reasonably well educated religious persons ever accepted? (One widely used study to determine the belief structure of church members was taken by seminarians in this country and the results indicated that no ministerial students were really religious.)

Masula does recognize the slippery character of belief and

participation studies when he points to the changing functions of the church itself. Worship for the entire community of believers was the primary form of church participation in the past, but that has declined to nearly 1% participation. Instead the worship function of religion has been displaced from the center and, where it does take place, occurs in the context of a number of other functions that appear less formal. Small-group, communal circles where conversation and discussion are the order of the day increasingly predominate. These can be organized according to age, sex, or vocation. Doctrinal issues fade into the background in these groups and themes from ethics, science, art, and literature come to the fore as ways by which people can orient their lives to the process of social change. Masula sees this entire trend as a strong piece of evidence for transition to full secularization, but occasionally he appears to be a bit baffled by it. In any case, he doubts that his trend will produce many lifetime faithful believers, and thus almost hints a legitimacy for such religious activity on the ground that such groups build attitudes of personal trust and psychological security that can allow fuller participation in the transformation of society.

Particular focus on the problem of youth occurs elsewhere in the volume in a more predictable paper by a Hungarian scholar. Ivan Varga, a social research expert from the Hungarian Academy of Science, investigated three villages — one industrialized, one agra-industrial, and one agricultural and traditional — according to a five-fold scale of belief structure: traditional, religious (vague but discernible Deism or Pantheistic beliefs), indifferent, nonreligious (loyalty to no particular world view but morally concerned), and atheist. Half of the village youth he studied fall in the middle three groups, and one-fourth at each end of the spectrum. As expected, the most "religious" were in the traditional village, and the fewest in the industrial. This clearly indicates the transitional character of the social matrix in which these youth find themselves, and Varga concludes that there are still numerous moments of alienation that occur in the whole social system. It is irrelevant whether the subjects were Catholic or Protestant, he found, but the social circumstances did make a

894

difference, with highest religiosity in least socialized centers. Still, when one looked at the goals of life that were held by the youth, there are very small distinctions between those at various points of the scale. Most wanted quiet, stable lives, material goods, or perhaps fame, in a socialized country.

Thus he concludes that wider study of the sociology of religion must not only include religious views but their relation to moral and social views and circumstances. Religion is still, for many, the guarantee of morality. Nevertheless, religion has lost its institutional basis of power for social regulation and the behavior of the youth is determined by other factors.

In Poland, according to the reports of Tadeusz Jaroszewski, director of the research project on "Contemporary Christianity" sponsored by the Party Academy in Warsaw, there are trends afoot that are not incompatible with the decline of religiosity in other Eastern European countries. The numbers involved in formal religious activity are declining at an increasing rate, although they remain high among the elderly, the women, the uneducated, and those farthest from industrial-urban society. However, Poland is shaped by a number of factors that give its development particular forms and problems. First of all, it has a long although not really scientific sociological tradition that has shaped the way it thinks about these matters. Second, Poland has been until recently a land with an almost monolithic religious structure in which Roman Catholicism traditionally represented a rich spiritual integration. At the same time, it has had a series of changes of revolutionary character that rendered a relative degree of scientific freedom, a division of church and state, and a tolerance for different confessions and world views — all of which preceded and led to the radical changes of industrialization, urbanization, and social consciousness in the socialist revolution. Further, the challenge of socialistic views of the world has been met by the development of a Catholic intellectual elite that still influences the situation. Thus, Poland represents both general trends in social development and particular trends that shape its uniqueness.

On the basis of several thousand representatively selected

anonymous questionnaires, Jaroszewski finds that 78% identify themselves as Catholics and 21.6% as atheists. While there seems to be a decline in total religious participation or membership, much more interesting is the comparison of these total figures with responses to basic Catholic teachings. Of the Catholic respondents, 70% did not disapprove of abortion, 37% were not critical of divorce, and 14.5% did not believe that God created the world. When asked about the primary responsibilities of Catholicism today, more definite answers were given to such matters as "securing freedom" and "utilization of thermonuclear energy for peaceful purposes" than to such answers as "the extension of Christianity." Jaroszewski cites other studies by Judenko, Podgorecki, and Legowski that concur with his results and suggest both that only 7% of the population defends the laws of the church in regard to marriage and the family and that self-confessed "believing" people are reading forbidden books of an anticlerical slant.

Such divergence of confessed believers from the standards of the belief, Jaroszewski suggests, can be best clarified if one arranges a typology to deal with those who are attached to Catholicism for traditionalistic, emotional, or intellectual reasons. On the basis of such discriminations, he finds that genuine loyalties to, and the intellectual defense of, religion is much less significant than traditional attention to feast-days. One must consequently make a fundamental distinction between the secularization of consciousness that is taking place, and the feeling of belonging to the church as a matter of tradition.

Secularization in Poland in the last twenty years, therefore, takes two forms. Among the intelligentsia, trained workers, youth, and the urbanized there is a slackening of church ties. But in the villages, small towns, and suburbs where there is comparatively little visible exodus from the traditional and cultic functions, there is a subtle but persistent internalization of new sets of values that derive from sources outside the church and are at odds with the church. For these groups the cultic and aesthetic dimensions of religion are in fact divorced from questions of dogma, credo, and social orientation.

896

The massive shift is being created by several factors. In place of the believer, and even in the midst of religious practice, a technological man who is anti-speculative is coming to the fore. The new man has lost confidence in the possibility and fruitfulness of intuitive and purely spiritual modes of cognition. He has little patience with the subtleties of personalism and mysticism. The whole foundation of religious psychology is called into question. According to Jaroszewski, man has come to a point where he feels himself to be nature's lord and he now engages in what one Polish publicist has called the "intentional dissection of the mysterious."

Second, in earlier stages of social and economic development, Polish Catholicism was the essential factor in social integration. It linked an ideological and cultural unity to actual foundations in the community. Indeed, there was a confessional monopoly on nearly all cultural functions. Now, philosophy, legal theory, science, art, and entertainment have all been emancipated from that control. The church simply could not keep pace and now actually performs no essential social function.

Third, citing Robertson-Smith's typology of groups — natural, local, and free — Jaroszewski claims that religious grouping was determined according to naturalistic and localistic group formations. In this situation belief and world view were supported by local pressure of the social group toward full solidarity. Industrialization and urbanization have undercut the power of local communalism and freed the individual from the tyranny of the natural and localistic groups. The infiltration of city life into the local situation has even there displaced the confessional as the center of social and cultural life. Thus a whole new range of models for life has been imported: they accelerate the rhythm of life, they shorten the drudgery of workaday life, they provide more freedom and, perhaps most important, they supply a sense of access to, not distance from, fundamental cultural forms. Religion is thus neutralized.

These things are terribly important to know, concludes the author, for the socialist ideal to Polish Marxists involves not only the ending of private ownership and of the exploitation of the

897

masses by man, not only the planning of production and the establishment of the security and well-being of the workaday masses, but also entails the establishment of a society in which man feels more free and the social situation is humanized and transparent to every man in his practical life. It points toward a social organization in which man feels himself ready to be creator of history; and all sides of his personal potentialities can be developed.

In spite of the fact that there seem to be moments of stretching to prove the wide extent of secularization in the face of stubborn data on the adherence to Catholicism, Jaroszewski's paper conveys the impression that he has *felt* the data, not just seen them. Although he deals with material that celebrates the decline of intuitive thought precisely his own stretching has allowed a genuine humanism to cut through the mechanical and the reductionistic. He has sensed the lives of men and the flow of history behind the data in a direct way. His analysis of religion in Poland is supplemented by his colleague's report on religiosity in the Polish village.

Konstanty Judenko rehearses both the sociological tradition that informs his analysis and the deprovincialization process that is occurring in the Polish backwaters. He traces the development that has led from a situation so parochial that most peasants were sure that God spoke Polish and where the Polish patriarchal family structure was seen as part of God's order of creation, to the present revolution in social situation and in consciousness. The development has produced a crisis in the parish. He too sees the practices remaining, although the defection rates are growing, but suggests that they have a moral or aesthetic function, helping people to appreciate the good or the beautiful. In general the day of the dominance of religion is already past and the change in consciousness has already been accomplished. Only the forms hang on.

The contributions from the Soviet Union are less interesting from the standpoint of what they tried to do but fascinating from the standpoint of the observations made in passing. A.F. Okulow, Professor and Director of the Institute for Scientific

Atheism in Moscow, spent a good bit of his time telling about the activities of the Institute — especially a study that was in its early stages. The results of that study, when available, may well be of considerable significance if only because of its vastness and attempted comprehensiveness. But what is interesting to me are his observations on why the study should be made. Tucked around his general line that we should know the enemy, the more readily to defeat it, were suggestions that religion is considerably more persistent than had been expected and that in order to understand why, one had to look both at the motives of persons and the changing, refined, and modified character of religion in the period of its own decline. Religion according to ordinary expectations, Okulow seems to hint, should be a fixed and rigidified constant that will decline as its social base alters. Instead it is changing in both social function and ideology. Indeed, the process of overcoming religious ideology cannot be reduced to presenting the believer with an alternative ideology. It must be tied to seeing the whole style of life of people. Many who are involved in the social and cultural construction of a communist society evidently have latent Deistic and Pantheistic elements in their thought that make it impossible to classify them as either believers in the ordinary sense or spontaneous atheists in the orthodox sense.

His countryman Nikolai Krasnikov, who is Director of the Museum of the History of Religion and Atheism in Leningrad, hints at something of the same sort. He suggests that religion is not being overcome as totally or as quickly as expected, although on the basis of research done by the Museum in 1962, he follows the pattern set by most of the presentations to show that the overwhelming majority of the religious are rural dwellers, women, old men, pensioners, the uneducated; in short, they are those least integrated into the new society. Yet he also points out that growing evidence points toward a kind of believer whose belief is blended with numerous forms of secular knowledge. This believer in fact knows that his belief is different, but he preserves his relationship to the tradition after a fashion. These modern believers have the same interests as the whole

899

people in that they see the sense of life in the building up of communism, yet they preserve a belief commitment. The new belief pattern is not only found in personal attitudes, but also in the widespread modernization and simplification of the cultic patterns. Still further, there is frequently the attempt to relate and even to identify Christianity and communism, science and religion. All this means, for the most part, that residual Christianity is being incorporated into a more advanced view. But Krasnikov seems also to be suggesting that such shifts show the lack of integrity in a religion that will do almost anything to survive. At other moments there is the hint that religion serves a prophetic function in Marxist society, indicating areas that need attention; religionists tend to fasten upon those areas of life and culture where people are not satisfactorily cared for. Thus Krasnikov thinks the study of religion is important for it helps uncover faults in the cultural and material well-being of the citizens.

The reports of research in Czechoslovakia were divided according to region. Erika Kadlecova of the Sociological Institute, Academy of Science, Prague, reported on research in Moravia. In her carefully controlled study it was shown that the number of believers declines from 45% among those over 61 to 25% among those in the 20 to 30 age group, a significant decline of 20%. At the same time the number of confessed atheists increased by 8% and the number of undecided by 12%. As with previous studies, the larger percentages of believers were found among the women, the farmers, the least educated and least urbanized or industrialized. Overall, 30% of the population was religious, 30% atheist, and 40% was indifferent or indeterminate because of ambiguous responses (for example, did not believe in God, but thought that He probably existed).

Several aspects of her study are of special interest: first, her clear statement on the basis of her data that the exodus from Christianity under the impact of social and economic change does not lead necessarily to subscription to Marxist or scientific orientation. Many seem to become more free-floating and are not strongly committed to any clear system of thought. Second, she attempts to measure the functions that religion performs when held by people. She delimits three levels of intensity: 48% of the confessed religious population are of the church conforming type, although only about half of these find in religion their central values and life orientation. The latter are the truly religious. The others merely recognize the basic Christian dogmas and fulfill their church obligations. The majority of believers, however, are non-conforming. Religion is a residual form that is rooted in social grouping and traditional practices. Third, she asks how we are to understand those who engage in private devotions and prayer. In what way is such activity a reflection of false social relations and not an expression of deep personal religious need? And, finally, she asks why those not intensively committed continue to call themselves believers.

Religion must be understood, responds Kadlecova to her own questions, not as a basic conception or idea, but as a way of dealing with problems. The basis of religion is pragmatic. Religion is not valuable to the overwhelming majority of believers because of its intrinsic worth or its supernatural aspects, but as a means to bind man to man, or as a means for solving difficulties or as a way of postulating values for society. Religion, thus, is not something that provides the goal and meaning of life. It is a means to the end of attaining goals and senses of meaning derived elsewhere. Religion supplies a source of trust, strength, and inner calm that compensates for its absence in other aspects of life. Further, religion makes what is outside itself seem valuable. Religion thus is a substitute for unfulfilled human personal and social development and a defense mechanism against those aspects of life that threaten its meaning and purpose.

To reinforce her view, Kadlecova points out that by far the greatest numbers of reasons that were given for believing in religion were of the moral kind. Religion points man to the good and helps to cultivate man. Indeed, 64% saw value in religion because of its service to men, not because it was intrinsically valuable. Among the respondents to her questionnaire 12% took special note of its positive effects on the young.

In short, religion has lost its integration function in most of contemporary society, but it has not as yet lost its compensation function. Still it has been shown that people do not consider religion intrinsically valuable, but only useful as a tool, and thus it will probably be dispensed with when the new society is secured.

The second paper from Czechoslovakia, prepared by Peter Prusak and Bohumir Kvasnicka of the Department of Scientific Atheism in the Slovakian Academy of Science in Bratislava, portrays the rather complex picture in southern Czechoslovakia.

Deeply influenced by the political and nationalistic use of religion for most political movements in the past, much of which has led to the discrediting of the church and its leadership, the religious picture is quite variegated. The most powerful group, of course, is the Catholic. But the Church of the Augsburg Confession, the Lutheran Church, is strong in the West and North. In the South, where a number of citizens of Hungarian extraction live, the Calvinistic population is strong. In the East there exists in addition to the Catholics a sizable number of Orthodox. And finally, scattered throughout many communities are numerous sect groups — Bohemian Brothers, Adventists, Baptists, Methodists, and so on. Perhaps because of this complexity, the authors suggest that great subtlety is needed to sort out the various kinds of social conditions that make for such divergence. Here religion serves not so much as a means of social integration, but a means of social differentiation. Declaring it to be a residue of the past really doesn't seem to lead to its release. Instead the point of departure for victory over religion in its various forms must be the establishment of new socialistic forms of consciousness based on new forms of social and economic organization. The differences of religion only indicate the persistence and varieties of alienation that must be overcome.

Hungary also has a variegated religious picture, but treatment of the situation there is handled in a quite different way by Istvan Konya, Chairman of the Professorships of Marxism-Leninism in the University at Debrecen. Konya raises a whole set of problems scarcely dealt with by the colloquium outside this paper. The chief question that concerns him is: how does it happen that in a predominantly Catholic country bounded on one side by a sea of Lutheranism, on another by Eastern Orthodoxy, and next to the world of Islam, there have developed relatively large centers of Calvinism, "the most western form of Christianity"? The answer that is usually given to this question, which was first posed by a theologian, Mihaly Bucsay, is disposed of by Konya; it simply doesn't explain anything to answer that the Hungarian people turned to Helvetian Calvinism in order to find a view that corresponded most closely to their already well developed views.

Konya points out that Calvinism is strongest in those areas where the Turks were in control at earlier stages of Hungary's history and that the Turks had in fact allowed and encouraged the development of an early capitalism. The system of large Hungarian land owners was disturbed and a relatively free atmosphere for trade and industry opened up. Opposition to the Hapsburgs by the Hungarian patriots made the adoption of Catholicism hardly possible. The conditions for the adoption of Calvinism were thus created. Calvinism had already developed, during its time in West Europe, an adequate religious ideology for a society in the stage of early capitalism. Konya is indirectly turning the tables on Max Weber by an argument that accounts for the extension of Calvinist motifs into the nationalist and urbanizing development of particular countries. The broad implications of his paper are not in any way stated, and he confines himself to a rather orthodox Marxist interpretation of Calvinism in Hungary. But the implications assert themselves: Why do forms of religion quite like Calvinistic Christianity continue to expand in some of the developing countries?

With the above synopsis of the data and some of the most interesting features of their interpretation before us, we can begin to ask the questions tentatively posed at the outset. Are religious belief and practice rapidly declining in Communist lands? The answer is clearly yes, especially if we mean by religion what the researchers seem to mean: inherited cultic practice, traditional doctrine as the singular mode of interpretation of life, and clerical dominance of cultural activity. But what is unexpected to the observers is the persistence of religion in its less traditional forms. There is here and there a backhanded recognition that religion stands as a judgment against socialistic society precisely in its attraction to the still alienated and in it its capacity to bear aesthetic, moral, and interpersonal values in a rapidly changing environment. On the one hand, there is almost the recognition that communism has not yet succeeded in bringing all it has promised and that the deficiency can be measured by the frequency of religious orientation and participation. On the other hand, the fact that it is the elderly, the least industrialized and urbanized, the illiterate, and the women who are most attached to religion portends the further decrease of religion as the older generation dies off, and as industrialization, urbanization, education, and the equality of women are extended. Still, the new developments of small group formation, of modified and modernized religious belief and practice, of the adaptation of Christian motifs to Communist circumstances on the part of some, and of the lack of enthusiastic commitment to a scientific atheism on the part of many — and all this occurring among those who are young, educated, and urbanized with enough frequency that it shows in several studies — bears marks that are not at all bleak to liberal theologians of the West. If all this means the death of some of the idolatrous, magical forms of religion that have held sway in the Eastern European countries, many Christians can, with only modest difficulty, participate in the funeral conducted by the Marxists.

But how successful are efforts at intentional secularization? Clearly, the efforts to overcome religion by rational argumentation or polemical counterposition have not been successful modes of intended secularization. It is not possible to tell whether it is frustration or theoretical "orthodoxy" that causes nearly all authors to observe that religion is not overcome by antireligious propaganda. Yet all the scholars who gave papers at Jena are convinced that it is possible for man intentionally to secularize by extending economic security, technology, education, political consciousness, and socialization. Thus can man be fully humanized and ultimately separated from his illusions of dependency. Of course, it will be a long slow process.

The Christian is tempted to see a familiar pattern at this point. The *parousia* has failed, but the faith is not dead. Marxism to these scholars represents an institutionalized means of redemption as much as an eschatological vision. They are already far along the road of "routinization of charisma." And it is at this point that the socially concerned religious man both celebrates the advances that have been made and warns of moral pretension. It is difficult to weep because an "anti-religious" movement has been shattering idolatrous myths that have made man accept the tyranny of exploiting groups who wrap themselves in sanctity. But it is difficult not to warn of the utopianism that does not recognize the stubbornness of the human propensity to exploit.

Nevertheless, it seems quite clear that the specific forms of religion that are the most noxious to the Marxists are being stamped out in a process not greatly different in result from the way the same forms are being outgrown in the West. Like industrialism and urbanism, which emerged slowly and painfully in the West and convulsively in the East, new forms of religiosity that are open to the world are displacing closed, complete, and controlled forms of religious belief and practice — emergently in the West, suddenly in the East.

These observations on the effectiveness of intentional secularization thus lead to a partial answer to the question of whether religion is purified by such efforts or whether it looses its import. The deprivation of religion of its social basis has forced a reassessment in certain circles of what theology and religion are about and seems to be producing religious activity that is clearly compatible with some of the prophetic trends throughout the history of the church. It may be more than vain hope that sees the possible emergence in Christianity of a prophetic and innovative orientation that has often been only a minority report. But it is highly likely that without any social base whatever it can neither stand as a judgment against actual inadequacies in the more fully socialized system nor participate in processes of social and cultural creativity on even ethical, aesthetic, and small-group grounds. Any effective conceptual framework requires an organized constituency. It is simply too soon to see with what social grounding the new forms of religious consciousness will find secure affinity and whether they will be strong enough to endure in contemporary circumstances. But without some *religious* practice and organization, it does not look as though Christianity can survive in any recognizable form. Religionless Christianity dies.

We turn, then, to the third question posed at the outset of this interpretive report, and ask whether Marxist social science is conceptually capable of dealing with religious phenomena. To answer, we must look at another set of papers delivered at the Jena conference. Nearly one-third of the material prepared for the Jena conference had to do with the theoretical problems of Marxist sociology of religion and its relation to the basis and results of "bourgeois sociology."

Marxism understands religion, according to the presentation of the East German Olaf Klohr who also edited the volume, not according to the question of the truth or untruth of its creed, but as a social, economic, and historical phenomenon. Religion must be understood first in its sociological dimensions rather than in terms of a theory of cognition. Ethics, religion, metaphysics, and other forms of ideology or consciousness can no longer take on the appearance of independence. They have no history and no development separable from the material ground and circumstances of their origins. Consciousness does not determine existence; existence determines consciousness.

Having stated this fundamental viewpoint that is echoed throughout the theoretical papers, Klohr states five theses that represent the basis of a "Marxist-Leninist sociology of religion":

1. Religion is a specific *form of social consciousness* which, in the *final* analysis, is conditioned by material, social conditions, and determined as to its contents.

906

2. Religion in its contemporary expression is primarily a *social phenomenon* which derives from a class society.

3. Religion is therefore only a social factor insofar as it is institutionalized in a church with all its accoutrements and forms of life.

4. Religion and the church are, nevertheless, in no way only *passive* products of social relations, but in turn influence politics, morals, law, and philosophy and thereby play an *active* role in social life.

5. Insofar as religion and the church are finally determined by social relations, attention must be given to the relatively independent developments so that they do not develop determinative social power.

On the basis of these five theses, Klohr looks at Christianity, paying particular attention to modern theologies in which concern for one's fellow man is a central theme. He concludes that the decisive difference between humanitarian theologies and Marxist atheism is that the former obscures fundamental human relations by placing them on a mysterious undergirding, whereas the latter forms such relations on a primarily rational basis.

He goes on to point out that religion is not a natural or spontaneous thing, but a convention growing out of specific conditions. Atheism is not a spontaneous matter either. The theoretical and practical affirmation of the world is something that must be attained and is not gained by mere negation of religiousness or faith. One must actually free man from the conditions of slavery and suppression and make it actually possible for him to become lord of his world. Then the old dream of humanism, of which one finds many traces in Christianity, can become a reality. Only then will scientific atheism as the theoretical expression of practical relations be fully possible. In an oblique way, Klohr then moves briefly to an argument for tolerance. It is foolish to suppress religion, he suggests quoting Engels, for the *need* still remains.

He also attempts to articulate what he means by atheism. Most certainly he is not referring to the intellectual and bourgeois atheism of the eighteenth and nineteenth centuries. That sort of atheism was directed against clericalism and cultural Christianity that was inhibiting the development of bourgeois individualism. It is thus a product of the milieu that is very similar to many conservative theological orientations. It was in no major way related to the transformation of the environment by the oppressed. Atheism in the form of Scientific Marxism developed in connection with the workers' movement and thus has a social ground that gives it particular import. It is the failure to distinguish between these forms of atheism that has led theologians to miss the mark almost totally when they attempt to characterize modern scientific atheism, for they see only a new edition of the intellectual denial of God that occurred in bourgeois atheism.

Klohr states the major criteria by which one can establish, in contrast to bourgeois atheism, a genuinely scientific, socially grounded, atheistic standpoint:

A. In regard to its world view and political basis, it holds that:
   1. The course of human life and world history is finally dependent upon natural law and human dealings. Only science can correctly and fully enlighten the processes in nature and society.
   2. Man can rule the natural powers and social relations without divine help.
   3. Man can consciously and systematically fashion the life of society in socialism, which will extend itself throughout the whole world.
B. In regard to its critique of religion and relations to the church:
   1. It endures no belief in God and his revelation through Jesus Christ.
   2. The results of science are not compatible with religious faith.
   3. Man needs no religion in our times. Religion will die.
   4. Nonaffiliation with a religious community is essential.
C. In regard to its relation to the practical social situation:
   The church loses its ordering function in society under so-

cialism and cannot bind man to specific religious norms. The new norms grow out of the social-economic, political, cultural and ideological realities of socialist society. These norms are increasingly binding not only for Marxist and nonreligious citizens, but also for the Christian.

To reinforce his view, Klohr argues that religion is not a constant anyway, and that one need only look at the history of Christianity to find how variegated it is and how in each case religion has changed as social conditions have changed. Indeed, he notes, even today modern theology claims that until the beginning of the twentieth century the Christian message has been falsified, and thereby claims that it has only now been discovered what Christianity really is. This theology persists in denying that even the contemporary form of theology is a transition phenomenon in our time, a transition to knowledge by scientific means and a response to the irresistible secularization process.

One expects that Klohr's insights, couched unfortunately in a rather wooden and "official sounding" understanding of Marxist sociology and of religion, provide few guidelines for either the alert Marxist, the honest sociologist, or the serious believer as they separately or jointly try to come to grips with the modern world. Yet he has in the course of his presentation raised some hard questions that can serve as a point of departure for subsequent presentations that deal with the problem of Marxist sociology of religon.

J. A. Lewada of Moscow's Academy of Science, for one, points out the fundamental relation between social conditions and the formation of religious belief, but sees the process of dealing with religion as more complicated than Klohr's view reflects. A religious complex, whether a concept, a person, or a doctrine, has many aspects — epistemological, psychological, religious-historical, and sociological. It is, in Lewada's view, the function of sociology of religion to deal with the social needs which call the religious complex into life. And, because this sociological dimension is of such fundamental significance, it can show that what appears to be a psychological or epistemological "fiction" is in fact based in certain social needs or conditions.

He suggests that there are two important sociological problems that need attention. One is the structure of religiosity among the masses, a question on which his views differ little from views already presented. The other is an understanding of ritual.

From a rationalistic standpoint, it appears that ritual is merely an affirmation of a religious *idea*. But when one understands ritual from a social perspective, one sees that it is in fact a particular expression of sanctified social relationships which cannot be fully inferred from the theological conception alone. Ritual is a complex of actions whose goal is to reinforce and stimulate the religious connection. In ritual one sees an apparent overcoming of the real contradictions of life — suffering, death, need, etc. — by group formation.

However, ritual appears to have a stability that does not occur in society. If ritual and belief are mere reflections of the social situation, how does it happen that ritual does not change very rapidly while the social situation seems to have been in continual flux? Ritual, points out Lewada, is for the most part devoid of informational content and is thus not so directly tied to the changing information of the social scene. Indeed, he implies that it finds its meaning in the inarticulate, unconscious aspects of the social relations that are very deeply rooted and quite persistent. Ceremonial is of course not eternal, but it does teach us that the overcoming of religion is not only tied to the triumph of conscious values and critical scientific thought in decisive acts, but also to the relatively slower, progressive conversion and the re-evaluation of the customary and traditional relations and dependencies expressed in ritual relations.

Lewada's countryman D.M. Ugrinovitsch, Professor of Dialectic and Historical Materialism in Moscow, and Johann Klügl, like Klohr a Professor of Scientific Atheism at Jena, conclude the theoretical section of the book with comparisons of the way Marxists deal with sociology of religion to the efforts of western sociologists. Ugrinovitsch agrees with Klohr that religion is a social phenomenon that draws its content from the particular forms of each society, but he wants to focus on the degree of independence that religion has from its social ground. The criticism of religion should be able to give reasons for religion's long historical existence as well as its origins. Nor, Ugrinovitsch suggests, should Marxists ignore the fact that bourgeois sociologists have acknowledged the relationship of religion to social conditions. Max Weber, for example, whom Ugrinovitsch sees as the founder and prototype of bourgeois sociology continually acknowledges the interaction and exchange between social phenomena and religion. But religion for Weber is not grounded in the social order itself. Indeed, religion is seen as a "meta-social" phenomenon, although Weber has agnostic and positivistic elements in his work. Such attitudes toward religion, held still by his followers, betray a fideist bias in bourgeois sociology irrespective of the figleaf of agnosticism that never quite covers their nakedness. Joachim Wach, Gustav Mensching, Van der Leeuw, and others quite clearly state that the essence of religion is transcendent, nonsocial, and not accessible to sociological analysis. Sociology, for them, does not touch the center of religion but only its social manifestations. Ugrinovitsch does, of course, find discussions of a two-way exchange; such sociologists as Milten J. Yinger see their task in understanding the ways in which society, culture, and personality affect religion. But for the most part, the failure to acknowledge the social foundations of religion perpetuates a dualistic relationship between religion and society. Bourgeois sociology of religion is thus itself a reflection of a bourgeois society. Even Durkheim, who acknowledges the social origins of religion, sees religion taking on a more independent role than actually exists, and concludes that every society must produce some form of "religious" formulation. He too ends in an apologetic for religion.

For Ugrinovitsch, the Marxists see religion as a reflection of social conditions, although it behooves them to make an analytical distinction, not an existential distinction, between the reflection and the objective reality that it reflects. Especially critical is the question of how a reflection can take upon itself such ruling power for men. Unfortunately, many try to answer this question by saying that religion is either a false picture of the real world or a real reflection of a false world. In fact, it is a question of a distorted picture of a distorted world. Only when one sees both facts can one begin to deal with sociology of religion on a fundamental basis.

With copious quotations from Marx and Lenin, Ugrinovitsch goes on to show that an undistorted picture of an undistorted world is required, thereby implying that every society needs symbolic expression.

Ugrinovitsch has opened a door that remains closed throughout the remainder of the papers. He comes almost to a point of acknowledging what many Western sociologists and theologians consider to be the case: every society, to be a society, requires some form of ritual and belief pattern. The debate is an ethical one: is the social foundation a just one, is the articulation of it an honest one and is it better or worse to have the ritual and belief pattern totally integrated with economic and political structures?

On the other hand, Ugrinovitsch leaves unanswered the question of the degree of independence of the "reflection" from its "object," a question raised first by Klohr. Supposing that one took the view that various social forces did deeply influence or even determine the erection of a particular religious belief and cultic pattern, does not the question of Durkheim still stand? Is it not the case that religion becomes, once generated, a social fact that has considerable independence? Is it not the case, further, that Marxism once generated became a symbolic structure that transcends and surpasses in its calculations of the future, in its attempted wholeness of explanation, the actual social foundation upon which it rests? It seems clear that the persistence of religion in the Eastern European countries indicates that the whole of the social order has not been transformed. Should not scientific atheism, then, present itself as a partial picture of social reality reflecting a partially accomplished social transformation? The "bourgeois" notion that Marxism can in part be understood as secular faith may not be wholly wrong.

Johann Klügl touches on several of these themes in his wide-ranging survey and evaluation of western sociology of religion as it attempts to come to grips with secularization. Bourgeois sociology of religion is rooted in the idealistic philosophy of history and in the neokantianism of Max Weber and Ernst Toeltsch. It came to fruition because of a number of factors, not the least of which are the industrial development, urbanization, the extension of science and technology, and a radical this-worldly orientation of the people that further and further contradicted the religious outlook of preceding ages. Protestantism, which was most allied with the small bourgeois and farmer strata of society and alienated from the working population had to find a way to explain the environment. Another branch of social research founded by Father LeBras, is seen by Klügl to be quite clearly an effort to find strategic locations where the interests of the church could be extended. The fact that much contemporary sociology of religion is dominated by theologians is cited as certification of this motivation.

Nevertheless, western sociologists have themselves acknowledged the decline of religiosity. In England, in Scandinavia, in America, reports continue of the departure of people from the church and the departure of the church to the periphery of society. What is most interesting, says Klügl, is the search for the causes for this phenomenon on the part of western scholars. They attribute it to such things as the privatization of religion in conjunction with the increasing complexity of society, the development of alternative modes of thought brought about by science and technology, and the shifting social and interpersonal needs of the people. Thus, bourgeois sociology has acknowledged a whole series of important causes of the contemporary crisis, although they still do not focus on the question of the relationship of the people to the means of production and of the connections of the church, especially the clergy, to the values and interests of the middle class.

Nevertheless, the Eastern European sociologists believe that the turn to sociology of religion in the West has occasioned considerable self appraisal and has caused a great number of sociologists of religion and theologians to come to several conclusions:

913

1. The necessity of a break by Christianity and the church with its own social past.
2. The necessity of changing the methods and organization of the church, putting "dialogue" always in the center, and deemphasizing cultic action.
3. The necessary inclusion of the results of science.
4. The concentration on ethics, including an attempt to provide a point of tension against a completely rationalized society.

Such shifts, however, are believed to represent a defensive position of the church which runs with "breathless gasps and flapping tongue" behind the times. The shifts also display a lack of theoretical perspicacity in contemporary bourgeois sociology of religion, and indicate the degree to which sociology of religion is dependent upon apologetic theology, pastoral care, and apostolic preservation. Where it seems to have broken from its past orientation, it has degenerated into a micro-sociological empirical position that is too often used as a tool for church strategists. In any case it is incapable of making any major contribution to society (although it *seems* to represent a transition to a more scientific view).

In short, bourgeois sociology of religion is incapable of accounting for the nature of religion itself, or the basis of the rapid secularization which it reports itself, or the development of sociology of religion in western forms. Socialism, however, can show both how sociology of religion arose in the West and why the processes of secularization are taking place (at the same time finding a grounding in actual social relationships that move toward the creation of a new man and a new consciousness that will have no need of either religion or bourgeois apologies for it).

Klügl has forced the issues to a point where such perspectives often lead. A generation ago, the academic trick was to see who could "out-psych" the other. Klügl has tried to "out-soc" his fellow sociologists. One is tempted at times to out-Marx the Marxist in response, for there is a conspicuous absence of reference to Marx' deeply rooted notion that the fundamental criticism of a society begins in the criticism of religion. With that notion in mind, the efforts of Max Weber are very hard to get around, in spite of the way they have often been systematically misrepresented. It is not mere defensiveness to ask why some are and some are not willing to engage in action that extends them beyond what is already present in their environment — indeed intentionally to transform that environment before they have the social conditions undergirding them. What period of history could Klügl point to in which the church did not spin off new groups and techniques the more readily to deal with the real and changing needs of man — groups and techniques that acknowledged and accented the break with the dominant practices of the church while still claiming continuity with the church? But this is not the place to give a full-fledged response.

One can, however, attempt answers to the remaining two questions posed many pages ago. Is the Marxist frame of reference capable of dealing with religious phenomena in other than a reductionist fashion? And are there grounds for a Christian-Marxist dialogue through the social sciences? Much of the time we have to answer with a disappointed "no" to both questions. Far too often the Marxist definition of religion, and of secularization for that matter, is so narrow that very, very little of the human attempt to define and organize around that which is deemed ultimately worthy and valuable is included. Secularization is not then seen as a new chapter in a long human narrative, but a conclusion that ends the drama. Never is the question asked whether religion ever tried to deal seriously with real dilemmas of existence. No search is made to see how a tradition that speaks continually of a new man and a new creation gives rise to a humanist ethic and a transformationist ethic. And seldom is account taken of the secular forms of myth, ritual, and symbol that have to be created to supplant those rooted out. Such lacks are unhistorical and unempirical.

But there are numerous moments when the answer is a promising "maybe." That the entire industrialized world is undergoing a shift in group formation and consciousness under the name of secularization is manifest. Some of these papers demand the rec-

ognition, where it is not already present, of the fact that changing social and ideological conditions (which religion has itself
partially engendered) can force strong belief and organizational
commitment, Christian or Marxist, into indifference to the conditions of others. What then are believers in a whole humanity
reconciled to that which is ultimately worthy and powerful to
do? Shall we romantically glorify the past? Shall we write our
own obituary? Shall we retreat to personal piety and cure of
souls? Shall we rejoice that the whole society is now performing
what was once the special responsibility of the *ecclesiola* and
congratulate ourselves on the "christianization" of society? Or
shall we ecumenically join with those Marxist "separated brethren" who are willing to use social analysis *and* symbolic constructs to create a prophetic body of believers that transcends
scientist or religious reductionism? These are the questions that
the so-called religiously biased social analyst of the West must
ask.

Second, there are several specific areas open for joint research.
In discussions of the role of religion in youth culture, in analysis
of the role of religion among the alienated and as a center for
new group formation, in social research into why people are
religious and how they use religion in their lives, and in study of
the ways in which religion changes and perennially baptizes aspects of worldly knowledge and life without apparent embarrassment, much can be learned from serious exchange with the
growing discipline of sociology of religion in the Eastern European countries.

Third, as long as there is the honest, if theoretically tenuous,
recognition that religion exercises a relatively independent power
in society, and that symbolic and ritual expressions are necessary
to the building and maintenance of human relationships, there
are openings for non-reductionistic treatment of religious phenomena. There will remain vigorous debates as to which symbols
are most adequate to that which is ultimately powerful and
worthy of final loyalty, and disagreement as to how that is to be
discerned. But serious conversation with the "secular theologians" of modern society is possible, and no view will be seri-

916

ously considered unless it represents a sense of truth, justice, and compassion for people, supported by a group policy and polity directed to those ends. By their fruits ye shall know them.

None of this, however, mitigates the shock that materials from Jena will induce among many believers, especially those who understand Christianity not as a movement, but as a set of eternal ideals and ideas. Those who have a historical understanding of Christianity will not be threatened. And a movement that understands history in terms of crucifixion and resurrection should not be so shocked. It is highly unlikely that a tradition that is not a constant, but a pattern of constant change, should be shattered by a cultural shift that it helped to generate. The symbols of the Christian theological tradition have an expansive, flexible character that points toward historical phenomena more persistent than momentary crises. The present rod of Cyrus may actually represent that which is most powerful and worthy of loyalty. But the rod of chastisement does not exhaust that which is ultimately worthy and powerful.

REFERENCE

1. Klohr, Olaf, ed: *Religion und Atheism heute. Ergebnisse und aufgaben marxistischer Religionssociologie* (VEB Deutsches Verlagder Wissenschaft, Berlin) 1966.

EASTERN EUROPE AND THE DEATH OF GOD
by Norman Birnbaum

IN HIS BOOK on the German Peasants' War, Friedrich Engels observed that in a religious epoch, even revolutionary ideas have to be expressed in a religious rhetoric: the very thoughts which anticipate the future assume old forms. I was reminded of Engels' remark when, last December, I attended a conference of Marxist sociologists of religion in Prague. The participants, nearly all of them from Eastern Europe, were troubled by the persistence of religion among the populations of the communist countries. A few reacted dogmatically: as the case was put by one scholar from the German Democratic Republic who held to a rather narrow version of Marxism, if religion did not decline under socialism, then the Marxist theory would have to be considered false. Other participants who took a much more subtle, comprehensive, and comprehending view of religion in history (including their own recent history) did so in different Marxist terms. I believe that their utilization of Marxism to explore the social and spiritual realities around them may anticipate new developments in Eastern Europe.

Engels was writing, in fact, about the great Reformation theologian and Christian communist Thomas Muenzer, who died a horrible death at the hands of vengeful German (Protestant) princes for having taken seriously the doctrine of the Imminence of the Kingdom in early Protestant theology. My colleagues at Prague were sociologists and philosophers, not theologians, and none spoke directly against his own princes. Yet some of the things they said in the course of the meeting reflected deep changes in Eastern Europe, and these may very well portend new developments in other spheres — not least in politics.

Ever since the end of Stalinism, the communist parties of Eastern Europe have been seeking a *modus vivendi* with the populations they rule. Janos Kadar's *bon mot*, "all who are not against us are with us," typifies one prevalent attitude. The peoples of Eastern Europe cannot yet be described as enthusiastic about socialism in its Eastern European version. A less hostile and more sophisticated view of the religious beliefs and communities to which these peoples remain attached is a consequence of the new communist awareness of this fact. It is true that the communists (or some of them) remain most hostile to religion where the churches have been strongest: above all, in Poland, where the Primate is about as stubborn as the General Secretary of the Communist Party, both being old men who grew up in a different world; and in Germany, where the Protestant Church has been the one functioning all-German institution. In general, however, Eastern European regimes have now learned to distinguish between the political views of certain ecclesiastical leaders and the religious convictions of their peoples — if only the better to split the two. Indeed, the regimes have found some politically compliant churchmen, and there are groups of theologians (the most distinguished of whom are at the Comenius Faculty of Protestant Theology at Prague) who see no scriptural warrant for depicting communism as the work of the devil.

In addition to setting off a general attempt at discussion between Christians and Marxists, the demise of Stalinism has also entailed the development of empirical social research in the Eastern European communist countries. Instead of deducing the contours of reality from a few exceedingly primitive political postulates, communist parties and governments have begun to rely on social inquiries and occasionally on broader sociological analyses. In some countries, such inquiries and analyses were first undertaken by politically courageous thinkers (like Djilas and others) who had a clear revisionist intent — to demonstrate that the official picture of reality was grotesquely untrue. There seems, however, to be a law at work in both East and West by which ideas and techniques originally meant to create new social possibilities serve only to consolidate old ones. Empirical social inquiry in our own societies was devised as an instrument of social reform; it has become very largely another piece of administrative technology. The same thing seems to be happening, in a much more compressed period of time, in Eastern Europe. Ten years ago, "sociology" was a politically dubious term in much of Eastern Europe: it evoked fears of the penetration of "bourgeois science." (We may define "bourgeois science" as science done by bourgeois professors who are *not* Marxists.) Today, communist parties and governments alike look with great favor on sociology. As for "bourgeois science" — speaking of the intense interest shown by his colleagues in sociology in the work of Talcott Parsons, a "revisionist" Czech philosopher told me with some feeling that "if this goes on, Marxism in eighteen months will become a revolutionary doctrine again."

At any rate, the scholars who met in Prague were interested in developing an empirically grounded sociology of religion from a Marxist point of view. They had met together once before, at Jena in Germany, the university which gave Karl Marx his doctorate. I have termed them scholars, and the description is exact: most were teachers at universities or research workers at the Academies of Science in their respective countries. There was a professor of the sociology of religion from the German Democratic Republic, Olof Klohr, even if his chair was designated as the *"Lehrstuhl für wissenschaftlicher Atheismus"* (Chair of Scientific Atheism). There were also two or three publicists from party institutes for the struggle against religion; even they acknowledged the necessity for an empirically founded approach to religion, and indeed the institute attached to the Central Committee of the Soviet Communist party has actually conducted sociological research on a large scale. My own presence was accounted for by my position as secretary of the International Sociological Association's Committee on the Sociology of Religion. Actually, there had been certain hesitations about inviting me, but these probably had less to do with my status as a "bourgeois" scholar than with the fact that I was known in some Eastern European countries as a "neo-Marxist." What, precisely, this may mean, and whether or not it is true, in parts of Eastern Europe the accusation is a grave one.

The conference, and particularly the lively spontaneous discussions of the prepared papers, made national differences among the participants very evident — differences which resulted from local intellectual traditions, the particular shape of the problem of religion in the various countries, and the degree of intellectual freedom permitted by the individual regimes.

The Bulgarians, for example, were quite rigid intellectually, and I must confess that I did not always sense that they followed the contributions of some of the others with sympathy, or even with total comprehension. The Czechs, our hosts, were there in large numbers (some fifteen, whereas there were only three or four from each of the other countries). Czechoslovakia at the moment enjoys a considerable amount of intellectual freedom, and the Czech contributions showed this: they were direct, even blunt, and did not circumvent real problems with empty formulations. The East Germans were solid and thorough, precisely like scholars from the other German state. They came, however, from working-class families in a society in which workers' children had rarely gone to the universities in ages past. Not surprisingly, their Marxism coincided almost exactly with the Marxism of the German Social Democratic party in the Wilhelminian Empire. It was a doctrine of the sovereignty of applied science, in which socialism was reason triumphant. By contrast, the Hungarians evinced great imagination and subtlety: their group included Ivan Varga, who is a pupil of Georg Lukacs and has inherited the critical humanism which is the best side of his teacher. The Polish group was divided between scholars from the Academy of Sciences and anti-religious publicists.

The Soviet participants were extraordinary. Fully in possession of their own intellectual tradition, they seemed also to have recaptured the long Russian tradition of mastery of Western thought. About the Yugoslavs, finally, little need be said. In that country, Marxism is not obligatory in the universities: one of the Yugoslavs present struck me as a positivist and rationalist. When the Yugoslavs do work with Marxism, they often make something interesting of it.

The conference went on for three days, in what was once the chapel of a Franciscan cloister, now converted into the headquarters of the municipal Communist Party. (The building is next to the old Opera House, where Mozart himself conducted the premiere of *Don Giovanni*.) There were Baroque religious paintings on the ceiling, and stern busts of Marx, Engels, Lenin, and Gottwald stared fixedly at us from the front of the room. The discussion returned to a number of central themes which were systematically — I am inclined to say dialectically — interrelated. The findings of a number of research projects pointed to the difficulties of a Marxist interpretation of religion under Marxist regimes. Discussion of such difficulties soon enough turned into a reexamination of the moral experience of these societies.

The sessions began, straightforwardly enough, with a lucid exposition by our chairwoman, Dr. Kadlecova of the Czechoslovak Academy of Sciences. She had studied the religious consciousness of a group of her compatriots, in a locality in which religious affiliation was still rather strong. Among those who said that they were religious, nominal adherence to the Church and traditional ritual participation far outweighed deep inner conviction; the belief in immortality, or in the divinity of Jesus, was conspicuously absent from their affirmations. Seventy-five per cent of her sample, however, said that religion was a means to master life. They consciously saw religion, in other words, as an instrument of adaptation and were therefore outside the religious experience or historically past it. These results, of course, correspond almost exactly to those found in many Western countries.

Professor Ugrinovtisch of the Lomonosov University in Moscow was the next speaker. A humorous and sympathetic scholar who had impressed many of the Western scholars at the World Congress of Sociology in France in September by the suppleness and sharpness of his mind, Ugrinovtisch suggested that studies in the Soviet Union yielded much the same findings as those of Dr. Kadlecova. I was reminded that at the World Congress of Sociology, Ugrinovtisch had insisted that religion was strongest in the Soviet Union among those least integrated into Soviet society: older persons, rural communities relatively untouched by urban currents. At Prague, however, he added some new dimensions to his argument. He held that there were secular or non-religious, indeed even anti-religious, cultic and ritual observances in socialist society; ritual alone, therefore, was not necessarily connected with religion. What he intended was to support his contention that studies of religious comportment by itself were meaningless — we had to study the psychological and spiritual content of religious beliefs. What in fact he did was to raise the vexed question of the spiritual status of civic belief in the socialist societies. For the moment, this passed unremarked; the participants argued about other matters.

Dr. Kadlecova pointed out that an ideal community had not yet been constructed under socialism. In the circumstances, she felt it justified to ask if there were social grounds for the continuance of religion, in some form, in socialist society. Ugrinovtisch carried this argument further. He described as "an old dualism" the view that men controlled their own destinies under socialism but did not do so under other social systems. We required concrete inquiries into the precise degree of control over the social process exercised by specific individuals and groups. To begin with, we already knew that in socialism some individuals could exert far more influence on the social process than others. These remarks seemed to be unexceptionable, yet they quickly led to controversy. Professor Klohr, from Germany, strenuously denied that religion and what he called a high degree of educated consciousness could coexist. Klohr and his colleagues proceeded to present statistics which showed, to their satisfaction at least, that religion declined as socialism advanced.

The East German researches rested on the assumption that there is nothing universal about religion, or about human consciousness in general. Indeed, neither religion nor atheism was a primary form of consciousness: both, rather, were derivatives of more fundamental modes of thought. The sources of these, in turn, were in class relationships and the relationships of production. Atheism arose when a materialistic view developed, quite spontaneously, as a result of social changes which increased society's conscious power over social and natural processes. It followed, the East Germans insisted, that there had to be a sociology of religion specific to socialist societies: the identical categories could hardly deal with religion in different social systems.

The evidence they introduced to support these contentions did not entirely convince many of their colleagues. Klohr and his group found, to be sure, that many with religious convictions had a "progressive" (by which they meant positive) attitude to the East German state. But they also insisted that those who were most engaged in "constructive" social activity were most remote from religion. I found their mode of inference curiously devoid of psychological penetration: they seemed to care little about what people thought, and even less about what they felt, and to concentrate on what they said. "Socialist" science in this case was rather like the more backward sectors of "bourgeois" research. In one respect, however, it was true to old traditions in classical sociology. August Comte enjoined the European elites after the convulsions of the French Revolution to use sociology as an instrument of domination. Klohr and his colleagues made their own aims quite clear: "The analysis of this entire complex . . . gives a further basis for a differentiated educational and pedagogic activity."

The response to the German presentation was vigorous. Dr. Kadlecova declared that different categories were not needed for the same religious systems in the same cultural areas, despite political differences. This was an interesting way of insisting on the unity of European culture, an idea more Gaullist than "orthodox" Marxist. Varga of Hungary doubted that the actual content of religious beliefs was different in the different types of society. The East German categories, he continued, referred to the sociology of politics and not of religion: he doubted that it was useful to make the strengthening of socialism the direct aim of study. In any case, Hungarian inquiry had shown that young Catholics and young communists were quite identical with respect to social engagement. Moreover, Varga observed, a materialist world-view did not always lead to positive social action. He did not elaborate on this point.

Klohr defended himself against his critics rather well. He noted that "bourgeois" sociology also dealt with the political correlates of religious conviction, that it too had shown that the same Christian convictions gave different results in different political contexts. I myself took the floor at this point, to say that the interpretation of Marxism as a doctrine of man's mastery of nature and society with the aid of science and technology was not absolutely true to Marx's philosophic intentions. We in America also had a doctrine of the use of science and technology for mastery of the human environment. Perhaps its most conspicuous current proponent was our secretary of defense, Mr. McNamara, himself a former professor of economics. (Many at the conference, if not our German colleagues, appreciated the point.) I also said that those who had the most radical and revolutionary ideas about society in the West were often theologians. "Theologians, perhaps, but the churches not. Socialism is always the doctrine of the working class," objected Klohr. "In America," I responded, "socialism is more likely to be found in seminaries of Protestant theology or in the universities generally than in trade unions."

The argument about the fate of religion in Eastern Europe quickly touched upon a critical theme: the persistence of an alienated human condition under socialism. Alienation, in the early writings of Marx, was the stunted and unfulfilled human condition which resulted from the subjugation of men to powers outside themselves. These powers were in fact the products of their own labor, but in the class society men could not enjoy the fruits of their labor. Rather, they were ruled over by them in the form of the laws of the market, and the coercive might of the state. In the sphere of consciousness, men were haunted by the phantasmagoria of their own minds: they made an eschatology of their unrealized yearning for fulfillment, and the idea of God expressed at once their desperate hope in the beneficence of a world become strange and their awful submission to it. Religion was therefore also a product of alienation.

The participants were aware that the term alienation has come in the West to cover practically every spiritual disease known to man. They were also fully conversant with the early Marxist texts, and they knew that until very recently, discussion of these as anything but youthful aberrations had been officially discouraged in Eastern Europe. The elimination of market relationships, or so the official doctrine went, rendered all talk of alienation gratuitous. This attitude, along with much else, has changed. Dr. Kadlecova declared directly that the future ought not to be confused with the present — alienation had not yet been eliminated from socialist society. Varga remarked that other forms of alienation besides the "fetishism of commodities," perhaps political ones, could also account for the persistence of religion. "There are also in socialist society phenomena of alienated consciousness capable of evoking the so-called substitute religions." He mentioned the mythologizing of technique as a religious substitute — which provoked an immediate protest from Klohr, who found the notion of substitute religion extremely dubious. Klohr went on to say that the class roots of religion had been eliminated in socialist society, and to deny that there was any religious continuity between capitalist and socialist society. Finally, an Austrian Marxist, Walter Hollitscher, objected that the present and future difficulties of life under socialism need not engender a recourse to religion.

In the end, historical developments may prove Hollitscher right. For the moment, he received little support from those at Prague who reported on psychological researches into religion in Eastern Europe. A Czech scholar said that despite the general decline in religious belief and feeling, sentiments of passive dependence and of homelessness in the universe persisted. His studies have shown that among students, those who sought a harmony unobtainable in their daily lives turned to religion. Another participant from Czechoslovakia, but this time a Russian lady who worked at the Slovak Academy of Sciences in Bratislava, noted that religion could be derived from hope as well as from anxiety. Ugrinovtisch concluded this part of the discussion by observing that there was no specifically religious psychology, only a general human one.

The entire discussion was moved onto another plane by a second Soviet participant, Dr. Levada of the Academy of Sciences. Levada began by noting that Marx and Lenin had treated the economic roots of religion as fundamental, but not as the only ones. Religion was not simply a matter of social classes, and socialism was not just a global negation of the previous class system. Socialist society was undergoing a process of secularization which had to be compared to the same process in capitalist society. An entire culture was being secularized, certain values had become desacralized. Meanwhile, those affected by religious influences in the secularized culture were not always aware of the fact. Perhaps this was because the distinction between religious and non-religious rituals was not always clear. Sometimes, non-religious rituals had the same social function as the religious ones they replaced, even if the values attached to them were different. Levada found the entire discussion of alienation too general and abstract: we required studies of new forms of consciousness in socialist society before we could say whether these were religious or not. He himself did not think of the mythologizing of technique mentioned by Varga as religious, but simply as an illusory solution to social and psychological problems.

If I understood Levada correctly, he took the view that the antithesis of socialist society and capitalist society was too ahistoric to be of very much use. Rather, he proposed that the antithesis should be translated into specific terms for each social type before we generalized further about it. And he did insist on the common element in the religious situation across ideological frontiers.

Levada's contribution did not quite evoke the discussion it merited, possibly because it moved in historical and spiritual dimensions otherwise touched at the conference only by his immediate colleague, Ugrinovtisch, and by Varga. I was genuinely surprised, however, that an excellent historical contribution by a Hungarian, Jozef Lukacs, produced almost no discussion at all. Lukacs presented a panoramic view of the difference between oriental and occidental religion, the one fatalistic and resigned, the other activistic and world-changing. "It would be an error, of the sort that occurs not only in propagandistic activity but also in scholarly work, to ignore this active element in Christianity and to exaggerate the quietistic-contemplative element which is always present in religion, and it would be particularly an error to do so for the Western forms of Christianity." Lukacs did not directly raise the possibility that Marxism might be thought of as descended, spiritually, from the more activistic elements in the Judaeo-Christian tradition. The suggestion, however, was not very far from the surface of his paper. Indeed, many of the most interesting things about the Prague conference were not quite on the surface — but they were not very far below it either.

What was said at the conference was important enough, and I have tried to give a sense of it. There were no visible constraints on our colleagues, and the discussion was quite free. The things which were not quite said bespoke an underlying movement of thought which has not yet been completed: a search for new general ideas, their outlines barely discernible but their substance still obscure. The constraints under which the participants labored, in other words, were inner ones: the difficulty of altering a set of assumptions, a fixed structure of thought. The contradictions, differences, and disputes at Prague, the schematism of some and the tentativeness of others, point to a new spiritual future in Eastern Europe. In trying to explain how, let me take four major areas of discussion.

The continuity of European culture, across all political boundaries, was very much emphasized at Prague. Our Czech chairwoman said quite explicitly that we lived in a common culture, and the Soviet participants touched upon similar themes. The participants were familiar with religious tradition, and their familiarity was not the familiarity associated with contempt or the deep hostility born of fear. It would be vulgar (and, above all, wrong) to suppose that the dispute with China has suddenly brought Eastern Europe to the realization of its common heritage with Western Europe. Rather, the historical force of that heritage itself, the population's stubborn attachment to it, the equally strong attachment of the intellectuals, have made another view of religion inevitable — following the removal of these questions from control by the police. A sense of the concrete, of national particularity, of the value of tradition: these are now emphasized by the Communist regimes as part of a new political strategy. (I would also say that these are values congenial to new Communist leaders well aware of the perversion of "internationalism" under Stalinism.)

The Jewish participants no less than the others seemed to share in this temper — although Jewishness, Judaism, and Jewish communal life in Eastern Europe were not discussed at the Prague conference. I have the impression, from other experiences in Eastern Europe, that a number of Jewish intellectuals in the communist movement now identify themselves with things Jewish. It will be recalled that Professor Adam Schaff, member of the Central Committee of the Polish party, recently published a book which among other matters dealt with the problem of the continuation of anti-Semitism in Poland. (I have dealt with this book in an essay in the May–June, 1967, issue of *Dissent*.) At any rate, the situation of Judaism and the Jews in Eastern Europe is perhaps best understood in the light of newer developments in these countries.

The rather more explicit discussion of alienation under socialism entailed more delicate questions. If fifty years of socialism in the Soviet Union, and twenty years elsewhere, had not brought appreciable progress toward the end of alienation, then clearly second thoughts were in order. The possibility was broached at Prague that there may be forms of alienation peculiar to socialist society, but this possibility was not thoroughly explored. The participants tended to insist on the general human problems which socialism had not yet eliminated (and which it might not eliminate in the foreseeable future), rather than on oppressive elements in Eastern European socialism. They did, however, prepare for a thorough critique of the quality of life in socialist society — by showing that the persistence of religion, in some cases at least, had real roots in human distress.

The discussion of alienation was rather general, but the exploration of the question of secular derivatives of religion was somewhat more specific. The participants from the Soviet Union were quite prominent in this discussion: they came, after all, from a country which has a religious tradition rich in ritual and litany. I was glad to see that the Eastern European states were depicted as resting on psychological forces somewhat more subliminal than the insight of their citizens into the high degree of political perfection they had attained. The participants did *not* say that there were civic or state religions prevailing in Eastern Europe (religions which used the Marxist rhetoric without having much connection with Marxism in its original form). I myself find the notion of Marxism as a substitute religion very debatable: Marx intended to end a transcendental form of human thought in favor of a humanism immanent in the world. I do think that the communist sociologists of religion are beginning to approach the terrain on which this debate has been conducted elsewhere. They will have to cross it before they can find convincing answers.

Finally, I was struck by the repeated references at the conference to secularization as a universal process in Western culture.

929

Some of the participants shared that nostalgia for the religious past of mankind which is so curious a part of the current discussion of the death of God, among the religious and non-religious alike. I wonder whether this aspect of the exchanges at Prague may refer, if obliquely, to Marxism as much as to Christianity. In the Constantine epoch, Christianity became a fixed part of the social order — and lost its prophetic qualities as a result. In due course, the social order itself began to dispense with Christianity. What of a Constantine epoch in Marxism? Having become a state doctrine, it has legitimated a system which seems no less problematical than those it has replaced — and in which the universal reign of justice and fraternity, reason and human sovereignty, seems remote. These are familiar enough ideas outside Eastern Europe, and familiar enough experiences inside it. The persistence of religion must strike many Marxists as not unlike the persistence of Marxism: a stubborn perseverance of a belief in a better world, despite the experience of a worse one.

This places the discussion of alienation at Prague in a somewhat different light. Talking about unfulfilled human needs under socialism, some of the participants may have been attempting to say that religion was but one historical solution to the absence of human fulfillment. Marxism may offer another — but not in its present, its own Constantine form. A rediscovery of other elements and possibilities in Marxism, perhaps related to the chiliastic tendencies in Christianity noted by one of the speakers, might offer an alternative to that official Marxism which has become a state doctrine. From a consideration of the fate of religion under state socialism, the Marxist sociologists at Prague were edged by the nature of the theme itself toward critical reflection on the fate of Marxism under their regimes. The process of reflection has begun, and although it is as yet tentative and usually covert, its continuation and enlargement is a certainty for the future.

24. A REPORT ON CHURCHES AND TAXATION

by the Guild of St. Ives

What follows is a report on the results of investigation and thinking undertaken by the members of the Guild of St. Ives, an informal organization of Episcopal lawyers and clerics in the New York City area. This project was undertaken in the belief that too much of what has been said and written on the significant subject of churches and taxation has been productive of more heat than light. It is our hope that this report will both clarify and stimulate further and better thinking on the subject. We regard this as no more than a beginning.

While there are two rather modest recommendations contained in this report, we wish to emphasize that the conclusions we have so liberally stated are but statements of a consensus among various people with divergent views. We have no wish to impose these conclusions on anyone; at the same time, we humbly suggest that these conclusions and the reasons underlying them are entitled to the respect of careful consideration even by those who may disagree with them.

TAX EXEMPTIONS accorded churches have been described as "the most important governmental recognition of religion in America" [4:60]. This recognition has been accorded in a number of ways, and, as will be seen, indications are that it is very substantial.

On the Federal level, this recognition is most significantly extended in two ways. First, corporations operated for religious purposes are exempt from the income tax (I.R.C. §501). Second, contributions by individuals and corporations to such tax exempt organizations are, within limits, deductible from income for tax purposes (I.R.C. §170). Income earned by employees of religious organizations is not generally tax exempt.

On the State and local level, real and personal property owned by religious organizations is generally exempt from taxation. In a number of states, such property is exempt by Constitution. (See, for example, N.Y. Const., Art. XVI, §1. The New York State Constitution is presently being revised.) The availability of the exemption in some states is based on religious use of the property, and in others only on ownership by a religious organization. Local sales and similar taxes are usually not applied to purchases or sales by religious organizations (see, for example, N.Y. Tax L., §1116). Local taxation of income of religious organizations is generally consistent with Federal practice.

The total wealth of organized religion and of other tax exempt institutions is growing while the needs of government, particularly at the local level, are increasing. Tax burdens are also increasing, and would probably be increasing faster except for the vague limits of political expediency. With growing tax burdens producing increasing discomfort and discontent, it is not surprising that the tax shelters accorded organized religion (among others) by existing tax laws have already come under criticism. This criticism seems bound to increase, since none of the above trends appears to be reversible in the immediate future.

As a practical matter, then, the question of taxation and religion should be re-examined. Even if political pressure to end present tax exemptions were not increasing, religious organizations themselves have a moral obligation to re-examine the question under current conditions. (This report is not intended to address itself, except incidentally, to the uses or possible abuses by others of their tax exemptions.)

CONSTITUTIONALITY

The First Amendment to the United States Constitution provides that "Congress shall make no law respecting an establishment of religion, or prohibiting the free exercise thereof. . . ." Though hardly indisputable, it is settled that the Fourteenth Amendment's prohibition against a State's depriving "any person of life, liberty, or property, without due process of law

. . ." similarly inhibits State action with respect to either the establishment or free exercise of religion. *Cantwell v. Connecticut,* 310 U.S. 296 (1940).

The most vigorous assaults on present tax exemptions thus far have been directed at the issue of constitutionality; these attacks seem likely to continue. (See the note, Constitutionality of Tax Benefits Accorded Religion, 49 Colum. L. Rev. 969, 985 [1949]: "It is clear that the exemption of religious organizations from . . . taxes . . . affords financial aid to such institutions. Moreover, analysis dispels distinctions between outright grants to religious organizations, clearly invalid under the [Supreme Court] decisions, and tax exemptions to such organizations." [Footnotes omitted.])

The exemption of religious organizations from taxation has generally been attacked on two constitutional grounds. *First,* it has been said that the present scheme tends "to infringe the constitutional provision of separation of state and church." (*E.g.,* the 1966 Resolution of the Diocesan Commission on Civil Rights submitted to [but not adopted by] the Diocese of Massachusetts.) This argument is of dubious historical and legal merit. The constitutional prohibition is not so worded, though the abstract principle is often referred to, even by the Supreme Court. The language of separation appears to have originated as a constitutional principle in private correspondence of Thomas Jefferson in 1802, long after the adoption of the Bill of Rights [1:191]. (We note, however, that the following has been attributed to Roger Williams: "When they have opened a gap in the hedge or wall of separation between the garden of the church and the wilderness of the world, God hath ever brake down the wall itself, removed the candlestick, and made his garden a wilderness, as at this day" [Howe, *The Garden and the Wilderness,* Univ. of Chicago, 1965, p v].) We also have the authority of the Supreme Court that "separation" does not, even if strictly applied, require taxation of churches.

> . . . The First Amendment, however, does not say that in every and all respects there shall be a separation of Church and State. Rather, it studiously defines the manner, the specific

ways, in which there shall be no concert or union or dependency one on the other. That is the common sense of the matter. Otherwise the state and religion would be aliens to each other — hostile, suspicious, and even unfriendly. *Churches could not be required to pay even property taxes.* . . . (*Zorach v. Clauson,* 343 U.S. 306, 312 [1952], emphasis added.)

Second, there are those who believe that any tax exemption in favor of religious organizations constitutes an establishment of religion. The Court of Appeals of Maryland recently rejected this argument, and on October 10, 1966, the Supreme Court declined to review the question. (Murray v. Goldstein, 241 Md. 383, 216 A. 2d 897, *cert. den.,* 385 U.S. 816 [1966].) Judicially speaking, therefore, the question is still open.

The argument that present tax exemptions constitute a forbidden "establishment" of religion is perhaps best expressed as follows: (i) Current exemptions are in effect a subsidy of religion; (ii) this subsidization has the effect of taxing non-believers to support the institutions of believers; (iii) this result constitutes an "establishment" of religion. Though one of the undersigned subscribes to this view, the rest do not.

Conceding that direct governmental subsidization of religion would be unconstitutional, we believe it invalid constitutionally to equate tax exemptions with subsidies for several reasons: (i) they are mechanically different; a subsidy is "a *direct* pecuniary aid furnished by a government to a . . . charity organization, or the like" [3] (emphasis added), while tax exemption is indirect. The difference between the direct and the indirect or incidental often gives rise to different results in law, particularly constitutional law. (ii) Subsidization would be government sponsorship of religious organizations on behalf of all the people, while tax exemption represents only a governmental accommodation to the past and present sponsorship of such organizations by those individual citizens who have freely chosen to undertake such sponsorship, and an implicit recognition that the choice of these individuals was a reasonable and socially beneficial one deserving of encouragement. (iii) The purposes for which subsidies are employed are normally more strictly defined and controlled than are the purposes for which the tax savings resulting from exemptions may be employed. (iv) The amount of a subsidy is determined by the government granting it, while the benefit accorded by tax exemptions is measured by past and present contributions by millions of individuals.

The majority also differ, as a practical matter, with the belief of one of the undersigned that the present system of exemptions has the effect of taxing non-believers to support believers. While, in theory, the taxes of non-believers as well as believers may be higher than they would be if religious organizations were accorded no tax exemptions at all, this objection is more theoretical than real. In this era of increasing governmental needs, deficit financing by most governments, and constant pressure for still greater governmental involvement in society, it appears that tax rates and revenues are limited primarily by the bounds of political expediency, not by governmental needs. At least at present, the possibility that full taxation of religious organizations would lower the taxes of either non-believers or believers seems remote, and the possibility that it would delay future tax increases seems unlikely.

The Supreme Court, the final authority on the subject, has offered no concrete guidance on this point. Its most comprehensive exposition of the meaning of the "establishment" clause provides little insight into the present problem:

> The "establishment of religion" clause of the First Amendment means at least this: Neither a State nor the Federal Government can set up a church. Neither can pass laws which aid one religion, aid all religions, or prefer one religion over another. Neither can force nor influence a person to go to or to remain away from church against his will or force him to profess a belief or disbelief in any religion. No person can be punished for entertaining or professing religious beliefs or disbeliefs, for church attendance or non-attendance. No tax in any amount, large or small, can be levied to support any religious activities or institutions, whatever they may be called, or whatever form they may adopt to teach or practice religion. Neither a State nor the Federal Government can, openly or secretly, participate in the affairs of any religious organizations or groups and

vice versa. . . . (*Everson v. Board of Education of Township of Ewing*, 330 U.S. 1, 15–16 [1947].)

Lest the above proscriptions upon laws "which . . . aid all religions" and taxes "levied to support any religious activities" be thought to read upon the present problems, it should be pointed out that the quotation was from the Supreme Court 1947 decision upholding the use of tax funds to subsidize bus fares for parochial school children.

A more troublesome test was set forth in 1963:

> . . . The [establishment of religion] tests may be stated as follows: what are the purpose and the primary effect of the enactment? If either is the advancement or inhibition of religion then the enactment exceeds the scope of legislative power as circumscribed by the Constitution. (*Abington School District v. Schempp*, 374 U.S. 203, 222 [1963].)

The majority of the undersigned believe that the "advancement" of religion is neither the purpose nor primary effect of laws granting tax exemptions to religious organizations. Tax laws enabling religious organizations to function more effectively than they otherwise might are not believed to be a governmental sanction or compulsion of religion which would amount to an establishment. (*Cf.* "We are a religious people whose institutions suppose a Supreme Being. We guarantee the freedom to worship as one chooses. We make room for as wide a variety of beliefs and creeds as the spiritual needs of man deem necessary. We sponsor an attitude on the part of government that shows no partiality to any one group and that lets each flourish according to the zeal of its adherents and the appeal of its dogma. When the state encourages religious instructions or cooperates with religious authorities by adjusting the schedule of public events to sectarian needs, it follows the best of our traditions. For it then respects the religious value of our people and accommodates the public service to their spiritual needs. To hold that it may not would be to find in the Constitution a requirement that the government show a callous indifference to religious groups. That would be preferring those who believe in no religion to those

936

who do believe . . ." [*Zorach v. Clauson, supra,* 343 U.S. at 313–14].)

The proliferation of tax benefits to churches thus must be regarded in part, at least, as a manifestation of a political consensus that aid to organized religion, in non-discriminatory form at least, has a special tendency to enhance (to use John Stuart Mill's phrase) "The first element of good government . . . to promote the virtue and intelligence of the people themselves." (Van Alstyne, Tax Exemption of Church Property, 22 Ohio St. L.J., 1959, pp 462–63.)

The undersigned also recognize that it can be argued that the "free exercise" clause compels tax exemptions in favor of religious organizations. A minority of the undersigned question whether religious tax exemptions could constitutionally be repealed if similar educational and charitable ones are retained. With respect to property and most other taxes, however, the majority are inclined to accept the distinction which concludes the following argument.

The [Supreme] Court has held, for example, that a license tax validly exacted for the privilege of engaging in a common occupation denies free exercise to one whose practice of religion necessarily involves performance of the licensed activities [door to door solicitation]. The apparent effect of this line of cases has been to require tax exemption in certain situations where other persons who receive the same protections and benefits as the exempt individual must pay taxes. Could it then be said that the application of a general property tax to houses of worship and the land they occupy would be an interference with the constitutional right of churchgoers to freely exercise their religion? For there can be no doubt that the financial burden thus imposed would seriously curtail religious worship by many groups, to the point even of jeopardizing the existence of many churches. *It is possible to distingiush the property tax situation on the ground that the tax is levied on the institution itself, and not on the individual worshipper, and does not, therefore,* directly *interfere with the latter's exercise of religion.* (Note, Constitutionality of Religious Tax Benefits, 49 *Colum. L. Rev.,* 1949, vol 49, pp 968, 988–989, emphasis added.)

937

For various reasons, we all agree that different taxation of different religions by the same taxing authority would be unconstitutional.

The opinion of the majority of the undersigned is, therefore, that the United States Constitution neither forbids nor compels the present favored treatment of religion under our tax laws. The question being constitutionally neutral, we believe that it should be resolved in the exercise of sound legislative discretion.

ECONOMIC CONSIDERATIONS OF TAXATION OF RELIGIOUS ORGANIZATIONS

It would be helpful in discussing the problem of taxation of religious organizations and institutions if there were reliable data available which illustrated the extent of the problem. Unfortunately, we find little. Taxing authorities do not require reporting, even of an informational variety, by religious organizations, and few, if any, religious organizations voluntarily disclose data concerning their financial condition; there seems to be no central collection agency for the collation of available information. *So that more information may be available to the presently uninformed public, the majority strongly recommend that informational reports* (see Internal Revenue Service Form 990-A) *be required from religious organizations by all taxing authorities. In the absence of such requirements, the majority recommend that such information be made available voluntarily.* Such reports should be similar to those required from educational and charitable organizations, and should be made a matter of public record. We can see no justification for keeping the dimensions of this entire problem a secret from the public.

If there are no comprehensive data with respect to the extent of the tax exemptions granted religion, however, there are unverified indications that the amount is considerable. For example, it has been estimated that the real estate held by organized religion in the United States is worth 79.5 billion dollars $79,500,000,000.00). That real estate, if taxed, could at present rates produce up to 4.0 billion dollars in local tax revenues annually [2]. It has also been estimated that Federal income tax exemptions for organized religion cost the Federal Government roughly the same amount annually [2]. The real estate and assets of the largest religious institution in the United States, the Roman Catholic Church, have been estimated to exceed the total *combined* assets of A.T. & T., U.S. Steel and Standard Oil of New Jersey, or to exceed 51.4 billion dollars [2].

Certain facts have come to our attention which indicate that the dimensions of the problem are no less impressive. Well documented sources state that the appraised value of property in the City of New York which is tax exempt because it is dedicated to religious purposes is nearly 700 million dollars. (This is about 25% of all exempt private property in the City, 4.5% of all exempt property in the City, and 1.5% of all property in the City. The only exempt classes of property which are larger are properties owned by the City Board of Education and Higher Education, the Department of Marine and Aviation (piers and airports are its most substantial assets), the Department of Public Works and the Department of Parks. [Citizens Budget Commission, Inc., "Real Estate Tax Exemption in New York City — a Design for Reform," April, 1967.]) If taxed at the current rate of 5%, this property could produce about 35 million dollars in revenues for the City (about 7/10 of one per cent of the City's reported 1967 budget).

LEGISLATIVE CONSIDERATIONS OF TAXATION
OF RELIGIOUS ORGANIZATIONS

This nation was founded upon the belief that the free expression of religious convictions and the free pursuit of spiritual ideals are essential to both the well being of the people and the fullness of national life. Since the nation's constitutional beginnings it has been recognized that the religious sector of our nation, in contrast to the commercial, would not be profitable, or even economically self-sustaining, without gifts, and that the

939

survival of this religious and spiritual aspect of the national life, and the continuation of its benefits to society at large, depend upon a governmental policy which does not exact from religion taxes which it cannot afford to pay.

More pragmatically, religious teaching imparts moral and ethical values and standards which when observed undoubtedly benefit society as a whole. In their ministries, most religions exercise their vocation to summon the nation to perfect the rights of all men in a just society. A religious faith also offers insights and confidence to many persons which sustain them throughout life.

One example would appear to be religion's involvement in the civil rights movement. Without comment on the merits of the movement itself, it seems safe to say that its course to date has been less violent, less tumultuous, and less disruptive to civil order than it would have been without religious involvement and the adoption of certain religious ideals as part of the movement.

Religious organizations also do, at times, stand against social injustice, inhumanity and the suppression of individual rights, thereby serving as a corrective to some of the ills of society.

Organized religion performs numerous other beneficial functions which can only be alluded to here. A substantial educational establishment is supported wholly or partly by organized religion. The abandonment of any part of this activity would either throw a heavier educational burden on government or would decrease the total education effort of the community, an undesirable result in either case. The same can be said with respect to that medical establishment which is sponsored or supported in part or in whole by organized religion. The undersigned question that there is any social advantage to be achieved by disturbing the status quo in these areas.

Organized religion also underwrites and operates a number of charities. Some of these are highly desirable to the communities in which they operate; there may be others which government would not feel obliged to assume. The supposed benefit to society of an increase in tax revenues cannot be considered in the ab-

stract. The probable uses of such tax revenues must be considered. To the considerable extent that the services now performed by religious institutions would in fact be continued in some form by the state, the situation would improve only if one believes (which the majority of the undersigned do not) that it is more efficient and politically sounder to have a service performed by the state than by a private institution.

No one really knows what the effect of religion's loss of its tax exemptions would be, but reasonable predictions can be made. Were organized religion to lose all of its present tax benefits, it would have no alternative but to curtail its activities drastically. It is reasonable to suppose that religion's educational, medical, and charitable activities would bear the brunt of these curtailments.

It is likely that organized religion's beneficial, non-religious activities are presently supported in the main by a rather small minority of all the churches and congregations in this country. Among these activities are those which are imaginative and innovative, some of which are later adopted on a broader social level by governments favorably impressed by their results. As to these relatively few, relatively wealthy, religious organizations, an end to present tax exemptions would probably signal a reduction in their non-religious programs, particularly those of a more experimental nature.

As to the relatively larger number of churches and congregations whose operations are barely marginal in an economic sense, any significant reduction in present tax exemptions would inevitably cause the closing of a number of churches, chapels and synagogues, particularly in depressed or deprived areas where they are needed most, and the elimination or curtailment of the useful social programs of many other such churches.

On the other hand, there are considerations which mitigate against tax exemptions for organized religion. The tax loss is substantial. Popular support for religion is apparently declining (which is evidently well documented: Pike, in *Playboy, supra,* asserts that from 1958 to 1965 church attendance dropped roughly 10% while population increased 13%. Gallup, in a poll

942

released April 12, 1967, reports that weekly attendance declined from 49% of the adult population in 1958 to 44% in 1966, and that increasingly large portions of the population feel that religion is losing its influence). The wealth of organized religion, and consequent tax loss, appears to be increasing (Pike, in *Playboy, supra,* cites *Christianity Today* for the extreme proposition that any church utilizing present tax exemptions could parlay $1,000,000.00 into ownership of America in sixty years.) It is widely said that, therefore, current tax exemptions increase an already heavy burden on the average taxpayer, be he religious or not. While, for reasons stated previously, most of us do not agree with this, we do agree that if the exemptions were removed there would be available to government more money to increase services to the people or decrease operating deficits; it seems likely that not all of this money would be needed simply to replace services formerly rendered by religious institutions.

Perhaps the most objectionable result of tax exemptions given religious organizations is that these exemptions create a competitive advantage in the business world. Tax exemptions accorded churches with regard to the operation of unrelated businesses create a substantial economic benefit which allows such businesses to compete unfairly with non-exempt businesses. (We call attention to the fact that the unrelated business income of educational and charitable organizations, unlike such income of religious organizations, is subject to taxation. I.R.C. §511.)

To a lesser degree, church-owned corporations have an advantage over other competing corporations. (Because dividends received by religious organizations are tax-free, while dividends received by non-exempt organizations are not, a church-owned corporation need not pay as high dividends as other corporations to produce the same net return to its stockholders. Therefore, church-owned corporations can retain more earnings for internal expansion and/or charge lower prices than their non-exempt competitors.) A similar advantage arises to the extent that rental income is exempt from taxation.

It has also been suggested that tax exemptions lead to centers of power which are not responsible to the people as a whole,

943

and that such undemocratic centers of power are repugnant to our American way of life. (The Very Reverend Sherman Johnson, Dean of the Church Divinity School of the Pacific, views tax exemptions as a recognition by the sovereign that there are and should be independent centers of power able to level unpopular criticisms and uphold unpopular standards. "[Tax exemption] symbolizes a permanence and sacrosanct character like that of the state. The question is whether or not the people are willing to limit their own power . . . in the interest of the future, realizing that there are principles which justify this limitation, so that they may be preserved from the dangers of total exercise of their power in the immediate moment." [Memorandum to the Guild of St. Ives, February, 1967.]) The majority of the undersigned believe this problem to be of greater future than immediate concern (see Pike, *infra.*) While it has some economic validity, most economic centers of power in our society are neither responsible to the body politic nor particularly powerful on a popular political (as opposed to legislative) level. To the extent churches represent moral centers of power, they do so relatively independent of economic power (witness the civil rights movement again), and only because they command a significant amount of popular respect.

PROBABLE EFFECTS ON RELIGION OF CHANGE IN
TAXATION OF RELIGIOUS ORGANIZATIONS

The most immediate and direct effect of an end to the tax exemptions currently enjoyed by organized religion would be the reduction in services performed by them, and inevitably, the closing of many churches and the curtailment of the church's mission. The extent of this effect would undoubtedly depend upon the extent of the taxes newly imposed.

Some have found comfort in this prospect of an end to current tax exemptions for various reasons which they believe would be beneficial to the church. Bishop Pike has suggested at least one sound long-term reason for the reduction at least of current tax benefits:

Several times in history, the churches have become so wealthy and powerful from the geometric growth of tax-free wealth, without carrying their share of the public expense, that the whole economy was imperiled, and the governments feared the political power which concentrated wealth can buy. In each case, acting almost in self defense, the state has seized a substantial amount of church property. This happened in 16th Century England, in 18th Century France, in 19th Century Italy and in 20th Century Mexico (where, prior to the 1910 revolution, 80 per cent of all arable land was church-owned) . . . . [2].

In the long run, of course, organized religion cannot afford to ignore this history.

Bishop Pike and others envision a number of more immediate consequences of benefit to religion from the abolition of many present tax exemptions: (i) A reduction in funds available to religious organizations will require economies, lessen waste and bring about a greater emphasis on assigning priorities. (ii) This change will serve as an impetus to ecumenism, at the very least with regard to the sharing of facilities which are now widely and unnecessarily duplicated. (iii) Greater expenses will tend to divorce the church from its historic addiction to property, particularly real property, which is not necessary for the legitimate function of religion. The majority of the undersigned have reservations as to all three of these arguments.

Some waste and inefficiency are inevitable in any institution, but it is doubted that what waste and inefficiency there may now be within the religious establishment is tolerated because of any over-abundance of funds. They would seem more probably attributable to the (i) calibre of presently available administrative personnel, which seems unlikely to improve if available funds to be administered should be reduced, and (ii) resistance at the local level to moves toward consolidation. Therefore, a revenue reduction would probably not serve to promote any significant economy or efficiency. Lower revenues will not necessarily cause more efficient utilization of property, or ecumenism, or a greater willingness to separate religion from the physical structures we call churches, chapels, and synagogues. What seems more likely to occur is that activities not specifically religious in nature will be curtailed, and that only as a last resort will many churches be driven to sharing of facilities. Finally, however desirable it might be to take religion out of the churches and into society (and we question whether these are really alternatives), the abolition of tax exemptions would appear to be better calculated to drive religion back into the churches because of the curtailment of such other activities.

One concern all of us share relates to an at least occasional reluctance on the part of religious institutions to take stands on contemporary problems which might alienate their most substantial contributors. We believe there to be an understandable feeling on the part of large donors that their contributions entitle their views to greater consideration by the church than they might otherwise receive. We view this situation with misgiving, and would regret any aggravation of it. Yet any elimination of tax exemptions would seem necessarily to increase organized religion's reliance upon contributions.

Similarly, it has been suggested that present tax exemptions tend to mute the voice of the church for fear of offending the government which gives these exemptions. We doubt this and point out that (i) to the extent, if any, that this suggestion is valid, the problem is a far more profound one for organized religion than is the mere question of tax exemptions, and (ii) the same problem appears to concern the educational establishment, which is similarly favored, hardly at all.

CONCLUSIONS

The majority recognize that there is a minority of one who does not concur with the majority insofar as the majority favor any preferential treatment for any religious institution. This minority also questions the wisdom of many of the charitable and educational exemptions which are outside the scope of this report.

Property Taxes. The undersigned believe that real and personal property owned by religious institutions should be subject

946

to taxation to the extent that it is used for business purposes in either actual or potential competition with secular persons, or if it is unused and not definitely committed in the immediate future to some exempt use. Such property appears to constitute a significant portion of the "wealth" of organized religion which is currently subject to criticism. Such tax treatment is believed to accord, at least generally, with existing practice.

The majority believe that real and personal property owned by religious institutions which is used for educational, charitable and other social purposes should not be taxed any more or less than such property would be taxed if owned by secular organizations. In short, there is no reason to deny church schools, hospitals and other charities the same tax treatment they would receive if they were owned and operated the same way by someone else.

The majority believe that property owned by religious organizations which is used for religious purposes should remain exempt from taxation. This category primarily encompasses churches, chapels, parish houses and synagogues. They are believed to constitute the greatest part of the "wealth" of most religious congregations in this country, a significant number of which are only marginal operations in an economic sense. The repeal of this exemption, resulting in repeated annual assessments which would bear no necessary relationship to current cash flow, would constitute a major hardship to organized religion as we know it today in its broadest and most basic sense. We believe that legislators should continue this exemption to religious institutions in recognition of their overall beneficial role in our society. These tax exemptions have, historically, been accorded to organized religion (as well as education and charity) as a public recognition of public services rendered. We are all in agreement that this exemption should not extend to taxes, charges or assessments which are rationally measured by benefits demonstrably conferred upon the property — paving assessments, utility charges, etc.

Income Taxes. Present effective corporate tax rates (most religious organizations are corporations) are roughly 48% on inter-

947

est and other income (the rate on the first $25,000 of income is 22%), 7.2% on dividend income, and 25% (maximum) on profits from the sale of business assets, property or securities held for more than six months. Expenses reasonably incurred to produce such income are normally deducted before the taxes are applied. The undersigned are fully aware that such taxation of such income of religious organizations will have a serious financial effect on the economy of organized religion. For this reason, we suggest that any *new* taxation of income of religious organizations be phased in progressively over a five to ten year period. Such a time of transition should give religious organizations a better opportunity to adjust to their changed circumstances.

Income from unrelated businesses owned by religious organizations is not now taxed (except to the extent such businesses are operated as independent, taxable corporations). In this respect, religious organizations are favored over even educational and charitable ones. The undersigned disagree with such treatment in principle. Such unrelated businesses are operated in actual or potential competition with secular businesses and should, we feel, be accorded similar tax treatment.

The majority also believe that religious organizations should recognize the unfairness of their competitive business advantage. To reduce this advantage, religious organizations should operate their businesses in the corporate form, thereby subjecting those businesses to the same income taxes as their competitors.

The undersigned are of more than one mind on the subject of what is sometimes called "passive" investment income. About half would exempt such income (as is presently done) on the grounds (i) that such income is normally spent for religious and charitable purposes, and (ii) that the tax exemption has no adverse competitive effect on others. (There is a difficult problem in this connection — at what point does a church "investment" become church ownership and operation of a business venture? Obviously, outside ownership of a minute part of the stock of a corporation or a single issue of debt securities which are otherwise church-owned should not change the tax treatment of churches with regard to income from such stock or securities.

948

Somewhere, a line must be drawn; we merely point out that defining the location of this line poses practical problems.) About half of the undersigned believe that such "passive" investment income should be taxed. While some who favor such taxation believe it should be at ordinary corporate rates, a number believe that such a tax (i) should, perhaps, be at lower than generally applied rates in recognition of the religious, educational and charitable uses to which such income is put, or (ii) should, perhaps, be applied only to income in excess of a certain specified amount so as not to penalize religious organizations with relatively modest investment incomes, or (iii) should, perhaps, in some other way be tailored to prevent the future accumulation of investments as a result of tax-free income, yet permit present uses of such income from current investments on a tax-free basis. Those who accept the principle of taxation of investment income do so because they recognize that this is the area in which the "wealth" of organized religion is growing fastest, and which is subject to the most pervasive and persuasive criticism.

Whatever wealth organized religion may possess, of course, is mainly attributable to contributions which would be tax deductible (and tax exempt to the recipient) under today's tax laws. Viewing the question of income taxation from this starting point may be helpful in understanding the views of those who would tax "passive" investment income.

The original contribution, though tax exempt, does not in and of itself permanently remove any funds from what might be called the taxable wealth of the nation. To the extent the contribution is utilized to meet operating expenses of the religious organization (salaries, maintenance, etc.) it is quickly returned to the taxable wealth. To the extent it is used to build churches and other exempt structures, its amount, for what we believe are good reasons, is removed from the taxable wealth of the nation. To the extent such a contribution is turned into an investment and/or business operation, it is probably returned to the taxable wealth of the nation, but only in exchange for other property which is simultaneously removed from that taxable wealth. Those of us who would tax investment income believe that any in-

949

creased value of such investment or business operation upon sale, and the income derived therefrom, should remain part of the taxable wealth for two reasons. *First,* such investments and businesses are uses to which contributions are frequently put only in the absence of more pressing and immediate religious needs. *Second,* it is here that pyramiding of such investments poses the most serious threat of erosion of the national tax base.

One exception should be made to the above. To the extent such business income or investments are realized or owned by educational or charitable institutions which are operated or sponsored by religious organizations and would not be taxed if owned or operated by secular educational or charitable institutions, there should be a tax exemption. Again, we can see no reason why the tax treatment of church and secular-owned educational and religious institutions should not be the same, though we have obviously touched upon an even broader question of tax policy here.

Sales, Franchise, License, Excise, and Other Similar Taxes. Miscellaneous taxes, such as sales, license, and excise taxes, are normally imposed in relatively nominal amounts, and frequently are imposed to regulate, supervise or facilitate the commercial activity with respect to which they are imposed. Subject to the above-stated caveat that church-sponsored educational and charitable activities should be treated the same as any other such activities, we see no pressing reason why any exemptions should be granted in this area.

Salaries Paid by Religious Institutions. These are generally taxed the same as any other salaries earned in our society, and we see no reason for change.

Deductions for Gifts to Religious Institutions and Organizations. Within limits, these gifts are generally deductible just as are contributions to educational and charitable institutions. Since we believe that the social value of organized religion to our society is at least comparable to that of educational institutions and of charitable organizations, and that it is appropriate to encourage such contributions, we propose no change in this regard.

One Final Recommendation. Present tax laws, particularly real property tax laws, may limit exemptions in various ways — e.g., to the extent of actual religious use of the property in question. It has come to our attention that certain religious institutions, like many businesses, take a somewhat relaxed view of such limitations. Specifically, they tend to be lax in reporting changed uses of property which would remove their exemptions, and wait for the taxing authorities to catch up to the change. It is respectfully submitted that the morals of the market place are not appropriate to organized religion, that the public which has given organized religion its favored tax status has a right to expect better, and that organized religion should in all good conscience offer it better. *It is therefore recommended that the various financial officers of the religious establishment voluntarily undertake a program of periodic self-policing of all claimed tax exemptions, and that they be directed by higher ecclesiastical authorities to do so.*

New York, New York
May 6, 1967

> Respectfully submitted,
> THE GUILD OF ST. IVES
> By   Stephen B. Clarkson, Esq.
>   Rev. Canon Walter D. Dennis
>   Anthony L. Fletcher, Esq.
>   John F. Geer, Esq.
>   Robert F. Gibson, III, Esq.
>   Rev. Francis C. Huntington
>   Edward S. Moore, III, Esq.
>   Robert W. Pleasant, Esq.
>   Rev. James Proud*
>   Rev. Neale A. Secor*
>   William Sherman, Esq.
>   Paul Taylor, Esq.
>   Floyd W. Tomkins, Jr., Esq.
>   Bradley Walls, Esq.
>
>   *Also an attorney

REFERENCES

1. Corwin, W: *The Constitution and What It Means Today* (Atheneum, New York, New York) 1963.
2. Pike, James A: Tax Organized Religion, *Playboy*, April 1967, vol 14, no 4.
3. *The Random House Dictionary of the English Language* (Random House, New York, New York) 1966 (unabridged edition).
4. Sperry, W L: *Religion in America* (Cambridge University Press, Cambridge, England) 1946.

COMMENTARY

by Jack Mendelsohn

I F THE ancients believed that a picture was worth a thousand words, our contemporary public relations sense convinces us that a succinct word surpasses a score of catechisms. The appropriate potent word points, needles, motivates, and galvanizes. Religionists in our time possess and are possessed by such a word.

In the Winter 1967 issue of *Daedalus*, Daniel Callahan observed that a hortatory "relevance" now sets the task for believer and church alike, compelling "a fresh function, a new impact, and a contemporary appeal." When used in its contrary form, this word becomes a castigating engine. To be guilty of *irrelevance* is to stand condemned of feebleness and insignificance in a world hungering for radical, creative reform. Yet, as Dr. Callahan wisely reminds us, "the use of *relevance* also reveals . . . a number of anxieties and unanswered questions that exist within the churches today."

Can organized religion keep its moral passions in one compartment and its tax, investment, and purchasing policies in another?

The report of the Guild of St. Ives is a pioneering position

952

paper on the tax dilemma. Carefully thought out and ploddingly written, it responds to an increasingly dyspeptic issue. For some years, Eugene Carson Blake, James A. Pike, and numerous lesser ecclesiastical lights have been imploring church bodies to begin rendering the tax dollars to Caesar that are legitimately his before Caesar comes to take them with a sword. The efforts of the St. Ives Guild demonstrate that the fervent prophets are not entirely without honor in their own country. Yet the Guild group settles for mincing steps rather than manly strides, an outcome that is probably inescapable when the issue is looked upon chiefly as a "constitutional" one. Thus, the report does not wrestle vigorously enough with the concerns of a Blake or a Pike, who insist that the problems are primarily *situational*, not constitutional. Pike, for example, claims that tax shelters have already made church wealth a "menace" to church and society. One looks through the report in vain for adequate treatment of the contention.

Moreover, the report treats in cool establishmentarian fashion Bishop Pike's fascinating existential description of a church as "a club for its members" that should be taxed like any other club. The report simply ignores such impudence.

Regarding "relevance," the Guild majority obviously feels weighted down by the conservative predilections of church bodies. Pike rhapsodizes over the institutional revolutions "fair church taxation" would launch. He relishes the prospect that a "recognition of tax liability could give a tremendous stimulus to an approach that is now just on the horizon of church thinking: the radical notion that the existence and effective functioning of a community of faith does not really depend upon properties or buildings at all." The Guild report is of the lugubrious opinion that far from inducing revolutionary thrusts, increased tax responsibilities would more likely result in sharp curtailment of what modest innovative and "relevant" church activity there is. Any significant increase in the tax-paying responsibilities of churches, according to the St. Ives men, is more likely to cause things as they are to deteriorate than to become as they ought to be. A suitable rebuttal, presumably, is that the sooner things as they are deteriorate, the sooner things as they ought to be will emerge.

But if the report is tepid before the full force of arguments of the Bishop Pike kind, it nevertheless attests to a church conscience that sickens at remaining a sacred cow in the eyes of the tax collector. While the report mirrors what is unquestionably the tax creed of most American religious communities — continued exemption for religious activities — it bravely identifies initiatives churches may take to become accountable for a fairer share of taxes. Who knows how many alive and intelligent people might be willing to give the church a searching look if it should begin to lobby effectively for a dismantling of some of its own tax shelters?

Taxes, however, are only one side of the coin of the religious-economic realm, and the more passive side at that. The truly active-aggressive question is whether or not religious communities should deliberately manipulate their resources as investors and purchasers in order to advance moral and social aims.

When an assembled congregation hears a canvass chairman intone the Biblical text "where your treasure is, there will your heart be also," the bite for pledges and contributions traditionally comes next. But an increasing number of churchmen are applying this text to quite another objective, social action, arguing that a church's treasure — endowments and purchasing power — should not be used to perpetuate social injustices, indeed must be used to foster social justice.

The possibilities are anything but conjectural. The investment portfolios of religious bodies add up to billions of dollars. Annual purchases of goods and services run to billions more. Church construction alone amounts to something like a billion a year. The economic biceps of organized religion are Samson-like. Yet, how to flex them for specific moral objectives in the market place? Indeed, should they be flexed in this way at all? These questions, as never before, are becoming the focus of soul-searching and tension within congregations and denominations as the quest for relevance goes on.

A few years ago there came into being an organization known

954

as the National Committee on Tithing in Investment, with an impressive and lengthy list of celebrities as sponsors, including many of the country's most noted churchmen. Its proposal was simple and direct. Investments can be an eloquent voice for equal opportunity in housing. Money talks. If churches and other eleemosynary institutions, and their individual members, would invest ten per cent of their investable resources in open housing they could not only sabotage housing discrimination but earn a respectable financial return as well. Reasoning that there are entrepreneurs, brokers, and bankers who would be delighted to make money from open housing if the necessary investment capital was available, N.C.T.I. proposed the obvious: let churches, colleges, labor unions, and foundations earmark a fraction of their investment resources for equal housing.

The goading of N.C.T.I. and the organization of a number of investment-seeking local and national corporations with fair housing goals have brought some congregations and denominational bodies to their first modest investments of a non-traditional, high social utility type, others to the brink of apoplexy and schism.

The issue found another focus when a group of churches voted to withhold proxies on some 30,000 shares of Eastman Kodak Company stock in order to question the company's disavowal of an agreement to employ and train several hundred unskilled Negroes in Rochester. The action was taken at the urging of a militant civil rights organization known as F.I.G.H.T. (Freedom, Integration, God, Honor – Today).

F.I.G.H.T. and a Kodak assistant vice-president, after extensive bargaining, signed an agreement providing training and jobs for six hundred Rochester Negroes. Within forty-eight hours, the company announced that the agreement was "unauthorized" and that company policy forbade a binding arrangement with an outside organization.

The churches that voted to withhold proxies sent representatives to the annual shareholders' meeting in Flemington, New Jersey, to challenge the company's action. With more than eighty million Kodak shares outstanding, the gesture was admittedly symbolic, but a great deal of dust was stirred. Several weeks later, Kodak did reconsider, and worked out a new agreement with F.I.G.H.T.

An additional dimension is provided by the ferment over ten major U.S. banks which together provide a $40 million revolving loan fund to the government of South Africa. The profits are handsome, yet the fund undeniably bolsters one of the world's most oppressive racial tyrannies. Indeed the level of American investment in South Africa may be approaching the point where American business pressures could deflect U.S. diplomatic strategy against the South African *apartheid* system.

Several churches and denominational bodies use the revolving fund banks as depositories, and some hold their stocks in investment portfolios. Should the deposits be transferred to other banks? Should the stocks be sold, or should concerned religious representatives, as shareholders, maneuver to persuade bank managements to change their South African policy? How are churchmen to decide in the face of certain ambiguous factors? At least some of the banks involved are providing financial support to efforts churches warmly approve. For example, does abhorrence of Chase Manhattan's South African business outweigh that same bank's admirable interest in Latin American development? If so, would the gesture of church disengagement and protest be only a grandstand play, or could it make a real difference? The issues are complex, yet they are genuine. The only unthinkable course is that churches should not wrestle with such issues and accept the contamination of decisions about them.

Still another frontier is the church's vast role as consumer of goods and services. Here a highly sophisticated bit of pioneering is to be found in the ecumenical effort known as Project Equality. Project Equality's theory is that religious bodies can use their spending power to command more than fair prices and dependable merchandise. They can demand positive action to end discriminatory employment practices as well.

After initial scrutiny and reform of their own employment practices, the participating religious groups ask businesses and unions with which they have dealings to pledge unremitting affirmative efforts toward equal opportunity recruiting, training, hiring, and upgrading. Annual, statistically detailed reports are required. A confidential list of cooperating firms, regularly revised, is distributed to those who do the purchasing for religious bodies.

Initially launched in St. Louis, Detroit, and San Antonio on a pilot basis, the program spread rapidly to other metropolitan and state-wide areas. The project directors expect that thirty fully-staffed offices will be in operation by the end of 1968, at which time the buying power of the participating religious groups will be a multi-billion dollar matter.

If faith is communicated by witness, Project Equality stands out as a powerful example of how religious institutions can create candid and responsible dialogue with the business community, productive of positive social change. Yet some churchmen, and not merely moss-backs, view such use of church economic leverage as teeming with potential abuses. *The New York Times* quoted the Rev. John L. Reedy, Editor of the Ave Maria Press in South Bend, Indiana, as saying, "Churches aren't at home with this sort of method and can easily foul up their own purposes. The power that is used to promote equal employment today might easily be used to enforce censorship tomorrow." He then added, "What does the liberal who backs Project Equality say to someone else who thinks that Catholic hospitals should boycott pharmaceutical firms that manufacture birth control pills?" Still, Father Reedy concluded, "We must find some way of responsibly confronting the fact that when churches don't recognize their economic power, they simply re-enforce the status quo."

All of these issues transport church members and denominational leaders into strange territory. There are no maps. On the question of investment policy, with its staggering stakes, there is no carefully worked out rationale, let alone fiduciary law support, for novel social approaches. The investment policies of church groups are guided by a traditional design of "prudence, intelligence, and discretion," all admirable traits. Three factors are weighed and mixed in a pattern of investment decisions: the relative safety and liquidity of the capital involved, the pressing need of income to meet budgets, and reasonable growth of capital and income over the years. All of these factors assume that the economic system is autonomous or independent of human problems other than those concerned with the production and distribution of goods and services.

What some people are now proposing is the addition of a fourth factor which views the economic system as part of a total effort to combat specific social evils and to improve the quality of human living in concrete ways. Traditional church investment philosophy places itself entirely within the economy as it is, and avoids looking beyond it, believing that this is the most prudent way to serve the financial welfare of the investing institution. The proposed innovation is that churches as investors also look at the economy from the outside to see how the church's participation in it aids or damages other major human concerns. What is suggested, then, is that in the total pattern of investment decision-making, consideration be given to particular purposes of human good or ill. It is a call for adding a dimension of purposeful social objectives to the present rubrics of investment philosophy.

Church investment philosophy is now more insulated from comprehensive concerns of human living than much of industry and commerce. Among those bearing chief responsibility for our greatest business enterprises there is widespread alertness to the need for creativity and innovation in meeting broad human aspirations. One wonders if it doesn't border on the ridiculous for churchmen to go on ignoring the impact a social-utility expansion of their investment philosophy might have, say, on housing patterns or ghetto economic development.

The potential investment resources exist, the technology exists, the devices of propaganda exist, the mechanisms of organization and skills of management are available, for molding human life in many distressed realms closer to the likeness of an ideal. Or, to put it in classical economic language, opportunities abound for solving human problems with a fair return on investment, if only the investment philosophy of church members and bodies can

958

expand to embrace such opportunities. Among our most efficiently managed business enterprises are those that have learned to strive for the best possible balance of profits and social accountability. Progressive business management does not simply try to maximize profit, knowing that in the long run the effort to do so is sterile and self-defeating. It becomes increasingly difficult to explain why church investment policy should cling to a lesser standard. Given the rapidly increasing competence of technologically oriented business management, it is constantly harder to argue that some portion of church investment should not be deliberately committed to influence the social vision of such competence. Admittedly, the concrete details will be complex, but they will also be considerably more exciting, requisite of ingenuity, and much more involving of church memberships than the present investment litany of safety, income, and growth.

Since the investment resources of churches come mainly from contributions and bequests, the question naturally arises whether the future flow of such gifts and legacies will be choked off. What is more likely to happen is a redistribution of donors and bequeathers. Some would rewrite their wills or reinstruct their financial advisors to "disinherit" experimenting churches, while others, intrigued by new means of multiplying the fruits of their largesse, would be attracted to placing more of it at the disposal of church bodies of demonstrated social imagination.

In addition, most individual church members are not well-enough off to figure significantly in the investment field. However, as participants in an investing church body with a developing social utility know-how, they can gain an entirely new sense of personal sharing in creative economic goals.

Money, as an investing and purchasing resource of religious institutions, is patently a means of extending and amplifying communal wishes, motives, concerns, and values. It is not now conceived in this fashion except as the buying of stocks, bonds, goods, and services supports and undergirds a church's budgetary programs. Beyond the prevailing conception, however, are new possibilities of economic relevance, and to the extent that there is response to these opportunities there is likely to be a rising

959

counter-pressure, not from the Pikes and Blakes, to shrink the churches' tax-exempt status. Realism dictates, in a social order as tax and money conscious as ours, that untaxed church wealth is tolerated partly because it is viewed as being relatively benign in the economy. If, and as, churches become more economically partisan and aggressive, Mammon's sufferance will diminish. Clemency granted to a cross that dwells in a realm essentially different from that of the wallet can be withdrawn with startling swiftness if the cross starts behaving as if it and the wallet share a common turf. A sacred cow becomes rapidly less sacred and less a cow when it turns from grazing to goring. There is, as an Episcopal bishop is reputed to have said, "that magical substance which men pursue relentlessly for six days a week and refuse to discuss on the seventh." A more militant church flexing its economic muscle in behalf of social change must reckon with a severe scrambling of such familiar symbolic relationships, and with a widespread rise in blood pressure both within and without parochial preserves. But this is precisely what *relevance* is all about: confrontation, engagement, impact, maybe even new birth.

NOTES ON CONTRIBUTORS

THOMAS J. J. ALTIZER is associate professor of religion at Emory University. His published writing in theology includes *The New Apocalypse: The Radical Christian Vision of William Blake* (1967).

HASAN ASKARI is chairman of the Department of Sociology, Osmania University, Hyderabad, Andhra Pradesh.

ROBERT N. BELLAH is Ford Professor of Sociology and Comparative Studies at the University of California, Berkeley. He has published a number of theoretical and comparative essays on religion, and edited *Religion and Progress in Modern Asia* (1965).

LOWELL L. BENNION is associate dean of students and lecturer in sociology at the University of Utah. The second edition of his *Religion and the Pursuit of Truth* is forthcoming in 1968.

NORMAN BIRNBAUM is professor of sociology at the New School for Social Research. His book *The Theory of Industrial Society* is forthcoming.

ROBERT T. BOBILIN is associate professor of religion at the University of Hawaii and will also be a senior colleague in the Institute for Advanced Projects at the East-West Center in 1968–69.

DAVID L. BREWER is assistant professor of sociology at California State College at Hayward.

D. W. BROGAN is emeritus professor of history at Cambridge University. He is the author of many books and articles, including *Worlds in Conflict* (1967). His publications about the American scene include *Politics in America* (1954) and *The American Character* (1956).

DANIEL CALLAHAN is executive editor of *Commonweal* magazine. Mr. Callahan edited *The Secular City Debate* (1966) and has written, among other books, *The New Church: Essays in Catholic Reform* (1966).

JOSEPH CAMPBELL is a member of the Literature Department at Sarah Lawrence College. The fourth volume, *Creative Mythology*, of his work on mythology, *The Masks of God*, is scheduled for publication in 1968. He has also written *The Hero with a Thousand Faces* (1949).

JOHN B. CARMAN is assistant professor of comparative religion at the Harvard Divinity School. He is presently engaged in three years of resident research in South India.

GONZALO CASTILLO-CARDENAS is a doctoral candidate in the "Religion and Society" program at Columbia University and Union Theological Seminary. He expects to return to Bogota, Colombia, at the end of 1968 to teach at the Ecumenical Center.

ARTHUR A. COHEN is vice president, and editor-in-chief of the General Book Division, of Holt, Rinehart and Winston. His first novel, *The Carpenter Years*, was published in 1967; he is also the author of *The Natural and the Supernatural Jew* (1964).

HARVEY COX is associate professor of church and society at the Harvard Divinity School. Mr. Cox is the author of *The Secular City* (1965) and *On Not Leaving It to the Snake* (1967).

ARTHUR J. DYCK is assistant professor of social ethics at Harvard Divinity School and a member of the Harvard Center for Population Studies.

ERIK H. ERIKSON is professor of human development and lecturer on psychiatry at Harvard University. Among his publications are *Childhood and Society* (1950), *Young Man Luther* (1958), *Identity and the Life Cycle* (1959), and *Insight and Responsibility* (1964).

EMIL L. FACKENHEIM is professor of philosophy at the University of Toronto. He is the author of *The Religious Dimension in Hegel's Thought*, forthcoming in 1968.

EDWIN S. GAUSTAD is professor and chairman of the Department of History at the University of California, Riverside. He is the author of *Religious Issues in American History*, forthcoming in 1968, as well as of the already published *A Religious History of America* (1966) and *A Historical Atlas of Religion in America* (1962).

CLIFFORD GEERTZ is professor of anthropology at the University of Chicago. In addition to editing *Old Societies and New States* (1963) he has written *The Social History of an Indonesian Town* (1965), *The Religion of Java* (1959), and *Peddlers and Princes* (1963).

962

IRVING GREENBERG is associate professor of history at Yeshiva University and rabbi of the Riverdale Jewish Center, Riverdale, New York.

THE GUILD OF ST. IVES was founded in February, 1966, by a group of Episcopalian lawyers and clergy in New York City. Its purposes embrace both legal aid and the preparation of reports on matters of church and public concern.

PHILIP E. HAMMOND is Associate Professor of Sociology at the University of Wisconsin. Mr. Hammond has co-authored *Religion in Social Context* (in press), has edited *Sociologists at Work* (1964), and has written *The Campus Clergyman* (1966).

VINCENT HARDING is chairman of the History Department at Spelman College. His writings on the Negro in America also include the forthcoming *Black Radicalism in America* and "Religion and Resistance among Antebellum Negroes, 1800–1860" in a volume edited by Meier and Ruderick to be published in 1968.

RICHARD SHELLY HARTIGAN is assistant professor of political science at Loyola University, Chicago.

MILTON HIMMELFARB is director of the Information Service of the American Jewish Committee, editor of the *American Jewish Yearbook*, and a contributing editor to *Commentary* magazine.

ROBERT G. HOYT is editor of the *National Catholic Reporter*. He has also edited the forthcoming *Issues That Divide the Church*.

SIR JULIAN S. HUXLEY has had a distinguished career both as a scientist and as a humanist. He lives in Hampstead. His many published works include *The Human Crisis* (1964), *Essays of a Humanist* (1963), *Evolution in Action* (1952), and *Man in the Modern World* (1947). Among his varied contributions has been a term (1946–48) as Director-General of UNESCO.

EUGENE IRSCHICK, presently in India studying late nineteenth and early twentieth century South Indian history, is assistant professor of history at the University of California, Berkeley.

DIMITRY KONSTANTINOV was a printer and publisher in the Soviet Union before World War II. Now a priest of the Russian Orthodox Church in the United States of America, he contributes articles on religious subjects to publications of the Institute for the Study of the USSR.

ALLEN LACY is assistant professor of humanities at Michigan State University. His published writings include *Miguel de Unamuno: The Rhetoric of Existence* (1967).

DAVID LITTLE is assistant professor of Christian ethics at Yale Divinity School. He is the author of *New Order in Old England* (tentative title) forthcoming in 1968.

KONRAD LORENZ is director of the Max-Planck–Institut for behavioral physiology in Bavaria. His many books and scientific papers include *On Aggression* (1966), *Man Meets Dog* (1965), *Evolution and the Modification of Behavior* (1965), and *King Solomon's Ring* (1952).

WILLIAM F. LYNCH, S.J., is a writer in residence at St. Peter's College, Jersey City, New Jersey. He is completing a study of the religious image of secularity; his published works include *Images of Hope* (1966), and *Christ and Apollo* (1960).

MARTIN E. MARTY is chairman of the Church History Field at the University of Chicago Divinity School and associate editor of *The Christian Century*. Mr. Marty co-edits *Church History* and the annual *New Theology*. He has written, among many titles, *Varieties of Unbelief* (1964), *Religion and Social Conflict* (1964), and *The New Shape of American Religion* (1959).

JACK MENDELSOHN is senior minister of the Arlington Street Church in Boston. He is preparing a biography of William Ellery Channing. Mr. Mendelsohn's published works include *The Martyrs* (1966) and *The Forest Calls Back* (1965).

REINHOLD NIEBUHR is professor emeritus of Union Theological Seminary. He lives and writes in New York City. Among his many published books and articles are, more recently, *Man's Nature and His Communities* (1965), *A Nation So Conceived* (with Alan Heimert, 1963), and *The Structure of Nations and Empires* (1959).

MICHAEL NOVAK is assistant professor of theology at Stanford University. He has written *A Time To Build* (1967), *Belief and Unbelief* (1965), and, with Robert McAfee Brown and Abraham Heschel, *Vietnam: Crisis of Conscience* (1967). Mr. Novak also writes frequently on religion and world affairs in national journals and magazines.

THOMAS F. O'DEA is professor of sociology and director of the Institute of Religious Studies at the University of California, Santa Barbara. He has written *The Sociology of Religion* (1966), *The American Catholic Dilemma* (1958), and *The Mormons* (1957). *The Catholic Crisis* is forthcoming in 1968.

TALCOTT PARSONS is professor of sociology at Harvard University. Among his extensive list of published works are *Sociological Theory and Modern Society* (1967), *Societies: Evolutionary and Comparative Perspectives* (1966), and *Structure and Process in Modern Societies* (1959).

LEO PFEFFER is professor of constitutional law at Long Island University. Mr. Pfeffer is the author of *Church, State, and Freedom* (rev. ed. 1966) and *This Honorable Court* (1965).

RALPH B. POTTER, JR., is assistant professor of social ethics at the Harvard Divinity School and a member of the Harvard Center for Population Studies.

RICHARD L. RUBENSTEIN is director of B'nai B'rith Hillel Foundation and university chaplain to Jewish students at the University of Pittsburgh and Carnegie-Mellon University. He is the author of *After Auschwitz* (1966) and *The Religious Imagination* (forthcoming).

ZALMAN M. SCHACHTER is associate professor and head of the Department of Judaic Studies at the University of Manitoba, Winnipeg.

EDWARD SHILS is professor of sociology and social thought at the University of Chicago and fellow of King's College, Cambridge. He and Talcott Parsons jointly edited *Toward a General Theory of Action* (1951), and he has written, among other works, *The Torment of Secrecy* (1956) and *The Intellectual Between Tradition and Modernity: The Indian Situation*.

PHILIP E. SLATER is associate professor of sociology at Brandeis. He is the author of *Microcosm* (1966) and, with Warren G. Bennis, *The Democratic Revolution* (1967). *The Glory of Hera* is to be published in 1968.

HUSTON SMITH is professor of philosophy at the Massachusetts Institute of Technology. Mr. Smith has written *Condemned to Meaning* (1965) and *The Religions of Man* (1958).

MAX L. STACKHOUSE is assistant professor of Christian ethics at Andover Newton Theological School. He has edited a previously unpublished work of Walter Rauschenbusch, *The Righteousness of the Kingdom.*

NIKITA STRUVE is an associate lecturer at the Sorbonne. He is the author of *Christians in Contemporary Russia* (1967).

GUY E. SWANSON is professor of sociology at the University of Michigan. His published works include *Religion and Regime: A Sociological Account of the Reformation* (1967) and *The Birth of the Gods: The Origin of Primitive Beliefs* (1960).

JOHN R. WHITNEY is instructor in religious studies at the Pennsylvania State University. He is director of a project to produce courses in religious literature for Pennsylvania public secondary schools.

BRIAN WICKER is staff tutor of the Department of Extramural Studies of the University of Birmingham. He has written *First the Political Kingdom* (1967), *Culture and Theology* (1966), and *Culture and Liturgy* (1963).

M. YAMUNACHARYA is director of the Research Department of the Gandhi Peace Foundation, New Delhi.

INDEX

986